16.00

20296531
v6

MAGILL'S
SURVEY
OF
SCIENCE

MAGILL'S SURVEY OF SCIENCE

EARTH SCIENCE SERIES SUPPLEMENT

Volume 6
2805-3199
A–Xenoliths
CUMULATIVE INDEX

Edited by
ROGER SMITH

SALEM PRESS

Pasadena, California   Englewood Cliffs, New Jersey

Managing Editor: Christina J. Moose
Project Editor: Robert McClenaghan   *Production Editor:* Joyce I. Buchea
Copy Editor: Rowena Wildin   *Layout:* William Zimmerman

Library of Congress Cataloging-in-Publication Data
Magill's survey of science. Earth science series. Supple-
ment / editor, Roger Smith.
    p. cm.
    Includes bibliographical references and index.
    1. Earth sciences. I. Smith, Roger, 1953-   .
QE28.M33   1990   89-10923
550—dc20   CIP
Supplement
ISBN 0-89356-606-3 (set)
ISBN 0-89356-933-X (volume 6)

First Printing

PRINTED IN THE UNITED STATES OF AMERICA

PUBLISHER'S NOTE

The original five volumes of *Magill's Survey of Science: Earth Science Series*, published in 1990, contained 377 articles examining a broad array of subjects in the earth sciences. This one-volume supplement expands and updates the coverage of the original set by providing expert commentary on fifty-five additional topics of interest. Included in the present volume are articles covering important recent developments in the earth sciences—such as the 1991 eruption of Mount Pinatubo and the launching of the Mission to Planet Earth program—as well as additional descriptive and theoretical essays providing a yet fuller picture of the planet, its features, its fundamental processes, and its history.

Each article retains the familiar Magill format: All the entries begin with ready-reference top matter, including an indication of the relevant discipline or field of study and a summary statement in which the writer explains why the topic is important to the study of the earth and its processes. A listing of principal terms and their definitions helps to orient the reader to the essay. A summary section forms the major part of each article, providing necessary background and a description of the features of each topic. Two types of summaries are provided, depending on the subject matter. The first type, "Summary of the Phenomenon," describes the characteristics of the particular earth science phenomenon under discussion: the nature of a geologic process, the composition and origin of a geologic feature, or the background of a public policy or health issue such as global warming or ozone holes. The other type of essay, "Summary of the Methodology," examines the techniques and approaches used in earth science research and analysis, including tools, technologies, and problem-solving strategies—for example, satellite meteorology or seismic tomography. Following "Summary of the Phenomenon" is a description of how the topic is studied in the field and laboratory; following "Summary of the Methodology" is an overview of the topic's applications by researchers, engineers, or technicians for academic, commercial, or social purposes. "Context," the concluding section of both types of essay, presents the conclusions, applications, and implications derived from investigation of the topic. An annotated Bibliography is provided to refer the reader to external sources for further study that are accessible to the student or nonspecialist. "Cross-References" directs the reader to other articles in all six volumes of the *Earth Science* series that offer additional information on the same or a related topic.

At the end of the volume, three additional tools are provided to assist in the retrieval of information. The Alphabetical List of contents is followed by the Category List, which groups article titles by general area of interest. Finally, the comprehensive Index directs the reader to appearances of important names, terms, and topics throughout the text. Each of these reader aids is cumulative, referencing the entire six volumes of the complete set.

Many hands went into the creation of this work. Special mention must be made of editor Roger Smith, who played a principal role in shaping the book's contents. Thanks are also due to the many academicians and professionals who worked to communicate their expert understanding of the earth sciences to the general reader; a list of these individuals and their affiliations appears at the beginning of the volume. The contributions of all are gratefully acknowledged.

CONTRIBUTORS

Richard W. Arnseth
Science Applications International

Alvin K. Benson
Brigham Young University

John L. Berkley
State University of New York, College at Fredonia

Habte Giorgis Churnet
University of Tennessee at Chattanooga

Robert G. Corbett
Illinois State University

Loralee Davenport
Mississippi University for Women

Ronald W. Davis
Western Michigan University

René De Hon
Northeast Louisiana University

Albert B. Dickas
University of Wisconsin

George J. Flynn
State University of New York, Plattsburgh

Daniel G. Graetzer
University of Washington/Seattle

Clay D. Harris
Middle Tennessee State University

Charles D. Haynes
University of Alabama

Robert M. Hordon
Rutgers University

Louise D. Hose
Westminster College

Stephen Huber
Beaver College

Jeffrey A. Joens
Florida International University

Richard C. Jones
Texas Woman's University

Karen N. Kähler
Independent Scholar

Christopher Keating
Angelo State University

Ralph L. Langenheim, Jr.
University of Illinois

David W. Maguire
C.S. Mott Community College

Randall L. Milstein
Oregon State University

Otto H. Muller
Alfred University

C. Nicholas Raphael
Eastern Michigan University

Charles W. Rogers
Southwestern Oklahoma State University

Neil E. Salisbury
University of Oklahoma

Virginia L. Salmon
Northeast State Technical Community College

Panagiotis D. Scarlatos
Florida Atlantic University

Kenneth J. Schoon
Indiana University Northwest

R. Baird Shuman
University of Illinois at Urbana-Champaign

Paul P. Sipiera
William Rainey Harper College

Roger Smith
Independent Scholar

Joseph L. Spradley
Wheaton College

Robert J. Stern
University of Texas at Dallas

Dion C. Stewart
Adams State College

Leslie V. Tischauser
Prairie State College

CONTENTS

EARTH SCIENCE

MAGILL'S
SURVEY
OF
SCIENCE

AFRICAN RIFT VALLEY SYSTEM

Type of earth science: Geology
Field of study: Tectonics

The African rift valley system is characterized by its elongated basins, which cut across a region that is dotted with domes and that extends from South Africa to the Red Sea. Most lakes of the region are located in the rift basin.

Principal terms
ASTHENOSPHERE: the layer of the earth that lies beneath the lithosphere and is partly composed of melt
CARBONATITE: an igneous rock with abundant carbon in its makeup
CINDER CONE: a cone-shaped mound made up of volcanic granules
FAULT: a fracture in a rock associated with rock movement or sliding
GRABEN: a linear topographic depression caused by subsidence along faults
HALF-GRABEN: a basic structural element by which a rift system is formed, consisting of an arcuate ridge that bounds a depression and is formed by normal faulting
HYDROTHERMAL FLUID: a natural hot steam that seeps through the ground
LITHOSPHERE: the top rock layer of the earth, ranging from 70 kilometers in depth in the African continent to 21 kilometers in the African rift
MAGMA: a melt from which igneous rocks are formed
NORMAL FAULT: a fault in which the rock block on top of an inclined fracture surface, also known as a fault plane, slides downward
PYROCLASTICS: fragmentary igneous rocks that are formed by the forceful ejection of volcanic materials into the atmosphere
RIFT PROPAGATION: the lateral movement of a rifting process that leads to the prying open of a section of the lithosphere, accompanied by the formation of igneous rocks

Summary of the Phenomenon

A continental rift is a linear topographic depression that may develop into an ocean as the bounding regions drift into two separate continental fragments. The African rift valley system is one of several continental rifts; others include the Rio Grande, the Baikal, and the Rhine Graben. It is a long system that extends from South Africa to the Red Sea coast.

The African rifts are marked by depressions that cut across domes, such as the East African and the Afro-Arabian domes. The East African dome encompasses parts of Tanzania, Uganda, and Kenya and is dissected by two rift branches. The eastern branch is discontinuously traceable to the Main Ethiopian Rift, which is one of three rifts of the Afro-Arabian dome. The other two rifts are the Red Sea and the Gulf of Aden. The three rift arms of the Afro-Arabian dome meet in a triangular depression, the Afar. Actually, the central structures of the three rifts overlap in the Serdo Block, a roughly square area of about 90 kilometers per side.

The rift basin margins may be distinct and marked by cliffs in some places. At Dalol, about 100 kilometers north of the Serdo Block, the rift floor is about 3,000 meters below the rift rim, and there is a 5,000-meter-thick layer of salt that was deposited in the last 4 million years. Since salt forms at sea level, the Afar floor must have been slowly sinking (subsiding) about 5 kilometers in 4 million years. Clearly, the rift floors have formed by subsidence relative to the rim.

Subsidence occurs as the rock block on top of an inclined fracture surface slides downward, a movement that geologists call "normal faulting." Rift basins are formed by a series of normal fault movements that generally produce grabens and half-grabens. A half-graben consists of an arcuate ridge that bounds a depression and is formed by normal faulting; it is the basic building unit of continental rifts. A typical half-graben is about 100 kilometers long and less than 4 kilometers wide. Half-grabens might be arranged facing or opposite or staggered in the rift basins. The thickness of the rock layer (lithosphere) at the rift basins ranges from 21 to 30 kilometers, less than half its thickness elsewhere on the continent.

Geologists believe that the lithosphere lies above a partially molten layer, the asthenosphere. The melt, also known as "magma," from the asthenosphere rises through fractures and flows to form layered basalt, or it oozes to form volcanic domes and cones, or it is ejected explosively to spray volcanic ash and fragmental rocks that geologists call "pyroclastics." Some volcanic rocks that geologists call "carbonatites" are formed from magmas that originate at great depths and that contain abundant carbon dioxide. Also, from deep within the mantle, sodium- and potassium-rich magma forms volcanic rocks that geologists term "alkaline igneous" rocks. However, the dominant igneous rocks of the rift basins are tholeiites, which are comparatively rich in magnesium and the magma of which originated at comparatively shallow depths. Some of the rift volcanoes issue substantial quantities of volcanic gas. Actually, volcanic gases and steam (hydrothermal fluids) also seep through fractures unrelated to volcanoes.

Igneous and volcanic activity is not restricted to rift basins. Huge volcanic edifices are formed outside the rift basins. A string of such volcanic structures is found on either side of the rift rims. Examples of such volcanoes include Mount Kilimanjaro of Tanzania and Ras Dashen of Ethiopia. The rift-related volcanic activity started some 23 million years ago outside the rift, although most of it has been limited to the rift basin in the last 6 million years.

In addition to igneous rocks, the rift basin is covered by sediments and sedimentary rocks. At cliffed rift basins, boulders, cobbles, gravel, and granules accumulate at the bottoms of the cliffs. Rivers descend into rift basins and wind along the rift until they empty into lakes. Such rivers transport detrital sediments such as sand, silt, and mud, which are deposited within the river channel, in overbank floodplains, and at the lakes. In addition to detrital sediments, evaporation of rift lakes produces chemical sediments such as salt and gypsum. Rift basins, particularly the parts that are close to seas, such as the Afar, can be flooded by the sea. Before volcanic rocks isolated it, the northern part of the Afar was covered by a shallow sea. Evaporation of that sea yielded copious amounts of salt deposits and underwater volcanic flows. Thus, rift deposits include chemical and detrital sedimentary rocks that may be interbedded with volcanic flows or pyroclastics.

Geologists have suggested that the origin of the rifts can be explained by plate tectonic theory. According to this theory, the lithosphere is segmented into discrete plates. The plates move, and the boundary type of the plates is identified by the direction of movement of neighboring plates. Thus, in divergent plate boundaries neighboring plates move away from each other; in transform boundaries, neighboring plates slide alongside each other; and in convergent boundaries, the plates collide against each other. The movement of the plates is considered to be guided by convection within the asthenosphere, which in turn results from movement of molten material to equalize the temperature within the asthenosphere. Hot molten material from the deeper part of the asthenosphere rises, pushes on the lithosphere above, and then diverges beneath the lithosphere. The lithosphere is carried along by the diverging asthenosphere, as if it is luggage placed on a conveyor belt. Geologists believe that the African rift system is a divergent plate boundary at which Africa is tearing apart. According to this bulge-rift model, the rift borders are elevated from the surrounding areas because of the initial bulge before the rifting process was established. The discrete domes along the rift would then indicate areas at which randomly rising deeper and hot asthenosphere encountered the lithosphere that was expanded and buoyed because of the heat.

The Afro-Arabian dome, with its higher elevation and shape and its triple rifts, has attracted the attention of many geologists. Much as the crust of a pie placed in an oven would bulge up and form three fractures, the rifts of the Afro-Arabian dome are considered to have formed as a result of the heat of the ascending plume. This theory is proposed by geologists as an explanation of why triple rifts are present in many places before a continent is split apart and an ocean fills the gap. According to this dome-rift model, the Red Sea and Gulf of Aden, which are now occupied by seas, have begun to open up as Saudi Arabia is splitting and drifting away from Africa, whereas the third rift, the Main Ethiopian Rift, is not. While the dome-rift model requires that the Main Ethiopian Rift is a failed arm of a rift, there is evidence that shows that it is a divergent boundary with a spreading rate of about 1 centimeter per year. Moreover, the exact triple point, the Serdo Block, is on land. The Serdo Block is linked by a line of volcanoes to the Red Sea and the Gulf of Aden, which mark plate boundaries between the Saudi Arabian plate to the north, the Ethiopian plate to the southwest, and the Somalia plate to the southeast.

The central rift system of the Gulf of Aden is connected to a mid-oceanic rift system, the Carlsberg Ridge, in the Indian Ocean southeast of Saudi Arabia. Scientists have found that the average age of igneous rocks along the central Gulf of Aden Rift is progressively younger toward the Serdo Block. They suggest that the origin of the Gulf of Eden Rift is to be explained by a rift-propagation model. That is to say that a rifting, once begun somewhere, will move laterally. According to geologists, the submarine Carlsberg Rift might have initiated the "burn" of the African continent on the east side of where the Gulf of Aden is currently located, and that rift has propagated toward the Serdo Block.

In the northern Red Sea, geologists have found that sedimentary rift deposits contain older rock particles in younger strata. It is as though, initially, young rocks from a source area were eroded, and their particles were deposited in the rift. Subsequently, the rim of the rift was uplifted, older rocks were exposed in the source area, and their particles were deposited in the rift basin atop sedimentary layers that contain younger rock particles. Geologists propose that rifting probably arose because the Arabian plate collides with Eurasia to form the Zagros Mountains in the north, and that the lithosphere is tearing apart to form the Red Sea as a consequence. The comparatively thin lithosphere at the Red Sea is then heated by the asthenosphere and made buoyant so that the rift borders rise to higher elevations. This is called the "rift-bulge" model.

Clearly, the African rift system is a laboratory for geologists to explore and understand the characteristics of continental rifting. Several geological processes likely operated simultaneously to produce the northern part of the rift system.

Methods of Study

Scientists have used a diverse set of instruments to study the different aspects of the African rift system. Aspects studied include the shape and structure of the landscape, the thickness of the lithosphere, the magnetic properties of the rocks, and the mineral and chemical composition of the rocks.

Instruments used to study landscape and structure include the plane table and alidade, used for ground surveys, and cameras and other sensors mounted on airplanes and satellites, used for taking aerial photographs and satellite images. The alidade is a special telescope that is placed on a plane table and is used to measure both horizontal distance and height from a ground station by sighting at a stadia, or surveyor's stick. At a ground station, a plane table is mounted on a tripod and set in a perfectly horizontal position. A stadia person stands at separate locations so that the surveyor at the ground station can sight at the graduated stadia and read the stadia lines that match crosswire lines in the alidade. That information is converted by use of suitable equations or tables to determine the distance and elevation of the ground surface between the plane table and stadia stations. That information is then placed on a paper that covers the plane table. This survey is taken from different ground stations until a whole region is surveyed. The data can then be used to produce contour maps that show the landscape on a two-dimensional piece of paper.

Mapping of remote areas awaited the use of aerial photographs. Overlapping photographs of a region are taken by cameras mounted on airplanes that fly along parallel lines. The overlapping photographs are then viewed under stereoscopes that have suitably mounted mirrors and lenses that permit the viewing of the region in its three dimensions. The locations and heights of the ground are measured from the photographs. Topographic maps are made from these measurements after checking some of them by actual field examination, a process also called "ground truing."

Satellite images of various sorts help delineate structures and textures. Basically, energy-sensing devices mounted on satellites are used to detect the energy that is emitted from the ground. The type of emitted energy is identified by its wavelength, and the data are converted into numbers, or "digitized." The digitized data along with the coordinates of the source region are transmitted to receivers on the ground. Maps produced from these data are enhanced by false colors or shading and patterning to highlight particular features. Linear arrangements of volcanic cones and their relationships to other structures, the presence of major fault zones, and other features across a region can be identified from satellite images.

A primary instrument used to study the thickness of the lithosphere is the gravimeter, which is a mass suspended by a spring and encased in a suitable container. The attraction between the mass in the gravimeter and the earth helps to determine the gravity values of a region. Since rocks have lower densities than the asthenosphere, a thick lithosphere has a lower gravity value than a thin lithosphere. Scientists have found that the rift basins have high gravity values, and they have used these values in conjunction with suitably devised models to estimate the thickness of lithospheres. The African continent has a lithosphere that is generally 70 kilometers thick, but in the African rift basins the lithosphere is between 30 and 21 kilometers thick, the thinnest part being in the Afar.

Context

According to many scientists, the African rift system is where human beings first evolved from apes. Lucy, the famous hominid fossil long thought to be the link between apes and humans, was exhumed in Hadar, about 60 kilometers south of the Serdo Block. Other hominid fossil sites abound in the southern part of the Main Ethiopian Rift and in the Eastern African Rifts of Kenya and Tanzania. Although more recent findings have suggested the existence of still older hominids, the origins of all these have remained within the African rift system.

The northern part of the rift system, the Afar, offers rocks and structures that are found under oceans elsewhere. Within the Afar, the junction point of the triple rifts, the Serdo Block essentially belongs to three plates; it is therefore rotated in response to the movement of neighboring plates. At this place, geologists and other students of the earth sciences have opportunities to field-examine three separate plate boundaries exposed over a small area.

The rift system offers economic development opportunities for the countries of the region. The hominid sites can be cordoned off for tourists to examine their origin. These are international treasures.

Salt deposits that accumulated when the northern Afar was covered by a shallow sea are economic deposits in their own right. Moreover, the mixing of the deeper waters of the Red Sea with shallow water that covered the northern Afar led to the formation of potash deposits that are interlayered with the salt deposits at Dalol. Potash is an economic deposit and is used as a fertilizer. The salt deposits are even more extensive in the Red Sea and the Gulf of Aden.

Igneous rocks, particularly cinder cones composed of gravel-sized igneous particles called "lapilli," are quarried for surfacing roads. Other rocks such as basalt are used for building homes and industrial complexes. Moreover, since freshly formed volcanic rocks weather rapidly to form rich soil, the rift basins are good agricultural areas.

The hot steam of the rift system can be harnessed to generate electricity (geothermal energy). That energy can be used for irrigation and other purposes. The hot water itself can be circulated to buildings for uses that require warm water. Public bath houses in Addis Ababa, the capital city of Ethiopia, use natural hydrothermal water.

The lakes are used for recreation, and the water is also pumped and distributed through suitable conduits for irrigation and other purposes. The lakes are sources of freshwater aquatic foods, notably fish, for animals as wells as humans. In fact, since many birds and wild land animals visit the different lakes at different seasons, the rift system and its biology are excellent laboratories for both tourists and scientists to watch or study.

The Gulf of Aden and the Red Sea are areas of sea transport for merchant and military ships and submarines. The ports along the coasts are important sources for economic development, and the coastal areas can be developed to attract tourists to bask in the warm climate. Furthermore, these seas are sources of saltwater aquatic fishes.

Bibliography

Baker, B. H., P. A. Mohr, and L. J. Williams. *Geology of the Eastern Rift System of Africa*. Geological Society Special Paper 136. New York: Geographical Society, 1972. Gives a good description of the landscape and the evolution of igneous rocks of the rift.

Chernicoff, S., and R. Vekatakrishnan. *Geology*. New York: Worth, 1995. Chapter 9 gives an excellent and well-illustrated description on faulting. Chapter 12 covers plate tectonic theory and discusses how continents split apart and drift to form oceans. This is one of many introductory geology texts offering excellent reviews on plate tectonic theory and the formation and deformation of rocks.

Compton, R. C. *Geology in the Field*. New York: John Wiley & Sons, 1985. Provides excellent descriptions of a variety of geologic field methods. Chapter 7 describes the use of aerial photographs and other remotely sensed data. Chapter 8 explains the method of mapping by using the plane table and alidade.

Moores, Eldridge M., ed. *Shaping the Earth: Tectonics of Continents and Oceans*. New York: W. H. Freeman, 1983. Provides an excellent review of various aspects of plate tectonic theory. Chapter 5, "How Continents Break Up," gives a fine description of the rift-propagation model as it applies to the Gulf of Aden.

Verbyla, D. L. *Satellite Remote Sensing of Natural Resources.* New York: Lewis, 1995. Chapters 1 and 2 of this well-written and authoritative book give the basics of satellite imaging and processing. Chapter 3 deals with spectral regions; chapters 4, 5, 6, and 7 describe corrections and classifications; and chapter 8 discusses accuracy assessment. In an age of computer application and the expanding use of satellite data, this book provides an excellent source on methodology and information.

Habte Giorgis Churnet

Cross-References

Archaeological Geology, 86; The Basin and Range Province, 157; Continental Drift, 2863; Continental Rift Zones, 275; Geysers and Hot Springs, 929; Gravity Anomalies, 997; Human Evolution, 641; Igneous Rocks: Carbonatites, 1173; The Ocean Ridge System, 1826; Plate Margins, 2063; Plate Tectonics, 2079; Volcanism at Spreading Centers, 2607.

AMAZON RIVER BASIN

Type of earth science: Hydrology
Field of study: Sedimentology

The Amazon River basin is the largest in the world, covering an area of more than 1,850,000 square miles. It is home to more plant and animal species than any other region in the world and contains thousands of species that have not yet been discovered or named.

Principal terms

BASIN: the region drained by a river system, including all of its tributaries

DELTA: the area at the mouth of a river that is built up by deposits of soil and silt

FAUNA: the animal population of a region

FLORA: the plant species of a region

TRIBUTARIES: rivers that flow into larger rivers

VÁRZEA: the part of the rain forest that is flooded for up to six months per year

Summary of the Phenomenon

The Amazon River of South America is the world's largest river, though not quite the longest. Africa's Nile River is 4,150 miles long, about 150 miles longer than the Amazon. The amount of water flowing down the Amazon is, however, about sixty times greater than that of the Nile. The Amazon carries more water than the Nile, the Mississippi, and China's great Yangtze River combined, a total that adds up to more than one-fifth of all the river water in the world. Its basin, the region drained by a river and its tributaries, includes parts of Brazil, Bolivia, Peru, Ecuador, and Colombia and measures more than 1,850,000 square miles, an area about three-fourths the size of the continental United States. More than a thousand tributaries flow into the Amazon, and the basin contains about 14,000 miles of navigable water.

There are two different types of tributaries, so-called black-water and white-water rivers. The black-water rivers, such as the Urubu, the Negrō, and the Uatama, come from very old geologic areas that are poor in salts, very acidic, and filled with sediments. They are avoided by fishermen because they have small fish populations. The water is actually tea-colored because of heavy concentrations of tannic acid. The black-water rivers have few nutrients and carry much decaying vegetation from river banks. The decaying matter, chiefly leaves and branches, consumes much of the oxygen in the water. Because of low oxygen levels, these rivers support few forms of life; they are so muddy that little light can penetrate and few plants can live in them, further reducing the food supply for fish. Indians living along these rivers call them "starvation rivers" because little food can be obtained from them. On the other hand, they can also support fewer insects and mosquitoes, making the areas around them more livable for human beings. The white-water, or clear-water, tributaries come from areas of little erosion. The waters from these streams, such as the Xingu and the Tapajos, are clear enough that the bottom is visible in many places.

The Amazon begins high in the Andes Mountains in Peru, less than 100 miles from the Pacific Ocean. There, the elevation is about 17,200 feet; for its first 600 miles, the Amazon headstream, known as the Apurímac River, drops through the mountains at a rate of about 27 feet per mile. It passes through grasslands used for grazing sheep and alpaca and by Cuzco, the old capital of the Inca Empire and the region's largest city. After passing through the Montana, an area of dense forests and steep valleys, the Apurímac flows into the Urubamba, forming a river called the Ucayali. It then heads north for about 200 miles, where the stream is joined by several smaller tributaries coming from Peru and Ecuador.

Where the Ucayali joins the Maranon, about 100 miles above the city of Iquitos, the middle course of the Amazon begins. There, the elevation is about 348 feet, and the river is 2 miles wide. It then travels through 250 miles of unpopulated territory before it enters Brazil. For the next 800 miles, the Amazon becomes a slow-moving, meandering stream, forming many huge lakes. There the Río Negrō, named for its very dark waters, enters from the north. The Río Negrō is 4 miles wide and carries water from Colombia and Venezuela. A few hundred miles downstream, the Madeira, the Amazon's longest tributary, enters from the south. Its waters come from as far away as La Páz, the capital of Bolivia, to the Paraguay River in far southern Brazil. Below the Madeira, the Amazon narrows to little more than a mile wide, but it is about 430 feet deep. It still has about 500 miles to go before it reaches the ocean.

The Xingu is the last major river to enter the Amazon, and its junction is considered the place the delta—the triangular part of a river formed by soil deposits just before it enters the sea—begins. The Xingu is about 1,000 miles long and rises in the Brazilian highlands. The Amazon Delta stretches along the Atlantic coast for about 200 miles to the north and inland for about 300 miles. The delta contains the island of Marajó. The city of Belem, population 500,000, is in the delta and is the official port of entry for the Amazon basin.

Most of the basin has a rainy tropical climate. Annual rainfall in the delta averages about 85 inches per year, with 70 inches in the middle region and 120 to 160 inches per year in the upper course. The middle course and the delta have a rainy season that lasts from December through May, during which as much as 18 inches of rain can fall every month. During this time, the floodplain, called the *várzea*, is soaked and becomes a giant lake that can be anywhere from 30 to 125 miles wide. Above the mouth of the Madeira, the Amazon flows through a different type of floodplain called the *terra firme*. There the soil is generally very poor in nutrients and unsuitable for agriculture. Even in the *várzea*, however, less than 2 percent of the floodplain can be used for farming. Mostly, there is a tropical rain forest of light woods, brush, wild cane, and grasses. The soil is poorly drained and often clayey. Cattle are grazed on Marajó Island, and Japanese farmers have brought in water buffalo, but little else can be grown or raised in the region.

There are more than thirty thousand flowering plant species in the basin. That number represents about one-third of all the flowering plants found in South America and three times the number found in all of Europe. The amount of vegetation in various areas of the river is influenced by the rise and fall of the water. Some plants are drowned during floods, while others thrive. During periods of low water, the floodplain has little vegetation. There are, however, grasses and wild rice that grow at low water. The grasses become floating islands during flood season, sometimes reaching sizes of more than a mile in length and several hundred yards wide. The islands are home to passionfruit, morning glories, and giant water lilies more than 2 feet in diameter. Ants, spiders, and grasshoppers also live on the islands. The root zone becomes a home for insects and an important source of food for fish. Many fish also eat the fruit of the plants. At low water, the islands are trapped in bushes and trees and the plants begin to rot, turning the water a deep, murky brown.

In the *várzea*, forest trees and bushes must adapt to survive during the flood season, which reaches its peak from May until July. During this period, plants become waterlogged, and the forests, or *igapo*, constantly are under water from 3 to 6 feet deep. In some cases, the shoreline is swamped all year, and many plants and trees will die. Young plants are often under water from seven to ten months per year. There, growth is also limited by lack of light, as bigger trees block out the light. In many cases, it takes seedlings ten to twenty years to reach a size that will enable them to survive. There are also other problems; for example, *kapok*, or silk-cotton trees, have been among the most successful plants in the *várzea*. In recent years, however, the species has been almost entirely destroyed by loggers cutting down trees to be made into boxes.

About nine hundred species of birds live in the Amazon, about 10 percent of the total number of bird species on the planet. About 50 percent of these species are endemic, meaning that they are found in this region and nowhere else. The bird population includes hummingbirds, macaws, owls, parakeets, parrots, toucans, and many others. Most species favor a particular level of rain forest, either on the ground or in the lower, middle, or upper level of trees. Only a few kinds of birds move between levels. The Amazon is the richest bird region in the world. There is also an enormous population of another kind of flying animal, bats, with more than fifty different species represented, making it the most diverse group of mammals in the region.

There are no crocodiles in the Amazon, but there is a smaller relative, the caiman. The black caiman can reach a length of 18 feet. Unfortunately, it is rapidly disappearing because of overhunting. Its shiny black skin, which is used for handbags and expensive shoes, is very valuable and sought by hunters.

There are believed to be somewhere between 1,300 and 2,000 species of fish in the river; in comparison, the Congo River in Africa has an estimated 560, and the Mississippi River has fewer than 300. There are so many species in the Amazon because there were no mass extinctions in the river caused by glaciers or ice ages. The huge size of the basin also provides for numerous kinds of different environments, each of which can be exploited by a unique species. There are rapids, waterfalls, lakes, and streams, each with different types of water and vegetation. Both freshwater and saltwater species are found. Lungfish, which have survived from the Paleozoic era 150 million years ago, are common.

About 43 percent of the fish are characoids, including species such as piranhas and neons that are familiar to many aquarium owners. Piranhas are a diverse group of twenty species; they are red-bellied and very dangerous. They hunt in groups of up to a hundred fish, and they are constantly in search of food. Normally, they are found in the floodplain lakes of the *várzea*. Various kinds of catfish and twenty species of stingrays are found in deeper water. One species, the piraiba catfish, is the largest fish in the river, reaching a length of 15 feet and a weight of 500 pounds. The Amazon River is also home to many dolphins, which can reach lengths of 8 feet.

Insects are by far the most diverse group in the Amazon region, with a million or more species in the area, a large number of them still unclassified. They are without a doubt the most successful animals in the rain forest. About 90 percent are arthropods, jointed invertebrates (animals without backbones); 9 percent are spiders, and 1 percent are other, more obscure kinds of insects. Insects include flies, beetles (the most diverse group), ants, scorpions, millipedes, centipedes, and symphylans. The latter are centipede-like animals that live on the floodplain floor. The floor-dwelling species generally migrate upward into the trees when the rainy season begins. In the middle and upper tree levels are spiders, moths, butterflies, and various other winged species. The most abundant species at all levels are the ants, many of them adapted to living on one particular kind of tree or plant at one specific level. Millions more live on the ground, where huge numbers of mollusks, segmented worms, and flatworms also thrive.

Several types of lizards live in the basin, iguanas being the most well known. Iguanas are typically green in color but can quickly change color to blend in with their background. They have long toes and sharp nails that enable them to climb trees, and most live at the tops of trees. Iguanas are vegetarians and can reach a size of more than a foot in length. Another kind of lizard, the teiid, can reach lengths of 5 feet. There are only a few frog species in the region, primarily because they have difficulty competing with fish for food and are easy prey for piranhas and other flesh-eating fish. There are more toads than frogs in the Amazon, as toads can more easily hide in the leaf litter that covers the ground.

The Amazon is home to the world's largest rodent, the capybara, which looks something like a large guinea pig and lives in groups of a dozen or more along the riverbanks, feeding on grasses and other plants. The capybara is being rapidly reduced in numbers, however, because it is intensively hunted for food by native peoples. Other rodents include the torospiny rat, a common night hunter; tree-dwelling porcupines; anteaters, which also eat termites; leaf-eating sloths; five species of opossums; and several species of armadillos. Most of these groups migrated into the basin from the north when Central America became connected to South America via Panama from 3 million to 4 million years ago.

There are some hoofed mammals in the basin, but most species of this type have become extinct. The tapir is the oldest hoofed mammal in the basin and the only one that enters the river, usually for bathing and to eat fish. Monkeys are abundant in the region, with more than forty species found. There are two main groups. Marmosets and tamarins form one group; they live in small groups in trees and are most active during the day. Cebids, the other major group, include capuchins and howlers. They are much larger than species in the first group, have large brains, and resemble African apes.

There are 160 species of snakes in the Amazon; most live on the floodplain or on the riverbank. Only the coral snakes and vipers are poisonous. The area's pit vipers are among the most dangerous snakes in the world. They hunt at night, reach lengths of 3 feet, and live on a diet of small animals. The anaconda is the largest snake in the basin, reaching a length of 20 feet. It is not poisonous but kills by squeezing its victims to death. It is most active at night, grabbing birds, rodents, turtles, or caimans by the neck and coiling around and crushing them until they are soft enough to digest. Boa constrictors use the same method of capturing their food and are common in the water and on the shore.

Manatees, the largest animal in the Amazon, weighing 1,000 pounds or more, are found in large numbers. These relatives of the elephant eat grasses and plants and live in the water. They can stay under water for more than an hour before coming to the surface to breathe. Other animals include coatis, which resemble raccoons; several kinds of deer; and peccaries, or wild hogs. Human beings were the last species to enter the basin, perhaps about ten thousand years ago.

Methods of Study

The European discovery of the Amazon took place in 1500, when Vincenté Yáñez Pinzón, a companion of Christopher Columbus, sailed past the river along the Atlantic coast. Recent investigations by geologists have shown that prior to the rise of the Andes Mountains, perhaps 20 million years ago, the Amazon flowed to the west into the Pacific. The river reversed its course during the drastic changes taking place during the Miocene era and began draining large areas of its new floodplain all the way to the Atlantic.

Indians lived in the Amazon Basin for perhaps nine thousand years before Pinzón made his discovery. It was not until 1541, however, that a Spaniard, Francisco de Orellana, made the first European exploration of the river. Orellana began his expedition in Peru and sailed down the river until he reached the Atlantic. Along the way, his party was attacked by Indians—who, the Spaniards later said, were all female. Hence, they called them "Amazons," a name given to a legendary group of female warriors by the ancient Greeks. The name was later given to the entire river.

For the first three hundred years after European exploration began, the Amazon remained virtually empty of settlements. In the 1850's, however, Portuguese settlers found rubber trees in the region, and the basin became the world's most important source of rubber. Nearly a century later, the invention of synthetic rubber during World War II almost wiped out the demand for organic rubber and destroyed the region's economy. In the 1960's, the government of Brazil began building thousands of miles of highways in the region to promote economic development. Airports and railroads were also developed, and a population boom ensued. New towns and farms were established, and thousands of Japanese immigrants were brought in to raise crops and graze beef cattle.

The cities and towns of what is now called Amazonia grew at spectacular rates. Belém, at the gateway to the river region, had almost a million people in 1990, while Manaus, the region's second-largest city, had more than 600,000. This huge increase in human population and development has had a sometimes devastating impact on the environment. Logging operations have proven particularly disastrous for the rain forest. Thousands of square miles of trees have been cut down for timber, paper, and manufacturing since the beginning of development. The clearing of forest in the *várzea* to open new cropland has also harmed the river's ecology. Thousands of fish have died because the cutting of trees has reduced their chief supply of food, the flowers and fruits of the trees. The building of hydroelectric dams on the river has also led to the destruction of millions of acres of forest and has endangered the future of thousands of species of animals.

Context

The Amazon River basin has the world's most diverse population of animals and plants. An estimated 11 percent of the total amount of the world's fresh water flows down its course. The rapid destruction of the region's rain forest also affects the world's climate. Still, the demands of economic development for Brazil require use of the vast resources available in the basin. Some mineral deposits, including gold, have been discovered there, and mining of these resources has led to further habitat destruction. Yet it is logging, frequently done without any restrictions or concern for the environment, that has caused the greatest problems. It is estimated that an area of rain forest about the size of the state of Maryland is destroyed every year. Even given the tremendous size of the Amazon basin, such large-scale cutting cannot be sustained without major consequences for the region's flora, fauna, and habitat.

Bibliography

Davis, Wade. *One River: Explorations and Discoveries in the Amazon Rain Forest.* New York: Simon & Schuster, 1996. A history of human exploration of the region. Includes much information on local peoples and the impact of modern economic development. Well written, with many photographs, and a useful index.

Furneaux, Robin. *The Amazon: The Story of a Great River.* New York: Putnam, 1970. A still-useful resource, with many photos and detailed descriptions of major plant and animal species. Recounts the history of human settlement and exploration in the region.

Malkus, Alida S. *The Amazon: River of Promise.* New York: McGraw-Hill, 1970. Especially written for younger readers. Contains a wide amount of useful and interesting information about the major plant and animal species in the area.

Moran, Emilio. *Developing the Amazon.* Bloomington: Indiana University Press, 1981. An economist's view of development in the river basin. Pays some attention to the ecological losses caused by development. Written mainly for specialists in development; however, contains some excellent maps and descriptions of the region's geography.

Smith, Nigel J. H. *Man, Fishes, and the Amazon.* New York: Columbia University Press, 1981. A brief but detailed exploration by an anthropologist who lived in the basin for several years. Contains a lengthy discussion of the different kinds of fish found in the river and how they are trapped and caught by local Indians. Ends with a plea for respect for the traditional lives of native peoples. Also has information on climate and the impact of industrialization on the region. Interesting descriptions of traditional ways of life, some photographs, and a detailed index.

Leslie V. Tischauser

Cross-References

The Andes, 54; Deltas, 332; Floodplains, 712; Nile River, 3024; River Bed Forms, 2196; River Flow, 2203; River Valleys, 2210.

ASTEROID IMPACT

Type of earth science: Planetology
Field of study: Geomorphology

Projecting what would happen if an asteroid struck Earth occupies the time of a number of scientific researchers. Geologic evidence indicates that Earth has been struck by large asteroids and meteorites numerous times in the past. The chances of an asteroid colliding with Earth again are quite high. The energy from a large asteroid impact would equal the explosion of five billion atomic bombs and would transform Earth into a bleak and devastated planet.

Principal terms

AMOR: one of a class of asteroids with orbits that approach, but do not intersect, the orbit of Earth

APOLLO: one of a class of asteroids with orbits that intersect that of Earth

ASTEROID: any small, rocky, airless body that orbits a star; three main kinds have been identified in the solar system: carbonaceous, siliceous, and metallic

HYPERVELOCITY: a speed with a Mach number greater than five

IMPACT CRATER: a large, bowl-shaped depression in a planet's surface made by the impact of a large meteoroid, asteroid, or comet

MEGATON: a unit of explosive force equal to one million tons of TNT

RAREFACTION: the process by which high pressure in a shock wave is relieved by the propagation of release waves from free surfaces into the shocked material

SHOCK METAMORPHISM: a term used to describe changes in rocks and minerals resulting from the passage of transient, high-pressure shock waves

SHOCK WAVE: a very sharp, thin, compression wave front generated when energy is suddenly released or deposited into a medium occupying a limited space

TSUNAMI: a giant, long-period sea wave caused by oceanic disturbances, such as earthquakes, volcanic eruptions, and hypervelocity impacts

Summary of the Phenomenon

Asteroids are small, rocky bodies, less than about 1,000 kilometers in diameter, with a heliocentric orbit in the inner solar system. There are more than two hundred known asteroids with diameters greater than 100 kilometers, about one thousand with diameters greater than 30 kilometers, and another million with diameters greater than

1 kilometer. The three largest asteroids to be identified are Ceres (1,025 kilometers in diameter), Pallas (583 kilometers in diameter), and Vesta (555 kilometers in diameter). Their combined mass is about half of the combined total mass of all known asteroids.

The asteroids lie mostly between Mars and Jupiter in a zone called the Asteroid belt, where a tenth planet might have formed during the formation of the solar system; however, asteroids were apparently too strongly influenced by the gravitational pull of Jupiter to combine to form a planet. The gravitational acceleration caused by Jupiter creates asteroid velocities that are too fast, and individual collisions that are too energetic, to allow colliding asteroids to unite and form a planet.

Asteroids orbit in concentrated belts separated by gaps. The gaps occur at distances related to the orbit time of Jupiter. Asteroids rarely collide, but when they do, the collisions may be at speeds up to 30 kilometers per second. The force of these collisions may nudge an asteroid into one of the gaps in the Asteroid belt. An asteroid nudged into a gap experiences additional gravitational acceleration from Jupiter, making its orbit path more eccentric and, thus, more likely to collide with a planet or moon.

There are more than thirteen hundred asteroids, called "Apollos," with highly elliptical orbits that periodically bring them inside the orbit of Earth. All asteroids with Earth-crossing orbits threaten collision with Earth. Another group of asteroids, called "Amors," pass near Earth but intercept the orbit of Mars. These two groups of asteroids are the suspected source of large asteroids and meteorites that occasionally strike Earth.

The amount of energy released by an asteroid colliding with Earth would depend upon the asteroid's speed and mass. Incoming objects in excess of 350 tons may impact Earth at speeds as high as 30 to 40 kilometers per second. In the first few milliseconds after the asteroid entered Earth's atmosphere, friction between the asteroid and the air would raise the temperature of the outer layers of the asteroid to several thousand degrees centigrade, vaporizing and ablating some of the asteroid's surface but doing little to decelerate the object. The kinetic energy of such an asteroid would be so great that the speed would be only slightly reduced, and only a small fraction of its total mass would be ablated prior to impact. For truly large asteroids, this scenario would have little bearing. An asteroid with a diameter of 10 kilometers would be comparable in thickness to the main portion of Earth's atmosphere, so aerodynamic drag would have little decelerating effect. When the front of the asteroid reached the surface of Earth, the trailing edge of the asteroid would still be in the stratosphere.

The impact process is similar to a water drop falling into a still body of water. At the moment of impact, water springs upward, ripples and troughs surround the impact point, and a spray of fine water moves upward and outward. Although water quickly returns to its normal state, rocks altered by impact remain broken, melted, and shocked for the rest of their existence. At the moment of an asteroid's impact, a number of complicated processes would begin, starting with the formation of shock waves traveling down into the target rocks and simultaneously upward into the asteroid. The shock waves formed on impact would travel through both target and projectile at speeds greater than 10 kilometers per second, but as the asteroid would be traveling downward quicker, it would continue on a downward course. As the shock waves traveled through the target rocks, they would instantly cause temperatures reaching many thousands of degrees centigrade and pressures exceeding 100 gigapascals, a value more than the weight of a million atmospheres. In less than a thousandth of a second, the shock waves would penetrate several hundred meters from the point of impact and engulf the asteroid and the target region in very high pressure.

One of the most interesting by-products of impact-generated shock waves is the effect they have on rocks and minerals. When a rock or mineral is exposed to a high-pressure shock wave, its state is often altered by a process known as shock metamorphism. Natural shock metamorphism is produced by the nearly instantaneous transfer of kinetic energy by means of intense shock waves directly into the rocks. The results of this quick energy transfer have distinct and dramatic effects on the density, crystal structure, and composition of the rock.

Within the initial second of the impact, a rarefaction wave would follow the shock front into the target, eventually catching up with the shock-accelerated target rocks. The enormous pressures behind the expanding initial shock wave would be much greater than the strength of the asteroid or the target rocks, and neither could remain solid. Initially, the asteroid and the target rocks would liquefy, but as the angle of ejection increased, they would jet upward and outward from the point of impact. Rarefaction waves always travel behind shock waves, their effect being confined by the pressure of surrounding material; when they approach the surface of an impacted target, however, the pressure of the air above ground is inadequate to contain them. After a large impact, the rarefaction waves burst from the ground and expand the shock-compressed target materials, hurling them in all directions at speeds approaching 80 kilometers per second. This ejection process is responsible for the formation of bowl-like impact craters.

During the formation of a crater, the ground hundreds of meters below the crater begins to move, rebounding upward after the passage of the shock waves formed on impact. Blocks of rock hundreds to thousands of meters below ground, free from overlying pressure, lift toward the surface to form a domed uplift near the crater's center.

More than 70 percent of Earth's surface is covered by water; as a result, it is most likely that an impacting asteroid would strike an oceanic target. The average depth of Earth's oceans is roughly 5 kilometers. If an asteroid 10 kilometers in diameter were to strike the ocean, in the fraction of a second that it would take to reach the ocean's floor, half the asteroid would still be above sea level. The impact of the asteroid with seawater would compress the water to several times its normal density, and its temperature would rise to many thousands of degrees centigrade, producing a steam bubble that could have a volume of many hundreds of cubic kilometers and enough explosive power to eject debris to the upper reaches of the atmosphere. The energy of this rock and water-vapor explosion would be equal to about 10 million megatons of trinitrotoluene (TNT). The tsunami resulting from the impact and the atmospheric blast waves would affect millions of square kilometers of territory surrounding the impact site. Shock waves from the impact would heat the air to more than 3,000 degrees Fahrenheit and generate winds many hundreds of kilometers an hour, blowing for up to twenty hours and reaching several thousand kilometers from the impact site. The tsunami created by such an oceanic impact might reach 5 kilometers above sea level as it raced toward shore. If such a wave reached a shoreline unbroken, massive flooding of coastal regions would result. The destructive powers of post-impact winds and tsunamis are probably not globally significant, but anything within about 1,000 kilometers of the impact area would be destroyed. Objects above ground would face the possibility of being shredded by an expanding fireball of steam and high-speed molten ejecta from the crater; a large-scale firestorm would result as superheated rock and debris rained from the sky, igniting anything flammable. A massive earthquake with an estimated Richter scale magnitude as high as thirteen, followed by numerous powerful aftershocks, would follow the impact. The total area directly affected by the impact of a 10-kilometer asteroid would be approximately three million square kilometers, or about 1 percent of Earth's surface.

On a global scale, huge amounts of nitrogen oxides circulating in the atmosphere would eventually fall as acid rain; a massive dust cloud and ejecta plume injected into the atmosphere would block sunlight and make photosynthesis nearly impossible, at the same time lowering global temperatures to winter-like conditions; and water vapor and carbon dioxide remaining in the atmosphere long after the dust cloud settled would result in a reversal of winter conditions and lead to a dramatic warming of global temperatures. The problems resulting from added carbon dioxide would be greatly increased if the asteroid struck target rocks rich in limestone ($CaCO_3$). The vaporizing limestone would inject enormous amounts of carbon dioxide into the atmosphere, many times more than that needed to cause even a modest raising of global temperatures. Large amounts of added water vapor in the atmosphere could also dramatically reduce atmospheric ozone, which filters harmful ultraviolet radiation from the Sun.

Methods of Study

The odds are extremely small that an asteroid will hit Earth in the near future. Yet so many people would be killed if such an event did happen—an estimated one and a half billion human casualties—that the probabilities become skewed. Because the risks from asteroid impact are high, the situation has been evaluated for defensive actions that humans might take.

The problem presented by a possible asteroid impact was addressed at an international workshop in 1991-1992 by the National Aeronautics and Space Administration (NASA) at the request of the U.S. Congress. The risks analyzed were those presented by objects with diameters greater than 1 kilometer. About 90 percent of the potential impactors are near-Earth asteroids. There are more than two thousand known near-Earth objects, and between 25 and 50 percent are expected to strike Earth eventually; however, the average estimated time interval between impacts is thought to exceed one hundred thousand years. The risk of an individual on Earth being killed by the impact of an asteroid with a diameter of 1 kilometer or greater in any fifty-year period is estimated to be about one in twenty thousand.

At present, research into impact-cratering processes is conducted experimentally by use of high-velocity guns and high-speed cameras, such as those at the NASA Vertical Gun Range at the Ames Research Center, or by observing the effects of high-energy explosions, most notably the detonations of nuclear devices. By applying basic physical principles and scaling laws to observations of craters produced in the laboratory or on the test range, researchers can make extrapolations and assumptions concerning the outcome of an asteroidal impact with Earth.

Because the possibility of an Apollo asteroid striking Earth is relatively high, identifying and tracking asteroids is a high astronomical priority. The development of high-technology observational equipment has resulted in the Spacewatch camera. Spacewatch is a joint project of NASA, the Steward Observatory, and the University of Arizona. The Spacewatch camera uses a normal, computer-controlled telescope combined with an advanced electronic detector known as a charge coupled device, or CCD. The CCD is more sensitive than a photographic plate or film and can detect fainter objects, but its main advantage is that its electronically formed images can be directly inputted into a computer. To discover a moving object, all the Spacewatch camera does is take repeated images of the same region of the sky a few hours apart, then use the computer to search for any objects that may have changed position between exposures. If movement is detected, the computer, which already knows the positions of the asteroids and the times at which the images were taken, can immediately attempt to calculate the object's orbit and advise astronomers whether the object is a new discovery or an imminent threat to Earth.

If an asteroid were discovered to be on a collision course with Earth, the warning would most likely be measured in days, not months or years. As no true asteroid defense system exists on Earth, it is almost certain that nothing could be done to avert an impact. The only realistic option would be to try to predict the point of impact and attempt to evacuate the region. Since the impact would produce a crater more than 100 kilometers in diameter, and since the shock waves would devastate an area of thousands of square kilometers, evacuation would not be practical. In fact, attempts to minimize the immediate loss of life from such an impact might be almost irrelevant because of the severe long-term ecological effects such an impact would have. Natural factors quite beyond human control would determine whether or not humankind survived.

At present, three options are being considered to defend Earth from the catastrophe of an asteroid impact: to divert the asteroid so that it would miss Earth; to break it into pieces in the hope that the fragments would miss Earth, accepting the risk that the remaining pieces might still do damage; and to try to blast the entire asteroid into dust-size particles that would burn up upon entering Earth's atmosphere. In each case, the need for swift decision making, precise timing, political consensus, global cooperation, mutual trust, and the use of nuclear weapons would make such options extremely difficult to put into practical effect.

Context

Asteroids abound in the belt between Jupiter and Mars. The strong gravitational force of Jupiter sends asteroid fragments outbound on collision courses with nearby planets, including Earth. Statistically, the risk of being killed by an asteroid impact is about the same as that of dying in an airplane crash, and about three times greater than that of dying as the result of a flood or tornado. Humankind has the ability to locate incoming asteroids, but altering their courses or destroying them prior to impact is beyond present technological and political capabilities.

If struck by an asteroid, Earth would be subjected to great stress. Such an impact would generate large-scale earthquakes, cause wide-ranging firestorms, and inject the atmosphere with dust, ash, and gases that would result in major changes in atmospheric composition. These changes to the atmosphere would alter global temperature regimes, solar radiation and sunlight reception, the chemical composition of precipitation, and the overall chemical composition of the atmosphere. The results of these global stresses would have a profound effect on living organisms on Earth. Those organisms unable to adapt to the rapid global changes would become extinct.

The resulting dust cloud from an asteroid impact would be as much as seventeen miles thick and would envelope the entire planet in twenty-four hours. Computer simulations indicate that no sunlight could penetrate such a dust-filled atmosphere. The surface of Earth would be shrouded in a darkness thirty times darker than a moonless night for as long as six months. Such a period of extended darkness would halt photosynthesis in all plant life except for the hardiest Arctic plankton. This die-off of plant life would trigger a collapse of the marine and terrestrial food chains.

Earth's surface, shielded from the Sun's rays, would rapidly radiate away its store of heat. Within weeks of the impact, temperatures would plummet to subfreezing. The darkness and cold would prevent most large animals from finding adequate food stocks, and they would starve. In addition, those creatures unprepared for such a drastic environmental change and unable to locate sufficient food would weaken and be subjected to increased risk of disease.

As water vapor in the atmosphere gradually condensed and mixed with the nitric oxides ejected during impact, falling precipitation would become as corrosive as battery acid. The toxic snow and rain would defoliate plants, acidify water, and leach highly toxic metals from soils and rocks; they would then migrate to other bodies of water, poisoning them. It is also theorized that the influx of these strong acids into marine waters would dissolve carbonaceous sediments and organisms, resulting in a massive release of carbon dioxide into the atmosphere. This gaseous release would alter atmospheric composition for a considerable period of time, at least until solar radiation and renewed plant life could begin the long, slow renewal of an atmosphere conducive to life.

Bibliography

Gehrels, T., ed. *Asteroids*. Tucson: University of Arizona Press, 1979. A collection of scientific papers on asteroids. This book, while not for general audiences, is a good reference for college readers or those with basic knowledge of astronomy.

Grieve, R. A. F., et al., eds. *Astronaut's Guide to Terrestrial Impact Craters*. Houston: National Aeronautics and Space Administration, 1988. Contains black-and-white remote-sensing images and topographic maps showing the locations of known terrestrial impact craters. Little text, but a useful bibliography.

Hodge, Paul. *Meteorite Craters and Impact Structures of the Earth*. New York: Cambridge University Press, 1994. Catalogs more than one hundred fifty known impact craters on Earth. The descriptions of the craters are based on published accounts and personal experiences. Many illustrations.

Lewis, S., et al., eds. *Comets, Asteroids, and Meteorites*. Alexandria, Va.: Time-Life Books, 1990. A richly illustrated general reference book on the subject of "celestial visitors." For general audiences; contains a wealth of information.

Melosh, H. J. *Impact Cratering: A Geologic Process*. New York: Oxford University Press, 1989. The most complete publication available on impact cratering. While somewhat technical, the book is suitable for college-level readers with a basic background in physics. Indispensable for anyone interested in impact-cratering processes.

Silver, L. T., and P. H. Schultz, eds. *Geological Implications of Impacts of Large Asteroids and Comets on the Earth*. Boulder, Colo.: The Geological Society of America, 1982. Contains topical papers from a conference on large-body impacts and terrestrial evolution. Contains many of the most important research papers published on crater identification and impact processes.

Randall L. Milstein

Cross-References

ATMOSPHERIC THERMODYNAMICS

Type of earth science: Atmospheric sciences and meteorology

Atmospheric thermodynamics involves the process by which energy from the sun is absorbed and deposited on the earth, oceans, and atmosphere. The processes of solar radiation and infrared radiation are approximately balanced globally, but they are often transiently out of balance locally, accounting for everyday changes in the weather.

Principal terms

ADIABATIC TEMPERATURE CHANGE: the cooling or warming of air caused by its expansion or compression

AIR POLLUTANTS: airborne particles and gases that have the potential to disrupt the normal thermodynamics of the atmosphere and endanger the health of organisms

ATMOSPHERE: the gaseous environment that surrounds a planet; Earth's atmosphere is divided vertically into four layers on the basis of temperature

ENVIRONMENTAL LAPSE RATE: the general temperature decrease within the troposphere; the rate is variable but averages approximately 6.5 degrees Celsius per kilometer

GROWING DEGREE-DAY INDEX: a measurement system that uses thermal principles to estimate the approximate date when crops will be ready for harvest

LATENT HEAT: the energy absorbed or released during a state of change

MESOSPHERE: the atmospheric layer above the stratosphere where temperature drops rapidly

NET RADIATIVE HEATING: the driving force for atmospheric thermodynamics, basically computed as the difference between solar heating and infrared cooling

SENSIBLE HEAT: heat that can be felt or measured with a thermometer

STRATOSPHERE: the atmospheric zone above the troposphere that has the greatest ozone concentration and exhibits isothermal conditions followed by a gradual temperature increase

TEMPERATURE GRADIENT: the change in temperature with displacement in a given direction

TEMPERATURE INVERSION: an abnormal increase in air temperature with increasing elevation from Earth's surface

THERMODYNAMICS: a scientific field concerned with equilibrium states and changes in system properties following transformations from one state to another

THERMOSPHERE: the atmospheric zone beyond the mesosphere in which temperature rises rapidly with increasing distance from the earth's surface

TROPOSPHERE: the lowest atmospheric layer, marked by considerable turbulence and a decrease in temperature with increasing altitude

WET BULB GLOBE TEMPERATURE: a heat-stress index that includes measurements of relative humidity, radiant heat, and ambient temperature

WINDCHILL: a measurement of apparent temperature that quantifies the effects of ambient wind and temperature on the rate of cooling of the human body

Summary of the Phenomenon

Atmospheric thermodynamics can be described as the process by which energy from sunlight is absorbed and deposited on Earth's surface, in the oceans, and in the atmosphere. This energy must be returned to space in the form of infrared radiation in order for the planet to maintain a cyclic range of ambient temperatures within normal limits. Even though solar radiation and infrared radiation must be approximately balanced on a global level, they are frequently out of balance on a local level, accounting for the ambient weather changes seen on a day-by-day basis.

Solar absorption is most concentrated on Earth's surface, particularly in tropical regions, whereas most of the infrared radiation going out to space originates in the middle troposphere and is more evenly distributed between equatorial and polar regions. Time-averaged temperature distribution is maintained by the system by transporting heat from regions where solar heating dominates over infrared cooling to regions where radiative cooling is able to dominate. In this way, the atmosphere transports heat from the ground to the upper troposphere, and the atmosphere and the ocean work together to transport heat toward the Arctic and Antarctic poles from the equatorial belt.

Net radiative heating, the difference between solar heating and infrared cooling, is the driving force for atmospheric thermodynamics. Solar radiation reaches the top of the atmosphere, where about 30 percent of it is reflected back into space. The remaining radiation is absorbed. About 70 percent of solar absorption happens at the surface, and about 40 percent of that leaves the surface as net infrared radiation. This serves to leave a net surface radiative heating of about 150 watts per square meter. On a global and annual average, the net radiative heating of Earth's surface is equivalent to the net radiative cooling of the atmosphere; normal thermodynamics within the atmosphere thus maintains an appropriate balance between the two. A prolonged and severe imbalance between these two systems would result in global warming, which could melt the polar ice caps and raise the elevations of the oceans.

Over the oceans, most of the net radiative heating of the surface is used in the process of water evaporation. Energy is removed from the surface as latent heat; when this vapor condenses, it deposits almost all of its latent heat into the air rather than into the condensed water, which returns to the surface as precipitation. The result is that heat is transported from the surface to the air, where the potential for condensation takes place. On a global average, about 70 percent of the net radiative heating of the surface is removed by latent heat flux, and the remaining 30 percent leaves the surface by conduction of the sensible heat to the overlying air. The atmosphere thus experiences diabatic heating or cooling from four ongoing processes: latent heating, sensible heating at the surface, solar absorption, and infrared heating or cooling.

Earth's atmosphere is divided vertically into four layers on the basis of temperature: the troposphere, the stratosphere, the mesosphere, and the thermosphere. The troposphere is the layer closest to the surface, where temperature increases with an increase in altitude. The term "troposphere" literally means the region where air "turns over"—an accurate description of the process of vertical mixing. The general temperature decrease within the troposphere is called the "environmental lapse rate," which is variable but averages approximately 6.5 degrees Celsius per kilometer.

The occurrence of shallow layers where temperatures actually reverse this normal pattern and get hotter with increasing height is known as a "temperature inversion." Temperature inversions are often seen in cities located at high altitudes with a low partial pressure of oxygen, and in basins surrounded by mountains that serve to block winds and trap industrial pollutants. A "greenhouse effect" inversion causes a reversal of an ecosystem's normal atmospheric temperature gradient, cooking harmful chemicals and enhancing their negative effects on organisms living below. A notable example is the strong eastern wind that blows toward Denver, Colorado, and traps a brown cloud of pollutants against the Rocky Mountains. This requires the daily broadcast of air-quality reports on radio and television and leads to the frequent calls for weak and elderly residents to stay indoors during hotter parts of the day. Trapped carbon monoxide, coming mainly from automobile tailpipes via the incomplete combustion of gasoline, combines quickly with hemoglobin, the oxygen-carrying compound in the blood in humans and animals. By taking up binding sites on the hemoglobin molecule, carbon monoxide impairs oxygen delivery to the tissues. Elderly persons with heart disease are at special risk of any restrictions in oxygen delivery.

Of all common air pollutants, ozone is the most toxic and presents the greatest danger to the body. A high-ozone environment can cause lung irritation and coughing, shallow breathing, headaches, and nausea. Long periods of breathing ozone combined with hydrocarbons, aerosols, and other pollutants may contribute to the production of allergies, asthma, pulmonary emphysema, bronchitis, and lung cancer.

In the vast majority of areas where a temperature inversion does not take place, the normal temperature gradient in the bottom layer continues to decrease to an average height of approximately 12 kilometers. However, the thickness of the troposphere around Earth's surface is quite variable. The troposphere reaches heights in excess of 16 kilometers in the tropics as compared to less than 9 kilometers at the poles. Warm surface temperatures and a greater rate of thermal mixing are responsible for the greater height of the troposphere near the equator, in addition to accounting for the hotter ambient temperatures experienced at the surface. The troposphere is under continual observation by meteorologists, who attempt to predict the weather. This "weather sphere" contains almost all the clouds and all the precipitation that falls to the surface and is the area where potentially disastrous weather patterns such as lightning storms, tornadoes, and hurricanes are born.

Atmospheric thermodynamics are continually evident within the troposphere, but the layer just above it, the stratosphere, does not exhibit this large-scale turbulence and mixing. The temperature remains nearly constant within the stratosphere up to an altitude of about 20 kilometers, where a sharp temperature increase occurs until a height of approximately 50 kilometers. Higher temperatures occur here because the stratosphere is the region where ozone, which absorbs ultraviolet radiation from the Sun, is most concentrated. Just above the stratosphere is the mesosphere, where temperatures again decrease until a distance of about 80 kilometers from the surface. Temperatures in the mesosphere approach −90 degrees Celsius and extend upward to the thermosphere.

The thermosphere, which does not have well-defined limits, exhibits another increase in temperature as a result of the absorption of very short-wavelength solar energy by atoms of oxygen and nitrogen. Although temperatures rise to values in excess of 1,000 degrees Celsius in this outermost layer, it is difficult to compare the temperature here with that seen on the earth's surface. Temperature is directly proportional to the average speed at which molecules are moving, and because gases within the thermosphere are moving at very high speeds, ambient temperature remains very high. However, the gases in this region are so sparse that only a minimal amount of these fast-moving air molecules collide with a foreign body, thus causing only a minimal amount of energy to be transferred. For this reason, the temperature of a satellite orbiting Earth in the thermosphere is determined by the amount of solar radiation it absorbs and not directly by the temperature of the surrounding environment. Thus, if an astronaut in the space shuttle were to expose his or her hand outside into ambient space, it would not feel hot.

Methods of Study

While historians continue to debate whether Christopher Columbus was the first to discover America, he was undoubtedly the first to document the winds that were able to blow a ship there. During the 1700's, the wind was not merely a part of the weather; it provided the necessary energy source for a craft to sail the ocean. The cause leading to Columbus' discovery when the wind blew him west has since been determined to be uneven atmospheric temperature and pressure in combination with the rotation of the earth and turbulence caused by the roughness of the ground's surface. Intense solar heating along the equator causes uneven hot and cold temperatures in the earth's "hot belt" as it rotates. This region is known as "the doldrums" because prolonged stretches of calm weather often stalled sailing ships for weeks at a time, leaving sailors with dwindling food and water supplies. In the Northern Hemisphere, heated air rises and moves northward until it enters the polar regions, where it cools, sinks, and gradually rotates back to the equator. As the air warms, its density is reduced, and the barometric pressure drops. Pressure differences caused by atmospheric thermodynamic changes are the driving force behind wind movement, which pushes cooler and denser air from regions of high pressure to warmer and less-dense regions of low air pressure.

The greater the difference in pressure, the stronger the wind. Thus, a westerly wind means that the wind is blowing toward the east, typically because of a higher barometric pressure in the west. In general, a high-pressure system will produce fair weather, while a barometer reading that is steadily falling for several days will enable the wind to bring in cloudiness, a rise in humidity, and possible rain or snow. The real question regarding thermodynamics and its effect on wind and weather is not what the average barometric pressure is but whether the pressure is rising or falling and, if so, how fast.

If barometric pressure were the only force affecting the wind, it would simply move in a straight line from high to low pressure. The only point where this can theoretically occur, however, is close to the equator, because of the influence of the rotation of the earth. The counterclockwise eastward rotation of the earth, which completes one rotation every twenty-four hours, causes different wind velocities in various global locations depending upon their distance from the equator. The further one gets from the equator, the greater the effect of rotation on wind speed.

The "trade winds" that Columbus and other early explorers discovered blow from the edge of the equator to about 30 degrees north and south latitude. These north-easterly winds are formed as heated air in the equatorial belt rises and embarks toward the polar regions, as the earth's rotation sends it on a curving path. This air is cooled quickly, drops to lower altitudes as its density increases, and makes a southwestern turn back to the equator.

Not all the rapidly cooling air is reversed to a southern direction by the time 30 degrees latitude is reached. Some continues northward and passes through a band lying between 30 and 60 degrees north latitude. There, the rotation of the earth turns the flow so that the winds travel from the southwest, becoming the "prevailing westerlies."

The final point of thermodynamic deflection occurs at about 60 degrees as the winds enter a third band and are shifted for a final time. These "polar easterlies" become heavy with increasing cold and sink to low altitudes, generating considerable force as a consequence of their distance from the equator as they begin the journey back to the earth's midline. The same winds as are also seen in the Southern Hemisphere, with the difference that the north/south direction of flow is reversed. The southern trade winds flow toward the equator from the southeast, the prevailing westerlies come from the northwest, and the polar easterlies rise from the southeast.

Wind speed and direction are also affected by altitude and the roughness of the earth's surface. As a general rule, wind speed increases greatly with higher altitudes, because the difference in pressure between two barometric pressure systems increases with height. Aircraft flying between North America and Europe use this to their advantage as they cruise in the jet streams at thirty-one thousand feet. Because of the prevailing westerlies, airplanes can fly eastbound from New York to Europe about two hours faster than they can make the return trip against the wind. Mountains, hills, forests, skyscrapers, and other obstructions that cause roughness in the earth's surface create irregular eddies of moving air. The intensity of these erratic gusts, or "turbulence," increases considerably over cities and mountains and decreases considerably over level plains.

Context

By the late twentieth century, much thermodynamic information had been collected describing the air close to the earth's surface, but upper atmospheric conditions could be estimated only using indirect methods. Data from balloons and kites could only reveal that air temperature dropped with increasing elevation from the immediate surface and that ambient air temperature experienced regular fluctuations. Without the ability to take measurements, early scientists estimated that air temperature continued to drop with increasing height to a value of absolute zero (−273 degrees Celsius) at the outer edge of the atmosphere. The French scientist Leon Philippe Teisserenc de Bort disproved this theory through use of balloon experiments, which revealed that ambient temperature tended to level off at altitudes between 8 kilometers and 12 kilometers. In the decades to come, radio waves and rocket-sounding techniques were employed to further document the temperature structure of the atmosphere and its changes.

There are many practical applications of the knowledge of thermodynamic data, one of which is regularly utilized by the agricultural industry to estimate the approximate date when crops will be ready for harvest. The growing degree-day index estimates the number of growing degree-days for a particular crop on any given day as the difference between the daily mean temperature and the minimum temperature required for growth of a particular crop. For example, the minimum growing temperature for corn is 50 degrees Fahrenheit (10 degrees Celsius), which means that on a day when the mean temperature is 75 degrees Fahrenheit, the number of growing degree-days for sweet corn is estimated at twenty-five. Starting with the onset of the growth season, the daily growing degree-day values are added. If two thousand growing degree-days are needed for corn to mature in a particular region, the corn should be ready to harvest when the accumulation reaches that figure.

Heat-stress index and windchill factor are other examples of the use of regularly changing environmental data. One heat-stress index developed by the military is called the "wet bulb globe temperature" (WBGT), which is derived from measurements of relative humidity, radiant heat, and ambient air temperature. The American College of Sports Medicine recommends that sponsors of athletic events warn participants of possible heat illnesses and dehydration problems beyond certain levels of WBGT. At the other end of the spectrum, windchill factor shows that even if environmental temperature is well above freezing, a chilling 35-mile-per-hour wind will reduce a temperature of 40 degrees Fahrenheit to an apparent temperature of 10 degrees Fahrenheit. Similarly, windchill factor will decrease a 10 degree Fahrenheit temperature to an apparent temperature of −30 degrees Fahrenheit with a 25-mile-per-hour wind speed. These are only a few examples of the practical importance of the understanding of atmospheric thermodynamics.

Bibliography

Ahrens, C. D. *Meteorology Today: An Introduction to Weather, Climate, and the Environment*. Minneapolis, Minn.: West Publishing, 1994. A useful text designed for college-level students taking an introductory course on atmospheric science.

American Meteorological Society. "Policy Statement of the American Meteorological Society of Global Climate Change." *Bulletin of the American Meteorological Society* 72 (1991): 57-59. A review of current knowledge and a call for more research into the nature of climate variability.

Burroughs, W. J. *Watching the World's Weather*. New York: Cambridge University Press, 1991. A very readable text with helpful explanations regarding weather changes in all parts of the world.

Campbell, I. M. *Energy and the Atmosphere: A Physical-Chemical Approach*. New York: John Wiley & Sons, 1986. An excellent text on the physical and chemical nature of the atmosphere and the effects of pollution.

Eagleman, J. R. *Air Pollution Meteorology*. Lenexa, Kans.: Trimedia Publishing, 1991. Describes the role of the earth's atmosphere in dissipating industrial air pollution, with regard to thermodynamic principles.

Grotjahn, R. *Global Atmospheric Circulations: Observations and Theories*. Oxford, England: Oxford University Press, 1993. An advanced text that provides a useful presentation of old concepts and new theories regarding atmospheric thermodynamics.

Iribarne, J. V., and W. L. Godson. *Atmospheric Thermodynamics*. Boston: D. Reidel, 1981. An excellent, well-referenced text on atmospheric thermodynamics. Contains geophysics and astrophysics monographs.

Lutgens, F. K., and E. J. Tarbuck. *The Atmosphere: An Introduction to Meteorology*. Englewood Cliffs, N.J.: Prentice-Hall, 1995. Contains excellent chapters on the atmosphere, meteorology, and weather patterns.

Schneider, S. H. *Global Warming*. San Francisco: Sierra Club Books, 1989. Discusses the causes and possibilities of enhanced global warming and the greenhouse effect in the light of atmospheric thermodynamic principles.

Williams, J. *The "USA Today" Weather Book*. New York: Random House, 1992. An excellent guide to the interpretation of weather reports. Gives numerous applied examples of thermodynamic principles.

Daniel G. Graetzer

Cross-References

AVALANCHES

Type of earth science: Urban geology and geologic hazards

An avalanche is a large mass of snow, ice, rock, or earth that moves rapidly down a slope or over a precipice. The term is most often used to refer to movements of snow, and often only to movements large and rapid enough to endanger life or property.

Principal terms

AVALANCHE: a large mass of rock, soil, mud, snow, ice, or other material that descends rapidly down an incline

LANDSLIDE: a massive downward and outward movement of material that has previously formed the slope of an incline

LOESS: silt deposited by wind along a hillside

PRECIPICE: a very steep or overhanging area of earth or rock

SNOW: precipitation which takes the form of small tabular or columnar white ice crystals formed directly from the water vapor of the air at a temperature of less than 32 degrees Fahrenheit (0 degrees Celsius)

Summary of the Phenomenon

The term "avalanche" refers to large masses of rock, soil, mud, snow, ice, or other materials that move rapidly down a hillside or mountain slope. The unqualified use of the word "avalanche" in English typically refers to snow movement and often applies only to movements large and rapid enough to endanger life or property.

Landslide avalanches are massive downward and outward movements of material that has previously formed the slope of a hillside or mountain. The term "landslide" is usually restricted to refer to the movement of rock and soil; the term can connote a broad range of velocities, from slow, gradual movements to high-velocity events that can require immediate evacuation of an area.

A landslide begins when a portion of a hillside becomes weakened to the point where it is no longer able to support its own weight. This weakness is generally caused when rainfall or flood waters elevate the overall water content of the slope, thereby reducing shear strength of the slope materials. Landslides are most common in areas where erosion is actively wearing away at the terrain; they can be initiated by earthquakes and loud acoustics. Some landslides move only sporadically or during certain seasons of the year and may lie dormant for decades or millennia, so that their extremely slow movements go unnoticed. Slow-moving landslides are distinguished from the geological phenomenon of "creep" in that they have distinct boundaries and adjacent stable ground.

Ground that has remained relatively stable for several hundred or even several thousand years may begin to slide following alteration of the natural slope by human development, such as grading for roads or building on hillsides. Landslides can be started by cutting into the slope, thereby removing support necessary for materials higher up the slope, or by overloading the slope below with the excavated materials.

Some landslides have occurred where development altered groundwater conditions, especially around potential landslide masses that had previously been dormant.

Landslides can be classified into slides, falls, and flows. Slides move as large bodies of earth and rock that slip along one or more unstable surfaces known as "failures." "Slumps" are those slides that move largely by rotation along cylindrical surfaces. The resulting backward rotation of the slide mass commonly produces hillside flats in otherwise sloping terrain. Slumps and block glides, which slide along inclined planar slip surfaces, move up to two meters per day and often involve large amounts of material. Falls of rock or soil originate on cliffs or steep slopes and can be catastrophic events, as evidenced by a 1970 earthquake in Peru that started a relatively small rockfall that gained more and more material as it accelerated, finally reaching estimated speeds of more than 280 kilometers per hour; the quick-moving mass eventually buried more than eighteen thousand people. "Flows" are landslides that behave like fluids and involve damp mud and debris. "Earthflows" are composed of wet, claylike material, with slow earthflows generally moving as slowly as a few meters per year. "Solifluction" is the slow downslope flow of soil that occurs on Arctic alpine hillsides when thawed ice or snow saturates the soil cover. "Dry" flows occur where great kinetic energy, as from an earthquake or a fall from a steep slope, initiates the flow of dry materials. A large, rapid flow of dry loess accompanying an earthquake in 1920 in Gansu Province, China, quickly killed more than 100,000 people. Dry-flowing rockfall avalanches may also occur with large rockfall deposits on gentle slopes and have been observed to have occurred on the Moon.

Snow avalanches require a snow layer that has the potential for instability and a slope that is steep enough to enable a slide to continue moving once it has started. Slope inclines between 25 and 55 degrees represent the broadest range for avalanche danger, but a majority of avalanches originate on inclines between 30 and 45 degrees. When a layer of snow lies on a sloped surface, the constant force of gravity causes it to creep slowly down the slope. When a force imposed on a snow layer is large enough, a failure is triggered somewhere within the snow, and an avalanche may begin to move rapidly. Angles above 55 degrees are generally too steep to collect significant amounts of snow, as the snow tends to roll down the hillside soon after falling. Slope angles of less than 25 degrees are generally quite safe, except for the remote possibility of very slow snow avalanches in extremely wet conditions. Participants in winter activities often overestimate the angle of a slope, so it is recommended that outdoor enthusiasts purchase a clinometer, which is built into some compasses, to assist in assessing potential danger.

Two distinct types of failures can occur within the snow prior to an avalanche. When a cohesionless snow layer rests on a slope steeper than its angle of repose, it can cause a loose-snow avalanche, which is often also called a "point-release" avalanche. This type of avalanche can be started by one grain of snow slipping out of place and dislodging other grains below it, causing a chain reaction that continues to grow in size as it slips down the hill. A point-release avalanche generally appears as an inverted "V" shape on the snow and is typically limited to the surface layer of snow cover. The snow in this situation has little internal cohesion, no obvious fracture line, and no clear layer where the sliding snow separates it from the layers underneath. By contrast, when snow fails as a cohesive unit, an obvious brittle fracture line occurs, and an entire layer or slab of snow is set in motion. Because creep formation has caused the snow layer to be stretched out along the slope, the brittle fracture releases stored elastic energy. The release of this energy may cause the fracture to propagate across an entire slope or basin. Failure may occur deep within the snow layer, allowing a good portion or nearly all of the snow thickness to be included in the avalanche. Slab avalanches are often larger and more destructive than point-release avalanches and can continue to slide on the ground or on weaker layers underneath.

Natural avalanches can be triggered when additional stress is provided in the form of the added weight of additional snow, either fresh snowfall or wind-blown snow, or when the cohesive strength of the snowpack naturally decreases, serving to weaken the bonds between grains. Artificial avalanches are triggered when humans, animals, or vehicles begin the downslide by adding stress to the snow. Many avalanches in outdoor recreation areas are triggered by the weight of a skier or the impact of small masses of snow or ice falling from above. Avalanches have presented a danger to military troop movement, as was evident in the Dolomites of Italy during World War I, when six thousand troops were killed in a single day by snow avalanches. Explosives can also trigger an artificial avalanche, either intentionally or unintentionally. When explosives are detonated to knock down potentially dangerous snow at a prescribed time and location, such as for maintenance of highways or ski areas, the public is temporarily evacuated from the area.

Avalanches can be very destructive, particularly if they are able to generate extremely high speeds. Precise measurements have shown that highly turbulent dry snow or dry powder can create avalanche speeds averaging between 35 and 45 meters per second, with velocities as high as 85 meters per second occasionally attained. These high speeds are possible only in "dry" avalanches because these avalanches entrain large amounts of air within the moving snow, serving to reduce internal frictional force. In "wet" avalanches, the snow is very dense and actual liquid may be present, creating less-turbulent movement once the slide begins. With the reduction in turbulence, less air is entrained; a more flowing motion is generated, and speeds are generally no higher than 30 meters per second.

The impact pressures resulting from high-speed avalanches can threaten both life and property. Small to medium-sized avalanches can hit with impact pressures of one to five tons per square meter, enough power to damage or destroy wood-frame structures. Larger avalanches can generate forces that can exceed 100 tons per square meter, which is easily enough to uproot mature forested areas and destroy concrete structures.

Methods of Study

Snow avalanches are one of the main hazards facing winter enthusiasts who are hiking, climbing, snowshoeing, hunting, skiing, or driving through a mountain pass in an automobile or snowmobile. The degree of avalanche hazard and the conditions that create it at any particular time are relatively easy for a trained professional to identify and are generally reported through the local media in populated and well-traveled areas. However, there is no completely valid and reliable way to predict precisely where and when a dangerous avalanche might occur. Outdoor enthusiasts and others who traverse snow-covered areas can certainly benefit from learning to identify different types of snow crystals and to recognize hazardous terrain and weather; however, even well-trained people should not be lulled into a false sense of security regarding avalanche safety, as overconfidence in such circumstances can lead to a devastating confrontation with nature.

Avalanche research has consistently shown that approximately four out of five avalanches strike during or just after a storm. The danger increases rapidly when snowfall exceeds one inch per hour or builds up an accumulation of twelve inches or more in a single storm. Quick changes in temperature and wind also significantly increase avalanche danger. Storms that start when there is a low ambient temperature and dry snow on the ground and that are followed immediately by a rapidly rising temperature are likely to set off avalanche conditions. The dry snow tends to form poor bonds and does not possess the strength to support the heavier, wet snow that accumulates on top. Rainstorms or spring weather with warm winds and cloudy nights can cause a percolating effect, mixing water into the snow and creating the danger of a wet-snow avalanche.

The shape of the slope also reflects avalanche danger, with common sense dictating that hazards are highest when snow accumulates on straight, open, and moderately steep slopes. One classic law of avalanches is that mountaineers face the least danger on ridges, more danger on the valley floor, and most danger when directly on the slopes. Snow on a convex slope is more prone to avalanches, because it comes under tension as it stretches tightly over the curve of the hill. When coming down a convex slope, mountaineers may not know how steep the slope is until they have passed the curve that obstructs their view and find themselves quite far down on the face.

Bowls and cirques have a shape that invites snow deposited by the wind. Once an avalanche starts, it often spreads to the entire face and dumps large amounts of snow into the area below. Couloirs (gorges) are very enticing for climbers because they offer direct routes up mountainsides, but they also create natural avalanche chutes. Forested slopes offer some avalanche protection, but it is important not to put too much trust in trees. While slides are less likely to originate within a dense forest, they have been known to crush through them from above. Shattered trees that appear to be shaped like a fan constitute clear evidence of previous avalanche penetration. A slope that has only bushes and small trees growing on it may indicate that the slope has experienced avalanches so often than the timber is not being given a chance to regrow. Grass can increase the flow of an avalanche by providing a slick surface for a slide. When traversing a valley, one must keep in mind that an avalanche can sweep on the level for more than one mile after it reaches the bottom of the slope. Good advice for winter travelers is to always stop for lunch or set up camp outside of the potential reach of an avalanche.

The way the sun and wind hit a slope can provide valuable clues for potential avalanche danger. In the Northern Hemisphere, slopes that face the south receive more sun. This makes the snow settle and stabilize faster than on northern slopes. Generally speaking, southern slopes are safer in winter, but there are certainly many possible local exceptions to this rule. South-facing slopes also tend to release their avalanches sooner after a storm; slides beginning on southern slopes, therefore, may indicate that slides on slopes facing other directions may soon follow. As warmer days arrive near the end of winter, southern slopes may actually become more prone to wet-snow avalanches, making the northern slopes safer. North-facing slopes receive little or no sun in the winter, so consolidation of the snowpack takes longer. Colder temperatures may create weak layers, thus making northern slopes more likely to slide in midwinter. It is important to note that these guidelines should be reversed for mountain areas south of the equator.

Windward slopes that face into the snow tend to be safer, because they retain less snow as the wind blows it away. The snow that remains tends to become more compacted by the blast of the wind. Lee slopes, which face the same direction the wind is blowing, collect snow rapidly during storms and on windy days as the snow blows over from the windward slopes. This condition results in cornice formations on the lee sides of ridges, snow that is deeper and less consolidated, and the formation of wind slabs that can be prone to avalanches. Snow formation often indicates the prevailing wind direction, following the general rule that cornices face in the same direction in which the wind is blowing.

Avalanche hazard can be assessed by examining the snow for new avalanches in the area. Cracks in hard snow may outline an unstable slab, as may snow that settles with the weight of a person moving on it. The sound of a loud thump may indicate that a hard slab is ready to release. Snow stability can be tested by probing with a ski pole to feel for layers of varying solidity or by digging a pit to examine the layers for weakness.

Attempts have been made to prevent avalanche damage by building artificial supporting structures or transplanting trees within anticipated avalanche zones. The direct impact of an avalanche can be effectively blocked by diversion structures such as dams, sheds, and tunnels in areas where avalanches repeatedly strike. Structural damage can be limited by the construction of various types of fencing and by the construction of "splitting wedges," V-shaped masonry walls that are designed to split an avalanche around a structure located behind it. Techniques have been developed to predict avalanche occurrence by analyzing the relationships between meteorological and snow-cover factors, lay versions of which are often reported through the media. Zones of known or predicted avalanche danger are generally taken into account during development of a mountainous area. The avalanche danger of unstable slope accumulations is often prevented by the detonation of explosives or by the sending out of controlled acoustical waves.

Context

Avalanche damage may seem to be small when compared to the destruction caused by other hazards such as tornadoes and floods. However, the frequency of accidents resulting in destruction, injury, or death has risen tremendously in direct proportion to the increased popularity of winter recreational activities in the mountains. In countries where avalanche data are systematically and accurately recorded, there are approximately 150 to 200 avalanche-related deaths per year.

Although avoiding dangerous areas is obviously the best way to reduce avalanche hazards, search-and-rescue agencies have offered a number of emergency safety tips for anyone caught in an avalanche. These include making as much noise as possible to alert potential rescuers, throwing off any equipment such as packs and skis, and grabbing onto anything stable, such as large rocks or trees, to avoid being swept away. Anyone caught in a slide should attempt to stay on the snow surface by making swimming motions with the arms and legs or by rolling. It is important to close the mouth if the head goes below the surface. A person who is about to become buried should try to create a breathing space by putting hands and elbows in front of the face and inhaling deeply before the snow stops in order to expand the ribs. A person who is completely buried should conserve oxygen and energy if he or she anticipates that rescuers will immediately begin appropriate search-and-rescue efforts.

Avalanche rescue efforts should begin immediately by companions of the victim, who should assume that there is not time to go for help. Rescuers are advised to note three spots—where the victim was first caught, where the victim disappeared beneath the snow, and where the moving surface of the avalanche finally stopped—to reduce the area to be searched. Rescue beacons, small electronic devices that should be carried by all persons in a winter travel party, are effective tools for finding buried victims. Beacons can transmit or receive signals at a radio frequency that is set during the climb. Searchers who switch their beacons to receive after an incident can often locate a buried victim in a matter of minutes. Beacons that utilize a frequency of 2,275 hertz are most common in North America. Procedures for avalanche rescue have been established by search-and-rescue organizations and should be reviewed by all persons participating in winter activities in an avalanche zone.

Bibliography

Armstrong, B. R., and K. Williams. *The Avalanche Book*. Golden, Colo.: Fulcrum Press, 1986. An excellent text highlighting the post-disaster assessment of major avalanches in North America.

Daffern, T. *Avalanche Safety for Skiers and Climbers*. Seattle, Wash.: Rocky Mountain Books, 1983. A basic text for novice and advanced skiers and climbers.

Fawcett, R., J. Lowe, P. Nunn, and A. Rouse. *The Climber's Handbook*. San Francisco: Sierra Club Books, 1987. A basic introductory handbook for advanced climbers who expect to encounter dangerous terrain.

Graydon, E. *Mountaineering: The Freedom of the Hill*. Seattle, Wash.: The Mountaineers, 1992. A presentation of both introductory and advanced information on the sport of mountaineering. Includes much practical information on avalanches and other hazards of snow travel and climbing.

LaChapelle, E. R. *The ABC of Avalanche Safety*. Seattle, Wash.: The Mountaineers, 1985. Discusses different types of avalanches, how they form, and where they can be predicted to occur. Also contains general guidelines on safety for people traveling in mountainous regions.

National Research Council Panel on Snow Avalanches. *Snow Avalanche Hazards and Mitigation in the United States*. Washington, D.C.: National Academy Press, 1990. Edited by committee chairman D. B. Prior and panel chairman B. Voight, this government report assesses avalanches and related natural disasters in the United States and evaluates the efficiency of government relief efforts.

U.S. Department of Agriculture. Forest Service. *Snow Avalanche: General Rules for Avoiding and Surviving Snow Avalanches*. Portland, Oreg.: U.S.D.A. Forest Service Pacific NorthWest Region, 1982. Provides general guidelines for both recreational and serious outdoor enthusiasts for avoiding and surviving snow avalanches.

Daniel G. Graetzer

Cross-References

CASCADES

Type of earth science: Mountain ranges
Field of study: Tectonics

The Cascade mountain range extends from northern California through western Oregon and Washington into British Columbia in Canada. The loftiest peaks of this range are stratovolcanoes, the highest being 4,392-meter Mount Rainier in Washington. The history of the Cascades goes back about twenty-five million years, but the periodic eruption of once-dormant volcanoes such as Mount St. Helens shows that the range is still evolving.

Principal terms

ANDESITE: a type of volcanic, igneous rock, typically gray in color; the predominant lava expelled by stratovolcanoes such as those in the Cascades

BASALT: a dark, iron-rich, silica-poor volcanic rock

DACITE: a volcanic rock similar to andesite but containing more silica, typically gray in color

LITHOSPHERIC PLATES: massive horizontal slabs consisting of crust and the uppermost upper mantle, capable of movement by sliding over a semifluid layer in the mantle

RHYOLITE: a light-colored, silica-rich volcanic rock, commonly violently erupted as ash deposits

STRATOVOLCANOES (COMPOSITE VOLCANOES): lofty volcanoes composed of alternating layers of volcanic ash and lava or mudflows

SUBDUCTION ZONE: a linear area representing the line of collision between two lithospheric plates

Summary of the Phenomenon

The Cascade mountain range, named for the great cascades (waterfalls) of the Columbia River, spans 1,139 kilometers through the northwestern United States and southwestern Canada. Its highest peaks are a string of lofty volcanoes that extend from northern California through Oregon and Washington and terminate in British Columbia. The Cascades lie about 160 to 240 kilometers inland from the Pacific coast and are separated from the northwestern coast ranges by a broad valley called the Puget Trough in Washington and the Willamette Valley in Oregon. The range is divided into western and eastern sections; the western side consists of older, eroded volcanic rocks of relatively low topographic relief, but the east side, popularly known as the "high Cascades," sports more spectacular—and much younger—volcanic peaks. Because the Cascade range creates a major climatic barrier, the western slopes are heavily forested, nourished by abundant rainfall. In contrast, the eastern slopes are dry scrublands covered mostly by grass and low bushes. The rugged scenery of the Cascades, including numerous deep valleys, lakes, and ridges, has been sculpted both by stream erosion and by glaciation, which began in the Pleistocene ice age but which has continued even in recent times.

The high Cascades give the range its highest peaks and grandest mountain scenery. They consist of a string of stratovolcanoes that extend from northern California (Mount Shasta, 4,317 meters; Lassen Peak, 3,187 meters) to British Columbia (Meager Mountain, 2,679 meters; Mount Garibaldi, 2,678 meters). Other important volcanoes in the Cascades include Mount Hood (3,426 meters; near Portland) and Mount Jefferson (3,199 meters) in Oregon, and Mount Adams (3,751 meters), Mount Rainier (4,392 meters; near Seattle), and Mount Baker (3,284 meters) in Washington. Mount St. Helens (2,500 meters) in southwestern Washington is one of the youngest and the most active of the Cascade volcanoes, having erupted violently in May, 1980, and more than sixty times during the last fifty thousand years. Oregon's famous Crater Lake was created by a volcano that literally blew itself out of existence nearly seven thousand years ago. The crater, the remains of once-mighty Mount Mazama (estimated elevation of more than 3,500 meters), is now an eight-kilometer-wide bowl-shaped collapse depression (caldera) filled with water.

Stratovolcanoes (also known as composite volcanoes) occur worldwide, mostly along continental margins and in near-continent island arcs such as the Aleutian Islands, Japan, and the Philippines. They tend to form lofty, cone-shaped peaks, commonly snow-packed because of their high elevations above sea level. The Andes in western South America, like the Cascades, also exist as a coast-hugging, linear chain of stratovolcanoes.

Stratovolcanoes owe most of their impressive height to the composition of the volcanic magma they emit. This magma is rich in silica (silicon dioxide), the most common chemical component of rocks and minerals in the earth's crust and mantle. High-silica magmas have high viscosities and thus are generally thick and sticky upon eruption. As a result, erupted concentrations of high-silica volcanic materials tend to pile up in a single area, producing tall mountain peaks. Less viscous basaltic magmas tend to spread out, creating broad, low "shield volcanoes" such as those that make up the islands of Hawaii.

The volcanic rocks produced by the high-silica magmas of stratovolcanoes are called andesite. Dacite is an especially siliceous (silica-rich) variety of andesite; stratovolcanoes commonly eject one or both of these magma types. Stratovolcanoes are noted for their explosive eruptions, and this proclivity, too, can be attributed to the nature of their magmas. Andesite and dacite magmas generally contain significant quantities of water, which, when trapped as steam within this sticky magma, may suddenly explode with the power of several atomic bombs. For example, the 1980 eruption of Mount St. Helens released the estimated explosive energy of about five hundred Hiroshima-type atomic bombs. For this reason, stratovolcanoes, including those in the Cascades, are the most dangerous volcanoes in the world, at times causing catastrophic death tolls and property damage.

The geologic history of the present Cascade range is complicated, especially as it relates to other major geologic terrains in the Pacific Northwest. For example, the Cascades can be considered a younger northern extension of the Sierra Nevada range in eastern California. The thick, layered accumulations of basalt (a dark, low-silica, high-iron rock) lava flows of the Columbia River Basalt Plateau also have a relationship to the Cascades, as do the Willamette and Puget valleys and the Pacific coast ranges. The Cascades, especially the high Cascade volcanoes, represent one of the most recent additions to the geology of the Northwest; most of these volcanoes have initial eruption ages of less than one million years, making them very young by geologic standards. The eruptions of Mount Lassen between 1914 and 1917 and Mount St. Helens in 1980 show that these volcanoes are still actively adding to the mass of the range. On the other hand, the north-south-trending volcanic field on which the current volcanoes are built was first established about twenty-five million years ago, during the Miocene epoch. Much of the western Cascades consists of the eroded remnants of volcanoes that once dominated the region's skyline but that are now extinct.

To fully appreciate the origin of the Cascade range, it is necessary to go back in geologic time about 150 million years, a time when the dinosaurs dominated life on Earth. At that time, much of northwestern Oregon and southwestern Washington were covered by an embayment of the Pacific Ocean that extended nearly to the present state of Idaho. Paralleling the coastline of this embayment was a subduction zone, a linear terrain representing the collision line of two lithospheric plates. The earth is broken up into "plates," averaging about one hundred kilometers thick, that consist of the crust and a part of the upper mantle. These plates move horizontally over the earth's surface, carrying the continents with them. Where they collide, one plate will slide under the other (a process known as "subduction"). When this process involves a thinner but denser oceanic plate colliding with a thick, buoyant continental plate, the oceanic plate always dives under the continental plate. This movement creates a narrow trench in the ocean off the coast of the continent that fills with sediments scraped off the ocean floor as the plate descends. These crumpled sediments eventually are pushed upward to become coastal ranges. Inland from the coastal ranges about one hundred kilometers will be volcanoes produced by the melting of former surface materials sinking to ever deeper and hotter depths. Magma produced by the partial melting of subducted rocks powers the volcanoes of the present Cascades and most other stratovolcanoes.

One hundred fifty million years ago, subduction was occurring along the Oregon coast, parallel to the northeast-trending ocean embayment. This movement produced a northeast-trending mountain range consisting of coastal ranges (including the current California, Oregon, Washington coast ranges) and a string of volcanoes, now mostly eroded away. These old mountains are now represented by the Blue and Wallowa ranges in eastern Oregon and southeastern Washington and the Klamath range in southwestern Oregon and northern California. Also at this time, a subduction zone paralleled much of the California coast, producing the present California coast ranges and active andesite stratovolcanoes in the area of the Sierra Nevada in eastern California. As in Oregon, these old volcanoes in the Sierra are now eroded away, but the underlying magma chambers, now crystallized to granitic rocks, provide evidence of their former existence. Yosemite National Park is an excellent place to view the massive granitic plutonic bodies that once fed volcanoes similar to those in the present-day Cascades.

About thirty-five million years ago, a strange event occurred that altered the pattern of mountain building and volcanic activity in the Pacific Northwest. The subduction zone that had been trending northeast across Oregon straightened out into a new north-south trend, an orientation it has maintained. About twenty-five million years ago, a new north-south trending line of volcanoes sprang up parallel to the subduction zone. These volcanoes were similar to the present Cascade volcanoes, but they spewed out an even more siliceous and explosive variety of magma called rhyolite, the volcanic equivalent of granite. This began a very impressive era of explosive volcanism, with the widespread deposition of volcanic ash, that continued for about ten million years. The remnants of these ash deposits can still be observed in the John Day formation of northern Oregon. All during this time, the volcanic range was gradually being uplifted by the buoyancy of the hot crustal rocks below. To the east, the areas of the present Willamette and Puget valleys were downwarped as they were squeezed between the uplifting coast ranges to the west and the volcanic arc to the east. These valleys originally were shallow seas that eventually filled with sedimentary rocks and later were covered by basalt lava flows.

During much of the time that volcanoes were erupting in Oregon and Washington, they were also erupting in a nearly continuous band down the length of California in the present area of the Sierra Nevada. About thirty million years ago, however, volcanism suddenly ceased in the Sierra as the former subduction zone transformed into the current San Andreas fault system. The San Andreas, famous for the earthquakes it has wrought in California, is another form of plate boundary called a "transform fault." In a transform fault, the lithospheric plates slide past each other but do not subduct. Thus, volcanic activity is limited at such boundaries. The Sierra volcanoes, which had once formed a continuous chain with the early Cascade volcanoes, died with the formation of the San Andreas system. They have since eroded away, leaving behind the granitic rocks that crystallized below them.

About twenty million years ago, volcanism in the present western Cascade area suddenly stopped, replaced some time later by the extrusion of voluminous quantities of very fluid basalt lava that flooded wide areas in Oregon and Washington. This was the event that created the present Columbia River Basalt Plateau. About twelve million years ago, volcanism resumed in the western Cascades but never achieved the level of activity of their explosive early history. The current eastern Cascade volcanoes have resulted from a renewed burst of volcanism over only the last million years; however, the infrequent rate of volcanism in the Cascades probably is signaling a decline in subduction activity, which may eventually lead to the extinction of the Cascade volcanoes in a manner similar to what befell the Sierra Nevada volcanoes.

Methods of Study

The Cascades are perhaps the best-studied volcanoes in the world. From a scientific standpoint, they are of interest for what they reveal about how continental subduction-zone volcanoes originate and evolve over time. They also have important implications for how continents in general grow and evolve. From a human-interest standpoint, the study of Cascade-type volcanoes may lead to methods of predicting their potentially devastating eruptions. Scientists—principally volcanologists, geophysicists, and other geologists—study volcanoes by first performing field studies of their lava flows or pyroclastic (explosively ejected) ash deposits. These rock units are investigated by field parties who chart their surface distribution on geologic maps. This information may be used to correlate volcanic materials with tectonic features such as faults, folds, uplifted or down-warped areas, and plate boundaries, or it may be used to estimate the energy of eruptions and the amount of material involved. The history of a volcanic area can be determined by noting the number and order of interlayered deposits of volcanic ash (indicating an explosive event) and lava flows (indicating a relatively quiet event). Samples are also analyzed by radiometric means (potassium-argon, carbon-14, and other techniques) to produce the ages of the rocks. Rock ages allow the precise determination of just when volcanoes were most active and for how long. Other chemical data collected from volcanic rocks can be used to suggest what kinds of parent rocks were melted to produce the magmas and under what conditions.

The prediction of volcanic eruptions is difficult because volcanoes seldom produce warning signals in a reproducible pattern that can be universally applied. Previous experience with volcanic eruptions shows that earthquakes generally precede eruptions, but the strength and frequency of quakes varies from one eruption to the next. Many volcanoes show an actual rise in elevation (caused by rising magma) shortly before an eruption, and such changes can be measured with precision laser transits. Also, the earth's magnetic field around volcanoes may show a change in intensity shortly before an eruption. These measurements rely on having sophisticated instruments and well-trained operators observing the volcanoes on a nearly constant basis. Highly technical prediction strategies may not be financially or practically feasible in all circumstances in which the threat of volcanic eruptions is a constant concern.

The May 18, 1980, eruption of Mount St. Helens provided an excellent opportunity for intense close-up study of an active volcano. Not only did this volcano provide a spectacular show of volcanic fury when it finally erupted (with the loss of fifty-seven lives), but it also was located in a uniquely accessible area, close to established government and university facilities with expertise in volcanology. The U.S. Geological Survey made thorough scientific studies of the volcano before, during, and after the catastrophic eruption. One encouraging result of these studies was the discovery that a certain frequency (vibration rate) of earthquake wave called a "harmonic tremor" provided a fairly reliable warning that an eruption was imminent. Harmonic tremors are believed to be generated by magma rising within the central feeder conduit of the volcano. As the magma moves upward, it rubs against the rocks lining the conduit, producing the characteristic vibration of the harmonic tremor. Detection of this special earthquake wave allowed the prediction of five subsequent minor eruptions of Mount St. Helens between 1980 and 1982. It remains to be seen whether or not this technique has applications beyond this one volcano.

Context

The Cascade mountain range provides some of the most uniquely resplendent mountain scenery in North America. It is the only place in the contiguous United States where visitors can explore active volcanoes, some of which also contain glaciers (particularly in the northern Cascades, including Canada), numerous lakes, and clear mountain streams. Some of the rivers in the Cascades have been dammed for hydro-electric power.

Much of the economic value of the Cascades comes from the tourist industry. They are a favorite resort for hunters, hikers, campers, boaters, and other outdoor enthusiasts. Four national parks and monuments have been established in the Cascades: Crater Lake National Park in Oregon and Mount St. Helens National Volcano Monument, Mount Rainier National Park, and North Cascades National Park in Washington. In addition, most of the rest of the Cascades is devoted to national forests and recreational areas. Ski resorts are a popular attraction in the winter.

Few economically exploitable ore deposits have been discovered in the Cascades; those that have include pulverized volcanic rock, used as construction gravel, and larger stones sold as garden ornaments. Gold in some quantity was discovered in the mid-nineteenth century in the Blue and Klamath mountains of Oregon, but the Cascades are devoid of notable metallic ore deposits. Probably the most valuable economic commodity in the Cascades is timber, with many thousands of trees harvested each year, particularly from the heavily forested western slopes.

From a philosophical standpoint, the Cascades provide a dramatic demonstration of the awesome internal energy of the earth and its ability to render considerable modifications to the planet's surface, both constructive and destructive. Appreciation of these powerful forces should begin with the contemplation of huge "plates" colliding with such force that, over millions of years, mountains rise, adding to the dry land of the continent. Continental mass is also augmented by the explosive fury of stratovolcanoes depositing ash and lava over wide areas. The recent eruptions of Mount St. Helens and Mount Lassen show that plenty of energy remains below the Cascades that will, no doubt, be unleashed again in the future. The eruption of Mount St. Helens destroyed all life in an area measuring about 180 square kilometers, wiped out many resorts and private residences, and reduced the size of once-popular Spirit Lake to that of a large pond. On the other hand, soil in the area of the volcano and in a band of wind-blown ash extending to the East Coast received the benefit of a potassium- and phosphorous-rich fertilizer. Many of the huge trees blown down by the force of the explosion were harvested for lumber, and the scientific study of the eruption has provided information useful in predicting future eruptions in the Cascades. Thus, the violent expenditure of energy in Cascade volcanoes is not without benefits to humans and wildlife.

Bibliography

Alt, David D., and Donald W. Hyndman. *Roadside Geology of Oregon*. Missoula, Mont.: Mountain Press, 1994. One of a series describing informal geology tours that can be conducted by automobile. Other recommended books in the series pertaining to the Cascades are the volumes for California and Washington. The Oregon volume has the best description of the nature and geological history of the Cascades and their volcanoes. All volumes are illustrated with clearly labeled diagrams, maps, and monochrome photographs and include a glossary and recommended reading list.

Decker, Robert W., and Barbara B. Decker. *Mountains of Fire*. New York: Cambridge University Press, 1991. The writers of this book, professional volcanologists, are well qualified to explore the nature of world volcanic terrains, the latest scientific findings, the anatomy of volcanoes, and the reasons why volcanoes erupt where they do. Cascade volcanoes are covered, particularly Mount St. Helens. A nontechnical, highly readable, in-depth treatment. Illustrated with more than one hundred color and monochrome photographs and drawings. Features eyewitness accounts of major volcanic eruptions.

King, Philip B. *The Evolution of North America*. Princeton, N.J.: Princeton University Press, 1977. By a renowned veteran geologist with the U.S. Geological Survey. This is the best book to consult for the geologic history of any major geological terrain in North America. Chapter 9 (part 3) deals with the origin and evolution of the Cascades; other sections deal with related areas such as the coast ranges, the Sierra Nevada, and the Columbia Plateau. Illustrated with monochrome maps, diagrams, and sketches. Aimed at readers with some knowledge of geology, but not overloaded with jargon; should be intelligible to college students and college-educated readers.

McKee, B. *Cascadia: The Geological Evolution of the Pacific Northwest*. New York: McGraw-Hill, 1972. Contains one of the most comprehensive treatments of the history, evolution, and interpretive problems associated with geological features in the Pacific Northwest. The author skillfully explains the relationships between the major geological features of the area, with an extensive section on the Cascades. Illustrated with maps, geological cross sections, and diagrams.

Wood, Charles A., and Jurgen Kienle, eds. *Volcanoes of North America: United States and Canada*. New York: Cambridge University Press, 1993. A major compendium of North American volcanoes, including those of Alaska and Hawaii. Every entry contains information on the type of volcano and its location, dimensions, eruptive history, and composition. The introduction has sections that show the methods used to study volcanoes. The Cascade volcanoes are well represented in this book; the introductory section to the chapter "Volcano Tectonics of the Western U.S.A." has a subsection with a discussion of the Cascades. Illustrated with monochrome photographs, maps, and diagrams. Easily comprehensible by the general reader.

John L. Berkley

Cross-References

The Andes, 54; Continental Growth, 268; Igneous Rock Bodies, 1131; Igneous Rocks: Andesitic, 1146; Island Arcs, 1261; Lithospheric Plates, 1387; Mountain Belts, 1725; The Origin of Magmas, 1428; Pyroclastic Rocks, 2131; The Sierra Nevada, 2357; Subduction and Orogeny, 2497; Volcanic Hazards, 2601; Volcanoes: Flood Basalts, 2630; Volcanoes: Mount St. Helens, 2659; Volcanoes: Recent Eruptions, 2673; Volcanoes: Stratovolcanoes, 2688; Volcanoes: Types of Lava Flow, 2701.

CATASTROPHISM

Type of earth science: Paleontology and earth history
Field of study: Large solar system bodies

Historically, catastrophism was the doctrine that a series of sudden and violent events caused widespread or even global effects, producing the differences in fossil forms and other features found in successive geological strata. More recently, a new school of catastrophism has arisen, prompted by growing evidence that much of the geological record, including mass extinctions of living organisms, has been greatly influenced by rare events of large magnitude, such as widespread flooding, volcanic activity, and asteroid impacts.

Principal terms

ASTEROID: one of the numerous small rocky bodies bigger than about ten meters in size orbiting the Sun, mostly between Mars and Jupiter; some, however, cross the earth's orbit

CRATER: an abrupt circular depression formed by extrusion of volcanic material or by the impact of an asteroid or meteorite

CRUST: the outermost solid layer or shell surrounding the earth

FOSSIL: naturally preserved remains or evidence of past life, such as bones, shells, casts, and impressions

GEOLOGICAL COLUMN: the order of rock layers formed during the course of the earth's history

METEORITE: a fragment of an asteroid (less than ten meters in size) that survives passage through the atmosphere and strikes the surface of the earth

STRATIGRAPHY: the study of rock layers to determine the sequence of layers and the information this provides on the geological history of a region

UNIFORMITARIANISM: the doctrine that geological events are caused by natural and gradual processes operating over long periods of time

VOLCANISM: the processes by which magma is transferred from the earth's interior to produce lava flows on the surface and the ejection of gases and ash into the atmosphere

Summary of the Phenomenon

Although the term "catastrophism" is usually associated with the work of Georges Cuvier near the beginning of the nineteenth century, most theories of earth history before that time involved various ideas of catastrophism, emphasizing sudden and violent events rather than gradual processes. Based on the biblical account of creation in six days and genealogies of the descendants of Adam, most writers assumed that the earth was only about six thousand years old. Early theories of the earth's surface features were based on the biblical account of Noah's flood. In early eighteenth century

England, Thomas Burnet and John Woodward used the idea of a universal flood to explain geological phenomena such as the formation of mountains and valleys, irregularities in strata, and the existence and location of fossils. These ideas stimulated the collection of fossils as evidence of biblical veracity.

In Italy, where volcanoes were active, the Venetian priest Anton Moro suggested in 1740 that Noah's flood was a more localized event and that rock strata formed from a series of violent volcanic eruptions that entombed plants and animals, forming fossils in the rocks. These catastrophic ideas were sometimes viewed as complementary; by the late eighteenth century, however, they led to a controversy between the Neptunists, who stressed the role of water and floods, and the Vulcanists, who emphasized fire and heat.

In 1749, Georges Buffon, keeper of the King's Gardens in Paris, suggested a speculative natural history of the earth with a vastly expanded time scale. Instead of a recent six-day creation, he proposed seven epochs of development over a span of about seventy-five thousand years. Using a calculation devised by Sir Isaac Newton for estimating the cooling of comets, Buffon experimented with the cooling of a red-hot globe of iron; he extrapolated his findings for a mass the size of the earth, arriving at an estimate that it would have taken 74,832 years for the earth to cool to its present temperature. By the time he finished his *Épochs de la Nature* (1779), Buffon had divided his history of nature into seven "epochs" as metaphors of the seven "days" of creation.

Although he did not refer to catastrophism, Buffon's epochs included catastrophic events of both fire and water. In the first epoch, the earth formed out of matter ejected from a collision of a comet with the Sun. As the earth solidified in the second epoch, its crust wrinkled to form the mountain ranges. In the third epoch, vapors condensed as the earth cooled, covering the earth with a flood in which fishes flourished and sediments formed, enclosing fossils and organic deposits such as coal. The fourth epoch began after further cooling produced subterranean openings, causing a rush of waters, earthquakes, and volcanoes that produced dry lands. Land animals and plants appeared in the fifth epoch, and the continents moved apart in the sixth after migrations of animals had separated various species. Finally, wrote Buffon, humans appeared in the seventh epoch.

By the end of the eighteenth century, the Neptunists and Vulcanists became more sharply divided. The British geologist Sir William Hamilton developed in more detail the implications of Vulcanism from the action of volcanoes. He identified basalt and other rocks found near volcanoes as products of lava flows. He argued that volcanic action played a constructive role in uplifting new land from the sea, shaping the landscape, and providing a safety valve for excess pressure below the crust.

A purely Neptunist school was established by the German mineralogist and geologist Abraham Werner. He accepted the idea of geological succession in sedimentary deposits but did not develop its historical implications, since he classified rocks by mineral content rather than by fossils. Secularizing earlier theories based on the biblical flood, Werner held that rock strata formed from a universal primeval ocean, which produced four types of rocks by sequential processes. Primitive rocks, such as granite, crystallized out of the primeval ocean and contained no fossils. Transitional rocks, such as micas and slate, contained only a few fossils. Sedimentary rocks such as coal and limestone were next and were rich in fossils. Derivative rocks such as sand and clay formed from the other three by processes of weathering. Werner believed that volcanoes resulted from the burning of underground coal and were not an important geological force.

Although Werner's theory about the origin of sedimentary rocks was largely upheld, most other rocks were eventually shown to have an igneous origin from a molten state. This idea was developed by the Plutonist school of geology, which stressed the geological activity of the internal heat of the earth, in addition to the volcanic eruptions of the Vulcanists. This view was developed by the Scottish amateur geologist James Hutton in his *Theory of the Earth* (1795). Hutton believed that the geological forces seen in the present operated in the same way and at the same rate in the earth's past and that this principle should be the basis of geological explanation: The present is the key to the past.

Hutton's "uniformitarian principle" contrasted with Werner's idea of a primeval ocean, which involved catastrophic events confined to the past and unobservable in the present. Hutton carefully observed the slow and steady erosion of the land as rivers carried silt into the sea. He examined the weathered beds of gravel, sand, and mud brought down by the rivers, as well as the crystalline granites of the Scottish mountains. He concluded that sedimentary rocks formed from beds of mud and sand compressed by overlying seas and heat pressure from below, while crystalline rocks came from molten material inside the earth brought to the surface by volcanic action.

Developing the idea that the interior of the earth is molten, Hutton suggested that molten rock pushes into cracks beneath the earth's crust, tilting up sedimentary strata and solidifying to form granites. Thus mountains were built with a crystalline core and sedimentary surface. This principle of injection was apparent in some granite intrusions into crevices in sedimentary rocks above, indicating that the granite was younger. The existence of granites of differing ages was contrary to Werner's assumptions. In some cases, Hutton found horizontal sedimentary strata covering tilted strata near the base of mountains, suggesting long periods of time since the strata tilted. The age of the earth appeared to be so long that catastrophic events did not seem to be necessary to account for its surface features.

Although these uniformitarian ideas found some early support, it was not enough to overcome religious objections to a theory that required such an ancient earth, delaying its eventual acceptance. In France, Georges Cuvier opposed Hutton's idea of slow geological processes with his theory of "catastrophism" in the introduction to his *Researches on Fossil Bones* (1812). Since there was no apparent continuity between successive strata and their fossils, he believed that a series of catastrophic floods must have occurred—rather than continuous forces—with each flood wiping out many species and eroding the earth. These catastrophes also tilted strata left by earlier floods, ending with Noah's flood some six thousand years ago. Cuvier's catastrophism applied

Neptunism to the vast time scale of Hutton. His influence delayed the acceptance of both biological and geological ideas of evolution in France for several decades.

In England and France, the study of strata was made easier by many well-exposed horizontal layers rich in fossils. These were systematically studied in France by Cuvier and in England by William Smith, who discovered in 1793 that each stratum had its own characteristic form of fossils. Their work revealed that strata near the surface were younger than those farther down, and a history of life forms could be worked out from their fossils. Further stratigraphic studies by Adam Sedgwick and Roderick Murchison identified the Cambrian series of strata with the oldest fossil-bearing rocks, the Silurian series with the earliest land plants, and the Devonian series dominated by fish fossils.

The discoveries of this "heroic age of geology" (1790-1830) were summarized by the Scottish geologist Charles Lyell. Reviving Hutton's uniformitarian ideas, Lyell published three volumes entitled *The Principles of Geology: Being an Attempt to Explain the Former Changes of the Earth's Surface by Reference to Causes Now in Operation* (1830-1833). Assuming indefinitely long periods of time, he insisted that geological forces had always been the same as they are now. Yet few of Lyell's contemporaries accepted his ideas before Charles Darwin developed them in his theory of organic evolution. The combined influence of Lyell and Darwin caused many scientists to shift away from Cuvier's catastrophism.

One of Cuvier's later associates, the Swiss-American naturalist Louis Agassiz, helped to modify the extreme uniformitarianism of Lyell. From the distribution of boulders and the grooves scratched on solid rock in the Swiss Alps, he showed in 1837 that Alpine glaciers had once stretched from the Alps across the plains to the west and up the sides of the Jura Mountains. In 1847, he accepted a position at Harvard University, and in North America, he found evidence that glaciers had also overrun that continent's northern half. Agassiz's Ice Age theory gradually won acceptance over more catastrophic flood theories, and evidence for several long ages of advancing and retreating ice over millions of years was eventually found.

Methods of Study

By the end of the nineteenth century, uniformitarian logic had become the primary method of studying the history of the earth's surface. Early in the twentieth century, the development of radioactive dating techniques confirmed the enormous age of the earth, revealing some 4.6 billion years during which the same slow processes of erosion, eruption, sedimentation, and ground movement visible today could account for everything from the Grand Canyon to marine fossils in the Alps. Yet this very method has identified discontinuities and anomalies that reveal the importance of catastrophic events in earth history. It now appears that the planet and its life forms have been shaped by more than gradual processes still operating today. Evidence has accumulated that many sudden and violent events in the past had widespread consequences, including torrential flooding, massive volcanic activity, and huge asteroid impacts causing global disasters. A "new catastrophism" uses uniformitarian methods to show that past catastrophes may be the key to understanding the present.

An early attempt to revive catastrophism was made by J. Harlen Bretz in 1923 to explain certain landscape features. He suggested that some of the world's largest floods poured down the Columbia River Gorge from melting glaciers into the Pacific Ocean, scouring much of the Columbia Plateau down to bedrock and creating the Channeled Scabland of eastern Washington. His ideas were finally vindicated from aerial and satellite photographs. It was then shown that glacial Lake Missoula in Montana produced as many as seventy floods from about fifteen thousand to twelve thousand years ago, matching legends of several native American tribes in the Pacific Northwest. At that time, a glacial ice dam impounded a body of water some 250 miles long. Repeated emptying of Lake Missoula occurred when the ice dam floated and broke, releasing as much as ten cubic miles per hour for at least forty hours. This deluge, some ten times the combined flow of all the world's rivers, removed soil as deep as one thousand feet, inundating three thousand square miles as deep as 350 feet.

More obvious catastrophic events are associated with volcanic activity. The most devastating volcanic eruption in recorded history was that of the Tambora volcano on Sumbawa Island, Indonesia, in 1815. The explosion killed twelve thousand people, and another eighty-two thousand died of starvation and disease. Tambora ejected so much volcanic ash into the stratosphere that Europe and North America experienced a year without a summer. Snow blanketed New England in June, and frosts blighted crops throughout the growing season.

Much larger volcanoes changed the landscape in prehistoric times. Volcanic activity in the Yellowstone region began about two million years ago as the continental crust moved westward. Subterranean melting of the crust produced a large underground reservoir of magma that resulted in three major explosions over a period of a million years. The first produced one of the largest eruptions to occur on earth, ejecting more than 620 cubic miles of magma. After the roof of the magma reservoir collapsed, it subsided several thousand feet, producing a caldera (giant crater) that covered an area of a thousand square miles. The volcanic ash canopy from the last eruption annihilated life over much of the western United States, and its fallout is preserved in strata from California to Kansas.

Recent discoveries have revealed that asteroid or comet impacts are the probable source of even more widespread annihilation of life and may be associated with extensive volcanic activity. In 1958, the Estonian astrophysicist Ernst Öpik suggested that a sufficiently large asteroid collision could penetrate the continental crust, triggering the formation of huge areas of lava floods such as the Deccan Traps in western India and the Columbia River Plateau in the Pacific Northwest. In 1973, the American chemist Harold Urey proposed that a comet collision could cause sufficient heating of the biosphere to explain global extinctions. More recently, University of Montana geologists have shown that an asteroid impact 17 million years ago could account for the immense lava flows of the Columbia River Plateau, spreading as far as three hundred miles from their source to form the largest volcanic landform in North America. As the North American continental plate moved westward, the resulting hot spot shifted to form the Yellowstone volcanic region.

In 1980, a team of physicists and geologists headed by Luis Alvarez and his son Walter discovered that the thin global sediment that separates the end of the Cretaceous era (age of dinosaurs) from the Tertiary era (age of mammals) contained anomalous quantities of the element iridium, rare on the earth but common in meteorites. They suggested that this K-T boundary layer, dated at 65 million years ago, was evidence of an asteroid collision that ejected enough matter into the atmosphere to produce a "cosmic winter," killing the dinosaurs and many other species. Their estimate of at least a ten-kilometer asteroid was confirmed in 1990, when a two-hundred-square-kilometer crater was identified in the Yucatán region of Mexico, dating from 65 million years ago. Such a collision could have produced shock waves that came to a focus on the opposite side of the earth, explaining the 65 million-year-old eruptions that formed the earth's largest lava fields in the Deccan Traps. Satellite surveys have revealed at least a hundred large but weathered craters on the earth known as "astroblemes."

Context

The "new catastrophism" now seems to be fairly well established, giving rise to new concerns about threats to modern civilization from asteroid collisions, as well as volcanoes, earthquakes, and floods. Estimates indicate that asteroids about fifty meters in size and comets about one hundred meters in size penetrate the earth's atmosphere about once per century. Theoretical models show that such intruders, traveling at more than fifteen kilometers per second, tend to explode about ten kilometers above the surface of the earth as a result of shock waves generated by the atmosphere. Such an explosion seems to account for the Tunguska event that occurred over Siberia in 1908, flattening trees over an area more than one hundred kilometers in diameter in the biggest impact catastrophe of the twentieth century. Similar events have probably occurred in recent centuries, but few if any have entered the historical record.

Asteroids more than about one hundred meters in size can strike the earth before the shock wave propagates far enough to cause them to explode above the surface. Lunar studies show that such asteroids hit the earth about once every one thousand to two thousand years and can produce craters from one kilometer to two kilometers in diameter. Meteor Crater in the Arizona desert is of approximately this size, but most such craters can no longer be detected as a result of weathering effects. The greatest damage from such collisions would occur if such an object hit the ocean. Such an impact could produce a tidal wave that would rise to as much as two hundred meters in height, killing millions of inhabitants in coastal cities.

Asteroids of between one and two kilometers in size are expected to hit the earth about once every one hundred thousand years; such an impact could fill the stratosphere with enough light-reflecting dust to lower the surface temperature by several degrees for a few months to years. The resulting collapse of agricultural production could kill perhaps half of the world's human population. If temperatures fell far enough, mass annihilation of carbon-dioxide-consuming ocean plankton would cause a rapid increase of carbon dioxide in the atmosphere, causing enough global warming to melt glaciers and the polar icecaps and flooding coastal areas.

The greatest damage to the biosphere could be caused by asteroids of ten or more kilometers in size, such as the one believed to have killed the dinosaurs 65 million years ago. These are estimated to strike the earth about once every 100 million years. There is growing evidence in the fossil record that mass extinctions of species have occurred every 26 million to 31 million years, leading to theories that such large asteroids or comets are periodically disturbed by some regular astronomical event. One theory suggests that the sun is accompanied by a companion "nemesis" star, too dim to be seen but with a highly eccentric orbit that periodically brings it near enough to the solar system to send comets on Earth-crossing orbits. In spite of these possible catastrophes, analysis shows that the risk of dying from asteroid impact in an average life span is roughly one chance in ten thousand—compared to one chance in a hundred of being killed in an automobile accident, and one chance in thirty thousand of dying in a flood.

Bibliography

Chapman, Clark, and David Morrison. *Cosmic Catastrophes*. New York: Plenum Press, 1989. A good review of classical catastrophism and uniformitarianism. Includes an authoritative discussion of the "new catastrophism" associated with asteroid collisions. The book is well illustrated and contains a good glossary.

Clube, Victor, and Bill Napier. *The Cosmic Winter*. Oxford, England: Basil Blackwell, 1990. A good history of meteorite collisions and their effects, including a chapter on assessing the risk from meteorite and asteroid collisions.

Harris, Stephen L. *Agents of Chaos*. Missoula, Mont.: Mountain Press, 1990. A good geological description of catastrophic events that have shaped the earth's crust, including earthquakes, volcanoes, floods, and asteroids. Many interesting illustrations and a good glossary are included.

Huggett, Richard. *Catastrophism: Systems of Earth History*. London: Edward Arnold, 1990. A careful geological assessment of the rise and fall of classical catastrophism and its modern neocatastrophist revival. Includes an extensive bibliography.

Lewis, John S. *Rain of Iron and Ice*. New York: Addison-Wesley, 1996. A survey of impact cratering in the solar system and the implications for bombardment of the earth by comets and asteroids. Includes a dozen photographs.

Raup, David M. *The Nemesis Affair: A Story of the Death of Dinosaurs and the Ways of Science*. New York: W. W. Norton, 1986. An excellent history of catastrophism and its revival in the light of asteroid-collision evidence, including a discussion of possible sources of periodic extinctions and the nature of scientific controversies.

Steel, Duncan. *Rogue Asteroids and Doomsday Comets*. New York: John Wiley & Sons, 1995. An interesting discussion of asteroid and comet impacts, past and future, including speculations about their historical influence and precautions that could be taken in the future. Contains a good glossary and bibliography.

Joseph L. Spradley

Cross-References

Archaeological Geology, 86; Asteroids, 98; Astroblemes, 106; The Cretaceous-Tertiary Boundary, 303; The Fossil Record, 760; Impact Volcanism, 3136; Mass Extinctions, 1514; Meteorite and Comet Impacts, 1623; Nemesis Theory, 3017; Tsunamis, 2548; Uniformitarianism, 2571; Volcanoes: Stratovolcanoes, 2688.

CAVES AND CAVERNS

Type of earth science: Geology
Field of study: Geomorphology

Caves, large natural holes in the ground, are part of the earth's plumbing system. Groundwater passes through most caves at some point in time, creating many unusual features.

Principal terms

CALCITE: a common, rock-forming mineral that is soluble in carbonic and dilute hydrochloric acids

GROUNDWATER: water beneath the earth's surface

KARST: a landscape formed by the dissolution of rocks; characterized by sinking and rising streams, caves, and underground rivers

LAVA: molten rock extruded from a volcano

LIMESTONE: sedimentary rock, usually formed on the ocean floor and composed of calcite

PHREATIC: a zone in the ground below the level of complete water saturation

SPELEOLOGIST: a scientist who explores and studies caves

SPELEOLOGY: the exploration and scientific study of caves

SPELEOTHEM: a mineral deposit formed within a cave

SUPERSATURATED SOLUTION: a solution that contains more of the dissolved material (solute) than the water or other liquid (solvent) can hold in equilibrium

VADOSE: a zone in the ground above the level of complete water saturation

Summary of the Phenomenon

Caves, or caverns, are natural cavities in rock large enough for a person to enter. Most caves develop by the process of groundwater dissolving limestone, a common rock deposited on ocean floors. Gypsum, dolomite, and marble (metamorphosed limestone) are other rocks that dissolve readily to form caves. Rain and snow pick up a trace of carbon dioxide as they travel through the atmosphere. Where the ground has a thick layer of decaying vegetation, more carbon dioxide combines with the water, and a dilute solution of carbonic acid forms. (Carbonic acid, carbon dioxide dissolved in water, is also present in soda pop.) The water soaks into the ground and finds its way into cracks in the soluble rock (limestone, dolomite, gypsum, or marble). The acid dissolves the rock in a process similar to that of water dissolving table salt. Groundwater removes what was previously solid rock, and a hole, or cave, remains.

The longest cave in the world is the Mammoth-Flint Ridge Cave System, a solutional cave near Bowling Green, Kentucky. More than 560 kilometers of cave passage have been surveyed and mapped.

In mountainous areas such as the Alps in Europe or the Sierra Madre Oriental in Mexico, groundwater moves hundreds or even thousands of meters downward through cracks in the rocks. The resulting passageways are mostly vertical, with deep shafts. The deepest explored cave in the world is the 1,602-meter-deep réseau Jean Bernard in the French Pyrenees. Scientists have shown that water passes through a 2,525-meter-deep cave in southern Mexico, but explorers have not yet successfully followed much of its course.

Streams flow into or out of the entrances to many actively growing caves. Scientists refer to entrances where water flows into caves as "insurgences." Entrances that have streams or rivers flowing out are called "resurgences." Insurgences and resurgences often mark the boundary between soluble and insoluble rocks. Where water reaches insoluble rock, it flows onto the surface and the cave ends. Similarly, streams flowing over insoluble rocks commonly sink into caves upon reaching a limestone terrain.

In some places, acid-charged water comes from deep in the earth and not from rainwater. Pockets of carbon dioxide and hydrogen sulfide in the earth's crust can combine with deep flowing water to form carbonic acid and sulfuric acid, respectively. Caves form when these deep waters rise through cracks in soluble rocks. Water charged with hydrogen sulfide rose up through limestone and dissolved the spectacular Carlsbad Cavern in New Mexico.

Lava flows on the flank of a volcano can create another type of cave, commonly called a "lava tube." As lava flows down the slope of a volcano, the surface cools and solidifies while liquid lava continues to flow under the crust. As the flow cools, self-constructed pipelines under the crust continue to pass fast-moving, hot lava down the slope. Tubes drain when no more lava passes through, and a cave remains. The deepest known cave in the United States, which is 1,099 meters deep, is the 59.33-kilometer-long Kazumura Cave, a lava tube on the island of Hawaii.

A few caves are in insoluble rocks such as granite, sandstone, and volcanic tuff. These features are generally small and have varied histories leading to their development. In many cases, groundwater has carried individual grains of sand, one at a time, from the base of a cliff where a spring emerges. With time, the resulting hole at the cliff base is deep enough to be called a cave. Other caves have formed under blocks of rocks that fell or slid down adjacent hillsides. Pounding waves excavate caves in cliffs along some ocean shorelines. These caves are usually referred to as "sea caves."

Ice caves sometimes form under glaciers near their toes. Melt water flowing under a glacier during summer may enlarge a passageway large enough to form a cave. Ice caves, however, are usually short-lived and are constantly changing size and shapes. Solutional caves are often divided into three categories: phreatic caves, vadose caves, and dry caves. Most phreatic caves are still actively forming. Their passages are below the water table and completely filled with water. Vadose caves are above the water table, but water passes through them as rivers and streams. Some caves form under vadose conditions. Other caves in the vadose zone were saturated when they formed. They now provide convenient paths for water to flow through unsaturated zone. Dry caves are no longer actively enlarging. The water that formed them has withdrawn.

The air in a dry cave is usually humid, but the cave does not act as a conduit for water.

Water levels in caves commonly respond quickly to rain. A river may pass through an otherwise dry passage during the spring snow melt. A vadose passage with a small stream can become completely filled with water within a few minutes after a heavy rain commences. Tops of phreatic zones in caves have been observed to rise more than 50 meters within a few hours after the start of a surface deluge.

Once the void forms, nature commonly starts to fill caves. While most of the limestone (or dolomite or gypsum) dissolves, some impurities in the rock always remain as sediments on the cave floor. In addition, sand, mud, and gravel brought into the cave from outside by streams add to these sediments. Over hundreds, thousands, or even millions of years, caves can become completely choked by sediments.

If too much rock is dissolved and the rock is not strong enough to support the void, the ceiling collapses. Failure can occur one small rock at a time or in massive blocks. If the cave is still actively forming, groundwater may eventually dissolve the debris, and the passage will continue to grow upward. However, if the debris is not removed, the passage can completely fill with rubble, ending the existence of the cave.

Attractive deposits of minerals, called "speleothems," form from supersaturated water in a cave. Supersaturated waters contain more dissolved minerals, usually calcite, than they can maintain in solution. Supersaturation can occur when water evaporates and the dissolved minerals stay behind in the remaining liquid water. More commonly, supersaturation happens when cave water releases dissolved carbon dioxide. The less carbon dioxide dissolved in the water, the less acidic the water, and the less mineral the water can hold in solution. Cave water loses carbon dioxide—in the same manner that carbon dioxide bubbles escape from soda pop—when the surrounding pressure on the water drops (like opening a soda can) or when the temperature of the water rises. In both cases, dissolved minerals solidify—a process called "precipitation"—as speleothems.

The most common speleothems are soda straws, stalactites, stalagmites, and flowstone. Soda straws look like their namesakes and hang from the ceilings of caves. Water is fed from a hole at the top of the soda straw, flows down through the hollow speleothem, and hangs on the end before falling. Calcite precipitates around the edges of the water as it slowly drips from the soda straw's end. Stalactites are typically cone-shaped deposits that hang from the ceiling. Originally soda straws, they grow as water deposits calcite around the outside of the speleothem. Stalagmites grow when drops of water from the ceiling hit the ground, lose carbon dioxide when they splash (like shaking a soda can), and precipitate calcite. They look almost like upside-down stalactites, but their ends usually are more rounded. Stalactites and stalagmites that grow together result in a "column." Flowstone, a sheet of calcite coating a sloping wall or floor of a cave, forms under flowing water.

Gypsum, composed of calcium sulfate, is commonly deposited within limestone, dolomite, and gypsum caves. Gypsum precipitates in a similar manner as calcite, but the process involves dissolved hydrogen sulfide instead of carbon dioxide. Gypsum speleothem shapes differ from those of calcite speleothems. One type of speleothem, a gypsum flower, looks like clear or white rock flowers growing out of cave walls. They form at the base of the "petals" and extrude earlier-formed deposits away from the wall in a manner similar to the squeezing of toothpaste out of a tube.

Ice forms many of the same speleothems as calcite. Ice stalactites (icicles), stalagmites, and flowstone are displayed in cold caves, particularly in winter and spring. Some caves in the Austrian Alps have moving glaciers and massive ice columns.

The temperature of most caves is the mean (average) annual temperature of the local area above ground. Temperatures typically fluctuate slightly near entrances and usually are a constant temperature a short way from the entrance. Thus, caves usually seem cool in summer and warm in winter. The moisture in the ground makes most caves very humid. Like temperature, humidity remains nearly constant year round away from entrances.

Caves try to adjust to changes in local barometric conditions. When the outside atmosphere changes from higher barometric pressure to a lower pressure, strong winds blow out the entrances of large, air-filled caves as they also try to lower their atmospheric pressure. When an area changes from lower pressure to higher pressure, large caves will suck air in from the outside. Just as on the surface, the temperature and air pressure of caves increase at greater depths. The change can be substantial in caves of more than 1,000 meters in depth. "Blowing caves" have entrances at different elevations. A chimney effect causes cold air to drop through the cave and blow out the lower entrance throughout the winter. The effect reverses as air blows out the upper entrance during the summer.

Methods of Study

Studying caves is one of the few scientific endeavors that still requires original geographic exploration. Although the continents' surfaces are almost thoroughly explored, most of the world's caves have never been entered. Exploration in caves can be hazardous. Since caves are the earth's natural storm sewers, flooding is common, and many inexperienced cave explorers have drowned. Falling is the second most common cause of serious accidents. Visits to undeveloped caves should always be in the company of an experienced caver. Cave diving is extremely hazardous, and only experienced scuba divers with extensive specialized training should enter a water-filled passage or cave.

Geologic research starts with exploring, surveying, and drawing detailed maps. Well-trained amateur explorers largely do this work. Using compasses, inclinometers (instruments that measure slope), and tape measures or similar devices, explorers measure the width, height, length, and depth of cave passages while drawing a detailed sketch of the floor, walls, and ceiling. Experienced explorers also record the geology of the passage, standing and flowing water, and speleothems.

The collected data must be adjusted using trigonometry to scale the true horizontal and vertical distances on the final map. Adjusted or "reduced" data are plotted to scale. Then, a cartographer uses the notes and sketches made in the cave to draw a plan and vertical cross sections. These maps give scientists important information about the unique qualities of the cave and provide a base for recording further observations.

Understanding water flow in caves is important to people living on the surface. Groundwater in karst areas behaves differently from groundwater elsewhere. Because water passing through a cave is, in effect, passing through a pipe rather than through sand or other soil, there is no opportunity for the ground to filter out pollutants. Contamination dumped in a stream that enters a cave may come out in a spring tens of kilometers away.

When speleologists cannot follow the water in a cave for part of its underground journey, they use non-toxic dyes or other markers to determine where the water goes. Before pouring dye into a disappearing stream, scientists put traps in all springs and wells that may be fed by the stream. The traps are monitored during the weeks and months following the injection of dye to detect it. In karst regions, one cave can be the source of several springs many kilometers apart.

Speleothems are sources of important information about the climate in the past. Molecules that make up calcite contain oxygen. Most oxygen atoms have eight neutrons, but some oxygen atoms have ten neutrons in their nuclei. Both types are "isotopes" of oxygen. These isotopes do not decay, but the ratio of the two oxygen isotopes to each other indicates the temperature of the water that precipitated the speleothem. Since the temperature of the cave water is generally the mean surface temperature, speleologists can learn about the past temperatures of an area.

Many speleothems contain trace amounts of a uranium isotope that decays to lead. Using radioactive dating techniques, speleologists can calculate the age of a speleothem. If the oxygen isotope ratio is also known, the past average temperature of the area at a specific time can be determined. Radioactive dating of speleothems near coastlines also gives information on sea-level rises and falls. Stalactites and stalagmites only grow in air-filled environments. Some Caribbean "blue holes," caves under the ocean floor, have stalactites and stalagmites. The ages of these speleothems prove to scientists that the ocean in the area was lower thousands of years ago.

Caves are particularly delicate environments. Once damaged, most caves will never return to their natural state. Scientists are very careful to avoid damaging a cave. Even touching many speleothems will harm or destroy them. Speleologists collect speleothems only when they have a specific purpose and permission from the landowner. They then collect the smallest piece necessary for the job. Samples for radioactive dating and oxygen isotope analysis are usually small cores drilled into the speleothem. Amateurs should never touch, break, or remove a speleothem. One of the greatest values of caves is their pristine beauty.

Context

Caves are sites of great beauty and adventure. They are the only continental areas left where individuals can truly be the first to explore and map. Underground streams sculpt beautiful, smooth walls. Bizarre and spectacular speleothems sparkle against the brown and gray walls of rock. A visit to a cave is an escape from the civilized world.

The constant temperature and humidity and protection from rain, snow, and wind in caves made them valuable resources to early humans. Earlier people used caves as art galleries, temples, shelters, refrigerators, sources of minerals, burial sites, and fortresses. The protected environment of caves preserves their paintings, shrines, pottery, baskets, and skeletal remains. Many of the world's most important archaeological sites are in caves. Animals also seek the shelter of caves. Much of the knowledge of many extinct mammals is based on the remains left in caves. Cave explorers have found bones, feces, and even mummies of extinct animals. Knowledgeable speleologists do not touch or remove archaeological (ancient human) or paleontological (ancient animal) material. Such items may have been preserved for hundreds or even thousands of years, and removing them from the cave environment will usually destroy them. Instead, experienced explorers work with specialists from a museum or college to document their finds.

Today, caves are used as sites of recreation, natural science classrooms, and preserves for endangered animals such as bats. In caves, scientists collect information about past climates and sea levels and examine the interior of the earth firsthand.

Caves can also affect human lives on the surface. When the roof of a cave collapses, a sinkhole develops. Homes and businesses are occasionally lost over a period of a few hours when a cave collapses underneath them. While caves are generally stable and roof collapses are rare, the process is often greatly accelerated in urban areas when a town pumps groundwater out faster than it is replenished. As a previously filled cave drains, water no longer partially supports the ceiling. This is the time when a cave is most vulnerable to roof collapse.

Water traveling through caves moves through the ground much faster than water moving through insoluble rocks. Polluted water entering a cave can travel through a natural pipeline without experiencing the filtration and cleansing that occurs when water passes through sand. The contaminated water may cross under surface drainage divides and re-emerge at a spring tens of kilometers away. Learning the course of water flowing through caves can help prevent a town from drinking contaminated water after a toxic spill into a distant source stream. Researchers in a karst area with a contaminated water supply may learn the source of the contamination by tracing the path of the underground water through caves.

Many endangered species, particularly bats, depend on the unique environment of caves to live. If the atmosphere of their cave home is altered by closing or enlarging of entrances, these animals may die or be forced to try to find another home. Earth scientists working with biologists determine the conditions necessary for the welfare of the animals. They strive to ensure that cave habitats are not adversely affected by the gating of an entrance, by quarrying near the cave, or by developing it as a public attraction.

Bibliography

Courbon, Paul, et al. *Atlas: Great Caves of the World.* St. Louis, Mo.: Cave Books, 1989. Describes and provides maps of the deepest and longest caves in the world.

Includes all countries and all types of caves. An essential reference book for understanding the world's greatest caves.

Davies, W. E., and I. M. Morgan. *Geology of Caves*. U.S. Geological Survey, 1991. A brief, inexpensive brochure published by the U.S. government. Explains how most caves form and discusses the common speleothems within them.

Erickson, Jon. *Craters, Caverns, and Canyons: Delving Beneath the Earth's Surface*. Chicago: Facts on File, 1993. Covers structural geology and geomorphology, including caves, at a high-school level. A basic explanation of caves.

Exley, Sheck. *Caverns Measureless to Man*. St. Louis, Mo.: Cave Books, 1994. Sheck Exley was the greatest scuba diver ever to explore caves. This book documents his explorations and the water-filled caves he explored. Although the book focuses on his explorations, a good feeling for how caves develop and their significance can be achieved by reading about his adventures.

Hill, Carol A., and Paolo Forti. *Cave Minerals of the World*. Huntsville, Ala.: National Speleological Society, 1986. The definitive book on speleothems. Describes them and explains how they form; filled with beautiful pictures.

Jagnow, David H., and Rebecca Rohwer Jagnow. *Stories from Stones*. Carlsbad, N.M.: Carlsbad Caverns-Guadalupe Mountains Association, 1992. Describes the geology of the Guadalupe Mountains in New Mexico and gives an excellent description of how the spectacular caves in the area evolved. Carlsbad Cavern and other area caves formed in an unusual manner, and the Jagnows are experts on their origins.

Middleton, John, and Tony Waltham. *The Underground Atlas: A Gazetteer of the World's Cave Regions*. New York: St. Martin's Press, 1986. Describes the major caves and karst areas of nearly every country in the world. The potential for finding caves in countries without presently known caves is also discussed.

Moore, George W., and G. Nicholas Sullivan. *Speleology: The Study of Caves*. 2d ed. St. Louis: Cave Books, 1978. Small, easy-to-read book clearly explains the fundamentals of cave geology and biology. Excellent, brief discussions on cave atmospheres, speleothems, evolution of blind cave animals, interactions of microorganisms with the cave walls, and human uses of caves.

Rea, G. Thomas, ed. *Caving Basics: A Comprehensive Guide for Beginning Cavers*. 3d ed. Huntsville, Ala.: National Speleological Society, 1992. A comprehensive book on the geology, biology, archaeology, and exploration of caves written by members of the world's largest organization dedicated to caves. Each chapter was written by a leading expert on the subject. Useful bibliographies accompany each chapter.

Louise D. Hose

Cross-References

Aquifers, 71; Carbonates, 190; Dolomite, 2889; Groundwater Movement, 1020; Groundwater Pollution, 1028; Karst Topography, 1310; Limestone, 2980; Paleoclimatology, 1993; Water-Rock Interactions, 2462; Weathering and Erosion, 2723.

CONTINENTAL DRIFT

Type of earth science: Geology
Field of study: Tectonics

Continental drift is the modern paradigm that describes and accounts for the distribution of present-day continents and associated geological formations and phenomena, including mountain ranges, mineral deposits, volcanoes, and earthquakes.

Principal terms

CONTINENTAL DRIFT: the horizontal displacement or rotation of continents relative to one another

CONVECTION (CELL): a mechanism of heat transfer in a flowing material in which hot material from the bottom rises because of its lesser density while cool surface material sinks

CONTINENTAL CRUST: the outermost part of the lithosphere, consisting of granite and granodiorite

OCEANIC CRUST: the outer part of the lithosphere, consisting mostly of basalt

EARTHQUAKE: the violent motion of the ground caused by the passage of a seismic wave radiating from a fault along which sudden movement has occurred

FAULT: a fracture in the earth's crust along which there has been relative displacement

GONDWANALAND: a hypothetical supercontinent made up of approximately the present continents of the Southern Hemisphere

LAURASIA: a hypothetical supercontinent made up of approximately the present continents of the Northern Hemisphere

LITHOSPHERE: the outer layer of the earth, situated above the asthenosphere and containing the crust, continents, and tectonic plates

PANGAEA: a supercontinent, made up of all presently known continents, which began to break up in the Mesozoic era

PALEOMAGNETISM: the science of reconstruction of the earth's former magnetic fields and the former positions of the continents from the magnetization in rocks

PLATE: a large segment of the lithosphere that is internally ridged and moves independently over the interior, meeting in convergence zones and separating at divergence zones

PLATE TECTONICS: the study of plate formation, movement, and interactions

TECTONICS: the study of the movements and deformation of the earth's crust on a large scale

Summary of the Phenomenon

Continental drift is the guiding model for the mechanisms driving the geologic forces near the surface of the earth. This theory is the simplest explanation for the behavior of the earth's crust and the distribution of continents and their associated topographic features. The theory is useful not only in decoding the history of the earth but also in predicting future observations.

The idea that continents may have occupied different geographies in the past was developed by Alfred L. Wegener as early as 1910. Wegener observed that the coastlines of the Americas corresponded with those of Europe and Africa in a jigsaw-puzzle fashion. He was encouraged to learn that similar fossils had been discovered on both sides of the Atlantic Ocean, and he proposed that the splitting up of a supercontinent and the drift of its pieces could explain this data. He continued to refine his ideas and published a book, *The Origins of Continents and Oceans*, in 1915. By his account, about 200 million years ago, at the end of the Permian period, there existed a single supercontinent that Wegener called "Pangaea." This supercontinent, he theorized, broke apart, and the various pieces drifted; for example, North America and South America moved westward from Europe and Africa, creating the Atlantic Ocean.

Wegener had an American rival, Frank B. Taylor, who in 1910 published his own theory of mobile continents. Interestingly, Taylor's starting point was not the physical similarity of the Atlantic coastlines but the pattern of mountains belts in Eurasia and Europe. Yet Taylor's hypothesis, like Wegener's, soon faded from scientific memory.

There was, however, much physical evidence to suggest that continental drift was a feasible theory. First, the physical fit was a good one; in addition, the discovery of similar fossils, mineral deposits, glacier deposits, and mountain ranges seem to show a correlation across the oceans. Wegener described these correlations: "It is just as if we were to refit the torn pieces of a newspaper by matching their edges and then check whether the lines of print run smoothly across." Efforts to confirm the hypothesis were interrupted by World War I and, soon thereafter, the Depression and World War II. The theory of continental drift thus retained its marginal status until the 1950's.

The major stumbling block to its acceptance was the need to describe a plausible mechanism for driving the continents. Pushing continents around requires a tremendous amount of energy, and no model proposed was acceptable to the geophysics community. The only plausible suggestion came from British geologist Arthur Holmes, who tentatively proposed that thermal convection within the mantle could split the continents and drive them across the surface. Holmes was one of the most respected geologists of his time, and the scientific community did pay attention to his idea. Yet he could offer no evidence to support it, and continental drift thus remained merely an interesting possibility in the eyes of most scientists.

Wegener had a more difficult time gathering an audience. To most of the geologic community, he seemed to be an outsider attempting to restructure the science. For example, in the publication of the 1928 American Association of Petroleum Geologists symposium, R. T. Chamberlain quotes a remark made by a colleague: ". . . if we are to believe Wegener's hypothesis we must forget everything which has been learned in the last 70 years and start all over again." (This, however, is exactly what happened in the 1950's, as the strength of the hypothesis eventually became evident.) The hypothesis thus lived on the fringes of the scientific community and was supported by a minority of geologists, most of whom worked in the Southern Hemisphere.

Worldwide interest in the origins and evolution of the planet's features culminated in the observation of the International Geophysical Year from July, 1957, to December, 1958. The result of this effort was that in almost every area of research, and especially in geology, scientists found the earth and particularly its oceans to be very different from what they had imagined. One of the most interesting features studied was the Mid-Atlantic Ridge, an investigation that would lead to the understanding of plate tectonics.

The existence of a submarine ridge in the Atlantic had been recognized in the 1850's by Matthew Maury, director of the U.S. Navy's Department of Charts and Instruments. The British expedition aboard HMS *Challenger* (1872-1876) also recorded a submarine mountain. The next advance came in the 1920's with a German expedition led by Nobel laureate Fritz Haber. The expedition utilized an echo sounder to map the ocean floor. In 1933, German oceanographers Theodor Stocks and Georg Wust produced a detailed map of the ridge, and they noted a valley that seemed to be bisecting it. In 1935, geophysicist Nicholas H. Heck found a strong correlation between earthquakes and the Mid-Atlantic Ridge.

Oceanic exploration resumed after World War II as a predominately American venture. The data collected pointed to an array of seemingly unrelated phenomena. In 1950, Maurice Ewing of the Lamont-Geological Observatory discovered that no continental crust existed beneath the ocean basins. In 1952, Roger Revelle, the director of the Scripps Institute of Oceanography, and his student A. E. Maxwell measured the heat flow from the earth's interior and discovered that it was hotter over the oceanic ridges. Additional data from Jean P. Rothe, director of the International Bureau of Seismology, revealed a continuous belt of earthquake centers associated with this submarine mountain range, which extends from Iceland through the mid-Atlantic, around South Africa, and into the Indian Ocean to the Red Sea. In 1956, Maurice Ewing and Bruce C. Heezen mapped a large area of this submarine mountain range and confirmed the existence of a rift valley bisecting the mountain crest. A peculiar faulting style was discovered in association with the range in 1959 by Victor Vacquier. The mountain range was offset by a large transverse fault that ran for hundreds of miles but did not extend into the continents. In 1961, Ewing and Mark Landisman discovered that this ridge system extended throughout the world's oceans, was seismically and volcanically active, and was mostly devoid of sediment cover.

The paleomagnetic researches of University of Manchester scientist Patrick M. S. Backett and his student Keith Runcom proved central to understanding the relationships among these phenomena. Their studies of fossil magnetism suggested that the position and polarity of the earth's magnetic field had once been very different than its present orientation. This data could only make sense if one assumed that the continents had shifted relative to the poles and to one another.

By the end of the 1950's, it was clear that then-current geologic theories had failed to predict or explain these seemingly unrelated phenomena, and the new data required a new theory. In 1960, Harry Hammond Hess proposed a simple model to explain the data. He suggested that seafloor spreading powered by convection currents within the mantle might be the cause of the motion of the continents. Hess's theory, though simple, was radical; it bore out Chamberlain's earlier insight that previous geologic models would have to be discarded and that the geologic community would have to reinterpret and test all of its data in the light of the new model. This did not come easily to the science community; eventually, however, the theory of continental drift did emerge as the dominant paradigm for the earth sciences.

Methods of Study

The lengthy process leading to the acceptance of the theory of continental drift is not unusual in the history of science. Often, a hypothesis has to wait upon the development of technology or upon accidents of timing for its observations to be tested.

The observation that there was a relationship between the coastlines of the Americas and those of Europe and Africa can be traced to Francis Bacon, who in 1620 noted the similarities of shape. The idea was further enhanced by a French monk, François Placet, who in 1666 suggested that the earth's land masses had split as a result of the biblical flood, thus separating Europe and Africa from the Americas. The idea was repeated by a German theologian, Theodor Lilenthal, in the 1700's. In 1800, Alexander von Humbolt suggested that the oceans had eroded the land to further divide the continents. The drift theory was then supported by Evan Hopkins, who in 1844 proposed the existence of a "magnetic fluid" that circulated to drive the continents. In 1857, American geologist Richard Owen published *Key to the Geology of the Globe*, in which he proposed that the earth was originally a tetrahedron that had expanded in a great cataclysm, breaking the crust and expelling the moon from the Mediterranean.

These ideas and hypotheses were interesting but largely unsupported by physical evidence; Wegener's and Taylor's hypotheses proposed in the early twentieth century were thus fundamentally different from those of the past. Still, it was the development of new technological tools that illuminated the phenomena and eventually supported the drifting-continent theory. Much of this new technology was developed as a result of World Wars I and II and the technological race of the Cold War.

Wegener collected data from paleontology to show a correlation between continents and to illustrate that the continents had been in different latitudes in the geologic past. Further, he suggested an experiment to confirm the theory; the experiment failed not because the idea was inappropriate but because the experimental error resulting from his crude equipment was greater than the phenomena he was trying to measure. His experiment, conducted in 1922 and again in 1927 and 1936, involved the measurement of the time it took radio signals to travel across the Atlantic. The measurements failed to reveal a widening of the Atlantic through progressively longer travel times.

Upon the advent of satellite and laser technology, however, widening was detected.

Eventually, wartime technology such as sonar was applied to scientific applications. Sonar is the underwater version of radar; an energy pulse is sent out, and its reflection from the seafloor is recorded. This data can be translated via computers (another new technology) to create either a profile or contour map. Literally thousands of soundings were made over thousands of kilometers of ocean in an effort to construct a map of the ocean floor in the greatest possible detail. These data began to produce a map that revealed rather remarkable features, including a continuous 64,000-kilometer mountain range that had a valley running along its crest. Princeton's Harry Hess realized the significance of the valley on top of the mountain range: It was a tensional, or "pull-apart," feature. The same forces that formed the mountain chain were also pulling it apart.

Other technologies were also contributing to the investigation. After World War II, a worldwide network of seismographs was deployed, not so much for recording earthquakes as to listen for atomic explosions. These new and sensitive instruments mostly recorded earthquakes at plate boundaries and revealed their outlines. (Interestingly, no nuclear powers camouflaged their atomic blasts as earthquakes by detonation at a plate boundary). The earthquake pattern was a fingerprint of plate activity and evidence of a dynamic crust.

Other compelling data were those of monitoring internal heat flow. The temperature of the earth increases with depth. At the core, the temperature is above 4,000 degrees Celsius. This heat flowing from the interior can be measured; the hottest crustal areas were found to be above the junction of plates that are spreading centers.

More traditional geologic sampling of the subsurface was conducted by retrieving core samples from below the ocean depths. These physical samples were analyzed according to the type of sediment and the age of fossils present. The findings were surprising: The oceans are very young compared to the continents, and the sediments on the midoceanic ridges is thin to nonexistent, while the sediments next to the continents are kilometers thick. Therefore, not only are the oceans young, but they are also youngest in the middle and oldest next to the continents.

The straw that broke the back of opposition to the theory of continental drift came with the study of fossil magnetism. Sedimentary and igneous rocks offer a record of the orientation of the earth's magnetic field through time, as iron particles within them are incorporated into their structures as they form. The decoding of these fossil magnetic fields suggested that the magnetic poles have reversed themselves and that the continents have wandered through the latitudes. If the poles reversed and the continents wandered, then a mirror image of polar reversal correlating with submarine topography should be present on both sides of a spreading center such as the Mid-Atlantic Ridge. This was exactly what was observed. The model was no longer merely an explanation of previously observed phenomena; it had also been shown to be capable of predicting future observations. Earth scientists thus came to perceive the idea of drifting continents and plate tectonics as the unifying model of geologic phenomena.

Context

The development of the continental drift theory is a story of how science works in a period of paradigm revolution. This period began with Alfred Wegener's work in 1912 and ended with Harry Hess's discoveries in 1960. The model Hess developed gave a new explanation of virtually all geologic phenomena at or near the surface of the earth. Within its field, the theory has had an impact comparable to that of Charles Darwin's theory of evolution in the field of biology. In essence, the theory of continental drift accounts for the global distribution of the continents, the birth and death of oceans, the distribution of earthquakes, volcanoes, and mountain ranges, and leads explorers to mineral and fossil-fuel deposits.

Bibliography

Engle, A. E., H. L. James, and B. F. Leonard, eds. *Petrologic Studies: A Volume in Honor of A. F. Buddington*. New York: Geological Society of America, 1962. The primary source for Hess's theory of continental drift.

James, Harold Lloyd. *Harry Hammond Hess*. National Academy of Sciences Biographical Memoirs, vol. 43. New York: Columbia University Press, 1973. This biographical sketch yields insight into Hess and his synthesis of the oceanic data to form a new paradigm.

LeGrand, H. E. *Drifting Continents and Shifting Theories*. New York: Cambridge University Press, 1988. Traces the development of the continental drift paradigm and the work of people who contributed to the data collection and debate.

Scientific American. *Continents*. San Francisco: W. H. Freeman, 1973. An excellent resource for landmark papers from 1952 to 1970. Illustrates the progression of the geologic "revolution."

Sullivan, W. *Continents in Motion: The New Earth Debate*. New York: McGraw Hill, 1974. Well written and illustrated with drawings and photographs. Develops like a detective story rather than a textbook.

Young, P. *Drifting Continents, Shifting Seas*. New York: Impact Books, 1976. An introductory book to the story of continental drift. The emphasis is on the researchers involved and the chronological development of an idea.

Richard C. Jones

Cross-References

CONTINENTS AND SUBCONTINENTS

Type of earth science: Geology
Field of study: Tectonics

Continents are large land masses with elevations that are considerably higher than that of the surrounding crust. Subcontinents are smaller land masses that converged over time to form the large continents familiar today. Because of this, continents have a wide variety of terrains and landforms.

Principal terms

CONTINENT: a large land area consisting of a variety of terrains
CRATON: a stable, relatively immobile area of the earth's crust that forms the nucleus of a continental land mass
CRUST: the thin layer of rock covering the surface of the earth; solid and cool, the crust makes up the continents and floor of the ocean and may be covered with thick layers of sediments
DENSITY: the weight per unit volume of a substance
MAFIC ROCKS: rocks that contain large amounts of magnesium and iron, found mainly in the oceanic crust and upper mantle
MANTLE: the region of the earth between the dense core and the thin crust; the mantle makes up most of the volume of the earth
OROGENIC BELT: an area where mountain-forming forces have been applied to the crust
PLATE TECTONICS: the process that causes the continents and large unbroken land areas within the oceanic crust, called "plates," to move slowly along with currents of rock in the upper mantle
SEDIMENTS: rocks and soil that have been eroded from their original position by forces of weather
SUBCONTINENT: an area of land that is less extensive in size and has a smaller variety of terrains than a continent

Summary of the Phenomenon

The word "continent" comes from the Latin *continere*, which means "to hold together." Continents are the large land masses composed of lighter rocks that ride on top of the more dense rocks in the mantle, somewhat like a cork in water. This results in areas on the earth's surface that are higher than sea level, producing dry land. The earth was not formed with these continents in place; a long, complicated process resulted in the formation of the land masses familiar today.

When the earth was first formed approximately 5 billion years ago, it was a molten ball composed of all the elements. The high temperature of the planet was the result of the heat released from several sources: the process that formed the planet; decay of radioactive elements; and intense meteoritic bombardment. This molten state allowed the different elements, and the compounds they form, to differentiate, or separate.

This differentiation process is similar to mixing different kinds of oil with water in a bottle. Shake up the bottle, and the different liquids will be mixed together. Let it sit, and they will begin to form layers. The water is densest and will form a layer on the bottom. Each of the different oils will then form a separate layer above the water, with the layer of the densest oil being on top of the water and the least-dense oil forming the uppermost layer.

Similarly, when the earth underwent differentiation, the densest material, mainly iron and nickel, sank toward the interior and formed the planetary core. Compounds and elements that were medium in density would lie on top of the denser core and form the layers of the planetary mantle. The least-dense compounds floated to the surface and eventually formed the crust, seawater, and atmosphere. These least-dense compounds consisted principally of the elements silicon, oxygen, aluminum, potassium, sodium, calcium, carbon, nitrogen, hydrogen, and helium, with lesser amounts of other elements.

The earth today has two kinds of crust: the heavier, thinner crust under the oceans and the thicker, lighter continental crust. The oceanic crust was created between 4.2 billion and 4.5 billion years ago, has an average density of 2.9 grams per cubic centimeter, and consists mainly of mafic rocks. Mafic rocks are made of minerals that consist mainly of magnesium and iron. The most common kind of mafic rock in the oceanic crust is basalt, a dark, hard stone. The dark maria on the face of the Moon are the result of basalt that was able to reach the Moon's surface after large meteor impacts. Beneath the crust is the upper mantle, which has a density of approximately 3.3 grams per cubic centimeter and consists of mafic rocks that contain an even larger percentage of magnesium and iron; hence, they are called "ultramafic." This layer formed at about the same time as the oceanic crust.

Mixed with these two layers were even lighter materials, mainly compounds of silicon, oxygen, and aluminum, but the high temperature of the planet would not allow these materials to start solidifying until about 4 billion years ago. When this occurred, the first continental rocks began to form, although they were being continuously broken up. The oceanic rocks were mainly basalt; the continental rocks were mainly granite with a density of about 2.7 grams per cubic centimeter. The cooling process was slowed by the formation of crystal structures within the oceanic crust and upper mantle that forced out certain rare-earth elements, including the radioactive elements. These elements had to go somewhere and are thus found concentrated in continental rocks. Continental granites contain about ten times as much uranium as the oceanic basalts and about a thousand times as much as the upper mantle rocks. Heat released by the decay of this concentration of radioactive elements helped keep the continental rocks molten longer than the oceanic rocks.

This period in the earth's history was also characterized by a large amount of volcanic activity; large chains of volcanoes formed archipelagoes of islands. As a result of plate tectonics, these islands would move around on the surface of the earth and would eventually be reabsorbed back into the earth's interior at subduction zones.

Subduction zones occur where one plate in the earth's crust meets another. The denser, heavier plate will be forced under the other plate and into the upper mantle, where it will be melted and returned to the surface through volcanic activity. Given enough time, this process will completely recycle the oceanic crust; today there is none of the original oceanic crust remaining.

Sometime about 4 billion years ago, the intense meteoritic bombardment suddenly came to an end; the surface of the planet began to cool more quickly, and more island chains were formed. However, the still-molten, lighter continental rocks would sometimes flow into large cracks, called "fissures," in the volcanic islands and provide them with additional buoyancy. When these islands, riding on the surface of a plate, reached the subduction zones, they would be too light to be subducted and would instead be scraped off by the other plate. As the other plate continued to move along, it would continue to scrape off more of the light islands; over time, a large amount of this lighter material would accumulate in front of the plate. Eventually, that plate would be subducted by another plate, and the light continental material it had collected would be added to any collected by the new plate. In this way, the size of continental crustal material grew until it was large enough to be a subcontinent.

A subcontinent is an area of land that is too large to be pushed simply by the movement of oceanic crustal plates. Instead, these large pieces of land ride on top of moving mantle rock deep beneath the surface. Yet while subcontinents are extensive, they are still not large enough to be considered continents. Modern examples of subcontinents include the island of Greenland and the Indian subcontinent. The importance of subcontinents is that they will eventually collide with one another. When they do, they can stick together, forming even larger areas of land and, eventually, continents. This process is called "accretion."

When subcontinents or continents collide, the event is something like an automobile crash in very slow motion. The two large bodies are moving and do not stop immediately; they continue to plow into each other, causing the rock to bend, fold, and lift, forming mountain ranges. Areas where this has occurred in the past are called "orogenic belts." The Himalayas are an example of the result of this process. The Indian subcontinent took millions of years to move from southeast Africa to its current position on the southern side of Asia. When it collided with Asia, the force was enough to raise a giant plateau, with the towering Himalayas on top. Large areas between the orogenic belts are called "cratons." The American Midwest between the Appalachian and Rocky Mountains is an example of a craton.

This movement of the land masses continues even after the formation of continents. The continents continue to ride on top of currents of rock in the mantle, slowly making their way across the earth's surface. Currently, continents are moving at a rate of about five to ten centimeters (two to four inches) per year, but this rate was faster in the past. Over millions of years, the continents have been able to move great distances, and the shape and distribution of continents in the past did not resemble the global features of today. At times, the continents have been together to form supercontinents that last for millions of years before breaking apart.

In addition to accretion, two other major forces at work on continents are volcanism and erosion. Volcanism is a result of plate tectonics, and most volcanism thus occurs along the edges of the land masses where subduction is occurring or where fault lines are found. Volcanism recycles material that has been subducted and adds to the mass of the continents.

Erosion, meanwhile, wears down landforms. Rain, ice, heat, wind, and flowing water all work to break apart the rocks and slowly wash the surface material away. Some of these sediments are washed to sea, while others collect in low-lying areas on the land. These sedimentary deposits can be several kilometers thick and will eventually turn into sedimentary rock.

Continents are complicated structures consisting of a patchwork of a large variety of landforms. The processes that formed the continents of today have been going on for billions of years and are continuing. The forces of plate tectonics are still slowly moving the continents, forming mountains, subduction zones, fault lines, and volcanoes, while the effects of weather work to wear down the land masses.

Methods of Study

Continents are vast in size and complexity. Likewise, the study of these land masses is also vast and complex. Much of the work in learning about continents is hampered by the fact that scientists can easily sample only the thinnest top layer of the crust; moreover, much of the evidence of past activity is destroyed through erosion. As a result, the study of the continents is a slow process involving many scientists using a large variety of techniques and instruments.

The most basic method of studying the continents involves studying the layers of rocks. Sometimes these layers can be seen from the surface, and other times scientists must use drills to remove core samples. Sometimes these layers lie flat, while other times they are at all angles. By studying these layers, it is possible to learn what they are made of, how they were made, and even when they were made. Eventually, it becomes possible to conclude that various layers are related and sometimes even constitute the same layer. For example, it is possible that a layer of rock found in North Dakota is identical to a layer of rock found in Nebraska, hundreds of miles away. In this way, geologists are able to build maps showing where these layers of rock can be found.

Maps like this then reveal much about the past of the land. If a type of rock found in the desert is made of material found only on the bottom of swamps, geologists can deduce that the desert was once a swamp and that the climate in the area was once different. It might even be possible to track the change from swamp to desert by examining the different layers, although sometimes the layers are destroyed through erosion. If the ages of the different layers are known, it is possible to build a storyline showing how the swamp changed to desert over a period of time.

Also, the angle of the layers tells about what happened to the land. If the layer is horizontal, then it has probably been undisturbed since it formed. If it is tilted or folded over on itself, then some kind of forces were applied to the rocks. Also, if a layer of rock is found on one continent and also found on another continent, then it can be concluded that the two continents were together when the layer was formed.

Rocks themselves also provide clues. What are the rocks made of? If they are sedimentary rocks, then the material in them existed in some other rocks before. Where were those rocks? If the rocks are basalts, it is possible to conclude that there was volcanic activity in the area at one time. The chemical structure can tell much about the temperatures and pressures to which rocks have been exposed over the years.

Today, instruments on spacecraft can make measurements over very large regions. This not only speeds up the process but provides new views and evidence not possible before.

All this information can be included into computer models in attempts to determine the forces at work in the formation of continents. In this way, clues can be found that were previously unsuspected. Once something is suggested by a computer model, scientists can investigate it to find scientific evidence to support or refute it. Through these and other processes, geologists gradually learn more and more about the earth and its history.

Context

Continents are obviously an important part of everyday life, as the vast majority of the world's population lives on them. Yet they are also important in less obvious ways.

Continental landforms such as mountain ranges strongly influence the weather, which affects nearly every aspect of daily life. The extent of these effects can be graphically demonstrated by comparing the weather over land masses to the weather over the oceans. People on continents may be having freezing weather, while people on islands at the same latitude may be enjoying tropical weather.

With ever-increasing populations, proper management of increasingly strained freshwater resources becomes more and more important. Knowledge gained through the study of continental landforms makes it possible to determine where underground water is and how fast it can be replenished when it is tapped. The shape of the surface of the land also helps to determine where water will flow. This not only helps people better to use the water that is available but also helps to minimize the damage caused by floods and droughts.

Continents also have a great effect on the oceans. The very existence of continents helps to determine the nature of oceanic currents, and most marine life lives in the shallow waters of the Continental Shelf. Increased understanding of the continents therefore increases the understanding of these and other phenomena.

How the land is used is also of great importance. The effects of human activities on the earth are vitally important. By improving the understanding of how continents are formed and how they fit within the global environment, scientists make it possible to predict the planet-wide results of human actions with greater accuracy.

Likewise, the processes of the continents have a great impact on human life. By understanding the nature of earthquakes and volcanic eruptions—phenomena that result from plate tectonics—researchers can suggest ways to minimize the damage such events cause. Increased understanding also increases the ability to provide warning that eruptions or earthquakes are likely to occur.

Satellites in space make it possible to use natural resources more efficiently. Satellites can track the motion of sediments as they are washed away by storms, providing information that helps to manage valuable soil resources more efficiently. It is also possible to use scientific instruments from space to identify the nature of mineral deposits, simplifying the process of prospecting for necessary minerals.

Bibliography

Dott, Robert H., Jr., and Donald R. Prothero. *Evolution of the Earth*. 5th ed. New York: McGraw-Hill, 1994. Chapters 6 through 8 provide a good account of the early history of the planet and the formation of the crust. Chapters 10 and 11 discuss the formation of cratons and orogenic belts. A well-written, well-illustrated text suitable for college and advanced high-school readers.

Moores, Eldridge, ed. *Shaping the Earth: Tectonics of Continents and Oceans*. New York: W. H. Freeman, 1990. This collection of readings from *Scientific American* magazine presents a variety of well-written articles by experts in their respective fields. Individual articles are devoted to plate tectonics, mountain forming, and crustal formation, among other topics. Good illustrations and an index covering all articles is provided. Suitable for college and advanced high-school readers.

Stanley, Steven M. *Earth and Life Through Time*. New York: W. H. Freeman, 1986. Chapter 7 provides a good discussion of plate tectonics, while chapter 8 covers mountain building. The formation of the earth, the crust, and the continents is discussed in chapters 9 through 11. Well written and well illustrated; also has a good index and several appendices that provide additional details about specific topics. Suitable for college and advanced high-school students.

Taylor, S. Ross, and Scott M. McLennan. "The Evolution of Continental Crust." *Scientific American*, January, 1996, p. 274. A comprehensive discussion of the origin of the continental crust and the evolution of the continents. Suitable for high-school readers.

Weiner, Jonathan. *Planet Earth*. Toronto: Bantam Books, 1986. This companion volume to the Public Broadcasting Service television series *Planet Earth* covers many aspects of the earth. Well illustrated; suitable for high-school readers.

Christopher Keating

COSMIC RAYS AND OTHER BACKGROUND RADIATION

Type of earth science: Atmospheric sciences and meteorology
Field of study: Large solar system bodies

Cosmic rays are highly energetic protons and heavier atomic nuclei that continually rain down upon the earth from space. Ranging in energies up to 10^{20} electronvolts (about 20 joules), cosmic rays are not well understood. Primary cosmic rays can produce a secondary "cosmic-ray air shower"—a plethora of secondary particles reaching the earth's surface as a result of collisions of primary rays with atoms in the atmosphere.

Principal terms

ALPHA PARTICLE: a helium-4 nucleus, consisting of two protons and two neutrons

ELECTRONVOLT (eV): a unit of energy used for atomic and subatomic measurements; 1 eV is the kinetic energy acquired by an electron accelerated through a potential difference of 1 volt

FLUX: the number of particles striking a unit of surface area per unit time

ISOTOPES: atoms of a given element with the same number of protons but different numbers of neutrons

NEUTRINOS: massless (or nearly massless) particles given off in certain types of nuclear reactions

PHOTON: the smallest energy packet of light for a given frequency; X rays and gamma rays are examples of high-energy photons

POSITRON: the antiparticle to the electron

PROTON: the nucleus of the hydrogen-1 atom; a proton carries one unit of charge, and the number of protons in the nucleus of an atom determines what element it is

Summary of the Phenomenon

Cosmic-ray particles are fast-moving subatomic particles that are continually striking the earth's atmosphere. They are mostly highly energetic, completely ionized nuclei. About 90 percent of primary cosmic rays are protons, 9 percent are alpha particles (helium-4 nuclei), and the rest are nuclei of heavier elements and electrons. Most cosmic rays are moving so fast that they must be described in relativistic terms—that is, their kinetic energies are comparable to or much greater than their rest mass energies. Sources of cosmic rays include the Sun, other sources believed to be in this galaxy (for example, supernovas), and other galaxies, particularly active galactic nuclei.

The flux of cosmic-ray particles decreases approximately exponentially with increasing energy. The highest-energy cosmic rays are in the range of 10^{20} electronvolts

(100 million million million electronvolts, or approximately 20 joules). This energy is about eleven orders of magnitude greater than the rest mass-energy of the proton.

Cosmic rays are generally divided into two categories: primary and secondary. The primary rays strike the earth's atmosphere; secondary rays are the resulting cascading showers of particles produced by collisions of the primary rays with atoms in the atmosphere. Primary rays have the following characteristics: Their intensity seems to be essentially constant; their flux and spectrum appear to be isotropic in space (the same in all directions); they are anomalous in composition; and their spectrum includes very energetic particles.

An important feature of cosmic rays is that their chemical abundance is significantly different from that of the Sun. Likewise, their chemical abundance is significantly different from that of the universe in general. Cosmic-ray composition is particularly rich in heavier elements. However, even with the lighter elements, cosmic rays contain about one million times as much lithium, beryllium, and boron relative to hydrogen as does the Sun.

Not only are cosmic rays individually energetic, but, given their high spatial particle density, they also represent a large fraction of the total energy associated with astrophysical phenomena. The energy density of cosmic rays is comparable to that of photons, interstellar magnetic fields, and the turbulent motion of interstellar material, each of which is approximately 1 electronvolt per cubic centimeter.

Since their discovery in 1911 by V. F. Hess, cosmic rays have presented scientists with an enigma. The fundamental questions with regard to cosmic rays—where do they come from, and how are they accelerated to such high energies—have yet to be fully understood. Although the Sun is a source of some of the lower-energy cosmic rays, it is clear that it cannot be responsible for the higher energy of the cosmic-ray spectrum. As yet, there has not been a satisfactory mechanism developed that can realistically account for the high acceleration necessary to account for the higher-energy rays. However, some promising models have recently been developed whereby cosmic rays may be repeatedly accelerated by shock waves from violent astrophysical phenomena. Sources for these shock waves would include exploding galaxies and supernovas (exploding stars). It is well known that supernovas are rich in heavier elements. Indeed, this is presently thought to be the primary mechanism whereby heavier elements are synthesized.

The flux of primary cosmic rays incident upon the earth's atmosphere is about 1 particle per square centimeter per second. However, the earth's magnetic field effectively prohibits cosmic rays of less than 10^8 eV (100 million electronvolts) from reaching the surface, the radius of curvature of the path of the charged particles being sufficiently short that they are turned away by the earth's magnetic field.

There is a measured latitude effect in the flux of cosmic rays reaching the earth. This effect is caused by the earth's magnetic field, which manifests a higher cutoff energy (the minimum kinetic energy required for the cosmic rays to reach the atmosphere) at the geomagnetic equator than at higher latitudes. For example, the energy cutoff for vertically arriving protons at the geomagnetic equator is about 15 gigaelectronvolts (GeV), whereas at geomagnetic latitude 50 degrees, the cutoff energy is 2.7 GeV.

Furthermore, there is a significant east-west effect in the flux of cosmic rays incident upon the earth, also the result of the earth's magnetic field. The cutoff energy for cosmic rays reaching the earth's surface is less from the west (about 10 GeV) than from the east (about 60 GeV) for positive charges interacting in the earth's magnetic field.

High-energy gamma-ray photons have also been observed in cosmic rays. Gamma rays and X rays produced by the interaction of primary cosmic rays with interstellar material yield information on the distribution and composition of matter in the galaxy.

Several point sources of X rays and gamma rays have been observed, for example, the Crab Nebula, Hercules X-1, and Cygnus X-3. These sources have been observed to emit gamma rays in the range of 10^{12} eV.

Intense gamma-ray burst events (about five per year) have also been observed. These bursts are characterized by an initial intense pulse of 0.1 seconds to 4 seconds duration followed by one or more pulses, the entire event taking place within one minute.

Researchers have also begun to investigate the ability of shock waves to accelerate cosmic rays to some of the higher energies observed in the cosmic-ray spectrum. Shocks are common in the solar system. For example, "bow" shock waves are produced when the solar wind is deflected by planetary magnetic fields, from solar flares, and when fast solar-wind streams overtake slower streams (somewhat like the effects that produces tsunamis in the earth's oceans). Some solar-wind particles attain high energies through this mechanism, which is generally referred to as "diffusive shock acceleration." Furthermore, mathematical models have shown that the shock waves generated by supernova explosions can dramatically accelerate charged particles.

The resulting acceleration from shock waves may also account for the anomalous component of cosmic rays. Thought to originate from neutral particles in the interstellar medium that become ionized via collisions with the solar wind or by solar photons, anomalous cosmic rays may then be further accelerated at their termination by the shock of the solar wind. However, this is still a very speculative model, and spacecraft have yet to detect the termination shock of the solar wind. Hence, its properties and effects are currently somewhat conjectural; the ultrahigh energies observed in the range of 10^{20} eV still defy a clear understanding as to their production and acceleration mechanisms.

The nuclear composition of cosmic rays enables scientists to sample matter that comes to the earth from remote parts of the galaxy. Indeed, some cosmic rays are thought to be of extragalactic origin as well. Data on the composition of cosmic rays suggests that they may well have experienced similar nuclear conditions as the interstellar medium in the distant past. The cosmic-ray spectrum contains abundances of heavier nuclei in approximate proportion to their nuclear charge. For example, iron-56 (atomic number 26) is about twenty-six times more abundant than would otherwise be expected. Likewise, this observation extends to elements as heavy as lead and uranium. The lighter elements lithium, beryllium, and boron are present in cosmic rays by a factor of about 100,000 times greater than that found in typical universal abundance. In contrast, the relative proportions of nuclei of odd-even charge are similar to those of universal abundance for those nuclei from carbon to iron.

The extremely high proportions of lithium, beryllium, and boron can be accounted for by collisions of the more abundant heavier nuclei, carbon through iron, with protons—the overwhelmingly most populous nuclei present in the interstellar medium. If most cosmic rays are confined to the galactic disk, then this process, known as "spallation," can be used to calculate a mean galactic age of the cosmic rays of several million years.

One radioactive species, beryllium-10, is particularly suitable as a radioactive clock when compared with its stable neighbor, beryllium-9. The results of this comparison yield a mean age for galactic cosmic rays of greater than 20 million years.

The "leaky box" model of galactic cosmic rays assumes that spallation is not complete by the time cosmic rays reach the earth and, hence, leads to the prediction that most cosmic rays in fact leave the galactic disk at a relatively young age. The galactic magnetic field has an energy density slightly less than that of cosmic rays. Hence, it is thought that galactic gravity also plays a role in confining cosmic rays within the galactic halo.

Given the energy density of cosmic rays and the requisite confinement energies, it appears that the principle source of cosmic-ray energy is supernovas—events that are also the source for the synthesis of nuclei heavier than helium and lithium.

Methods of Study

There are a variety of methods for observing cosmic rays: ground-based arrays of detectors both at low altitudes and on mountain tops, balloons carrying a detector payload, and rockets and satellites carrying payloads designed for cosmic-ray research.

Ground-based instruments can employ a variety of detection techniques. Some of the more traditional techniques use cloud chambers, scintillation detectors, and photomultiplier tubes. Usually, these instruments are networked into an extensive two-dimensional array (or, in some cases, with limited three-dimensional information). Computer modeling of the arrival times at the various detectors then can be used to reconstruct a shower front, yielding the approximate direction of origin of the shower. A more recent technique detects the Cherenkov radiation given off by fast-moving electrons through the earth's atmosphere.

Ground-based detectors rarely observe a primary cosmic ray. Rather, they detect the shower of secondary particles produced by the interaction of the high-energy primary ray with atoms in the earth's atmosphere. Primary particles with energies in excess of a few hundred million electronvolts (MeV) per nucleon will readily interact with atmospheric nuclei, mainly producing neutral pions, charged pions, protons, and neutrons. The neutral pions decay into gamma-ray photons which in turn produce electron-positron pairs in a cascading process known as an "extensive air shower." The charged pions decay into muons, some of which can be very penetrating. A case in point is the muon detector one mile underground at the Homestake Detector in South Dakota. The nucleons (neutrons and protons) produced by primary cosmic rays are sufficiently energetic to produce additional nucleons, resulting in neutron-proton cascades, which are also detected at ground-based array detectors. Production of these cascades is very sensitive to atmospheric conditions, in particular, temperature and pressure.

The use of rockets and satellites beginning in the 1960's enabled researchers to establish crucial characteristics of cosmic rays not directly discernible from ground-based detectors. In particular, scientists were able to determine the energy spectra and particle abundances of primary cosmic rays. For example, gamma-ray emissions from the plane of the galaxy were first detected by the OSO III satellite in 1967. The SAS-2 satellite then detected the diffuse gamma-ray background, and the COS-B satellite provided a detailed map of gamma-ray emissions in the galaxy. In addition, COS-B discovered twenty-five discrete gamma-ray sources, including 3C273 (a quasar) and the pulsars in the Crab and Vela supernova remnants. The Einstein X-Ray Observatory was launched in 1978, making high-resolution surveys of selected areas of the sky. The Einstein Observatory provided detailed images of many X-ray sources.

Context

Cosmic rays are a significant tool for the astrophysical investigation of the galaxy. Cosmic rays represent the only sample of matter that reaches the earth from the rest of the galaxy outside the Solar System. Furthermore, some of these rays may originate or be accelerated by the most energetic events that occur both within the galaxy and, perhaps, from within the galactic nucleus as well. This sampling from outside the solar system is vital to the understanding of the evolution of the earth, the solar system, the galaxy, and, indeed, the universe.

Radioactive isotopes created by cosmic rays interacting with atoms in the atmosphere have been used for a variety of terrestrial dating methods, the best-known of which is carbon-14 dating. Since the isotope carbon-14 has a half-life of 5,730 years, there is essentially no population of this isotope remaining from the initial formation of the earth approximately five billion years ago. Rather, the presence of carbon-14 on the earth is the result of its continuous production from cosmic-ray interactions with atoms in the atmosphere. With a steady production rate, an equilibrium abundance of carbon-14 is established. Experimental measurements strongly suggest that the flux of cosmic rays—and, consequently, the production rate of carbon-14—has been fairly constant for hundreds of thousands of years. Living organisms must continually replenish carbon for cell production. When an organism dies, the fraction of its carbon that is carbon-14 decays, reducing the ratio of carbon-14 to stable carbon. This change in ratio can then be used to determine when the organism died. Additionally, radioactive dating methods have been used to measure geophysical effects such as oceanic sedimentations and the deposition of glacial and polar ice.

Solar cosmic rays play a significant part in a variety of geophysical phenomena, including modifications of ionospheric structure, modifications of the atmospheric ozone layer, and influences on the weather. Perhaps the best-known of the effects of solar cosmic rays are the aurora borealis and the aurora austrailis (the northern lights and the southern lights). These displays are the result of charged solar particles (mostly electrons) interacting with the magnetosphere of the earth. The particles lose their energy in inelastic collisions with atoms in the atmosphere, and less than 5 percent of their incident energy actually goes into producing the visible light seen in the auroral displays. More than 95 percent of the incoming electron energy is converted to ionizing, dissociating, and heating the atmosphere.

There appears to be a strong correlation between solar cosmic-ray activity and weather and climatic conditions on the earth. However, because of the complex interconnection among various factors affecting climatic conditions, the nature of the interaction of solar cosmic rays with the climate is not yet clearly understood.

Bibliography

Darrow, K. K. "Cosmic Radiation: Discoveries Reported in *The Physical Review*." In *The Physical Review: The First 100 Years*. New York: American Institute of Physics, 1996. The lengthy introduction provides an overview of the development of cosmic-ray physics. Includes an excellent bibliography for further investigation.

Davies, P., ed. *The New Physics*. New York: Cambridge University Press, 1990. Several chapters in this excellent book include discussion of cosmic rays. In particular, the chapter "The New Astrophysics," by Malcolm Longair, is strongly recommended.

Gaisser, Thomas K. *Cosmic Rays and Particle Physics*. New York: Cambridge University Press, 1990. Although this text can be somewhat technical at times, it is an excellent overview of the discipline of cosmic-ray astrophysics. Should be readily intelligible to a general audience.

Murthy, R., P. V. Wolfendale, and A. W. Wolfendale. *Gamma-Ray Astronomy*. New York: Cambridge University Press, 1986. An good overview of gamma-ray (high-energy photon) astronomy.

Silberberg, R., C. H. Tsao, and J. R. Letaw. "Composition, Propagation, and Reacceleration of Cosmic Rays." In M. M. Shapiro et al., eds., *Particle Astrophysics and Cosmology*. Boston: Kluwer Academic Publishers, 1993. An excellent, though somewhat technical, discussion of cosmic-ray astrophysics.

Stephen Huber

Cross-References

Earth-Sun Relations, 399; Geochronology: Radiocarbon Dating, 840; Nucleosynthesis, 1764; Van Allen Radiation Belts, 3129.

DISCONTINUITIES

Type of earth science: Geology
Field of study: Structural geology

Discontinuities are boundaries within the earth that divide the crust from the mantle, the mantle from the core, and the outer core from the inner core. The term is also used to describe the less dramatic boundaries within layers.

Principal terms

CRUST: the top layer of the earth, composed largely of the igneous rock granite; it ranges from 3 to 42 miles in thickness

DISCONTINUITY: a boundary between two adjacent earth layers, such as the Mohorovičić Discontinuity between the crust and the mantle

EARTHQUAKE: a tremor caused by the release of energy when one section of the earth rapidly slips past another; earthquakes occur along faults or cracks in the earth's crust

EARTHQUAKE WAVES: vibrations that emanate from an earthquake; earthquake waves can be measured with a seismograph

INNER CORE: the innermost layer of the earth; the inner core is a solid ball with a radius of about 900 miles

MANTLE: the largest layer of the earth, about 1,800 miles in thickness; the mantle is within 3 miles of the earth's surface at some locations

OUTER CORE: the outer portion of the core, about 1,300 miles in thickness; it is believed to be composed of molten iron

SEISMOGRAPH: a device that measures earthquake waves

Summary of the Phenomenon

Discontinuities are underground boundaries between layers of the earth. The closest discontinuity to the earth's surface is the Mohorovičić Discontinuity, which divides the earth's crust from the mantle underneath. Other discontinuities divide the mantle from the outer core and the outer core from the inner core. Minor discontinuities are found within these layers.

The interior of the earth has been the object of much speculation and interest for thousands of years. Because direct observation of the earth's interior is usually impossible, however, inferences about its structure and characteristics must be made from phenomena seen or felt at or near the earth's surface. Several phenomena do give indications of the subsurface earth: caves that are often cool and damp, cool water emanating from springs and artesian wells, hot water spewing upward from geysers, and volcanoes from which extremely hot lava erupts. These phenomena give a mixed and incomplete picture of the earth beneath the surface.

The structure and composition of the interior of the earth can, however, be inferred from the study of earthquake waves. Seismographs can detect three types of vibrations: surface waves (the ones that can cause damage when there is an earthquake),

P (primary) waves, and S (secondary) waves, which are also generated by every quake. P waves are compressional (pushing) waves, in which earth or rock particles move forward in the direction of wave movement; S waves are shear waves, in which the particle motion is sideways or perpendicular to the direction of wave movement. The more efficient P waves travel twice as fast as S waves and thus are always detected first by a seismograph. Seismographs record these waves on charts, called "seismograms," attached to moving drums. By noting the arrival times of the various waves, seismologists can determine the distance to an earthquake and can see the effects on these waves caused by the type of rock through which the waves have moved.

Seismic waves travel through rock layers at specific speeds, which are different for each type of mineral or rock. For example, waves travel through basalt at 5 miles a second and through peridotite at 8 miles a second. Seismogram study has shown that the earth's interior is not homogeneous, but rather is composed of several major layers and many sublayers.

In 1906, Richard Oldham discovered that S waves are never detected on the opposite side of the earth from any earthquake. As he already knew that S waves cannot travel through liquid substances, Oldham postulated that the center of the earth must be composed of a molten core and that the materials above this core are not molten. The depth of the boundary between this core and the material above it was discovered eight years later by Beno Gutenberg. Now called the "Gutenberg Discontinuity," it is located about 1,800 miles beneath the earth's surface.

When Oldham made his discovery of a central core, Andrija Mohorovičić was the director of the Royal Regional Center for Meteorology and Geodynamics at Zagreb, one of the leading seismological observatories in Europe. In 1909, his meticulous study of a Croatian earthquake showed that some of the P waves from that quake had traveled faster than others. He already knew that other waves speed up or slow down when they move from one medium into another (as when light moves from air into water) and that this change in speed can result both in reflection, a bouncing back of waves, and in refraction, or a change in wave direction through the new medium. He deduced that the faster-moving P waves had traversed down through the earth, through a discontinuity to a material of a different density, and then had come back up to the surface. Deep in the earth was a material that allowed for faster transmission of P waves. Above this discontinuity, seismic waves travel at about 4.2 miles a second; below the boundary, they travel at about 4.9 miles a second.

When Mohorovičić's results were replicated by other seismologists, it was concluded that the discontinuity was a global phenomenon. Data from these studies showed that there were two very distinct layers of the earth: an upper, less-dense layer now called the "crust," and a denser layer below called the "mantle." Thus Andrija Mohorovičić had discovered what is now called the Mohorovičić Discontinuity, the boundary between the earth's crust and mantle (it is often called the "Moho").

The crust of the earth is made up of continents and ocean basins that are very different from one another. Continental crust is made primarily of granite. Covering this granite over much of the earth's continents may be found layers of younger sedimentary rock such as sandstone, limestone, and shale. Ocean basins, on the other hand, are composed of the dark, heavy rock basalt.

Mohorovičić believed the discontinuity between the crust and mantle to be about 30 to 35 miles below the surface of the earth. Subsequent studies have shown that it is usually at a depth of about 21 miles. However, the Moho has an irregular shape that is roughly a mirror-image of the surface of the earth. Under the continents, the Moho is much deeper; under the oceans, the crust is very thin, and the Moho is as close as from 3 to 5 miles from the surface. The greatest depth of the Moho is probably beneath the Tibetan Plateau, where it reaches a depth of 42 miles.

The continents are higher because they are composed of granite, which is a lower-density rock than basalt or the materials of the mantle. Even though the mantle is composed of solid rock, under long-term stresses, the rock moves slowly like a liquid. Thus, just as ice floats in water, the continents actually are floating upon the heavier mantle rock. The Moho is the boundary between continental granitic rocks and the denser peridotite rock of the mantle.

The mantle extends from the bottom of the crust to a depth of 1,800 miles. It appears to be made of the rocks somewhat similar chemically to those in the earth's crust but more "basic,"—that is, having more of the heavy iron and magnesium minerals such as olivine, and less lightweight aluminum. The mantle also appears to be composed of layers with discontinuities about 220 and 400 miles beneath the earth's surface. Although mantle rock is solid, it can, under certain conditions, behave somewhat like a liquid. Under long-term pressures, the molecules of this solid rock can move like liquids, but under sharp, short-term stresses, mantle rock fractures like a brittle solid.

Heat within the earth is created through the decay of radioactive isotopes. Although this generated heat is very small when compared to the heat received from the Sun, it is well insulated and is enough to create volcanoes and the convection currents of the mantle. Mantle rock is extremely hot; because of the pressure on it from the crust above, however, it cannot melt, except where there is a decrease in this pressure.

Studies at the surface of the earth have revealed areas where great heat flow comes from the mantle. Near the center of the Atlantic Ocean, the basaltic ocean bottom has split; the two sides are being pulled away from each other as Europe and Africa move away from the American continents. At this split, a decrease in pressure allows the hot mantle rock to melt and well upward, filling the gap between the dividing ocean bottoms. Thus the new ocean basin is made of material directly from the mantle. Within the mantle are large, slow-moving convection currents where hot mantle rock moves upward, cools off, and slowly sinks. These currents are believed to be the driving forces of continental drift.

At the bottom of the mantle, beneath the Gutenberg Discontinuity, is the earth's core. Seismic studies have shown that the outer core, which extends from roughly 1,800 to 3,100 miles beneath the earth's surface, is not a perfect sphere. The core rises in areas where hot mantle rock is moving upward and is depressed where cooler mantle rock is moving downward. The density of the core is much greater than that of the mantle. It is believed that this core is made of molten nickel and iron and that its motion generates the earth's magnetic field and aurora borealis.

In 1936, Danish seismologist Inge Lehman discovered evidence for a solid core within the molten center of the earth by detecting seismic waves that had been deflected back to the surface from within the core. When she realized that these waves, though very weak, travel faster through this most-central part of the earth than through the rest of the molten core, she was able to infer that this inner core was composed of solid material completely surrounded by the molten outer core. This most central layer of the earth extends from 3,100 miles beneath the earth's surface to the center of the earth, 4,000 miles down.

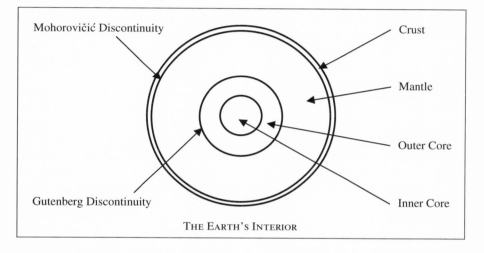

Mohorovičić Discontinuity — Crust — Mantle — Gutenberg Discontinuity — Outer Core — Inner Core

THE EARTH'S INTERIOR

Seismograms have shown that the earth is composed of four major layers: the crust, mantle, outer core, and inner core. The crust is the only layer of which scientists have any direct evidence. In 1957, a project was conceived to drill a hole through the thin oceanic crust down past the Mohorovičić Discontinuity to bring up rock from the mantle. Although the "Mohole" project was approved and funded by the National Science Foundation, funds for it were cut off by the U.S. Congress in 1966.

Methods of Study

Although the deep interior of the earth cannot be seen or examined directly, earthquake waves can give an indirect picture of the earth's interior. These waves, formed by an earthquake or when artificial explosions are set off, go through the earth at speeds determined by the type of rock through which they pass. Like sound and light waves, earthquake waves may be reflected and refracted when they move from one medium to another if the media are of different densities.

The seismoscope is an ancient instrument that shows earth movements. A Chinese seismoscope of the second century a.d. had eight dragon figures each with a ball in its mouth. When the earth trembled, a ball would fall from the dragon's mouth into the mouth of a frog figure underneath it. European seismoscopes often used bowls of water that would spill when agitated. In 1853, Luigi Palmieri designed a seismometer that used mercury-filled tubes that would close an electric circuit and prompt a recording device to start moving when the earth vibrated.

In 1880, British seismologist John Milne invented the first modern seismograph, which employed a heavy mass suspended from a horizontal bar. When the earth would quake, the bar would move, and that movement would be recorded on light-sensitive paper beneath. Most seismographs employ a pendulum, which, because of inertia, remains still as the earth moves underneath it.

When seismographs measure shock waves from nearby earthquakes, they first receive the P waves, which vibrate in the direction in which the waves are moving. S waves, which vibrate perpendicular to the direction in which the waves are moving, then arrive, followed by surface waves. When seismographs record more distant earthquakes, the results are complicated by the reflection and refraction of seismic waves resulting from the various discontinuities underground. As the complications were deciphered, seismologists realized that the recordings described the rock layers below and between the quake and the seismograph.

Once geologists realized that they could learn about the earth by examining seismograms, some researchers became impatient when they wanted to study a particular area but had to wait for an earthquake to occur. This became particularly difficult in areas where earthquakes did not occur frequently. Milne solved the problem by dropping a one-ton weight from a height of about 25 feet. The impact of this weight on the ground generated seismic waves that were weaker than, but similar to, those generated by earthquakes. To create stronger waves, seismologists explode charges of dynamite. These artificially induced shock waves have enough energy to reach deep into the planet. Since the 1970's pistons on large trucks have been used to strike the earth and create artificial seismic waves.

When charges are exploded and the vibrations recorded by several nearby seismographs, a detailed description of rock layers can be detected. Since 1923, when a seismograph was first used to locate a large underground pool of petroleum, seismology has played a large part in the oil and gas industries. Earthquake waves artificially produced by explosions are also able to determine the location of underground geologic structures that may contain mineral deposits.

With the advent of the space age, seismographs connected to radio transmitters have been placed on the surfaces of the moon and Mars. There are more than a thousand seismographs in constant operation gathering seismic data around the world. Data from the National Earthquake Information Center is updated daily and is available on the Internet.

Context

The same technology that has indicated the location of discontinuities deep within the earth has also provided a greater knowledge about the crust. Whereas ancient civilizations feared earthquakes as manifestations of angry gods, quakes are now seen as results of energy released when plates of the earth's crust move past one another.

Although earthquakes do occur in many places on the earth's crust, they are most common in certain areas such as the "Ring of Fire" around the Pacific Ocean. Most earthquakes are linked directly to the movement of the earth "plates," or sections of the crust. The Pacific plate and the North American plate meet along the San Andreas fault, which runs from western Mexico through California to the Pacific Ocean. The two plates are moving past each other along this fault. Each time there is movement along the fault, tremendous amounts of energy are released, and the earth quakes. Quakes along this fault and others have caused untold damage.

One of the primary goals of seismologists is to determine a way to predict exactly when earthquakes will occur. If this information were known in advance, people could prepare for quakes, and far fewer deaths would occur. Many phenomena have been observed before quakes, such as increased strains upon bedrock, changes in the earth's magnetic field, changes in seismic wave velocity, strange movements of animals, changes in groundwater levels, increased concentrations of rare gases in well water, geoelectric phenomena, and changes in ground elevation. However, none of these dependably occurs before every quake, and thus these signs have not become reliable indicators.

Seismologists cannot prevent earthquakes from occurring, nor can they yet predict the exact time of a major quake, but they can predict where earthquakes are likely to occur. It is believed that certain active faults where there has been no earthquake activity for thirty years or so are about ready for an earthquake. With this information, urban and regional planners can provide for quake-resistant roads, bridges, and buildings.

Seismology and the search for minor discontinuities play a great part in the search for oil, gas, and mineral resources. Since much petroleum is retrieved from off-shore locations where the crust of the earth is thinner, knowing the location of the Mohorovičić Discontinuity sets the lower boundary for exploration.

Seismic studies are used regularly to assist in the search for oil and gas reservoirs. Natural gas and petroleum both can become trapped under some geologic formations. Seismologists routinely create a survey of an area before drilling to find minor discontinuities or boundaries between two different rock types, such as shale and sandstone. These surveys are made by measuring the reflection of seismic waves from the underlying rock layers. Geologic structures that can contain petroleum, natural gas, or mineral deposits can be identified from these surveys. Seismic surveys can show the distance and direction to these structures.

Bibliography

Calder, Nigel. *The Restless Earth: A Report on the New Geology*. New York: Viking Press, 1972. A companion book to the television program "The Restless Earth," this book emphasizes how geologists came to the conclusion that the continents are moving. Illustrated with black-and-white and color photographs and diagrams. Indexed.

Cromie, William J. *Why the Mohole?* Boston: Little, Brown, 1964. A 1960's view of the never-finished American and Soviet plans to drill holes through the entire crust of the earth in order to reach the mantle. The author was public-information officer for the American project. Several diagrams and photographs, a bibliography, and an index.

Emiliani, Cesare. *Planet Earth: Cosmology, Geology, and the Evolution of Life and Environment.* Cambridge, England: Cambridge University Press, 1992. A large, comprehensive book containing basic information about matter and energy, many aspects of the physical and historical earth, and a large section about the earth's relationship to the universe. The last section is a brief history of the earth sciences.

Erickson, Jon. *Rock Formations and Unusual Geologic Structures.* New York: Facts on File, 1993. An easy-to-read description of the earth's crust, including the creation, deformation, and erosion of rock. Clear black-and-white photographs, diagrams, and maps along with a large glossary, bibliography, and index.

Lambert, D., and the Diagram Group. *Field Guide to Geology.* New York: Facts on File, 1988. A profusely illustrated book about the earth, its seasons, rocks, erosional forces, and geological history. Contains a list of "great" geologists (including Mohorovičić) and a list of geologic museums, mines, and spectacular geologic features. Indexed.

Miller, Russell. *Continents in Collision.* Alexandria, Virginia: Time-Life, 1983. A thorough text describing how earth motions have created geologic features. Profusely illustrated with color and black-and-white illustrations. Bibliography and index.

Tarling, D., and M. Tarling. *Continental Drift: A Study of the Earth's Moving Surface.* Garden City, N.J.: Anchor Press, 1971. A small paperback book with black-and-white photographs and diagrams that help the reader to understand the principles of earth structure and plate tectonics.

Vogt, Gregory. *Predicting Earthquakes.* New York: Franklin Watts, 1989. A good text on the earth's interior and on how earthquakes are generated, detected, and measured. The last chapter discusses the prediction of earthquakes and efforts to control their effects. Black-and-white photographs and diagrams, glossary, and index.

Weiner, Jonathan. *Planet Earth.* New York: Bantam Books, 1986. A companion volume to the television series "Planet Earth," this book is well illustrated with both black-and-white and color pictures and diagrams. No glossary, but a comprehensive bibliography and index.

Kenneth J. Schoon

Cross-References

Earthquake Distribution, 421; Earthquake Prediction, 461; Earth's Core, 504; Earth's Core-Mantle Boundary, 511; Earth's Crust, 518; Earth's Mantle, 555; Earth's Structure, 589; Heat Sources and Heat Flow, 1065; Oil and Gas Exploration, 1878; Plate Tectonics, 2079; Seismic Reflection Profiling, 2333; Seismometers, 2340.

DOLOMITE

Type of earth science: Economic geology
Field of study: Mineralogy and crystallography

Dolomite is a common rock-forming carbonate mineral of uncertain origin. Its chemically basic nature makes it a useful raw material for industrial applications; its refractory properties render it invaluable for metallurgical uses.

Principal terms

CARBONATE MINERAL: a mineral compound with a fundamental structure that includes the CO_3^{-2} anion

CONNATE WATER: water trapped in the pore spaces of a sedimentary rock at the time of its deposition

DEAD-BURNED: a term used to describe a carbonate material that has been heated until it contains less than 1 percent carbon dioxide

DIAGENESIS: the conversion of unconsolidated sediments into rock after burial; the process includes compaction, cementation, and replacement

DOLOMITIZATION: the process by which a deposit of calcite or aragonite reacts with magnesium-rich waters to become partially or wholly replaced with dolomite

DOLOSTONE: a sedimentary rock composed chiefly of the mineral dolomite; this rock is often associated with or interbedded with limestone

METEORIC WATER: water derived from atmospheric origins; rainwater and snowmelt

PENECONTEMPORANEOUS: formed shortly after sediment deposition and before sediments consolidate into rock

PROTODOLOMITE: a form of dolomite in which magnesium and calcium cations share the same crystallographic planes; an order-disorder polymorph of dolomite

REFRACTORY: a material able to withstand contact with corrosive substances at high temperatures

SABKHA: an arid or semiarid coastal environment just above high-tide level, characterized by evaporite-salt, tidal-flood, and wind-borne deposits

Summary of the Phenomenon

Dolomite, or calcium magnesium carbonate ($CaMg(CO_3)_2$), is a common rock-forming mineral. It derives its name from Déodat de Dolomieu, the eighteenth century French geologist who first studied the rocks of the Dolomite Alps of northern Italy. Dolomite belongs to a family of minerals called "carbonates," compounds with a fundamental structure that includes the carbonate anion (CO_3^{-2}). Dolomite is one of the most common varieties of carbonate mineral, along with calcite and aragonite (both calcium carbonate, $CaCO_3$); together, these minerals make up approximately 2 percent of the earth's crust. Pure dolomite contains almost equal amounts of calcium and magnesium, making it intermediate in composition between calcite and magnesite (magnesium carbonate, $MgCO_3$).

Dolomite's crystal structure resembles that of calcite. Both have a rhombohedral crystal structure; however, in calcite, layers of calcium cations (atoms with a positive charge) separate parallel layers of CO_3 anions (groups of atoms with a negative charge), whereas in dolomite, the cation sites are alternately occupied by calcium and magnesium. Some forms of dolomite, called "protodolomites," exhibit a disordered structure, with calcium and magnesium sharing the same crystallographic planes. This phenomenon, in which two crystalline substances have the same composition but differing states of order within their atomic arrangements, is known as "order-disorder polymorphism." Protodolomites occur in younger deposits (those formed within the past ten thousand years), while older dolomites have the more orderly structure.

A number of cations are known to substitute within the dolomite structure. A portion of the magnesium in dolomite may be replaced by ferrous iron or, to a lesser extent, by manganese. Zinc and cobalt may also substitute for magnesium in minor quantities. Small amounts of barium and lead may substitute for the calcium. Boron, rubidium, strontium, and uranium are other elements that have been known to occur within the dolomite structure.

Dolomite may be colorless, white, pale pink, gray, green, brown, or black, with a glassy, pearly, or dull luster. It occurs as crystals or as granular masses. Its crystal faces are often convexly curved; aggregates of small, curved crystals sometimes form a distinctive saddle shape. Dolomite has a perfect rhombohedral cleavage, a hardness ranging from 3.5 to 4 on the Mohs scale, and a specific gravity of 2.86. The mineral may be identified by its weak effervescence (fizzing) in dilute hydrochloric acid. Some dolomites exhibit a property called "triboluminescence"; that is, they glow if crushed, scratched, or rubbed.

Rock made up principally of the mineral dolomite is also sometimes called "dolo-stone" or "dolomite rock." Dolostone is a sedimentary rock similar in composition and characteristics to limestone, and it is commonly found in association with or interbedded with limestone. A rock is classified as dolostone if dolomite accounts for more than 90 percent of its weight and calcite accounts for under 10 percent; by contrast, a rock is considered to be limestone if it consists chiefly of calcite, with or without magnesium carbonate. Intermediate rock compositions are often found in nature. A limestone containing at least 90 percent calcite and 5 to 10 percent dolomite, for example, would be considered a magnesian limestone, owing to its appreciable magnesium content. If a limestone includes a significant amount (10 to 50 percent) of dolomite in its composition, it is known as "dolomitic limestone." (The Dolomite Alps are actually composed of dolomitic limestone.) A dolostone in which calcite is conspicuous (10 to 50 percent) but dolomite predominates (50 to 90 percent) is a calcitic dolostone.

The intermediate compositions are believed to be the result of incomplete dolomitization. Dolomitization, the process by which dolomite replaces the aragonite and calcite in calcium carbonate sediment or limestone, is a topic of ongoing debate in the geologic literature. It is known that calcium carbonate precipitates from seawater as calcite or aragonite, either inorganically or through marine organisms, to be deposited as sea-bottom sediment. This material undergoes diagenesis, a series of changes including compaction, cementation, and replacement. Calcite replaces most or all of the aragonite, and ultimately the sediments harden to become limestone. While the conversion of this sediment or rock to dolomite is generally accepted in the scientific community, the exact mechanism by which this secondary replacement occurs has yet to be determined. However, because direct precipitation of dolomite from seawater under natural conditions has never been observed or chemically demonstrated and is believed to contribute relatively minor amounts of the mineral at best, most researchers focus on secondary replacement of calcium carbonate as the most likely mechanism for the formation of extensive dolostone deposits.

Modern protodolomites are known to form in sabkhas, arid or semiarid coastal environments just above high-tide level. Sabkhas are characterized by evaporite-salt, tidal-flood, and wind-borne deposits. Dolomite formation has also been observed in association with hot springs and with the precipitation of calcite, aragonite, magnesium calcite, gypsum, and anhydrite in highly saline lagoons (that is, in bodies of water that are rich in mineral salts). These localities where modern dolomitization is taking place are geographically restricted, relatively rare depositional environments; yet somehow, thick, extensive deposits of dolostone and other dolomitic carbonate rocks have developed throughout the geologic record, particularly in major sequences of marine strata, and no indication has been found to suggest they developed under unusual geologic conditions. It is worth noting that the relative proportion of dolostone to limestone increases with age in carbonate rocks. It is unknown whether this trend indicates that past environments were more conducive to dolomitization or that limestones are more likely to become dolomitized the older they grow. The exact relationship between ancient dolostones and today's protodolomites is one geologists and geochemists are still trying to determine.

Several models explaining dolomitization have been proposed; most involve seawater, an obvious, plentiful source of magnesium for the replacement reaction. Some models require this seawater to be concentrated by evaporation into a highly saline brine. Magnesium-charged meteoric waters (those derived from the atmosphere as rain or snow) have also been suggested as a possible dolomitizing fluid, as have connate waters (the waters trapped in the interstices of a sedimentary rock at the time of its deposition). Some theories of dolomitization suggest that a combination of waters (for example, meteoric and sea waters, or fresh and salt waters) in certain ratios is an important part of the process. The fluids that bring about dolomitization must be able to carry magnesium cations to the calcium carbonate deposit and remove excess calcium cations from it.

Fluid flow is another key component of these models; there must be a way for the magnesium-rich solutions to reach the parent materials and to move on, carrying with them the excess calcium cations. Proposed fluid-flow mechanisms include sea-level fluctuations, gravity-driven percolation through permeable material, periodic tidal influx, and density differences between fluids. An example of the latter is evaporative reflux, a process by which the evaporation of highly saline waters eventually produces magnesium-rich brines dense enough to sink, displacing connate waters and seeping through the underlying sediment or rock.

Whatever its origin, dolostone is generally more lithologically uniform that limestone, more even-grained, and more coarsely crystalline. Because recrystallization tends to obliterate minor features present in the original seafloor sediments or limestones, smaller features such as shell fragments and thin layering structures may not survive dolomitization; however, grosser features such as bedding and chert nodules often carry over from the parent material into the dolostone. There are a few well-stratified, finely crystalline dolostones, typically found interbedded with evaporites, in which many of the parent limestone's original textures and structures are preserved. These finely textured dolostones are sometimes called "primary dolostones." These dolostones were at one time thought to be the result of direct precipitation from sea or lake water; now it is considered more likely that dolomitic alteration of calcium carbonate is taking place penecontemporaneously—that is, almost immediately after the original materials are precipitated, and well before they consolidate into rock.

Dolomite also occurs in dolomitic marble, a metamorphic rock formed from dolostone and other dolomitic carbonates, and in talc schists. It is sometimes found as a cement in various sedimentary rocks. Its presence in dolomite-rich veins has been ascribed to hydrothermal activity and to the percolation of meteoric waters. A minor constituent of igneous rocks, dolomite is a chief component of dolomitic carbonatites. These relatively rare rocks are believed to be magmatic (derived from molten rock) in origin.

Methods of Study

In the field, geologists often use dilute hydrochloric acid in identifying dolomite. Like other carbonates, dolomite effervesces in dilute hydrochloric acid: The rock fizzes as the acid's hydrogen reacts with the carbonate ions to produce water and carbon dioxide. In the case of dolomite, however, the reaction proceeds relatively slowly, whereas calcite effervesces rapidly and strongly. In some cases, the dolomite must be powdered or the acid heated before a reaction is evident. This characteristic difference in effervescence is often used as a quick and easy method for distinguishing dolomite from calcite.

In the laboratory, staining techniques are a common method used in dolomite identification. In fact, one of the earliest rock-staining methods, developed by J. Lemberg in the late 1800's, was designed for the study of dolomite and other carbonates. Staining techniques employ a dye or reagent, or a series thereof, to stain a rock sample selectively, coloring only those components having a certain composition or chemical property. Many staining methods are best suited for use on a hand specimen with a polished surface, or on rock sliced and ground down to a thin section; however, some staining methods will accommodate rock chips or individual mineral grains. Staining used in conjunction with microscopy is particularly helpful where dolomite and calcite are intimately interlayered within a carbonate rock.

X-ray diffraction is another laboratory method commonly employed in identifying and studying dolomite. Different crystal structures will diffract a beam of X rays in different, characteristic ways, depending on the spacing of the planes of atoms within the crystal. An older dolomite with a well-ordered crystal lattice will yield an X-ray diffraction pattern distinctly different from that of a structurally similar calcite crystal.

Field observations and laboratory experiments have both been used in the efforts to ascertain dolomite's origins. To determine whether dolomite can precipitate directly from seawater, geochemists have conducted laboratory experiments with various temperatures, pressures, and degrees of saturation. Conditions found in modern marine environments do not appear to support precipitation; in the laboratory, precipitation has occurred only at temperatures over 100 degrees Celsius or under conditions of abnormally high saturation or pH. X-ray diffraction shows that precipitates formed under ambient conditions in the laboratory lack dolomite's characteristic structural order. Careful observation of localities where modern marine dolomites are forming has produced evidence that what might appear to be direct deposition of dolomite is in fact a penecontemporaneous alteration of calcite and aragonite, occurring almost immediately after these original materials are precipitated.

Laboratory investigations into the dolomitization process have identified catalysts and inhibitors that are consistent with observations of naturally formed dolomites. These catalysts include an increase in temperature, in the ratio of magnesium cations to calcium cations in the parent solution, and in the surface area of the material being replaced. The precipitation of evaporite minerals may encourage dolomitization by positively affecting the cation ratios. Experiments have also found that dolomitization occurs more readily with aragonite than with calcite.

Fluid inclusions, minuscule cavities within a mineral that contain liquid or gas, have yielded additional insights into dolomitization. Fluid inclusions within a dolomite crystal provide geochemists with a sample of the spent solution from which the dolomite crystallized. Through laboratory analysis of fluid inclusions, researchers gain information on the origin and timing of the dolomitization and learn what temperatures and pressures are linked to the process.

Context

Dolomite and dolomite-containing rocks are important natural resources that are used for a variety of purposes. Like limestone, dolostone and rocks of intermediate composition are quarried, cut, and shaped into blocks and slabs that are widely used for construction and ornamentation. Coarsely crushed, they become aggregate, used as a component of concrete and other construction materials, as railroad ballast, as fill material, and as sewage filter beds. In agriculture, ground dolostone and similar calcium-containing materials are applied to soil to deacidify it, improve its texture and stability, and enhance its nitrogen-fixing capabilities.

Dolostone and rocks of similar composition are a source of dolomitic quicklime (calcium and magnesium oxides) and related compounds, such as type N and type S dolomitic hydrates. Dolomitic quicklime is similar to lime (calcium oxide), a well-known basic industrial compound obtained from limestone, and shares many of its uses. Dolomitic quicklime is produced by heating crushed dolostone or other dolomitic carbonate rocks to above 1,000 degrees Celsius. This process, called "calcining," causes the rock to dissociate; it loses carbon dioxide and yields dolomitic quicklime. Adding water to stabilize dolomitic quicklime yields the slaked, or hydrated, forms. The glass, paper, chemical, construction, and waste-treatment industries are among the major consumers of these compounds. Dolomitic carbonates are also a key component in the ferrosilicon (Pidgeon) process for obtaining magnesium metal.

Another industry in which dolomite and dolomite-containing rocks are extensively used is metallurgy. Dolostone and similar rocks are commonly employed as flux stone in smelting operations such as the blast-furnace process that produces pig iron from iron ore. Flux is a material that lowers the melting temperature of the metal and purifies it. In iron smelting, dolomitic flux is introduced into the blast furnace along with the iron ore and coke. It combines with incombustible impurities from the ore and ash from the coke to form a liquid waste material called "slag." The slag floats on top of the molten iron and is drawn off separately. Limestone was previously the more widely used flux stone, because dolostone was believed by some to be less effective as a flux and purifier, to impede the fluidity of the slag, and to necessitate higher furnace temperatures. However, environmental considerations have helped to increase dolostone's popularity as a flux. Unlike limestone, which produces a hardened slag that disintegrates in water, dolostone forms a solidified slag that can be employed as a lightweight aggregate or for other uses.

Additional metallurgical applications for dolomitic materials make use of their refractory properties. A refractory is a substance that can withstand a corrosive and high-temperature environment, such as that found within a metallurgical furnace. Heating dolostone or rocks of similar composition in a blast furnace or special kiln at about 1,650 degrees Celsius drives away the little carbon dioxide that might remain in ordinary dolomitic quicklime, yielding what is called "dead-burned" dolomite. This material is used for manufacturing refractory brick to line the basic open-hearth furnaces and converters used in producing steel.

Dolomite and dolomitization are also significant because of their relationship to other economic minerals and fuels. The dolomitization process can often increase a rock's permeability and porosity. Thus a "tight" limestone is transformed through dolomitization into an excellent reservoir for petroleum, natural gas, or groundwater. Higher permeability and porosity provide a means for mineralizing fluids to enter the rock, as well. Dolomitized rocks throughout the world host what are known as Mississippi Valley-type deposits, lead or zinc ores found with associated barite and fluorite as veins and replacement bodies within carbonate rocks.

Most important, dolomitic carbonates play a role in the earth's carbon cycle. Some of the vast amounts of carbon dioxide that pass from the atmosphere into the oceans ultimately become bound up in carbonate rocks and minerals. Dolostones and the other carbonate rocks serve as the largest repository of carbon in the cycle. The carbon remains locked in these rocks until they are subducted, in which case the carbon may be vented to the atmosphere in volcanic gases, or until they are uplifted to the earth's surface, in which case the carbon is released during erosion. The slow turnover in the carbonate-rock reservoir helps to regulate the composition of the earth's atmosphere and oceans.

Bibliography

Bates, Robert L. *Geology of the Industrial Rocks and Minerals.* New York: Dover, 1969. The subchapter on limestone and dolomite compares and contrasts dolostone with limestone and describes dolomite's uses and physical and chemical properties. Although primary deposition is given more emphasis than is found in many recent works, this remains a useful, clearly written overview. Includes extensive references.

Brownlow, Arthur H. *Geochemistry.* 2d ed. Upper Saddle River, N.J.: Prentice-Hall, 1996. The chapter on sedimentary rocks includes a straightforward, comprehensible discussion of dolomitization and dolostones within the context of diagenesis. Includes references.

Hubbard, Harold A., and George E. Ericksen. "Limestone and Dolomite." In Donald A. Brobst and Walden P. Pratt, eds. *United States Mineral Resources (U.S. Geological Survey Professional Paper 820).* Washington, D.C.: U.S. Government Printing Office, 1973. Discusses dolomite and dolostone as natural resources. Summarizes the occurrence, geologic environments, desirable properties, and uses of dolomitic carbonates and limestone. Includes references.

Klein, Cornelius, and Cornelius S. Hurlbut, Jr. *Manual of Mineralogy.* 21st ed. New York: John Wiley & Sons, 1993. The subchapter on carbonate minerals includes a description of dolomite's crystallography, physical properties, composition, structure, occurrence, and uses. A later chapter on mineral assemblages discusses dolostones and other carbonate rocks. This lucid, classic college text includes references and suggested reading.

Krauskopf, Konrad B., and Dennis K. Bird. *Introduction to Geochemistry.* 3d ed. New York: McGraw-Hill, 1995. The chapter on carbonate sediments includes a brief but helpful discussion of "the dolomite problem." Includes references and suggestions for further reading. Suitable for the college-level reader.

Morse, John W., and Fred T. Mackenzie. *Geochemistry of Sedimentary Carbonates.* Amsterdam: Elsevier, 1990. Dolomite, dolostone, and dolomitization are discussed throughout the text; chapter 7 in particular provides a good overview of what is known regarding dolomite formation. While the material is technical in nature, it is clearly presented.

Purser, Bruce, Maurice Tucker, and Donald Zenger, eds. *Dolomites: A Volume in Honor of Dolomieu.* Oxford, England: Blackwell Scientific Publications, 1994.

Although many of the articles in this volume are highly technical, the general college-level reader should find the introductory articles accessible, particularly the opening discussion of the problems, progress, and future research regarding dolomites and dolomitization.

Selley, Richard C. *Applied Sedimentology*. London: Academic Press, 1988. The chapter on autochthonous sediments includes a substantial section on carbonate rocks and minerals. Primary and secondary dolomites and the chemical constraints on dolomite formation are discussed. Suitable for the college-level reader.

Tucker, M. E. *Sedimentary Petrology: An Introduction to the Origin of Sedimentary Rocks*. 2d ed. Oxford, England: Blackwell Scientific Publications, 1991. The chapter on limestone includes a section that discusses dolomite and the various theories of dolomitization. A technical text appropriate for the college-level reader.

Zenger, Donald H., and John B. Dunham. "Concepts and Models of Dolomitization—An Introduction." In *Concepts and Models of Dolomitization*, edited by Donald H. Zenger, John B. Dunham, and Raymond L. Ethington. Tulsa, Okla.: Society of Economic Paleontologists and Mineralogists, 1980. A good overview of various proposed models for dolomitization, suitable for the college-level reader. Includes copious references.

Karen N. Kähler

Cross-References

Carbonates, 190; The Geochemical Cycle, 818; Igneous Rocks: Carbonatites, 1173; Industrial Nonmetals, 1225; Limestone, 2980; Reefs, 2158; Seawater Composition, 2282; Sedimentary Mineral Deposits, 2296; Sedimentary Rock Classification, 2304; Sedimentary Rocks: Chemical Precipitates, 2318.

DROUGHT

Type of earth science: Atmospheric sciences and meteorology
Field of study: Analytical techniques

Drought is an unusually long period of below-normal precipitation. It is a relative rather than an absolute condition, but the end result is a water shortage for an activity such as plant growth or for some group of people such as farmers.

Principal terms
ADIABATIC: a change of temperature within the atmosphere that is caused by compression or expansion without loss of heat
EVAPOTRANSPIRATION: the combined water loss to the atmosphere from evaporation and plant transpiration
PALMER DROUGHT INDEX: a widely adopted quantitative measure of drought severity that was developed by W. C. Palmer in 1965
POTENTIAL EVAPOTRANSPIRATION: the water needed for growing plants
PRECIPITATION: liquid water or ice that falls from the atmosphere to the ground
SAHEL: the semiarid southern fringe of the Sahara in West Africa that extends from Mauritania on the Atlantic to Chad in the interior
SOIL MOISTURE: water that is held in the soil and is available to plant roots
SUBSIDENCE: air that is descending and getting increasingly dry

Summary of the Phenomenon

Droughts have had enormous impacts on human societies since ancient times. The most obvious effect is crop and livestock failure, which have caused famine and death through thousands of years of human history. Drought has resulted in the demise of some ancient civilizations and, in some instances, the forced mass migration of large numbers of people. Water is so critical to all forms of life that a pronounced shortage could, and did, decimate whole populations.

Even in recent times, the effects of drought are profound. For example, the dry conditions in the Great Plains of North America in the early 1930's in conjunction with extensive farming activities resulted in the creation of the Dust Bowl, which at one point covered more than 200,000 square kilometers, or an area about the size of Nebraska. During the early 1960's, a severe drought affected the Middle Atlantic states. Parts of New Jersey had sixty consecutive months of below-normal precipitation, so depleting local water supplies that plans were actively considered to bring rail cars of water into Newark and other cities in the northern part of the state, since the reservoirs that usually supplied the region were practically dry. The Sahel region south of the Sahara in West Africa had a severe drought beginning in the late 1960's and continuing into the early 1970's, creating an enormous and negative impact on the local population, livestock, and vegetation. Hundreds of thousands of people starved, thousands of animals died, and many tribes were forced to migrate south to areas of more reliable precipitation.

Almost all droughts occur when slow-moving air masses that are characterized by subsiding air movements dominate an area. Often, the source of the air is from continental interiors where the amount of moisture that is available for evaporation into the atmosphere is scarce. When these conditions occur, the potential for precipitation is low for a number of reasons. First, the initial status of the humidity in the air is low, since the continental air mass is distant from maritime (moist) influences. Second, air that subsides undergoes adiabatic heating at the rate of 10 degrees Celsius per 1,000 meters. The term "adiabatic" refers to a change of temperature within a gas (such as the atmosphere) that occurs as a result of compression (descending air) or expansion (rising air), without any gain or loss of heat from the outside. For example, assume that air at a temperature of 0 degrees Celsius is passing over the Sierra Nevada in eastern California at an elevation of 3,500 meters. As the air descends and reaches Reno, Nevada, at an elevation of 1,200 meters, the higher atmospheric pressure found at lower elevations results in compression and heating at the dry adiabatic rate of 10 degrees Celsius per 1,000 meters, yielding a temperature in the Reno area of 23 degrees Celsius. Thus, adiabatic heating from subsiding air masses results in a decline in relative humidity and an increase in moisture-holding capacity. In addition, the movement of air under these conditions is usually unfavorable for vertical uplift and the beginning of the condensation process. The final factor that reduces precipitation potential is the decrease in cloudiness and corresponding increase in sunshine, which in turn leads to an increase in potential evapotranspiration demands, which favor soil moisture loss.

Another characteristic associated with droughts is that once they have become established within a particular location, they appear to persist and even expand into nearby regions. This persistence and expansion is apparently related to positive feedback mechanisms. For example, the drying out of the soil influences air circulation and the amount of moisture that is then available for precipitation further downwind. At the same time, the atmospheric interactions that lead to unusual wind systems associated with droughts can induce surface-temperature variations that, in turn, lead to further development of the unusual circulation pattern. Thus, the process feeds on itself to make the drought last longer and intensify. The problem persists until a major change occurs in the circulation pattern in the atmosphere.

Many climatologists concur with the concept that precipitation is not the only factor associated with drought. Other factors that demand consideration include moisture supply, the amount of water in storage, and the demand generated by evapotranspiration. Although the literature in climatology is replete with information about the intensity, length, and environmental impacts of drought events, the role of individual climatological factors that can increase or decrease the severity of a drought is not fully understood.

Methods of Study

Research in drought identification has been changing over the years. Drought was once considered solely in terms of precipitation deficit. Although that lack of precipitation is still a key atmospheric component of drought, sophisticated techniques are now used to assess the deviation from normal levels of the total environmental moisture status. These techniques have enabled investigators to better understand the severity, length, and areal extent of drought events.

Drought has been defined in numerous ways. Some authorities consider it to be merely a period of below-normal precipitation, while others relate it to the dangers of forest fire. Drought is also said to be occurring when the yield from a specific agricultural crop or pasture is less than expected; it has also been defined as a period when soil moisture or groundwater reaches a critical level.

Drought was identified early in the twentieth century by the U.S. Weather Bureau as any period of twenty-one or more days when the precipitation was 30 percent or more below normal. Subsequent examination of drought events that were identified by this method revealed that soil moisture reserves were often elevated during these events to the extent that there was sufficient water to support vegetation. It was also determined that the precipitation preceding the drought event was either ample or even heavy. Thus, it became apparent that precipitation should not be used as the sole measure to identify drought. Subsequent research has shown that the moisture status of an area is affected by factors other than the sole factor of precipitation.

Further developments in drought identification during the middle decades of the twentieth century began to focus on the moisture demands that are associated with the evapotranspiration of an area. Evaporation is the process by which water in liquid or solid form (snow and ice) at the earth's surface is converted into water vapor and conveyed into the atmosphere. Transpiration refers to the loss of moisture by plants to the atmosphere. Although evaporation and transpiration can be studied and measured separately, it is convenient to consider them in applied climatological studies as a single process, evapotranspiration.

There are two ways to define evapotranspiration. The first is actual evapotranspiration, which is the actual or real rate of water-vapor return to the atmosphere from the earth and vegetation; this process could also be called "water use." The second is potential evapotranspiration, which is the theoretical rate of water loss to the atmosphere if one assumes continuous plant cover and an unlimited supply of water. This process could also be called "water need," as it indicates the amount of soil water needed if plant growth is to be maximized. Procedures have been developed that enable one to calculate the potential evapotranspiration for any area as long as one has monthly mean temperature and precipitation values.

Some drought-identification studies have focused on agricultural drought, looking at the adequacy of soil moisture in the root zone for plant growth. The procedure involved the evaluation of precipitation, evapotranspiration, available soil moisture, and the water needs of plants. The goal of this research was to determine drought probability based on the number of days when soil moisture storage is reduced to zero.

Evapotranspiration was also used by the Forest Service of the U.S. Department of Agriculture when it developed a drought index to be used by fire-control managers. The purpose of the index was to provide a measure of flammability that could create forest fires. This index has limited applicability to nonforestry users, as it is not effective for showing drought as an indication of total environmental stress.

One of the most widely adopted drought-identification techniques was developed by W. C. Palmer in 1965. The method, which became known as the Palmer Drought Index, defines drought as the period of time—usually measured in months or years— when the actual moisture supply at a given location is consistently less than the climatically anticipated or appropriate supply of moisture. The calculation of this index requires the determination of the following environmental parameters: evapotranspiration, soil moisture loss, soil moisture recharge, surface runoff, and precipitation. The Palmer Drought Index values range from approximately +4.0 for an extremely wet moisture status class to −4.0 for extreme drought. Normal conditions have a value close to zero. Positive values indicate varying stages of abundant moisture, whereas negative values indicate varying stages of drought.

Although the Palmer Drought Index has been used for several decades and is recognized as an acceptable procedure for incorporating the role of potential evapotranspiration and soil moisture in magnifying or alleviating drought status, there have been some criticisms of its use. For example, the method produces a dimensionless parameter of drought status that cannot be directly compared to other environmental moisture variables, such as precipitation, which are measured in units (centimeters, millimeters) that are immediately recognizable. In addition, the index is not especially sensitive to short drought periods, which can affect agricultural productivity.

In order to address these shortcomings, other researchers use water-budget analysis to identify deviations in environmental moisture status. The procedure is similar to the Palmer method inasmuch as it incorporates the environmental parameters of precipitation, potential evapotranspiration, and soil moisture. However, the moisture status departure values are expressed in the same units as precipitation and are therefore dimensional. Drought classification using this index method ranges from approximately 25 millimeters for an above-normal moisture status class to −100 millimeters for extreme drought. The index would be close to zero for normal conditions.

Context

Drought is invariably associated with some form of water shortage, yet many regions of the world have regularly occurring periods of dryness. Three different forms of dryness that have a temporal dimension are known as perennial, seasonal, and intermittent. Perennially dry areas include the major deserts of the world, such as the Sahara, Arabian, and Kalahari. Precipitation in these large deserts is not only very low but also very erratic. Seasonal dryness is associated with those regions of the world where the bulk of the annual precipitation comes during a few months of the year, leaving the rest of the year rainless. Intermittent dryness is associated with those instances where the overall precipitation is reduced in humid regions or where the rainy season in seasonally dry areas does not occur or is shortened.

It is the absence of precipitation when it is normally expected that creates a major problem for people. For example, the absence of precipitation for a week in an area where daily precipitation is the norm would be considered a drought. In contrast, it would take two or more years without any rain in parts of Libya in North Africa for a drought to occur. In those areas of the world that have one rainy season, a 50 percent reduction in precipitation would be considered a drought. In those regions that have two rainy seasons, the failure of one could lead to drought conditions. Thus, the very word "drought" itself is a relative term, since it has different meanings in different climatic regions. The total amount of precipitation in one location is therefore not a good indicator of drought, as each location has its own set of criteria for drought identification.

User demands also influence drought definition. Distinctions are often made among climatological, agricultural, hydrologic, and socioeconomic drought. Climatological, or meteorological, drought occurs at irregular periods of time, usually lasting months or years, when the water supply in a region falls far below the levels that are typical for that particular climatic regime. The degree of dryness and the length of the dry period is used as the definition of drought. For example, drought in the United States has been defined as occurring when there is less than 2.5 millimeters of rain in forty-eight hours. In Great Britain, drought has been defined as occurring when there are fifteen consecutive days with less than 0.25 millimeters of rain for each day. In Bali in Indonesia, drought has been considered as occurring if there is no rain for six consecutive days. Other examples of this type of classification could be cited; it is obvious that the definition of drought for one region is not applicable to another region in a different climatic regime.

Agricultural drought occurs when soil moisture becomes so low that plant growth is affected. In this case, drought has to be related to the water needs of the crops or animals in a particular place, since agricultural systems vary substantially. The degree of agricultural drought also depends on whether shallow-rooted or deep-rooted plants are affected. In addition, crops are more susceptible to the effects of drought at different stages of their development. For example, inadequate moisture in the subsoil in an early growth stage of a particular plant will have minimal impact on crop yield as long as there is adequate water available in the topsoil. However, if subsoil moisture deficits continue, then the yield loss could become substantial.

Hydrologic drought definitions are concerned with the effects of dry spells on surface flow and groundwater levels. The climatological factors associated with the drought are of lesser concern. Thus, a hydrological drought for a particular watershed is said to occur when the runoff falls below some arbitrary value. Hydrological droughts are often out of phase with climatological and agricultural droughts and are also basin-specific; that is, they pertain to certain watersheds.

Socioeconomic drought includes features of climatological, agricultural, and hydrological drought and is generally associated with the supply and demand of some type of economic good. For example, the interaction between farming (demand) and naturally occurring events (supply) can and does result in inadequate water for both plant and animal needs. It is also worth noting that human activities, such as poor land-use practices, can create a drought or make an existing drought worse. The Dust Bowl in the Great Plains and the Sahelian drought in West Africa provide ready examples of the symbiotic relationship between drought and human activities.

In short, the definition of drought is complex and requires interdisciplinary attention. Most definitions stress the physical aspects of drought, but it must be recognized that the social aspects are also germane.

In a sense, droughts differ from other major geophysical events such as volcanic eruptions, floods, and earthquakes because they are actually nonevents: that is, they result from the absence of events (precipitation) that should normally occur. Droughts also differ from other geophysical events in that they often have no readily recognizable beginning and take some time to develop. In many instances, droughts are only recognized when plants start to wilt, wells and streams run dry, and reservoir shorelines recede.

There is wide variation in the duration and extent of droughts. The length of a drought cannot be predicted, since the irregular patterns of atmospheric circulation are still not fully known and predictable. A drought ends when the area receives sufficient precipitation and water levels rise in the wells and streams. Since the severity and areal extent of a drought cannot now be predicted, all that is really known is that they are part of a large natural system and that they will continue to occur.

Bibliography

Bryson, Reid A., and Thomas J. Murray. *Climates of Hunger*. Madison: University of Wisconsin Press, 1977. An interesting account of the profound effect of climate on human societies going back to ancient times. The treatment is nonmathematical and is suitable for a wide range of readers. Major climate changes and droughts for various regions in the world are discussed in separate chapters. The material is suitable for senior-level high-school students and above.

Dixon, Lloyd S., Nancy Y. Moore, and Ellen M. Pint. *Drought Management Policies and Economic Effects in Urban Areas of California, 1987-92*. Santa Monica, Calif.: RAND, 1996. This 131-page report examines the impacts of the 1987-1992 drought in California on urban and agricultural users. The purpose of the investigation was to assess the effects of the drought on a broad range of residential, commercial, industrial, and agricultural water users.

Frederiksen, Harald D. *Drought Planning and Water Resources Implications in Water Resources Management*. Washington, D.C.: World Bank, 1992. This relatively short report contains two papers on drought planning and water-use efficiency and effectiveness. The papers deal with policy and program issues in water-resources management from the perspective of the World Bank.

Garcia, Rolando V., and Pierre Spitz. *Drought and Man: The Roots of Catastrophe*. New York: Pergamon Press, 1986. Part of a larger series, *Impact of Climate Change on the Character and Quality of Human Life*, sponsored by the International Federation of Institutes for Advanced Study. The topics in this volume include the food insecurity and social disjunctions that are caused by drought. Case studies include northeastern Brazil, Tanzania, and the Sahelian countries.

Mather, John R. *Drought Indices for Water Managers*. Newark: University of Delaware Center of Climatic Research, 1985. A useful monograph on the variety of drought indices that have been developed by researchers. Examples are provided of the different types of methods used by investigators.

Oliver, John E., and John J. Hidore. *Climatology*. Columbus, Ohio: Merrill, 1984. A thorough, well-written textbook that discusses all aspects of climatology. Contains numerous black-and-white illustrations and maps. Suitable for college-level students. Although quantitative measures are included, no particular mathematical background is necessary.

Russell, Clifford S., David G. Arey, and Robert W. Kates. *Drought and Water Supply*. Baltimore: Johns Hopkins, 1970. An excellent, scholarly study of the losses experienced by municipal water-supply system customers in Massachusetts as a result of a 1962-1966 drought. The well-documented methodology discussed in the book has applicability to water systems in other areas.

Tannehill, Ivan R. *Drought: Its Causes and Effects*. Princeton, N.J.: Princeton University Press, 1947. A classic text on the climatology of droughts. Although the discussion is technical, it is nonmathematical and very readable and should appeal to the general adult audience.

U.S. Congress. House. *Effects of Drought on Agribusiness and Rural Economy*. 100th Congress, 2d session, 1988. This report contains the testimony of a variety of witnesses at a congressional hearing held July 13, 1988. In addition to the text and tables documenting the impacts of the drought of July, 1988, a map of the United States is included that illustrates the use of the Palmer Drought Index. The testimony also provides the flavor of a congressional hearing on drought issues.

Wilhite, Donald A., and William E. Easterling, with Deborah A. Wood, eds. *Planning for Drought: Toward a Reduction of Societal Vulnerability*. Boulder, Colo.: Westview Press, 1987. An extensive collection of thirty-seven short chapters on drought covering a wide range of topics ranging from the climatological to the institutional. The different authors provide a good background to the many issues pertaining to drought, social impacts, governmental response, and adaptation and adjustment. Suitable for college-level students.

Robert M. Hordon

Cross-References

The Atmosphere's Global Circulation, 121; Climate, 217; Clouds, 224; Earth-Sun Relations, 399; El Niño, 2911; Global Warming, 2932; The Greenhouse Effect, 1004; Precipitation, 2108; Weather Forecasting, 2717.

EARTH RESOURCES TECHNOLOGY SATELLITE (ERTS)

Type of earth science: Remote sensing

An earth resources technology satellite (ERTS) is an artificial satellite that assesses and monitors the earth's natural resources using remote sensing techniques. A wide range of disciplines in the earth sciences and other fields make use of the diverse data collected by these satellites.

Principal terms

ACTIVE SENSOR: a sensor, such as a radar instrument, that illuminates a target with artificial radiation, which is reflected back to the sensor

MULTISPECTRAL SCANNER (MSS): a passive scanning instrument that simultaneously records image data from a scene in multiple spectral bands

NEAR-POLAR ORBIT: an orbit that lies in a plane that passes close to both the North and South Poles

PASSIVE SENSORS: sensors that detect reflected or emitted electromagnetic radiation from a natural source

PUSHBROOM SYSTEM: a space-borne imaging system made up of a fixed, linear array of sensors that is swept across an area by the motion of the spacecraft

RETURN BEAM VIDICON (RBV): an imaging system consisting of multiple sensors, similar to television cameras, operating in different spectral bands

SUN-SYNCHRONOUS ORBIT: for an Earth satellite, a near-polar orbit at an altitude such that the satellite regularly passes over a point on the earth at the same local time

SYNTHETIC APERTURE RADAR (SAR): a space-borne radar imaging system that uses the motion of the spacecraft to simulate a very long antenna

THEMATIC MAPPER (TM): a passive, multispectral scanning instrument similar to a multispectral scanner but with a greater spectral range and superior sensitivity and performance

Summary of the Methodology

An earth resources technology satellite (ERTS) is an artificial satellite designed primarily to assess and monitor the earth's natural resources. Employing remote-sensing techniques, an ERTS obtains data that, once interpreted, can be a valuable tool for a variety of disciplines, including agriculture, forestry, ecology, fishery, oceanography, hydrology, meteorology, geology, mineral exploration, geography, civil engineering, archaeology, economics, land-use planning, and sociology. The data can be used to help scientists, planners, and others discover previously unknown resources, make informed decisions concerning resource use, and detect problems that endanger resources or people.

The importance and usefulness of observing the earth's resources from space became apparent after the early cosmonauts and astronauts brought back high-quality photographs they had taken from their spacecraft with hand-held cameras. It was found that individual images could hold an abundance of information about vast areas of the earth's surface. Through a technique called color-slicing, in which the colors within the spectrum printed on the film are separated, these photographs could be reconstituted to yield more data. Portions of the resulting images could be correlated with locations on Earth where known activities were taking place or certain conditions existed. This correlation, known as "ground truth," matched the separated colors in the images to a particular activity, condition, or feature on the earth's surface. Establishing a clear relationship between the separated colors and actual conditions provided a means for image interpretation.

Recognizing the potential of these early images obtained from space, the United States developed a series of satellites devoted to observing Earth on an ongoing basis. The first of these satellites, initially called ERTS-1 but subsequently renamed Landsat 1, was launched in 1972. More Landsats followed, with launches in 1975, 1978, 1982, and 1984. (Landsat 5 had to be launched ahead of schedule because of problems with Landsat 4's power supply and communications systems. Landsat 6, launched in 1993, failed to achieve orbit.) Landsats 1 through 3 each operated for five to seven years. As of early 1997, Landsats 4 and 5 remained in operation, and Landsat 7 was scheduled for launch in 1998.

The Landsat platforms use a combination of Earth rotation, satellite orbit, and instrument scanning patterns to provide the coverage necessary for observing changes in the earth's surface over time. The first three Landsats orbited at an altitude of approximately 920 kilometers in a near-polar orbit (a north-to-south orbit that passes near the earth's poles). This orbit was sun-synchronous, meaning that the satellite passed over all places on the earth having the same latitude twice daily at the same local time. Each satellite orbited the planet fourteen times a day; the orbit and field of view provided repetitive coverage—that is, the satellite acquired data from any given place on Earth—every eighteen days. The orbits of two of the satellites were phased to provide repetitive coverage every nine days. Landsats 4 and 5 orbit at an altitude of approximately 705 kilometers and provide repetitive coverage every sixteen days. The satellites transmit the data they obtain to ground stations located around the globe. When a satellite is able to "see" a ground station, it sends real-time data to the station; otherwise, it stores the data until it is within a station's transmitting range.

Imaging systems aboard the Landsats collect data from different parts of the electromagnetic spectrum, including wavelengths in the visible and infrared regions. The first three Landsats were equipped with a return beam vidicon (RBV) system and a multispectral scanner (MSS). The RBV systems consisted of multiple sensors that were essentially television cameras operating in different spectral bands. The MSS used an oscillating mirror to scan the earth's surface from west to east as the satellite moved in its descending (north-to-south) orbit over the sunlit side of the planet. The instrument recorded reflected and emitted energy from multiple regions in the electromagnetic spectrum: Landsats 1 and 2 recorded data from four bands in the visible and near-infrared spectral regions, while Landsat 3 added a fifth band in the thermal-infrared region. Landsats 4 and 5 are also equipped with a four-band MSS, but the RBV has been replaced with a more sophisticated sensor, the thematic mapper (TM). The TM is a multispectral scanner that, although similar to the MSS, is superior in spatial resolution (the ability to define closely spaced features), spectral range and resolution, and overall sensitivity and performance. The TM records data from seven bands in the visible, reflective-infrared, middle-infrared, and thermal-infrared regions of the spectrum. It obtains data on both west-to-east and east-to-west scans, in contrast to the MSS's single-scan approach. Landsat 7 is to carry an enhanced TM instrument.

The United States has developed other satellites to monitor Earth resources. These include Seasat and the Heat Capacity Mapping Mission (HCMM), both launched in 1978. Seasat, designed specifically to observe Earth's oceans, included radar systems among its instrumentation; unlike the Landsats' passive sensors, which record radiation reflected or emitted from the terrain below, Seasat's active sensors sent signals to a target location and recorded them as they bounced back. Among Seasat's instruments was a synthetic aperture radar (SAR), a radar imaging system that used the motion of the spacecraft to simulate a very long antenna, thereby creating a "synthetic aperture" of view. From its nearly circular, near-polar orbit approximately 800 kilometers above the earth, Seasat collected data on sea-surface winds, sea-surface temperatures, currents, tides, wave heights, atmospheric water vapor, sea ice, ocean topography, oil spills, coastal features, and coastal storm activity. A malfunction ended the satellite's operation after only three months of activity, but during this brief period it collected a wealth of oceanographic data. The HCMM, which operated until 1980, provided thermal surveys of the earth's surface. Its sensor, called a heat capacity mapping radiometer (HCMR), operated in a visible and near-infrared band and a thermal-infrared band. The satellite's circular, sun-synchronous orbit at an altitude of approximately 620 kilometers allowed it to sense surface temperatures near the maximum and minimum of the daily cycle. The satellite's records of temperature changes revealed such information as mineral resource location, soil moisture, thermal pollution sites, snowfield conditions, and the effects of urban areas on climate.

Other countries have joined the United States in establishing their own programs for viewing Earth resources from orbit. In 1986 the French space agency launched the first of the Système Probatoire d'Observation de la Terre (SPOT) series of satellites, placing it into a sun-synchronous, circular, polar orbit at an altitude of approximately 830 kilometers. The SPOT satellites are equipped with two identical high-resolution visible (HRV) sensors that can be operated in either of two modes: panchromatic mode, which scans in only one band within the visible range to provide images with very high spatial resolution; or multispectral mode, which records data from three spectral bands in the visible and near-infrared spectral regions. Unlike the MSS and TM systems with their oscillating mirrors, the HRV sensors are linear "pushbroom" arrays that are swept across an area by the motion of the platform. These sensors have an off-nadir viewing capability; that is, their sensors can pivot to view locations to either side of the satellites' ground track. In 1991, the European Space Agency launched its first Earth Remote Sensing Satellite (ERS-1) to investigate climate and surface features. ERS-1's sensors include an SAR, a wind scatterometer to measure wind velocity at the sea surface, a radar altimeter to determine surface elevations, and a scanning radiometer to measure temperature and water vapor. Russia, Japan, and India also have satellites devoted to monitoring Earth resources.

There are several advantages to observing Earth resources from space using satellites. Unlike aircraft, satellites are a relatively vibration-free platform from which to obtain high-resolution images. A single image can cover a large area, making possible the recognition of large-scale features while alleviating the technical problems of assembling mosaics from aerial photographs. Satellites provide regular, repeated coverage of areas, so that changes over time may be observed. Sun-synchronous orbits permit consistent lighting conditions for an area. Satellites also cover remote areas that are beyond the practical range for aircraft-based photographic operations.

Applications of the Method

Monitoring Earth's resources from space has yielded a wealth of diverse data at relatively low cost. These data, gathered on an ongoing, repetitive basis, provide a means for observing changing phenomena and conditions. Collected predominantly in digital form, the information can be readily manipulated digitally and integrated with other data. ERTS imagery, with enhancement and interpretation, can provide information pertaining to a wide range of interests, including soil and rock types, plant health, water quality, fires, floods, human and animal populations, traffic patterns, and urban development.

In particular, information from satellites has contributed greatly to an increased understanding of the earth's oceans. Data collected by radar instruments aboard Seasat and other satellites have been used to map the shape of the ocean surface. Different gravitational pulls from ridges, troughs, and other structures on the ocean floor create an ocean-surface topography, with water collecting above submarine mountains and forming surface troughs over ocean-floor trenches. Satellite radar altimeters were used to measure the distance between the satellite and the ocean surface. The difference between the altimeter reading and the distance from the earth's center of mass to the satellite at any one point represented the height of the ocean, relative to an ellipsoidal reference surface. Ocean-surface relief was found to deviate from this reference surface by as much as 100 meters. Surface depressions up to 60 meters deep were found over submarine trenches. Less dramatic features, some with an amplitude of only a few centimeters, were also detected, notably above fracture zones cutting through mid-oceanic ridges. From this ocean-surface information, inferences can be made about unexplored regions of the ocean floor.

Context

Data from earth resources satellites have revealed information about less remote environments as well. The American Forestry Association used Landsat imagery taken between 1972 and 1993 to evaluate the urban ecology of Atlanta, Georgia, with particular attention to the effects of the city's expansion during this period. It was found that forested areas in the study area decreased by 65 percent over the twenty-one-year period, giving way to a built environment. An increase in the temperature difference between downtown and the surrounding countryside was observed during this period. Water quality in the city's Chattahoochee River was assessed, based on its reflectivity. As tree cover along the river decreased and development increased with time, an increase in river sediment and organic matter (presumably sewage or fertilizer residue) was noted.

Earth resource information from satellites has also been used in exploration for mineral resources. Such exploration generally involves selecting an area to investigate, mapping it, collecting and analyzing samples, conducting geophysical surveys, and drilling. Remote sensing data help to maximize the effectiveness of exploration efforts and reduce field costs. Satellite images reveal major geological structures that may not be apparent when viewed in the field or from aircraft. In areas that have not been mapped or where existing maps are of poor quality, satellite data are used to create maps of geographical and geological features. Routes of access are plotted, and existing roads are identified. Satellite information on vegetation and soil type is used to assess the vulnerability of the environment to exploration activities or to monitor the impact of those activities over time. Remote sensing data are particularly valuable when images are manipulated to enhance desired features and combined with other information, such as geochemical, geophysical, or seismic data. For example, the spectral data from Landsat TM scanners can be combined with higher-resolution SPOT panchromatic data to produce sharper images of structural features, and additional data can be overlain to enhance the image further. Locations where different data sets show coinciding anomalies are potential sites for mineral deposits. Also, some mineral signatures associated with valuable mineral deposits are recognizable in satellite images, notably in arid, well-exposed terrains where cloud cover and vegetation provide minimal interference. For instance, certain hydrothermal gold deposits often have a conspicuous "alteration halo" of clay minerals that is readily detected in infrared TM scans. Another indicator of possible economic mineral deposits that satellite imagery can detect is stressed vegetation. High concentrations of some metals in soil can adversely affect plant health. While this stress is not always visible to the naked eye, TM imagery readily "sees" a reduction in leaf pigment or water content as an increase in plant-canopy reflectance in the visible and short-wave spectra and a decrease in the near-infrared.

Likewise, petroleum exploration efforts have benefited greatly from ERTS data. Petroleum exploration also uses satellite information for basic operational planning, environmental assessment, and the like. Satellite imagery provides information on geotechnical elements such as an area's landforms, drainage, soil, and vegetation, all of which are considered during a search for likely oil trap locations. In offshore exploration operations, radar data are used to locate oil slicks on the ocean surface, which are indicators of possible areas of natural hydrocarbon seepage from the ocean floor. Satellites provide information on offshore locations where expensive, time-consuming ship-borne surveys are impractical. ERTS images, which recognize no corporate security considerations, are also a convenient way for companies to keep track of a competitor's oil wells and pipelines.

Bibliography

Barrett, E. C., and L. F. Curtis. *Introduction to Environmental Remote Sensing*. New York: John Wiley & Sons, 1976. Although the information on the Landsat program is dated, the chapters discussing satellite data applications in global climatology, hydrology, soil science, mineral exploration, agriculture, land use, forestry, ecology, urban studies, and other disciplines remain useful.

Colwell, Robert N. *Manual of Remote Sensing*. 2d ed. Falls Church, Va.: American Society of Photogrammetry, 1983. Volume 1, *Theory, Instruments, and Techniques*, includes a chapter on the Landsat program and information on Seasat and the HCMM satellite. Volume 2, *Interpretation and Applications*, is dedicated to various applications. This thorough manual includes a glossary, copious references, and examples of satellite imagery.

Drury, S. A. *Image Interpretation in Geology*. London: Allen & Unwin, 1987. Focusing on the interpretation of satellite imagery and other remote sensing data, this text includes thorough discussions of electromagnetic radiation and materials, human vision, and sensors, as well as a glossary. While intended for the geoscientist, it is suitable for a nontechnical audience.

Elachi, Charles. "Spaceborne Imaging Radar: Geologic and Oceanographic Applications." *Science* 209 (September 5, 1980): 1073-1082. This overview of the characteristics and applications of space-borne imaging radar includes an explanation of the synthetic aperture imaging technique, a discussion of potential applications in geologic mapping and oceanography, and Seasat radar images collected over oceans and land.

Gupta, Ravi P. *Remote Sensing Geology*. Berlin: Springer-Verlag, 1991. Includes discussions of electromagnetic radiation and the spectra of minerals and rocks, descriptions of the Landsat and SPOT programs and other Earth resources satellites, and a substantial chapter on geological applications.

Lillesand, Thomas M., and Ralph W. Kiefer. *Remote Sensing and Image Interpretation*. New York: John Wiley & Sons, 1979. Provides detailed information on multispectral scanners, radar sensing, and Earth resource satellites such as Landsat, HCMM, Seasat, and SPOT.

Porter, Richard W. *The Versatile Satellite*. Oxford, England: Oxford University Press, 1977. The first chapters focus on the challenges of designing and launching satellites in general. The chapter entitled "Surveying the Oceans and the Land" includes a detailed description of the imaging devices with which Landsat 1 was equipped.

Richason, Benjamin F., Jr., ed. *Introduction to Remote Sensing of the Environment.* Dubuque, Iowa: Kendall/Hunt, 1978. This accessible text includes chapters on the Landsat program and the application of ERTS and other remote sensing data in such areas as industrial analysis, regional planning, urban analysis, forestry, agricultural analysis, and landform analysis.

Strain, Priscilla, and Frederick Engle. *Looking at Earth.* Atlanta: Turner, 1992. Copiously illustrated with images taken from orbit by Landsat, SPOT, and other satellites, this appealing book provides a continent-by-continent look at Earth. It includes an introductory essay on the history of remote sensing, detailed descriptions of the images, and a brief guide to space-based sensors.

Karen N. Kähler

Cross-References

Aerial Photography, 17; Earth Resources, 2175; Future Resources, 2182; Landsat, 1358; Mission to Planet Earth, 3003; Remote Sensing and the Electromagnetic Spectrum, 2166; Satellite Meteorology, 3090; Skylab, 2375.

EL NIÑO

Types of earth science: Atmospheric sciences and meteorology; oceanography
Field of study: Heat flow

El Niño is a series of linked atmospheric and oceanic events in which a reduction or reversal of the normal large-scale pressure systems acting in the equatorial regions of the Pacific Ocean results in dramatic changes in precipitation, currents, and wind patterns. Repercussions occur over wide areas from the interior of North America to India. Although not regularly periodic, El Niño phenomena generally occur every two to seven years.

Principal terms
> CONVECTION CELL: the path taken when an air parcel is heated in one location, expands, rises through the atmosphere, cools, contracts, descends through the atmosphere to arrive at a different location, and then moves along the surface to return to its original location
> EL NIÑO: warm extreme of the El Niño Southern Oscillation cycle, with unusually warm surface water in the equatorial Pacific Ocean and subdued trade winds
> ENSO: acronym for El Niño Southern Oscillation, used to denote the complete linked atmospheric/ocean phenomenon
> LA NIÑA: the cold extreme of the El Niño Southern Oscillation cycle, with unusually cold surface water in the equatorial Pacific Ocean and enhanced trade winds
> SOUTHERN OSCILLATION: an atmospheric "seesaw" that tilts between atmospheric pressure extremes at Tahiti and Darwin, Australia
> THERMOCLINE: the depth interval at which the temperature of ocean water changes abruptly, separating warm surface water from cold, deep water
> TRADE WINDS: winds blowing from the northeast in the Northern Hemisphere and the southeast in the Southern Hemisphere and converging at the intertropical convergence zone, which wanders back and forth across the equator during the course of a normal year

Summary of the Phenomenon

El Niño is the term used for the oceanic aspects of one phase of a climatalogical phenomenon more generally referred to as an El Niño Southern Oscillation (ENSO) event. *El Niño* is a Spanish term meaning "the Christ child" that was used by Ecuadoran and Peruvian fishermen to refer to unusually warm surface currents that arrived—if they did at all—around Christmastime. ENSO events typically recur every two to seven years and involve nutrient upwellings and dramatic changes in sea surface temperatures and precipitation and wind patterns. Such environmental fluctuations influence and in some cases may control the ecology of large areas of the earth where the effects of the ENSO events are most pronounced.

The large-scale wind patterns of the earth result from the different amounts of solar energy received at the equator and at the poles. Generally, a low-pressure region of ascending air can be found at the equator. This air rises, cools, and releases its water vapor as rain, giving us equatorial rain forests. High in the atmosphere, this dry air spreads out, eventually returning to earth near the latitudes of the tropics, between 23 degrees and 30 degrees north and south latitudes. Most of the earth's large deserts are located in this latitude band. To finish its circuit, this air travels across the surface of the earth toward the equator. Because of the earth's rotation, however, its path is deflected. In the Northern Hemisphere, deflection is to the right, and in the Southern Hemisphere, it is to the left. Such a deflection causes the air to travel obliquely toward the west in both hemispheres, resulting in the system of winds that are known as the trade winds. (Most of the United States lies north of this area and is under the influence of a similar set of winds blowing in the opposite direction, the prevailing westerlies.) This convection system is called Hadley circulation and dominates the global wind system, but additional systems are superimposed on it.

In one system called Walker circulation, warm, wet air rises over Indonesia, spreads out, and then falls as cool, dry air on the eastern Pacific Ocean and the coast of Peru. The existence of this cell became apparent to British scientist Sir Gilbert Walker as he collected data from Tahiti and Darwin, Australia, during the early part of the twentieth century. He found that the atmospheric pressures in these two locations varied together but out of phase with each other. That is, if the pressure rose in Darwin, it fell in Tahiti. Sometimes conditions were normal, with high-pressure zones over Tahiti and lows over Darwin, at other times they were reversed. Walker called this phenomenon the Southern Oscillation and showed that many other meteorological phenomena from around the world seemed to be tied to it. His particular goal, predicting when the monsoons would fall in India, has yet to be achieved.

As the trade winds move across the Pacific Ocean, they drag along great quantities of water. This water is at the sea surface, is warmed by the sun, and piles up in the western Pacific, in the vicinity of Indonesia. The elevation of the sea there can be forty centimeters higher than in the eastern equatorial Pacific. The temperature of the sea changes rather abruptly between the water that has been warmed by the sun and the water beneath it. The depth at which the change occurs is called the thermocline. Because the density of water varies with temperature, this abrupt temperature change corresponds to a density contrast, and mixing of water across the thermocline does not readily occur. The piling up of warm surface water in the area east of Indonesia causes the thermocline to get deeper—as much as two hundred meters deep. Off the coast of Peru, the thermocline is typically fifty meters deep. The difference of forty centimeters of water at the surface is balanced by a difference of one hundred fifty meters on the thermocline because the density contrast across the thermocline, between the cold water and warm water, is much less than the density contrast between the water and air at the surface.

Every few years, for reasons that are not well understood and may be quite complex, the strength of the trade winds decreases. Often this is accompanied by an eastward spreading of the surface pool of warm water. These two phenomena are linked: each can and probably does to some extent cause the other. As the trade winds collapse, a major readjustment of the thermocline occurs. As the small surface slope dwindles, the much larger slope on the thermocline also disappears. As the thermocline rises, it generates Kelvin waves, which are large-scale gravity waves. These race across the Pacific Ocean, deepening the thermocline to the east as they go.

The deeper thermocline and warmer surface water reduce the effectiveness of upwelling in supplying nutrients to the surface water. This causes dramatic decreases in the primary productivity of the oceans off the coast of Peru and often spectacular die-offs in many species of fish and the seabirds and other animals that rely on them. During the 1972 El Niño, die-offs resulted in the collapse of the anchovy fishing industry, although its decline was exacerbated by questionable fishery management policies.

As the thermocline deepens and warmer surface waters move east, the area in the Pacific equatorial region where the ascent of warm, moisture-laden air produces intense precipitation shifts to the east. This area, called the intertropical convergence zone, is generally found over the warmest water. During strong ENSO events, the Walker circulation may be completely reversed, with warm, moist air rising over coastal Peru, where cool, dry air normally falls. Suddenly, regions that have not received a drop of rainfall for years are inundated.

The paths and severity of many storms tracking across the continental United States are affected by the location of the intertropical convergence zone. During ENSO events, the jet stream is often moved or disrupted by the heavy storm activity above the zone. Sometimes this results in more precipitation across certain sections of the United States and sometimes less, but typically the result is abnormal weather.

Eventually, the condition begins to reverse. Trade winds pick up and begin to push the warm surface water back across the Pacific Ocean. Cold water wells up from the depths to replace it, bringing nutrients to reestablish the high productivity of the waters off Peru's coast. As warm surface water piles up in Indonesia, the thermocline there deepens again, and the intertropical convergence zone moves toward its earlier location. If, as often happens, the return of the trade winds cools the surface waters beyond their normal temperatures, a phase called La Niña begins.

Apparently, the ocean/atmosphere system oscillates between two states, La Niña and El Niño. What drives it from one state to the other remains a matter of considerable speculation. Although the complexities of the ocean/atmosphere system would seem more than adequate to produce almost any sequence of events, some researchers have suggested the involvement of yet another complex system, the earth's tectonic engine. ENSO events may be correlated with eruptions of large equatorial volcanoes, which inject dust into the air and can have dramatic impact on the atmospheric components of the cycle. Alternatively, fluctuations in hydrothermal or igneous activity at the ocean floor, which can apply huge amounts of heat directly to the oceanic components of the cycle, may control the timing or intensities of ENSO events.

There is a great deal of interest—scientific and general—in learning more about ENSO events. Computational capabilities and theoretical developments have progressed rapidly, and although scientists are not yet on the verge of understanding this complex interaction of air and water, they may very well be on the verge of developing the right tools to study it.

Methods of Study

El Niño Southern Oscillation events are huge. They last more than a year, involve massive amounts of air and water, and affect a substantial percentage of the earth's surface. During the course of an ENSO event, the changes that have already occurred in the system influence the changes that will occur as it progresses. Winds affect sea surface temperatures, and sea surface temperatures affect the winds. Such feedback and interactions make it difficult to develop models with predictive capability. Until recently, computer models used for atmospheric studies often oversimplified the ocean, and those used for oceanic studies oversimplified the atmosphere. ENSO events involve a tight coupling of the ocean and atmosphere, and any successful model will need to treat both with sophistication and detail.

Large computer models are being developed to try to study ENSO events. As they evolve, deficiencies in the available data set are being identified, and additional data is being acquired. Much of the necessary data is of the type normally gathered during almost any routine oceanographic study: temperatures, salinities, and surface wind velocities and directions. Researchers would like to have such data from before, during, and after an ENSO event. Because these events recur so frequently, almost any data must be within a few years of an event. The difficulty lies in figuring out which data are important. Although there is agreement on what typically happens during an ENSO event, the specifics vary widely from event to event. Just when one group of scientists think they understand it well enough to venture forth with a predictive model, nature comes along and shows them that their model is faulty.

Models, whether sophisticated computer models or simple physical models, can further understanding of ENSO events. This simple physical model uses a clear Pyrex baking pan as the ocean basin, water as the deep, cool, ocean water, vegetable oil as the warmer, less dense, surface water, and a hair dryer (set to blow unheated air) as the trade winds. If the flow of air produced by the hair dryer is directed across the oil, the oil piles up at the far side of the baking pan. The surface of the oil will form a slight slope, with the higher elevation at the far side of the baking pan. A more pronounced, readily visible slope will form where the oil meets the water. Friction from the air produced by the hair dryer pushes surface oil toward the far side of the pan, but as it piles up, it increases the pressure on the water beneath it. This causes the water beneath the oil to move back toward the near side of the baking pan. Eventually a wedge of oil sits over the water, its upper slope maintained by the hair dryer "wind," and its lower slope positioned where the pressures at depth are the same. (The fraction of an inch of additional oil instead of air at the top surface is compensated by a considerably greater deflection of the oil-water boundary because the density contrast between oil and water is much less than that between oil and air.) This represents the normal state in the equatorial Pacific: a shallow thermocline off the coast of Peru; winds moving off the South American continent at Peru, preventing rainfall; a deep thermocline in Indonesia; and air moving from east to west across the ocean, becoming warm and moist, rising over Indonesia, and drenching it in rain.

In the model, an El Niño can be produced by turning off the hair dryer. The forces that maintained the slope on the upper surface of the oil are gone, so the oil sloshes down and its surface becomes horizontal. A wave forms where the oil meets the water, a boundary that corresponds to the thermocline. Such a wave is called an internal wave because it occurs between two layers of water with contrasting densities but in general is not visible at the surface. The wave races across the baking pan just as the waves race across the Pacific during an El Niño.

Although this physical model demonstrates many of the basics of an ENSO event, no physical model is capable of capturing the entire natural event because its scale is so enormous. The rotation of the earth plays a very important role, and the peculiar nature of currents and waves as they move directly along the equator is also quite significant. Computer models can incorporate these effects, however, and developing such models is an active area of research.

Additional data on the ocean is also required. The Pacific Ocean between Indonesia and Peru has not been studied in enough detail to enable scientists to refine their models as much as they would like. The processes that occur during an ENSO event involve large areas and take place over a considerable period of time. Monitoring the sea to detect gradual changes in sea surface temperatures, depth of the thermocline, and surface wind velocity and direction is a complex, expensive project. As more data is acquired, understanding of ENSO events is certain to improve.

Context

The El Niño Southern Oscillation cycle is as much a part of the earth's weather and climate as the cycle of seasons is. Just as people spend about a quarter of the year in winter, people spend about a quarter of their lives in an El Niño phase. Therefore, El Niño events are not truly anomalous. Unlike winter, however, the timing of the ENSO cycle is not regular. For example, from 1991 through 1994, three El Niños developed. Analysis of historic records shows that El Niños have occurred at nearly the same frequency since at least 1525 when record keeping began in Peru. In addition to historic records, evidence for ENSO events is found in tree rings, flood deposits, ice cores, and other geological and biological record keepers. These, too, suggest that the frequency and severity of ENSO events has been fairly constant for at least several thousand years.

The severity of El Niños can vary remarkably. Substantial effort has been made in trying to identify predictors that would permit an early estimate of the occurrence and severity of ENSO events. Several promising predictors of the timing or intensity have emerged but have been abandoned as additional events transpired in which the predictor was present but the expected development did not occur.

Sir Gilbert Walker's suggestion that local weather in widely separated parts of the planet might be closely related was ridiculed by some of his contemporaries. However, his belief has been borne out by the data and understanding acquired subsequent to his early work. ENSO-related changes can also be seen in the Indian and Atlantic Oceans. Some droughts in Africa and India and most droughts in Australia seem connected to ENSO events. For example, weak floods on the Nile River, records of which have been kept since A.D. 622, seem directly related to El Niño events.

Droughts and floods can probably never be prevented. However, many of the ensuing hardships could be avoided or reduced if they could be predicted a year or so in advance. People and governments in affected areas could take preventive measures: Drought-resistant or flood-resistant varieties of crops could be planted, dikes could be reinforced, and water could be temporarily impounded. Before these measures are taken, however, considerable confidence in any prediction is required. Preparing for a flood will make the effects of a drought correspondingly worse. Someday, however, it may be possible to predict ENSO events with the same degree of accuracy that meteorologists predict the arrival of a significant winter storm.

Understanding of the interactions of the atmosphere and oceans is still in its infancy. As it develops, however, people may be able to apply the knowledge quickly and directly to some of the most vexing problems that nature presents.

Bibliography

Davidson, Keay. "What's Wrong with the Weather? El Niño Strikes Again." *Earth,* June, 1995, 24-33. Reviews the anomalous 1991-1994 period when El Niños of various strengths occurred in three out of the four years. Effects in the Indian Ocean are also described. Includes some discussion of Rossby waves from earlier El Niños bouncing around the Pacific basin. No equations, several diagrams. Suitable for readers at the high-school level.

Diaz, Henry F., and Vera Markgraf, eds. *El Niño: Historical and Paleoclimatic Aspects of the Southern Oscillation.* Cambridge, England: Cambridge University Press, 1992. A collection of twenty-two papers dealing with historical aspects of El Niño. These papers cover a variety of climate indicators from ice cores to tree rings to records of floods on the Nile River and seek to reveal the long-term characteristics of El Niños. Most have useful summaries and concluding sections. Suitable for college-level readers.

Knox, Pamela Naber. "A Current Catastrophe: El Niño." *Earth,* September, 1992, 31-37. Provides an easy-to-read overview of many aspects of El Niño events. Some historical perspectives are presented along with various theories on causes, including possible tie-ins with volcanic eruptions. No equations, several good diagrams. Suitable for high-school readers.

Open University Oceanography Course Team. *Ocean Circulation.* Oxford, England: Pergamon Press, 1989. This carefully written textbook provides an introduction into the analysis and understanding of all sorts of circulation in the world's oceans.

Intended for an undergraduate college-level reader, it provides the mathematical background needed to understand many of the aspects of geophysical fluid dynamics. Although treatment of El Niño is brief, it builds on many other discussions of topics such as Kelvin waves and Rossby waves, which are presented very well.

Philander, S. George. *El Niño, La Niña, and the Southern Oscillation.* San Diego, Calif.: Academic Press, 1990. Although it contains some quantitative material beyond the grasp of the average reader, this book covers its subjects thoroughly and with enough qualitative discussions to make it worthwhile. Plenty of diagrams back up the material. Includes visual representations of much of the math. Suitable for most college-level readers, particularly those with some background in science.

Ramage, Colin S. "El Niño." *Scientific American*, June, 1986, 76-83. This balanced, scientific paper avoids throwing all of the vagaries of weather into the El Niño basket and presents several different theories on what causes and sustains these events. It is careful to distinguish between the generally accepted model of El Niños and the actual course taken by any particular event. Several excellent diagrams and maps. Suitable for high-school readers.

Otto H. Muller

Cross-References

The Atmosphere's Global Circulation, 121; Climate, 217; Deep Ocean Currents, 1792; Ocean-Atmosphere Interactions, 1779; Precipitation, 2108; The Structure of the Oceans, 1871; Surface Ocean Currents, 1798; Wind, 2730.

FALLOUT

Type of earth science: Atmospheric sciences and meteorology
Field of study: Analytical techniques

Fallout consists of radioactive particles that settle out of the atmosphere. Nuclear explosions, nuclear reactor accidents, and improperly contained nuclear wastes are all possible sources of fallout particles. Fallout can carry hazardous radioactivity far from the site of its release.

Principal terms

GROUND ZERO: the point on the ground that lies directly beneath a nuclear device when it explodes

HALF-LIFE: the time it takes for half a sample of a radioactive isotope to decay

ISOTOPE: a variant form of an element having the same number of protons but a different number of neutrons from the typical form

RADIOACTIVITY: the spontaneous decay of an unstable nucleus

REM: a traditional unit of measure of the radiation dose absorbed by a person

SIEVERT (Sv): the modern unit for the equivalent radiation dose absorbed by a person; one sievert equals 100 rem

YIELD: the explosive power of a weapon, stated in terms of how many tons of dynamite would be required to produce the same explosive power

Summary of the Phenomenon

Fallout is the name given to radioactive particles that rain down from the debris cloud of a nuclear explosion. The first nuclear weapons were fission bombs incorporating the radioactive isotopes uranium 235 or plutonium 239 (isotopes of an element are denoted by the total number of neutrons and protons in an atom.) In the process called fission, neutrons striking nuclei of these particular isotopes cause these nuclei to fragment into two roughly equal pieces. Three hundred isotopes of thirty-six elements have been identified in fission fragments. Many of these isotopes are radioactive, and they make up the primary source of radioactive fallout.

In less than one-millionth of a second after detonation, a nuclear explosive changes from a solid material into an expanding fireball with a temperature of 100 million degrees Kelvin and a pressure of 100 million atmospheres. As the boundary of the fireball expands outward, it vaporizes the remaining parts of the bomb. The fireball cools as it grows; eventually, it cools enough so that the bomb vapor condenses into the solid particles that will become fallout. The particles are radioactive because they incorporate the radioactive ashes of the nuclear explosive.

Eventually, the expansion of the fireball slows, and then the simple phenomenon of hot air rising lifts the fireball and its burden of fallout particles high into the atmosphere. For explosions with yields of less than 100 kilotons, the fireball will remain in the troposphere, the lowest layer of the atmosphere. Precipitation along with the natural settling of heavier particles will clear the air of fallout in a time span of hours to days, although some very small particles may remain aloft longer. This fallout is called "local fallout" and may occur near the site of the explosion (often called "ground zero") to as far as a few hundred kilometers distant. After the Hiroshima and Nagasaki explosions, smoky fires started by the bombs caused black rains to fall about thirty minutes after the blasts, and these rains brought down fallout with them.

Modern nuclear weapons are generally three-stage devices that use fission, fusion, and fission in turn. In nuclear fusion, nuclei of lighter elements are fused to form nuclei of heavier elements. Typically, nuclei of hydrogen-2 (deuterium) and hydrogen-3 (tritium) are fused to form helium in a reaction that also produces high-energy neutrons. These neutrons can cause the common isotope of uranium, uranium 238, to fission. The detonation of a modern weapon's first stage causes plutonium to fission, and then the second stage uses the energy released by the plutonium to produce hydrogen fusion. In the third stage, neutrons from the hydrogen fusion cause uranium 238 to fission.

Since the fusion reaction products are mostly nonradioactive, a fusion weapon can be designed to produce more or less fallout. To make a "clean" bomb, care must be taken in choosing the nonnuclear explosive materials, because the fusion-produced neutrons can make many materials become radioactive. Choosing materials that will be made radioactive by fusion neutrons, on the other hand, produces a "dirty" bomb.

The ultimate fallout weapon is perhaps the cobalt bomb, made by placing a blanket of cobalt around a fission-fusion weapon. Radioactive cobalt has a half-life of about five years, and it emits a very penetrating gamma ray. At one hour after detonation, a cobalt bomb's fallout radiation would be fifteen thousand times less intense than that of a conventional nuclear bomb; however, the conventional bomb's radioisotopes decay faster. After six months, the fallout levels from the two types of weapons would be equal; after five years, cobalt fallout radiation would be 150 times more intense. The detonation of thousands of cobalt bombs would constitute a "doomsday weapon," since it would make large areas uninhabitable for many years. Any nation launching such a doomsday attack would likely also suffer from it as radioactive cobalt dust blew onto its own territory. Fortunately, cobalt bombs have never been built.

In an air burst, the fireball does not touch the ground. For air bursts of weapons with yields between 100 kilotons and 1 megaton, less fallout is deposited locally, and more goes into the stratosphere as the explosive yield increases. Because missiles and bombs were not very accurate in the 1950's and 1960's, nuclear powers made weapons with large yields. For example, the Titan II missile carried a 10-megaton warhead, and the Soviet SS-18 missile carried either a 10-megaton or 20-megaton warhead. Such missiles need only to hit somewhere near their targets to destroy them. As accuracy improved, nuclear stockpiles were downsized to weapon yields of 100 to 700 kilotons.

Perversely, these downsized weapons produce more local fallout than the larger weapons they replace.

For yields above one megaton, the fireball will punch its way up into the stratosphere; in the case of an air burst, the fireball will carry most of the radioactive fallout with it. Fine particles can remain in the stratosphere for years, circling the globe many times. Most of these particles will not cross the equator and so will remain in either the Northern Hemisphere or the Southern Hemisphere depending upon their point of origin. Fallout that takes several days to a few years to settle to the ground is called "global fallout." A fireball that touches the ground sucks up dirt and debris and mixes them with the radioactive bomb vapor. This greatly increases fallout. While an air burst causes the most widespread damage, the greatest damage at ground zero is caused by a ground burst, and therefore ground bursts would be used against hardened targets such as missile silos. For a one-megaton ground burst, about half the fallout will be deposited locally, and the other half will rise into the stratosphere.

The length of time it takes for fallout to reach the ground depends largely on the size of the particles and on how high they are lofted. Since radioactive nuclei decay, the longer they remain aloft, the weaker the radioactivity will be when the fallout reaches the ground. Half-lives of radioactive isotopes from nuclear weapons range from a fraction of a second to billions of years, but the total mix obeys a simple rule: For each factor-of-seven increase in time, the intensity of radioactivity decreases by approximately a factor of ten. For example, seven hours after a blast, the radioactivity will be only 10 percent of what it was one hour after the blast. Forty-nine hours after the blast, the radioactivity will be only 1 percent of what it was at one hour, and so on. After about six months, the radioactivity decreases even more rapidly.

Short-lived isotopes are intensely radioactive, but only for a brief time; long-lived isotopes are only weakly radioactive, but they are active for a long time. Those with intermediate half-lives are the most dangerous fallout isotopes. Two other important considerations are the type of radiation emitted and the human body's affinity for certain elements. Fallout radiation is usually gamma rays or beta particles. Gamma rays are similar to X rays, but they have higher energies and are more penetrating. Staying inside a frame house will reduce gamma radiation from fallout by a factor of two or three. A basement will reduce the radiation by a factor of ten to twenty, and a below-ground shelter covered with a meter of dirt will reduce the radiation by a factor of five thousand. Beta particles are electrons emitted by a radioactive nucleus. Heavy clothing can block much of the beta radiation. Beta emitters are most harmful if left on the skin for long times or if they are ingested. If fallout dust is not rinsed off, people and animals may receive skin burns. Because of their cause, such burns are sometimes called "beta burns."

The most hazardous elements in fallout include the short-lived isotopes of iodine that emit both beta particles and gamma rays. Cows eating fodder contaminated with radioactive iodine pass it on in their milk. When humans consume this milk, the radioactive iodine is concentrated by the thyroid gland, which consequently may receive a very high radiation dose. Radioactive strontium is a beta-particle emitter and is chemically similar to calcium, so it is readily absorbed by the body. Radioactive cesium emits both beta particles and gamma rays. It is chemically similar to potassium, and so it is also readily taken up by the body. In the ground burst of a fusion weapon, neutrons will make some elements in the soil radioactive. The most hazardous of these include the short-lived isotopes of sodium, manganese, and silicon.

Consider an event that would qualify as a worst-case scenario for local fallout: a one-megaton ground burst. Such a blast would form a crater at least 300 meters in diameter and 60 meters deep. Much of the crater material would be sucked into the rising fireball, while the rest would be flung into a wide ring around the crater. The first fallout would likely begin within minutes of the blast, as radioactive pebbles rained down near the stem of the mushroom cloud. Fallout of ever-finer particles would continue to rain out over the next hours and days in a region beginning near ground zero and extending downwind for a hundred kilometers or even a few hundred kilometers. Hot spots would exist in the fallout pattern where a lethal dose might be received within a few hours. As much as a few thousand square kilometers might receive enough radioactive fallout to be lethal to anyone remaining in the open for a week.

Radioactive fallout can also be produced by a nuclear reactor accident, as happened when the Soviet reactor at Chernobyl exploded in 1986. Because of operator error coupled with a poor design, two chemical explosions rocked the core of the Unit 4 reactor early in the morning of April 26. The explosions lifted the 1,000-ton cover plate from the reactor core, blasted radioactive particles more than 7 kilometers into the air, and started several fires in and around the reactor. Emission from the fires formed a radioactive cloud 1.5 kilometers high. News of the accident did not reach the West until the morning of April 28, when workers contaminated by Chernobyl fallout set off radiation monitors as they entered the Forsmark Nuclear Plant north of Stockholm. It is estimated that all the radioactive xenon gas, about half the radioactive iodine and cesium, and from 3 percent to 5 percent of the remaining radioactive material in the core was released in the accident.

Methods of Study

Most of the fallout from the atomic bomb detonated at Nagasaki seems to have been carried by the wind to a suburb called Nishiyama, three kilometers from ground zero. In 1981, thirty-six years after the bomb, researchers still found traces of plutonium in the soil there. Most of it had not migrated very far through the soil; in fact, 97 percent of it was found in the top thirty centimeters. The researchers also found an area of contamination near the Nishiyama reservoir with an activity of thirty times the normal background level. Someone continuously exposed to such a radiation level would receive approximately the maximum dose thought to be safe.

During 1948, American scientists developed a method to detect low levels of fallout. "Sniffer" planes equipped with ducts that scooped air through paper filters were used to collect samples from various parts of the world. The filter papers were taken to a laboratory, and the small particles that they picked up were analyzed for radioactivity.

The ratios of various isotopes in a dust particle can be used to determine its age. Particles from natural sources are not very radioactive, and they have varying ages. The sample recovered from a sniffer plane flying near the Kamchatka Peninsula on September 3, 1949, was different. Its radioactivity was several times background, and the uniform age of its most radioactive particles implied formation at zero hours Greenwich Mean Time on August 29. The analysis of the sample was the West's first signal that the Soviet Union had exploded its first atomic bomb; the time deduced was off by only one hour. Further analysis showed that the bomb had a plutonium core surrounded by a natural uranium blanket. Fallout analysis thus became an important component in following the nuclear-weapons progress of nations and, later, of monitoring compliance with the ban on atmospheric testing.

Since much radioactivity decays before global fallout settles to the ground, and since such radioactivity is spread over a wide area, global fallout poses less danger to individuals than local fallout does. However, if enough weapons were exploded at once, global fallout might become very dangerous. How many would be enough? Various tracer materials were incorporated into several atmospheric nuclear tests in the late 1950's. These materials were then tracked with sniffer planes, balloon measurements in the stratosphere, and ground measurements. Mathematical models based on these measurements show that even after a large-scale nuclear exchange between superpowers, global fallout is likely to increase cancer fatalities from the current approximately 15 percent to perhaps 16 percent to 18 percent. This is consistent with the total excess cancer mortality of 3.4 percent seen in the Hiroshima and Nagasaki survivors through 1978. (Those victims who received high radiation doses died not long after exposure and are not included in these statistics.)

Context

Radiation damage occurs to body cells. Cells can normally repair themselves, but if they are too damaged, they die. This is a normal occurrence, and unless too many die at once, the body replaces them. Cells repaired incorrectly may become cancer cells. Rapidly dividing cells are very susceptible to radiation damage, and thus the cells of children and, in adults, the lining of the digestive track, bone marrow and lymphatic tissues, red and white blood cells, hair follicles, and cancer cells are especially sensitive to radiation.

The average radiation dose received by a person from natural background sources is estimated to be 3.0 millisieverts per year. Artificial sources such as medical X rays add another 0.6 millisieverts. Fallout from atmospheric tests conducted by the nuclear powers adds another 0.01 millisieverts. Since this is three hundred times less than that received from natural background sources, it has no measurable effect. Unfortunately, some people have been exposed to higher levels of fallout. "Downwinders" living in southern Nevada and southern Utah were exposed to fallout from nuclear tests conducted in Nevada. The inhabitants of Saint George, Utah, may have received as much as 200 millisieverts, which is enough to cause leukemia in a small percentage of the population. Evidence suggests that one dozen or more children died of radiation-induced leukemia. After lengthy legal battles, the U.S. government agreed to pay some compensation for those injured by the fallout.

The United States tested hydrogen bombs in the Marshall Islands. Perhaps because of a higher-than-expected bomb yield and a change in the wind, the Bravo test of March 1, 1954, produced local fallout up to 500 kilometers away. Some inhabitants of Rongelap Atoll received as much as 2 sieverts before they were evacuated. Several showed signs of radiation sickness such as nausea and vomiting. Most of the local children eventually developed lesions of the thyroid and required surgery. A Japanese fishing boat, the *Fortunate Dragon*, was also showered with fallout from the blast; the crew suffered from radiation sickness, and one crew member died.

After the Chernobyl accident, 237 patients were treated for acute radiation sickness, and twenty-eight of them died not long after. During the ten years following the accident, several more died of causes linked to radiation. Many patients suffered from radiation-induced damage to the skin and to the digestive and respiratory tract caused by contamination with radioactive cesium and strontium. Children are particularly susceptible to radiation-induced thyroid cancer, and nearly seven hundred cases linked to radiation from the Chernobyl explosion have been diagnosed and treated. Ten deaths have been attributed to this cause. The distribution of iodide tablets to children at risk may have prevented a higher toll, as thyroid saturated with nonradioactive iodine is less likely to absorb radioactive iodine. Another helpful practice is to convert contaminated milk to powdered milk or to cheese, which can then be stored until the radioactive iodine has decayed away. The amount of radioactive cesium passed on in the milk and meat of cattle can be reduced by factors of two to eight by feeding the cattle Prussian Blue, an iron-based chemical that binds cesium into a compound that is then excreted.

The general decrease in health of the people following the breakup of the Soviet Union has added to the difficulty in determining which effects are attributable to fallout from Chernobyl; according to the World Health Organization, however, there has not yet been a marked increase in leukemia or other cancers as a result of the accident. Some increase is still expected. Almost 200,000 emergency and recovery workers received significant radiation doses during 1986 and 1987 at Chernobyl. Normally, about 41,500 of them would be expected to die of cancer; estimates are that an additional two thousand will die of cancer induced by radiation. Normally, about 800,000 of the 6.8 million residents of the regions contaminated by fallout would be expected to die of cancer. It is estimated that fallout exposure will increase that number by approximately 4,600. The numbers of those who suffer debilitation because of radiation but do not die because of it, however, are expected to be far greater.

Bibliography

Ball, Howard. *Justice Downwind: America's Atomic Testing Program in the 1950's.* New York: Oxford University Press, 1986. The author uses newspaper accounts and recorded interviews to carefully trace changes in public attitudes toward atmospheric nuclear tests. He documents the exposure of the "downwinders" to fallout and traces their efforts to win redress through the courts and through

Congress. He gives evidence for and against the existence of fallout-induced cancer and describes the settlement finally agreed to by the government.

Chernousenko, Vladimir M. *Chernobyl: Insight from the Inside*. Berlin: Springer-Verlag, 1991. An interesting collection of personal anecdotes, pictures, reports, evaluations, and recommendations. Begins with an account of the accident and carries through to the medical problems caused by fallout. The author faults the government for being more concerned with managing the news than with dealing with physical problems.

Chivian, Eric, Susanna Chivian, Robert J. Lifton, and John E. Mack, eds. *Last Aid: The Medical Dimensions of Nuclear War*. San Francisco: W. H. Freeman, 1982. Sponsored by the International Physicians for the Prevention of Nuclear War, this is a calm, factual report on the effects of nuclear weapons. It discusses fallout, including that which fell on the inhabitants of Rongelap Atoll and on the fishermen aboard the *Fortunate Dragon*. The appendix includes an extensive book list for suggested reading.

Katz, Arthur M. *Life After Nuclear War: The Economic and Social Impacts of Nuclear Attacks on the United States*. Cambridge, Mass.: Ballinger, 1982. A classic work on the problems that would arise after a nuclear exchange. Katz concludes that in addition to the casualties caused, fallout would lead to denial of rescue services, fire control, and distribution of food and other supplies, would contaminate farm-land, and would drive people to make irrational decisions as a consequence of fear.

Schell, Jonathan. *The Fate of the Earth*. New York: Alfred A. Knopf, 1982. An eloquent, even poetic treatment of how nuclear explosions and fallout might reduce life on Earth to a republic of insects and grass, both of which are relatively radiation tolerant. While Schell's predictions may be extreme, his concerns merit considera-tion.

Solomon, Fredric, and Robert Q. Marston, eds. *The Medical Implications of Nuclear War*. Washington, D.C.: National Academy Press, 1986. Sponsored by the National Academy of Sciences Institute of Medicine. Somewhat technical in places, but written for a general audience and includes a helpful glossary. An excellent, authoritative source of information on fallout and on the effects of radiation on humans.

Charles W. Rogers

Cross-References

The Atmosphere's Global Circulation, 121; Cosmic Rays and Other Background Radiation, 2876; Environmental Health, 615; Nuclear Power, 1749; Nuclear Waste Disposal, 1758; Radioactive Decay, 2136.

THE GEOID

Type of earth science: Geology
Field of study: Geodesy

The shape of the sea-level surface, over the oceans and under the continents, is given by the geoid. This shape differs from the best-fitting ellipsoid by amounts ranging up to approximately one hundred meters, and these variations provide valuable information concerning models of the convection and tectonics of the planet.

Principal terms

ELLIPSOID OF REVOLUTION: a three-dimensional shape produced by rotating an ellipse around one of its axes

EQUIPOTENTIAL SURFACE: a surface on which every point is at the same potential, used here to include gravitational and rotational effects; no work is done when moving along an equipotential surface

GLOBAL POSITIONING SYSTEM (GPS): a group of satellites that go around Earth every twenty-four hours and that send out signals that can be used to locate places on Earth and in near-Earth orbits

LEGENDRE POLYNOMIALS: mathematical functions used to describe equipotential surfaces on spheres

MANTLE CONVECTION: thermally driven flow in the earth's mantle thought to be the driving force of plate tectonics

Summary of the Phenomenon

The geoid is an imaginary surface that is at sea level everywhere on the earth. Over the oceans, it is generally at mean sea level; under the continents, it is the elevation the sea would have if all of the continents were cut by narrow sea-level canals. It is usually represented as the difference in elevation between sea level and some ellipsoid representing the average shape of the earth, and its relief is on the order of 100 meters. It is important in surveying and geodesy because elevations are measured above or below this surface, and it is important in geology and geophysics because its departures from a perfect ellipsoid reveal information about the earth's interior.

The shape of the earth can be approximated, with varying degrees of complexity and with different levels of success, by different mathematically defined shapes. If represented as a sphere with a radius of 6,371 kilometers, the shape is very simple, but it will have a radius that will be 7 kilometers too small at the equator and 15 kilometers too large at the poles. Nonetheless, this is adequate for many purposes. To get an idea of how well this shape fits the earth, picture the biggest circle possible on a basketball court. This circle will have a radius of 25 feet. If the circle is drawn with a 1-inch-wide line, this line will contain all the errors in the approximation.

For some purposes, however, a spherical shape is entirely inadequate. Gravity varies with the radius of the earth. Surveys seeking to detect density variations beneath the surface using sensitive measurements of gravity need a way to account for the gradual increase in radius from the poles to the equator. This change in radius, usually called the earth's "flattening," is obtained by dividing the difference between the equatorial radius and the polar radius by the equatorial radius. A modification to the spherical shape is obtained by letting the radius vary slightly with latitude, using a straightforward function that includes the value for flattening. This shape is the spheroid, sometimes known as the "niveau spheroid," and for many years was used in gravity surveys. It permitted data reduction at a time when computers filled rooms, if not buildings. This simple formula is actually an approximation of a slightly more complex shape, the ellipsoid.

An ellipsoid of revolution is the shape of a solid produced by rotating an ellipse about one of its axes. If an ellipse with a minor axis equal to the polar diameter and a major axis equal to the equatorial diameter is rotated about the poles, the resulting shape is the earth's ellipsoid. This ellipsoid is used in studies when the sphere or spheroid is inadequate, and it forms the basis for the geoid.

The geoid is an example of an equipotential surface. If there was some way of sliding a mass around on its surface without any friction, no work would be done in moving that mass from place to place, because the mass would stay at the same potential. It is not difficult to calculate the shape of this surface for various idealized situations. It is also possible to measure the shape of the geoid. Much can be learned by comparing the observed shape with the shapes generated by the models.

If the earth were a stationary sphere of uniform density, the geoid would also be a sphere. If the earth were a rotating sphere of uniform density, the geoid would become an ellipsoid. This is because the rotation produces centrifugal force. (Rotation involves an acceleration, which, when multiplied by a mass, must be balanced by a centripetal force, in this case one supplied by gravity. For these purposes, using the non-Newtonian centrifugal force will prove simpler.) This centrifugal force acts in a direction perpendicular to the rotation axis. At the equator, it would be directly opposed to the gravitational pull of the earth. An equipotential surface would need to be higher there to make up for this. The equator would be farther from the center of the earth, and the poles would be closer to the center of the earth, but because the geoid is an equipotential surface, traveling from the equator to one of the poles would not involve going downhill. If the earth formed a rigid sphere, oceans would be much deeper at the equator than at the poles. The scale of the earth and its billions of years of existence, however, have allowed it to deform much as if it were a fluid.

Suppose this model is allowed to assume the equilibrium shape of a fluid with the earth's mean density, rotating in space once a day. In 1686, Sir Isaac Newton determined that such a model would form an ellipsoid with a flattening of 1 part in 230. His solution piqued considerable interest. This much flattening would result in differences in the length of a degree of latitude between the equator and the poles, which should have been measurable using the techniques available in the early part of the eighteenth century. Expeditions were made to Lapland and Peru to do just this. The results showed a flattening, but of only about 1 part in 300. The current value is

1 part in 298.257, and many geoids are presented in terms of elevation above or below this reference ellipsoid.

As additional geodetic surveys, gravity surveys, and satellite orbit determinations were done, knowledge of the geoid evolved. It is now known that the Indian Ocean just off the southern tip of India is about 100 meters beneath the ellipsoid. Other ocean lows exist in the western North Atlantic Ocean (−50 meters), the eastern North Pacific Ocean (−50 meters), and the Ross Sea near Antarctica (−60 meters). On the continents, lows are present in central Asia (−60 meters) and northern Canada (−50 meters). High areas of the geoid occur over New Guinea (+75 meters), southeast of Africa halfway to Antarctica (+50 meters), in the North Atlantic Ocean (+60 meters), in western South America (+40 meters), and in southern Alaska (+20 meters). These highs and lows dominate the geoid. Their existence and locations have been known since the 1970's.

The huge areas over which individual highs and lows extend require that they be produced by large, deep-seated density variations. Their existence suggests an Earth that is not in hydrostatic equilibrium, which in turn suggests that they result from density variations that do not persist for more than a few hundred million years. Therefore, mantle convection seems to be the most likely cause of these undulations, and many geophysical studies of the long-wavelength undulations of the geoid have concentrated on determining what they tell us about this convection. In general, lows on the geoid are above areas of rapid spreading, and highs are above subducted slabs. Although still evolving and hence subject to change, most of these investigations seem to suggest that mantle convection is driven by descending, not ascending, plumes; that convection involves the whole mantle, not just the seismically active (less than 670 kilometers deep) mantle; and that viscosity increases by a factor of about ten at some depth, probably 670 kilometers.

Other research involves the smaller-wavelength geoid anomalies, particularly over ocean areas. The data are filtered to remove the larger effects, and what remains is usually an excellent indicator of sea-bottom topography. The additional mass produced by a mountain on the seafloor attracts extra water, which piles up and causes a high on the geoid. The geoid is depressed above trenches because trench areas have less mass than the normal seafloor, so they attract less water. This small-wavelength low, with an amplitude of ten meters or so, is usually superimposed on a much larger wavelength high produced by the huge mass excess of the cold slab descending into the mantle nearby.

Undulations of the geoid give some of the best evidence for lateral density variations in the mantle. Seismic data also reveal lateral variations within the mantle, but these are variations in seismic wave velocities, which may or may not correspond directly to density variations. Eventually, the two lines of investigation promise to reveal the inner workings of the planet.

Methods of Study

Because gravity depends on the shape of the geoid, if there were enough accurate determinations of gravity at sea level, mathematical manipulations could be performed to find the shape of the geoid. However, gravity measurements taken above sea level can be adjusted in ways that convert them to equivalent values for sea-level readings. By the middle of the twentieth century, great progress had been made in mapping the gravity field over much of North America and Europe. This gave some indication of how the geoid undulated locally, but accurate determinations of geoid heights actually require considerable knowledge of gravity from around the entire earth. When the first satellite was launched in 1957, a new technique suddenly became available that permitted global gravity—and geoid height—to be calculated.

A satellite's orbit is influenced by the distribution of mass beneath it. The motion of the satellite in its orbit and the precession (gyration) and nutation (wobble) of the orbit are all influenced by the gravitational field it experiences. If the orbit is carefully tracked, it reveals much about the earth's shape and gravity. This requires a considerable mathematical effort, seeking solutions to a partial differential equation called Laplace's equation. These solutions take the form of coefficients of Legendre polynomials and associated polynomials. To see how they can describe the geoid, consider a surface suspended in space above a chessboard.

To describe the topography of this surface, each square could be designated by its row and column number and its elevation listed. However, there is another way to do this. The description can begin with the average elevation for the whole surface. Once that is determined, the surface is divided into quarters labeled "1" through "4"; the difference between the average elevation for each quarter and the average for the whole surface is then listed. Each quarter is then divided into four parts labeled "A" through "D," and the difference between the average elevation for each part and the average for the whole quarter is again listed. If this is done once more, labeling the divisions "a" through "d," elevation data will exist for all sixty-four squares of the chessboard. If the quarters are numbered clockwise from the upper left, then the square in row 3, column 7 would be designated 2Ca, and its elevation would equal the total surface average plus the difference for quarter 2, plus the difference for sixteenth 2C, plus the difference for sixty-fourth 2Ca.

One advantage this system has is that the earlier results do not change as the description gets more and more detailed. The geoid uses a similar system; however, it divides a spherical grid rather than a square one, so instead of repeatedly quartering, it uses Legendre polynomials. Instead of dividing the board horizontally, the geoid goes to the next degree; instead of dividing the board vertically, the geoid goes to the next order. A geoid determined to degree and order 12 will have much more detail than one determined to degree and order 6, but the coefficients for the first six degrees and orders should be the same.

As satellites have been tracked through more orbits by better technology, the geoid has become known to increasingly better precision. It was known to degree and order 8 by 1961, 16 by 1971, and 20 by 1985. Current models use supercomputers to work through 10,000 parameters, yielding some results to degree and order 360. There are differences between them; however, typically they vary on the order of half a meter at degree and order 50 or so. Much of the difficulty lies in correctly merging data from more than thirty satellites and tens of thousands of individual gravity measurements made on land.

Satellite data are influenced by factors such as atmospheric drag and refraction effects, and considerable thought and engineering have gone into finding ways around such problems. Geodetic satellites must be in near-Earth orbits in order to be influenced significantly by the undulations in the geoid, and in such orbits atmospheric drag is significant. One approach has been to design satellites out of uranium, which is denser than lead, giving them a great mass for a small cross-sectional area. Another solution has been to suspend a massive core inside a spherical shell. Atmospheric drag will act on the shell, pushing it closer to the core on the side experiencing the drag. Appropriate use of thrusters built into the shell can then ensure that these effects are perfectly canceled. Refraction effects also result from the atmosphere and can be minimized by determining the satellite's position relative to other satellites in higher orbit. Lasers are used for this, reflecting off corner cubes embedded in the outer shell of the satellite.

Ground-based gravity data are influenced by instrument design, operator expertise, and the care with which topographic effects have been removed. Accurate elevations are essential, and much of the earth's land surface has not been mapped with sufficient topographic precision to provide this control. This, combined with political and economic realities, has resulted in a data set that includes very little information from Asia and not enough from South America. The Global Positioning System (GPS) constellation of satellites promises great improvement in the data set by providing better satellite tracking as well as better elevation control in poorly mapped areas.

Context

Better knowledge of the geoid will lead to better understanding of plate motions and convection in the mantle, permit more accurate placement of satellites in orbit, and provide an enhanced base for surveys on Earth. One of the outstanding questions in geophysics concerns the scale of convection in the mantle. No one knows if the convection cells extend throughout the entire mantle or if there are two convection regimes, one above a depth of 670 kilometers, the other below it. Unequivocal answers have yet to be found, but the study of the geoid offers great promise. Models for most of the highs of the geoid use the mass of the descending slabs to generate them. It appears that a slab reaching only to depths of 670 kilometers may not have sufficient mass. This somewhat tentative result favors deep mantle convection. As knowledge of the geoid improves, particularly in continental areas for which only sparse gravity data exist, the validity of this result may be established. An improved grasp of convection in the mantle will increase understanding of the plate-tectonic theory. As that develops, it may well produce a capability to predict earthquakes and volcanoes and to mitigate the death and destruction they cause.

As communications technology develops, the need for many more satellites to relay the ever-increasing traffic will grow. Just as minor perturbations in satellite orbits help us to define the geoid, a better understanding of the geoid will permit much better predictions of just how a satellite will behave in orbit. This is true even for the very high communications satellites. As the population of satellites grows, the need for such refinements in orbit calculations will become necessary to avoid collisions.

Ocean currents such as the Gulf Stream are powered by differences in elevation of the sea surface. These differences, on the order of a meter or so, occur because huge, warm lenses of water float on denser water below. Water at the surface, which in this case is not an equipotential surface, tries to flow down the slope, is affected by the earth's rotation, and ends up going around the lens of warmer water instead. Measuring such tiny variations in the level of the sea is difficult. As our knowledge of the geoid improves, however, we should be able to observe these discrepancies. This should provide important data from which changes in ocean currents can be predicted. Finally, because all surveys on land measure elevations with respect to sea level, improvements in charting sea level will make the elevation measures on land much better.

Bibliography

Fowler, C. M. R. *The Solid Earth*. Cambridge, England: Cambridge University Press, 1990. This college textbook contains a brief but easily understood treatment of the geoid and examples of geoid height-anomaly calculations.

Garland, G. D. *The Earth's Shape and Gravity*. Oxford, England: Pergamon Press, 1977. An excellent, easy-to-read general treatment that describes the geoid and the techniques and data manipulations needed to obtain it. Although somewhat dated (the geoid map included is from 1961), the treatment is thorough. Potential theory is discussed in an appendix, and the book tries to avoid higher math as much as possible, making this the best source for a quantitative introduction to the subject.

Heiskanen, Weikko A., and Helmut Moritz. *Physical Geodesy*. San Francisco: W. H. Freeman, 1967. The standard text on this subject for many years, this book presents a thorough treatment of the techniques and theoretical bases for classical geodesy. Somewhat heavy with equations.

King-Hele, Desmond. *Scientific American*, October, 1967. This easy-to-read paper captures the excitement and sense of discovery shared by scientists working with the early satellites. Although the data set has grown tremendously since this paper was written, most of the major features of the geoid can be seen on the map.

Lambeck, Kurt. *Geophysical Geodesy*. Oxford, England: Clarendon Press, 1988. The best book available on the subject, it includes a detailed treatment of the geoid and how it is obtained. Considerably better than other references in explaining satellite techniques and dynamic ocean topography. Although rich in equations, many containing Legendre polynomials, most of the relevant concepts and results are also described in words. Contains many maps, including one of global gravity and one of geoid heights from 1985.

Stacey, Frank D. *Physics of the Earth*. 2d ed. New York: John Wiley & Sons, 1977. A standard geophysics textbook for many years, this book examines the geoid and its implications for geophysical models of Earth. Contains a map of a geoid of 1971.

Tsuboi, Chuji. *Gravity*. London: George Allen & Unwin, 1983. A remarkable book by an accomplished Japanese scientist. The geoid is given unusual treatment, using Cartesian, cylindrical, and spherical approaches. Although quantitative and rigorous, many of the treatments are practical, drawn from work done by the author in the first half of the twentieth century. Almost entirely devoted to presatellite work.

Otto H. Muller

Cross-References

GLOBAL WARMING

Type of earth science: Atmospheric sciences and meteorology
Field of study: Heat flow

Global warming is the phenomenon of rising global temperatures that may be caused by air pollution from human activities. This rise in temperature has the potential to cause drastic changes in climate and weather patterns worldwide.

Principal terms
CLIMATE: the long-term weather patterns for a region, distinct from the
day-to-day weather patterns
GREENHOUSE EFFECT: the trapping of heat in the atmosphere by certain
gases
GREENHOUSE GAS: gases that absorb infrared radiation more efficiently
than other gases; examples include carbon dioxide, methane, and
water vapor
INFRARED RADIATION: electromagnetic radiation emitted by warm
objects; it is frequently confused with heat but is actually a different
phenomenon

Summary of the Phenomenon
"Global warming" is the term for the rise in the earth's average temperature. Scientists know that the earth's average global temperature has been rising since the beginning of the Industrial Revolution in the second half of the 1700's. Increases in temperature could alter precipitation patterns, change growing seasons, result in coastal flooding, and turn some areas into deserts. Scientists do not know the cause of this phenomenon but believe that it could be part of a normal climate cycle or be caused by natural events or the activities of humankind.

When the ground is heated by sunlight, it gives off the heat as infrared radiation. The atmosphere absorbs the infrared radiation and keeps it from escaping into space. This is called the "greenhouse effect" because it was once believed that the glass panes of greenhouses acted similarly to the atmosphere, capturing the infrared radiation given off by the earth inside the greenhouse and not allowing it to pass through. Although it has subsequently been shown that greenhouses work by trapping the heated air and not allowing it to blow away, the name has stuck.

The atmosphere eventually releases its heat into space. The amount of heat stored in the atmosphere remains constant as long as the composition of gases in the atmosphere does not change. Some gases, including carbon dioxide, water vapor, and methane, store heat more efficiently than others and are called "greenhouse gases." If the composition of the atmosphere changes to include more of these greenhouse gases, the air retains more heat, and the atmosphere becomes warmer.

Global levels of greenhouse gases have been steadily increasing and in 1990 were more than 14 percent higher than they were in 1960. At the same time, the average global temperature has also been rising. Meteorological records show that from 1890 to the mid-1990's, the average global temperature rose by between 0.4 and 0.7 degrees Celsius. About 0.2 degrees Celsius of this temperature increase occurred since 1950. In comparison, the difference between the average global temperature in the 1990's and in the last ice age is approximately 10 degrees Celsius, and it is estimated that a drop of as little as 4 to 5 degrees Celsius could trigger the formation of continental glaciers. Therefore, the rise in average temperature is significant and already beginning to cause some changes in the global climate. Documented changes include the melting of glaciers and rising sea levels as the ocean gets hotter and its waters expand. Measurements of plant activity indicate that the growing season has become approximately two weeks longer per year in the middle latitude regions.

A common misunderstanding is that global warming simply means that winters will be less cold and summers will be hotter, while everything else will be basically the same. Actually, the earth's weather system is very complicated, and higher global temperatures will result in significant changes in weather patterns. Most changes will be observed in the middle and upper latitudes, with equatorial regions witnessing fewer changes. The areas that will experience most of the changes include North America, Europe, and most of Asia. The Southern Hemisphere will experience less severe effects because it contains more water than the Northern Hemisphere does, and it takes more energy to heat water than land.

It is difficult to predict precisely what these changes will be, but observation of the changing climate and scientific studies allow researchers to make some rough estimates of the kinds of changes the earth will experience. Summers will be hotter, with more severe heat waves. Because hot air holds more moisture than cool air, rain will fall less frequently in the summer. Droughts can be expected to be more common and more severe. Through the late 1980's and into the early 1990's, annual temperatures climbed higher and higher, and summer heat waves became more frequent. This is a particularly troubling problem in areas where homes are typically built without air conditioning. The air in a closed-up house during a heat wave can reach temperatures well over 40 degrees Celsius. Because these temperatures exceed people's normal body temperature, which is about 36.5 degrees Celsius, it becomes very difficult for the body to cool down. For this reason, heat waves are particularly dangerous for the very young or old and the sick. More frequent heat waves will cause increases in the use of air conditioning, which requires more energy and will release additional greenhouse gases.

Global warming will also produce severe autumn rains. The overheated summer air will cool in the autumn and will no longer be able to hold all of the moisture it was storing. It will release the moisture as heavy rains, causing flooding. This phenomenon has already been observed, but not for a period of time that is scientifically significant. It is difficult to tell the difference between long-term changes and short-term fluctuations with only a few years of observations.

These changing rain patterns—droughts and severe autumn storms—will certainly have an effect on the earth's landscape. Some areas may be turned to deserts, and others may be transformed from plains to forests.

One of the strange aspects of global warming is that it is predicted to result in not only hotter periods during the summers but also colder periods during the winter. It takes energy to move large cold-air masses from the polar regions in winter, so it is possible that large winter storms will be colder, more violent, and more frequent. This pattern has been evident since about the mid-1970's. Winter storms have brought record low temperatures and enough snow to close cities for days. However, this time span is too short to determine if this is a temporary phenomenon or a trend. It is possible that some smaller, less permanent event than global warming is responsible for the more severe winter storms. A shorter (although more severe) winter may create a surge in pest populations and diseases that are normally controlled by long winters.

Global warming will cause ocean levels to rise, because water expands when heated and also because of the melting of glaciers on Greenland and Antarctica. The melting of the ice in the northern polar areas will not contribute to rising ocean levels because that ice, unlike the ice on Greenland and Antarctica, is already in the ocean. Just as the melting of the ice in a drink does not cause the level of the drink to rise, the melting of the northern oceanic ice sheets will not affect sea levels.

Although many scientists are convinced, based on the abundant evidence, that global warming is occurring, they are less sure of why. One significant factor, the rise in greenhouse gases, can be attributed to the activities of humankind. Burning forests to clear land and operating factories and automobiles produce carbon dioxide and water vapor. Livestock herds and rotting vegetation release methane, and fertilizers used on farms also release greenhouse gases. Power plants that consume fossil fuels such as coal, oil, or natural gas release massive amounts of carbon dioxide into the air. However, no one knows if humankind's activities are the real or only reason for the increase in global temperature. The last ice age ended very recently in geologic terms, and a number of changes are still taking place as the globe recovers from the presence of huge ice sheets. It is possible that the world's climate is still warming up from the last ice age. In addition, volcanoes are another major source of greenhouse gases, and the level of volcanic activity has been increasing since approximately the beginning of the Industrial Revolution.

Global warming could also be part of a natural cyclical change in the climate. Evidence indicates that the earth's climate varies between warmer and colder periods that last a few centuries. History provides many stories of dramatically changing climate, including one period from 1617 to 1650 that was so unusually cold that it is called the "Little Ice Age." Therefore, the earth may be merely experiencing another cyclical change in its climate.

Methods of Study

The problem with studying global warming is that no one can be sure of its extent, and some scientists debate whether it actually exists. They argue that the observed changes may only be a warm phase of a climatic cycle that will make the earth warmer for a few years, then cooler for a few years. If this is true, then the coming decades may see average temperatures leveling off or even dropping.

A major source of the confusion involves the way global warming is studied. It would seem easy to record temperatures for a number of years and then compare them. However, detailed records on the weather have not been kept for more than a few decades in many areas. Scientists are forced to rely on interpretations of historical accounts and the clues left in fossil records. The analysis of tree rings, sedimentary deposits, and even very old ice from deep within glaciers can provide data about the climate in the past.

In addition, the existing records must be reviewed carefully to identify local changes that may not reflect global ones. For example, as towns grow into cities, the temperature climbs simply because larger cities are warmer than smaller ones. Measurements taken years ago in a more rural environment should be lower than those taken after the population around the measuring station increased. This problem can be overcome with balloons. By sending instruments high in the atmosphere on weather balloons, air temperatures can be measured without being affected by urbanization. Although data recorded this way show a consistent rise in global temperature, such measurements go back only a few decades.

Measurements of the level of greenhouse gases in the atmosphere are also affected by urbanization. As a small town becomes a city, levels can be expected to rise. However, recording stations located in regions far removed from cities and factories show an increase in the level of greenhouse gases. One station on the island of Hawaii has shown a rise in the amount of carbon dioxide present in the air since early 1958, with similar reports coming from stations in Point Barrow, Alaska, and Antarctica.

Another important variable in looking at global warming is sea surface temperature. Measurements can be skewed by local effects that have no impact on the global climate. One method used to make detailed measurements of seawater temperature is to broadcast a particular frequency of noise through the water and measure it at distant locations. The speed and frequency of the sound is affected by the temperature of the water.

However, more accurate and more global data are becoming available through the Mission to Planet Earth program of the National Aeronautics and Space Administration (NASA). The program places satellites in orbit to study the earth and make a variety of detailed measurements, many of which are of factors that contribute to global warming. This data will help immensely in enabling scientists to understand the global climate and the changes it is undergoing.

Context

The global climatic environment is very complicated, and many factors contribute to it. All these factors together produce the climate in which people live. For this reason, it is impossible to say that any changes are attributable simply to a particular natural event or to the activities of humankind. However, at the same time, the activities of humankind are so large-scale and widespread that it is safe to conclude that they have definitely changed the world. Unfortunately, the effect of these changes is still not clear. People have generated massive amounts of greenhouse gases and released them into the air, but no one really knows the extent of their effect on the environment.

If scientists determine that humankind's activities are responsible for the observed changes in the environment, then people can identify what they must do to preserve the environment and take measures to change the way they live. People may eventually gain enough knowledge to plan the changes in the climate to occur in such a way as to provide maximum benefit to the environment and themselves. Even if researchers determine that global warming is caused by natural events beyond human control, people still must evaluate their role. Humankind's activities are likely to contribute to the problem, so altering behavior and ways of life might lessen the negative effects of global warming. For example, although global warming might not be caused by emissions of greenhouse gases, these emissions might worsen the droughts and severe rainstorms. If so, then by reducing emissions, people might be able to counteract some of the effects of the climatic changes.

If the changes in the climate approach what is expected based on scientific models of global warming, the impact on the environment and humanity will be staggering. The changes are such that virtually every person on Earth would be affected. If rain patterns change drastically, it is possible that the food supplies of the world will be sharply reduced. In some areas, if the average temperature increases, certain diseases associated with warmer climates will begin to affect the people. An increase of a few meters in the ocean level will inundate many of the world's coastal areas and the large cities found in those areas. In addition to these large-scale changes, changes in the weather will have a great impact on the day-to-day lives of the majority of the world's people. Any solution to the problem of global warming will also probably dramatically affect people's lives.

Bibliography

Abrahamson, Dean Edwin, ed. *The Challenge of Global Warming*. Washington, D.C.: Island Press, 1989. This detailed examination of what global warming is and how it occurs is suitable for all readers. Also discusses greenhouse gases and policy-making decisions regarding global warming.

Bach, Wilfrid, Jurgen Pankrath, and William Kellogg. *Man's Impact on Climate*. Vol. 10 in *Developments in Atmospheric Science*. Amsterdam: Elsevier Scientific, 1979. A well-written but technical account of research into changes in the atmosphere and their effects. Suitable for more advanced readers.

Gates, David M. *Climate Change and Its Biological Consequences*. Sunderland, Mass.: Sinauer Associates, 1993. This excellent book examines the effects that climatic changes would have on life on Earth, discussing many of the models used in making predictions. Suitable for high-school students and up.

Magill, Frank N., and Russell R. Tobias, eds. *USA in Space*. Pasadena, Calif.: Salem Press, 1996. This three-volume set consists of an extremely well-written series of articles on U.S. space activities. A number of pieces discuss data collection on the environment and detecting people's effects on the environment. Suitable for all levels.

Nance, John J. *What Goes Up: The Global Assault on Our Atmosphere.* New York: William Morrow, 1991. This is a clearly presented documentation of the investigation into the changes occurring in the atmosphere. Topics covered include global warming and the depletion of the ozone layer. Suitable for all readers.

Weiner, Jonathan. *Planet Earth.* Toronto: Bantam Books, 1986. This exceptionally well-written book is the companion book to the *Planet Earth* series developed by the Public Broadcasting Service. It covers many aspects of the planet and devotes a chapter to its climate. Suitable for all audiences.

Wyman, Richard L., ed. *Global Climate Change and Life on Earth.* New York: Chapman and Hall, 1991. A collection of articles on various aspects of climate change and the effects of these changes. Suitable for high-school students and up.

Christopher Keating

Cross-References

Air Pollution, 24; The Atmosphere's Structure and Composition, 128; Climate, 217; Earth System Science, 407; El Niño, 2911; The Greenhouse Effect, 1004; Mission to Planet Earth, 3003; Ozone Holes, 3039; Paleoclimatology, 1993; Satellite Meteorology, 3090.

GREAT LAKES

Type of earth science: Hydrology
Field of study: Geomorphology

The Great Lakes represent the largest freshwater lake complex on Earth. Created by continental glaciers over the past eighteen thousand years, the five lakes provide significant resources for Canadians and Americans occupying the surrounding basin.

Principal terms

EPILIMNON: a warmer surface layer of water that occurs in a lake during summer stratification; during spring, warmer water rises from great depths, and it heats up through the summer season

GREENHOUSE EFFECT: a natural process by which water vapor and carbon dioxide in the atmosphere absorb heat and re-radiate it back to Earth

ISOSTATIC REBOUND: a tendency of Earth's surface to rise after being depressed by continental glaciers, without faulting

PLEISTOCENE: a geologic era spanning about two million years that ended about ten thousand years ago, often considered synonymous with the "Ice Age"

SEICHE: rocking motion of lake level from one end of the lake to the other following high winds and low barometric pressure; frequently, a seiche will follow a storm event

STORM SURGE: a rapid rise in lake level associated with low barometric pressure; the water level is frequently "pushed" above a shoreline on one end of the lake and depressed on the opposite end

THERMOCLINE: a well-defined layer of water in a lake separating the warmer and shallower epilimnon from the cooler and deeper hypolimnon

WETLANDS: areas along a coast where the water table is near or above the ground surface for at least part of the year; wetlands are characterized by wet soils, water-tolerant plants, and high biological production

Summary of the Phenomenon

The Great Lakes are superlative features on the North American landscape. They make up the largest freshwater lake complex on Earth and represent about 18 percent of the world's water supply. Covering a total area of 245,000 square kilometers, the Great Lakes have a shoreline length of 17,000 kilometers. Lake Superior (82,100 square kilometers), Lake Huron (59,600 square kilometers), and Lake Michigan (57,800 square kilometers) are among the ten largest lakes on Earth.

The rocks forming the foundation of the Great Lakes date back some 600 million years. On the northern and northwestern shore of Lake Superior are remnants of the Canadian Shield, which is composed of igneous rocks of the Precambrian era, some one billion years ago. Following volcanic activity and mountain building during the Precambrian era, the central region of North America was repeatedly covered by shallow tropical seas. At this time, the Paleozoic era (600 million to 230 million years ago), sediments transported by rivers from adjacent eroding uplands were deposited in a shallow marine environment, and lime, salt, and gypsum were precipitated from seawater. All these soft materials were eventually hardened into sedimentary rock layers such as sandstone, shale, limestone, and halite. A multitude of fauna colonized the submarine environment, including corals, brachiopods, crinoids, and several species of mollusks.

As the layers of sediments accumulated over millions of years, the basin began to subside at its center. The Great Lakes basin structure may be compared to a series of bowls, one stacked on top of another. As viewed from above, only the top bowl is completely visible; however, the rims of the progressively deeper bowls are visible as a number of thin concentric rims along the perimeter of the basin.

The Paleozoic era was followed by the Mesozoic era (230 to 63 million years ago), a time of little deposition. In spite of the great age of the rocks making up the foundation of the Great Lakes, the lakes themselves were created in the relatively recent Pleistocene epoch. Between the 220 million years that the basin's bedrock was deposited and the onset of Pleistocene glaciers, the landscape now occupied by the individual lakes was occupied by streams. The streams sought and eroded the softer bedrock. The divides between and parallel to the eroded valleys were more resistant to erosion and are represented by higher elevations.

Streams excavated shales, and weaker limestones now occupied the Lake Michigan and Lake Huron basins. An arc, composed of hard dolomite rock, separates the east side of Lake Huron from Georgian Bay (the Bruce Peninsula). The same structure continues counterclockwise across Michigan's upper peninsula, separating Lake Michigan from Green Bay as the Door Peninsula. The ancient stream channels were favored by the glaciers because they were at lower elevations and composed of more erodable bedrock. The linear shape of the lower Great Lakes is clearly related to the initial erosion by streams followed by the continental ice.

Lake Superior is partly located on the Canadian Shield, and its geologic origin is less obvious. East-west faults underlie Lake Superior, and the rocks form a structural sag, or syncline, oriented along the long axis of the lake in an approximately east-west direction.

The glacial origin and development of the Great Lakes is complex for several reasons. Each lake has a unique history and time of formation, making generalizations difficult. For example, the glaciers repeatedly advanced and retreated from many directions, covering and exposing each lake basin. There is abundant evidence regarding the size, elevation, and precise geographical distribution of each ancestral lake; this historical information is documented by coastal landforms such as higher ancient shorelines and relict wave-cut features. Yet the changing of the lakes' outlets to the ocean, and reversals of drainage patterns, complicate the sequence of events. Furthermore, because of the weight of the ice, the Paleozoic bedrock subsided. As the glaciers receded, exposing different segments of the basin, the land began to rise. This process, isostatic rebound, is active today, causing elevation changes of many fossil shorelines. Although uplift has slowed since the ice exposed the newly created Great Lakes, the process is continuing.

As the ice began to retreat from the region, glacial landforms were deposited. Along many shorelines, moraines—composed of fragments of rock, sand, and silt—form spectacular bluffs. Along Lake Superior, the ice scraped and removed much of the soil, exposing the bedrock, which now forms high cliffs. Sand eroded from glacial sediment was transported by rivers to the lakes and deposited as beaches. The exposed beach sand was then transported inland by the wind to form coastal dunes.

Weather and climate are related to several processes occurring in the Great Lakes, including changing lake levels, storm surges and related seiches, and lake stratification and turnover. Through the hydrological cycle, moisture is evaporated from the lake surfaces and is then returned as precipitation over the water and as runoff from the land. During cooler and wetter years, evaporation is retarded and more water is contributed to the lakes by excess precipitation, causing lake levels to rise. In warmer and dryer years, evaporation increases and precipitation is retarded, causing lower lake levels. Such changes in water levels are not cyclic and occur over several years. In 1988, Lake Huron and Lake Michigan had record levels of 177.4 meters above sea level. In 1995, the average water level was 176.3 meters above sea level, a difference of 1.1 meters.

Unstable weather conditions generate storms that pass over the region, generally from west to east. When strong winds persist for several hours from a constant direction over a lake, the water level is "pushed" from one side of the lake to the other. This storm surge, accompanied by low atmospheric pressure, may elevate the water level as much as 2 meters along a shoreline in a matter of a few hours. Gale-force winds on October 30-31, 1996, over Lake Erie raised the lake level 1.25 meters at Buffalo, New York. Concurrently, as the water rose at Buffalo, it was lowered in Toledo, Ohio, at the opposite end of the lake, by 2.25 meters. The total difference of water level was 3.50 meters. Following a storm, the level of a lake rocks back and forth as a "seiche" before settling to its normal level.

In turn, the lake waters dramatically affect the local weather. As winter approaches, lake-effect snows commonly occur. The effect is most common in the fall, before the lakes cool and freeze. Cold winds from the north or west pass over the basin, picking up moisture from the relatively warm lakes. The water vapor is then condensed, forming clouds that, in turn, dump heavy snows in coastal zones, especially along eastern Lake Michigan and southern Lake Superior, Lake Huron, Lake Erie, and Lake Ontario. From November 9 to November 12, 1996, 1.2 meters of snow fell along Lake Erie's south shore, paralyzing local communities.

With the exception of Lake Erie, the lake bottoms were scoured by glaciers to depths below sea level. The lakes thus have variable temperatures from the surface to the bottom. As the water temperature changes from season to season, water density is altered. During winter as ice forms over the lakes, the water beneath the ice remains warmer. As the ice cover breaks up in spring, the deeper warmer water rises, or "turns over," to the surface. It heats up through the summer months, causing stratification of warmer water (or "epilimnon") above colder denser water. The contrasting water layers are separated by a thermocline, demarcating a rapid temperature transition between the warmer epilimnon and cooler subsurface water.

An issue of concern to scientists regarding the Great Lakes is the impact of the "greenhouse effect" on the lakes' water levels. The increase of greenhouse gases in the atmosphere, especially carbon dioxide, appears to cause warming at unprecedented rates. Although climatologists differ in their opinions as to the impact of a warmer atmosphere over the Great Lakes, there is general agreement that both evaporation and precipitation will increase and stream runoff will decrease over many years. Based on general circulation models, it appears that lake levels will be from one-half meter to two meters lower than present levels if the climate continues to warm.

Wetlands along the shorelines of the Great Lakes are significant ecological zones located at the meeting of the land and lake. Although many wetlands around the basin have been lost or degraded, the remaining habitat has multidimensional functions as part of both upland and aquatic ecosystems. The wetlands are exposed to both short-term (storm surges and seiches) and long-term changes in water levels that constantly change the biogeography of these habitats. Because of the state of constant water-level change, or "pulse stability," the distribution and types of wetland plants shift dramatically. Thus, a constant renewal of the flora is occurring. Furthermore, because of the flushing action of the rise and fall of lake levels, peat accumulation in Great Lakes wetlands does not commonly occur, as it does in marine settings.

The coastal wetlands serve significant ecological, economic, and social functions. They provide spawning habitat and nursery and resting areas for many species, including fishes, amphibians, reptiles, ducks, and fur-bearing mammals. Largely because of the sport fishing industry, these habitats contribute significant revenue to the surrounding states and to the province of Ontario. Furthermore, pollution control and coastal erosion protection are additional benefits provided by these habitats. In 1978, the annual value gained by Michigan's coastal wetlands was estimated to be $5,066 per hectare.

Methods of Study

The creation and development of the Great Lakes have, in terms of geologic time, occurred relatively recently. Also, modifications such as erosion and deposition of coastal features are continual, active processes. To unravel the events leading to changes in the Great Lakes, scientists use techniques that include varve analysis and radiocarbon dating. A common theme of both techniques is that they express time in numbers of years within a reasonable range of accuracy, rather than in a relative or comparative way. Varves consist of alternating light and dark sediment layers deposited in a lake. A light-colored mud is deposited during spring runoff; a dark-colored mud is deposited atop the lighter-colored layer during the following winter, as ice forms and there is less agitation of the lake water. One light and one dark band together represent one year of deposition. Numerous layers can be counted, like tree rings, and the number of years that were required for a sequence to be deposited can be determined. To obtain numerous undisturbed varve layers, researchers use a piston-coring device, which consists of a hollow pipe attached to a cable that is released vertically into the lake. As it free falls to the bottom, it plunges into the soft sediment. A piston allows the sediment to remain in the pipe as it is raised by an attached cable. The mud can then be extracted from the tube, cut open, and analyzed.

Radiocarbon dating of carbon-rich material such as peat, lime, coral, and even bone material is useful for absolute dating back to about fifty thousand years ago. Carbon's abundance in nature, coupled with the youthfulness of the Great Lakes, makes this tool very useful, because many glacial, coastal, and sand dune landforms frequently contain some form of carbon suitable for absolute dating.

To map and detect recent changes in the landscape such as coastal erosion or the rate of dune migration, old maps, navigation charts, and aerial photographs are used. Charts and maps of the coastal zone have been available for more than a century, and aerial photographs of the region have been taken since the 1930's. By observing the position of a shoreline on historical sets of detailed aerial photographs over a ten-year period, for example, the changes in the shoreline can be detected, and the erosion rate per year can be determined.

Geographic positioning systems (GPS) can accurately locate the latitude and longitude of a point on a shoreline, store the information, and compare the shoreline position with the position at some future time. Satellite pictures help to detect wetland types and determine acreage; this information can then be compared to a later environmental condition, such as a period of higher lake level, to see if species or acreage have changed.

Because of a geological process known as "isostatic rebound," fossil shorelines are uplifted. Elevations retrieved from older topographic maps reveal how much uplift has occurred. If the age of a relict shoreline can be determined with radiocarbon analysis, the rate of glacial rebound in millimeters per century can be assessed.

Context

The Great Lakes—Superior, Michigan, Huron, Erie, and Ontario—are significant resources and have important physical and cultural heritage values to the United States and Canada. A recurring theme in geology is the enormity of time it takes for landscapes to develop and change. The Great Lakes, however, were created in only about eighteen thousand years, which suggests that even major landscape elements can be created rapidly. Historically, the Great Lakes waterway provided an avenue for exploration of North America. A significant stimulus for the exploration of these freshwater seas was their abundance of resources. French and English explorers sought furs such as those of the beaver and muskrat, which occupied the basin's wetlands.

Loggers exploited the timber. Industry utilized the area's iron ore and copper, which was combined with local limestone and nearby coal to create North America's industrial heartland. All these products were moved through the region by the most economical means possible: water transport.

The shoreline is the site of numerous regional and federal parks. Sites of national prominence include several national seashores and an underwater national park. Tourism and related activities, including fishing, hunting, coastal recreation, and boating, are added amenities of the basin, providing annual revenues of $14 billion to state and provincial governments. More than 30 million people live and work in the Great Lakes basin, and the region's largest urban centers—Chicago, Detroit, Buffalo, and Toronto—are ports in the coastal zone. The Great Lakes thus attract many people and much investment in coastal property. Today, about 8 percent of the American and 20 percent of the Canadian shore of the lakes is privately owned. The high demand for shore property, combined with the availability of shore land, has contributed to dense populations and much development in the area. This is particularly significant in the southern part of the basin, which is nearest to the large urban centers, because the shorelines there are composed of less-resistant materials such as glacial moraine and sand dunes. During storm surges, and especially during years of high water levels, bluff erosion and coastal flooding frequently occur. In southeast Lake Michigan, erosion rates of 2 meters per year have been documented. Based on recession rates and property values, a 1990's U.S. Army Corps of Engineers study determined that a $247,887,000 loss can be anticipated in just one Lake Michigan county during the next fifty years.

The lakes provide a manageable model for the study of the relationships between global warming and rising sea levels in the world's oceans, in spite of differences—such as water-freezing points, salinity, and wave conditions—between the oceans and the lakes. The effects of rising ocean levels on the world's shorelines are difficult to study except under laboratory conditions. However, the higher water levels to which the diverse shorelines of the Great Lakes are exposed every few years do provide insights into what might happen to the world's marine shorelines if the process of global warming continues unabated.

Bibliography

Biggs, Donald L., ed. *Centennial Field Guide, North-Central Section of the Geological Society of America.* Vol. 3. Boulder, Colo.: Geological Society of America, 1987. Includes twenty-four papers on the geology and landforms of the Great Lakes basin. Features are treated in detail, the discussion is well supported by good maps, photographs, and tables. Suitable for college-level students.

Bolsenga, S. J., and C. E. Herdendorf. *Lake Erie and Lake St. Clair Handbook.* Detroit: Wayne State University Press, 1993. A thorough description of the natural history of Lakes St. Clair and Erie. Included are well-illustrated sections on geology, climate, hydrology, and wetland flora and fauna. A useful reference manual, with numerous maps, tables, and diagrams and a glossary.

Dorr, J. A., Jr., and D. F. Eschman. *Geology of Michigan*. Ann Arbor: University of Michigan Press, 1970. A college-level treatment of the geology of Michigan. Also included are chapters on sand dunes, shorelines, glaciation, and the creation of the Great Lakes. The text includes many photographs keyed to locations on inset maps.

Douglas, R. J. W. *Geology and Economic Minerals of Canada*. Report Number I. Ottawa: Geological Survey of Canada, 1970. Details the regional geology of Canada. Chapters on the Canadian Shield and the geology of the Great Lakes are included. Black-and-white aerial photographs illustrate significant glacial landforms. Intended as a reference work for professionals.

Hough, J. L. *Geology of the Great Lakes*. Urbana: University of Illinois Press, 1966. This 313-page book is a synthesis of research up to the mid-1950's. It includes sections on the present processes in the lakes and their glacial history. The text is jargon-free; it is intended for college students yet suitable for the general reader.

Leverett, Frank, and F. B. Taylor. *The Pleistocene of Indiana and Michigan*. Washington, D.C.: U.S. Geological Survey, 1915. This 529-page tome is the classic publication detailing the origin of the Great Lakes. A professional publication, yet suitable for a cross section of audiences.

Paull, R. L., and R. A. Paull. *Geology of Wisconsin and Upper Michigan*. Dubuque, Iowa: Kendell/Hunt, 1977. A readable presentation of the geology of the region. Also included are sections on unique features such as minerals, fossils, and karst topography. Includes a glossary of some three hundred terms. A good introduction to the Great Lakes.

U.S. Environmental Protection Agency. *The Great Lakes: An Environmental Atlas and Resource Book*. Chicago: Great Lakes Program Office, 1995. A free soft-cover publication designed for anyone interested in the lakes. Designed as a public-education tool; the material briefly addresses the physical and cultural environments of the basin. Includes colored maps, tables, and charts.

C. Nicholas Raphael

Cross-References

Alpine Glaciers, 960; The Cenozoic Era, 202; Continental Glaciers, 967; Drainage Basins, 384; Geochronology: Radiocarbon Dating, 840; Glacial Deposits, 937; Glacial Landforms, 946; Isostasy, 1269; Lakes, 1318; Waterfalls, 3171.

GULF STREAM

Type of earth science: Oceanography
Field of study: Heat flow

The Gulf Stream is a geostrophic surface current that constitutes the Northwestern part of the North Atlantic gyre. It moves huge quantities of water at remarkably fast velocities through vast distances with many geological, physical, and biological repercussions. By itself, however, it is not responsible for the mild climate of Western Europe.

Principal terms

CORIOLIS FORCE: a non-Newtonian force acting on a rotating coordinate system; on Earth this causes things moving in the Northern Hemisphere to be deflected toward the right and things moving in the Southern Hemisphere to be deflected toward the left

GEOSTROPHIC CURRENT: a current resulting from the balance between a pressure gradient force and the Coriolis force; the current moves horizontally and is perpendicular to the pressure gradient force and the Coriolis force

GYRE: the major rotating current system at the surface of an ocean, generally produced by a combination of wind-generated currents and geostrophic currents

PRESSURE GRADIENT: a difference in pressure that causes fluids (both liquids and gases) to move from regions of high pressure to regions of low pressure

THERMOHALINE CIRCULATION: a mode of oceanic circulation that is driven by the sinking of denser water and its replacement at the surface with less dense water; not caused by winds or geostrophic currents

WIND-DRIVEN CIRCULATION: the surface currents on the ocean that result from winds and geostrophic currents; not driven by differences in water density

Summary of the Phenomenon

It is convenient to consider any systematic movement of water at sea as being part of either a wind-driven circulation system or a thermohaline circulation system. In the former, the linkage with atmospheric movement is direct, the currents are usually at or near the sea surface, and the velocities of the flows are often in the range of several centimeters per second (or several knots). In thermohaline circulation, the driving force is gravity, which causes denser water to sink and flow to the deepest parts of the sea, and the currents are usually much slower. In the North Atlantic Ocean, thermohaline circulation occurs on a vast scale as saline surface water gives up its heat, sinks, and eventually flows across the bottom of both the North and South Atlantic basins.

Wind-driven circulation develops a gigantic clockwise circular motion called the North Atlantic gyre. The most intense flow of this gyre is along its northwestern boundary and is called the Gulf Stream. Because the flow is circular, it does not actually have a beginning or end. As it is usually geographically defined, however, the Gulf Stream begins in the straits of Florida, where water leaving the Gulf of Mexico and the Caribbean joins with water continuing to go around the gyre. There the Gulf Stream moves about 30 million cubic meters per second past any point. The volume of water entrained in this flow continues to increase, and by the time it reaches Cape Hatteras, there are about 85 million cubic meters moving by any point every second. When the Gulf Stream reaches longitude 65 degrees west, off the Grand Banks, it moves 150 million cubic meters per second.

To put this in perspective, consider that a cubic meter of water has a mass of 1,000 kilograms. A 150-pound person has a mass of sixty-eight kilograms. Therefore, a cubic meter of water has the mass of about fifteen people. The flow off of Cape Hatteras would be equivalent to 1.2 billion people, roughly the population of China, streaming by every second. By the time it gets to the Grand Banks, the flow would be larger by 65 million cubic meters, or 975 million more people. The Gulf Stream truly dwarfs most of nature's other wonders. The total hydrological cycle, which includes all the rain, snow, sleet, and hail that falls on the earth (oceans plus continents), moves an average of only 10 million cubic meters of water per second.

The secret to maintaining such huge flows of water lies in their circular nature. A hill of warm, low-density water sits over the core of the North Atlantic gyre. Water on or within this hill is driven by gravity or a pressure gradient to move down the slope or away from the center of this hill. This moving water is deflected by the Coriolis force, which is a consequence of the earth's rotation. In the Northern Hemisphere, the Coriolis force causes things moving with a horizontal velocity to move to their right. Therefore, the parcels of water trying to move out from the center of this hill are deflected to move around the gyre instead. Eventually a balance is achieved between the Coriolis force and the pressure gradient forces. As a result, the parcels of water do not move away from the center of the hill but instead circle it in a clockwise fashion. This kind of current is called a "geostrophic" current.

The earth's spherical shape means that the effects of the Coriolis force vary with latitude. One result is that the flow within the North Atlantic gyre varies with location. The hill is not symmetrical but has its steepest slopes on its northwest edge. Because currents must balance slopes, the gyre is most intense there. The center of the gyre is in the western Atlantic not far from Bermuda. The hill also slopes away to the east, but very gradually, so that the southern flows of the gyre are slow and spread out over a very large region.

Driving the gyre and maintaining the hill are the winds over the Atlantic Ocean. These are dominated by a subtropical high-pressure region of descending, dry air near the center of the North Atlantic Ocean. After descending, this air pushes out across the ocean. It, too, is deflected by the Coriolis force, developing into somewhat circular, clockwise winds. Near the center of this system, winds are weak, and precipitation is uncommon. Early sailors, faced with long, dry periods of calm, sometimes made their thirsty horses walk the plank. This is the origin of the term "horse latitudes," sometimes used to describe this region.

With little cloud cover and a subtropical latitude, this region receives intense solar radiation that warms the surface water and causes intense evaporation. This causes the water of this area, the Sargasso Sea, to become saline and very warm. Just as oil floats on vinegar in a salad dressing, this warm, saline water floats on cooler water below.

It is this warm water that forms the hill driving the Gulf Stream. The warm water tries to spread out and flow over cooler surface waters far from the center of the gyre. The Coriolis force makes it move around the hill, not down it, and the boundary between this warm, rotating mass of water and the cooler water it is trying to flow over is where the currents are most obvious. This is the Gulf Stream, a distinct boundary between the productive coastal waters, which are green and teeming with life, and the dark blue, nearly lifeless Sargasso Sea waters.

For decades, schoolchildren have been taught that the mild climate of the British Isles and Western Europe gets its heat from the Gulf Stream. The Gulf Stream is often presented as a river of warm water, moving north and then east to deliver its heat to the European continent. The significance of the Gulf Stream as a source of heat changes when it is recognized for what it is, just a boundary current. It separates the huge hill of warm, saline, Sargasso Sea water from surrounding waters.

The Gulf Stream can be compared to the cowboys of the Old West. A few dozen cowboys on horseback would circle the herd, making sure that the thousands of cattle within it would make their way toward the market. Much has been written about those cowboys and their actions, attitudes, and even apparel; much less has been written about the cattle. Similarly, the Gulf Stream is a very active boundary region, with motions driven by the wind and geostrophic currents, that surrounds the huge quantity of surface water, heated by the sun in subtropical high-pressure zones and made especially salty by accompanying evaporation. The Gulf Stream gets all the press, but it is this huge quantity of water that conveys heat to Europe.

In the North Atlantic, beyond the northern extent of the circulating gyre, cold winds remove heat from the surface waters. In the process, these winds are warmed and bathe Europe in the pleasant temperatures to which the continent is accustomed. However, by removing heat, these winds cool the saline surface waters until they become dense enough to sink to the bottom of the sea. This is the thermohaline circulation. The sinking waters are replaced by a gradual northward flow of surface water. It is likely that most of this surface water spent time in the North Atlantic gyre, but its transport northward was independent of that circular motion. If the gyre were to stop tomorrow, the thermohaline circulation would continue, and Europe would stay just as warm as it is today. In fact, some researchers have suggested that the strength of the Gulf Stream actually reduces the warming effects of this thermohaline circulation. If they are correct, were the Gulf Stream to stop, Europe might grow warmer.

Although its role as a heat-delivery system may have been overstated, the Gulf Stream is still an incredibly powerful element of oceanic circulation and as such greatly influences the biology and chemistry of the surface ocean. This significance is easily seen where meanders develop on the Gulf Stream, typically beyond Cape Hatteras. Just as meanders can grow and develop on a slow-moving river, they also grow on the Gulf Stream. Whereas a stream meander may form an oxbow lake if the course of the stream closes in upon itself, a meander in the Gulf Stream produces a circulating eddy, separated from the rest of the stream, when one closes upon itself. These eddies will have a core of warmer, less fertile water and rotate in a clockwise manner if they close off on the southeastern side of a meander. They will have a core of cooler, more fertile water and rotate in a counterclockwise manner if they close off on the northwestern side of a meander. These rings persist for months to a year or more and establish their own ecosystems during their lifetimes.

As a biologic agent, the Gulf Stream disperses eggs, seeds, and juvenile and adult organisms. As a chemical agent, it stirs up the surface waters, keeping its warm waters well mixed. As a physical agent, it moves enormous quantities of water. It is clearly a remarkable current and a very important part of the global ecosystem.

Methods of Study

The Gulf Stream is studied by directly measuring the strength of its currents at different depths and locations, by examining the effects of its currents through monitoring the position of floats released within it and designed to stay at particular depths, and by exploring the causes of its currents through measuring the topography of the sea surface.

Floating current meters can be moored to anchors at the bottom of the sea. Their depth is controlled by the length of the tether keeping them attached to the anchor. They can record data electronically, storing it in computer memory. When a vessel is at the surface, ready to retrieve the meter and its data, it transmits a special coded sound pulse. This instructs the meter to release itself from the tether and rise to the surface, where it transmits a radio signal allowing the vessel to home in on it and recover it. The data is incorporated in complex computer models that tie together the results obtained from hundreds of current meters deployed during overlapping time periods. Snapshots of the current system can then be obtained, and sequences of these snapshots reveal the behavior of the currents over time.

Floating objects can be released at sea and tracked by satellite. To ensure that these objects are being moved by ocean currents rather than surface winds, they usually have a large parachute or sail deployed in the water beneath them. Because the density of seawater increases with depth, floats can be designed to be neutrally buoyant at some particular depth (neither sinking below, nor floating above that depth). A layer of the ocean (the SOFAR channel) acts as a wave guide for sound waves. Floats in this layer can transmit sounds over tremendous distances, permitting them to be tracked efficiently by a small number of surface ships with sonar receivers suspended into this layer.

Because geostrophic currents are driven by the slopes of the ocean's surface, any technique that can measure those slopes can provide valuable insight into the driving forces behind the Gulf Stream. These slopes are very gradual—total dynamic relief over all the world's oceans is about two meters—and, consequently, direct measurement is difficult. Satellite techniques, coupled with computer models to filter out waves, tides, and dozens of other confounding effects, are approaching the point where they will be able to measure this topography. Yet the dynamic topography is generally determined indirectly, by measuring temperature and salinity as a function of depth and position. These data are used to determine the density of the seawater as a function of depth and position. By assuming that at some depth the horizontal pressure gradients have disappeared, it is possible to reconstruct the differences in the height of the water column needed to accommodate these variations in density. Then the velocities and directions of the resulting currents can be calculated. When the theoretical models are compared with currents measured by moored meters or revealed by the paths of floating objects, the results are in agreement. This gives strong support to the theoretical concepts underlying the study of ocean currents.

Many of the approaches to study of the Gulf Stream are exercises in applied mathematics. That computed and measured results agree so well is a triumph of geophysical fluid dynamics. As the mathematical models improve, they will be applied to help understand this current and its awesome power.

Context

The North Atlantic gyre, which has the Gulf Stream as its northwest boundary current, dominates surface flow in the Atlantic Ocean. Voyages of discovery, exploration, conquest, and exploitation all were affected to some extent by this system and the winds that accompany it.

Like a great atmospheric front, the Gulf Stream separates water masses of different character. Just as winds often move along a front, vast quantities of water move within the Gulf Stream currents, the ocean's counterpart to winds. Just as pilots pay close attention to frontal systems as they plot their routes, so mariners need to include the Gulf Stream in their planning.

The Gulf Stream, studied since the eighteenth century, has provided the basis for much of what scientists know of ocean currents. Elaborate mathematical constructs, including the entire concept of geostrophic currents, have been invented to describe, analyze, and comprehend this mighty system.

As scientists have learned more about the Gulf Stream, they have discovered many new areas of study, including branches in the stream, countercurrents at the surface and at depth, and fluctuations in flow and velocity with time and place. Some researchers devote their entire careers to studying just the rings of the Gulf Stream, which contain entire ecosystems. Others investigate the location and strength of the Gulf Stream in the distant past, during and even before the ice ages. There is evidence that at times the current has taken different paths across the continental shelf, perhaps scouring out valleys in the ocean floor in the process.

Scientists' understanding of the dynamics of the planet relies on comprehending the transfer of energy from the equator to the poles. The Gulf Stream is an important component of this transfer. As people have become more aware of the fragility of the environment and become more concerned about issues of global climate change, the role of the Gulf Stream and thermohaline circulation in influencing temperatures in Europe and elsewhere on the planet has taken on a new importance.

Bibliography

Briggs, Peter. *Rivers in the Sea*. New York: Weybright and Talley, 1969. A very easy-to-read book, suitable for a high-school student. The author includes a fair amount of history and lore, with anecdotes and some sketches related to early scientific expeditions.

Chapin, Henry, and F. G. Walton Smith. *The Ocean River*. New York: Charles Scribner's Sons, 1952. A popular source of both information and misinformation. In attempting to review all of Earth's history before taking on the Gulf Stream, it describes many theories now considered groundless. Although the book is loaded with many discussions of atmospheric and oceanic dynamics, it is not clear that the authors ever grasped the nature of the North Atlantic gyre or the importance of thermohaline circulation. Still, the book contains considerable information of historical interest and is important because of the influence that it has had. Suitable for high-school readers.

Gaskell, Thomas Frohock. *The Gulf Stream*. New York: John Day, 1972. An interesting overview from a slightly technical perspective. The book emphasizes history and anecdotes but includes some well-chosen excerpts of original reports from some early expeditions. Good descriptions of many oceanographic techniques and excellent summaries of some of the biological consequences of the Gulf Stream.

MacLeish, William H. *The Gulf Stream*. Boston: Houghton Mifflin, 1989. Compelling reading, this book offers a personal approach to the Gulf Stream and many of its repercussions. Organized as a narrative rather than a scientific tome, it is easy to read, suitable for a high-school reader. It has no equations and few technical discussions but represents an obviously thorough research effort.

Open University Oceanography Course Team. *Ocean Circulation*. Oxford, England: Pergamon Press, 1989. This carefully written textbook provides an introduction to the analysis and understanding of all sorts of circulation in the world's oceans. Intended for an undergraduate college-level reader, it provides the necessary mathematical background to understand many aspects of geophysical fluid dynamics.

Stommel, Henry. *The Gulf Stream*. Berkeley: University of California Press, 1958. The author of this book is one of the leading pioneers in the study of the Gulf Stream. Based on geophysical fluid dynamics, this book is likely to challenge most undergraduate college students. Contains much qualitative information, however, that is accessible to even a high-school reader. Although much has been learned since this book was written, the essentials are all here.

Otto H. Muller

Cross-References

The Atmosphere's Global Circulation, 121; Climate, 217; Deep Ocean Currents, 1792; Ocean-Atmosphere Interactions, 1779; The Structure of the Oceans, 1871; Surface Ocean Currents, 1798; Wind, 2730.

HYDROTHERMAL VENTS

Type of earth science: Oceanography
Field of study: Heat flow

Hydrothermal vents are openings on the seafloor where hot water is released. This hydrothermal water forms when cold seawater percolates down into and is heated by hot rocks. Both rocks and water are changed by this interaction. Deposits rich in metals form around these vents, and many ore deposits represent similar ancient activity. Numerous kinds of organisms live around hydrothermal vents, supported by bacteria that derive their energy from reduction of sulfide to sulphate.

Principal terms
ANHYDRITE: a mineral with the formula $CaSO_4$
BASALT: a typical volcanic rock of the oceanic environment
CONVERGENT PLATE MARGIN: an area where the earth's lithosphere is returned to the mantle at a subduction zone, forming volcanic "island arcs" and associated hydrothermal activity
DIVERGENT MARGIN: an area where the earth's crust and lithosphere form by seafloor spreading
ENDOSYMBIONT: an animal hosting autotrophic bacteria, with both host and bacteria enjoying the benefits of symbiosis
HYDROSTATIC PRESSURE: the pressure resulting from an overlying, continuous column of water, approximately 1 bar for every 10 meters of water
MAGMA: molten rock generated by melting of the earth's mantle
MIDOCEAN RIDGE: a region of the seafloor where new oceanic crust is created by seafloor spreading
OPHIOLITE: a section of oceanic crust and upper mantle that has been thrust out of the ocean floor and up onto the continental crust

Summary of the Phenomenon

The late 1970's discovery of hydrothermal vents and the unique communities that live around them astounded scientists. Studies of these unique features have provided important and exciting research opportunities for biologists, geologists, and marine chemists. Almost all of the deep seafloor is a cold and quiet place, but this is not true where hydrothermal vents are found. In contrast to the homogeneous and stable environment of the deep sea, hydrothermal vents are constantly changing, and scientists have seen many changes in hydrothermal vents and their associated communities even over the short period that these have been studied. Hydrothermal vents are easily the most spectacular features, both geologically and biologically, on the floor of the abyss. There is still much to learn about hydrothermal vents, and there are almost certainly many more hydrothermal vents remaining to be discovered than are known.

Only about 10 percent of the midocean ridges where hydrothermal vents are concentrated have been surveyed for these features.

Hydrothermal vents are hot springs on the ocean bottom, the exhaust pipes of seafloor hydrothermal systems. These vents are the most visible and spectacular parts of seafloor hydrothermal systems, which are driven by heat sources that lie several hundred meters or even kilometers beneath the ocean bottom. Hydrothermal systems form where near-freezing seawater from the bottom of the ocean penetrates deep into the crust along fissures until it comes into contact with hot rocks. The water may be heated to as high as 400 degrees Celsius before it rises back up through the crust and jets back into the deep sea at the vents. Development of hydrothermal systems requires two things: hot rocks and a way for seawater to percolate along cracks in the hot rocks and return to the surface. How vigorous the resulting hydrothermal system is depends on both these factors. The hottest rocks are found at midocean ridges and other submarine volcanic centers such as Loihi Seamount off the coast of Hawaii, where frequent eruption of basalt lavas maintains conditions that are most favorable for developing and maintaining hydrothermal systems.

Yet it is not enough for hot rocks to lie beneath the surface; there must also be a way for seawater to be brought into contact with the hot rocks and kept there until the water is sufficiently heated. This requires just the right configuration of fractured hot rocks: If the cracks are too wide or the hot rocks are not deep enough below the seafloor, the water will not be heated enough before it returns to the surface. Similarly, if the cracks are too narrow, not enough water will flow through the system to develop a robust hydrothermal system, or the channels may be easily blocked by minor earth movements or mineral deposits. The sensitivity of deep-sea hydrothermal systems to the subseafloor circulation geometry may be why hydrothermal events experience rapid changes and are generally short-lived features.

Seafloor hydrothermal systems are similar to hot springs or geysers found on the continents in that both form as hot rocks heat and chemically modify cold water. Seafloor hydrothermal systems differ, however, in the much higher temperatures that are typical. This is because the boiling temperature of water increases as pressure increases, and pressures on the seafloor are several hundred times greater than they are on the surface. This effect is well known to most cooks, who are familiar with the fact that water boils at a lower temperature in the mountains, where the pressure is lower, than it does at sea level. Hydrothermal systems on land, such as those of Yellowstone National Park, have a maximum water temperature of not much more than about 100 degrees Celsius; at greater temperatures, the water "flashes," or turns to steam. This is what makes a geyser such as Old Faithful erupt, as the water in contact with the hot rock turns to steam and violently forces out the colder, overlying water. The greater pressure of the seafloor prohibits flashing and allows water to be heated to much greater temperatures.

Although most hydrothermal systems are found along the midocean ridges, where magma lies not more than a few kilometers beneath the ocean floor, hydrothermal water is not heated by magma; water heated by magma would be much closer to magmatic temperatures of 1,200 degrees Celsius. Instead, the water is heated as it passes through hot but solid rocks, although the hot rocks may be kept hot by underlying magma. The upper limit of about 400 degrees Celsius for seafloor hydrothermal systems may reflect the maximum rock temperature at which fractures can form and remain open, or it may reflect separation of the fluid into immiscible fluids. It may be that at temperatures much higher than 400 degrees Celsius, rocks begin to slowly flow, closing any fractures that do form. Another possibility is that, at pressures corresponding to typical depths of midocean ridges (about 300 bars), seawater separates into two fluids at about 400 degrees Celsius. One phase is enriched in salt relative to seawater, while the other fluid contains a lower concentration of salt than seawater. The more concentrated phase will be the denser phase, and this may be why it is not found among waters issuing from hydrothermal vents. About one-third of the total heat lost from the earth's interior through the seafloor is lost as a result of seafloor hydrothermal systems.

The seawater moving through a seafloor hydrothermal system is chemically changed as it is heated, and it alters the rocks through which it passes as well. All of the magnesium and sulphate in the seawater is absorbed by the hot rocks, and large amounts of metals such as manganese, cobalt, copper, zinc, and iron are lost from the hot rocks to the circulating water. In fact, magnesium is so completely removed from seawater that the depletion of this element in seawater can only be explained by seafloor hydrothermal activity. Oxygen-rich seawater is transformed into oxygen-poor hydrothermal water, and a high concentration of metals can be dissolved in such water. Seawater, for example, contains negligible magnesium and iron, whereas hydrothermal waters contain up to 1 millimole of magnesium and 6 millimoles of iron per liter.

When hot, chemically transformed water returns to the ocean at hydrothermal vents, the result is often spectacular. Near the vent, the hot, oxygen-poor, hydrogen-sulfide-rich hydrothermal water mixes with cold, oxygen-rich, hydrogen-sulfide-poor seawater. This may cause the metals in the hydrothermal fluid to precipitate. Some of it may precipitate in fractures just beneath the seafloor. These "stockwork" deposits are most likely to be preserved and many ore deposits represent ancient stockwork deposits. Some metals precipitate around the vent itself, forming metal-rich chimneys. These chimneys are typically composed of an outer layer of anhydrite and inner deposits of copper-iron sulfides. These chimneys can have fantastic shapes, resembling spires, columns, cones, and beehives. Scientists visiting these chimneys give them fanciful names: "nail," "fir tree," and "moose" are names given to vent features from one hydrothermal field. Chimneys have been found that are up to 30 meters in diameter and up to 45 meters tall. These growth rates can be on the order of a meter a year, and vent chimneys are thus among the fastest-changing of all geologic phenomena. Fast-growing vent chimneys rapidly become unstable and collapse, then rise again. Cycles of growth and collapse continue as long as the hydrothermal fluids continue to issue from the vent.

Metals that do not precipitate as stockwork or vent chimneys will rise with the hydrothermal water issuing from the vent. Because this water is so hot, it is less dense than seawater and jets out of the vents. The vent is the base of a hydrothermal plume, and the plume becomes larger as it rises. The plume becomes larger as it rises because cold seawater mixes turbulently with the hydrothermal water, and these waters quickly become well-mixed. The hottest hydrothermal fluids (those heated to 300 degrees Celsius or more) are sufficiently metal-rich and acidic that they precipitate large quantities of microscopic grains of iron sulfides, zinc sulfides, and copper sulfides upon mixing with seawater. Much of this precipitates as the plume rises, producing a sulphide "cloud." The rapid precipitation of sulphides darkens the hydrothermal plume, giving it the appearance of smoke. Those vents releasing the hottest fluids have the greatest density of sulfide precipitation and are therefore often referred to as "black smokers." In contrast, vents releasing cooler water (100 to 300 degrees Celsius) do not contain sufficient sulfide or metals in solution to cause this effect. Instead, mixing of these hydrothermal waters with seawater causes white particles of silica, anhydrite, and barite to form, forming a white cloud in the mixing plume and giving rise to the name "white smoker." White smokers may reflect mixing just below the surface, with the result that most of the metals associated with white smoker vents may be deposited just below the seafloor. Because the original hydrothermal vent waters are cooler and thus denser, plumes from white smokers rise less far than those from black smokers before obtaining neutral buoyancy and spreading laterally.

Mixing progressively dilutes the hydrothermal water until the mixed water cools to the point that it has the same density as ambient seawater and no longer rises. A tremendous amount of seawater must be mixed with the hydrothermal fluids before the plume attains neutral buoyancy. This may ultimately involve 10,000 or even 100,000 times as much seawater as hydrothermal water. During dilution, the mixture rises tens to hundreds of meters to a level of neutral buoyancy, eventually spreading laterally as a distinct hydrographic and chemical layer, recognizable hundreds or even thousands of kilometers away from the hydrothermal vent. Continued settling of hydrothermal iron and magnesium from these layers is the source of most of the metals in manganese nodules of the abyssal seafloor, far away from the midocean ridges.

Vast quantities of metals are deposited as sulfides around hydrothermal vents, especially as stockwork and in sediments around chimneys. These are particularly rich in iron, copper, zinc, and lead, and the exact composition of these deposits reflects several controls, including temperature of the hydrothermal fluid, water depth, composition of the source rock, and flow regime in the portion of the hydrothermal system that lies beneath the seafloor. Many of the world's great ore deposits seem to be fossil seafloor hydrothermal systems, with the possible exception that these may have mostly formed at convergent plate margins instead of divergent plate margins, where most modern hydrothermal systems are known. This may be part of the reason why ancient massive sulfide deposits are typically much larger than modern ones.

Methods of Study

To a marine biologist, hydrothermal vents are the oases of the deep seafloor. In contrast to most of the ocean bottom, which supports few animals, hydrothermal vents teem with life. In fact, the analogy to a desert oasis falls short because there is much more life around a hydrothermal vent. Life in most of the deep sea is scarce because food is scarce. There is no sunlight, so plants, the basis of most food chains, cannot grow. In contrast, food is abundant around hydrothermal vents; often, life is so crowded that the animals obscure the seafloor.

Vent fields can be divided into three biotic zones reflecting distance from the hydrothermal vents: the vent opening, the near-field, and the periphery. The bulk of the biomass is at the vent openings, where the density of life is so great that it appears to be limited by space, not food. Around hydrothermal vents on the East Pacific Rise and Galapagos Rift, vent openings are dominated by endosymbionts such as tube worms, clams, and mussels. These endosymbionts can grow to great size; some tube worms are a meter long with three-meter tubes, while clams up to 30 centimeters long are common. Other animals live with these, including limpets, polychaete worms, bresiliid shrimp, crabs, and fish. Vent chimneys at several Mid-Atlantic Ridge vents are almost entirely populated by bresiliid shrimp.

Autotrophic bacteria are the primary producers around hydrothermal vents. These use sulfur to convert carbon dioxide, water, and nitrate into essential organic substances, in a fashion similar to the way in which plants use sunlight during photosynthesis. This process is called "chemosynthesis." Autotrophic bacteria live within the subsurface plumbing system of the vents, on the seafloor, and suspended in and around the hydrothermal plume itself, sometimes in such abundance that they color the water a milky blue or carpet the seafloor in white or bright yellow mats. Some of these bacteria can tolerate incredibly high temperatures, up to 110 degrees Celsius or more. All the other life around a hydrothermal vent ultimately feeds off the autotrophic bacteria. Some of the autotrophic bacteria are symbiotic, living within larger vent animals in a mutually beneficial relationship. The bacteria provide food, and the animals provide essential inorganic nutrients.

The flow of water around hydrothermal vents controls the distribution of life. Because cold water mixes with the hydrothermal plume, cold seawater flows in from all directions to converge on the rising plume. This means that the sulfur on which the autotrophic bacteria depend is not distributed around the vent. For a similar reason, the animals that feed or depend on the bacteria cannot survive away from the vent opening. The near-field is mostly populated by suspension feeders, animals that capture bacteria and other organisms that drift away from the vent opening. It is presumed that these animals live as close as possible to the vent but are forced to maintain a certain distance because of toxic effects resulting from very high concentrations of heavy metals. Animals living on the vent periphery include scavengers and other types that sustain themselves from bacteria that settle out of the hydrothermal plume.

Most of the animals that live around hydrothermal vents live nowhere else except in other sulfur-rich, reducing environments, such as in the rotting carcasses of whales or in "cold seeps," where cold, chemically altered seawater percolates up through the seafloor. Many vent animals may be ancient, originating in Mesozoic or earlier times.

These animals may have been insulated from the effects of surface catastrophes, such as the meteor collision hypothesized to have killed the dinosaurs about 65 million years ago.

There are a number of fascinating features about the life around hydrothermal vents, but one of the most intriguing is the suggestion that this environment is similar to what existed when life was just developing about 4 billion years ago. It is very likely that the development of life involved synthesis of organic chemicals in vents and that the first autotrophic life-forms were chemosynthetic, not photosynthetic.

Context

The events leading up to the discovery of seafloor hydrothermal vents provide useful insights into how advances in the natural sciences are made. Mining geologists knew that some ophiolites contained rich deposits of massive sulphides, and by the early 1960's, marine geologists were increasingly recognizing that many sediments from around the midocean ridges were rich in metals. In the early 1970's, marine chemists were aware that the seawater contained less magnesium than could be expected as the result of river influx alone. Measurements of conductive heat flow made in the late 1960's and early 1970's indicated that there was another way of losing heat from the oceanic crust, and that this alternate mode of heat loss was particularly important near the midocean ridges. Work in the eastern Pacific during the late 1970's detected water that was about 0.2 degrees Celsius warmer than expected, part of a hydrothermal plume. This finding focused work efforts and ultimately led to the 1979 discovery of black smokers and hydrothermal vents.

Bibliography

Anderson, R. N. *Marine Geology: A Planet Earth Perspective.* New York: John Wiley & Sons, 1986. A textbook intended for college undergraduates, with an excellent chapter on metal deposits and marine geology. This well-written chapter (chapter 7) and other parts of the book are accessible to a general, scientifically interested audience.

Francheteau, J. "The Oceanic Crust." *Scientific American* 249 (1983): 114-129. A good overview of the nature, composition, and mode of formation of the oceanic crust.

Humphris, S. E., et al., eds. *Seafloor Hydrothermal Systems.* American Geophysical Union, Geophysical Monograph 91. The most technically comprehensive overview of physical, chemical, biological, and geological interactions. A wealth of pictures, figures, and references are included in this volume. Technical but useful.

Macdonald, K. C., and B. P. Luyendyk. "The Crest of the East Pacific Rise." *Scientific American* 244 (1983): 100-118. Provides a good look at an outstanding example of a midocean ridge.

Rona, P. A., and S. D. Scott. "A Special Issue on Sea-Floor Hydrothermal Mineralizations: New Perspectives." *Economic Geology* 88, no. 8 (1993): 1933-2249. Deals with how mineral deposits form around hydrothermal vents, with many examples of individual vent fields from around the world. The preface includes a complete listing and summary of all known seafloor hydrothermal systems. Intended for the scientist, but abundant pictures, figures, and references make it useful to all who are interested in the topic.

Robert J. Stern

Cross-References
The Abyssal Sea Floor, 1; Crystallization of Magmas, 1420; Geysers and Hot Springs, 929; Heat Sources and Heat Flow, 1065; Hydrothermal Mineralization, 1108; Igneous Rocks: Basaltic, 1158; Manganese Nodules, 1459; Ocean Basins, 1785; Ocean-Floor Drilling Programs, 1805; Ocean-Floor Exploration, 1813; Ophiolites, 1954; The Origin of Life, 1961; Plate Tectonics, 2079; Seawater Composition, 2282; Sub-Sea-Floor Metamorphism, 1614; Water-Rock Interactions, 2462.

IGNEOUS ROCKS: PLUTONIC

Type of earth science: Geology
Field of study: Igneous petrology

Plutonic rocks crystallize from molten magma that is intruded deep below the earth's surface. Exposed at the surface by erosion, they occur mainly in mountain belts and ancient "shield" areas of continents. Many of the world's principal ore deposits are associated with plutonic rock bodies; the rocks themselves may be also exploited economically, as in the production of granite for building stone.

Principal terms
ANORTHOSITE: a light-colored, coarse-grained plutonic rock composed mostly of plagioclase feldspar
BATHOLITH: the largest type of granite/diorite pluton, with an exposure area in excess of 100 square kilometers
FELDSPAR: an essential aluminum-rich mineral in most igneous rocks; two types are plagioclase feldspar and alkali feldspar
GABBRO: a coarse-grained, dark-colored plutonic igneous rock composed of plagioclase feldspar and pyroxene
GRANITE: a coarse-grained, commonly light-colored plutonic igneous rock composed primarily of two feldspars (plagioclase and orthoclase) and quartz, with variable amounts of dark minerals
MAGMA: a molten silicate liquid that upon cooling crystallizes to make igneous rocks
STOCK: a granite or diorite intrusion, smaller than a batholith, with an exposure area between 10 and 100 square kilometers

Summary of the Phenomenon

Plutonic rocks crystallize from molten silicate magmas that intrude deep into the earth's crust. This same magma (molten silicate liquid) may eventually flow out onto the surface of the earth as lava that crystallizes to produce volcanic rocks. Volcanic rocks can be distinguished from plutonic rocks by the relative size of their mineral grains. The rapidly cooled volcanic rocks have nearly invisible crystals (or glass), while the slowly cooled plutonic rocks have larger crystals clearly visible to the naked eye. The popular building stone granite is probably the best known plutonic rock, but many other plutonic rock types are used in the construction and monument trades. Plutonic magmas may also serve as the source for economic deposits of certain metallic ores, either within the bodies themselves or as hydrothermal (hot water) veins and other deposits injected into adjacent "country rocks." Many of the world's ore deposits of copper, silver, gold, lead, zinc, tin, uranium, and other valuable commodities are derived directly or indirectly from plutonic rock bodies.

Because they form deep underground, plutonic rocks require special circumstances to become exposed at the surface. Uplift of the crust in a mountain range or high plateau accompanied by nearly constant erosion by streams or glaciers may eventually uncover once-buried plutonic rocks. Therefore, the best places to see excellent exposures of these rocks are in mountain ranges such as the Rockies, Sierra Nevada, and Appalachian ranges of North America, the Alps of Europe, and the Himalayas of Asia, among many others. Another major plutonic rock terrain exists in "shield" areas found on all the world's major continents. These areas comprise the ancient cores of the continents and consist of rocks that are billions of years old, most of the rocks having once existed in ancient mountain ranges now eroded down to relatively flat plains. In North America, this area is called the "Canadian Shield" and covers most of Canada and the northern portions of the states of Minnesota, Wisconsin, Michigan, and New York. Comparably ancient plutonic rocks, mostly granites, also occur in the center of the Ozark Plateau of southeastern Missouri.

Plutonic rocks come in many varieties depending upon the chemistry of the parent magma and their mode of emplacement in the crust. Igneous magmas vary chemically between two major extremes: "felsic" magma, in which the concentration of dissolved silica (silicon dioxide) is high and the concentrations of iron and magnesium are relatively low, and "mafic" magma, in which the concentration of silica is low and the concentrations of iron and magnesium are relatively high. Granite and related (generally light-colored) rocks are produced by crystallization of felsic magmas. Their light color and the presence of the mineral quartz (silicon dioxide) distinguishes granitic rocks from the dark plutonic rock gabbro, which crystallizes from mafic magmas. Other rocks, such as diorite, crystallize from magma that is intermediate in composition between felsic and mafic extremes. Diorite and its relatives are generally gray-colored and are commonly mistaken for granite. For example, much of the Sierra Nevada range in eastern California is composed of diorite, although it is popularly known as a "granite" mountain range.

Plutonic rocks are emplaced in the crust as a variety of geometric forms, collectively called "plutons." By far the largest plutons are batholiths, huge masses of granite, diorite, or both with surface exposures exceeding 100 square kilometers. In western North America, some batholiths are exposed over a considerable portion of whole states, such as the Boulder and Idaho batholiths of Montana and Idaho and the Sierra Nevada and Southern California batholiths of California. Batholiths also occur in the Appalachian Mountains, particularly in the White Mountains of New Hampshire, and in parts of Maine. Most batholiths attain their large size by the successive addition of smaller plutons called "stocks." Stocks are generally exposed over tens of square kilometers but range between 10 and 100 square kilometers in surface area.

Minor plutonic bodies include dikes and sills, tabular intrusions that commonly represent magma that has filled in fractures that either cut across layers in country rock (dikes) or that intruded parallel to rock layers (sills). Some sills fill up with so much magma that they expand and force the overlying layers of rock to bow upward. Such plutons are called "laccoliths," and some, like the Henry Mountains of southeastern Utah, have attained the scale of small mountains.

Batholiths, stocks, and laccoliths are predominantly granitic or diorite bodies. Mafic (gabbroic) intrusions occur in their own particular geometric forms, mostly as dikes and sills. Some of these bodies reach enormous size and are exposed over areas that rival large stocks or even granitic batholiths. Many of these bodies show evidence of having concentrated layers of crystals that gravitationally settled after crystallization. Known variously as "gravity-stratified complexes" or "layered mafic-ultramafic complexes," these bodies are commonly rich sources of economically important metallic ores, particularly those of chromium and platinum. The best examples of these bodies are in South Africa (the Bushveld and the Great Dyke), Greenland (the Skaergaard Complex), and North America (the Stillwater Complex in Montana and the Muskox Complex and Kiglapait Complex in Canada).

Other mafic-ultramafic complexes may produce massive layers of metallic sulfides rich in copper, nickel, and variable amounts of gold and silver, among other metals. In North America, the Sudbury "nickel irruptive" in Ontario, Canada, is a well-known example of a rich sulfide ore body associated with gabbroic magma. Melting to produce this magma has been attributed to the ancient impact of a large meteoroid. Gravitational segregation of metallic oxides is also known from gabbroic magmas. The rich iron deposits in Kiruna, Sweden, are believed to form from the settling of large blobs of liquid iron oxide that later crystallized to the mineral magnetite. Titanium deposits in anorthosites (feldspar-rich gabbro) at Allard Lake, Quebec, may have formed by gravitational concentration of iron-titanium-rich fluids within the gabbroic magmas that also produced the associated anorthosite rock.

The origin of the magmas that create plutons depends in large part on their chemical compositions. Most granite-composition magma probably arises by partial melting of siliceous metamorphic rocks in the deeper parts of the continental crust. Rocks in these regions have compositions that are already close to granitic, so melting them leads inevitably to the production of granitic liquids. These liquids (magma), being less dense than the surrounding, cooler rocks, rise through the crust and join with other bodies to make stocks and, possibly, batholiths.

Mafic magmas of the kind that crystallize gabbro originate in the upper mantle, where they arise by the partial melting of mantle peridotite. Peridotite is the major constituent of the upper mantle and consists of the mineral olivine (iron-magnesium silicate) with minor pyroxene (calcium iron-magnesium silicate) and other minerals. Laboratory experiments have shown that partially melting peridotite at pressures like those in the mantle produces mafic liquids capable of crystallizing gabbro (or basalt at the surface).

A special kind of gabbro, anorthosite, is produced by the separation and concentration of plagioclase feldspar from the gabbroic magma subsequent to its production in the mantle. Because plagioclase commonly is less dense than the surrounding iron-rich gabbroic liquid from which it crystallized, plagioclase crystals may literally float to the top of the magma chamber to form a concentrated mass of feldspar. Anorthosite makes up most of the light-colored regions of the Moon (the lunar highlands), but also occurs as large intrusions on Earth, as in the Duluth Gabbro Complex of northern

Minnesota, in the Adirondack Mountains of New York State, and the Kiglapait, Nain, and Allard Lake Complexes in Labrador. Mysteriously, most of Earth's anorthosite bodies were generated during only one restricted period in geologic time, between about 1.1 billion and 1.3 billion years ago.

The origin of diorite magma is complicated by the fact that it can arise in a variety of ways. Diorite plutons, like those in the Sierra Nevada range, represent magma reservoirs under now-vanished volcanoes. The magma that produced these intrusions was generated by melting along a subduction zone, where the Pacific Ocean lithospheric plate (crust plus uppermost mantle) was diving under the North American plate in a zone roughly parallel to the West Coast. A similar process is currently producing the active volcanoes in the Cascade Range of the Pacific Northwest. Any number of parent materials being pulled down to great depth (and, thus, greater temperature) in a subduction zone may mix with subducted ocean water and subsequently melt to produce diorite-type magma. These materials include hydrated (water-saturated) oceanic basalt lava, and even some hydrated mantle materials (serpentine). Ample evidence suggests that some diorite is also produced by the physical mixing of granitic magma produced by melting of continental crustal materials, and gabbroic magma produced in the mantle. These contrasting liquids intermingle on their way upward, finally intruding as intermediate-composition diorite magmas.

One other group of plutonic rock is worthy of mention, even though surface exposures are relatively rare. These are the "alkaline" intrusives, so named because they tend to be enriched in the alkali elements potassium and sodium and relatively depleted in silica. Alkaline magmas originate by partial melting of mantle peridotite at extreme depths and high pressures (20 kilobars or greater). Because high pressure acts to discourage melting (even at high temperatures), special conditions are required—commonly tectonic rifting—to generate alkaline magmas, making them among the rarest of igneous rocks.

A fairly familiar variety of alkaline-type volcano-intrusive body is the kimberlite "pipe" that in some areas contains diamond. Diamond-bearing kimberlites are especially common in South Africa and other African countries, India, and Russia. North American localities include Murfeesboro, Arkansas, and the Arctic of Canada. Kimberlite rock itself is a complex mixture of mantle and crustal fragments, carbonate minerals, and silicate minerals crystallized from the alkaline magma. Diamonds, if present, were swept up by the magma from high-pressure areas of the mantle and propelled by expanding carbon-dioxide gas to the surface at speeds estimated to exceed supersonic velocities in some cases. Surface deposits (diatremes) of kimberlite consist of volcanic ash ejected during powerful volcanic explosions.

Other important alkaline plutons include the nepheline syenites, light-colored, coarse-grained rocks consisting mostly of the mineral nepheline (sodium aluminum silicate). Important North American localities include Magnet Cove, Arkansas, and Bancroft, Ontario. Depending on the particular locality, these rocks are potential repositories of rare elements and, thus, unusual minerals. Commercial exploitation of nepheline syenites has produced the metals beryllium, cesium, thorium, uranium, niobium, tantalum, and zirconium, to name just a few. These rock bodies may also be a fertile source of apatite (hydrated calcium phosphate), an ore of phosphorous, and the dark-blue mineral sodalite (sodium aluminum silicate chloride), used as a semi-precious gem stone and for sculpted carvings. Another alkaline plutonic rock rich in rare elements and minerals is carbonatite, a magmatic rock composed mostly of calcium, magnesium, and sodium carbonates. Like nepheline syenites, carbonatites are highly prized for their mineral treasures, although they are relatively rare and their individual surface exposures are limited in size. The best examples are in the East African rift and in South Africa.

Methods of Study

Plutonic rocks are igneous rocks; thus, their study entails the same methods that might also apply to volcanic rocks. Field studies of plutons include the construction of geologic maps showing spatial distribution and structure of the various rock types in the pluton. Most plutons contain more than one type of igneous rock or at least show some chemical and mineralogical variation from one locality to the next. During mapping or other field surveys, samples are normally collected to be chemically analyzed by various techniques, including atomic absorption analysis, X-ray fluores-cence, or neutron activation analysis. Individual minerals in the rocks may be chemi-cally analyzed using an electron microprobe, a machine that gives a full chemical analysis of a 1-micron spot on a single mineral in a matter of minutes. More sophisticated analyses include isotopic abundance ratios and radiometric ages deter-mined from mass spectrometry. Collected chemical data is normally plotted on diagrams that help show how and why the plutons may have changed over time, and may lead to an understanding of the ultimate origin of their parent magmas.

The identities, textures, and spatial orientations of minerals in rocks are assessed by preparing microscopic slides of thin slices of the rocks called "thin sections." A skilled igneous petrologist (geologist who specializes in igneous rocks) can determine much about the history of a plutonic rock merely by studying a thin section under a microscope. For example, the identification of constituent minerals under the micro-scope serves to classify the rock, and the relative volume of individual minerals provides hints about the rock's chemistry. For example, a rock with a high volume of dark, mafic (iron and magnesium-rich) minerals would suggest a high concentration of iron and magnesium in that rock compared to one with fewer dark minerals.

Economic geologists are interested in the usefulness of plutonic rocks as sources of ore minerals. Their first job after an ore deposit is discovered is to determine the nature of the deposit and to assess the origin of the ore minerals. They will also map ore structures such as veins, dikes, or sills in order to predict the extent and economic value of the ore body and to predict where more ore minerals might be found. An example of how economic geologists might conduct a field study is the search for the "mother lode" of gold deposits. Gold is commonly recovered from sand and gravel deposited by streams eroding granite plutons. "Mother lode" refers to the gold-bearing hydrothermal quartz veins injected into country rocks from parent granite bodies as they enter the late stages of crystallization. Tracing the path of gold up a stream valley may lead to the "mother" quartz vein and to a rich trove of concentrated gold and other precious metals.

Context

Plutonic rocks are the source of many of the raw materials that are used in industrial society. Granite and diorite are used as construction stones in buildings and monuments and as crushed stone for roadways and concrete. Gabbro, however, is generally shunned for decorative purposes because its high iron content causes it to oxidize (rust) over time. On the other hand, the special kind of light-colored gabbro called "anorthosite" (mostly plagioclase feldspar) is prized as a polished building facing stone; it is also used to grace floors or countertops in bank and office buildings.

In addition, many of the richest metallic ore deposits originate in or adjacent to plutonic bodies. The extensive list of metals from granitic deposits includes copper, gold, silver, lead, zinc, molybdenum, tin, boron, beryllium, lithium, and uranium. Gabbroic and related deposits contribute nickel, iron, titanium, chromium, and platinum as well as copper, gold, and silver.

Plutons are also the source of some of the most precious and semiprecious gemstones. For example, the precious gems topaz and emerald occur in ultra-coarsegrained granitic deposits called "pegmatites." Pegmatites also provide the semiprecious gems aquamarine (a blue-green form of emerald), tourmaline (elbaite), rose quartz, citrine (yellow quartz), amethyst, amazonite (aqua-colored microcline feldspar), and zircon (zirconium silicate). Also, large mica crystals from pegmatites are used as electrical and thermal insulators, and feldspar minerals are powdered to make porcelain products and potassium-rich fertilizer. The principal source of the element lithium, used in lubricants and psychoactive drugs, is granitic pegmatite. Lithium is obtained from spodumene (a lithium pyroxene) and lepidolite (a lithium mica), minerals that occur exclusively in pegmatites.

In addition to providing a highly desirable construction stone, anorthosite plutons may also be the source of the semiprecious gemstone labradorite. Labradorite is a high-calcium form of plagioclase feldspar (the major mineral in anorthosites) that displays a green, blue, and violet iridescence similar to the play of colors in the tail of a male peacock. Gem-quality labradorite crystals may be made into jewelry, and polished slabs of labradorite anorthosite are used as counter and desk tops and as building facings.

In a larger sense, plutonic rocks (particularly granitic and diorite plutons) form the bulk of the world's continents. During the early evolution of the earth, low-density granitic plutons rising from the early, primitive mantle coalesced to form the cores of the first continents. Some of these ancient plutons can still be observed in shield areas such as the Canadian Shield of North America. In later eras, continents have continued to grow, as plutons and overlying volcanic rocks have added new material to the margins. This process is well illustrated by the plutonic terrain of the Sierra Nevada range, the andesite (volcanic equivalent of diorite) volcanoes of the Cascades of the Pacific Northwest, and the Andes Mountains of South America. Were it not for the formation and expansion of continents by the continuing addition of plutons over geologic time, life on Earth would be considerably different. Without continents and the dry land they provide, life would be confined to the oceans, with obvious implications for the evolution of human beings.

Finally, plutonic rocks in natural settings enhance the beauty and general aesthetic value of the landscape. Deeply eroded plutons have produced some of the most striking landscapes in North America, Europe, and Asia, many of which have been set aside as parks and recreation areas. In North America, especially magnificent landscapes in eroded plutons occur at Yosemite National Park in the Sierra Nevada range of California, the Boulder batholith area of Montana, the high peaks area of the Adirondack Dome of New York State, and the White Mountains of New Hampshire.

Bibliography

Ballard, Robert D. *Exploring Our Living Earth*. Washington, D.C.: *National Geographic*, 1983. Aimed at the general reader and should be available in most public libraries. Covers the earth as an "energy machine," with sections on volcanism, mountain-building, earthquakes, and related phenomena. Richly illustrated with colored photographs and drawings. An excellent source of information on plate tectonics, the unifying theory that seeks to explain the origin of major Earth forces and surface features. Because plutonic rocks are involved in both mountain-building and volcanic activity, an understanding of plate tectonics is essential to understanding the origin of plutons. Glossary, bibliography, and comprehensive index.

Best, Myron G. *Igneous and Metamorphic Petrology*. 2d ed. Cambridge, Mass.: Blackwell, 1995. This is a college-level textbook, but it should be accessible to most general readers. Part 1 contains comprehensive treatments of all major plutonic rock bodies, complete with drawings, diagrams, and photographs detailing the essential features of each pluton type. Chapter 1 contains a section on how petrologists study rocks. The appendix contains chemical analyses of plutonic rocks and descriptions of important rock-forming minerals. One of the best books available for the serious student of igneous and metamorphic rocks.

Beus, S. S., ed. *Rocky Mountain Section of the Geological Society of America: Centennial Field Guide*. Vol. 2. Denver, Colo.: Geological Society of America, 1987. This field guide was produced for professional geologists but should also be of use to the general reader. It describes automobile field trips to geological localities in the Rocky Mountain states. Many of the stops on these tours are at plutonic localities, including the Idaho batholith and the Stillwater Complex of Montana. Illustrated with photographs, geological cross sections, various diagrams, and maps. Descriptions and explanations of the various localities allow an appreciation for the details of plutons and their relationships to associated rocks.

Jensen, Mead L., and Alan M. Bateman. *Economic Mineral Deposits*. New York: John Wiley & Sons, 1981. One of the most comprehensive single-volume treatments of world ore deposits available. Illustrated with abundant monochrome diagrams and photographs; includes tables listing statistics about major ore-bearing regions. All important ore deposits associated with plutonic intrusions are described in detail. Extensive index. This text should be available in most college libraries or in metropolitan public libraries.

Prinz, Martin, George Harlow, and Joseph Peters. *Simon & Schuster's Guide to Rocks and Minerals.* New York: Simon & Schuster, 1978. This field guide to rocks and minerals is readily available in most bookstores. It contains beautiful color photographs of museum-quality minerals and rocks, along with comprehensive descriptions. The introduction to the section on rocks contains a concise description of igneous processes, including plutonic bodies and intrusive processes. Explains how magmas are generated and emplaced in the crust and how they become differentiated. Includes a glossary and index. Highly recommended both for "rockhounds" and for professionals interested in exploring plutonic rocks in the field.

Smith, David G., ed. *The Cambridge Encyclopedia of Earth Sciences.* New York: Cambridge University Press, 1981. One of the best and most comprehensive resources on Earth processes available for the nonspecialist. Richly illustrated with colored photographs, drawings, and diagrams. Pertinent sections to plutonic rocks include chapters 10, 13, 14, and 16. Plate-tectonic concepts relevant to plutonic and volcanic processes are explored in depth, as are topics about plutonic rocks and minerals. Includes an extensive glossary and "further reading" section.

John L. Berkley

Cross-References

Building Stone, 178; Continental Crust, 261; Crystallization of Magmas, 1420; Earth Resources, 2175; Igneous Rocks: Anorthosites, 1152; Igneous Rocks: Batholiths, 1165; Igneous Rocks: Kimberlites, 1186; Mountain Belts, 1725; The Origin of Magmas, 1428; Pegmatites, 2025.

LAKE BAIKAL

Type of earth science: Hydrology
Field of study: Sedimentology

Lake Baikal in southeastern Siberia is the deepest lake in the world and the eighth largest. It has some of the cleanest, coldest fresh water in the world; until recent times, its waters have been among the most pollution free on the earth.

Principal terms
  BAYKALIA: the geographic region surrounding Lake Baikal
  ENDEMIC: found in a particular place and no other
  PHYTOPLANKTON: tiny plants that make up the lowest part of the food chain
  PLANKTON: forms of microscopic life that drift or float in water
  RIFT: a crack or split in the earth
  ZOOPLANKTON: tiny animals that feed on phytoplankton

Summary of the Phenomenon

Lake Baikal is found in the center of the east Siberian region of Russia. Most of the region is covered with forests of pine and larch trees, though much of the area is also covered with grasslands. The climate is harsh, and there are many areas of permanently frozen subsoil in the region.

Lake Baikal (also spelled "Baykal") is the oldest lake in the world. It is located in southeastern Siberia, about fifty miles north of Mongolia. Baikal is the world's eighth-largest lake in area, covering about twelve thousand square miles. It is 395 miles long and thirty miles in width at its widest part. No lake is deeper than Baikal, which has a maximum depth of 5,314 feet. It contains about one-fifth of all the fresh water on the earth's surface and about four-fifths of Russia's freshwater supply.

The lake occupies the deepest continental depression in the world, accounting for its great depth. It is surrounded by mountains that rise to 6,600-foot peaks. The mountain ranges around the lake include the Khamar-Daban, the Baykal, and the Barguzin. Two submerged mountain ranges are found beneath Baikal's surface. They cut across the width of the lake and separate it into three distinct basins. The northern basin depression reaches to 3,243 feet below the surface, the southern to 4,738 feet; the greatest depths are in the central basin, which goes down to 5,745 feet. The northern edge of the central basin is bordered by the Akademichesky Range, the peaks of which rise nearly a mile from the floor. Some peaks break through the surface to create islands, the largest being Olkhon, which contains 322 square miles and has a mountain peak reaching 2,624 feet.

Lake Baikal was formed about 80 million years ago in the late Mesozoic era, when dinosaurs still walked the earth. At that time, the region was made up of a broad basin of shallow lakes and marshes with a subtropical climate. It was then shaken and reshaken by a series of tremendous earthquakes. Earthquake after earthquake pushed the earth up, forming gigantic mountains and deep valleys. About 25 million years ago, water rushed into the deepest basin and began to fill it up. Since that time, earthquakes have continued to strike the region. There have been more than thirty major recorded earthquakes since the eighteenth century. In 1861, a particularly deadly quake killed 1,300 people in a village on the eastern shore. The quake created a new fracture in the earth, and billions of gallons of water rushed in to create a new part of the lake, Proval Bay.

Baikal has 336 rivers entering it, including the seven-hundred-mile-long Selenga River, which comes from northern Mongolia. The Selenga carries about one-half of all the water received by Lake Baikal. Other major tributaries are the Turka, the Barguzin, the Upper Angara, the Kichera, and the Goloustnaya. The tributaries drain an area of about 208,000 square miles. Only one river runs out of the lake, the 1,000-mile-long Angara. It eventually reaches the 2,364-mile-long Yenisei, which flows all the way north to the Arctic.

Baikal is among the cleanest lakes in the world. The lake's water is clear to about 130 feet because it contains few minerals and very little salt. Baikal's water level moves up and down about two to three feet a year, with the highest water in August and September and the lowest in March and April. Melting rain and snow from the surrounding mountains account for most of the change in water level. Rainfall averages about 12 inches per year. Other sources of the waters of Baikal are the vast underground streams that feed into it.

Baikal is usually free of ice only about 110 days a year. The lake is usually frozen over from January to late in May, though in the north the ice usually does not melt until early June. The ice reaches depths of three to six feet by spring. Water on the surface reaches about 48 degrees Fahrenheit by August, though at lower depths the temperature remains a relatively constant 37 degrees. Because of its immense size, the lake has a great influence on the climate of Baykalia, as the surrounding area is called. Summers along the lakeshore are usually much cooler than in the surrounding area, while winters tend to be warmer by the lake and colder away from the lake. June temperatures average around 64 degrees Fahrenheit in Irkutsk, a city about 36 miles from the lake. Irkutsk, on the Angara River, is Baykalia's largest city, with a population of about 600,000 in 1990. In February and March, temperatures in the city frequently reach −60 degrees. Altogether, about 2,500,000 people live in Baykalia.

Despite its generally cold climate, the lake is rich in life, and many forms of plants and animals thrive beneath the ice even in the coldest months of winter. Baikal is home to more than fifteen hundred species of animals, including more than three hundred types of birds and six hundred species of plants. Conditions are unusually superb for aquatic life, and the great age of the lake has allowed more than sufficient time for a great diversity of species to evolve. The lake has some thirteen hundred species of plants and animals that are found only in its waters and nowhere else, including the Baikal seal, a freshwater shrimp, and the golomyanka fish, which gives birth to live young. There is also a fish, the *comechorus baicalensis*, that lives at more than 3,000 feet below the surface. Other important and unique species include the Baikal oilfish, many varieties of mollusks, and the fish found in greatest numbers, the Baikal whitefish, a member of the salmon family.

Plant life is abundant; even in winter, sufficient sunlight breaks through the surface ice to keep plants alive at depths of 30 to 150 feet. Tiny plants, phytoplankton and algae, bloom by the millions at these depths, providing food for rotifers, copepods, and other kinds of freshwater zooplankton, the animal components of plankton. These lowest but important parts of the food chain can usually be seen only through a microscope and are found by the hundreds of millions in lakes and streams.

Baikal is unusual because of the vast amount of life found at its great depths. Most lakes are nearly lifeless below 1,000 feet, but because of the circulation of Baikal's waters, enough oxygen is carried to depths of 3,000 feet to support a variety of species. The lake can be divided into three major depth zones. The first is the shallow coastal waters, which extends to depths of from 60 to 70 feet and which is home to hundreds of species of plants and animals familiar to other Siberian lakes. However, several species of caddis flies found in the shallow waters of Baikal are endemic—that is, they are found there but nowhere else. These flies are adapted to bouncing from wave to wave in the lake. They have small wings shaped like paddles, and legs designed for swimming. Their bodies can float on the water. These "flies" have become so well adapted to the water that they no longer have the ability to fly.

The second zone, the intermediate depths, ranges from 70 to 660 feet below the surface. Further down is the abyssal zone, where life-forms become even more unusual. In these two zones, 80 percent of the species are endemic. In the 38-degree temperatures of the deepest region, there is eternal darkness; hence, many of the species have no eyes or only a minimal sense of sight. One kind of crustacean has a segmented body with seven pairs of legs. This amphipod has small indentations on the sides of its head where its eyes used to be found. The eyes disappeared over millions of years, and now the animal finds its way through the use of long antennae-like objects attached to its body. Many other species in the abyssal zone have made similar adaptations to the absence of light.

Of the fifty species of fish in Baikal, about half are found nowhere else. The largest is the lake sturgeon, ten feet in length and weighing up to five hundred pounds. The sturgeon are highly prized by local fishermen as a source of food and also for the caviar, or eggs, that the species produces. Sturgeon were almost fished out of existence, but recent limitations imposed by the Russian government have helped to restore the population.

Other species of fish include the omul, belonging to the salmon family, which reaches more than a foot in length and can weigh up to nine pounds. The omul is a predator, eating other fish. It is usually inactive until water temperatures reach 54 to 60 degrees in the summer. Omuls live in the upper zone, usually not more than thirteen feet below the surface, feeding on smaller fish and zooplankton.

The omul is the most important commercial fish in the lake. When it is taken from the icy waters, it sends out a piercing cry as air is expelled from its bladder. The shriek sounds like a bitter complaint; Siberian fishermen say that anyone who whines or complains "cries like an omul."

The golomyanka, endemic to Baikal, has no scales, grows to about eight inches in length and weighs only a few pounds. More than a third of its body weight is oil, however; the fish is so oily that it almost glows in the dark. The golomyanka feeds at the surface at night, eating zooplankton and algae. The fish has little tolerance for heat, however, and when temperatures reach above 45 degrees Fahrenheit it will die. When its body washes ashore, its fat is melted by the sun, leaving behind little but skin and bone. The golomyanka has another unique property: It gives birth to live larvae rather than laying eggs as most fish do, and the female can produce up to two thousand babies during the autumn breeding season. Frequently, the female's belly contains so many larvae that it explodes, killing the mother and most of the offspring.

The only mammal that feeds in the water is the Nerpa seal, one of only two freshwater seals in the world. The Nerpa's closest relatives live more than two thousand miles away in the Arctic. It lives among the rocks on the northeastern coast of Baikal. In the summer, it migrates south, where it sleeps on the shore and feeds on omuls and golomyanka fish. The population of Nerpa seals is estimated at about twenty-five thousand. Scientists believe that the seals originated in the Arctic and made their way to Lake Baikal by way of various tributary rivers about twelve thousand years ago. The Baykal hair seal is not as numerous as the Nerpa but is also found on the coasts of various islands in the lake.

Methods of Study

Though it has among the cleanest lake waters on Earth, Baikal is beginning to be endangered by industrial wastes, despite its great size. There are no major cities right on the lake, but economic development has brought increased pollution to the area. In the 1960's, two paper mills were built on the southern shore, and government officials in the Soviet Union, eager to expand Siberia's economic growth, called for the building of more mills. Protests from the Soviet Academy of Sciences helped stop the construction of two plants and prompted a redesign of another to make it less polluting. Still, in 1977, scientists studying Baikal's biology became alarmed at the decline in zooplankton. Especially serious was the killing of millions of *Epischura*, a tiny shrimplike species that is a major food source for larger fish. Quick action led to some changes in levels of chemical pollutants dumped into the lake by the paper mills. The crisis illustrated how even slight changes in the quality of the lake's water could eventually lead to disaster.

Industrial development began in 1905, after the completion of a railroad along the rocky southern shore. The new train replaced the existing ferry boat that previously was the only way across the lake. The advent of the great nine-thousand-mile trans-Siberian route in 1916 opened the region to contact with Russian territory from Moscow in the west to Vladivostok on the Pacific coast in the east. Still, the region had only a small population of mostly Mongolian peoples. The most important of these were the Buryats, population 353,000, a mostly Buddhist people who had settled in the area of Lake Baikal a thousand years before. It was not until 1938, however, with the completion of the Baikal-Amur trunkline that thousands of farmers and settlers came into the region. Since then, major industries have developed in the area; in addition to paper mills, mining, ship building, fishing, and timber cutting have emerged as local industries.

All the cities and industries of the area lie along the trans-Siberian railroad. Irkutsk is the center of the region and the major industrial city. Ule-Ude, east of Lake Baikal, and Chita are two other cities of more than 100,000 population. The trans-Siberian railroad has been the lifeline of this eastern part of Siberia since its completion. Ulan Ude has a rail link to the Mongolian capital of Ulan Bator. Since 1954, both cities have been linked to Peking and northern China.

Another problem created by the paper mills results from the cutting of huge numbers of trees to make into pulp. The loss of trees dramatically increased soil erosion, which led to severe problems of runoff and contamination of Baikal's once crystal-clear waters. Since 1969, the lake has been part of a water-conservation area decreed by the Soviet government. Regulations prohibiting logging in certain critical areas were imposed, and strict regulations ordering the treatment of industrial pollutants were issued to reduce the amount of contaminated water entering the lake from the paper mills. Unfortunately, these regulations have not been effectively enforced, and economic development has usually been placed before environmental concerns by local officials. Tougher regulations and stricter enforcement of existing laws have been promoted by defenders of the environment, but a lack of funding has limited the enforcement of antipollution laws.

Because of the harshness of the climate, agriculture is possible only in limited areas around Lake Baikal. Oats are grown in the region, however, and cattle, sheep, and horses are raised there. Food industries are limited to meatpacking, fish canning, and the processing of some dairy products, chiefly cheese and milk. Mining has a long history in the region, as there is a relatively wide range of metals and minerals such as gold, tin, graphite, mica, and zinc. There are large coal deposits west of Lake Baikal along the Angara River. The Angara is also the home of the giant Bratsk hydroelectric plant, the largest in the world, which supplies power to Irkutsk.

Context

The future of Lake Baikal, according to some scientists, includes the possibility of continuing geological turmoil. The great earthquakes that have been part of the history of the region are expected to continue to bring tremendous changes. Some geologists believe that the trench in which Baikal is found is part of a huge "rift system" that goes all the way from the northern part of the lake to the southern part of the Caspian Sea hundreds of miles away. This rift, or split, it is thought, will gradually deepen and grow wider. Eventually—perhaps in a few million years—the trench may become so huge that it will split eastern Siberia and China into two separate land masses. Lake Baikal would then become a new ocean lying between two new continents.

Efforts to save Lake Baikal from greater levels of pollution are led by scientists at the Russian Academy of Science in Irkutsk. The by-products of paper milling and various types of mining have changed the chemistry of the lake. Pollution from human-made toxic chemicals has posed a direct threat to the existence of fish and other forms of aquatic life, especially at the lower ends of the food chain. Yet some efforts to control discharges into the lake have proved successful. Much remains to be done if the lake is to escape the fate of the Aral Sea to the west, which has lost more than 40 percent of its water as the result of the diversion of many of its tributaries for irrigation and hydroelectric projects. One factor that may preserve the lake from such a fate is the simple fact that only a small percentage of the land in areas drained by rivers flowing into the lake is suitable for agriculture. The harshness of the climate may in the long run be the salvation of Lake Baikal and its waters.

Bibliography

Bogdanov, Uri. *Mysteries of the Deep: From the Depths of Lake Baikal to the Ocean Floor*. Moscow: Progress Publishers, 1989. By a geologist and underwater photographer. Includes illustrations and pictures of some of the more unusual animals that live in the abyssal zone of the lake. Also contains some information of the geological history of the area. No index.

Dapples, Edward C. *Beach Material from Lake Baikal, Siberia*. Miami: Field Research Projects, 1979. Contains photographs, a map, graphs, and drawings of material collected by the geologist and explorer Henry Field on a trip to the lake in 1973. Discusses the formation of the lake and the effect of earthquakes in the region.

Koptyug, Valentin A., and Martin Uppenbrink, eds. *Sustainable Development of the Lake Baikal Region: A Model Territory for the World*. New York: Springer, 1996. A collection of scientific papers from a conference hosted by the North Atlantic Treaty Organization Scientific Affairs Division. Describes the environmental impact of recent development and the ways in which pollution threatens the future of plants and animals in the region. Fairly technical, but includes an extensive bibliography of recent books and articles on the lake.

Sergeev, Mark. *The Wonders and Problems of Lake Baikal*. Translated by Sergei Sumin. Moscow: Novosti Press Agency, 1989. A brief book with many photographs and wildlife, fish, and plants of the region. Discusses the hazards and costs of industrial pollution and its impact on the lake. Also has a brief history of the geology and history of Baykalia. A detailed map is included.

Symons, Leslie. *The Soviet Union: A Systematic Geography*. Totowa, N.J.: Barnes & Noble, 1983. Contains some useful information on Lake Baikal and its effects on East Siberia. Includes many detailed maps describing the region's mineral, agricultural, and industrial wealth. Also contains a brief description and history of the impact and influence of the trans-Siberian railroad.

Leslie V. Tischauser

Cross-References

The Abyssal Sea Floor, 1; Earthquake Hazards, 437; Lakes, 1318; Surface Water, 2504; Weather Modification, 3186.

LAND BRIDGES

Type of earth science: Paleontology and earth history
Field of study: Tectonics

The theory that Earth's continents were once connected by land bridges that accounted for the migration of flora and fauna was considered viable by many leading geologists during the last half of the nineteenth century and for the first three decades of the twentieth century.

Principal terms

CONTINENTAL DRIFT: the theory that land masses separated and drifted apart in prehistoric times

CENOZOIC ERA: the geologic era dating from the present to about 65 million years ago

CRETACEOUS ERA: a geologic period ending some 65 million years ago, during which seas covered much of North America and the Rocky Mountains were formed

EOCENE EPOCH: part of the Cenozoic era, dating to about 37 million years ago

GLACIATION: the process of being covered by an ice sheet or glacier

ISTHMIAN LINKS: chains of islands between substantial land masses

LAND BRIDGES: narrow land formations that connect land masses

MESOZOIC ERA: the geologic era spanning the period from about 245 million years ago to about 65 million years ago

Summary of the Phenomenon

For geologists, Earth has long been a huge, complicated jigsaw puzzle waiting to be reconstructed. The difference between this jigsaw puzzle and the ones with which most people are familiar is that this one is constantly changing. Earth changes in small ways—and sometimes in larger ways, such as when a volcano erupts—on a daily basis. It changes more drastically over longer periods of time. It is now thought to be changing as global warming slowly melts the polar ice caps, with a resulting increase in the volume of ocean waters and a corresponding decrease in the shorelines adjacent to the rising oceans.

It has long been acknowledged that drastic climatic changes have occurred on Earth over millions of years. The Arctic and Antarctic, now solidly frozen, once had tropical and subtropical vegetation, as is evident from impressions of plants found in mineral deposits in these regions and from other paleontological evidence. Now-moderate regions were, during the Ice Age, much colder. Glaciation pushed debris unrelentingly from one region to another as the glaciers moved toward the equator.

Long baffled by the existence of similar flora and fauna in areas seemingly unrelated to each other climatically—Africa, Australia, and Antarctica, for example—geologists arrived at various conclusions regarding the phenomenon. It must be remembered that geologists talk in terms of hundreds of millions of years more often than they do in terms of a century or a millennium. Geological change often occurs so slowly as to be virtually unnoticeable within such geologically abbreviated time spans as thousands of years.

Among the theories promulgated to explain the presence of similar flora and fauna in widely disparate areas was that of land bridges. Some land bridges obviously existed, such as the one across the Bering Strait that linked Siberia to what is now Alaska. It is apparent that two continents, Asia and North America, were at one time linked by this broad bridge. Similarly, some geological conjecture also has it that land bridges existed between present-day Ireland and Scotland and between present-day Gibraltar and North Africa.

A Viennese geologist, Edward Suess, proposed an extensive land-bridge theory in his influential book *The Face of the Earth* (1885). Suess coined the term "Gondwanaland," named after Gondwana in east-central India, an area with rocks that revealed unique fossil plants and showed indisputable signs of glaciation dating from the late Paleozoic to the early Mesozoic eras.

As Suess pieced together the discrete elements of his geological puzzle, he found that separate continents had the sorts of fossil plants and glacial rocks that he found in Gondwana. He attributed these occurrences in widely separated areas to land bridges rather than to continental drift. Suess, and the scores of notable geologists who accepted his thesis, contended that the land bridges connecting the continents sank beneath the ocean at some time in prehistory.

Other geologists were trying to solve the same riddles with which Suess was confronted. In 1908, F. B. Taylor published a privately printed pamphlet in which he suggested that present mountain ranges occurred when enormous landslides advanced slowly and steadily from the polar regions toward the equator. He conceived of the world's great continents as originally consisting of huge sheets of rock that were torn apart by glaciation as gigantic fields of ice moved toward zero latitude.

Taylor advanced two fundamental ideas, both of which have been opposed by other geologists to the point that these two hypotheses have been discredited. First, he speculated that mountain ranges were products of thousands of miles of lateral movement; second, he believed that the Moon became associated gravitationally with Earth during the Cretaceous period, about one hundred million years ago. In this period, there was a considerable increase in the variety of flora and fauna found on Earth. Taylor suggested that in the earliest times, the Moon created phenomenal tidal forces that slowed the rate at which Earth rotated and pulled the continents away from the poles. Both of these theories were subsequently disproved.

H. H. Baker, an American geologist, considered the supercontinent of Earth's earliest years to have been split along the Atlantic and Arctic Oceans as the Miocene period neared its end some seven million to eight million years ago. He asserted that great tidal action had torn a huge piece from Earth. The resulting void, according to Baker, became the Pacific Ocean. The portion that was catapulted into space, he speculated, became the Moon.

In his landmark study *The Origin of Continents and Oceans* (1915), Alfred Wegener proposed that Earth had at one time consisted of a single land mass that he called "Pangaea," the Greek term for "all earth." He concluded that during the Mesozoic era, the single land mass was torn apart, with the southern continents (Africa, Australia, South America, Antarctica) being pulled away first. Looking at the globe as though it were a jigsaw puzzle, one can imagine that the east coast of South America would fit easily into the declivities in the west coast of Africa.

As this investigation into Earth's origins was ongoing, the fossil record uncovered during the 1870's and 1880's led to the inevitable conclusion that land links, either land bridges or isthmian links, had existed between Africa, India, Australia, South America, and Antarctica. These areas of vastly differing climates in modern times (geologically speaking) appeared to share a fossil plant record that suggested a close affinity among them.

F. H. Knowlton, speaking in 1918 about Mesozoic floral relations, supported the notion that land bridges from Antarctica once linked most of the southern land masses. Writing in 1947, however, after the land-bridge theory had been largely discredited, Theodor Just suggested that "the needs of animal and plant geographers . . . vary sufficiently with their respective interests and so do the land bridges assumed by them." Just discounted land links as deciding factors in the migration of flora.

During the Eocene epoch, the southeastern United States experienced an influx of tropical flora, suggesting to some that a land bridge or isthmian link had once existed between South America and what is now the United States, possibly between South America and southern Florida. Modern researchers suggest that this tropical foliage actually came to the southeastern United States from an intermediate region such as Central America or the Antilles.

During the Oligocene epoch, a considerable exchange of plant life appears to have taken place between present-day Panama and the Antilles. Petrified wood found on Antigua reflects several forms of flora found in both Panama and southeastern America. While the land-bridge or isthmian-link theory might explain this coincidence, other more viable theories exist to explain it. Among these is the theory that certain flora simply drifted on the open sea, perhaps hitchhiking on debris that eventually washed ashore in a place where the climate could support its germination and growth.

During the Pleistocene epoch, North and South America were connected. The Isthmus of Panama did not exist, and the region of what is now the Antilles was considerably higher than it is today, possibly with a land bridge to South America, less than a hundred miles away, and certainly with isthmian links to that continent. Vegetation common to the rain forests of the Amazon and Orinoco basins occurred in southern Florida, but most geologists consider it improbable that a land bridge existed between that region and the Antilles or South America.

On the other hand, those who dispute the existence of a land bridge between North and South America are on shakier ground than those who dispute a land bridge between Florida or the Antilles and South America. Vertebrate paleontologists have made a convincing case for animal migration (including human) in this area, as they have for animal migration between Asia and North America by way of the land bridge that is known to have existed between Siberia and present-day Alaska. In 1917, Edward W. Berry postulated that the Antilles were once a part of South America but that continental drift separated the region from that continent. Such a theory would explain much of the coincident flora and fauna in both places.

Numerous catastrophic theories regarding continental drift have been used to explain the separation of Earth's land mass into continents. Most of these theories have to do with the separation of the Moon from Earth, accompanied by the violent tidal action that followed this separation. As late as 1932, Charles Schuchert supported the notion that land bridges connected parts of an enormous supercontinent and that these bridges subsequently sank beneath the deep waters of the Atlantic, Pacific, and Indian Oceans, as suggested several decades earlier by Edward Suess.

The major portions of the jigsaw puzzle on which geologists have worked for the past century are now firmly in place. Other portions do not yet fit into any reasonable pattern. The land-bridge theory, although it explains certain animal migrations in a limited geographical range, has been displaced by other theories relating to diverse flora and fauna in such widely separated areas as India, Antarctica, Africa, and South America. The major importance of the land-bridge hypothesis is that it demanded testing, and this testing led to valuable insights about Earth's earliest history.

Methods of Study

As geologists during the past century have attempted to fit together the pieces of the vast jigsaw puzzle that Earth presents, they have informed their speculations with paleontological evidence. Such evidence is, however, subject to interpretation, and it is in this area that geology becomes highly speculative.

For example, it is known that the Bering Strait land bridge existed during the Ice Age. Paleontologists have recovered the remains of rhinoceroses that lived during that period in Siberia. Despite considerable searching, they have not found similar remains in Alaska, to which, presumably, at least some of the Siberian rhinoceroses would have migrated over the millennia.

The explanation for this lack of correspondence in the paleontological evidence is that the pasturage along the land bridge did not appeal to the rhinoceroses; therefore, they did not stray beyond their native Siberia. Obviously, such conjecture involves interpretation and may prove specious as further information and advanced technology make it possible for researchers to uncover and interpret future finds.

Geologists generally concede that Earth was originally a single land mass that over time fractured and divided into the modern continents. It is also evident that some land bridges and isthmian links existed and possibly accounted for such phenomena as the existence of identical forms of plant and animal life in places that are currently as far apart as South Africa and South America.

It is altogether possible that animal life that originated in South Africa over many millennia could have moved north, then across Asia to the Bering Straits, where a land bridge would have provided such animals with access to North America. Some geologists have pursued this possibility, concluding that once this animal life reached North America, it could, over time, have moved to South America and even Antarctica, possibly over isthmian links. It must be remembered that in these prehistoric times, Antarctica and the southern reaches of South America were not necessarily cold. Evidence of tropical vegetation has been found in both places.

Numerous geologists have speculated that after Earth ceased to be a single land mass, a large chunk of it was catapulted into outer space, leaving an enormous void that became the Pacific Ocean. The matter that flew out from earth into space, they speculate, became the Moon, which in time exerted a considerable influence over Earth by controlling the tides of Earth's major bodies of water. In early geological times, these tides were so violent that they rent huge portions of Earth, dividing them into the continents that are recognizable today.

For example, it seems clear that South America and Africa were once joined but that as the Central Atlantic Ocean became larger, it split these continents apart, eventually causing them to be separated by thousands of miles. Similarly, Europe and North America were once linked, but as the Atlantic Ocean asserted itself upon the land mass that linked these two continents, each became separate.

The methodology of geologists and paleontologists is essentially to unearth what artifacts they can from the past, exploring especially the frigid wastes of the polar regions, where past life has been frozen in time and preserved remarkably well. Once they have uncovered these artifacts, they then have to relate them to the larger picture, fitting them into the vast jigsaw puzzle they are working to complete.

Context

Because the land-bridge theory as advanced by Edward Suess and his followers has been discredited by such organizations as the American Geological Institute and the American Geophysical Union, it is of historical rather than practical importance today. Its real importance, nevertheless, is that as a hypothesis, it required testing; in doing that testing, other geologists evolved important theories that cast doubt upon the hypothesis but that advanced human knowledge.

Geologists who could not endorse the land-bridge/isthmian-link theory could not deny that some land bridges had existed. They did, however, deny that the migrations of plants and animals throughout prehistoric time was as dependent upon these links as their proponents suggested. Many of these dissident geologists and paleontologists attributed the coincidence of similar plant and animal life in disparate regions to continental drift or to other causes.

It was, for example, established that at one time the Tethys Sea extended from the Pacific Ocean to what is now the eastern shores of the Mediterranean Sea. Given this enormous surface, it is clear that debris could float easily over long distances and that, upon being washed ashore, the seeds of flora could germinate and flourish. Similarly, microscopic faunas could float over vast distances and reestablish themselves in venues far from where they had originated.

It is known that during the Triassic period, the dinosaurs that roamed Earth could walk from what is now southern Europe to Africa over land bridges. Dinosaur remains have been found on both continents, and their teeth have been dredged from the sea where sunken land bridges exist.

It is also known that reptile remains identical to those found in China have turned up in Antarctica. Although it seems implausible that such could be the case given the current climatic differences between the two places, one must remember that the climates of both places were not the same in the most ancient times as they are today.

It is clear that human migration took place over some of the land bridges. The physical characteristics of many Hispanic people in Central and South America are identical to those of people living in parts of Asia, most notably China. Clearly, the land bridge between Asia and North America accounts for some of these similarities, although it is equally clear that some early people reached South America by traveling there on rafts that were carried long distances by the currents, as Thor Heyerdahl illustrated by his trips on the *Kon Tiki*.

Researchers into Earth's origins consider every possibility as they work toward their conclusions. Most realize that no single explanation of a phenomenon as complex as plant and animal migration is consistently valid. There is probably a bit of truth in all the extant explanations relevant to migration, because these migrations took place in many ways at many times.

Bibliography

Brown, Hugh A. *Cataclysms of the Earth*. New York: Twayne, 1967. Brown examines various cataclysmic events that have shaped the development of Earth, not the least of which was the supposed creation of the Moon from a huge portion of the planet's surface and the effects of the violent tidal action that followed this event and changed forever the shape of Earth.

Carey, S. Warren. "A Tectonic Approach to Continental Drift." In *Continental Drift: A Symposium. Being a Symposium on the Present Status of the Continental Drift Hypothesis, Held in the Geology Department of the University of Tasmania, in March, 1956*. Hobart, Tasmania: University of Tasmania, 1958; revised 1959. Carey presents one of the most balanced overviews of the continental-drift/land-bridge controversy in this somewhat specialized article. Important, but not easily accessible to the beginner.

Fuentes, Carlos. *The Buried Mirror: Reflections on Spain and the New World*. New York: Houghton-Mifflin, 1992. Celebrating the five hundredth anniversary of Christopher Columbus' first trip to the New World, Fuentes traces with considerable skill the migration patterns that accounted for the presence on the American continent of a large population of people whose ancient ancestors were of Asian origins and who probably arrived in America by way of the Bering Sea land bridge. A most engaging book.

Glen, William. *Continental Drift and Plate Tectonics*. Columbus, Ohio: Charles E. Merrill, 1980. Although he devotes only two pages to a discussion of land bridges,

Glen provides excellent information about the Gondwanaland theory and about Edward Suess's original writings about land bridges. A worthwhile, succinct overview.

Marvin, Ursula B. *Continental Drift: The Evolution of a Concept*. Washington, D.C.: Smithsonian Institution Press, 1973. Despite its age, Marvin's book is timely. It evokes one's intellectual curiosity about the subject of land bridges and maintains a healthy skepticism about the various claims that have been made for this theory. Marvin writes extraordinarily well, with the result that this book is more readable than many that have been written in the field.

Ross, Charles A., ed. *Paleobiogeography*. Stroudsburg, Penn.: Dowden, Hutchinson, and Ross, 1976. Ross has gathered in one compendious volume the salient works of most of the geologists and paleontologists who worked toward evolving the land-bridge/isthmian-link theory, as well as the work of those who questioned and eventually discredited the theory.

Shea, James H., ed. *Continental Drift*. New York: Van Nostrand Reinhold, 1985. The section entitled "Gondwana" and Alfred Wegener's chapter "The Origins of Continents" are particularly valuable to those interested in the land-bridge theory. The presentations are clear and informative.

Suess, Edward. *The Face of the Earth*. Oxford, England: Oxford University Press, 1909. This translation of Suess's *Das Anlitz der Erde* (1885) is essential reading for anyone seriously interested in this field. Suess was the major early proponent of the land-bridge/isthmian-link theory. He presents his salient arguments, since discredited, in this book.

Sullivan, Walter. *Continents in Motion: The New Earth Debate*. 2d ed. New York: American Institute of Physics, 1991. Sullivan presents considerable information about land bridges and isthmian links, offering a comprehensive overview of the theory and its eventual loss of credibility. The presentation is well balanced and accessible to people not specifically trained in the field.

Wegener, Alfred. *The Origin of Continents and Oceans*. New York: Dover Books, 1966. This translation of Alfred Wegener's landmark book *Die Entstehung der Kontinente und Ozeane* (1915), in combination with Suess's *The Face of the Earth*, helps one to understand the considerable controversy that Suess's hypothesis evoked and some of the reactions to it. Fortunately, this relatively recent translation of the original work is available in many college and university libraries.

R. Baird Shuman

Cross-References

The Cenozoic Era, 202; Climate, 217; Continental Drift, 2863; Continental Glaciers, 967; Continental Rift Zones, 275; Continental Shelf and Slope, 281; Continental Structures, 290; Continents and Subcontinents, 2869; Earth's Oldest Rocks, 561; Earth's Structure, 589.

LIMESTONE

Type of earth science: Geology
Field of study: Sedimentary petrology

Limestone, the third most common sedimentary rock, is composed mostly of calcium carbonate, typically of organic origin. Limestone is usually fossiliferous and thus contains abundant evidence of organic evolution; it is also important as a construction material, groundwater aquifer, and oil reservoir.

Principal terms

CALCITE: the main constituent of limestone, a carbonate mineral consisting of calcium carbonate

CARBONATES: a large group of minerals consisting of a carbonate anion (three oxygen atoms bonded to one carbon atom, with a residual charge of two) and a variety of cations, including calcium, magnesium, and iron

CEMENTATION: the joining of sediment grains, which results from mineral crystals forming in void spaces between the sediment

DEPOSITION: the settling and accumulation of sediment grains after transport

DEPOSITIONAL ENVIRONMENT: the environmental setting in which a rock forms; for example, a beach, coral reef, or lake

DIAGENESIS: the physical and chemical changes that occur to sedimentary grains after their accumulation

GRAINS: the individual particles that make up a rock or sediment deposit

LITHIFICATION: compaction and cementation of sediment grains to form a sedimentary rock

TEXTURE: the size, shape, and arrangement of grains in a rock

WEATHERING: the disintegration and decomposition of rock at the earth's surface as the result of the exertion of mechanical and chemical forces

Summary of the Phenomenon

Limestones are a diverse group of sedimentary rocks, all of which share a common trait: They contain 50 percent or more calcium carbonate, either as the mineral calcite or as aragonite. Both are composed of calcium carbonate; however, they have different atomic arrangements. Other carbonate minerals may also be present; siderite (iron carbonate) and dolomite (calcium-magnesium carbonate) are especially common. Although carbonate minerals can form other rocks, limestone is easily the most common and important carbonate rock. Many geologists use the terms "carbonate rock" and "limestone" almost interchangeably, because most carbonate rocks are limestones.

Limestone may be of chemical or biochemical (organic) origin and can form in a wide variety of depositional environments. A limestone's texture and grain content are often useful clues for determining how and where it formed; however, diagenesis can easily obscure or destroy this evidence. Most limestones contain fossils, and many are highly fossiliferous. Limestones are perhaps our best record of ancient life and its evolutionary sequence. They are important sources for building and crushed stone and often contain large supplies of groundwater, oil, and natural gas. Weathering of limestone helps to develop distinctive landscapes as well.

Limestones form in one of three ways: chemical precipitation of crystalline grains, biochemical precipitation and accumulation of skeletal and nonskeletal grains, or accumulation of fragments of pre-existing limestone rock. Chemical precipitation occurs when the concentration of dissolved calcium carbonate in water becomes so high that the calcium carbonate begins to come out of solution and form a solid, crystalline deposit. The concentration of calcium carbonate in the water may change for a number of reasons. For example, evaporation, an increase in water temperature, or decreasing acidity can all cause precipitation. Crystalline limestone forms in the ocean, in alkaline lakes, and in caves.

Certain marine organisms are responsible for the formation of many kinds of limestone. Their calcareous (calcium carbonate) skeletons accumulate after death, forming carbonate sediment. Many limestones are nothing more than thousands of skeletal grains joined to form a rock. The organisms that contribute their skeletons to carbonate sediments are a diverse group and include both plants and animals. Among these are algae, clams, snails, corals, starfish, sea urchins, and sponges. Some marine animals also produce nonskeletal carbonate sediments. An animal's solid wastes, or fecal pellets, may accumulate to form limestones if they contain abundant skeletal fragments or compacted lime mud. Limestones composed of skeletal grains, or of nonskeletal grains produced by living organisms, are called "organic limestones."

Recycling of pre-existing limestones is a third source for carbonate grains. Weathering and erosion produce limestone fragments, or clasts, that may later be incorporated into new limestone deposits. Limestones consisting of clasts are clastic, or detrital, limestones; they are probably the least common of the three types of limestone.

The processes that turn loose sediment grains into sedimentary rock are known as "lithification." These may include either compaction, cementation, or both. The grains (crystals) in a chemically formed limestone are usually joined together into an interlocking, solid matrix when they precipitate; thus, they do not undergo further lithification. The grains in organic and clastic limestones, however, are usually loose, or unconsolidated, when they first accumulate and so must be lithified to form rock.

Limestones, unlike most other sedimentary rocks, are believed to undergo lithification during shallow burial rather than when deep below the earth's surface. Some may be lithified within a meter or two of, or even at, the surface. Therefore, lithification in most limestones consists of cementation without significant compaction of grains. In most cases, the cement is calcium carbonate. If the spaces, or pores, between the grains become cement-filled without much compaction, cement can be as much as 50 percent or more of the volume of a limestone. The cement forms by precipitation, much like the formation of a crystalline limestone.

A number of factors control the formation and preservation of carbonate sediments. These include the water temperature and pressure, the amount of agitation, concentrations of dissolved carbon dioxide, noncarbonate sedimentation, and light penetration. Cold, deep water with high levels of dissolved carbon dioxide tends to discourage the formation and accumulation of carbonate sediment. Warm, clear, well-lit, shallow water tends to promote formation and accumulation.

Certain periods of geologic history also favored limestone formation. Generally, the greatest volumes of ancient limestones formed when the global sea level was higher than today, so that seas covered large areas of the continents, and when global temperatures were also higher than at present. This combination of factors was ideal for producing thick, extensive deposits of carbonate rocks. Such limestones are exposed throughout the world today and provide a glimpse into Earth's distant past. Their abundant marine fossils are especially useful to paleontologists and biologists, as they allow them to piece together the sequence of biological evolution for a variety of plants and animals.

Modern carbonate sediments accumulate in ocean waters ranging in depth from less than a meter to more than five thousand meters and at nearly all latitudes. However, most ancient limestones now exposed at the earth's surface formed in low-latitude, tropical, shallow marine environments; for example, in reefs or lagoons. This is probably because elsewhere noncarbonate sediments, such as quartz sand or silt, diluted the carbonates so that limestone did not form. Carbonates from many other environments are also less likely to be preserved, so they are not a major part of the ancient rock record. This lack of preservation may result from weathering and erosion or from destruction by plate tectonic activities. Other factors may also play a role but are probably less significant.

One of the world's largest modern accumulations of carbonate sediment and rock is located in the Great Barrier Reef off the northeast coast of Australia. This reef tract, the largest in the world, contains thick sequences of carbonate sediment deposited during the last few thousand years draped over even older carbonate rocks formed by coral reef organisms in the more distant past. As long as these reefs continue to thrive, carbonate sediment production will also continue. As a result, this mass of limestone will grow even thicker, and the older rock will continue to subside, sinking deeper into the subsurface.

No matter where they form or what their origin, carbonate sediments are all subject to diagenesis. Diagenesis consists of those processes that alter the composition or texture of sediments after their formation and burial and before their eventual re-exposure at the earth's surface. Therefore, lithification is a part of diagenesis, and weathering is not.

One of the great mysteries of geology concerns the origin of dolomite, the calcium-magnesium carbonate mineral, and dolostone, the dolomitic equivalent of limestone.

Many geochemists believe dolomite and dolostone owe their origin to the diagenesis of limestone. Dolostones are relatively common in the ancient rock record, and yet the formation of dolomite by direct crystallization is rare. This creates a dilemma: Where did all this ancient dolomite come from? Many geochemists believe that the answer lies in alteration (diagenesis) of relatively pure limestone to form dolostone, which contains at least 15 percent dolomite. However, there is no general agreement as to how this process, known as "dolomitization," actually occurred.

As mentioned above, a limestone's texture and grain content tell geologists much about its environment of deposition. Numerous varieties of limestone have been named on the basis of their texture and grain content. These include dolomitic limestone, fossiliferous limestone, and crystalline limestone. Other common varieties include chalk, a very soft, fine-grained limestone; travertine, a type of crystalline limestone that forms in caves; and calcareous tufa, which forms by precipitation of calcium carbonate at springs.

Limestone weathers rapidly in humid environments. Rainwater, because of its content of dissolved carbon dioxide, is slightly acidic; it attacks and chemically weathers limestone quite readily. Since limestone is dense but of low strength, it also breaks, or fractures, easily. This characteristic allows even more rapid chemical weathering to occur, and the fractures quickly widen, becoming what are known as "joints."

In the subsurface, horizontal and vertical joints widen, as downward-flowing surface water and laterally flowing groundwater dissolve away limestone, creating increasingly large void spaces, or caves, in the rock. The largest and most extensive cave systems in the world, such as Mammoth Cave in Kentucky, form in limestones. The largest caves usually form where multiple joints intersect in the subsurface.

Where joints intersect at the earth's surface, conical depressions, or sinkholes, begin to form. Sinkholes may be exposed at the surface or covered by a layer of soil. Some sinkholes grow and subside only very slowly, while others may collapse in one rapid, catastrophic event. They range in size from a few meters wide and deep to sinkholes that are large enough to swallow several large buildings should they collapse. The resulting irregular, pockmarked landscape is called "karst topography." Karst topography is easily recognized by the presence of sinkholes, disappearing streams (which flow into sinkholes), caves, and springs.

Methods of Study

Geologists study limestones for a variety of reasons and at a variety of scales. Most early studies of limestones focused on their fossils. Many limestones contain abundant, well-preserved fossils; some are famous for the exceptional quality of the specimens they contain. Visible, or macroscopic, fossils provide evidence for the sequence of evolution of many invertebrate organisms. Fossils are clues to a limestone's depositional environment as well; however, more detailed information concerning depositional environments can often be gathered by examining limestones at either smaller or larger scales.

Carbonate petrography involves the study of limestones for the purpose of description and classification. This usually involves using a microscope to determine a limestone's grain content; that is, the types of carbonate and noncarbonate grains present and their mineral composition (mineralogy). Carbonate petrology deals with the origin, occurrence, structure, and history of limestones. This involves petrographic studies of limestone as well as field studies of one or more outcrops. Carbonate stratigraphy applies the concepts of petrology at even larger scales and attempts to determine the physical and age relationships between rock bodies that may be separated by great distances.

Carbonate petrography is commonly performed by observing a thin slice of a rock through a light microscope. A small block of the rock is cemented onto a microscope slide, then ground down and polished until the slice is about thirty microns (0.03 millimeters) thick. The slice is then thin enough for light to pass easily through it. Microscopic examination of a thin section can reveal a limestone's mineralogy and its microfossil or other grain content. Other observable traits include cement types, the presence or absence of lime mud, the purity of the limestone, and the types and degree of diagenesis. Use of special stains along with microscopy can reveal even more details of mineralogy. Stains allow easy identification of particular minerals—for example, Alzarin Red S colors calcite red and dolomite purple—so that their percentages can be determined.

Field study of exposures, or outcrops, of limestone also provides useful information. Along with the macroscopic fossil studies mentioned above, geologists can study sedimentary structures to learn about a limestone's depositional environment. Sedimentary structures are mechanically or chemically produced features that record environmental conditions during or after deposition and before lithification. For example, ripple marks indicate water movements by either currents or waves, and their shape and spacing suggests the depth of water and velocity of water movement. Careful study of sedimentary structures provides detailed information to methodical observers.

Outcrops also contain evidence of the lateral and vertical sequence of environments responsible for limestone deposition. By studying the lateral changes in a series of limestone outcrops, it is possible to interpret the distribution of environments, or paleogeography, in an area. For example, a researcher might determine in what direction water depths increased, or where a coastline might have been located. The vertical sequence of limestones at an outcrop indicates the paleogeography through time. By interpreting changes in sedimentary structures and other characteristics, a vertical sequence of limestones may indicate that, during deposition, a lagoon existed initially but gave way first to a coral reef and finally to an open ocean environment.

Many researchers conduct even larger-scale studies of limestone sequences. Using advanced technology developed for locating and studying petroleum reservoirs, geophysicists can produce cross sections showing limestone distribution in the subsurface. This research technique, sequence stratigraphy, allows geologists to see very large-scale features located thousands of meters below the surface and so provides even better insights into regional paleogeography.

Geochemists and mineralogists study limestones to determine their mineral composition. Simple techniques might involve dissolving a sample of limestone in stages, using a series of different acids. At each stage, the scientist weighs the remaining solid material. From this, approximate percentages of the limestone's mineral components can be determined. More advanced techniques can involve the use of X rays and high-energy particle beams to determine a mineral's atomic structure and precise composition. Such analysis might, for example, allow a chemist to suggest new industrial uses for a particular limestone deposit.

Engineers also study limestones, usually to determine their suitability as a construction or foundation material. Numerous tests are available; engineering tests generally involve determination of physical and chemical properties such as composition, strength, durability, porosity, permeability, solubility, and density. Results from such tests help to predict the behavior of limestones under certain conditions. For example, testing may indicate how a particular limestone would perform as a building foundation in an area with a humid climate and highly acidic soils.

Context

Limestone composes about 10 percent of the volume of the earth's sedimentary rock, and the understanding of the sequence of organic evolution is a by-product of this abundance. Nearly all limestones contain fossils, either those visible to the naked eye or microscopic fossils. These provide a record of life stretching back over billions of years, revealing details of early life-forms and the environments in which they lived. Without this record, scientists' knowledge of organic evolution would be spotty at best, and much of the detail of the sequence of life would be left to the imagination.

Some limestones preserve even fine details of the soft parts of organisms. The Solnhofen Limestone of Bavaria is famous for its fossils of *Archaeopteryx*, a Jurassic period fossil believed to be the remains of the earliest known bird. Details of *Archaeopteryx*'s feathers are visible in the Solnhofen Limestone. Although rare, some limestones contain fossils of organisms, such as worms and jellyfish, that contain no hard parts and yet were preserved as outlines with details of their internal organs.

The abundance of limestone makes it one of the most important stones for use in construction, especially as crushed and building stone. For many regions of the world, limestone is the rock of choice for building roads. People used limestone to construct both ancient structures, such as the Egyptian pyramids, and modern buildings, such as the Empire State Building in New York City.

Fine-grained, homogenous limestone is sculpted for use as an ornamental stone on building exteriors and interiors, for gravestones, or for statuary. Very fine-grained limestones are sometimes used in lithography. Porous limestone is a good host for some types of ores. For example, the Mississippi Valley lead-zinc district in Missouri is hosted in limestone.

Very pure, high-calcium limestones are used in producing masonry cement and in iron production. They are also crushed for agricultural uses. Powdered limestone may be spread on soil to increase fertility or fed to chickens to help them produce stronger eggshells. Limestone is also sometimes used as a pigment in industry, for example in producing whitewash.

The tendency of limestone to dissolve when in contact with rainwater and the ease with which it fractures causes large linear passageways, or joints, to develop. Below the surface, these joints permit water to move laterally and vertically, causing caves and karst topography to form. Although caves provide recreation to many, sinkholes are a hazard to landowners, especially in areas where these depressions tend to collapse catastrophically.

The joints in limestone also make it an excellent groundwater reservoir, or aquifer, and an excellent petroleum reservoir. In fact, about 50 percent of the world's petroleum is recovered from carbonate reservoirs, and carbonate rocks serve as a major source for groundwater in many parts of the world. However, joints may also allow groundwater supplies to become contaminated. Because water can flow easily and quickly from the surface down to an aquifer, the water may undergo little or no purification along the way. Therefore, people should exercise caution when using carbonate aquifers for domestic water supplies. This is especially true in areas where potential sources of pollution, such as septic tanks or landfills, overlie carbonate aquifers.

Bibliography

Brown, G. C., C. J. Hawkesworth, and R. C. L. Wilson, eds. *Understanding the Earth: A New Synthesis*. Cambridge, England: Cambridge University Press, 1992. Chapter 17, "Limestones Through Time," summarizes how limestone deposition, mineralogy, and diagenesis have changed through geologic time. Contains numerous small diagrams and photographs that help illustrate ideas presented in the text. A short bibliography of more advanced sources is included. Suitable for college-level readers.

Chesterman, C. W. *The Audubon Society Field Guide to North American Rocks and Minerals*. New York: Alfred A. Knopf, 1978. Well-written and organized, beautifully illustrated with color photographs, this is an excellent introduction to both rocks and minerals. Contains systematic descriptions of occurrences, chemical formulas, physical traits, and more. Also contains a mineral identification key, a glossary of terms, a short bibliography, and a list of localities from the text. Suitable for high-school readers.

Dougal, D. *The Practical Geologist*. New York: Simon & Schuster, 1992. An easy-to-read, well-illustrated book that covers all areas of geology at an introductory level. Related topics are presented in a methodical manner and are integrated with other concepts through illustrations and examples. Discusses the tools geologists use to investigate minerals, rocks, and fossils and how they use them. Contains a short glossary of terms. Suitable for high-school readers.

Grotzinger, J. P. "New Views of Old Carbonate Sediments." *Geotimes* 38 (September, 1993): 12-15. This short article discusses how ancient limestones, unlike modern ones that are produced primarily by organic activity, may contain evidence of inorganic carbonate production and a record of the development of carbonate-producing organisms. Suitable for college-level readers.

Prothero, D. R., and F. Schwab. *Sedimentary Geology: An Introduction to Sedimentary Rocks and Stratigraphy*. New York: W. H. Freeman, 1995. A thorough treatment of most aspects of sediments and sedimentary rocks. Well-illustrated with line drawings and black-and-white photographs, it also contains a comprehensive bibliography. Chapters 11 and 12 focus on carbonate rocks and limestone depositional processes and environments. Suitable for college-level readers.

Scholle, P. A., D. G. Bebout, and C. H. Moore. *Carbonate Depositional Environments, Memoir 33*. Tulsa: American Association of Petroleum Geologists, 1983. Well illustrated with color photographs, figures, and tables, this is an excellent treatment of limestone deposition. Each chapter covers a specific example of a different depositional environment and contains a general description of the physical traits of the environment and the limestones that form there, as well as a thorough bibliography for that environment. Suitable for college-level readers.

Wilson, J. L. *Carbonate Facies in Geologic History*. New York: Springer-Verlag, 1975. A comprehensive treatment of most aspects of limestone deposition throughout geologic time. Includes examples from a variety of environments and geographic locations. Contains many line drawings and black-and-white photographs, as well as a detailed bibliography. Suitable for college-level readers.

Clay D. Harris

Cross-References

MAGNETITE

Type of earth science: Geology
Field of study: Mineralogy

Magnetite is an iron oxide found in nature. Its dominant characteristic is its natural magnetism, and it is used as a raw material in the production of iron and steel. Magnetite occurs in many parts of the world, but it exists in unusually high concentrations in a few areas that support large mining operations.

Principal terms

FLOTATION: a method of separating pulverized ores by placing them in a solution in which some particles float and others sink

IRON OXIDE: a compound formed of the elements iron (Fe) and oxygen (O) in chemically stable combinations

MAGNETISM: the specific properties of a magnet, regarded as an effect of molecular interaction

MINERAL: a naturally occurring, homogeneous substance formed by inorganic processes and having a characteristic set of physical properties, a definite and limited range of chemical composition, and a molecular structure usually expressed in crystalline form

PELLETIZING: a method of rolling fine particles of iron ore under damp conditions into balls that are heated to become concentrated and durable

SINTERING: to make or become cohesive by the combined action of heat and pressure

TACONITE: an inferior grade of iron ore found in the Mesabi district in Minnesota, consisting of a very hard chert

Summary of the Phenomenon

Magnetite has several physical "signatures" that make it readily identifiable. To the eye, it is black and opaque, with a dull or metallic luster. Its most notable feature, however, is its natural magnetism, which distinguishes it among other metal minerals. A fine sliver of magnetite placed on water will float because of surface tension and will invariably move so that it has a north-south alignment, like a compass needle. It derives its magnetic properties from an internal flow of electrons, which produces magnetism just as magnetism, in reverse, produces electricity in electric generators. A molecule of magnetite contains two different ions of iron, which are located in two specific sites; this arrangement causes a transfer of electrons between the different irons in a structured path, or vector. This electric vector generates the magnetic field.

Magnetism can be induced by a magnetic field such that particular minerals are more susceptible than others. A few minerals have much stronger positive suscepti-bilites than others and may also exhibit a magnetism that remains after the magnetic field has been removed. These minerals are termed "magnetic" or, more correctly, "ferromagnetic." This characteristic has strong application in the concentration of magnetite iron ores.

Magnetite is an iron-oxide mineral. Iron is the world's most widely used metal and constitutes about 5 percent of the earth's crust. Precambrian iron-bearing deposits are distributed worldwide. They are found in the Lake Superior region of North America, in South America, in India, and in Sweden. The definition of an "iron formation," as deposits are known, is typically a chemical sediment, usually thin-bedded or laminated, containing 15 percent or more iron of sedimentary origin, commonly but not necessarily containing layers of chert. However, few iron-ore deposits containing less than 25 percent iron would be considered as commercial unless they existed in large amounts and could be concentrated to higher percentages of iron very inexpensively.

Two major sources of iron have been postulated. The first is the decomposition of rocks during weathering. The second is volcanic activity, from which the iron is obtained from magmatic emissions or contact of lava and seawater. For some time, it was assumed that a combination of these activities would be necessary for the very large accumulations of iron-bearing deposits observed. Later investigations of weathering under certain tropical or subtropical conditions have shown that there would be sufficient volumes of materials produced by weathering alone, without the necessity for the assistance of igneous activities.

Iron in solution is precipitated as various compounds, or facies, including oxide, silicate, carbonate, and sulfide. The oxide facies is subdivided into two parts: hematite-banded (nonmagnetic) and magnetite-banded (magnetic). The deposits of magnetite in North America are thought by some scientists to have been metamorphosed to a certain extent, although other opinions maintain that they are entirely sedimentary in origin. However, most authorities believe that a combination of metamorphism and sedimentation is responsible for magnetite and other iron-oxide formations that occur in nature.

Magnetite is the dominant iron-oxide mineral in what is referred to as "taconite" in the Mesabi range, or district, of Minnesota. The Mesabi is about 110 miles long and about 1.5 miles wide, having iron ore thicknesses between 400 and 750 feet. Characteristics of individual ore bodies in the Mesabi are lengths of up to 3.5 miles, widths from 0.5 to 1.0 miles, and thicknesses of 500 feet. Most of the world's magnetite is produced in the Mesabi and is thought to have been formed as a result of metamorphism and sedimentation. In mining parlance, "taconite" denotes an unenriched iron-oxide formation; it is characteristically a very hard material because of its high silica content.

There is a fundamental difference in a magnetite "reserve" and a magnetite "resource." Every deposit is classified as a resource, while reserves are only those deposits that can be extracted and utilized using current guidelines of technology, price, and cost. The commitment of funds for the development of magnetite reserves depends on the reliable estimation of recoverable deposits under current economic conditions. These estimates are used to predict the life of the mine and its cash flow and to project the manner and time in which the reserve will be extracted. The low-grade magnetic taconites of the Mesabi range in northeastern Minnesota are near the surface and typical of gently dipping ore bodies that can be assessed from ground and aerial surveys. These deposits have broad areal extent and usually have long productive lives.

Both conventional and computer methods are used in determining these magnetite reserves. In the conventional method, topographic maps are made from ground or aerial surveys. Cross sections are drawn to accommodate existing drill-hole patterns and extensions. Geologic information and test data are added to the cross sections, and the configuration and stratigraphic layering of the magnetite ore body are determined. For each drill hole, the minable taconite layer or layers are determined from core analyses or well logs (electrocardiograms for rocks), and the ore-to-waste ratio is calculated and compared to the cutoff-stripping ratio. This second ratio is the maximum amount of waste material that can be excavated and handled while still permitting economical operation. Incomplete data usually dictate the drilling of additional exploratory holes, which becomes a tug-of-war in maximizing data while minimizing expenses.

Using data from mining, metallurgical, and economic studies, a mining plan is developed that includes an approximation of the open-pit outline. Cross sections are prepared to include as much of the pit as possible. The information in these cross sections is weighted for influence, and an overall stripping ratio for the pit is determined. The pit outline is then adjusted to accommodate the overall stripping ratio, and refined economics using the current pit design are generated to determine profitability and directions for proceeding with the mine.

The computer method uses a series of computer programs to transform topographic elevations, drill-hole data, and geologic information into a three-dimensional model of the deposit and then performs calculations, as was done manually in the conventional method. In either method, these data are used to make formal proposals regarding funding sources, property leasing, equipment selection, and manpower requirements. In practice, both conventional and computer methods are used in determining these magnetite reserves.

Methods of Study

The taconite deposits of the Mesabi region of Lake Superior offer a typical example of the method of mining the dense magnetite ore. Very large open-pit excavations are deepened and widened from the surface through the use of blasting and bulk materials handling. The dense and abrasive nature of the deposit requires the use of wear-resistant drills and even flame drilling, a process called "jet piercing." Jet piercing is similar to using a blowtorch to burn a hole into the deposit through the differential expansion (spalling) of the silica and iron and the use of compressed air to expel the spalled material to the surface. The high cost associated with jet piercing, together with improvements in percussive drilling, has tended to render jet-piercing equipment obsolete.

The blast-hole drills are set up on benches, or flat areas, around the periphery of the open pit so that the blasted material will be expelled into the bottom of the pit. After drilling is performed to a depth just below the height of the bench, explosives are loaded into the hole for blasting. Either dynamite or a mixture of ammonium nitrate and fuel oil can be used as an explosive. The blasted material is loaded by power shovel or mobile loaders into large trucks having capacities between 80 and 200 tons for transportation out of the pit. Operations involving the mining of the raw magnetite are simple and straightforward. The problems center on equipment wear, operating cost, and economy of scale.

The Empire Mine, located in the Mesabi range and operated by the Cleveland-Cliffs Iron Company, is typical of large magnetite-producing operations. This mine has the capacity to produce more than 8 million tons per year of high-grade iron-ore pellets from a low-grade, magnetic ore. The pellets, containing about 65 percent iron, are sold to blast furnaces throughout the Great Lakes region.

The mine area, including open pits, waste stockpiles, tailing basins, water reservoirs, and pellet plant, covers 13,500 acres and extends over more than 50 square miles. In 1989, more than 62 million tons of material were removed from the active mining areas, including 26 million tons of iron ore. About 8 million tons of pellets were produced from this volume of iron ore. The mine is designed to operate 365 days per year. Total employment is more than 1,200 personnel, of whom about half are employed directly in pit operations and maintenance.

The magnetite ore grades within the minable zone vary from a low of 13 percent (the minimum, or cutoff, grade) to a high of 32 percent. The average mill feed in 1989 was about 23 percent magnetite. Mining is scheduled carefully to insure a uniform mill feed, and decisions are made as to cutoff waste percentages to determine whether certain material should be mined separately or included in the mill feed along with the iron ore.

Exploration drilling totaling more than 250,000 feet has been done on a 300-foot-by-300-foot grid pattern. This drilling has proved a reserve exceeding 787 million tons of magnetite ore. The mine is expected to last approximately 28 years.

Production drilling is performed with large, track-mounted rotary drills using bits between 10 and 16 inches in diameter, with the larger-diameter hole used to load blasting material. These drills are electric-powered, and the power is carried through trailing cables up to 5,000 feet in length. The average drilling rate is about 50 feet per hour.

Approximately 60 percent of the holes are loaded with bulk ammonium nitrate-fuel oil (ANFO) explosive and the balance with aluminized emulsions. Emulsions are primarily used in wet holes. Blast holes are fired with millisecond delays to improve efficiency. Electric shovels load the blasted material into trucks, which are dispatched by a computerized program to maximize utilization.

The magnetite ore is crushed, then ground to a powder. This material is upgraded by magnetic separators and flotation, then thickened and conveyed to a pelletizing mill, where it is balled and indurated in kilns at temperatures up to 2,300 degrees

Fahrenheit. The pellets are cooled and stockpiled for shipment. Tailings (waste materials) are pumped to a 3,050-acre impoundment, where the water is decanted, processed, and returned to the pellet mill for reuse.

Context

Considering that typical Mesabi taconite has an iron concentration less than 50 percent, the conversion of these raw ores to a product greater than 50 percent iron and without objectionable impurities is the greatest problem facing iron-ore producers. Typically, most iron ores are priced on a basis that they contain at least 51.50 percent iron at a specified "natural" moisture content.

Magnetite ore in its natural form is associated with waste materials, often silicates. The ore must be subdivided in order to liberate the magnetite and thus increase the iron concentration of the ore. Several concentration techniques are available, depending on the nature of the association of magnetite and its "gangue," or waste material, as well as the nature of the waste materials themselves. Common methods make use of physical and chemical properties of magnetite.

Common magnetite ore is sufficiently heavy that the magnetite, with a specific gravity of 5.1, can be easily separated from the relatively less heavy waste materials, which have specific gravities around 2.6. Heavy media separators using a ferrosilicon suspension in a rotary drum are most common for coarse particles. For medium-sized particles, heavy media separators using a magnetite suspension in hydraulic cyclones are used. For fine particles, machines known as "Humphreys spirals" are normally used; these machines use the tangential velocity differences between materials of different specific gravities to separate them.

Magnetite can also be separated from its waste material by using a low-intensity magnetic field. Such separation is inexpensive, because the process is very simple. Either electromagnets or permanent magnets can be used with equal efficiency. Rotary-drum separators utilizing permanent magnets are favored in this process, as permanent magnets provide freedom from electrical maintenance that is inherent in electromagnets.

Magnetite can also be concentrated by froth flotation, a process whereby the fine magnetite ore clings to bubbles formed by mixing a chemical reagent into water or a hydrocarbon, then frothing it. Froth flotation can be used to separate magnetite ores from waste material or to upgrade low-quality ore. Magnetite is also separated by cationic flotation, a process in which cationic reagents, often amines, are used as a medium for separation. In this process, the free quartz and locked quartz-magnetic particles are carried away from the free magnetite grains. The floated product can then be reground and reconcentrated magnetically. This process is carried out on a large scale by large batteries of flotation cells.

The process of blasting, loading, transporting, crushing, and grinding necessary to remove magnetite ore from its natural habitat and concentrate it for sale produces a considerable amount of dust-sized fine material, or "fines." Fines, if not utilized as sale material, can severely affect the profitability of a magnetite-concentration process. Blast furnaces are the usual endpoint for the magnetite concentrate. Such furnaces do not tolerate fine material very well, and thus a uniform-sized material without fines is necessary as feed material. It is necessary to utilize fines in a cost-effective manner, and this is done by agglomerating, whereby the fine material is pressed into various shapes by a variety of equipment.

The term "pelletizing" in the minerals industry refers to processes whereby the fines concentrate is rolled in a damp condition into balls that can be fired or indurated until they become hard. Fine-size ore concentrates are usually pelletized at the mine and shipped as pellets to the steel plant, although pelletizing processes are frequently constructed near transportation points, particularly in the Great Lakes region. Pellets are usually greater than $3/8$ inch in diameter. A common practice in some areas producing natural high-grade ores is to screen the ore at the mine to about $3/8$ inch, with the oversized material used for blast-furnace feed. The undersized material may be shipped for use as fines, pelletized at the mill site, or pelletized at the mine and shipped as pellets by the ore carrier. Pelletizing virtually revolutionized iron mining in North America. Although pelletizing had been known and pilot plants constructed before 1920, it was the exhaustion of the higher grades of ore that caused it to be reevaluated in the late 1940's. A decade later, pelletizing was firmly established as a normal operating practice in the Lake Superior iron ranges. Not only did pelletizing permit the economic use of ore fines, it prevented these fines from becoming stream sediments and therefore detrimental to the environment.

Magnetite ore fines may also be concentrated by the sintering process. In this process, the ore fines are mixed with fine carbonaceous material called "coke breeze," then fed on a moving bed grate across a heat source so that the coke breeze combusts and partially fuses the ore fines. The sintered product traveling off the end of the grate is crushed and sized for shipment to the blast furnace.

Since magnetite ore is a relatively inexpensive commodity, its transportation can frequently exceed the cost of mining and processing the ore. For effective commercial exploitation, therefore, it is necessary to find low-cost transportation, and this usually means that some form of bulk shipment on water is made. Typical are ocean-going vessels of 200,000 tons capacity that effect economies of scale over smaller vessels requiring about the same number of crewmembers.

Recent developments in ore transportation include the shipping of magnetite fines with enough moisture to bind them in the ship's hold but not enough to cause them to be fluid. After arrival at the destination, the mass is re-pulped by the addition of moisture and agitation, then pumped from the vessel to a dewatering facility onshore for pelletizing or sintering. Besides saving a costly dewatering operation at the shipping point, the cargo is shipped dust-free and can be unloaded at a reduced cost as compared to dry unloading operations.

Bibliography

Bateman, Alan M., ed. *Economic Geology*. Urbana, Ill.: Economic Geology Publishing, 1955. A classic text, often referenced by more recent writers. Discusses many of the principles of economic geology used today.

Kennedy, Bruce A. *Surface Mining*. Littleton, Colo.: Society of Mining, Metallurgical, and Exploration Engineers, 1990. A comprehensive treatment of the surface mining profession, including detailed descriptions of all phases of this endeavor. Case studies are mixed with topical descriptions. Extensive references are cited in the book.

Lamey, Carl L. *Metallic and Industrial Mineral Deposits*. New York: McGraw Hill, 1966. A comprehensive treatment of mineral formation and utilization. Includes a description of the formation of iron minerals, including magnetite, as well as all other known industrial minerals.

Tarling, D. H., and F. Hrouda. *The Magnetic Anisotropy of Rocks*. New York: Chapman & Hall, 1993. A complex book intended for use as a textbook at the college level or for reference by the practicing professional. An exhaustive treatment of a complicated and little-known phenomenon. Contains an extensive reference list.

Weiss, Norman L. *SME Mineral Processing Handbook*. New York: Society of Mining, Metallurgical, and Petroleum Engineers, 1985. This two-volume set provides a detailed description of mineral processing systems, equipment, and case studies. This is an advanced treatment of the subject of mineral preparation, but it is well illustrated and can be understood by the layperson.

Charles D. Haynes

Cross-References

Aluminum Deposits, 46; Iron Deposits, 1254; Meteorites: Nickel-Irons, 1652; Meteorites: Stony Irons, 1659; Mineral Supply, 2995; Mining Wastes and Reclamation, 1718; Physical Properties of Minerals, 1681; Rock Magnetism, 2217; Sedimentary Mineral Deposits, 2296; Surface Mining Techniques, 1703; Underground Mining Techniques, 1710.

MINERAL SUPPLY

Type of earth science: Economic geology
Field of study: Exploration geophysics

The mineral supply of any area—the entire earth, a nation, or small local place—is a function of the interaction between geology and the human definition of natural resources. Economic minerals, as natural resources of the earth's crust, require geologic processes to concentrate elements and compounds to proportions that are technologically and economically feasible to recover for human use.

Principal terms

BENEFICIATION: the concentration or purification of a mineral from an ore or rock as it is recovered from a mine

CLARKE: the average percentage content of an element in the earth's solid crust, which is roughly forty kilometers thick under mountains and only a few kilometers thick under ocean basins

HIGH-GRADING/LOW-GRADING: informal terms used to describe the mining practice of focusing on the richest or poorest part of a deposit

METALLOGENIC PROVINCES AND EPOCHS: provinces are regions of the earth's crust where particular ores have been deposited preferentially; epochs are the periods in geologic time when this occurred

ORE: a rock or concentration within a rock of a desirable substance that may be recovered profitably; the term originally referred to metals but has been extended to include industrial minerals

RECYCLING: the reuse of scrap or discarded minerals (chiefly metals) in mineral processing

RESERVES: economically recoverable minerals that have been identified by exploration in the earth's crust

RESOURCES: the total quantity of a mineral in the crust, including identified but subeconomic deposits and those deposits that are as yet undiscovered but are suspected to exist

STRATIFORM/NONSTRATIFORM: terms referring to the shape or form of mineral deposits and enriched zones: Stratiform deposits are large, continuous beds; nonstratiform deposits are small and discontinuous, as in veins or pods

SUBSTITUTION: the replacement of one mineral with another or with a nonmineral substance for some of a mineral's functions or uses

Summary of the Phenomenon

All economic minerals are the result of natural concentration by geologic processes of an element or compound that has been found to be useful and that can be recovered from the earth. The earth may be considered to be "neutral stuff" until both a need and the ability to utilize some portion of its materials coexist. What humans find useful changes with time and circumstances; some particular neutral stuff becomes a resource, while something else passes from usefulness and reverts to neutral stuff. Aluminum was little more than a laboratory curiosity until well into the twentieth century, despite the fact that its clarke, or degree of commonness in the earth's crust, ranks right behind oxygen and silicon (which combine to form silicates, far and away the most common rock type). Aluminum became a resource when humans found its physical properties useful and developed the technology of recovering it from earth materials. Flint was perhaps the most useful earth material throughout most of early human history, because its hardness was so valuable in making tools and weapon points. The development of metallurgy retired flint to a museum curiosity, and it is no longer an essential resource of humankind.

Human history is filled with similar stories that affect mineral supply; more often, though, it is not an element or compound itself that goes into or out of favor but rather the kinds of ore or deposits from which that mineral is recovered. Two sorts of technological advance are required to effect these changes: One is the scientific knowledge of type, form, and occurrence of deposits, together with the engineering advances in mining technology required to wrest the substance from the crust economically. The other advance lies in the manipulation of the substance as it comes from the earth; usually, a substance must be beneficiated to improve its properties or to increase the percentage of the desired element in the mineral. Metals rarely occur in nature as elements, placer deposits of the precious metals being the chief exception. Iron, for example, occurs mostly as oxides, silicates, carbonates, and sulfides; the oxygen, silicon, carbon, or sulfur must be removed in the beneficiation, milling, and refining process to increase the purity of iron. The relatively pure iron is then recombined with other elements to create the special characteristics modern industry desires, as alloys (including carbon steel, in which the amount of carbon is controlled by metallurgy).

Minerals are generally classified as metals, fuels, and industrial minerals (to call them "nonmetals" and "nonfuels" is cumbersome, although the use of the term "industrial" is confusing, as all minerals are used in industry; moreover, some industrial minerals are, chemically, metals, but they lack the strength and ductility that humans require from metals). In terms of world production and of potential supplies, industrial minerals are far and away the most important. Construction minerals account for the bulk of these, as aggregates, cement, and clays. Although construction materials usually require some beneficiation, it is generally of a minor nature; sand and gravel, for example, can be simply washed and sorted. Quality requirements of construction minerals are not especially severe, but they do exist. Iron content is frequently the impurity to be excised or avoided; iron oxidizes or rusts when exposed to the atmosphere, thus weakening the construction. Construction aggregates include sand and gravel as well as simple crushed rock, particularly limestone or granite. These are among the most common earth materials found at or near the surface, and while they are not spatially ubiquitous, their very bulk demands that they not be transported long distances. Large, expanding urban centers may exhaust local deposits, but otherwise there is little concern about future supplies.

Following the construction minerals in terms of quantity mined are the fuel minerals coal and oil. These are hydrocarbons, and neither hydrogen nor carbon appears near the top of the list in clarke, the percentage measure of the earth's crust composed of these elements. It would seem, therefore, that they might be rare, but they are found in tremendous quantities in the uppermost kilometer of crust, thus their clarkes are deceiving. The Industrial Revolution was built on coal and iron; oil is a twentieth-century phenomenon and will be shorter-lived in terms of potential supplies. It is not exaggeration to state that oil has been the most important mineral of recent decades, not only because of its contribution to human mobility but also because its availability has permitted industrialization to proceed rapidly in regions lacking significant coal and iron. Much more coal than oil exists in the earth's crust; coal is also is easier to find and easier to exploit. This is because it is stratiform—that is, it occurs as a strata or layer of rock. Determining the size of reserves—the amount of a mineral still in place that has been identified for future use—is significantly simpler for coal than for oil or most metals. Once a coal strata is located, usually because it crops out at the surface, it is a simple task to drill boreholes to determine its extent, quantity, and character.

Oil is also sedimentary material and has been concentrated naturally in environments that are similar to those of coal. However, oil and natural gas are fluids and thus move through the pores of rocks until they concentrate in reservoirs, called "pools" or "fields." Therefore, although oil and gas are found in sedimentary strata, they are more elusive than most stratiform deposits. Models of exploration and estimates of future probable supplies have been created more for petroleum than for other minerals; this reflects both oil's relative difficulty of exploration and its importance to modern society. In connection with petroleum, the terms "reserves" and "resources" as employed by mineral economists reflect circumstances; "reserves" indicates highly probable sources, while "resources" denotes all sources that might exist in the crust hypothetically. Reserves are said to be economically recoverable under present or foreseeable circumstances. Resources, on the other hand, can require significant technological advances to become viable sources for exploitation. It should be noted that the term "resources" as employed in most other economic contexts (in short, in most discussions of natural resources) is quite the opposite of the mineral connotation; "resources" are economic in most nonmineral discussions.

That being noted, it is clear that a knowledge of oil and gas deposits and reserves requires an understanding of their geologic conditions of occurrence. Success in the first decades of exploration required only a rather elementary knowledge of geologic structure and accompanying sedimentary rocks. After the easiest-to-locate pools and fields were exploited, the process became significantly more demanding of new technology; searching for an elusive pool of fluid thousands of feet down in the crust required sophisticated geophysical techniques. Compared to most other minerals, petroleum is geologically more recent. While some supplies have been recovered from

Paleozoic rocks hundreds of thousands of years in age, the largest deposits and the greatest reserves are found in much younger geologic terranes, especially in coastal environments only a few million or tens of millions of years old. Exploration has pushed offshore to seek these environments, frequently with conflict emanating from environmental concerns. In many instances, environmental activists have blocked effective exploration and development in promising geologic environments, placing a political constraint upon complete knowledge of the potential supplies of these commodities.

Metals and the less-common industrial minerals, with the exception of iron ore, are produced in much smaller quantities than either construction materials or fuels. This reflects their lower clarkes, for the most part, which in turn is an indication of more unusual geologic circumstances of concentration and the greater difficulties encountered both in exploration and in determining potential supplies. In this context, political geography is more important than it is with regard to the more common minerals, with the exception of oil. In other words, because these minerals are less common, it is less likely that the territories of smaller nations will include significant deposits. In any listing of mineral supply, the largest nations dominate; the larger the nation, the greater the probability that it will include within its borders the variety of geologic conditions that have created the concentrations that yield a variety of mineral deposits. Even fairly mundane industrial minerals such as fertilizers, salts, and clays require special geologic conditions to produce concentrations of a purity that permits economic recovery of the commodity. Salts and gypsum are evaporites; that is, they remain as solids after sea or lake waters have evaporated. Phosphates and other fertilizers are usually derived from sedimentary rocks of a somewhat unusual composition, which are consequently less common spatially. Clays concentrate in place as a residuum of chemical weathering of a variety of rocks; bauxite, the source of most aluminum metal, is a close cousin. This type of weathering is most effective in tropical climates, which do not have to be current; that is, past tropical climates have left bauxite and clay deposits in what are presently subtropical or midlatitude climates.

Metals pose the greatest problems in mineral supply. They occur naturally in the lowest clarkes and require the greatest concentrations in order to become economically recoverable as an ore. Most metals occur in a variety of circumstances, increasing the possibility that elements of which the richest deposits have been exhausted may still be recovered, perhaps as by-products of the mining of other metals from leaner or chemically more complicated circumstances. The richest deposits are most commonly nonstratiform, as veins, pods, and small inclusions. These deposits are often associated with mountain-building and the shifts occurring with the movements of continental crustal plates. Fluids may be pressed through the pores of rocks for hundreds of miles by plate tectonics, increasing the probability that the fluids' routes will collect and concentrate useful metals, depositing them in attractive environments such as limestone strata. This is a recent hypothesis for the formation of Mississippi Valley-type lead and zinc deposits, some of the world's richest. As a general rule, the richest deposits were discovered and exploited first, with leaner ores requiring the development of more sophisticated technology. This is the case with copper, one of the first metals placed in service by humans during the Bronze Age. The expansion of European settlement worldwide during the nineteenth century, coupled with the rapid rise of the Industrial Revolution, led to a virtual explosion of copper, lead, zinc, gold, and silver mining. These five metals frequently occur in association with one another, so that, for example, a prospector seeking silver may often end up with a rich lead ore. The richest lodes were discovered and exploited by the turn of the twentieth century, and the format and location of the major metallogenic provinces was well established. Leaner ores, including porphyry deposits, occurred in these same provinces and became the targets for exploitation as soon as the requisite technology was developed. Porphyry ores range downward to exceptionally lean, with by-products often making the difference in whether or not the mine would be profitable.

High-grading, or the skimming of the richest portion of a deposit, was common early in mining history. Low-grading, or deliberately mixing lower-grade with higher-grade ores in order to extend the life of the deposit, became common with the use of porphyry ores. Iron ore has had a more complex history, ranging from exploitation of small high-grade and low-grade ore bodies during the early days of the Industrial Revolution to a focus on high-grade Lake Superior ores in the latter part of the nineteenth century. This drove the exploiters of the small, low-grade deposits out of business. Exhaustion of the high-grade ores in the Lake Superior district forced a turn to lower-grade silicate deposits, which required costly beneficiation. Worldwide, high-grade banded-iron formations similar to those of Lake Superior remain, as well as extensive deposits of lower-grade ore. Recycling extends the life of iron deposits and those of most other metals. When possible, the substitution of one metal for a scarcer one, or of nonmetallic minerals for metals, promises to further extend mineral supply.

Methods of Study

Up to the end of the bonanza period of metals mining, around 1900, prospectors were inclined to scoff at the notion that academically trained geologists were required to discover new deposits; the high-grade finds they had developed up to that point required only the practical geologic knowledge they had accumulated in their careers. Much the same situation existed in the petroleum industry: The geology of the early, higher-grade deposits was comparatively simple. As lower-grade ores began to be sought following depletion of the highest-grade deposits, however, more complex knowledge was required. The ensuing century has seen an expansion of required information encompassing all branches of geology, and the blooming of two essentially new fields: geophysics, which aids in understanding subsurface rock structures, and geochemistry, which studies not only the chemical makeup of the ores, but the chemistry of earth materials that may serve as keys to future locations for development.

Economic geology is essentially applied geochemistry, rather than economics. Increasingly, determinations of mineral supply depend not merely upon the earth sciences but have become multidisciplinary. Engineering expertise is called upon not only to aid in decisions regarding the mining process itself but, especially, to develop technology that permits exploitation of lower-grade deposits. Biology has become significant, particularly in the quest for enhanced production of petroleum deposits. Economics and mathematical and statistical methods are essential in predictive models of future mineral supply, as well as in determining the probability of successful exploitation of a particular site.

Context

The ultimate limiting factor in mineral supply is that mineral deposits in concentrations rich enough to be not only economically attractive but also technologically feasible to recover are finite, at least in terms of the scale of geologic time. Many of the most important mineral deposits were created by geologic processes and conditions that no longer exist or that occur on a time scale that is profoundly longer than human life spans. This fact sets minerals apart from other natural resources. Humans may degrade land resources or cut forests, but these may be re-created or conserved. Conservation enters the mineral picture in the case of recycling, but there are always losses in the process, and eventually the desired element becomes too dispersed to be recoverable. Substitution is another savior; metals may be replaced by far more common materials, assuming that technology is up to the challenge.

To the extent that humankind continues to utilize the presently most important minerals, including iron, aluminum, copper, zinc, and other metals as well as fossil fuels, there are two overriding limiting factors. First, particularly for metals, is the limitation imposed by increasing energy costs as leaner and leaner ores are exploited, approaching the clarke of the elements rather than the rich concentrations that have supported industrialization to this point in time. The second limitation concerns technological development: Specifically, will it keep pace? Optimists point out that it always has; indeed, technology frequently expands or improves at a pace faster than the economy, and certainly faster than absolutely necessary for human survival. In this context, the role of rewards in the development of new technology cannot be overlooked. With the collapse or retrenchment of centrally-planned societies in the latter portion of the twentieth century, altruistic rewards seem less efficient than economic ones, raising social and political issues that philosophers, politicians, and, ultimately, society itself will have to decide.

A considerable body of opinion exists that suggests that the environmental degradation accompanying mineral exploitation represents the greatest limitation globally to continued or expanded industrialization. A certain amount of pollution or degradation of landscapes in the process of mining is inevitable, however great the strides made in reclaiming landscapes after miners have finished with them. Air pollution from beneficiation and refining of minerals, as well as oil spills from transporting fluids from production sites to markets, have captured public attention. These are controllable, but at a cost. More insidious and difficult to solve is the question of the role in global warming of carbon dioxide from fossil-fuel burning. This raises the specter of increased future dependence upon nuclear sources, however unpopular that choice is to many, or of increased development of alternative energy sources, which at the present state of development appear to be incapable of meeting society's energy requirements, especially if society is to remain as mobile as it has become in the twentieth century. Once again, improved technology will be required to solve these problems, with environmental regulation as the policing and driving factor.

Thus, issues determining future mineral supply assume an increasingly political bent, from local "not in my backyard" considerations to national and global decisions. The interrelationships of environmental regulation to globalizing industry are frequently straightforward; less stringent environmental regulations in developing economies encourage a shift of industry to these environments. In order to compete with lower-cost new locations, established industry is likely to turn to a form of high-grading. Mining may well follow suit, thus abandoning a considerable portion of the leaner resources that might be recoverable under a policy of low-grading. In the final analysis, mineral supply may be more a function of national and global political decisions and trends than of geologic constraints or technological developments.

Bibliography

Blunden, John. *Mineral Resources and Their Management*. London: Longman, 1985. Good coverage of world mineral production, including maps of distribution of production, which remain useful even though the relative importance of mining districts changes rapidly. Suitable for the college-level reader.

Brookins, Douglas G. *Mineral and Energy Resources: Occurrence, Exploitation, and Environmental Impact*. New York: Merrill, 1990. A nontechnical introduction to the occurrence of minerals and the factors involved in their recovery, including a discussion of world reserves. Suitable for the college-level reader.

Evans, Anthony M. *Ore Geology and Industrial Minerals: An Introduction*. 3d ed. Oxford: Blackwell, 1993. Chapter 1 on mineral economics and chapters 23 and 24 on metallogenic provinces and epochs are useful for the college-level reader, although the text is somewhat technical and assumes a knowledge of geology.

U.S. Department of the Interior. Bureau of Mines. *Minerals Yearbook*. Washington, D.C.: U.S. Government Printing Office, 1994. The standard reference, published annually, on U.S. and world production of nonfuel minerals. Earlier editions include useful information on new technology and other factors affecting production. Suitable for the general reader.

Vogely, William A., ed. *Economics of the Mineral Industries*. 4th ed. New York: American Institute of Mining, Metallurgical, and Petroleum Engineers, 1985. A comprehensive treatment of mineral economics, mineral models, and the industry. Intended for professionals in the field, it is frequently highly technical, but provides insight at greater depth than other references.

Wolfe, John A. *Mineral Resources: A World Review*. New York: Chapman and Hall, 1984. A somewhat dated but breezily interesting analysis, and a significant reference for its treatment of the world's major mineral commodities. Suitable for the college-level reader.

World Resources Institute. *World Resources, 1990-91*. New York: Oxford University Press, 1990. A biennial review, concentrating more upon energy sources than other minerals. Section 21 includes useful tables on energy, materials, and wastes. Suitable for the general reader.

Neil E. Salisbury

Cross-References

Earth Resources, 2175; Future Resources, 2182; Industrial Metals, 1216; Industrial Nonmetals, 1225; Mining Wastes and Reclamation, 1718; Oil and Gas Exploration, 1878; Strategic Resources, 2188; The Worldwide Distribution of Oil and Gas, 1923.

MISSION TO PLANET EARTH

Type of earth science: Remote sensing
Field of study: Large solar system bodies

Mission to Planet Earth is a long-term study of Earth. The project uses Earth-orbiting satellites to monitor the interactions between the atmosphere, the oceans, the solid planet, and the radiation from the Sun, with the objective of determining how these interactions influence the global climate.

Principal terms

AEROSOLS: very small particles of solid or liquid that are suspended in a gas such as the earth's atmosphere

GLOBAL WARMING: a long-term trend in which the average surface temperature of Earth is increasing

GREENHOUSE EFFECT: warming of the surface and lower atmosphere of a planet because of the presence of molecules in the atmosphere that transmit the Sun's radiation to the surface but reflect or absorb the infrared light emitted by the surface, trapping the Sun's energy

OZONE: a molecule consisting of three oxygen atoms

OZONE LAYER: a layer in the atmosphere, at a height of about twenty to thirty miles altitude, where atmospheric ozone absorbs the ultraviolet light from the Sun, shielding Earth's surface from this radiation

REMOTE SENSING: a technique by which some physical property is measured at a location different from the location of the instrument performing the measurement

STRATOSPHERE: the upper region of the atmosphere, generally above the region where weather occurs

TROPOSPHERE: the lowest and densest layer of Earth's atmosphere, the layer in which most of the planet's weather occurs

Summary of the Phenomenon

The National Aeronautics and Space Administration (NASA) is participating in the U.S. Global Change Research Program, an interagency research program to document and understand both natural and human-induced global change, through its Mission to Planet Earth program. The program employs a series of Earth-observation satellites to monitor the chemical composition, reflectivity, and other important properties of the planet's atmosphere, land, and oceans. The information thus gathered will allow researchers to document any changes and to observe patterns and interrelationships between such changes and the agents that cause them. It is the first coordinated effort to measure the interactions of the solid Earth, its atmosphere, and its oceans simultaneously.

Mission to Planet Earth is a recognition that Earth's climate is controlled by a complex interplay of factors. The atmosphere, the oceans, the land, and the biological activity on Earth all interact to produce changes in the global environment. For example, dust particles carried into the atmosphere absorb solar radiation, thus contributing to a warming of the planet—but those same dust particles can serve as condensation nuclei for clouds, which reflect sunlight back into space, giving rise to a cooling effect. Which effect is greater is the subject of debate; the answer may depend on the size, chemical composition, and altitude of the dust.

Humankind, in its efforts to improve the quality of life, may be altering the global climatic balance in ways that are not well understood. Industrial activity and the clearing of forested land for agricultural expansion may be altering the chemical composition and the abundance of aerosols in the atmosphere. Modeling of the atmosphere suggests these factors may give rise to "global warming" and the opening of an "ozone hole" stretching from the poles toward the equator, both of which have the potential for adversely affecting the habitability of the planet. Mission to Planet Earth will attempt to determine the extent to which the composition and aerosol concentration of the atmosphere is changing and to monitor the consequences of those changes.

A stratospheric layer of ozone, a molecule consisting of three oxygen atoms bonded together, absorbs much of the ultraviolet light emitted by the Sun, shielding the surface of Earth from this ultraviolet radiation. The continued habitability of Earth depends on maintaining the ozone layer, since the exposure of the skin to ultraviolet light has been implicated as a major cause of skin cancer. In 1985, the British Antarctic Survey announced the discovery of a large hole in the ozone layer over the South Pole. Since that time, modeling of the chemical reactions that take place in the atmosphere has suggested that the release of chlorofluorocarbons, such as the Freon used in air conditioning and refrigeration systems, may be responsible for the destruction of ozone in the upper atmosphere. NASA has monitored atmospheric ozone concentrations since 1978, using an instrument installed on the Nimbus-7 weather satellite. Mission to Planet Earth will continue to monitor ozone concentrations and will also attempt to determine the concentrations of the molecules that attack the ozone.

The balance between the solar radiation that strikes Earth and the energy radiated back into space determines the planet's temperature. Short-term variations in this energy balance provide local sources, or "sinks," of energy, driving the circulation of the ocean and the atmosphere. Long-term variations in this energy balance can bring about global warming or global cooling. Atmospheric modeling indicates that the abundance of carbon dioxide in the atmosphere exerts a controlling influence of this radiation balance through the "greenhouse effect." The radiation emitted by the Sun is strongest in the visible region of the spectrum, while the radiation Earth emits peaks in the infrared. Thus, if gases that transmit visible light but reflect or absorb infrared light are injected into the upper atmosphere, then the energy carried by sunlight will reach the ground; the energy reradiated by Earth, however, will be trapped, resulting in an increase in the average global temperature. Collectively, gases that have these properties are called "greenhouse gases," and an objective of the Mission to Planet Earth is to monitor the abundances of greenhouse gases and determine their sources.

The presence of aerosols and dust, particles ranging from one-billionth of a meter to one-hundred-thousandth of a meter in size, in the upper atmosphere also affects Earth's temperature. These particles scatter or absorb radiation from the Sun. If the particles are black, as is the case for the carbonaceous particles associated with sulfur emissions from the burning of coal and oil fuels, they can warm Earth by absorbing the Sun's radiation. Models indicate that concentrations of soot particles from terrestrial emissions could warm Earth by as much as 2 degrees Celsius. However, aerosols also serve as condensation nuclei for the formation of clouds, and these clouds can reflect sunlight back into space, resulting in a cooling effect.

The concentrations of aerosols in Earth's atmosphere are known to vary significantly over time. These particles come from a number of sources. The dominant aerosol in the upper atmosphere is sulfur dioxide, released by the burning of fossil fuels. However, other mechanisms contribute aerosols as well. Sulfides, released by biological activity in the oceans, provide a natural background level of sulfur aerosols in the atmosphere, which would remain even if the emissions from fossil fuels ceased. Volcanoes also inject dust and aerosols high into the atmosphere. Models indicate that major volcanic eruptions alter the radiation properties of the atmosphere for five years or more after an eruption. Determination of the sources, abundances, colors or reflectivities, and efficiencies with which these aerosol and dust particles serve as cloud nucleation sites is a major objective of the Mission to Planet Earth program.

Long-term variations in the energy output of the Sun also alter Earth's average temperature. Precise measurements by instruments on Earth-orbiting spacecraft indicate that the Sun's energy output dropped by about 0.1 percent over the interval from 1979 through 1986. Satellites in the Mission to Planet Earth program will monitor the radiation output of the Sun, determine the fraction of the radiation absorbed by Earth and the fraction reflected back into space, and try to correlate changes in Earth's absorption to the chemistry, cloud cover, and aerosol content of the atmosphere.

Global warming (or the related phenomenon of global cooling) has far-reaching implications for life on the planet. An increase of only a few degrees in the average surface temperature can shift precipitation patterns, induce extremes of weather variation (for example, flooding or droughts), and raise ocean levels. Changes in precipitation and temperature could shift agricultural production from its present locations to new regions of the world, while an increase in the sea level could put some coastal communities under water.

Methods of Study

Mission to Planet Earth will employ a diverse variety of sensors on a series of Earth-orbiting satellites to monitor the chemistry, aerosol content, wind direction, and velocity of the atmosphere, the temperature and strength of large-scale ocean currents, and the emissions of gases and particles by volcanoes, oceans, and other sources. NASA's first satellite in the Mission to Planet Earth series, the Upper Atmosphere Research Satellite (UARS), was launched on September 12, 1991, into a near-circular orbit 585 miles above Earth. The orbit is inclined 57 degrees to the equator, allowing the UARS sensors to view up to 80 percent of the planet's surface, excluding only the portions near the poles. The mission of the UARS was to carry out the first systematic and comprehensive study of the upper atmosphere, measuring its temperature, pressure, wind velocity, and chemistry. The goal of the UARS project is to understand the chemistry, dynamics, and energetics of the atmosphere.

Data obtained by the instruments on the UARS, coupled with measurements by ground-based instruments, have demonstrated that the ozone-depletion process depends on more than simply the release of chlorofluorocarbons into the atmosphere. A whole series of photochemical reactions involving oxygen molecules, water, and compounds containing nitrogen, chlorine, or bromine are implicated in controlling the atmospheric ozone content.

On August 10, 1992, the second satellite in the Mission to Planet Earth series, TOPEX/Poseidon, was launched into orbit from the European Space Agency's launch site in Kourou, French Guiana. The satellite, which was placed into a near-circular orbit at an altitude of 830 miles above Earth's surface, measures the height of the seas below its path to within an accuracy of about five inches; it provides measurements along the same ground path every ten days. These sea-level measurements provide information on ocean currents, which can then be related to changes in the atmosphere and climate monitored by other satellites and ground-based instruments. The TOPEX/Poseidon satellite has produced the first global view of the seasonal changes in the ocean currents, produced the most accurate maps of the ocean tides ever assembled, and provided global data to validate computer models of the ocean circulation. TOPEX/Poseidon's planned three-year mission ended in 1995, but the satellite's operation has been extended until a follow-up mission, Jason-1, can be launched to provide continuous monitoring of the ocean currents from space into the twenty-first century.

The Total Ozone Mapping Spectrometer (TOMS), built by NASA but flown on a Russian weather-observation satellite, provides a continuous global record of atmospheric ozone concentration, allowing scientists to map the annual development of the ozone holes over the poles and to correlate the severity of the hole with measurements, by other instruments, of the chemical variation of the upper atmosphere. This sensor is an updated version of an instrument that first flew on the Nimbus 7 weather satellite launched in 1978. The TOMS instrument also will be flown on the Japanese Advanced Earth Observation Satellite.

The Earth Radiation Budget Satellite monitors solar energy emission, the aerosol content of the upper atmosphere, and the reflectivity of the atmosphere. The intent is to determine the link between the types and abundances of aerosol particles and the degree of warming or cooling of the planet that these aerosols produce.

The Sea-Viewing Wide Field Scanner (SeaWiFS) is a color scanner designed to monitor the biological processes in the oceans. SeaWiFS measures ocean color, which is related to the abundance of phytoplankton chlorophyll. These phytoplankton are the major source of carbon dioxide released to the atmosphere by the oceans, and measurement of their abundance is an important factor in determining the amount of carbon dioxide added to the atmosphere by biological activity on the planet. Thus, the major objective of SeaWiFS is to investigate the interaction between marine biosystems and Earth's atmosphere.

El Niño, a periodic variation in the winds, rainfall, and heat from the Pacific Ocean, is known to modify the global climate. However, it has been difficult to monitor El Niño, since measurements of surface winds in the Pacific Ocean come from ships passing through the area, and the data is often inaccurate or widely scattered. NASA has developed two instruments to monitor marine surface winds and tropical rainfall in an effort to understand the El Niño phenomenon and how it influences global weather patterns. The NASA Scatterometer, which was launched on the Japanese ADEOS satellite, uses an active radar system to monitor wind speed and direction, covering at least 90 percent of the ice-free portion of the global oceans once every two days. The Tropical Rainfall Measuring Mission (TRMM), also a joint effort between the United States and Japan, has been designed to test the feasibility of monitoring the amount and spatial distribution of rainfall. Because the planned orbit of the satellite will be nearly equatorial, it will provide measurements between 35 degrees north and 35 degrees south latitudes using both microwave radar and infrared instruments. The TRMM mission is expected to provide a minimum of three years of data on tropical rainfall. After validating the instrument, NASA expects to fly it on future missions that will monitor worldwide rainfall.

Several Mission to Planet Earth experiments have been flown on the Spacelab module carried in the payload bay of the space shuttle. These experiments have measured the concentrations and compositions of atmospheric aerosols, gauged wind velocities in the atmosphere, used radar-mapping techniques to document environmental changes, and validated the performance of instruments under development for use on later satellites. The X-Band Synthetic Aperture Radar (X-SAR), flown on the space shuttle in 1994, observed the effects of tsunami damage to the coast of Japan, documented the long-term environmental effects of a volcano in Kamchatka, Russia, and monitored the extent of sea-ice development in the Wendell Sea in Antarctica. The development of sea ice impedes heat flow from the warm ocean to the colder atmosphere, impacting the global climate.

The LAGEOS 2 satellite employs lasers to provide precise measurements of positions on Earth. Using this satellite, scientists map the small motions of Earth's crust; such motions may lead to volcanoes and earthquakes.

These satellites are precursors to the Earth Observing System (EOS), a series of larger satellites to be launched into polar orbits, where they will be able to observe every point on the planet once every day, in the late 1990's. The EOS satellites are expected to have a fifteen-year operational lifetime, allowing them to monitor global conditions over a sufficiently large number of annual climatic cycles to help researchers understand the relation of climate to the changing chemical composition of the atmosphere. The instruments on these satellites will provide continuous monitoring of atmospheric concentrations of the greenhouse gases implicated in global warming and the concentrations of gases implicated in the seasonal depletion of the ozone layer. The EOS satellites will also carry sensors to document the interactions between geological and geophysical processes on Earth's surface, changes in ocean currents, and the climate of the planet.

Context

Mission to Planet Earth is a recognition of how the scientific understanding of Earth has been transformed during the second half of the twentieth century. The planet and its environment were once viewed as essentially static; now, Earth is seen as undergoing continual change, with an environment governed by an interplay of diverse factors. For example, the view of a static globe has been replaced with the dynamic view of continental drift and plate tectonics, and the motion of Earth's crust is being monitored by precise laser position measurements from the LAGEOS 2 satellite.

Prior to the development of Earth-observing satellites, measurements of the conditions of the atmosphere, oceans, and surface of the planet were restricted to specific sites where monitoring stations had been established. In the case of the atmosphere, many types of measurements required costly aircraft, balloon, or rocket flights, which provided observations over a limited time period and at only a few locations. Ocean measurements required the presence of a ship on site, and those measurements were frequently taken by crew members who were not experts in the equipment they were using, resulting in data of dubious quality.

"Remote sensing" is a technique by which measurements can be made from a considerable distance away. For example, the radar unit in the Earth-orbiting NASA Scatterometer can measure the wind speed and direction at points in the atmosphere. The use of Earth-orbiting satellites provides continuous, long-term monitoring of conditions over the entire globe. These satellite measurements are validated by comparison of their observations with the local measurements from traditional monitoring stations. The objective of the Mission to Planet Earth program is to develop a sufficiently good understanding of the planet as a system, and of the interactions between the atmosphere, oceans, and solid Earth, to allow the prediction of future changes to the global environment in the same manner that the comprehensive study of weather patterns now allows accurate short-term weather forecasting.

Bibliography

Bruning, David. "Mission to Planet Earth." *Astronomy*, May, 1995, 44-45. A well-illustrated account of the use of radar on the space shuttle to document geological activity on Earth. Focuses on observations of the aftermath of a volcanic eruption in the Philippines.

Evans, Diane, et al. "Earth from Sky." *Scientific American*, December, 1984, 70-75. A report on the results of the X-Band Synthetic Aperture Radar experiment flown on the space shuttle *Endeavour*. Includes photographs documenting the effects of a volcano in Kamchatka, Russia, floods in the Amazon, and ice floes in the Wendell Sea, Antarctica.

Holden, Constance. "UARS Launches Earth Mission." *Science*, September 20, 1991,

1352. An account of the launching of the Mission to Planet Earth's first satellite. Describes the satellite's instruments, the scientific objectives involved, and how this satellite fits into NASA's overall plan for the program.

Malone, Thomas. "Mission-to-Planet-Earth-Project." *Environment*, October, 1986, 6-11. A clear and well-illustrated account of NASA's plans for Mission to Planet Earth, focusing on how remote sensing from Earth-orbiting satellites can be used to measure atmospheric and oceanic phenomena and interactions.

_____. "Mission to Planet Earth Revisited." *Environment*, April, 1989, 6-11. A follow-up article describing the evolution of the Mission to Planet Earth project since 1986. Discusses how the scientific results from the project will be used for environmental management and how they may influence environmental policy. Also describes the international aspects of the program, including how satellites launched by other nations will obtain complementary measurements.

Space Science Board of the National Academy of Sciences. *Space Science in the Twenty-first Century: Mission to Planet Earth*. Washington, D.C.: National Academy of Sciences, 1988. An in-depth discussion of unsolved questions relating to the interactions of the solid earth, the oceans, and the atmosphere, combined with a discussion of how satellite measurements can address these questions.

Taubes, Gary. "Remote Sensing: Earth Scientists Look NASA's Gift Horse in the Mouth." *Science*, February 12, 1993, 912-914. Describes the uses of remote sensing in the Mission to Planet Earth program and explains some of the scientific controversy concerning the program.

Unninayar, Sushel, and Kenneth Bergman. *Modeling the Earth System in the Mission to Planet Earth Era*. Washington, D.C.: National Aeronautics and Space Administration, 1993. A 133-page account of the scientific questions to be addressed by the Mission to Planet Earth program and a description of the satellite instruments that will gather the data to address those questions. A comprehensive bibliography documents the complex interactions that determine the global climate.

Wickland, Diane. "Mission to Planet Earth: The Ecological Perspective." *Ecology*, December, 1991, 1923-1933. An extensive and well-illustrated description of how Earth-orbiting satellites make measurements relevant to biological and ecological systems. Discusses the ecological implications of the Mission to Planet Earth results, including measurements of the influences of agriculture and deforestation on the global environment.

George J. Flynn

Cross-References

The Atmosphere's Evolution, 114; The Atmosphere's Global Circulation, 121; The Atmosphere's Structure and Composition, 128; Atmospheric Ozone, 144; Clouds, 224; Earth-Sun Relations, 399; Global Warming, 2932; The Greenhouse Effect, 1004; Ocean-Atmosphere Interactions, 1779; Volcanic Hazards, 2601; Volcanoes: Mount Pinatubo, 3150; Volcanoes: Recent Eruptions, 2673.

MISSISSIPPI RIVER

Type of earth science: Hydrology
Field of study: Sedimentology

The longest river in North America, the Mississippi drains a major portion of the continent, with important historical and present-day effects.

Principal terms
    ALLUVIUM: a deposit of soil and mud formed by flowing water
    HYDROLOGY: the science that deals with the events of circulation and
       the properties of water and the earth
    SEDIMENT: matter that settles to the bottom of a body of water

Summary of the Phenomenon

The Mississippi River fascinates and amazes both residents and travelers. In North America, its 2,348-mile length (of which about 1,600 miles are navigable) is surpassed only by those of the Missouri River in the northern United States and the Mackenzie River in western Canada. The Mississippi has often been called the "Nile of North America." The comparison is appropriate; both rivers have deltas that hold fertile land and cliffs that dot their edges. Together with its two main tributaries, the Ohio and the Missouri, the Mississippi drains an immense area of thirty-one states and two Canadian provinces into the Gulf of Mexico. Altogether, the river drains an area of 1,245,000 square miles. It is the third-largest drainage basin in the world, exceeded only by the Amazon and Congo River basins. The Amazon basin, by far the world's largest, is more than twice as large as the Mississippi basin, draining an area of approximately 2,722,000 square miles. The Congo basin, however, is not much larger than the Mississippi's, draining some 1,425,000 square miles. The fourth-largest basin is that of the Nile, which drains about 1,105,000 square miles.

The Mississippi drains lands with greatly differing geologies and environments. The Mississippi and its tributaries flow over a wide variety of igneous, metamorphic, and sedimentary rocks. The sedimentary rocks are easily erodible, and the large amount of material constantly held in suspension by the Mississippi's waters helps explain its muddy appearance. The river flows through lands that have widely differing climates and vegetation covers. It drains diverse territories such as the complex mountain ranges in the West, the arid high plains, and the humid southern woodlands.

The geologic history of the Mississippi Valley has developed two distinct basins, the Upper and Lower Mississippi Valleys, with the mouth of the Ohio River as the dividing point. The Lower Mississippi would flood seasonally if it were not regulated by human activity. In the upper valley, the river is a shallower stream enclosed by high, rocky mountains that are geologically unlike the hills that create the borders of the lower valley. The lands over which the Lower Mississippi flows have alluvial surfaces and are only a few thousand years old. This area is marked by inliers, which are outcrops of a formation completely surrounded by another layer, with the older deposits basically engulfing the fresh alluvium of the present lower valley. In the lower valley, the Mississippi is, in fact, a deeper river than it is in the upper valley.

The Pleistocene buildup of ice in the Northern Hemisphere dropped sea levels throughout the world, and the mouth of the Mississippi River was once several hundred feet lower than it is today. The surface deposits that cover the lower valley are barely a thousand years old, and there is enough diversity in the alluvium of the lower valley to allow archaeologists to determine how long humans have been in the area. The variety of backswamps, natural levees, and crests that create a river sequence look like a winding chain. The prehistory of the very large Lower Mississippi River Valley before the appearance of Europeans is important, because the present flora and densely wooded areas are not like those the first human beings in the region saw thousands of years ago.

The Mississippi River system can be categorized into six main basins: the Upper Mississippi, the Missouri, the Ohio, the Arkansas-White, the Red-Ouachita, and the Lower Mississippi. The Lower Mississippi basin includes about 1,244,000 square miles. Of this area, 25,000 square miles are flat, while the rest is made up of rolling hills. The basin stretches from the mouth of the Ohio River at Cairo, Illinois, to the Mississippi's mouth below New Orleans. The majority of the Mississippi River floodplain is in the lower valley. Swamplands and timberlands are more common than cleared sections. The Lower Mississippi is a murky stream that is alluvial below Cape Girardeau, Missouri. The lower river receives the discharges of a number of smaller tributary streams, the basins of which are almost wholly within the alluvial valley of the river below Cape Girardeau.

Methods of Study

Like several other great rivers of the world, the Mississippi has formed an immense and fertile delta that has been created by the gradual deposition of sediment. Investigators disagree somewhat in their estimates of the river's depositions, but most believe that it amounts to about 260 million tons annually. The sediments largely consist of clay silt and fine sand, with different clays accounting for about 70 percent of the total sedimentary load.

These clays form the subsoils of most of the lower southern states. They vary greatly in their erodibility. The banks and beds of the Mississippi and its tributaries have also contributed greatly to complicating the work of hydrologists and engineers trying to control the flow of these rivers. Since at least Cretaceous times, the drainage basin of the Mississippi River system has been delivering sediments to the Gulf of Mexico. The deposition of materials was enhanced by the thawing of the glaciers in the Jurassic period. During this stage, sediment-filled streams submerged the Lower Mississippi valleys.

Throughout geologic time, the sites of maximum deposition (depocenters) have shifted along the Gulf Coastal Plain. The bulk of the sediments that make up the Gulf Coast geosyncline, which is a portion of the earth's crust subjected to downward warping during a large fraction of geologic time, have been derived in part from ancestral Mississippi River drainages. Over long periods of geologic time, the river has constantly fed sediments to the receiving basin, thus building up thick layers of deltaic sediments that have gradually enlarged the coastal plain shoreline seaward.

Deltas form in lobes; in modern times, the seaward progression of the different Mississippi delta lobes has constructed a deltaic plain that has a total area of 11,030 square miles. Of this, 9,228 square miles are subaerial, or periodically under water. In the past 7,000 years, the site of maximum sedimentation of delta lobes has shifted and has occupied many positions. One of the earliest deltas, the Sale Cypremort, created a deltaic lobe along the western borders of the Mississippi plain. This deltaic lobe was exceptionally widespread and thin. After approximately 1,200 years of build-out, the site of maximum deposition changed to another delta lobe, the Cocodrie system. A similar procedure of unseating developed, and the river abandoned the Cocodrie deposition, beginning a new delta lobe, the Teche. This process continued until the modern delta achieved its present form some 600 to 800 years ago. The result is a complex of deltaic arrangements stretching some 460 miles along the Louisiana coast and inland nearly 160 miles. The Mississippi Delta is the most recent, geologically speaking.

The soil deposits of the alluvial valley are of uneven thickness. Basins along the river at the north end of the valley hold only few feet of modern river deposits, whereas more than 200 feet of deposits exist beneath the flat-lying coastal marshlands near the mouth of the river. These modern deposits rest on a substratum of heavier sand and gravel. The top layers of land along the Lower Mississippi are extraordinarily fertile because of large amounts of organic material and nutrients contained in the sediment arriving from the north.

Rivers that flow through flat, sedimented deltas rarely have straight channels. In rivers that flow through mountainous areas, the steep slopes and the hardness of the rock force waters to take the shortest path downhill, which generally is a straight line. When rivers cross plains that have gentle slopes, however, the turbulence in the streams is constantly dislodging fragments of soft material and creating new channels, which are usually extremely winding. The channel can then form a sinusoidal pattern that in places comes almost full circle. This process is called "meandering." The meander is the natural response of a river by which it adjusts to the slope of the land through which it flows. Meandering expands stream length and reduces slope. During high flow in a freely meandering stream running over alluvial soil, the exterior concave bank bends erode, and the bed scours and deepens. At the same time, the eroded matter scoured from the bed and banks is dropped on the point bar in the next bend downstream. With the low flows, earth removal takes place in the bends. A meandering river can change the location of its main channel, or split into branches, thus creating islands.

As meandering continues and as concave banks continue to recede, old river bends become extremely elongated; a narrow strip of land is often all that remains between the two bends of the river. When a flood causes a river to exceed the capacity of its channel, water flows over the narrow neck at a steep slope and high velocity, thus eroding a new channel, or cutoff, across the strip of land. Eventually, as the new cutoff channel becomes wider and deeper, the old bendway becomes separated from the river by deposition on bars; it then becomes an oxbow lake. A fully developed stream will maintain much the same length over time, as the decrease in length caused by cutoffs is equal to the added length produced by the growth of other meanders. Each cutoff produces a new meander that climaxes in another cutoff.

The effects of a cutoff on a river and its surroundings can be dramatic. The cutoff shortens the length of the river bottom, which changes both the river-bottom profile and the water-surface profile. Immediately after the cutoff is made, a drawdown curve, or dip, in the water profile occurs in the area of the cutoff. This causes local erosion of the river-bottom upstream of the cutoff to start to take place. The increased erosion upstream will cause a temporary overloading of the river downstream from the cutoff and will result in deposition of the sediment that the river cannot carry. This effect, though temporary, may last for a long time, since the full length of the graded part of the river upstream involves the removal of tremendous quantities of bed material. During this period, the river downstream of the cutoff is overloaded. As a result of the consequent temporary aggravation, river stages and groundwater tables will rise. Because of the reduction in the river's length and loss in storage ability, flood peaks will increase in height. These downstream effects, although temporary, may well outweigh the long-term advantageous effects of the cutoffs that occur upstream.

A successful employment of a human-made cutoff can be found on the Lower Mississippi River, where a channel improvement project that began in 1932 resulted in a lowering of flood levels by 6 to 7 feet without creating extreme instability in the river channel. For a cutoff to be permanently successful, however, the hydraulic gradients must be such that the river can preserve them more or less naturally, without requiring periodic human-made adjustments at numerous intervals. To prevent the river from scouring upstream and depositing downstream, the cutoff needs to be planned in such away that the pilot cutoff channel diverts only the swift top water of the river, while the sediment-laden bottom water stays in the old river channel. This is best done by constructing the pilot channel in line with the upstream river channel and making the old river meander the branch channel of the new route.

The flatness of a delta, the meandering of the river channel, coupled with the great fertility caused by the continual deposition of new organic material, means that river deltas are natural wetlands. Marshes and swamps are areas of low, flat-lying wet earth open to daily or seasonal flooding, although they are not the same things. Physically, marshes and swamps have common traits; they differ primarily in the kind of vegetation that flourishes on the land. Marshes are covered with grasses and other grasslike plants such as cattails. Swamps commonly include hardwood forests. The Mississippi River Delta supports some of the most important wetlands in the world, and it includes about 40 percent of all coastal wetlands in the lower forty-eight states.

The delta wetlands support plant and animal populations that can adjust to shifting water levels. Annual floods supply the system with sediments containing dissolved organic matter and nutrients. Many species of fish feed or spawn in the wetlands. At the mouths of the rivers that drain the wetlands are estuaries that support marine life. The same flooding that brings life-supporting elements to the floodplain forests also flushes organic material of all kinds to the sea. This matter supports the food chains of the estuaries, which are especially complex because of the great gradations of temperature and salinity that exist where fresh river water meets the sea.

A natural part of the life cycle of a river delta is flooding, a phenomenon caused by the vast discharges associated with high-water levels that surpass the capability of the river channel to eliminate water. Floods are caused by melting snow, by rainfall mixed with snow melt, by glacial melts in mountain rivers, or by rainfall alone. Although modern floods produce heavy damage to human life and property, presettlement floods mainly served to rearrange the topography of riparian lands.

During annual floods, river stages will normally top adjacent natural levees. However, flood inundation is not continuous along all portions of a river; in many instances, during a single flood, various crevasse splays will form along low points in the natural levee. These small crevasses will be maintained for a year or more, until enough material is deposited in them to build them back up to the level of the natural levee. They will then cease to be active.

In a natural delta, distributary channels serve as flumes that direct a portion of the water from the parent river system to a receiving basin. With continued enlargement of the distributary channels, a point is reached at which the channel is no longer able to maintain its gradient advantage, and the process of channel abandonment begins. In the Mississippi Delta, where tidal flooding is not usually a factor, the distributary channels commonly fill with fine-grained material mixed with peats and transported organic debris. One of the major features of the Mississippi River basin is the large amount of silting caused by the formation of crevasses, which break off from the main distributaries and deposit materials in the numerous interdistributary bays. Eventually, deposits form in shallow bays between or adjacent to major distributaries and extend themselves seaward through a system of radial channels, similar in appearance to the veins of a leaf.

In essence, then, it is important to understand that the presettlement Lower Mississippi basin was a system that had functioned well throughout geologic time. The Mississippi River meanders carried runoff from its vast watershed to the Gulf of Mexico, and the sediments brought from the north created vast tracts of land that now form much of the gulf states. The sediments continually enriched this land, which supported an immense diversity of life by depositing new fertilizing organic materials. The river's floods did not destroy land but rather enlarged and enriched it. Once flood waters overflowed the Mississippi's natural levees, they flowed into distributaries or formed crevasses that directed them into the vast area of wetlands that surrounded the main channel.

Context

The Mississippi River built most of the state of Louisiana with silt and sand and would not have done so if the river had stayed in one channel. If the Mississippi had maintained only one channel, southern Louisiana would have been a peninsula stretching into the Gulf of Mexico. The Mississippi River has shifted and snaked within a 200-mile semicircle to form southern Louisiana. The river's main thrust is to reach the sea by the shortest route. As the mouth moves southward and the river grows in length, the slope drops, the current slows, and sediment accumulates on the bed. The building up of the bed will cause the water to overflow the banks.

The Mississippi River's primary channel of 3,000 years ago has become the Bayou Teche. Along the Bayou Teche, on the elevated ground of aged natural levees, are Jeanerette, Breaux Bridge, Broussare, and Olivier, a line of Cajun communities. Some 800 years B.C., the Mississippi channel was captured from the east. It switched swiftly and traveled in that path for another thousand years. During the second century A.D., the river again changed southward by the now-still Bayou Lafourche, which by the year 1000 was sending its waters to the present course through the area that would become known as Plaquemines. The Atchafalaya's course across the delta plain totaled 140 miles, much less than half the length of the route of the main river. For the Mississippi to make such a change was totally natural. It was during this transition that Europeans began to colonize the rivers' edges, and the "modern" history of the region began.

Bibliography

Coleman, James. *Deltas: Processes of Deposition and Models for Exploration*. Baton Rouge, La.: Burguess Publishing, 1981. This book contains an excellent overview of deltas. Provides a particularly good explanation of the changes that take place within a delta.

Dennis, John. *Structural Geology*. New York: Ronald Press, 1972. A good overview of the geology of North America. Useful background for anyone interested in the Mississippi and related rivers.

Foster, J. W. *The Mississippi Valley: Its Physical Geography*. Chicago: S.C. Griggs, 1869. A description of the geography of the Mississippi River in the 1860's. Provides an interesting historical perspective.

Harrison, Robert W. *Alluvial Empire*. Little Rock, Ark.: Pioneer Press, 1961. Notable for an excellent bibiography of works on the Mississippi Delta.

Miller, A. *The Mississippi*. New York: Crescent Books, 1975. Contains historical maps that allow the reader to trace the changes in the river's course over time.

Petersonn, Margaret. *River Engineering*. Englewood Cliffs, N.J.: Prentice-Hall, 1986. A good overview of the science of river engineering, including explanation of relevant terms.

Tompkins, Frank H. *Riparian Lands of the Mississippi River*. New Orleans, La.: Improvement and Levee Association, 1901. A collections of essays on the river from an engineering point of view.

Loralee Davenport

Cross-References

Alluvial Systems, 31; Amazon Basin, 2812; Aquifers, 71; Deltas, 332; Drainage Basins, 384; Floodplains, 712; Floods, 719; Groundwater Movement, 1020; Nile River, 3024; River Bed Forms, 2196; River Flow, 2203; River Valleys, 2210; Sediment Transport and Deposition, 2290; Soil Erosion, 2387; Soil Formation, 2394.

NEMESIS THEORY

Type of earth science: Planetology
Field of study: Large solar system bodies

The Nemesis theory proposes that a small, dim star orbits the Sun. Although unverified, the theory has excited interest among scientists and the public alike because it may help to explain mass extinctions such as that of the dinosaurs.

Principal terms

ASTEROID: a rocky celestial body; many are between 1 kilometer and 100 kilometers in diameter

COMET: a celestial body with a nucleus composed mostly of water and carbon dioxide ices surrounded by a cloud of gas and dust; nuclei average 10 kilometers in diameter

ELLIPSE: an oval; a closed curve with a long diameter (major axis) and a short diameter (minor axis)

IRIDIUM: a metallic element, atomic number 77, that is rare in Earth's crust

K-T BOUNDARY: the thin layer of clay sediment laid down between the Cretaceous and Tertiary geological periods 65 million years ago

MASS EXTINCTION: the die-off of a large percentage of species in a short time

PERIODICITY: the recurrence of related phenomena at regular intervals

RED DWARF: a small, dim, cool star that emits orange or red light

Summary of the Phenomenon

The Nemesis theory grew directly from attempts to solve a great mystery in paleontology: Why did the dinosaurs, the largest animals on Earth for 160 million years, suddenly die out? When fully developed, however, the theory treated the question of mass extinctions generally. It argues that a second star, much smaller than the Sun, circles the solar system in an immense orbit, occasionally deflecting comets so that they fall toward Earth. Some comets collide, and the catastrophic damage to the biosphere kills a large percentage of living organisms.

Seldom has science seen a proposal that generated as much contention in so many disciplines as the Nemesis theory. It evolved in three stages, each based on assertions more controversial than the last: that the impacts of asteroids or comets started mass extinctions, that the impacts and extinctions occur at regular intervals, and that a companion star to the Sun, a red dwarf dubbed "Nemesis," is responsible for the periodicity. The Nemesis theory remains unproved; however, most scientists now accept at least the relation between asteroid or comet impacts and some mass extinctions.

The original theory linking the demise of the dinosaurs and the collision of an asteroid appeared in a 1980 article by geologist Walter Alvarez, the Nobel laureate physicist Luis Alvarez (Walter's father), and two nuclear chemists, Frank Asaro and Helen Michel. During studies of sedimentation rates, Walter Alvarez collected samples from a 1.3-centimeter layer of clay deposited 65 million years ago between the Cretaceous (K) and Tertiary (T) periods. Because it separates the two geological ages, the layer is known as the K-T boundary. Chemical tests of the clay performed by Asaro and Michel revealed it to have three hundred times more iridium than the limestone layers immediately above and below it. A metallic element chemically similar to platinum, gold, and osmium, iridium is rare in Earth's crust; however, bodies formed early in the history of the solar system, such as asteroids and comets, have it in much higher concentrations. Accordingly, Luis Alvarez suggested that a large asteroid might have struck Earth and become part of the debris ejected into the atmosphere. The ejecta, with a high concentration of iridium, might then have settled to form the K-T boundary.

The asteroid impact would thus have occurred at the same time as the accepted date for the extinction of the dinosaurs. The Alvarezes believed it could not be a coincidence, especially since more than half of Earth's other animal species perished along with the dinosaurs. From the amount of iridium in the K-T boundary, they estimated the asteroid to have been about ten kilometers in diameter, the size of the largest mountains on Earth. It was moving at about 33 kilometers per second when it struck, and the impact released energy equivalent to 100 million megatons of trinitrotoluene (TNT), more than the combined explosive power of all existing atomic weapons. They further calculated that debris splashed above the atmosphere would quickly circle Earth and block sunlight for six to nine months, cooling the ground to Arctic temperatures. The passage of the asteroid through the atmosphere would cause fierce storms with acid rain and create toxic gases, and the impact, if in the ocean, would send a tsunami around the world several times. Such destruction to the global environment, the Alvarezes argued, could have brought about the K-T mass extinction.

In 1984, paleontologists David M. Raup and J. John Sepkoski claimed that mass extinctions have occurred every 26 million years for at least the past 250 million years. They based the claim on a computer analysis of the ages of fossils from thousands of species. This periodicity stunned scientists, most of whom believed the analysis was simply wrong because there was no known physical cause for regularly recurring extinctions.

Richard A. Muller, a colleague of the Alvarezes at the University of California at Berkeley, suggested that asteroids or comets caused all the catastrophes, not just the K-T mass extinction, and that a second star in the solar system could be responsible for regularly knocking comets toward Earth's orbit. While Muller developed this idea, the Alvarezes checked the dates of the one hundred largest craters on Earth. Those whose dates were most firmly established appear to indicate a periodicity of 28.4 million years. That figure seemed close enough to the 26-million-year mass extinction period to lie within the acceptable range of statistical variation, and so they believed they had found another periodicity coherent with that of the mass extinctions.

The double-star model was one of three explanations for the periodicity that various research teams offered in the British journal *Nature* in April, 1984. One article suggested that an undetected planet might orbit beyond Pluto in the Kuiper belt of asteroids and comets. The gravity of this "Planet X" could knock some of the Kuiper belt objects out of their orbit and send them Earthward. Although the Kuiper belt has been observed, astronomers later demonstrated that no such planet exists. A second article pointed out that as the Milky Way galaxy turns, the solar system rises and falls through the galactic plane on a regular path, like a car on a circular roller coaster. As the solar system passes through molecular clouds in the galactic plane, comets and meteors might be dislodged from their positions in the Oort cloud. The Oort cloud is thought to contain about two trillion comets at a distance from the Sun of twenty thousand to one hundred thousand astronomical units (AU, the distance from the Sun to Earth). However, the present position of the solar system in the galaxy and the period of its oscillations, 32 million years, does not fit the 26-million-year mass extinction period well.

Finally, two teams, working separately, contributed articles concerning the possibility that the Sun has a companion. Astronomers Daniel Whitmire and Albert A. Jackson IV theorized that the star was a red dwarf in a highly elliptical orbit that sent it through the Oort cloud, where its gravity would disturb comets. The orbit they calculated was later shown to be too elliptical to be stable; at the farthest reaches of its orbit, the red dwarf would be disturbed by the gravity of nearby stars. The orbit could not repeat long enough to cause the periodic mass extinctions. Yet the egg-shaped orbit described by the second team was stable enough. In their article, Muller, a physicist, and astronomers Marc Davis and Piet Hut based their theory on a slightly larger red dwarf than the Whitmire-Jackson model and a larger orbital ellipse. In a footnote, Miller suggested that this star be called "Nemesis" after the goddess in Greek mythology who punished crime and undeserved good fortune. Although other names were suggested, during the resulting debate and the widespread coverage in the popular press, the star was nearly always called Nemesis—or, because of its effect on life, the "death star."

The fully elaborated Nemesis theory holds that a companion star, between five thousandths and one-tenth the mass of the Sun, completes an orbit once every 26 million years. At the far point of its elliptical orbit, Nemesis is about 23.5 trillion kilometers (2.5 light-years, or 88,000 AU) from the Sun. At the closest approach, when Nemesis curves through the Oort cloud, it is five trillion kilometers (0.5 light-year, 17,600 AU) from the Sun. The orbit will be stable for another billion years. Its passage through the Oort cloud lasts about one to two million years, during which its gravitation throws some comets out of the solar system and sends others spiraling inward toward the Sun. As many as five of the comets strike Earth during some showers, while there may be no hits at all during some showers. Since the average size of cometary nuclei is about ten kilometers, the impacts devastate the environment. Right now, according to Muller, Nemesis is outward bound on its orbit, approximately two light-years away and nearing its most distant point.

Proponents of the Nemesis theory caution that comet impacts are probably not the only cause of animal extinctions. They point out that an impact, or a rapid series of impacts, might have given the coup de grâce to species in decline because of changes in the environment already underway for other reasons. Moreover, an impact may start widespread environmental alteration that eliminates species over the following hundreds of thousands or millions of years, rather than suddenly. They add that some mass extinctions probably have had nothing to do with comet or asteroid impacts at all.

As a reputable scientific theory should, the Nemesis theory contained several testable predictions. The recurrent million-year-long comet showers incited by Nemesis must have produced more craters on Earth than had then been found. The impact should leave iridium-rich boundary layers that coincide with mass extinctions. Most important of all, there should be a dim red dwarf lurking somewhere near the solar system.

Methods of Study

By the mid-1990's, astronomers had yet to find direct evidence that Nemesis exists. Meanwhile, support for the theory, never extensive, declined. Not everyone gave up on it, however, because there is good reason for the lack of direct evidence. At the estimated distance of two light-years, Nemesis would be nearly invisible to telescopes, and red dwarfs are so common in the stellar neighborhood of the Sun that picking out the right one would require an exhaustive survey of the sky and much patience.

Luis Alvarez and others searched star catalogs for candidate stars on the chance that someone had already located Nemesis without realizing that it belongs to the solar system. The catalog searches were unsuccessful. Astronomers looked for it with visible-light and infrared telescopes, also unsuccessfully. A University of California at Berkeley astronomy team under Muller's direction, checking about ten red dwarfs nightly, eliminated 3,100 candidates by 1996. They looked for stars that shift position from previous sightings against the background of distant stars, a technique known as parallax; the bigger the shift, the closer is the star to the Sun. Also, because Nemesis should be near the turn-around point in its orbit, it would have little velocity relative to the Sun; as a consequence, it would not have the redshift or blueshift apparent in the spectra of stars approaching or moving away at typical stellar speeds. No suitable parallax or spectrum has been found for a star close enough to the Sun.

Most stars belong to systems in which two or more stars orbit each other, and this fact bolsters the argument for the existence of Nemesis. Astronomers have long wondered why the Sun is a loner when its nearest neighbors are not. Still, the preponderance of multiple star systems is not proof, and it may even be that Nemesis is not a red dwarf at all. The other possible varieties of star—brown dwarf, neutron star, and small black hole—would be extremely difficult to detect with available technology.

Considerable indirect evidence for the Nemesis theory exists from the effects of large impacts on Earth. The most solid evidence, confirming one of the theory's predictions, is the discovery of two craters that match the dates of mass extinctions and are large enough to have instigated them. In 1990, geologists found a 65-million-year-old crater near the town of Chicxulub on Mexico's Yucatán Peninsula. Extending into the Gulf of Mexico, the crater is about 200 kilometers in diameter and was made by a body about 10 kilometers wide moving 20 to 60 kilometers per second. Ejected material found in Mexico and Belize, including microtektites, soot, and calcite sphericules, are all characteristic of the extreme high pressures of an impact. Geologists also found deposits from tsunami waves of the same age, and at least sixty-six deposits from the K-T boundary worldwide show the telltale concentrations of iridium from a comet. The crater's properties match the estimated size of the comet associated with the K-T mass extinction so well that, after the crater's discovery, few scientists completely rejected the Alvarez impact theory. The Manicouagan Crater in Quebec, Canada, about 100 kilometers in diameter, coincides with the mass extinction between the Triassic and Jurassic eras 208 million years ago.

In the case of the K-T boundary, the fossil record provides striking confirmation of the time relation between the impact and extinctions. Dinosaur fossils are regularly found below the boundary layer but never above it, although at some sites a two-meter gap between fossils and the layer exists, representing tens of thousands of years of difference in age. Microscopic fossils provide clearer evidence. The remains of foraminifera, shell-forming protozoans, are abundant immediately below the boundary layer and are rare above it, testifying to a thoroughgoing extinction of tiny animal species. Moreover, the pollen count in the limestone above the layer is three hundred times less than that in the limestone below it, which is evidence for major damage to plant life.

In addition to the K-T boundary, five other boundary layers contain some degree of iridium concentrations above the normal level for ordinary earth and so may record a comet impact. The dates of these layers coincide with mass extinctions of varying extents between geological periods: the Eocene-Oligocene, 38 million years ago; the Jurassic-Cretaceous, 145 million years ago; the Permian-Triassic, 250 million years ago; the late Devonian, 365 million years ago; and the Precambrian-Cambrian, 570 million years ago. Large impact craters of these ages have not been found, perhaps because the majority of craters have been weathered away or erased by the movement of Earth's tectonic plates.

Periodicities in the dates of mass extinctions and large craters, as determined by stratigraphy and radioisotope dating techniques, also support the 26-million-year comet impact cycle of the Nemesis theory; however, the analyses producing this figure have been controversial. Scientists reanalyzing the Raup-Sepkoski mass extinction data have calculated 28-million-year, 31-million-year, and 32-million-year periods. Some doubt the data reflect any periodicity at all; it could be merely an illusory result of the analytical techniques. Others have questioned the definition of mass extinction relied on by Raup and Sepkoski or have pointed out that the fossil record is too spotty and difficult to interpret for precise dating. Likewise, the analysis of crater ages made by the Alvarezes has been faulted for drawing from too little data to be meaningful.

Context

When the impact theory and Nemesis theory were published in the early 1980's, earth scientists assumed that species die out and geological features change only over vast stretches of time. This "uniformitarianism" arose from the writings of the English geologist Charles Lyell, especially his *Principles of Geology* (1830). Lyell overthrew an earlier theory propounded by the French geologist and botanist Georges Cuvier. Cuvier had argued that change comes suddenly because of great catastrophes. A century and a half of uniformitarianism made paleontologists and geologists skeptical of the Nemesis theory because it seemed to be a naïve resurrection of Cuvier's catastrophism. Still, the theory jolted their complacency and made them rethink basic assumptions.

The Nemesis theory also affected other scientific disciplines. Because the K-T impact's influence on mass extinction has gained wide acceptance, biologists reexamined the theory of evolution. Clearly, the idea of natural selection must be modified if cometary impacts are held responsible for extinctions; since an impact suddenly alters the biosphere and destroys many ecosystems, a species' survival would not depend solely upon its superior adaptation to an ecological niche. Chance is also a factor. Furthermore, some paleontologists believe catastrophes may be healthy for evolution; even though they obliterate much life, in doing so they clear out old species that may be overadapted, making room for surviving species to expand and diversify.

In general, astronomers have been more open to the Nemesis theory than have earth and life scientists. Because of the search for Nemesis, they have had reason to pay more attention to nearby red dwarfs, an undersurveyed type of star, and the effort played a small part in the discovery of the first brown dwarfs in 1996. More important, the possibility that comets and asteroids occasionally crash into Earth alarmed several governments enough that they investigated how to defend Earth from the collisions and encouraged or even financed programs to detect near-Earth objects. While searching for Planet X, astronomers scored another major discovery: In 1992, they spotted large objects in the Kuiper belt for the first time, although these objects are too small to be planets.

The Nemesis theory and the theories that led to it have engaged an extraordinary variety of specialists. Astronomers searched for the companion star or planet; astrophysicists calculated possible orbits; geologists looked for boundary layers and craters; chemists analyzed Earth's boundary layers; geophysicists determined the damage inflicted by impacts; biologists considered the effects on life; and paleontologists combed the fossil record. Even if the Nemesis theory is finally disproved, it has benefited modern science not only by drawing attention to Earth's plight in its cosmic environment but also by motivating scientists from many disciplines to scrutinize the same phenomena.

Bibliography

Alvarez, Luis W. *Alvarez: Adventures of a Physicist*. New York: Basic Books, 1987. In chapter 15 of this autobiography, the Nobel laureate relates how he and his son

Walter put together the asteroid-impact theory to explain the extinction of dinosaurs and its relation to the Nemesis theory.

Baugher, Joseph F. *The Space-Age Solar System*. New York: John Wiley & Sons, 1991. A sophisticated review of solar-system studies for readers with a college-level understanding of science. Bauger briefly summarizes the arguments and evidence for Nemesis and periodic cometary impacts.

Dauber, Philip M., and Richard A. Muller. *The Three Big Bangs: Comet Crashes, Exploding Stars, and the Creation of the Universe*. Reading, Mass.: Addison-Wesley, 1996. In chapter 8, the authors review the basic evidence for Nemesis and describe the attempt to locate it. Other chapters discuss comets, asteroids, and impacts.

Goldsmith, Donald. *Nemesis: The Death-Star and Other Theories of Mass Extinction*. New York: Walker, 1985. By a science writer and Public Broadcasting Service consultant, this well-written book concentrates on Luis Alvarez's impact theory and periodic mass extinctions. Goldsmith describes Nemesis as one of several possible causes of the phenomenon.

Lewis, John S. *Rain of Iron and Ice: The Very Real Threat of Comet and Asteroid Bombardment*. Reading, Mass.: Addison-Wesley, 1996. Lewis informs general readers about the threat to Earth of asteroid, meteor, and comet impacts. He devotes two chapters to the relation of impacts and geological ages, mentioning Nemesis skeptically.

Muller, Richard. *Nemesis*. New York: Weidenfeld & Nicolson, 1988. An originator of the Nemesis theory, Muller narrates the complex genesis of the idea from the impact theory of dinosaur extinction and periodicity. Abundantly detailed, the book presents scientific concepts and procedures clearly for general readers.

Norton, O. Richard. *Rocks from Space: Meteorites and Meteorite Hunters*. Missoula, Mont.: Mountain Press, 1994. An entertaining introduction to meteorites and the history of meteorite science for general readers. The text concludes with a discussion of mass extinctions and the Nemesis theory.

Raup, David M. *The Nemesis Affair*. New York: W. W. Norton, 1986. In a conversational style, Raup examines the evidence for mass extinctions, periodicity, asteroid impacts, and extraterrestrial influences on the impact rate in order to explain the development of "the Nemesis Affair" and to illustrate how science is conducted.

Roger Smith

Cross-References

Asteroid Impact, 2819; Catastrophism, 2848; Comets, 253; The Cretaceous-Tertiary Boundary, 303; Dinosaurs, 370; Impact Volcanism, 3136; Mass Extinctions, 1514; Meteorite and Comet Impacts, 1623; Paleobiogeography, 1984; Paleoclimatology, 1993.

NILE RIVER

Type of earth science: Hydrology
Field of study: Geomorphology

The Nile River is an interesting and important hydrologic system. Its complex geologic evolution began with the drying up of the Mediterranean Sea about 6 million years ago. The Nile carries water northward across the Sahara Desert from high-rainfall regions of equatorial Africa; it nurtured one of the great civilizations of ancient times and sustains millions of people in modern Egypt.

Principal terms

CATARACT: rough water or a waterfall in a river, generally obstructing navigation

HYDROLOGY: the science that deals with the properties, distribution, and circulation of water on land

MANTLE PLUME: a rising jet of hot mantle material that produces tremendous volumes of basaltic lava

MONSOON: a seasonal air current affecting eastern Africa and southern Asia; in the Northern Hemisphere's winter, dry winds flow from the continents to the ocean, whereas in summer, moist winds flow from the ocean to the continents and cause heavy rains

PYROXENE: a rock-forming mineral, commonly found in igneous rocks such as basalt or gabbro

RIFT: a portion of the earth's crust where tension has caused faulting, producing an elongate basin; rifts fill with sediments and, sometimes, volcanic rocks

TECTONIC: relating to differential motions of the earth's crust, usually associated with faulting and folding of rock layers

Summary of the Phenomenon

The Nile River is by some measures the longest river on Earth, extending 6,650 kilometers from Lake Victoria to the shores of the Mediterranean Sea. Only the Amazon River in South America approaches its length. The river follows a generally south-to-north path; both the source of the White Nile in equatorial Africa and its mouth on the southern shore of the Mediterranean Sea lie within one degree of longitude. The Nile crosses 35 degrees of latitude, a distance comparable to the width of the continental United States, and flows across a greater variety of regions than any other river.

In spite of its great length and large drainage basin (3,000,000 square kilometers, or about 10 percent of the area of Africa), the Nile carries relatively little water; during the twentieth century, annual flow ranged from a low of 42 cubic kilometers in the drought year of 1984 to a high of 120 cubic kilometers in 1916. This comparatively small flow results from the fact that no water is added to the river for the final half of its journey to the sea. Most rivers merge with increasingly large streams as they approach the sea, joining their waters into an ever-swelling stream. The Nile flows instead through the Sahara Desert, the largest and most desolate tract of land on Earth, matched only in size and desolation by the icy wastes of Antarctica.

Passage through the Sahara increases the importance of Nile water while reducing its volume. Its greatest value is reached as it nears the sea, where it has for more than five thousand years allowed the conduct of agriculture in Egypt. The rich soil, constant sun, and abundant water of the Nile Valley in Egypt result in one of the most productive agricultural regions of the world. The ancient civilizations of Egypt were built on this firm economic foundation. Without the Nile, Egypt would be as barren as the rest of the Sahara; with the Nile, Egyptian farms can produce two or even three crops every year. Egyptian civilization was nurtured by the Nile and protected from invasion by the sea to the north and the desert to the east and west. Egypt—and, consequently, much of world culture—thus truly is the "gift of the Nile."

Dramatic changes in the amount of water flowing through the Nile occur annually, reflecting the fact that two independent streams, the Blue Nile and the White Nile, join at Khartoum, the capital of Sudan. The White Nile issues from Lake Victoria, the second-largest freshwater lake on earth. The White Nile tumbles down a series of falls and rapids to Lake Kioga and Lake Albert before spilling out into a huge swamp, known as "the Sudd," in southern Sudan. The Sudd was the great barrier to European explorers seeking the source of the White Nile. The vast swamps caused explorers traveling in boats up the Nile to lose their way, forcing them to turn back or perish. As a result, the source of the White Nile was discovered in 1862 by an explorer, John Speke, who traveled west from Zanzibar to Lake Victoria.

In the Sudd, the White Nile—there known as the Bahr el Gebel—gains several tributaries. From the west flows the Bahr El Arab, and the Sobat flows from the east. The vastness of the Sudd results in huge losses by evaporation; about 50 percent of the water flowing into the Sudd is lost by evaporation. The Sudd acts as a buffer, so that greater water flow into the Sudd causes the swampy area to expand, resulting in increased evaporation. Efforts to plan for expected increases in water demand, especially in Egypt, have focused on reducing these losses by building a 350-kilometer diversion, the Jonglei Canal, around the Sudd. Civil war in southern Sudan has stopped its construction, but growing environmental concerns render it unlikely that the canal will be quickly finished even if the war ends. The combination of relatively constant rainfall over the Lake Victoria region, the vastness of Lake Victoria, and evaporative losses in the Sudd result in a relatively constant flow of water down the White Nile to Khartoum. North of Malakal, the Nile flows over a flat stretch in a well-defined channel without swamps; the river drops only 8 meters in elevation over its 800-kilometer length from Malakal to Khartoum.

In contrast to the White Nile, the Blue Nile and its little sister, the Atbara River, are seasonal streams. For about half of the year they flow as feeble trickles, contributing negligible water to the Nile from January to June. In mid- to late summer, the monsoons sweep large amounts of moisture evaporated from the Indian Ocean toward the Horn of Africa. As the water-laden air flows up over the Ethiopian highlands, it cools, and torrential rains fall. These rains so swell the Blue Nile that its waters overwhelm the smaller White Nile at Khartoum and cause it to flow back upstream. Between 70 and 80 percent of the Nile's total annual water budget results from the flood phase of the Blue Nile and Atbara Rivers. These raging rivers also erode large amounts of black sand and silt from the basaltic highlands of Ethiopia and carry these sediments north. In his 1899 book *The River War*, Winston Churchill described the Nile in flood: "As the Nile rises its complexion is changed. The clear blue river becomes thick and red, laden with the magic mud that can raise cities from the desert sand and make the wilderness a garden." The historic fertility of the Nile Delta and Valley in Egypt owe as much to the new layer of this rich soil added to the inundated fields as to the deep soaking. This annual flooding and delivery of sediment no longer occurs downstream of the Aswan High Dam, which was constructed in the 1960's to ensure that the water needs of Egypt could be met in spite of drought in the Nile headwaters.

Like the White Nile, the Blue Nile issues from a large lake, Lake Tana. It initially flows to the southwest, but progressively turns to the southwest and then northwest as it descends through the Blue Nile Canyon. It leaves the mountains about at the border between Sudan and Ethiopia and continues on a northwestward track across the Sudanese lowlands until it joins the White Nile at Khartoum.

For a distance of 1,850 kilometers from Khartoum to Aswan, the Nile is defined by two features: the cataracts and the great bend. The cataracts are sections where the river tumbles over rocky outcroppings, creating serious obstacles to navigation. There are six "classical" cataracts, but in reality there are many more, and as much as 565 kilometers of this portion of the Nile—referred to as the "Cataract Nile"—are affected by cataracts. The cataracts are also significant because these define river segments where granites and other hard rocks come down to the edge of the Nile. The floodplain in this region is narrow to nonexistent, and opportunities for agricultural development is correspondingly limited. These two factors—navigational obstacles and restricted floodplain—are the chief reasons that this part of the Nile is thinly populated and why the historic border between Egypt in the north and Nubia or Sudan in the south is found not far from the First Cataract at Aswan.

The great bend is one of the most unexpected features of the Nile. For most of its course, the Nile flows inexorably to the north; at one location in the heart of the Sahara, however, it turns southwest and flows away from the sea for 300 kilometers before resuming its northward journey. This deflection of the river's course is the result of tectonic uplift of the Nubian Swell that has taken place during the past few hundred thousand years. This uplift is also responsible for the cataracts; if not for the recent uplift, these rocky stretches would have been worn away long ago by the abrasive action of the sediment-laden Nile.

The northernmost segment is the Egyptian Nile, extending for 1,200 kilometers between Aswan and the Mediterranean Sea. It consists of two parts, the Nile Valley and the Delta. The Nile Valley consists of the broad floodplain that is imprisoned between steep limestone or sandstone hillsides. The boundary between the lush valley floor and the flanking desert is stark and sudden; a visitor can stand with one foot on the black mud, brought 3,000 kilometers from Ethiopia, and the other foot on desert sand or barren limestone. The floodplain widens progressively to the north until it opens up just north of Cairo into the Delta. The mouth of the Nile is where the term "delta" was first applied; the ancient Greeks were impressed by the triangular shape of the land around the Nile's mouth and the similarity that it had to the fourth letter of the Greek alphabet. The Nile splits into two branches at the south end of the Delta, the western, or Rosetta, branch (where the famous Rosetta Stone was discovered) and the eastern, or Damietta, branch. Up to the time that the Aswan High Dam was built, the Delta continued to grow as annual floods laid down their loads of silt. These sediments are now deposited in Lake Nasser, with the result that the sediment-starved Delta is slowly sinking and its shoreline is retreating.

The evolution of the Nile is an important area of scientific research. The river consists of a series of steeper and flatter segments, and this is thought to indicate that several independent drainage systems existed in the region now drained by the Nile. Much is known about when and how the course of the Nile came into being, but much remains to be learned.

A critical event in the formation of the Nile was the evaporation of the Mediterranean Sea about 6 million years ago. Because of the climatic zone in which it lies, more water evaporates from the Mediterranean than is supplied by the rivers that flow into it. This water deficit requires that replenishing seawater flow into the Mediterranean from the Atlantic. When the Straits of Gibraltar pinched shut as a result of the collision between Africa and Europe, the Mediterranean slowly dried up. The Dead Sea of Israel and Jordan at about 400 meters below sea level is presently the deepest spot on the continents, but the Mediterranean seafloor, lying as much as 3,000 meters below sea level, was a mile deeper and a thousand times more vast than the Dead Sea region. This may have been the greatest sea ever to evaporate completely, and the event profoundly affected the streams that flowed into it. A north-flowing river existed in what is now Egypt; as sea level dropped, the stream became steeper and steeper as it cut down into relatively soft limestones. The enhanced erosive power allowed its upper tributaries to extend into the headwaters and capture upstream drainages. The increased water from the captured streams further increased the stream's erosive power, further stimulating the expansion of the drainage system upstream. This led to the development of the "Eonile," which flowed through a huge canyon that was deeper than the Grand Canyon of Arizona and many times longer. This canyon is buried beneath all of the Egyptian Nile, but it cannot be traced south of Aswan.

In time, the barrier at Gibraltar ruptured, and a tremendous waterfall brought Atlantic seawater to refill the Mediterranean basin. The "Grand Canyon of Egypt" became a drowned river valley or estuary, similar to the fjords of Norway but very different in origin. Slowly, this estuary filled with sediments brought in by rivers flowing from the south, and a landscape not too different from the present was established by 3 million years ago.

Methods of Study

It is much more difficult to discern the development of the Nile upstream from Aswan, but there are some clues. Lake Victoria did not exist prior to about twelve thousand years ago. Before this time, the streams of the Ugandan highlands flowed west to join the Congo, which drains into the equatorial Atlantic. Recent tectonic activity lifted and tilted the region to make the lake and direct its overflow to the north. Similarly, recent tectonic activity caused the Nubian Swell and the Bayuda Uplift to be more or less of an obstacle, with the result that northward flow across Nubia is sometimes permitted and sometimes blocked. Probably the oldest parts of the Nile drainage are those associated with the Sudd. These follow the axes of sediment-filled rifts that formed more 65 million years ago and that have continued to sink and to fill with sediments since that time.

The Ethiopian highlands began to form about 30 million years ago as a result of tremendous volcanic activity, as a mantle plume punctured the crust, but the contribution of the distinctive black sediments from these highlands is not recognized in the Egyptian Nile until about 650,000 years ago. This may be the result of increased rainfall on the Ethiopian highlands accompanying the development and intensification of monsoonal circulation in the recent past. Monsoonal circulation is caused by the change position of atmospheric low-pressure cells, which lie over the equatorial Indian Ocean during northern winter and over south-central Asia during northern summer. The result is that cold, dry winds blow south from Asia during northern winter, but warm, moist winds blow from the sea toward Asia in northern summer. The westward deflection of summer winds resulting from the Coriolis effect brings part of the moisture-laden air currents over Ethiopia, where the air cools as it rises. Cool air can hold less moisture than warm air, so clouds and then rain form as the monsoon rises over the Ethiopian Plateau. This brings the long, drenching rains in Ethiopia that cause the annual Nile flood. The monsoonal circulation has intensified over the last few millions of years as a result of continued uplift of the Tibetan Plateau. The mystery of the Nile flood that puzzled the ancient Egyptians can thus best be understood by knowing about mountain-building events occurring thousands of miles away. Water from the Ethiopian highlands may not have reached Egypt because the Nubian Swell acted as a barrier, perhaps deflecting the water to the west. It may be that only with the additional water provided as a result of the intensifying monsoon that the upstream Nile was able to erode its way through the Nubian Swell and continue north to the Mediterranean Sea.

The history of the Nile is mostly inferred from sedimentary deposits in the Delta and Egyptian Nile. We know that great river systems carried sediments—preserved today as the Nubian Sandstone—north from central Africa as long ago as the Cretaceous period, about 100 million years ago, but the course of these rivers is poorly known. No link can be established between the Cretaceous rivers and the Nile. The sea invaded Africa from the north toward the end of the Cretaceous period, and much of northeast Africa was a shallow sea during much of the early Tertiary period, about 70 million to 40 million years ago. River deposits from the late Eocene and early

Oligocene (about 35 million years ago) are known from west of the present Nile, but these sediments did not travel far, indicating that they came from a relatively small river. This may have been the precursor of the stream that carved the great canyon following evaporation of the Mediterranean Sea about 6 million years ago.

Context

Five main episodes in the evolution of the Nile since the carving of the Grand Canyon of Egypt can be distinguished. From oldest to youngest, these are the Eonile, the Paleonile, and three Pleistocene Niles: the Protonile, the Prenile, and the Neonile. The deposits of the Neonile are indistinguishable from those of the present river.

The Eonile was the river that 6 million years ago cut the canyon deeper and deeper as the level of the Mediterranean Sea fell, until it lay 2,500 meters below the desert floor just north of modern Cairo. As the Mediterranean Sea filled again beginning about 5 million years ago, the canyon became an estuary that slowly filled with sediments. As the estuary filled, it was occupied by the Paleonile flowing in from the south. Sediments deposited by the Paleonile were not derived from Ethiopia; the distinctive mineral pyroxene, which is common in Ethiopian basalts, is not found in them. The Paleonile was probably fed by a drainage basin that was much more limited in size than that of the present Nile; it was probably restricted to southeast Egypt. Paleonile sediments are very fine-grained, suggesting that the river drained a moist and vegetated area very different from the desert now found in northeast Africa. The Paleonile flowed through Egypt from about 4 million to 1.8 million years ago.

The interval between the Paleonile and the Protonile was marked by a dramatic change in climate. This was the beginning of the Pleistocene, a period of widespread glaciation in Northern Europe and North America but a time when a harsh desert was first established in North Africa. The Nile stopped flowing north during this transition, and sand dunes drifted into the abandoned river channel. Torrential winter rains occasionally filled the channel, but no water reached the Egyptian Nile from south of the Nubian Swell until the flow regime of the Protonile was established about 1.5 million years ago. Coarse sediments, including conglomerate, gravel, and coarse sand, characterize the deposits of this time. There is no hint of material eroded from the Ethiopian highlands.

The Prenile flowed from perhaps 700,000 until about 200,000 years ago, when a desert occupied North Africa; it was a vigorous river with a wide floodplain. Its sources lay south of Egypt, and the presence of abundant pyroxene in these sediments indicates that the Ethiopian highlands were sediment sources for the first time. A large proportion of sediments in the Nile Delta were deposited by this phase of the river. It can be safely said that the Prenile was the largest and most vigorous of the Nile precursors. Its development marked the dawn of the present transcontinental river system, establishing flow from Ethiopia to the Mediterranean Sea and probably also from the Sudd.

The Neonile began about 120,000 years ago and was established at a time when North Africa was well-watered, with numerous lakes. Crude stones fashioned by humans are found in these sediments. The Neonile was significantly less vigorous than the Prenile. Several episodes when North Africa was wetter or drier can be identified. It was after the last wet period, sometime after ten thousand years ago, that hungry nomads migrated to the Nile Valley and Delta and took up farming. This process led in turn to the establishment of civilization in Egypt about five thousand years ago, a development with profound consequences for humankind.

Bibliography

Churchill, Winston. *The River War*. New York: Longmans, Green, 1899. An account of the Mahdi's rebellion in Sudan and the British expedition against it during the late nineteenth century. Accounts of military operations can be skimmed over, but the trials of navigation up the Nile provide the best account of the river upstream from Aswan. Provides a good understanding of why Egypt stops near Aswan. Suitable for the general reader.

Hillel, D. *Rivers of Eden*. New York: Oxford University Press, 1994. A wonderful account of the history of water use in the Middle East and the problems that the future holds for the region. Hillel is an environmental scientist and hydrologist, and his account is based on sound technical considerations, but he enlivens the tale with a generous spice of history, religion, and personal experience. Chapter 6 is entitled "The Mighty Nile." Suitable for the general reader.

Howell, P. P., and J. A. Allan, eds. *The Nile: Sharing a Scarce Resource*. Cambridge, England: Cambridge University Press, 1994. Overview of the history of the Nile, with special emphasis on how its flow has changed in the past. Discussion of the future utilization of the river and the problems facing planners. Comprehensive, excellent text, suitable for college students and professionals.

Moorehead, A. *The White Nile*. New York: Harper & Row, 1960. An account of the exploration and development of the White Nile, with emphasis of the discovery of Lake Victoria and the source of the White Nile during the mid-nineteenth century by Speke, the search of Henry Stanley for David Livingstone, and the Sudanese revolt and British reaction. An excellent overview of the land and the people, suitable for the general reader.

_____. *The Blue Nile*. New York: Harper & Row, 1962. Similar to *The White Nile* in its approach. An account of the exploration and development of the Blue Nile and parts of the Egyptian Nile, including the journey of James Bruce to the headwaters of the Blue Nile, Napoleon's invasion of Egypt, the empire of Mohamed Ali, and the collision of Ethiopian and British cultures at the end of the nineteenth century. These stories are told within a context of the land and the people of the Blue Nile basin and Egypt. Suitable for the general reader.

Said, R. *The Geological Evolution of the River Nile*. New York: Springer-Verlag, 1981. Outlines the geologic history of the Nile, with particular emphasis on the record from Egypt. This is the best source for those interested in the history of the Nile Valley and Delta in Egypt. Excellent figures and abundant references. Suitable for geologists and archaeologists.

Robert J. Stern

Cross-References

African Rift Valley System, 2805; The Amazon Basin, 2812; Dams and Flood Control, 309; Drainage Basins, 384; Earth System Science, 407; Floodplains, 712; Freshwater Chemistry, 795; The Geomorphology of Dry Climate Areas, 882; The Geomorphology of Wet Climate Areas, 890; Lakes, 1318; Mississippi River, 3010; Paleoclimatology, 1993; Precipitation, 2108; River Bed Forms, 2196; Sand, 2253; Sand Dunes, 2259; Sediment Transport and Deposition, 2290; Surface Water, 2504; Volcanoes: Flood Basalts, 2630; Watersheds, 3178.

NUCLEAR WINTER

Type of earth science: Atmospheric sciences and meteorology
Field of study: Analytical techniques

Nuclear winter is a model of the projected consequences of nuclear war, wherein smoke and dust concentrated in the upper atmosphere drastically reduce surface temperature and light by blocking solar radiation over several seasons or years, leading to collapse of the food chain, mass starvation, and possible human extinction. This model has drastically altered thinking on the survivability of humanity following a major nuclear exchange.

Principal terms
AEROSOL: a suspension of microscopic solid or liquid particles in a gas
GREENHOUSE EFFECT: various mechanisms for increasing the absorptive capacity of radiated energy by the atmosphere
THERMAL BUDGET: the balance of incoming and outgoing radiative energy in the earth's ecosystem

Summary of the Phenomenon

The theory of "nuclear winter" proposes that massive quantities of smoke and dust injected into the atmosphere by multiple nuclear detonations would drive temperatures on the earth's surface below the freezing point of water for extended periods and would diminish sunlight reaching the planet's surface, creating a period of prolonged cold and darkness. Atmospheric circulation could distribute the smoke and dust veils from even a moderate-sized nuclear exchange to make the effects global, rather than confined only to the regions of the detonations. Secondary effects from radioactive fallout and toxic substances carried by the smoke and dust veils also would be extremely widespread. The combined effects of nuclear winter could be sufficient to cause the eventual extinction of plant and animal life, and possibly of humanity itself.

The key factor in the nuclear-winter scenario is that the combined effects of smoke and dust injected into the atmosphere by multiple nuclear detonations could severely reduce the amount of sunlight reaching the surface of the earth, throwing the "thermal budget" of the ecosystem into imbalance and sending surface temperatures well into the subfreezing range. Over time and across latitudes, the thermal budget of the earth is more or less in balance, with the amount of thermal radiation incoming from the Sun more or less equal to the amount of energy radiated back into space. (Low latitudes characteristically receive more thermal radiation than they emit, and higher latitudes less, creating large-scale atmospheric and oceanic circulation patterns that balance the thermal budget and account for major weather patterns.)

Radiation from the Sun reaches the earth mostly in the visible-light wavelengths of the electromagnetic spectrum, but thermal radiation emitted from the earth's surface back into space is mostly in infrared wavelengths. If the earth did not have an atmosphere, the thermal budget would balance out at a level substantially below the freezing point of water. Fortunately, components of the atmosphere—primarily water and carbon-dioxide molecules—are excellent absorbers of solar radiation; consequently, they help to maintain ambient temperatures on most of the earth's surface above the freezing point of water, making possible a biological regime based on liquid water.

Nuclear winter is a kind of "anti-greenhouse" effect. The greenhouse effect is produced by increases in the amount of infrared-absorbing carbon dioxide in the atmosphere, increasing ambient temperatures at the earth's surface by reducing the amount of infrared energy being emitted into space. In the nuclear-winter scenario, changes in the atmosphere reduce the amount of incoming solar radiation reaching the surface by absorbing greater quantities of solar radiation in the upper atmosphere, with no reduction in surface infrared radiation to maintain a thermal balance. Surface temperatures would drop significantly; since any appropriate atmospheric agent responsible for such a reduction would have to absorb primarily visible light, continuous darkness would result at the earth's surface.

Depending upon the extent of a general nuclear exchange, from 100 million to 300 million metric tons of smoke and soot particles might be injected into the atmosphere, enough to diminish sunlight reaching the earth's surface by more than 90 percent if it were distributed uniformly throughout the atmosphere. The smoke would come from immense firestorms generated by detonations over urban or large industrial centers, so powerful that they would generate hurricane-like convective winds similar to those experienced by the victims of the Allied incendiary bombing of Dresden, Germany, in World War II.

The convective energy of these firestorms would drive the smoke and soot clouds beyond the dense troposphere into the stratosphere. The higher these clouds are injected, the longer they are likely to persist, since smoke and dust are cleansed from the atmosphere mostly by rainfall, and there is little water vapor in the stratosphere. Research suggests that this material would remain aloft long enough to become distributed throughout the stratosphere, with global rather than merely regional repercussions. Firestorms in modern urban centers, burning not only structures and material life but also huge quantities of plastics, light metals, and a host of synthetic chemicals of still unknown potential, would be far more dangerous over much greater areas than anything previously experienced. Additional smoke accumulation would come from forests and grasslands ignited by nuclear explosions.

The almost unthinkable loss of human life from the immediate effects of a nuclear conflict remain in the nuclear-winter scenario, but the secondary, longer-term losses are even more sobering. Deprived of heat and light, much of the earth would descend into a multiyear state of subfreezing temperatures and continuous darkness even at midday. Deaths from cold and exposure, and extraordinary psychological stress, would continue to increase the fatality rate in the aftermath of nuclear war. Over several seasons, the result would be collapse of the food chain, the destruction of most plant life and the animal life that feeds on it, and mass starvation. All remaining order would likely break down as survivors fought for food, water, and shelter.

Interruption of sunlight to the surface would result in breakdown of the process of photosynthesis in plants and, therefore, destruction of crops. Wild plant species would also be affected, and those susceptible to small changes in the environment would be driven to extinction. Large-scale extinction of vertebrate species dependent on plant matter for food would soon follow. At sea, the phytoplankton population that anchors the food chain for many large species would collapse; many of the larger species of aquatic life would face extinction as well.

Moderate-size thermonuclear explosions are capable of perforating the ozone layer of the earth's atmosphere; a significant number of such explosions could lead to massive ozone depletion. In addition to radioactive fallout from the explosions themselves—a hazard now judged to be more serious than previously believed, as a result of the long-term suspension of matter in the atmosphere—survivors of a nuclear war could be exposed to massive ultraviolet radiation from the Sun that is ordinarily blocked by atmospheric ozone.

The impact of radioactive fallout, once presumed to be localized in the vicinities of the nuclear explosions themselves, would become global and prolonged as these substances circulated in the upper atmosphere. Water and food sources hundreds or thousands of miles distant from actual detonations would be contaminated by atmospheric circulation of radioactive matter and toxic substances from burning cities. Human populations could decline to prehistoric levels, making the species vulnerable to eventual extinction.

Possible consequences of nuclear winter include long-term climatic disruption. For example, deposition of dust and soot over much of the earth's surface could lower the albedo, or reflective value, of the surface, with unknown climatic consequences over time. Coastal areas—in contrast to continental interiors, where convection would be almost nonexistent for years—might suffer storms of unprecedented magnitude, as warm air currents from over the oceans collided with chilled air masses on land.

Phenomena associated with the nuclear-winter scenario may vary considerably depending upon the magnitude of a nuclear exchange and the nature of selected targets; catastrophic results are possible far short of a full-scale thermonuclear war. In a "medium-range" exchange, for example, involving some 5,000 megatons of detonations, including a thousand ground bursts—the sort of exchange that might be envisioned should one superpower attempt to eliminate the first-strike capability of another—the resulting smoke and dust veils could create a global atmospheric inversion that would essentially stop wind currents near the surface. As the smoke and dust absorbed visible sunlight and blocked it from reaching the surface, the upper atmosphere would be heated as much as from 30 to 80 degrees Celsius. As the ground cooled, these hot layers would rise and expand, blanketing the planet in an unbroken cloud of smoke and dust. Even several months after the exchange, the lowest levels of the atmosphere would receive only enough radiation to drive very weak convective currents. This temperature inversion would inhibit the rise of moist air from the surface and thereby inhibit cleansing rainfall, increasing the time that the smoke and dust veils would remain suspended in the atmosphere.

One of the most significant features of the nuclear-winter model is the ability of its climatic consequences to involve the tropics through atmospheric circulation. Tropical plant and animal species are far more vulnerable than others to even minor shifts in temperature or rainfall. Prolonged cold and darkness over the tropics could result in the extinction of the majority of species on the planet. At the very least, destruction of the forest regions of the tropics, major absorbing agents for solar energy, would further alter the earth's thermal balance toward long-term subfreezing conditions. Widespread destruction of forests would also lead to further large-scale fires.

The nuclear-winter model predicts much more severe radiation hazards, spread over wider areas, than those estimated by earlier projections. Most radioactive isotopes in a nuclear explosion condense onto aerosols and dust sucked in by the initial fireball. Inasmuch as the model predicts very large quantities of dust aerosols in the atmosphere for longer periods of time, the dangers of transport or dispersal of radioactive materials would multiply, particularly with respect to intermediate and prolonged fallout. Although not immediately lethal, this fallout could lead to chronic radiation sickness, depressed immune systems, genetic defects, and delayed death for millions from cancer or other radiation-induced causes.

Methods of Study

Formulation of the nuclear-winter scenario, and its widespread discussion in the scientific, military, and political communities, resulted largely from the work of a research team appointed in 1982 by the National Academy of Sciences (NAS). The NAS requested that Richard B. Turco, Owen B. Toon, Thomas P. Ackerman, James B. Pollack, and Carl Sagan (a team subsequently known by their last initials as "TTAPS") investigate the possible effects of dust raised by nuclear detonations. The TTAPS team comprised scientists who already had investigated a variety of atmospheric effects of dust particles, including the consequences of volcanic explosions, the behavior of dust storms on Mars, and theories of mass extinction caused by asteroid or comet impacts in the geologic past.

Computer modeling represents the only feasible means of studying the consequences of a nuclear exchange. The TTAPS researchers had access to advanced models for atmospheric circulation, particle microphysics, and radiative-convective behavior. Also used were models of nuclear-exchange scenarios of varying size and geographical complexity. Other researchers, including Paul J. Crutzen at the Max Planck Institute for Chemistry in West Germany and John W. Birks at the University of Colorado, persuaded the TTAPS team to include in their research the possible effects of smoke from massive fires caused by nuclear explosions.

Prior to the TTAPS research, little was known about potential large-scale smoke-and-dust pollution except as the consequence of volcanic explosions. The TTAPS team was able to study firsthand results of the explosion of El Chichón in 1982, which generated a significant dust veil and possibly some short-term surface temperature reduction in some areas. The much larger explosion of Krakatoa in 1883 caused visible atmospheric effects around the world and, possibly, minor surface-temperature changes. Historically, several volcanic explosions far larger than Krakatoa are known from the eighteenth and nineteenth centuries, some of them comparable in energy to several multimegaton nuclear detonations. Yet none generated more than minor multiyear climatic effects.

The TTAPS team concluded that earlier attempts to judge the possible effects of nuclear explosions based on records and observations of volcanic explosions were misleading. No matter how large, volcanic events were episodic and localized. The clouds of soil-and-dust particles, or aerosols, created by these explosions consist mostly of relatively large and bright, light-scattering particles that can create dazzling displays but do not absorb much visible light. By including in their model the smoke and soot from fires generated by nuclear explosions, however, the TTAPS team identified the potential source of aerosols of very dark and very fine particles with average diameters smaller than the typical wavelength of infrared radiation. These smoke and soot particles would have a very high absorptive capacity for visible light but would not correspondingly increase infrared absorption in the atmosphere, thus bringing about surface darkness and temperature reduction.

One of the most unsettling results of the TTAPS research was to show that a full-scale nuclear exchange between the superpowers would not be needed to bring about the most serious nuclear-winter effects. Presuming that such an exchange would entail a total explosive yield of about 25,000 megatons, nuclear winter could be triggered by much smaller conflicts—in the range of from 3,000 to 5,000 megatons, depending upon the nature of the targets. Prior to the 1963 international treaty banning atmospheric testing of nuclear weapons, scenarios of nuclear conflict centered on massive atmospheric explosions of thermonuclear weapons in the 20-to-40-megaton range, principally over cities and refinery areas. Many of these weapons were to have been delivered by strategic bombers.

Subsequent development of ballistic missiles using multiple re-entry warhead configurations of from 1 to 5 megatons each, directed initially at the enemy's own silos, greatly increased the anticipated number of ground-level detonations in a nuclear war scenario, thereby increasing the expected amount of material injected into the atmosphere by the explosions. Ironically, the strategic use of much larger numbers of considerably smaller-yield warheads makes a nuclear-winter catastrophe even more likely, even if the nuclear exchange were limited to "surgical" strikes concentrated on missile silos and military installations.

Context

Prior to the development of the nuclear-winter scenario, it was generally assumed that humanity could survive a nuclear conflict. Granted that enormous loss of life, destruction of cities, and long-term radiation effects would occur, in the sort of nuclear exchange typically envisioned between superpowers, such damage would be confined mostly to the Northern Hemisphere. The Southern Hemisphere, the tropical areas of the earth, and even noncombatant areas in the Northern Hemisphere might be spared the worst. The dynamics of the nuclear-winter model suggest, instead, that the consequences would be global, climatic in a sense not previously foreseen, and probably sufficiently long-term to bring the survival of humanity into question.

The theme of nuclear winter became part of scientific and political debate at a unique juncture of human knowledge in atmospheric and climatic studies and the development of a new relationship between the United States and the Soviet Union. During the 1970's, global research established new links between tropical atmospheric circulation and climatic events. In the early 1980's, paleontologists formed a broad consensus that conditions similar to a nuclear winter some 65 million years ago, caused by a massive asteroid or meteor impact on the earth's surface, may have led to the demise of the dinosaurs. Space probes returned enormous amounts of new information concerning the likely histories of atmospheres on Venus and Mars.

In tandem with this new perspective on the potential fragility of life on the earth, international relations in the early 1980's took on new dimensions with a relaxation of tensions between the United States and the Soviet Union. In fact, some historians credit the TTAPS team itself with being instrumental in changing the superpower relationship, by reaffirming in the most somber terms that any significant exchange of nuclear weapons could lead to a climatic catastrophe threatening the survival of humanity. Realization that nuclear winter might result even from a limited nuclear exchange also led to renewed anxieties about nuclear proliferation and about potential regional nuclear exchanges in the future.

The interjection of the scientific debate about nuclear winter into the geopolitical and security considerations of actual and aspiring nuclear powers represents a distinctive example of the potential impact of new scientific findings on policy formulation. Nuclear winter made the first-strike strategy, even for those willing to consider it, unacceptable. It immediately depolarized international relations by suggesting that minor nuclear powers also held in their hands the potential for destroying civilization. Given that nuclear winter is a nonphenomenon, in the sense that it has not occurred, its impact on policymakers represents an acceptance of computer modeling more comprehensive than any previous one. Although no definitive study is available, early research suggests that contemplation of the nuclear-winter model was instrumental in moving the superpowers toward scaled nuclear-arms control. Nuclear winter therefore demands attention as a sociopolitical as well as potential physical phenomenon.

Bibliography

Diermendjian, Diran. *"Nuclear Winter": A Brief Review and Comments on Some Recent Literature*. Santa Monica, Calif.: RAND Corporation, 1988. An independent study of the first few years of debate about nuclear winter and policy implications. Covers some of the research literature outside the United States.

Ehrlich, Paul R., et al. *The Cold and the Dark: The World After Nuclear War*. New York: W. W. Norton, 1984. A summary of the TTAPS research for the general public.

Ehrlich, Paul R., et al. "Long-Term Biological Consequences of the Nuclear War." *Science* 222 (1983): 1293-1300. Confirms and elaborates upon the TTAPS team projections of the dangers of nuclear winter to plants and animals (and, hence, human food supplies) and projects likely conditions over several different time intervals. Together with a TTAPS article preceding it in the issue, this article announced the nuclear-winter scenario, and debate about it, to the scientific community.

Fisher, David E. *Fire and Ice: The Greenhouse Effect, Ozone Depletion, and Nuclear Winter*. New York: Harper & Row, 1990. Juxtaposes the twin hazards of global warming through the greenhouse effect and possible global winter resulting from nuclear war. Calls for more environmental and foreign-policy responsibility to avoid these dangers.

Greene, Owen. *Nuclear Winter: The Evidence and the Risks*. Cambridge, England: Polity Press, 1985. An independent confirmation of the TTAPS research that had a significant impact in Europe.

Harwell, Mark. *Nuclear Winter: The Human and Environmental Consequences of Nuclear War*. New York: Springer-Verlag, 1984. General survey of nuclear-winter conditions, with particularly good treatment of the potential hazards of widespread distribution of toxic materials by fires in bombed cities.

Nuclear Winter and National Security: Implications for Future Policy. Maxwell Air Force Base, Ala.: Air University Press, 1986. Papers from a military symposium that concluded that publicizing the nuclear-winter scenario would lead to increased international pressure for nuclear disarmament, thus affecting the capability of the military to respond to threats. Reflects a certain unwillingness on the part of military planners to accept the predictions of the nuclear-winter model.

Sagan, Carl. "Nuclear Winter and Climatic Catastrophe: Some Policy Implications." *Foreign Affairs* 62 (Winter, 1983): 257-292. A major contribution toward introducing the nuclear-winter issue into foreign-policy debates among the informed public, by the most prominent science writer on the TTAPS team.

Sagan, Carl, and Richard Turco. *A Path Where No Man Thought: Nuclear Winter and the End of the Arms Race*. New York: Random House, 1990. Two members of the TTAPS team tell the story of the research program and the campaign to bring the results to the attention of political and military authorities. Interesting speculations on how the findings may have influenced geopolitical and military thinking of major powers other than the United States.

Turco, Richard P., et al. "The Climatic Effects of Nuclear War." *Scientific American* 251, no. 2 (August, 1984): 33-43. Extraordinarily important article for its introduction of the TTAPS research to the scientifically educated public.

_____. "Nuclear Winter: Global Consequences of Multiple Nuclear Explosions." *Science* 222 (1983): 1283-1292. The key article announcing the TTAPS team findings to the scientific community.

Ronald W. Davis

Cross-References

The Atmosphere's Global Circulation, 121; Atmospheric Ozone, 144; Climate, 217; Fallout, 2918; Global Warming, 2932; Nuclear Power, 1749; Volcanic Hazards, 2601.

OZONE HOLES

Type of earth science: Atmospheric sciences and meteorology

The term "ozone hole" refers to the seasonal decrease in stratospheric ozone concentration occurring over Antarctica during early spring. The formation of the Antarctic ozone hole has been linked to migration of chlorofluorocarbons (CFCs) and related compounds to the stratosphere following their release in the lower atmosphere. Ozone-hole formation is evidence that human activities can significantly alter the composition of the atmosphere.

Principal terms

CATALYST: a substance that increases the rate of a chemical reaction without itself being produced or destroyed

CHLOROFLUOROCARBON (CFC): a chemical compound containing carbon, fluorine, and chlorine, used in air conditioners, refrigerators, and other applications

DOBSON SPECTROPHOTOMETER: a ground-based instrument for measuring the total column abundance of ozone at a particular geographic location

OZONE: an elemental form of oxygen containing three atoms of oxygen per molecule

OZONE LAYER: a region in the lower stratosphere, centered about 25 kilometers above the surface of the earth, which contains the highest concentration of ozone found in the atmosphere

POLAR STRATOSPHERIC CLOUDS: clouds of ice crystals formed at extremely low temperatures in the polar stratosphere

POLAR VORTEX: a closed atmospheric circulation pattern around the South Pole that exists during the winter and early spring; atmospheric mixing between the polar vortex and regions outside the vortex is slow

STRATOSPHERE: the region of the atmosphere between 10 and 50 kilometers above the surface of the earth

TOTAL COLUMN ABUNDANCE OF OZONE: the total number of molecules of ozone above a 1-centimeter-square area of the earth's surface

TOTAL OZONE MAPPING SPECTROMETER (TOMS): a space-based instrument for measuring the total column abundance of ozone globally

Summary of the Phenomenon

Ozone, although only a minor component of the atmosphere, plays a vital role in the survival of life on Earth. Ozone molecules absorb high-energy ultraviolet (UV) light from the Sun. Absorption of ultraviolet light in the ozone layer, a region of the stratosphere that contains the maximum concentration of ozone, prevents most such light from reaching the surface of the planet. Low levels of ultraviolet radiation are known to cause skin cancers, cataracts, and autoimmune disorders in humans, and similar disorders in other animals. In addition, exposure to low-intensity ultraviolet light can result in reduced crop yields in ultraviolet-sensitive plants and partial destruction of ocean phytoplankton, simple sea organisms at the bottom of the aquatic food chain. Higher levels of ultraviolet light have more drastic effects. If none of the Sun's ultraviolet radiation were blocked by the ozone layer, it would be difficult for most forms of life, including humans, to survive on land.

The concentration of ozone in the atmosphere is highly variable, changing with altitude, geographic location, time of day, time of year, and prevailing local atmospheric conditions. Long-term fluctuations in ozone concentration are also seen, some of which are related to the solar sunspot cycle. While long-term average ozone concentrations are relatively stable, short-term fluctuations of as much as 10 percent in total column abundance of ozone as a result of the natural variability in ozone concentration are often observed.

Beginning in the early 1970's, a new and unexpected decrease in stratospheric ozone concentration was first observed. The decrease was localized in geography to the southern polar region, and in time to early spring (which begins in October in the Southern Hemisphere). The initial decrease in ozone was small, but by 1980, decreases in total column abundance of ozone of as much as 30 percent were being seen, well outside the range of variation expected as a result of random fluctuations. This seasonal destruction of stratospheric ozone above Antarctica, which by 1990 had reached 50 percent of the total atmospheric ozone concentration, was soon given the label "ozone hole."

While it was unclear at first whether formation of the Antarctic ozone hole stemmed from natural causes or from anthropogenic effects on the environment, extensive field studies combined with the results of laboratory experiments and computer modeling of the atmosphere quickly led to a consistent and detailed explanation for ozone-hole formation. The formation of the ozone hole has two principal causes: chemical reactions that occur generally throughout the stratosphere, and special conditions that exist in the Antarctic region.

Under normal conditions, the concentration of ozone in the stratosphere is determined by a balance between reactions that remove ozone and those that produce ozone. The removal reactions are mainly catalytic chain reactions, in which trace atmospheric chemical species destroy ozone molecules without themselves being consumed. In such processes, it is possible for one chain carrier to remove many ozone molecules before being removed. The trace species involved in ozone removal include hydrogen oxides and nitrogen oxides, formed primarily from naturally occurring processes, and chlorine and bromine atoms and their corresponding oxides.

The main source of chlorine in the stratosphere is the decomposition of a class of compounds called chlorofluorocarbons (CFCs). Such compounds can be used in refrigeration and air conditioning, as aerosol propellants, and as solvents. Chlorofluorocarbons are extremely stable in the lower atmosphere, with lifetimes of several decades. The main fate of chlorofluorocarbons is slow migration into the stratosphere, where they absorb ultraviolet light and release chlorine atoms. The chlorine atoms produced from the breakdown of chlorofluorocarbons in the stratosphere provide an additional catalytic process by which stratospheric ozone can be destroyed. A similar set of reactions involving a class of bromine-containing compounds called halons, used in some types of fire extinguishers, leads to additional ozone destruction. By 1986, the average global loss of stratospheric ozone caused by the release of chlorofluorocarbons, halons, and related compounds into the environment was 2 percent.

While the decomposition and subsequent reaction of chlorofluorocarbons and other synthetic compounds explains the small general decline in ozone concentration observed in the stratosphere, additional processes are needed to account for the more massive seasonal ozone depletion observed above Antarctica. These processes involve a set of special conditions that in combination are unique to the stratosphere in the vicinity of the South Pole.

During daylight hours, a portion of chlorine present in the stratosphere is tied up in the form of reservoir species, compounds such as hydrogen chloride and chlorine nitrate that do not react with ozone. This helps slow the rate of removal of ozone by chlorine. Processes that directly or indirectly involve absorption of sunlight transform reservoir species into ozone-destroying chlorine atoms. During the Antarctic winter, when sunlight is entirely absent, stratospheric chlorine is rapidly converted into reservoir species.

In the absence of additional chemical processes, the onset of spring in Antarctica and the return of sunlight would convert a portion of the reservoir compounds into reactive chlorine species and reestablish the balance between ozone-producing and ozone-destroying processes. However, the extremely low temperatures occurring in the stratosphere above Antarctica during the winter months leads to the formation of polar stratospheric clouds, which, because of the extremely low concentration of water vapor in the stratosphere, do not form during other seasons or outside the polar regions of the globe. The ice crystals that compose the clouds act as catalysts that convert reservoir species into diatomic chlorine and other gaseous chlorine compounds that, in the presence of sunlight, reform ozone-destroying species. At the same time, the nitrogen oxides found in the reservoir species are converted into nitric acid, which remains attached to the ice crystals. As these ice crystals are slowly removed from the stratosphere by gravity, the potential for conversion of active forms of chlorine into reservoir species is greatly reduced. Because of this, when spring arrives, large amounts of ozone-destroying chlorine species are produced by the action of sunlight, and only a small fraction of this reactive chlorine is converted into reservoir species. The increased rate of ozone removal caused by the abundance of reactive chlorine present in the stratosphere leads to ozone depletion and formation of the ozone hole.

An additional process important in formation of the ozone hole is the unique air-circulation pattern in the stratosphere above Antarctica. During the winter and early spring, a vortex of winds circulates about the South Pole. This polar vortex minimizes movement of ozone and reservoir-forming compounds from other regions of the stratosphere. As this polar vortex breaks up in midspring, ozone concentrations in the Antarctic stratosphere return to normal levels, and the ozone hole gradually disappears.

While conditions in the Arctic stratosphere are similar to those found above Antarctica, important differences make formation of an Arctic ozone hole unlikely. Temperatures in the stratosphere during the winter months in the polar regions in the Northern Hemisphere are not as low as those found above Antarctica, making the formation of polar stratospheric clouds a less-favored process. In addition, the presence of mountain ranges at high latitudes in the Northern Hemisphere, such as the Rocky Mountains in North America and Ural Mountains in Russia, prevents formation of a stable polar vortex about the North Pole. While some ozone loss has been observed in isolated regions of the Arctic stratosphere in early spring, formation of an Arctic ozone hole has not occurred.

Methods of Study

The first instrument designed to measure atmospheric ozone was the Dobson spectrophotometer. Designed by Sir Gordon Dobson in 1926, this ground-based instrument measures the intensity of sunlight at several wavelengths in the ultraviolet region of the spectrum. By determining the fraction of sunlight absorbed by atmospheric ozone, the total column abundance of ozone at a particular geographic location can be found. Dobson also established the first global monitoring network to measure atmospheric ozone concentrations. Data from some of these early ozone-monitoring stations dates back to the early 1930's. The station at Halley Bay, Antarctica, from which Joseph Farman and coworkers obtained the data used to discover the existence of the ozone hole, was established in 1957 as part of the International Geophysical Year program of Earth and atmospheric observations.

The first space-based ozone monitoring instrument was carried into Earth orbit on the Nimbus 4 satellite in 1970. The instrument used measurements of the intensity of ultraviolet light scattered by the atmosphere to determine stratospheric ozone concentration and operated continuously for two years. An improved version of this instrument, which in addition to total column abundance of ozone also provided some information on the distribution of ozone in the atmosphere as a function of altitude, was included on the Nimbus 7 satellite launched into orbit in October, 1978. A second instrument on the Nimbus 7 satellite, the Total Ozone Mapping Spectrometer (TOMS), measured total column abundance of ozone on a daily basis at all latitudes illuminated with sunlight. This global coverage is the main advantage of space-based instruments over ground monitoring stations, which provide data for only a limited number of geographic locations. Data from the TOMS instrument confirmed the existence of the Antarctic ozone hole. Additional space-based instruments have provided a continuous record of global ozone concentrations since the late 1970's as well as improved data on the vertical distribution of ozone within the atmosphere.

In addition to ground-based and space-based ozone-measuring instruments, balloon-borne instruments can also be used to measure atmospheric ozone. Such instruments provide detailed data on the vertical distribution of ozone in the atmosphere. Balloon-borne instruments can also be used to measure concentrations of other trace atmospheric species, such as chlorine monoxide and chlorine nitrate, important in the mechanism for formation of the Antarctic ozone hole. Balloon measurements at the McMurdo Station in Antarctica in 1986 and 1987 provided key information confirming the mechanism for ozone-hole formation. Similar instruments carried in high-altitude aircraft have also been used to provide data on the distribution of ozone and trace chemical species in the stratosphere.

Context

The discovery of the Antarctic ozone hole in 1985 came at a time when efforts to limit the production and use of chlorofluorocarbons had stalled. Following the 1974 publication by F. Sherwood Rowland and Mario Molina of the theory that release of chlorofluorocarbons in the lower atmosphere would eventually lead to depletion of stratospheric ozone, with corresponding adverse health and economic consequences, Canada, Sweden, and the United States had banned the use of CFCs as aerosol propellants. However, because of uncertainties about the predicted effects of CFC release on atmospheric ozone and the lack of conclusive evidence of ozone depletion, more stringent regulations on CFCs were not enacted.

The discovery of the ozone hole and the rapid confirmation that its formation was a direct consequence of the release of CFCs into the atmosphere spurred scientists and environmentalists to renew efforts to place severe limits on the production and use of CFCs. In 1987, the Montreal Protocol, a multinational agreement to reduce the manufacture of chlorofluorocarbons and related compounds over the next two decades, was signed by representatives of forty-three nations. In the United States, passage of the 1990 Clean Air Act Amendments set a specific timetable for phasing out the production and use of CFCs by the year 2000. In response to these efforts, several chemical compounds such as hydrochlorofluorocarbons (HCFCs) and hydrofluorocarbons (HFCs) were developed for use as replacements for CFCs. These replacement compounds are far less stable in the lower atmosphere than CFCs and therefore have greatly reduced potential for destruction of stratospheric ozone. However, because of the long lifetime of CFCs in the lower atmosphere, the effects of CFCs on stratospheric ozone and the formation of the ozone hole are expected to continue until at least the middle of the twenty-first century.

The discovery of the Antarctic ozone hole represents the first concrete example of a major global environmental change directly linked to human activities. As such, it serves as a paradigm for other potential consequences of human activity such as the general decline in stratospheric ozone concentrations and the occurrence of global warming.

Bibliography

Bast, Joseph L., Peter J. Hill, and Richard C. Rue. *Eco-Sanity: A Common Sense Guide to Environmentalism.* Lanham, Md.: Heartland Institute, 1994. Highly critical of claims that human activities have the potential to degrade the global environment significantly. Although the authors are selective in the information they present, the book represents an interesting minority opinion on issues of global change. Ozone depletion and the ozone hole are briefly discussed in chapter 4.

Cagin, Seth, and Philip Dray. *Between Earth and Sky: How CFCs Changed Our World and Endangered the Ozone Layer*. New York: Pantheon Books, 1993. A history of chlorofluorocarbons. Beginning with the discovery of CFCs in 1928, the book goes on to discuss the increasing use of CFCs during the following decades, the establishment of the link between CFCs and stratospheric ozone depletion, and the subsequent restrictions placed on the use and manufacture of CFCs. Chapters 16 through 21 focus on the ozone hole.

Cogan, Douglas C. *Stones in a Glass House: CFCs and Ozone Depletion*. Washington, D.C.: Investor Responsibility Research Center, 1988. Provides a wealth of statistical information on the production and use of chlorofluorocarbons and the effects of such compounds on the atmosphere. Chapter 3 provides a brief history of the events surrounding discovery of the ozone hole.

Firor, John. *The Changing Atmosphere: A Global Challenge*. New Haven, Conn.: Yale University Press, 1990. An interesting and readable introduction to atmospheric science and global change. Complex scientific research is presented in a clear and balanced manner. Both scientific issues and the corresponding political challenges are discussed.

Fisher, David E. *Fire and Ice: The Greenhouse Effect, Ozone Depletion, and Nuclear Winter*. New York: Harper & Row, 1990. A thorough discussion of the real and potential effects of human activities on the global environment. Chapter 12 gives a brief history of the events surrounding the discovery of the Antarctic ozone hole.

Graedel, T. E., and Paul J. Crutzen. *Atmospheric Change: An Earth System Perspective*. New York: W. H. Freeman, 1993. An introduction to atmospheric science by two well-known workers in the field, one of whom, Crutzen, shared the 1995 Nobel Prize in Chemistry for his work in atmospheric chemistry. While portions of the book require an understanding of college-level mathematics and chemistry, most of the book can be understood without such a background. The large number of figures and tables are of particular interest.

Roan, Susan. *Ozone Crisis: The Fifteen-Year Evolution of a Sudden Global Emergency*. New York: John Wiley & Sons, 1989. A detailed account of the scientific and political events associated with the discovery of the connection between chlorofluorocarbons and stratospheric ozone depletion. Chapters 8 through 16 focus on the evidence linking the ozone hole to increasing atmospheric concentrations of CFCs, and the regulation of CFCs that followed.

Rowland, F. Sherwood. "Stratospheric Ozone Depletion." *Annual Review of Physical Chemistry* 42 (1991): 731. Although this article may be difficult to find, it is well worth the effort. Rowland, cowinner of the 1995 Nobel Prize in Chemistry for his work on ozone depletion, has written a thorough but highly readable review of stratospheric ozone chemistry and the role of chlorofluorocarbons and related compounds in ozone depletion. While some background in chemistry is useful for full understanding of the material, the essential points of the article can be understood by the layperson.

Somerville, Richard C. J. *The Forgiving Air: Understanding Environmental Change.* Los Angeles: University of California Press, 1996. A thorough investigation of the relationship between human activities and changes in the atmosphere and global climate. Written by a scientist involved in atmospheric research, but aimed at a nonscientific audience. Chapter 2 is a discussion of the ozone hole.

Jeffrey A. Joens

Cross-References

Air Pollution, 24; The Atmosphere's Evolution, 114; The Atmosphere's Global Circulation, 121; The Atmosphere's Structure and Composition, 128; Atmospheric Ozone, 144; Global Warming, 2932.

PALEOGEOGRAPHY AND PALEOCURRENTS

Type of earth science: Geology
Field of study: Geochronology

Paleogeography is both the geography of a past geologic time and the science of its determination. Paleocurrents are currents existing within a paleogeographic environment or region.

Principal terms

AZIMUTH: degrees of arc measured clockwise from the north
CORRELATION: the determination of identity in age, fossil content, or physical continuity of rocks observed in different areas
ENDEMIC SPECIES: species confined to a restricted area in a restricted environment
EPICONTINENTAL SEA: a sea overlapping continental crust, as opposed to a sea underlain by oceanic crust
ISOTOPES: forms of an element having the same atomic number but differing atomic weights
PLANETARY WIND SYSTEM: a global atmospheric circulation pattern, as in the belt of prevailing westerlies
REMANENT MAGNETISM: the magnetic field imposed upon a rock at the time of its formation in accord with the global magnetic field

Summary of the Phenomenon

Paleogeography is the geography or the study of the geography of a time in the past. Paleogeographic interpretations or maps may refer to any geographic phenomenon or group of phenomena, so there are many special types of paleogeographic maps. Paleobiogeographic maps show distribution of fossil species, ecological assemblages, floras, or faunas. Paleoclimatological maps plot ancient climatic realms, and paleo-physiographic maps depict ancient landforms. Paleotectonic maps outline regions of deformation, including crustal compression, crustal extension, persistent uplift or depression, and stable areas. Paleobathymetric maps describe the depths of ancient bodies of water. Maps defining past patterns of circulation in the sea, a lake, or stream are called "paleocurrent" maps. Any geographic property, in fact, may be the subject of a specialized paleogeographic map. Paleogeographic maps are, however, interpretive maps; that is, they are not maps of existing conditions or objects but describe conditions inferred from the rock record. They cannot be verified by direct observation in nature. Paleogeographic maps and interpretations may illustrate the geography of the entire globe, of whole continents, or merely of specific regions or features.

Global maps generally show continents and ocean basins as they are inferred to have existed during a major interval of time, such as a geologic period. The continents shown on these maps may be parts of present-day continents or may be composed of the merged parts of several modern continents. Furthermore, the ancient continents are not likely to be located in their present position in reference to latitude and longitude. On many of these maps, ancient continental land masses and archipelagos are plotted over the whole earth, with the outline of present continents and parts of continents superimposed. A series of such maps thus records the manner in which segments of continental crust have continually divided, split, merged, and moved about throughout geologic time. The maps for the Precambrian, which are least reliable, record the appearance of many "protocontinents," coalescing blocks of continental crust, lighter rocks of the composition of granite that form an incomplete outermost layer of the rocky earth. These protocontinents eventually gathered to form perhaps five ancestral continents. During the Early Paleozoic, these gathered in two large continents, one, Laurasia, in the Northern Hemisphere and one, Gondwanaland, in the Southern Hemisphere. During the Late Paleozoic, Laurasia and Gondwanaland coalesced in a single continental mass, Pangaea. A large embayment, the Tethys Sea, indented the eastern side of Gondwanaland and is the remote ancestor of the Mediterranean Sea. During the Mesozoic and Cenozoic, this single large continent, Pangaea, progressively separated into the modern suite of continents: North America, South America, Eurasia, Africa, Australia, and Antarctica. These continents gradually moved to their present positions relative to the poles and the equator. Global paleogeographic maps of this sort first appeared in the middle twentieth century, as the theory of plate tectonics and paleomagnetic concepts were discovered and accepted.

Knowledge of the global position, size, and interconnections of the continents and ocean basins is required to place past geologic events in a geographic context. It also is needed for full understanding of present global geologic relationships. The past position of crustal blocks, continents or parts of continents, and ocean basins may be inferred in part from the remanent magnetism of rocks of known age. Remanent magnetism is a magnetic field imprinted in a rock and conforming to the world's magnetic field existing at the time the rock was formed. This remanent magnetic field remains fixed, even if the rock is subsequently rotated or moved. It is, therefore, a permanent record of the original latitude and orientation of the rock. Thus, the azimuth direction of the remanent magnetism in a rock indicates the position of the pole with respect to the locality of a rock when it was deposited or intruded. The polarity of the remanent field reveals the polarity, normal or reversed, at the time the rock formed. The inclination of the vertical component of the remanent field gives the latitude at which the rock formed. Also, regions in which the remanent magnetic fields in rocks of common age are oriented uniformly may be considered parts of the same continental blocks or fragments. The remanent field is susceptible to destruction only by heating the rock to near-melting temperatures. The longitudinal position of a rock cannot be determined by paleomagnetic analysis, so other phenomena must be called upon to place ancient continental crustal blocks in their proper positions on the globe.

Former continuity between separated continental blocks may be inferred from their shape, as in the apparent match between the eastern coastline of the Americas and the western coast of Europe and Africa. This pattern was noted and a relationship inferred as early as the first half of the nineteenth century. Such "jigsaw puzzle" techniques are a significant aid in continental placement. It should be noted, however, that the land area of a continent is not what is being matched; much of the continent is submerged, so the location of the continental margin and slope is essential.

Apparent continuity of ancient geologic features on the margin of separated continental masses suggested former connections before the advent of plate tectonics, however, and still reinforces paleogeographic reconstructions. For example, the apparent continuation of the Appalachian orogenic belt and the band of carboniferous coal deposits from Texas to Newfoundland, the British Isles, and Western Europe supports the idea of former continuity between the land masses involved. Common occurrence of glacial deposits, coal beds, similar volcanic extrusives, and disjunct occurrences of fossil organisms incapable of crossing open oceans in Australia, India, Antarctica, South America, and Africa all support reconstruction of the Gondwanaland continent. Before the advent of plate tectonics, now-submerged continent-sized land masses in the South Atlantic and Indian Oceans or long isthmian land bridges were postulated as crossing those oceans to explain the present distribution of the Gondwanaland fauna and flora.

Paleogeographic maps of continental masses may show the distribution of ancient geographic features on modern-day continents, or they may refer to continents as they existed at some former time. Maps of the distribution of the land, sea, and ancient mountain ranges on present-day continents have been produced since the mid-nineteenth century. These maps will show the epicontinental seas, seas consisting of marine waters overflowing continental crust, as opposed to seas in deep ocean basins. Such maps also show the continental shelf or inundated continental margin, the relatively steep continental slopes at the very edge of the continental crust, and dry-land areas. In addition, major belts of deformation, broad areas of uplift, and broad areas of subsidence, or basins, are frequently shown on these maps. More detailed, and generally more specific, maps will show such things as deltas, ancient volcanic tracts, coastal lagoons, estuaries, reefs, dune fields, mountains, and glaciers.

Regional maps may show the paleogeography of areas defined by geologic interest, or they may be bounded arbitrarily. Examples of the first would include a map of the Late Paleozoic Ancestral Rocky Mountains. A set of paleogeographic maps for a state would exemplify the second. Regional maps of smaller areas generally are more detailed than continental or global maps and are more directly derived from local geology and paleontology. Latitude and pole position may, however, be shown and are determined by the same techniques employed in producing global or continental scaled maps. At the regional level, paleogeography may be concerned with the distribution of land and sea, mountain ranges, volcanic regions, lakes, flora and fauna, and the climate.

Paleogeographic maps are constructed by correlating and establishing the extent of rocks of the age in question. The conditions under which contemporaneous rocks were deposited are then determined. In this way, areas of uniform or nearly uniform environment may be outlined and mapped. Areas lacking rocks of the age under consideration were regions of nondeposition or intrusion or were areas subsequently eroded to remove rocks of that age. Areas undergoing deformation and areas suffering igneous intrusion or extrusive volcanism also are defined and mapped.

Methods of Study

By far the most used and most definitive means of determining contemporaneity among rocks is by their fossil content. Thus, rocks containing fossils belonging to a defined period are assignable to the interval of time defined by the zone. The age of rocks lacking fossils for which a time range has been determined—such as, perhaps, deposits in an isolated sequence of lake beds in which all of the fossils represent endemic species not found elsewhere, or rocks completely lacking fossils, such as almost all igneous and metamorphic rocks—still may be determinable by physical means. Such rocks may be interspersed among rocks of paleontologically determined age. Lateral continuity with rocks of paleontologically determined age may serve to "date" unfossiliferous rocks. Unfossiliferous rocks may also laterally interdigitate; that is, they may undergo a process of lateral replacement in which wedges of fossiliferous rock penetrate between layers of unfossiliferous material. Structural relationships may also define the age of a rock body if it has been deformed by one episode of known age but antedates another dated event. Finally, rocks recording geologically instantaneous events, such as massive explosive volcanic eruptions, may leave a layer of rock throughout a very large region. Individual volcanic ash beds, such as those of Ordovician age found throughout the Mississippi Valley, are a good example. During times of continental glaciation, cyclical melting and freezing of glaciers caused short-lived advances and retreats of the sea. These are recorded in repetitive cycles of sediments representing terrestrial and marine or deep-water and shallow-water conditions throughout the seas and coastal regions of the world. Individual rock units there may have originated within a lapse of no more than ten thousand years or so, making them practically instantaneous on the scale of geologic time.

In addition, rocks of all ages, from most ancient to recent, are potentially dated according to the condition of radioactive isotopes incorporated or formed at the time of their deposition. Radioactive isotopes progressively decay to form daughter isotopes; radioactive isotopes of uranium, for example, decay at a known rate to produce lead. Thus, the ratio of daughter isotopes to undecayed radioactive material indicates the age of the rock containing the material, provided there has been no addition or loss of substances involved in the reaction. The ratio of uranium to radioactively generated lead in a crystal of known composition thus gives the age of that crystal and its enclosing rock. Similarly, the ratio of unstable carbon isotopes to stable isotopes is a measure of the time since that carbon was isolated in plant or animal tissue. Also, remanent magnetism indicates the position of the magnetic north and magnetic south poles at the time of formation of the rock, and rocks of a common age will generate a common pole position. Inasmuch as the polarity of the earth's field periodically reverses, rocks may be assigned to defined periods of normal or reversed polarity.

After rocks of equivalent age have been identified within an area, it is possible to map the distribution of materials formed in an identified environment and map the area accordingly. If rocks of the age in question are absent, then either the area was undergoing erosion at the time, or deposits of that age have been subsequently removed. Rocks of the age in question surrounding the spot on the map lacking rocks of that age may be examined to determine whether erosional debris derived from the "bald" spot were being deposited or whether there is no such evidence. In many cases, resolution of this question is impossible.

Once rocks of a given age have been correlated and recognized within the region to be mapped, petrographic and paleontologic analysis will refer them to a limited environment. Fossils of near-shore organisms identify near-shore conditions where they are found; lateritic deposits identify the extent of a high-temperature, alternately wet and dry climate, as now occurs in the high tropics; carbonaceous sediments, such as coal and black shale, identify regions of chemically reducing environment; and regions of highly deformed and metamorphosed rocks identify areas of deep burial and intense deformation. When plotted on maps, these data produce a paleogeographic map.

At the most general level, areas occupied by rocks of the age being studied are outlined, excluding areas where they are not present. Areas where there is no record are areas in which erosion was proceeding at the time in question or in which later erosion has removed the record. Areas in which rocks of the age in question occur, obviously, were environments in which deposition was underway. These regions will primarily be marine environments, so the simplest paleogeographic map is one in which areas presumably occupied by epicontinental seas are outlined and distinguished from areas of nondeposition or later erosion; these are generally taken to have been land at the time. If the areas of no record are surrounded by concentric bands of near-shore sediments, then it may be assumed that these regions were, in fact, land at the time of deposition. If, on the other hand, bands of rock representing diverse environments are truncated by the margin of the area of no record, then it may be assumed that the lack of record is a result of subsequent erosion.

The term "paleocurrent" generally refers to ancient marine currents but also can refer to currents in lakes and streams. It can also be extended to winds and flow paths in glaciers.

Ancient maritime current patterns may be inferred from the present response of ocean waters to the planetary wind system and to modification of the ideal planetary wind system by the distribution of continental land masses. This, of course, follows construction of a global paleogeologic map. The actual existence of such hypothetical currents, in some cases, may be evaluated by examination of paleobiogeographic patterns. Many marine organisms are involuntarily distributed by ocean currents, either as eggs or in the larval state. In this way, they may be carried across inhospitable bottom environments to isolated areas in which they are capable of living. A present-day example of this is the occurrence of reef corals in Bermuda, which is at the latitude of North Carolina. In this case, the Gulf Stream transports coral larvae to the island and keeps the water warm enough for them to thrive at an otherwise inhospitable latitude.

Context

Paleogeographic interpretations are important, and in some cases essential, aids in locating and exploiting mineral resources. Sand and gravel deposits, for example, are to be found in beach deposits, stream-channel deposits, and glacial outwash deposits. Paleogeographic maps showing the distribution of such ancient environments obviously are a guide to their discovery. Paleogeographic maps showing the known and presumed distribution of ancient swamps are a guide to coal discovery. More detailed maps showing the position of ancient river channels traversing the swamp and their associated natural levees are a guide to finding low-sulfur coal and to avoiding places where the coal may be presumed removed. Exploitable petroleum accumulations require porous, permeable reservoir rocks, organically rich source sediments, and suitable porous and permeable rock bodies that allow the petroleum to move from its point of origin to a reservoir.

Detailed paleogeographic maps showing ancient beaches, barrier bars, stream channels, reefs with porous flank beds, areas of carbonate sediment subjected to subaerial exposure, and other environments in which porous accumulations may occur are good guides to finding petroleum reservoirs, or, for that matter, groundwater supplies. Maps of areas in which sediments may be assumed to accumulate under reducing conditions, such as in confined deep basins, serve to predict the occurrence of petroleum source beds. Maps showing ancient saline basins and salt pans serve as guides to occurrence of potash salts. Some metallic mineral deposits are associated with intrusive or extrusive igneous rocks, so exploration for them may be guided by locating and predicting the occurrence of ancient mountain ranges. Other metals are deposited when water with metals in solution is expelled from deep structural basins through layered sedimentary rocks and encounters water of differing chemical character. This induces deposition of metallic salts.

Paleocurrent analysis may be used to track down the source of useful minerals. In this way, for example, occurrence of diamond deposits in Canada or northernmost Minnesota and Michigan has long been inferred from discoveries of a very few diamonds within glacial deposits in the Middle West. During the 1970's and later, exploration in these areas uncovered a few small but promising prospects.

Bibliography

Dott, Robert H. *Evolution of the Earth.* 5th ed. New York: McGraw-Hill, 1994. A geologic history, centering on North America. Includes a set of global paleogeographic maps, paleogeographic maps of North America for Precambrian through Cenozoic times, and regional paleogeographic maps of areas of particular interest. Maps are supported by summaries of the data upon which they are based. Paleocurrents are shown on many of these maps. Comprehensive index and a useful glossary of technical terms. Designed for use as a beginning college geology text.

Hughs, Norman Francis, ed. *Organisms and Continents Through Time*. London: The Palaeontological Association, 1973. Discusses the methods and principles of global paleobiogeography. Includes a set of paleobiogeographic maps.

Levorsen, A. I. *Paleogeologic Maps*. San Francisco: W. H. Freeman, 1960. Describes how to prepare and interpret every conceivable type of paleogeologic map and presents examples.

McElhinny, M. W. *Paleomagnetism and Plate Tectonics*. Cambridge, England: Cambridge University Press, 1973. Describes the phenomena of the earth's magnetic field and rock magnetism and the methods by which they are studied. Considers reversals of the earth's magnetic field and the location of paleomagnetic poles as paleogeographic indicators.

Potter, Paul Edwin, and F. J. Pettijohn. *Paleocurrents and Basin Analysis*. Berlin: Springer, 1963. Discusses the means of identifying and describing all sorts of paleocurrents and how they are used in paleogeographic interpretations.

Schuchert, Charles. *Atlas of Paleogeographic Maps of North America*. New York: John Wiley & Sons, 1955. Summarizes the work of the most important American paleogeographer of the first half of the twentieth century. Maps predate plate-tectonic concepts but reliably show shorelines and the names and locations of major paleogeographic features within the continent.

Seyfert, Carl K., and Leslie A. Sirkin. *Earth History and Plate Tectonics: An Introduction to Historical Geology*. 2d ed. New York: Harper & Row, 1979. Contains a set of global paleogeographic maps from the Precambrian through the present, along with more detailed maps of North America for the geologic periods. Discusses how paleogeographic maps are compiled using paleomagnetic, geologic, biologic, and climatic data. Written for beginning students of geology.

Shell Oil Company. Exploration Department. *Stratigraphic Atlas, North and Central America*. Houston: The Department, 1975. Maps of the distribution and lithologic character of rocks belonging to the major subdivisions of each geologic system. Also paleogeologic maps, isopachous (thickness) maps, and lithofacies (regional changes in rock character) maps. Directly interpretable as paleogeographic maps.

Smith, A. G., D. G. Smith, and B. M. Funnell. *Atlas of Mesozoic and Cenozoic Coastlines*. New York: Cambridge University Press, 1994. Global paleogeographic maps showing past positions of Mesozoic and Cenozoic epicontinental seas.

Wanless, H. R., and Cynthia R. Wright. *Paleoenvironmental Maps of Pennsylvanian Rocks, Illinois Basin and Northern Midcontinent Region*. Boulder, Colo.: Geological Society of America, 1978. Detailed regional paleogeographic maps for individual subunits of the coal-bearing rocks of middle America.

Ziegler, A. M., et al. "Paleozoic Paleogeography." *Annual Reviews of Earth and Planetary Sciences* 7 (1979): 473-502. Discusses the paleomagnetic, biogeographic, tectonic, and climatic evidence for global paleogeographic maps for each Paleozoic period. The most important work in this field of study.

Ralph L. Langenheim, Jr.

Cross-References

The Atmosphere's Global Circulation, 121; Continental Growth, 268; Continents and Subcontinents, 2869; Displaced Terrains, 377; Gondwanaland and Pangaea, 982; Land Bridges, 2973; The Origin of the Oceans, 1863; Paleobiogeography, 1984; Paleoclimatology, 1993; Plate Motions, 2071; Sediment Transport and Deposition, 2290; Supercontinent Cycle, 3121.

PALEOSEISMOLOGY

Type of earth science: Geophysics
Field of study: Seismology

Paleoseismology is the study of the evidence of past earthquakes. By studying the physical features of previous earthquakes, scientists gain knowledge of the forces operating within the earth, knowledge that may be used to develop a means of predicting future large earthquakes.

Principal terms

EARTHQUAKE: a shaking or trembling of the earth caused by a break or rupture in the rocks of the earth's outer crust

ELASTIC REBOUND: the process of the buildup and release of geologic stress; the release of the strain in the rocks results in earthquakes

FAULT: a fracture of the earth's crust along which rocks move

FAULT OFFSET: a feature such as a road, creek bed, or tree line across a fault that separates and becomes misaligned by the fault movement

FAULT SCARPS: a steep cliff or slope created by movement along a fault

PLATE TECTONICS: the theory that the earth's hard outer crust (lithosphere) is composed of sections, or plates, that are in constant motion

RECURRENCE PERIOD: the range of time between successive earthquakes

SEISMIC GAP: a fault region known to have had previous earthquakes but not within the area's most recent recurrence period

TSUNAMI: a series of large ocean waves caused by an earthquake in the ocean floor

Summary of the Methodology

Seismology is the science that deals with earthquakes and movement within the earth. Seismologists and geologists use the historic and prehistoric information about earthquakes in order to make better calculations of the probability of earthquakes occurring in a particular area. However, historical evidence from earthquakes—that is, information acquired from observation and instrumental measurements—is short and incomplete. Paleoseismology is a relatively new branch of earthquake science that uses archaeological techniques to find physical evidence of large ancient earthquakes and thus to expand the seismic history of the earth.

In the 1960's, the theory of plate tectonics was introduced. According to this theory, the earth's outer crust is composed of sections, or plates, that are in constant motion. When these plates collide or spread apart, the resulting forces produce deformations, or tectonics, of the earth's surface that are identified with earthquakes. When plates collide and one plate moves beneath the other, the resulting fault is called a "subduction zone." Subduction zones are under water and cause changes in land at the shoreline. Earthquakes at the subduction zones often cause tsunamis that are devastating to coastal areas. When the plates rub against one another, the resulting fault is known as a "plate interaction." The San Andreas fault in California is a well-known example of a plate-interaction fault.

The idea of elastic rebound is used to explain how earthquakes originate. Under normal circumstances, the rocks at a fault boundary move a few inches a year. If the rock cannot move, the force of the normal movement becomes stored (this is known as "strain energy"). When the force becomes too great, the fault slips to release energy. As the plate boundaries shift or rupture, earthquakes occur. By studying the historic record, scientists have found that the plate boundaries rupture in segments until the entire section is broken, and the cycle then begins again. Scientists believe that future earthquakes are more likely to occur in places where the segments have not recently ruptured. These places are called "seismic gaps."

With the discovery of plate tectonics, scientists believed that long-term and short-term prediction of earthquakes would be possible. Long-term prediction is based on the probability that an earthquake will occur. Paleoseismic evidence of past earthquake recurrence periods allows scientists to determine when a large earthquake is "overdue" for a particular area.

Short-term prediction involves specifying the future place, magnitude (or strength), and time of the earthquake. Short-term prediction relies on data collected from monitoring equipment on known faults as well as precursory signals such as an increase in fault movement, change in deep-well water levels, changes in surface elevations, an increase in minor earthquake activity, the occurrence of a moderate foreshock, or an increase in the release of radioactive radon gas. Since other environmental factors can cause some of these signals, there are no definitive predictors of an imminent earthquake.

The advantages of knowing when, where, and how strong an earthquake will be are numerous. The cost of an earthquake in terms of loss of human life and property is tremendous. In addition to the damage caused by the actual ground shaking from the earthquake, there is loss of life and property caused by structural collapse and secondary effects such as landslides, fires, and tsunamis. For example, the September 19, 1985, earthquake that struck Mexico City killed more than eight thousand people, injured thirty thousand, destroyed or severely damaged more than one thousand multistoried buildings, and caused an estimated five billion dollars in damage.

Scientists use several methods to study earthquakes. One of the methods is based on recorded observations. The earliest known scientifically collected observational data about earthquakes is a survey taken after a strong earthquake struck Lisbon, Portugal, on November 1, 1755. Local officials sent a list of questions to the affected areas asking about the duration of the shock, the times and intensities of aftershocks, the number of people killed, the structures destroyed, and the extent of damage from related fires. Firsthand accounts of death and structural damage, as well as obvious changes in the physical features of the land, allow scientists to judge the severity of an earthquake. This information is useful in identifying seismic gaps. Probability indicates that an area is more likely to have a large earthquake if a large earthquake has occurred there before.

Another method for studying earthquakes is through instrumentation. Tiltmeters and strainmeters are used to measure changes in the crustal movement in earthquake areas. Hidden faults are located using a device that relies on how sound waves are reflected. Satellites, aerial photographs, and surveying equipment also provide clues to the location of underground faults. Seismic activity is monitored worldwide with seismographs, which record the occurrence, direction, severity, and duration of earthquakes. Modern seismographs are extremely sensitive and can detect ground motions of very small earthquakes. Scientists estimate that approximately eighty thousand small tremors and fifteen to twenty severe earthquakes occur around the world annually.

In the late 1970's, Kerry Sieh, a geologist at the California Institute of Technology, conducted the pioneering work in paleoseismology at Pallet Creek on the San Andreas fault. Scientists could now gather additional information about earthquakes to supplement and expand the existing observational and instrumentation knowledge. With the prehistoric evidence of earthquakes, scientists can better calculate the probability of another large earthquake.

Paleoseismic techniques may involve digging a trench across a fault and examining the rock strata, or layers, for evidence of previous ruptures. Scientists also look for evidence of flooded forests or sheets of sand along coastlines, which would indicate tsunami activity. The evidence can be direct, such as fault offsets, or indirect, such as landslides or sand deposits, which occur with strong ground shaking. By measuring the distance separating the two rock segments in a fault offset, scientists can determine how much the fault has slipped. The samples can be radiocarbon dated in order to determine when the earthquakes occurred. When the time gap between the earthquakes is determined, the recurrence period and average interval can be established. The recurrence period is a range of time between earthquakes; the interval is the average time between earthquakes. For example, if earthquakes happened in a particular region in 1700, 1775, 1825, and 1925, the recurrence range is fifty to one hundred years, with an average interval of seventy-five years.

Applications of the Method

Seismologists need information about past earthquakes in order to study and prepare for future earthquakes. Paleoseismology has been very useful in North America because of the short historical record. Additionally, the techniques have helped establish the accumulation of stress in faults all over the world.

Paleoseismic data enables scientists to determine higher levels of earthquake hazard in a geographic area. Engineers and public officials use the information from scientists to revise building codes and redraw maps of earthquake-shaking hazard zones. The U.S. Uniform Building Code, which includes nationwide standards for designing structures, defines six levels of earthquake-shaking hazard. By convincing people to reinforce existing structures and adopt earthquake-resistant construction standards, loss of life and property can be greatly reduced.

In California, a 1971 earthquake in the San Fernando Valley killed sixty-five people and caused an estimated $500 million in damages. California has had earthquake-resistant building criteria since 1933, criteria that have been updated several times. In contrast, a 1972 earthquake of similar magnitude in Managua, Nicaragua, killed more than five thousand people and caused economic losses equal to the country's gross national product for that year. Managua had few buildings designed under earthquake-resistant standards.

Paleoseismology helps answer questions about faults, folds, secondary effects of prehistorical earthquakes, length of an earthquake cycle, the cycle's regularity or irregularity, and similarity of characteristics of an area's earthquakes. Scientists believe that earthquake processes of the past will probably be the same as those in the near future. The longer the record of earthquake occurrences in a particular area, the greater the predictive value of the knowledge. The ability to predict the likelihood and possible effects of future earthquakes enables people to take precautions to protect themselves against injury, death, and economic losses.

Paleoseismology initially studied active faults to help establish the rates of movement. The technique was then applied to interpreting earthquake crustal deformations or shaking effects. Although paleoseismology is usually used to examine surface faults, the technique is also used to examine subduction-zone earthquakes indirectly. Since subduction zones are underwater faults, scientists examine changes in the land at the shoreline for evidence of past activity. The sudden lowering of a shoreline or a series of terraced beaches are associated with major earthquakes.

In Alaska, scientists examined terraced beach lines near an island in Prince William Sound. This area was the site of the March 27, 1964, "Good Friday" earthquake, the second-strongest earthquake recorded. The earthquake killed 114 people and caused $350 million in property damage. The coastlines of nearby land masses bowed by as much as eight feet, flooding them with seawater and killing square miles of forest. Scientists discovered that large earthquakes have occurred in the area an average of once every 850 years during the past five thousand years. Because of this investigation, scientists believe that it is unlikely that a major earthquake will occur in this area in the near future.

Until the mid-1980's, scientists believed that the area off the coast of Washington, Oregon, and Northern California had a low probability of a massive earthquake, since there was no historical record of such an earthquake. Paleoseismic studies, however, show evidence of a sudden lowering of the shoreline associated with major earthquakes. In addition, scientists also found sheets of sand deposited by tsunamis and sand-filled cracks caused by strong earthquake shaking. Researchers have thus concluded that three massive earthquakes have struck this area in the past three thousand years; the most recent great earthquake struck about three hundred years ago. Based on this knowledge, measures have been taken to reinforce existing structures and toughen earthquake design standards. Without the paleoseismic data, a powerful earthquake would have taken the area by complete surprise.

Scientists have been gathering much information about faults at plate boundaries, since an estimated 95 percent of all earthquakes occur at these boundaries. The probability of occurrence for some earthquakes is more difficult to predict, because they do not occur near plate boundaries. Often, these inner-plate earthquakes are devastating, because they occur so infrequently that there may be no historical record of an earthquake in that area.

On September 30, 1993, ten thousand people in Killari, India, died when an earthquake devastated the area. Prior to the earthquake, the area was included in the lowest level of the earthquake-hazard map of India. The seismologists were wrong at Killari because the hazard map relied mostly on the historical record of earthquakes. In India, this record is only about 150 years old. Investigation following the earthquake suggested that the area had been seismically quiet for 65 million years or more. Scientists believe that the earthquake may have been triggered by an artificial, or human-constructed, reservoir that changed the stress on a fault. Understanding how such construction affects the stress on the earth's crust that triggers earthquakes allows more considered and intelligent decisions about building nuclear power plants, dams, reservoirs, and cities.

In the United States, the area east of the Rocky Mountains has faults that are buried deep and accumulate stress slowly. Earthquake risk estimates for the eastern United States are not as advanced as those for the West, where the faults break the surface and earthquakes occur more often. Eastern faults may be quiet for hundreds, thousands, or millions of years.

One of the most destructive series of earthquakes in American history, however, occurred in 1811 and 1812 in New Madrid, Missouri. At least one earthquake a day took place in the area for more than a year, with three extremely powerful ones; these quakes were felt over approximately 1 million square miles and caused tremendous physical changes to the land. Destruction was severe, but casualties and economic losses were low because there were few settlements in the affected area. The earthquakes triggered landslides, submerged islands, opened fissures in the earth, flooded lowlands, and caused areas of land to rise or sink.

Large earthquakes have also occurred in Charleston, South Carolina, in 1886, Newfoundland, Canada, in 1929, and New York State in 1988. Numerous small earthquakes have occurred over the past two hundred years, with at least twenty damaging earthquakes in the central Mississippi Valley alone. Eastern earthquakes are puzzling because they do not generate visible surface faults. Because of this lack of physical evidence and the infrequent occurrences of eastern earthquakes, determining the probability and location of another large earthquake in the region is very difficult.

Context

There is no doubt that earthquakes will continue to occur. Most earthquake research in the United States focuses on hazard reduction and the nature of earthquakes rather than prediction. Predicting the exact time, location, and magnitude of an earthquake is almost impossible because of the dynamic complexity of the earth. Scientists are not able to identify significant indicators of impending earthquakes conclusively and so can only make estimates based on past evidence. By concentrating on hazard mitigation, earthquake research is focusing on long-term planning, building construction, and design issues.

Most deaths, injuries, and damages from earthquakes are caused by the collapse of buildings and structures or resulting fires. With the knowledge gained through paleoseismic studies, in addition to information from historical accounts and instrumental records, scientists can predict the probability of an earthquake in a given geographic region. Armed with that information, people can make intelligent decisions to protect themselves and their property from the potentially devastating effects of a massive earthquake.

The West Coast, specifically California, Alaska, and Hawaii, is the most seismically active region of the United States. Government agencies in those states have taken numerous precautions, including stringent building codes and mandated reinforcement of existing buildings, dams, bridges, water systems, schools, and factories. The eastern part of the United States also experiences earthquakes, but on a much less frequent basis. Nevertheless, damaging earthquakes strike the region approximately every twenty-five years, with serious ones occurring every fifty to one hundred years. Several of the eastern earthquake-prone states include Massachusetts, New York, South Carolina, Missouri, Indiana, and Utah.

Earthquakes in the East affect larger areas than western earthquakes because seismic waves generated by the earthquake travel further with less diminishing of energy. The crustal rock in the East is more solid and less fragmented than the crustal rock in the West; thus, the potential for extensive damage over an extended area is greater in the East. On October 7, 1988, a moderate earthquake in upper New York State was felt from Montreal, Canada, to New Jersey. The Charleston, South Carolina, earthquake in August, 1886, caused minor damage in New York City, six hundred miles away, and in Chicago, 720 miles away.

The East lags behind in improving building standards to meet earthquake guidelines. Most buildings and human constructions in the East are not designed or built to resist the ground shaking that accompanies an earthquake. Should an earthquake occur in a crowded urban area of the East, numerous old and structurally weak buildings are likely to collapse. In addition, state and local planning for services to assist after a major earthquake are almost nonexistent in the region. Plans for medical services, food and shelter, and restoration of water, electricity, gas, transportation, and communication lines must be in place before a disaster to be effective, yet such planning has not taken place in much of the eastern United States.

Although the potential for casualties and huge economic losses is high when an earthquake occurs, it may be difficult for some areas to justify the expense of preparing for a major earthquake. The information gathered through paleoseismic studies will help people to make the difficult decisions associated with preparing for future earthquakes. By recognizing the changing nature of the earth's interior and understanding the potential risks of earthquakes, communities can be prepared to deal with disasters before they happen.

Bibliography

Adams, John. "Paleoseismology: A Search for Ancient Earthquakes in Puget Sound." *Science* 258 (December 4, 1992): 1592-1593. Introduces a five-article series on paleoseismology fieldwork in the Pacific Northwest. Explains what scientists look for and how they interpret physical evidence of prehistoric earthquakes at coastlines. Briefly discusses the history of paleoseismology. Easy to follow.

Bolt, Bruce A. *Earthquakes and Geological Discovery*. New York: Scientific American Library, 1993. Explains why earthquakes occur and how they are measured. Also discusses some of the most famous earthquakes and what can be done to minimize their destructive effects. Suitable for anyone interested in earthquakes.

Harris, Stephen L. *Agents of Chaos: Earthquakes, Volcanoes, and Other Natural Disasters*. Missoula, Mont.: Mountain Press, 1990. The first third of this book discusses earthquake hazards in the United States. Looks at historic earthquakes and explains why future earthquakes will occur in various geographic areas. Well-written and suitable for high-school readers. Includes a glossary and a lengthy bibliography.

Lay, Thorne, and Terry C. Wallace. *Modern Global Seismology*. New York: Academic Press, 1995. A complete text discussing seismology and its various applications. Includes a chapter dedicated to the earthquake cycle. Contains only brief information specifically on paleoseismology, but the overview of seismology is excellent.

McCalpin, James P., ed. *Paleoseismology*. New York: Academic Press, 1996. Includes an introductory chapter on paleoseismology and discusses field techniques and interpretation of data. Includes a bibliography and index. Suitable for more advanced readers.

Main, Ian. "Long Odds on Prediction." *Nature* 385 (January 2, 1997): 19-20. Brief article discussing the possibility of reliable earthquake prediction. Discusses why earthquakes are difficult to predict and suggests that efforts should concentrate on hazard mitigation.

Moseley, Charles. "Slow Progress in Earthquake Prediction." *Editorial Research Reports* 2 (July 15, 1988): 354-363. Well-written and easily understood overview of earthquake prediction and the role of paleoseismology. Includes examples of major earthquakes and a clear explanation of the need for and problems associated with prediction. Includes a bibliography.

Worsnop, Richard L. "Earthquake Research." *CQ Researcher* 4 (December 16, 1994): 1105-1128. A balanced discussion of the state of earthquake research. Discusses the issues of earthquake prediction and hazard-reduction preparedness; also gives background on faults and current risk areas and includes an explanation of how earthquake strength is measured. Includes a bibliography and suggestions for further reading. Suitable for high-school readers.

Yeats, Robert S., Kerry Sieh, and Clarence R. Allen. *The Geology of Earthquakes.* New York: Oxford University Press, 1997. Detailed information about the geological explanations for and effects of earthquakes. Includes a discussion of tectonics and faults as well as an assessment of seismic hazards. Suitable for college-level readers. Includes a bibliography and informative illustrations.

Virginia L. Salmon

Cross-References
Archaeological Geology, 86; Earthquake Distribution, 421; Earthquake Engineering, 430; Earthquake Hazards, 437; Earthquake Locating, 445; Earthquake Magnitudes and Intensities, 452; Earthquake Prediction, 461; An Overview of Earthquakes, 484; Thrust Faults, 683; Transform Faults, 690.

PERMAFROST

Type of earth science: Geology
Field of study: Geomorphology

Permafrost is a thermal condition existing in any type of earth material that is perennially frozen. It occurs in ground in which the temperature remains below 0 degrees Celsius for at least two consecutive years. Affecting about 25 percent of the earth's surface, the condition hampers construction in the far north in regions such as Siberia and Arctic Canada.

Principal terms

PERIGLACIAL: originally restricted to regions modified by frost weathering such as tundra

PINGO: a growth of ice in a permafrost body associated with frost heave; the result is an upthrusted dome of sediments forming a conical landform several tens of meters high

PLEISTOCENE: the geologic era between two million and sixteen thousand years ago, characterized by extensive continental glaciation and a colder climate

STONE POLYGON: an assemblage of boulders in a roughly polygonal shape ranging from a few centimeters to several meters across; occurring in clusters, they form honeycomb or netlike patterns covering several square kilometers

SUBSIDENCE: a downward vertical movement of the ground, commonly caused by land-cover changes of the surface

TALIK: a layer of unfrozen ground in permafrost; water under pressure frequently occurs in talik layers

THERMOKARST: a group of landforms in flat areas of degrading permafrost and melting ice

Summary of the Phenomenon

Permafrost, or permanently frozen ground, is a thickness of earth material such as soil, peat, or even bedrock, at a variable depth beneath the ground surface, in which a temperature below 0 degrees Celsius exists continuously for a number of years (from at least two years to several thousands of years). Permafrost is thus not a process or an effect but a temperature condition of earth material on land or beneath continental shelves of the Arctic Ocean. The occurrence of permafrost is conditioned exclusively by temperature, irrespective of the presence of water or of the composition, lithology, and texture of the ground. However, unfrozen water horizons may exist within a body of permafrost as the result of various conditions such as pressure or impurities in the water.

With regard to the climatic history of the earth, cold conditions and glaciers are the exception, not the rule. Because they are so rare, they are referred to as "climatic accidents." During the Pleistocene, advances of continental glaciers covered vast areas of Europe and North America. Glaciers continue to be significant landscape features, since they lock up as ice some 2.15 percent of the earth's waters. Permafrost is a relatively new condition introduced with the onset of the Pleistocene glacial events, and it will be maintained as long as the climate remains cold.

As the earth's climate warmed during the past twenty thousand years and the continental ice receded, the location, distribution, and thickness of permafrost have changed. Today, the area underlain by permafrost is vast; it has been estimated that about 25 percent of the earth's surface is underlain by permafrost. One reason why vast areas of the earth possess permafrost is that the continents widen toward higher latitudes in North America and Eurasia. In the Northern Hemisphere, Mongolia, Russia, and China contain about 12.2 million square kilometers of land underlain with permafrost. North America and Greenland have 8.8 million square kilometers of permafrost. In the Southern Hemisphere, Antarctica accounts for 13.5 million square kilometers of permafrost. During the Pleistocene, perennially frozen ground had a different distribution. Permafrost produces soil and sediment structures that remain after the climate warms. Relict features such as ancient ice wedges can be identified, and former permafrost areas can be mapped. Evidence of preexisting permafrost conditions, and thus a record of climate change, has been extensively documented in Britain, southern Canada, and the central United States.

In terms of aerial distribution and continuity, permafrost may be classified as either continuous or discontinuous. At higher-latitude land circling the Arctic Ocean, the lateral extent of permafrost is uninterrupted nearly everywhere, except in areas of recent deposition and under large lakes that do not freeze to the bottom. Discontinuous permafrost includes areas of frozen ground separated by non-permafrost areas. A transect from the Arctic Ocean southward, into Canada or Russia, reveals more and more permafrost-free areas. Further south, in central Canada and central Russia, only patchy or sporadic zones of perennially frozen ground are to be found.

Permafrost is a unique condition because it is maintained very close to its melting point. Several thousand square kilometers are warmer than −3 degrees Celsius. If global warming continues, as many scientists predict, most discontinuous permafrost would degrade. Russian scientists, in fact, have documented the northward retreat of permafrost near Archangel at a rate of 400 meters per year since 1837. In Canada, permafrost has retreated northward more than 100 kilometers since 1945, as ground temperatures have increased by 2 degrees Celsius in the northern prairie provinces. Changes in temperature may result from a local microclimate change, alteration of land cover, or changes in the atmosphere. Conversely, permafrost is not only degraded by global warming but may indeed contribute to atmospheric change. Scientists suggest that thawing of Arctic terrain, which is rich in peat accumulation, may affect the chemistry of the atmosphere. It has been determined that one-quarter of the earth's terrestrial carbon is stored in organic matter in the permafrost and active layer.

Long-term warming would release enormous quantities of greenhouse gases, methane and carbon dioxide in particular, accelerating global warming.

A cross section of excavated earth in the high Arctic reveals the vertical characteristics of permafrost. The thickness of permafrost is variable because of differences in air temperatures, occurrence of water, composition and texture of earth materials, and many other factors. The permafrost in Siberia may be at least 5,000 meters thick, whereas in Alaska thicknesses of 740 meters have been recorded. Further south, thicknesses decrease as discontinuous permafrost becomes more common. The thickness of permafrost is in part determined by a balance between the increase of internal heat with depth and the heat loss from the earth's surface. If the thickness and depth of permafrost remains unchanged for many years, the heat loss at the surface and the heat at the base of the frozen ground are in equilibrium, and a steady state is maintained. At the surface, the ground seasonally thaws and freezes; this section of the permafrost is known as an "active layer." Its thickness is controlled by numerous variables in addition to seasonal temperature variations, and it exhibits great variability in thickness. Vegetation, snow cover, albedo, water distribution, and human alteration of the surface can all act as insulators and affect the thickness of the active layer. However, in areas not disturbed by people, the ground will typically thaw to a depth of from 1 to 12 meters during the summer.

The deeper boundary separating the active layer from the permafrost is known as the "permafrost table" or "zero curtain." Within the permafrost, unfrozen lenses known by the Russian term *talik* occur. These unfrozen bodies frequently contain water and function as protected water sources or aquifers in the Arctic environment. Talik layers may be isolated bodies completely enclosed in impermeable permafrost and result from a change in the thermal regime in permafrost. Conversely, talik may be laterally extensive even in continuous permafrost and is frequently a valuable source of groundwater. Talik lenses are larger in discontinuous permafrost, and the active layer thickens at the expense of the permafrost.

Below the permafrost table, the perennially frozen ground has low permeability. Maps and photographs of the Arctic reveal many lakes, swamps, and marshes, suggesting high precipitation. However, evaporation rates are low because of the cold air temperatures, and standing water occurs because the ground is frozen at depth. Throughout the region, precipitation is probably less than 35 centimeters annually, equivalent to that of marginal deserts. The abundant water and poor drainage result from the occurrence of permafrost at depth, not to high atmospheric precipitation. As seasonal warming and cooling occur, the land surface expands and contracts, particularly in continuous permafrost areas. In essence, the lowering of the ground temperature causes thermal contraction of the ground, and vertical fissures or frost cracks occur. Water filling and freezing in these cracks creates ice wedges in the permafrost that widen with seasonal expansion and contraction. Ice wedges are often 3 to 4 meters wide and extend 5 to 10 meters into the perennially frozen ground below the active layer. In areas of degradation, ice wedges in the thawing permafrost begin to melt, creating thermokarst features characterized by numerous depressions similar to karst plains. As temperatures rise above freezing, the active layer extends deeper and deeper and eventually may intercept an ice wedge. If large ice wedges begin to thaw, the ground subsides, creating steep-sided conical depressions. The perimeter of a depression, often composed of very moist sediment, will slump into the depression, thus making it wider. Water then fills the depression, creating a thermokarst, or thaw lake. Averaging about 3 meters across, the lakes occur in clusters, are elliptical in shape, and are all oriented at right angles to the prevailing wind direction.

Methods of Study

To examine and obtain data on the characteristics of permafrost is difficult because of the isolation and hostile climatic setting of Arctic regions. Fieldwork is usually done in spring and summer, when conditions are warmer. However, wet conditions frequently exist; the thawed active layer above the permafrost is often poorly drained and boggy, making trekking difficult. Geophysical methods, various types of thermometers, and aerial images have helped to unravel the complexities of permafrost.

The application of electrical resistivity is an example of a geophysical method; this technique is most effective in continuous permafrost extending to depths of about 60 meters and with a temperature not lower than 15 degrees Celsius. Ice acts as an insulator, whereas unfrozen ground regions have a smaller specific resistivity. If a hole is bored into the ground, a probe may be lowered to record the electrical resistivity at depth, and this information can then be interpreted as a temperature profile on a chart. More recently, airborne geophysical methods, which are more suitable for reconnaissance surveys of large regions, have been put to use. Although less detailed than ground surveys, they do provide information on the thickness of taliks in continuous permafrost areas and the general distribution of discontinuous permafrost.

Shallow ground temperatures yield significant data. They establish, for example, the thickness of the active layer, the presence of taliks, the depth of seasonal fluctuation of ground temperature, and the temperature profile of permafrost. These and related data are important for engineers to have prior to the construction of buildings, airstrips, or oil and gas platforms.

Maximum and minimum thermometers positioned in a bore hole record permafrost temperature at a specific depth. Maximum temperature data are used in winter, when ground temperatures exceed air temperatures, and minimum data can be used in summer, when the permafrost is colder than the air.

Thermocouple thermometers work on electrical concepts and are especially suitable for permanent installation. As many as twenty thermocouples can be installed in a pit or a drilled hole and joined so that readings may be taken quickly at different locations.

Aerial photography and images are used to make maps of Arctic environments and to determine spatial relationships and land covers of vast and less accessible areas. The occurrence and thickness of the active layer—and, to some degree, whether permafrost is continuous or discontinuous—is revealed in the distribution of water, landforms, and vegetation types. In general, landforms in cold climates can be divided into those associated with the aggradation of permafrost and those related to the degradation of permafrost. "Paisas" are low conical mounds 1 to 50 meters in height that occur in discontinuous permafrost, whereas stone polygons are common landforms in continuous permafrost. Thermokarst lakes are transitional features sited on the boundary between continuous and discontinuous permafrost. By mapping these features, the aerial extent and type of permafrost in a landscape can be determined.

Context

Following World War II, two events stimulated the study of permafrost environments. With the onset of the Cold War, both Eastern and Western governments quickly realized that permafrost phenomena materially impeded the settlement and development of northern regions, particularly with regard to military early-warning systems and airbases. The lack of knowledge of appropriate construction techniques in the cold environment resulted in the deformation, in many cases beyond repair, of roads, bridges, and other structures that were not built to withstand frost heaving or subsidence. In addition, issues emerged regarding the resources of the north that required a clear understanding of the behavior and alteration of this thermally controlled environment, especially the exploration for oil and gas in the Arctic coastal zone, the construction of pipelines for oil transport, and rising environmental concerns.

Essentially, construction in permafrost areas requires that the sensitive permafrost table and active layer be considered so that the thermal conditions remain unchanged if possible. Construction of concrete runways and roads alters drainage and vegetation, and these structures absorb heat during long summer days. The heat is conducted to the active layer, which may become thicker, making the permafrost thinner. Such environmental disturbances can cause a structure to subside unevenly. If a house or building is constructed on a concrete slab that is placed directly on the active layer, the structure may subside as the active layer thickens at the expense of the underlying thawing permafrost. Should the thicker active layer encounter a water-charged talik lens, seepage into the building is likely to occur. To avoid the problem, structures are built above ground level and placed on pilings.

In 1977, the 1,285-kilometer Trans-Alaskan Pipeline was built from Prudhoe Bay southward to the Pacific port of Valdez, Alaska. Originally, a buried pipeline was proposed. However, since the oil is transported at a temperature of from 70 to 80 degrees Celsius, a buried pipeline would thaw the permafrost, causing the pipe to sag and possibly break. To avoid potential damage to the pipeline and to the environment, one-half of the structure was suspended above the ground. A thorough understanding of the sensitivity and the mechanisms of permafrost must thus be considered so that similar problems affecting structures and the environment can be avoided.

Thanks to an environment that is very cold or frozen most of the time, organic matter derived from the scanty Arctic vegetation does not decay readily. Peat deposits make Canada a top exporter of this resource. To scientists, the peat provides clues to the past environmental conditions of the Arctic. Seeds and pollen preserved in these organic layers or in lake sediments help researchers to reconstruct past climatic conditions.

Radiocarbon analyses reveal some peat beds to be as much as fifty thousand years old. This information, however, does not tell scientists how long the ground was frozen. In Siberia and in Alaska, numerous frozen mammoth carcasses have been discovered. The fossil remains include not only the bones but also the flesh of these elephant-like mammals. Radiocarbon tests indicate that the mammoths fall into one of two distinct age groups, one dating from about forty-five thousand to thirty thousand years ago, and a younger cluster ranging in age from fourteen thousand to eleven thousand years ago. The animals were frozen and were not eaten by scavengers. This suggests that they must have been rapidly covered, perhaps by mud flows, and frozen quickly. The stomach-content remains of examined mammoths reflect the past vegetative diversity of the Arctic. Included were larch needles, willow, tree bark, grasses, sedges, and even rare poppies. Since the animals were not decomposed, scientists were able to infer that the ground must have been continually frozen for thousands of years.

Bibliography

Ballantyne, C. F., and C. Harris. *The Periglaciation of Great Britain*. New York: Cambridge University Press, 1994. A good upper-level description of permafrost in Britain. The discussion ranges from basic freeze-and-thaw processes to permafrost conditions and distribution in the geologic past.

Clark, M. J., ed. *Advances in Periglacial Geomorphology*. New York: Wiley Inter-Science, 1988. A series of state-of-the-art reviews of numerous processes and landforms in cold climates. Emphasizes processes of formation; very technical. Suitable for advanced earth science students as a reference and literature source.

Davis, J. L. *Landforms of Cold Climates*. Cambridge, Mass.: MIT Press, 1969. A basic primer on permafrost and related topics. Permafrost conditions and distribution are well described, and the discussion is jargon-free.

French, H. M. *The Periglacial Environment*. New York: Longman, 1978. A descriptive account of permafrost and its environment in North America and Eurasia. Somewhat technical, yet readable and supplemented with numerous photographs and other graphics.

Harris, S. A. *The Permafrost Environment*. Totowa: Barnes & Noble, 1986. A primer on the consequences of construction in permafrost regions. Topics include the soil properties and methods of permafrost analysis. Written for contractors and environmental specialists.

Muller, S. W. *Permafrost or Permanently Frozen Ground and Related Engineering Problems*. Ann Arbor, Mich.: Edwards Brothers, 1947. A comprehensive account of permafrost by the man who coined the term. Emphasizes the problems of building in permafrost areas. Gives excellent examples of poor planning in a poorly understood environment.

Tricart, Jean. *Geomorphology of Cold Climates*. New York: St. Martin's Press, 1970. A translation of a classic work on cold climate processes and landforms. Includes glacial and periglacial phenomena. Somewhat advanced, but not overwhelmingly technical.

Williams, P. J., and M. W. Smith. *The Frozen Earth: Fundamentals of Geology.* New York: Cambridge University Press, 1989. A college-level textbook for science majors, emphasizing the physics of cold regions. Equations are used to illustrate significant physical ideas.

C. Nicholas Raphael

Cross-References

Aquifers, 71; Continental Glaciers, 967; Geochronology: Radiocarbon Dating, 840; Groundwater Movement, 1020; Karst Topography, 1310; Soil Liquefaction, 2402; Weathering and Erosion, 2723.

RING OF FIRE

Type of earth science: Geology
Field of study: Tectonics

The Ring of Fire is a relatively narrow band of land composed of parts of the continents and island chains that surround the Pacific Ocean; the region is characterized by extensive volcanic and earthquake activity. The ring represents the surface expression of a tectonic boundary in which oceanic crust is forced into the upper mantle, producing molten rock that rises to the surface and forms volcanoes. The stresses imparted to the crustal rocks as they are forced into the mantle provide the energy for numerous earthquakes. Geologic investigations of the Ring of Fire have helped scientists refine the theory of plate tectonics.

Principal terms

CONTINENTAL CRUST: near-surface rocks primarily composed of low-density, light-colored minerals and constituting the bulk of continental land masses

MANTLE: the zone of the earth immediately underlying the crust; the uppermost region of the mantle is composed of partially melted and melting rocks

OCEANIC CRUST: near-surface rocks primarily composed of dense, dark-colored minerals that underlie the ocean floors

PLATE: a relatively thin slab of crustal rock, either continental or oceanic, that moves over the face of the globe, driven by currents of circulating molten rock in the underlying mantle

PLATE TECTONICS: a theory that explains the distribution of geologic features and phenomena across the face of the earth based on the interactions of crustal plates

SUBDUCTION: the process occurring at colliding plate boundaries when denser oceanic crust is forced down into the upper mantle by overriding continental crust

TRENCH: a very deep portion of the ocean where oceanic crust is being forced beneath continental crust

Summary of the Phenomenon

The "Ring of Fire" is the dramatic name of a narrow band of the earth's surface surrounding the Pacific Ocean. This band extends from the islands of the South Pacific, through Japan, to the Aleutian Islands between Asia and North America, down the west coast of North America, and through Central America and the western portions of South America. The name was applied to the roughly circular region because of its many active volcanoes. In addition to volcanic activity, this region of the earth's surface exhibits a combination of geologic features that have intrigued earth scientists for years. The region is characterized by mountain chains with many active and dormant volcanoes that parallel coastlines. Another characteristic of the area is its numerous strong earthquakes. In addition, some of the deepest portions of the world's oceans lie just offshore the volcanically active mountain chains of the region's land masses. Geologists had noticed the correlation between the land masses surrounding the Pacific, the volcanic and earthquake activity, and the oceanic depths long before they had an explanation relating these phenomena. The advent of the theory of plate tectonics provided the mechanism to explain the relationships among these geologic features.

The theory of plate tectonics, developed during the 1960's, views the earth's surface as divided into a number of crustal plates. Like the pieces of a jigsaw puzzle, the plates fit together at their edges and cover the surface of the earth; however, these pieces are in motion. Each plate moves slowly over the surface of the earth, riding on currents of molten rock in the upper mantle, the layer within the earth immediately underlying the crustal plates. Geologists have long known that rock temperatures increase with depth in the earth; for example, temperatures at the bottom of the deepest mines are sometimes uncomfortably hot. Deeper into the earth—in the upper mantle and beyond—temperatures are so high that most rocks begin to melt. Sources of heat within the mantle are not evenly distributed, however, and circulation systems exist; in areas of high heat, the molten rocks are less dense because they are hotter, and they rise. In cooler areas of the mantle, the molten rocks become denser and sink. This circulation system acts as a conveyor belt, propelling the crustal plates across the surface.

The two major types of crustal plates are composed of either continental or oceanic crust. Because the types of rocks making up these crustal types are chemically different, they also differ in density, or the mass per unit volume of the rock. Continental crust is less dense than oceanic crust. Tectonic plates may be composed of oceanic crust (for example, the Pacific plate), continental crust (for example, the Arabian plate) or some combination of the two types.

There are three basic types of plate boundaries. Boundaries where two plates are moving away from each other are called divergent boundaries and are probably associated with the areas of rising molten rock within the mantle. A good example of a divergent plate boundary is found in the middle of the Atlantic Ocean, where an underwater mountain chain, the Mid-Atlantic Ridge, runs the length of the seafloor. Plate boundaries where two plates are moving past each other are called transverse boundaries and are characteristically marked by a major fault. An example of a transverse boundary is found in the San Andreas fault zone of Southern California.

The third type of plate boundary occurs where two plates are colliding. These are known as "convergent plate boundaries"; this type of plate boundary is characteristic of the Ring of Fire. At a convergent plate boundary, two plates being moved along on mantle currents collide. At the point of collision, something must give. In many cases where the plates are composed of different crustal types (such as continental and oceanic) the denser crustal type (oceanic) will tend to be pushed beneath the lighter, less-dense continental crust and into the upper mantle. An example of this type of convergent boundary exists along the west coast of South America. There, the denser oceanic plate is subducted beneath the lighter continental plate. The subduction zone, where the oceanic plate is pushed beneath the continental plate, runs parallel to the coastline. Immediately offshore, the subduction zone is characterized by extremely deep ocean water. As the oceanic plate is subducted, it is bent down into the mantle, and the bottom of the ocean in the subduction zone becomes very deep. These deep linear features in the ocean, called "submarine trenches," are some of the deepest parts of the ocean.

As the oceanic crustal plate sinks deeper into the upper mantle, temperatures rise, and the rocks begin to melt. The molten rock, which is much hotter than the solid oceanic crust it came from, is less dense than the surrounding mantle material, and it tends to rise, like a beach ball held under water. As the molten rock from the oceanic plate rises, it hits the bottom of the overlying continental crust. Working its way through cracks and other openings in the continental crust, the molten rock often forces its way to the surface, where it pours out from a volcano. The volcanic activity tends to occur in a narrow band within the continental plate some distance inland from where the oceanic plate is being subducted. Mountain chains on the continent, composed of many volcanic peaks, are characteristic of this zone.

Another type of convergent plate boundary is where two similar crustal types collide. In the case of the Ring of Fire, this type of convergence is found in the South Pacific, where plates of oceanic crust are colliding. The result is that one of the plates again sinks beneath the other. The subducted plate is heated and melts within the upper mantle, and rising melt finds its way through the overlying oceanic crust to the surface of the ocean floor. The molten rock that builds these volcanoes continues to spill onto the ocean floor until the volcano rises above sea level to form a volcanic island. Volcanic island chains, called "island arcs," form with a deep submarine trench offshore.

Another feature of volcanic areas in the Ring of Fire is the presence of hot springs and geysers at the earth's surface. The abundance of hot and molten rock at relatively shallow depths above a subduction zone provides a perfect setting for hot-spring formation. Water from surface precipitation enters the earth's surface to become groundwater. Some of this groundwater will penetrate deeply into the earth's crust and be heated by the rocks and melt associated with the Ring of Fire. When the water is heated, like the heated, molten rock rising from the subducted plate, it becomes less dense and rises toward the surface. It rises through cracks and fractures in the earth's crust to emerge as a hot spring or geyser.

In addition to absorbing heat from the surrounding rocks and melt, the circulating water may dissolve many chemical elements from the rocks. These dissolved metals are carried along with the water through the cracks in the earth's crust toward the surface. However, as the water rises, it cools, and its ability to keep the elements dissolved decreases. As a result, minerals containing specific elements, especially metals such as lead, zinc, and copper, are deposited along the path of the water. Mineral deposits being mined today are thought to have been deposited from just such hot (hydrothermal) waters.

Earthquakes are another common feature of the Ring of Fire. Rocks at plate boundaries are subjected to the stresses at that boundary. Rocks are either being forced apart, are sliding past each other, or are colliding. Under these pressures, all rocks tend to break along planes called "faults." Sometimes the movement along a fault is not smooth. The rocks along the fault get stuck, and the pressures driving the movements build up. Eventually, the built-up pressures become so great that the sticking point along the fault breaks free, and the stored energy is released. The energy release travels through the surrounding rocks as vibrations, like the vibrations from a bell after it is struck. The sudden release of energy produces an earthquake. The intensity of the vibrations are related to the amount of energy released along the fault. The vibrations from a strong earthquake can do severe damage to buildings and roads.

Earthquakes are common in the Ring of Fire because areas of converging plates are ideal locations for rocks to break and form faults. In addition, the pressures of collision are constant and can build up if movement along the faults cease. Deep earthquakes are characteristic of the Ring of Fire. Faults only occur in solid rocks. In a subduction zone, solid rocks are forced deep into the upper mantle, an area usually composed of molten or partially melted rock. The faults in the relatively cold subducted plate are the only places in the upper mantle where pressures can build up and be released as an earthquake.

Methods of Study

The explanation for the Ring of Fire has depended, in large part, on investigations into the processes of plate tectonics. Geologists have used a broad range of technologies to understand how plate tectonics operates, and that understanding has helped explain the association of geologic phenomena composing the Ring of Fire.

Geologists have mapped the ocean floor with tools as crude as a weighted rope and with more sophisticated tools such as sonar. Sonar uses sound waves generated within the water to measure the distance to any object that can reflect some of the sound waves back to a receiver. The time that elapses between when the sound is made and when the reflected sound is received can be used to calculate the distance to the reflecting object. A map of the ocean floor can thus be created by towing a sound source and sound receiver behind an oceanic research vessel as it crisscrosses the ocean. Data from many such surveys have been compiled into maps of the ocean floor, which clearly show the mid-ocean ridges and the submarine trenches characteristic of divergent and convergent plate boundaries.

Oceanic surveys also often involve the taking of heat measurements. Using a sensitive heat sensor towed near the ocean floor behind a research vessel, scientists are able to map the amount of heat entering the ocean through the oceanic crust. The results of these surveys show that the warmest oceanic crust and the areas where the most heat enters the oceans are associated with the mid-ocean ridges. Conversely, the coolest portions of the ocean floor are those associated with submarine trenches.

However, some of the highest heat-flow measurements taken on land are associated with the areas of volcanic activity in island arcs and continental mountain chains within the Ring of Fire.

Seismologists are geologists who specialize in the study of earthquakes. Seismologists use seismographs, sensitive instruments that measure vibrations in the earth's crust, to identify where an earthquake has occurred. Seismographs can be used to identify the time earthquake vibrations arrive at a seismic measurement station. Knowing the velocity of earthquake vibrations through rocks, seismologists can calculate the distance from their measuring point to the earthquake source. With only a single measurement point, a seismologist would know only that an earthquake could have been centered anywhere on a circle of that radius. However, with many seismographs around the world, seismologists at each station combine measurements from other stations to locate the point on the earth's surface directly over the source of the earthquake. This point is called the "epicenter" of the earthquake. Measurements showing the locations of many epicenters over the years were used to identify the Ring of Fire as an area of high earthquake activity.

Another characteristic of the Ring of Fire is the depth of the earthquake source. Earthquakes occur where two bodies of solid rock are moving past each other, separated by a fault plane, when that movement is temporarily halted. The rocks must be solid; within the earth's depths, however, temperatures increase rapidly, and solid rock is not thought to exist below a certain depth. The implication is that earthquakes cannot occur below the depths predicted for melting of continental or oceanic crustal rocks. However, seismologists can use seismograph data to determine the depth of an earthquake source. Examination of seismograph data from many earthquakes in the Ring of Fire clearly indicates that, in addition to relatively shallow earthquakes, there are many very deep earthquakes. The epicenters of the very deep earthquakes are centered inland away from coastlines and submarine trenches. In the context of plate tectonics theory, the data suggest that deep earthquakes are centered within the relatively cold, and solid, rocks of the subducting plate; researchers have theorized that the plate remains solid, and able to generate earthquakes, because it is being driven into the earth's depths rapidly enough that the rock does not heat up and melt, as geologists might otherwise predict. Additional analysis of the seismic data has allowed seismologists to differentiate between subduction zones where the subducting slab is entering the upper mantle at a sharp angle, therefore producing a relatively narrow zone of earthquake activity, with deep earthquakes closer to a submarine trench, and those entering the upper mantle at a shallow angle, producing a broader earthquake zone and deep earthquakes further inland.

Context

The Ring of Fire has been the focus of much geological investigation. The coincidence of dramatic geologic phenomena such as volcanism, earthquake activity, mountain building, and submarine trenches has spurred much research in the region. With the advent of the theory of plate tectonics, the geologic features of the area became the focus of even more intense investigation. The Ring of Fire has been a key component in the understanding of plate tectonics and, thereby, the understanding of other, less spectacular areas of the earth's surface.

The phenomena of the Ring of Fire also have practical implications for the people who live in the region. Despite the spectacular natural beauty of many parts of the area, the level of geologic activity threatens every day. With little or no warning, a dormant volcano may become active, or a powerful earthquake may devastate a large region. The countries around the Ring of Fire have thus been in the forefront of research on earthquake and volcanic-activity prediction. Seismic stations are sprinkled throughout the Ring of Fire to help seismologists measure every small movement in the earth's crust. Scientists hope that the collection of enough data will enable them to identify patterns of movements that precede either an earthquake or the resurgence of volcanic activity. There have been a few successful predictions; however, such predictions cannot pinpoint the exact time of an event, only the likelihood that it will occur. It is difficult to issue warnings of an impending disaster when the event may not happen for weeks or even months. Continuing studies in the geologically active Ring of Fire may, however, eventually enable scientists to refine their predictive capabilities to the point that damage from earthquakes and eruptions can be minimized.

In addition to its hazards, the Ring of Fire also serves as an important source for many of the metals relied on in everyday life. Such metals are found in distinctive minerals and in economic concentrations in rocks associated with either volcanic or hydrothermal activity. Geologists have studied the Ring of Fire in order to understand this relationship and have used that knowledge to identify areas within continents where ancient convergent plate boundaries are exposed. The models developed by studying the Ring of Fire thus have been, and continue to be, used to locate critical mineral deposits.

Bibliography

Ballard, R. D. *Exploring Our Living Planet*. Washington, D.C.: National Geographic Society, 1983. A comprehensive review of the evidence supporting the theory of plate tectonics. Illustrated throughout with excellent photos and graphics, which support text written by an oceanographer. Includes a chapter devoted to the Ring of Fire.

Erickson, Jon. *Plate Tectonics: Unraveling the Mysteries of the Earth*. New York: Facts on File, 1992. A comprehensive, technical review of plate-tectonics theory, from the initial development of the theory to more recent areas of investigation. The material is presented in the manner of a classroom textbook. Illustrated; includes an extensive bibliography for each chapter subject and a comprehensive index.

Levy, Matthys, and Mario Salvadori. *Why the Earth Quakes*. New York: W. W. Norton, 1995. A general, readable discussion of the forces creating earthquakes and volcanoes. The text is supplemented throughout with helpful illustrations. The last few chapters discuss case histories of earthquakes, some of the engineering aspects of building in an earthquake-prone area, and the social consequences of earthquake predictions. Includes a glossary of terms and an index.

Miller, R. *Planet Earth: Continents in Collision.* Alexandria, Va.: Time-Life, 1983. This volume in the *Planet Earth* series provides a clear and well-illustrated explanation of the development and investigation of plate-tectonic theory. All the various lines of geologic and oceanographic evidence that have supported plate tectonics are discussed.

Ritchie, David. *The Ring of Fire.* New York: Atheneum, 1981. A mixture of science and history devoted to the Ring of Fire. The author combines the history of the development of explanations for the Ring of Fire with descriptions of some of the dramatic, and catastrophic, events associated with the area. Contains a glossary of terms, a bibliography, and an index.

Vogel, Shawna. *Naked Earth: The New Geophysics.* New York: Dutton, 1995. A readable discussion of the role of modern geophysics in exploring the mysteries of the earth. The author focuses on the roles of individual scientists and the array of technologies used in solving geologic mysteries. The text reads like a mystery, with just enough details to satisfy the more knowledgeable reader. Includes an index.

Richard W. Arnseth

Cross-References

Earthquake Distribution, 421; Earth's Crust, 518; Earth's Mantle, 555; Earth's Structure, 589; Heat Sources and Heat Flow, 1065; Island Arcs, 1261; An Overview of Earthquakes, 484; Plate Margins, 2063; Plate Tectonics, 2079; Volcanic Hazards, 2601.

SALINITY AND DESALINATION

Type of earth science: Hydrology
Field of study: Sedimentology

Salinity is the total amount of solid materials (salts) dissolved per unit of water; the average salinity of seawater, for example, is 35 grams of salts per kilogram of water. Utilization of saline water for domestic purposes requires removal of the dissolved materials. The desalinization of saline or brackish water involves costly operations and is typically performed only in coastal or arid regions where alternative water resources are limited.

Principal terms

DISSOLVED MATTER: the amount of solid materials that are completely dissolved in water

EVAPORATION: the physical process occurring at the water-air interface where water changes its phase from liquid to vapor

FILTRATION: the removal of particulate matter from the water by passing it through a porous medium

POTABLE WATER: fresh water that is being used for domestic consumption

REVERSE OSMOSIS: the forced passage of seawater through a semipermeable membrane against the natural osmotic pressure

SODIUM CHLORIDE: the main chemical compound found as dissolved material in seawater

SUSPENDED SOLIDS: the solid particles that can be found dispersed in the water column

WATER RESOURCES: all the surface water and groundwater that can be effectively harvested by humans for domestic, industrial, or agricultural uses

WATER SUPPLY: the amount of water that is actually delivered to the various consumer groups

WATER-TREATMENT PLANT: a facility where water is treated by physical and chemical processes until its quality is improved to that of potable water

Summary of the Methodology

Salinity is one of the most important physical properties of seawater. "Salinity" is defined as the total amount of dissolved solids found in a unit of water; it is measured in grams (g) of dissolved matter per kilogram (kg) of seawater. The average salinity of seawater is approximately 35 g/kg, corresponding to a concentration of 35 parts of salts per 1,000 parts of seawater (35 ppt). The main ionic components of dissolved matter in seawater and the percentages in which they are found in a typical sample are as follows: chlorine ions (55.0 percent), sodium ions (30.6 percent), sulphate ions (7.7 percent), magnesium ions (3.7 percent), calcium ions (1.2 percent), and potassium ions (1.1 percent). One cubic mile of typical seawater contains 120 million tons of sodium chloride, 18 million tons of magnesium chloride, 8 million tons of magnesium sulphate, 6 million tons of calcium sulphate, 4 million tons of potassium sulphate, and 550,000 tons of calcium carbonate. Depending on the prevailing physicochemical conditions, salinity can vary significantly, from brackish water (2 to 15 ppt) in estuaries and riverine deltas to highly saline water such as in the Mediterranean Sea (38.5 ppt) or Red Sea (42.5 ppt). Atmospheric precipitation or freshwater discharges from inland waters (surface water or groundwater) reduce salinity, while evaporation increases salinity content. In spite of the fact that salinity levels vary from one water body to another, the relative abundance of the main dissolved components remains almost unchanged.

The presence of dissolved salts has an effect on the density of seawater. A salinity of 35 ppt amounts to a density difference between fresh and saline water of approximately 2 percent. Thus, whenever there is confluence of fresh and saline water, some interesting phenomena occur. Depending on the degree of energy input by the wind, currents, and tidal action, the fresh and saline waters can be thoroughly or partially mixed or remain stratified. Under quiescent conditions, if all other parameters (such as temperature and pressure) are the same for both the fresh and saline waters, then the heavier saline water will sink. In many estuaries with high riverine discharge and low tidal range (such as the Mississippi River), seawater can penetrate many miles in the upstream direction, moving near the bottom and under the fresh water. This phenomenon is known as "saline wedge"; the separating interface between fresh and saline water is called the "halocline." Mixing conditions between fresh and saline waters are important from an ecological point of view, since salinity levels control the diversity and population of aquatic flora and fauna.

Sea salt is also a major contributor to atmospheric aerosol particles. During wave breaking (the phenomenon of "white caps"), small droplets are carried upward by air currents into the atmosphere. When the droplets evaporate, sea-salt particles of very small sizes (0.5 to 20 millimeters) are transported by the wind over the continents. About 10 percent of the total annual amount of salt that is generated in the oceans (1.8 billion tons) is deposited as airborne sea-salt particles on the continents.

The total volume of the oceanic waters is about 1.37 billion cubic kilometers (km^3). This volume constitutes approximately 96.5 percent of the total water on Earth. The other major water resources are groundwater, of which 10.53 million km^3 (0.76 percent) is fresh water and 12.87 million km^3 (0.93 percent) is saline water, and the polar ice, which contains 24.02 million km^3 (1.7 percent) of water. The remaining amount of water is in lakes, rivers, marshes, soil moisture, atmosphere, and biota. Fresh water thus makes up only 2.5 percent of the total amount of Earth's water. Most freshwater supplies are in the polar ice (68.6 percent) and in groundwater (30.1 percent). The percentage of fresh water found in lakes is only 0.26 percent, while the amount found in rivers is even smaller (0.006 percent).

Not all inland water is fresh. The amount of the dissolved salts occurring in inland waters, surface or underground, depends on the composition of the soils through which the water passes. Streams and rivers flowing over rocks containing chloride and sodium compounds contribute significantly to the generation of salt. Therefore, some inland waters have a high salt content and are not suitable for any use unless properly pretreated. The most extreme examples of brine inland waters are the Great Salt Lake in Utah (salt concentration of about 120 ppt) and the Dead Sea in the Middle East (salt concentration of about 270 ppt). Salt is also found as surface crust or layers in swamps and dry lake bottoms, particularly in arid climate areas. In coastal regions, excessive pumping of groundwater can lead to seawater intrusion into the aquifer. This can have a long-term negative effect on the water resources of a region, with subsequent devasting impact on the regional economy.

The average amount of fresh water that falls daily on the United States is about 4,200 billion gallons. This water feeds the various surface water bodies (lakes and rivers), recharges the aquifers, evaporates back to the atmosphere, or flows into the oceans. Therefore, only 675 billion gallons of precipitated water can be used for beneficial purposes. From this amount, 336 billion gallons are used by industry, 141 billion gallons by agriculture, and 25 billion gallons by domestic and rural consumers. The daily per-capita water use in the United States is about 1,900 gallons. The average domestic water consumption ranges from 20 to 80 gallons per day. Thus, the average amount of water used by a person during a seventy-year lifespan is estimated at 1.5 million gallons.

Direct measurement of seawater salinity by evaporation or chemical analysis is too complicated to be used on a routine basis. In the past, salinity (known as "absolute salinity") was estimated in terms of chlorinity. Chlorinity is the amount of chlorine ions plus the chlorine equivalent of bromine and iodine ions. From chlorinity, salinity was estimated by multiplying the value of chlorinity by a factor of 1.80655.

Presently, salinity (known as "practical salinity") is estimated indirectly by measuring the electrical conductivity of the seawater. However, since electrical conductivity is strongly affected by both salinity and temperature, the conductivity readings are properly corrected to compensate for temperature effects.

Applications of the Method

Fresh water is a precious commodity that is used for a variety of domestic, rural, industrial, and agricultural purposes. Water is not distributed evenly throughout the world and is subject to temporal short-term and long-term variations. In many regions, the available freshwater resources cannot meet the water demands. After the Industrial Revolution, accelerated anthropogenic pollution added to the water resource problem. In situations of limited water resources, the only alternative solutions are either cleanup and reuse of domestic and agricultural wastewater or, for islands and coastal regions, desalination of seawater. Both of these operations are costly and require construction of appropriate water-treatment facilities. Several countries in the Middle East, including Israel and Saudi Arabia, depend heavily on water desalination for their drinking-water supplies. Under emergency conditions, fresh water is obtained via the use of portable water-purification equipment.

Fresh water contains a number of impurities that have to be removed or treated before it is available for any useful purpose. These impurities include calcium, magnesium, iron, lead, copper, chloride, sulfate, nitrates, fluorides, sodium, different organic compounds, and suspended solids. Impurities can be hazardous to human health or can give water a disagreeable taste, smell, or appearance. In addition, they can create scaling or corrosive problems in pipes or in machinery that uses water. Because saline water contains a large amount of dissolved salts, before use it is always subjected to desalination. Generally, the acceptable quality standards for drinking water are 0.5 micrograms per kilogram (mg/kg) of total dissolved solids and 0.2 mg/kg of chloride.

Water treatment for production of domestic water involves a number of operations such as filtration, softening, distillation, deionization, chemical disinfection, exposure to ultraviolet radiation, and reverse osmosis. The number and the type of operations required depend on the quality and properties of the water supplies. The problem of high salt content can be treated with a variety of methods. Desalination is the process by which dissolved salts are removed from the water; there are a number of desalination methods. Since no one method is applicable in all situations, selection of the most appropriate desalination method is based on such variables as the amount and type of dissolved salts in water, the degree of purification of the water to be produced, and the associated costs. More than one hundred cities worldwide use desalination plants to provide fresh water for their needs.

There are two general methods of desalination, thermal processing (distillation) and membrane separation. The main principle behind thermal processing is as follows: Saline water is heated until it boils; then the released steam condenses as it cools, forming pure water. Membrane separation is achieved by using reverse osmotic pressure, so that the water passes through a membrane while the salt ions are retained by the membrane.

Distillation, the earliest desalination method, was used in steamships as early as 1884. There are several different thermal processing methods for desalination such as the Thin-Film Multiple Effect Distillation (TFMED), Multi-Stage Flash Desalination (MSFD), Mechanical Vapor Compression Desalination (MVCD), and Thermal Vapor Compression Desalination (TVCD). At standard atmospheric pressure (measured at sea level), water boils at 100 degrees Celsius (212 degrees Farenheit). However, boiling temperature decreases with decreasing pressure. Also, if the water is heated under high pressure at 100 degrees Celsius and is suddenly released into a vacuum chamber, it flashes into vapor. This technique is used in both the TFMED method and the MSFD method, in which the pressure is continuously reduced in sequential stages. The number of sequential stages can range from fifteen to twenty-five. The MVCD and the TVCD methods use compression to increase the pressure and thus increase the temperature of a constant volume of steam. Heating of the steam stream facilitates the desalination process. Water obtained through thermal processing can easily have a purity of less than 0.1 mg/kg of dissolved matter. The brine wastewater resulting from desalination of seawater has a salinity of approximately 70 g/kg.

Membrane separation includes two major desalination methods: Pressure Membrane Processes (PMP) and Electro-Dialysis Reversal (EDR). In PMP, only pure water is able to pass through the membrane, while the majority of the dissolved material is detained by the membrane. The EDR method utilizes ion-specific membranes placed between anodic (positively charged) and cathodic (negatively charged) electrodes. Dissolved material is then collected as the salt ions move under the electric current. Although the Electro-Dialysis Reversal method is relatively common, the most widespread desalination methods involve PMP.

There are four pressure-membrane desalination processes: Microfiltration (MF), Ultrafiltration (UF), Nanofiltration (NF), and Reverse Osmosis (RO). The common principle of these methods is the forced passing (under high pressure) of saline water through a membrane. The main difference among the PMP methods is the size of the particles that are removed from the saline water. For example, MF removes particles larger than 10 microns (1 micron equals 0.000001 meters), UF removes particles of sizes from 0.001 to 10 microns, NF removes particles greater than 0.001 microns, and RO removes particles ranging from 0.0001 to 0.001 microns. Another difference among the PMP methods is the pressure needed for forcing the water through the membrane. MF operates at a pressure of less than 10 pounds per square inch (psi), UF at a range of 15 to 75 psi, NF at a range of 75 to 250 psi, and RO at a range of 200 to 1,200 psi.

Reverse osmosis is an energy-consuming method that can be used very effectively, particularly for production of domestic use water, whenever good-quality saline water is available. Reverse osmosis can be accomplished using different design modules such as the tubular, the plate-and-frame, the spiral-wound, or the hollow fiber. In all these designs, the water that is allowed to pass through the membrane, the "permeate," is collected as the product water, while the water retained by the membrane forms the so-called concentrate or reject.

There are various type of membranes used for reverse osmosis, such as the cellulose acetate group, which includes cellulose acetate (CA), cellulose acetate butyrate (CAB), and cellulose triacetate (CTA), or polyamide (PA). Production of CA membrane involves four stages: casting, evaporation, gelation, and shrinkage. During the first stage, a solution of cellulose acetate in acetone containing certain additives is casted into flat or tubular thin surfaces. Then the acetone evaporates, leaving a porous surface. During the gelation stage, the cast is immersed in cold water, forming a gel, while at the same time the additives dissolve in the water. In the last stage, the film shrinks, forcing reduction of the pore sizes. High temperatures result in smaller pore openings.

Electrodialysis is also an effective desalination process whereby ions are separated from the water by being forced through selective ion-permeable membranes under the action of electric current. The ion-permeable membranes alternate between those allowing only the passage of cations (such as potassium, Na^+) and those allowing only the passage of anions (such as chlorine, Cl^-).

Another potential methodology for desalination involves freezing of the water. Since ice is theoretically free of any dissolved material, various techniques have been proposed for application of freezing for desalination. However, this method does not have any widespread applicability.

Both the thermal and membrane methods require some form of energy to accomplish desalination. The energy efficiency of the desalination methods is expressed either as the Gained Output Ratio (GOR) or the Performance Ratio (PR). The GOR is defined as the ratio between the mass of distillate over the mass of the steam. The PR, also known as economy, is estimated as pounds of distillate per 1,000 British Thermal Units (BTU) or as kilograms of distillate per 2,326 Kilo Joules (KJ). Criteria for the selection of a desalination method include energy consumption, process efficiency, operational and maintenance costs, auxiliary services, and growth of demand. Energy is provided mostly by electrically driven pumps, but diesel engines can also be utilized.

Context

Domestic (potable) water is a valuable commodity. Population growth and high demand for water for industrial and agricultural practices have created severe water shortages in many parts of the world. In addition, increased water contamination and extreme hydrologic conditions, such as prolonged drought, can adversely affect the socioeconomic conditions and human health of a region.

In addition, there are other applications that require high-quality water. For example, high-purity water is required by pharmaceutical companies for processing drugs and medications, by hospitals for kidney dialysis, by power and other energy-intensive plants for low-scaling water, and by semiconductor manufacturing for production of high-performance chips.

Since most of the conventional water resources are already under stress, the only alternative solution to the water-resource problem is desalination of the vast oceanic water masses or reuse of wastewater. The various existing thermal or membrane methods can effectively provide fresh high-quality water. However, the high costs associated with these methodologies limit their applicability only to communities that can afford the financial burden. There is ongoing research into improving the efficiency and reducing the cost of existing desalination methods and developing new methodologies. What began as a small distillation process used to provide fresh water to a handful of ships' crew members has evolved into a complex water-treatment operation that supplies fresh water to large populations.

Bibliography

Henry, J. G., and G. W. Heinke. *Environmental Science and Engineering.* 2d ed. Upper Saddle River, N.J.: Prentice-Hall, 1996. Lengthy presentation of water quality and wastewater treatment technological issues, including desalination. Contains a discussion of case studies.

Ko, A., and D. B. Guy. "Brackish and Seawater Desalting." In *Reverse Osmosis Technology: Application for High-Purity-Water Production.* New York: Marcel Dekker, 1988. Detailed presentation of technological methods for desalination of brackish and saline waters.

Metcalf & Eddy, Inc. *Wastewater Engineering: Treatment, Disposal, Reuse.* 2d ed. New York: McGraw-Hill, 1979. A comprehensive discussion of wastewater properties, waste-treatment processes, and associated methodologies. Emphasis on engineering design.

Pickard, G. L., and W. J. Emery. *Descriptive Physical Oceanography: An Introduction.* 4th ed. Oxford, England: Pergamon Press, 1988. Thorough presentation of seawater properties and salinity distribution in the various seas and oceans.

Porteous, A. *Saline Water Distillation Processes.* London: Longman, 1975. Detailed presentation of the distillation methods used for desalination of saline water.

Shafer, L. H., and M. S. Mintz. "Electrodialysis." In *Principles of Desalination.* 2d ed. New York: Academic Press, 1980. Detailed description of the electrodialysis method for removal of dissolved matter.

Sincero, A. P., and G. A. Sincero. *Environmental Engineering: A Design Approach.* Upper Saddle River, N.J.: Prentice-Hall, 1996. Detailed presentation of water-quality principles and associated water-purification and cleanup technologies and designs.

Speece, R. E. "Water and Wastewater." In *Environmental Health.* 2d ed. Orlando, Fla.: Academic Press, 1980. Provides a brief but comprehensive description of water-quality characteristics and the methodologies used for treatment of both domestic and industrial waters.

Tebbutt, T. H. Y. *Principles of Water Quality Control.* Oxford, England: Pergamon Press, 1971. An introductory textbook on water properties and applied methodologies for water-quality control.

Twort, A. C., R. C. Hoather, and F. M. Law. *Water Supply.* 2d ed. London: Edward Arnold, 1974. A discussion of water-supply systems, including distribution and treatment methodologies.

Viessman, W., Jr., and M. J. Hammer. *Water Supply and Pollution Control.* 5th ed. New York: HarperCollins, 1993. A thorough quantitative coverage of water-supply issues, water-quality treatment methodologies, and engineering designs.

Panagiotis D. Scarlatos

Cross-References

SALT DOMES AND SALT DIAPIRS

Type of earth science: Economic geology
Field of study: Structural geology

These geologic structures, which can extend more than 7 kilometers in diameter with heights that exceed 12 kilometers, arch and vertically penetrate overlying sedimentary rock. In addition to their importance in the supply of minerals for the food processing and chemical industries, salt domes and salt diapirs are associated with economic reserves of crude oil, natural gas, and sulfur. They are also utilized as repositories for valuable and strategic materials and, potentially, for nuclear waste.

Principal terms

CAP ROCK: an impervious rock unit, generally composed of anhydrite, gypsum, and occasionally sulfur, overlying or capping any salt dome or salt diapir

EVAPORITE MINERALS: that group of minerals produced by evaporation from a saline solution; examples are gypsum, anhydrite, and rock salt

PRECIPITATION: a process whereby a solid substance is separated from a solution

RIM SYNCLINE: a circular depression found at the base of many salt domes and diapirs

SALT DIAPIR: a vertical column of rock salt that has flowed upward to the extent of piercing overlying sedimentary rock

SALT DOME: a vertical dome of rock salt that has, by flowing upward plastically, arched or penetrated overlying sedimentary rock

SALT STRUCTURE SEISMOLOGY: the application of refracted and reflected seismic waves in the discovery of salt domes and diapirs

SEDIMENTARY ROCK: any rock formed by the accumulation and consolidation of loose sediment, as in the precipitation of salt crystals from seawater

SHALE SHEATH: a variable thickness of ground-up sedimentary rock found along the flanks of many salt domes and diapirs

VISCO-ELASTIC: pertaining to the viscosity and elasticity properties of a substance; rock salt has high elasticity and low viscosity

Summary of the Phenomenon

Salt domes and salt diapirs are found throughout the world in association with bedded salt, an evaporative sedimentary rock known to be part of the rock record of every geologic time period. While salt deposits underlie at least twenty-six of the United States, salt domes and diapirs in North America are confined to the Gulf Coast basin, extending from central Mississippi and Louisiana and coastal Texas south into the Isthmus of Tehuantepec in Mexico. The Gulf Coast basin contains more than five hundred salt domes and diapirs, located within at least nine separate sub-basins. Other significant concentrations of salt domes or diapirs occur in Europe, in the Zechstein Basin of Germany and Poland and in Denmark, England, Spain, Portugal, France, and Romania; in Asia, in the Donets Basin of Russia and the northern regions of Siberia; in Africa, along the Mediterranean coast of Algeria and Morocco and in Gabon and Senegal; in South America, in Peru; and in the Iran, Aden, and Yemen sections of the Arabian Peninsula.

Worldwide, salt domes and diapirs are commonly associated with significant reserves of crude oil, natural gas, and sulfur. Human-made caverns within domes and diapirs are employed as storage sites of crude oil, low-pressure liquid gas, and volatile materials; such caverns have also been proposed as possible sites for the storage of nuclear waste.

Bedded salt deposits result from geological processes that have been in operation for several hundred million years. Precipitation of salt deposits occurs within modified marine environments whenever evaporation exceeds surface runoff and rainfall, and wherever restriction of the free circulation of seawater exists. The evaporation of a 300-meter column of seawater will theoretically result in the precipitation of 4.6 meters of evaporate minerals, of which 3.5 meters will be salt (chemically composed of sodium chloride). Bedded salt units are generally confined to a structural basin, a downwarped region of the earth's crust containing thick sequences of sedimentary rock. In North America, the Louann Salt, of Middle Mesozoic age (approximately 175 million years old), underlies more than 2 million square kilometers of the Gulf Coast basin and is several thousand meters thick.

While halite, the mineralogical term for salt, is the principal evaporite mineral in salt domes and diapirs, minor amounts of other evaporites exist. Gulf Coast basin salt domes are commonly composed of 97 percent halite and minor amounts of anhydrite (calcium sulphate). Trace amounts of gypsum (hydrous calcium sulfate), calcite (calcium carbonate), pyrite (iron disulfide), and native sulfur can also be present. In comparison, the rock salt of the Zechstein basin of Germany is composed of from 94 to 99 percent halite, accompanied by minor amounts of anhydrite, carnallite (hydrous potassium and magnesium chloride), and sylvite (potassium chloride).

The mechanism whereby bedded salt units are transformed into salt domes and salt diapirs has been generally known for decades. After precipitation from an evaporating body of saline water, pure, bedded rock salt has a specific gravity of 2.16 grams per cubic centimeter. When that salt bed is initially overlain by younger sedimentary rocks composed of sandstone, siltstone, shale, and clastic limestone—normal rock associations found wherever salt domes occur—the salt is in density equilibrium with the younger rocks, as their specific gravities range from 1.7 to 2.0 grams per cubic centimeter. Upon burial to depths of several thousand meters, however, the specific gravity of the overburden will increase to levels ranging from 2.4 to 2.8 grams per cubic centimeter, while the salt, being incompressible, remains at the 2.16 specific gravity level. Under these conditions, an upper force of buoyancy will act upon the salt, encouraging movement toward the surface of the earth. This potential for movement is accelerated below depths of 3,000 meters by conditions of increasing temperature and pressure, altering the visco-elastic properties of the salt as it changes from a solid to a consistency comparable to that of warm butter. Through this combination of density imbalance and altered visco-elastic condition, bedded salt will begin to arch overlying rocks at those sites marked by slight salt-surface irregularities. As long as the overlying rocks are arched or folded and thus remain mechanically intact, the resulting structure is termed a salt "dome." Should the overlying strata be broken and penetrated by the rising column of salt, the structure becomes a salt "diapir" (meaning "through-piercing"), a form of intrusive sedimentary rock. Studies of the thickness and age of salt basins suggest that the rate of salt movement and penetration, while variable, generally averages less than 2 millimeters per year. During periods of very active sedimentation and crustal folding, domal activity is most active. In the Aquitaine basin of France, the seven mapped phases of salt upwelling relate directly to periods of crustal deformation in the nearby Alps.

Once initiated, upward flow will continue until the causative forces of buoyancy and flow properties are altered by diminished pressure and temperature, or until the base of the salt dome or diapir is cut off from the bedded unit acting as the salt source. In general, the thicker the bedded salt source and the deeper it is buried, the higher the developing salt structure. A salt dome or diapir will usually not reach to the surface of the earth; occasionally, though, surface penetration occurs, as in the case of the salt domes of the Persian Gulf region. There, 40 percent of the nearly two hundred salt domes rise above the surrounding desert, often displaying salt "glaciers" that flow laterally away from the center of the exposed salt mass. One exposed dome, Kuh-i-Namak, has a surface elevation of 1,310 meters and a diameter of 9.6 kilometers.

Through the process of arching or penetrating overlying sedimentary rock, all salt domes and diapirs take on certain identifiable characteristics. These features are found within the interior of the salt structure, forming the top of the dome or diapir and associated with the sedimentary rock adjacent to the salt structure.

Studies of salt mines within near-surface diapirs of the Gulf Coast basin give direct evidence of vertical flowage. This flowage is demonstrated by stretched, elongated halite crystals and vertically oriented, tightly folded layers of salt accentuated by color changes between alternating pure and impure halite beds. Further evidence of vertical intrusion into overlying rock is seen in the occasional sighting of inclusions of sandstone and shale within salt structures; such foreign rock is identical in composition to adjacent intruded rock.

Topping most shallow salt domes and diapirs is an impervious mantle of minerals, on average 90 to 120 meters thick, termed the "cap rock." While found on domes up to 3,000 meters deep, cap rock thickness is greatest over the center of the dome, generally decreases with dome depth, and is absent along dome flanks. A typical, well-developed cap rock is mineralogically composed of anhydrite grading upward into calcite (calcium carbonate). Often, a transition zone containing varying amounts of barite (barium sulphate), gypsum, and sulfur separates the two principle layers. Some salt domes within the Poland section of the Zechstein basin of Europe have a cap rock composed of clay minerals. It is generally agreed that cap rock is gradually formed by upward-migrating salt structures encountering waters of decreasing salinity contained within the sedimentary rock being penetrated. Incomplete solution of the impure rock salt results in the accumulation of insoluble residues, principally anhydrite, along the leading edge of the salt intrusion. Transition minerals are believed to result from later alteration of the anhydrite.

The most common features external, or adjacent, to salt domes and salt diapirs include a shale sheath, an overlying domed structure accentuated by a central graben, an overall complex pattern of faulting, and a peripheral rim syncline.

Where encountered by drilling in the Gulf Coast basin, the shale (clay) sheath covers the flanks of a dome or diapir much like a cap rock covers the top. This sheath is of variable thickness and is composed of finely ground rock formed by the frictional drag of the upward movement of the salt structure against adjacent sedimentary sandstones and shales.

As bedded salt beds become mobile under conditions of deep burial, they form circular structures created by arching of the overlying sedimentary rock. Diapiric movement is accomplished by salt, and developing cap-rock, penetration of the rock cover along a complex system of fractures (faults) that radiate outward from the circular structure. As such movement actually extends (stretches) the overlying rock cover, the structure center is commonly interrupted by a graben, a depressed block bounded by faults. This combination of a regional arched structure interrupted by complex faulting and a localized central graben is what complicates the geologic interpretation of the upper portions of any salt dome or diapir.

The most significant aspect of the exterior base of a salt structure is the presence of a rim syncline, a structural depression that partially or completely encircles most domes and diapirs. This feature is caused by the downward movement of overlying sedimentary rock into the void formed by the lateral flow of bedded salt into the developing dome. Details of rim synclines are little known as a consequence of their association with the base of salt domes and diapirs.

Methods of Study

Under normal conditions, salt domes and salt diapirs are not exposed at the surface of the earth and therefore are not accessible for direct study. An exception would include the diapiric salt structures of the Persian Gulf region, which are surface exposed and which, because of arid climate, are preserved for long-term analysis. Salt domes and diapirs can also be directly studied where salt has been extracted from the upper levels of the structure, either by brine-well production, such as at the Bryan Mound Dome in Brazoria County, Texas, or by direct salt mining, as conducted at the Avery Island Dome in Iberia Parish, Louisiana. Analyses of the walls of such mines gives evidence pertaining to the layering and folding of salt beds, permitting development of theories of salt mobility and flowage.

The formation of a salt dome or diapir by long-term upward salt movement usually does not manifest itself in the development of surface relief effects identifying the presence of the shallow salt structure. Therefore, the discovery of the great majority of intrusive salt structures is accomplished by instrumentation designed to measure contrasting physical characteristics of the salt and adjacent sedimentary rock indirectly. In 1917, a buried salt dome was identified near Hanigsen, Germany, by a torsion balance, an early prospecting instrument designed to measure alterations in the gravitational field of the earth. Subsequent drilling into this dome verified the accuracy of the torsion-balance method, which was soon being employed worldwide in the discovery of salt structures. By 1935, the cumbersome torsion balance had been successfully modified in the form of the first practical gravimeter, a modern field instrument that directly reads gravity differences with an accuracy to one millionth part of the earth's total gravitational field. Because of density differences between the salt and adjacent rock material, such accuracy permits easy identification by gravimeter of a salt dome or salt diapir, as well as identification and thickness analyses of the cap rock.

After World War I, the invention of the refraction seismology process, which measures the change in velocity and deflection of an elastic wave moving from one rock formation to another, opened a new and very successful era of salt dome and salt diapir discovery in the Gulf Coast basin. By the second half of the twentieth century, improvements in the reflection seismology process using technology related to refraction seismology were being employed worldwide in the continued discovery of intrusive salt structures, especially within marine waters off the Gulf Coast of North America and offshore Africa. The seismic reflection process makes it possible to identify the overall geometry of intrusive salt structures with considerable precision. Adaption of three-dimensional reflection seismology during the 1990's, technology that is capable of documenting not only the geology of the base of salt domes and diapirs but also the structure underlying the source salt layer, is yet another major advancement in the identification and scientific study of intrusive salt.

Upon discovery and verification by drilling, details of domes and the sedimentary rock columns found adjacent to the salt column are determined by wire-line analysis. In this process, varying instruments are lowered down a borehole by a wire line to record physical properties, such as electrical resistivity, radioactivity, and temperature, of the salt and adjacent rock.

Context

The mineral halite has been a significant industrial material and article of world trade for thousands of years. In the United States, half of produced salt is employed by the chemical industry in the manufacture of caustic soda, polyvinyl chloride, hydrochloric acid, and household and industrial bleach. Large volumes are used in cold climates for traction control on highways. Other uses include water treatment, insecticide, medicine, aluminum, and steel manufacture, and food preservation and seasoning.

Extraction of halite from salt domes and diapirs is accomplished by two means: by conventional underground mining, as conducted, for example, in the Winnfield Dome in Winn Parish, Louisiana; and by means of brine (salt solution) wells, as practiced at the Barbers Hill Dome in Chambers County, Texas. Drilled wells are also used to extract economic volumes of sulfur from the cap rock of many salt domes. Production of sulfur from domes and diapirs utilizes the Frasch superheated water process to melt and dissolve the sulfur.

The discovery and exploratory drilling of salt domes and diapirs has been a worldwide priority for decades because of their association with crude oil and natural gas. The bulk of these fossil-fuel deposits, concentrated within sedimentary rock penetrated by diapiric upthrust, is found in a circular area up to 1,000 meters away from the salt periphery. With the dual discovery in 1901 of the Spindletop Dome in Jefferson County, Texas, and the presence of oil within its cap rock, the center of oil and gas production in the United States moved from the Ohio River Valley to west of the Mississippi River. More than several hundred million barrels of oil have been produced from the cap rock and sedimentary rock flanking this historic salt structure.

In addition to their association with hydrocarbon resources, solution-created and mined cavities in salt domes and diapirs are becoming increasingly important as possible depositories of volatile, strategic, toxic, and nuclear material. With the signing of the Energy Policy and Conservation Act of 1972, five salt domes of the Gulf Coast basin became part of the Strategic Petroleum Reserve, the United States' emergency plan for the storage of crude oil. As a typical part of this program, two levels of mined rooms approximately 21 meters high by 30 meters square within the Weeks Island Dome in Iberia Parish, Louisiana, held a capacity 72 million barrels of crude oil during the mid-1990's. Elsewhere in Texas and Louisiana, solution-developed and mined dome cavities have been used for the storage of low-pressure liquid gas, high-pressure ethylene, and refined hydrocarbon products ranging from gasoline to fuel oil. Intrusive salt structures are particularly amenable to the storage of such products because salt is generally impervious to the passage of liquids. Impermeability combined with a relative lack of humidity makes dome and diapir cavities particularly adaptable to the long-term storage of volatile and radioactive waste materials as well as of historic, legal, and financial records vital to industrial and national security.

Possibly the most unusual use of an intrusive salt structure is that of the Tatum Dome of Lamar County, Mississippi. The dome is employed by the U.S. Atomic Energy Commission to house an explosion as part of the study of peaceful applications of nuclear energy.

Bibliography

Halbouty, M. T. *Salt Domes: Gulf Region, United States and Mexico*. Houston, Tex.: Gulf Publishing, 1979. This presentation, written by the acknowledged salt-dome expert among American geologists and petroleum engineers, lists pertinent data for more than four hundred salt domes and salt diapirs within the U.S. and Mexican portions of the Gulf Coast basin. Numerous full-color figures illustrate salt-dome distribution, configuration, composition, classification, and economic significance. A very readable reference written for the general public.

Jackson, M. P. A., ed. *Salt Diapirs of the Great Kavir, Central Iran*. Boulder, Colo.: The Geological Society of America, 1991. A useful reference for salt domes of the Central Iranian basin, one of the most spectacular and well-exposed salt dome regions of the world. These salt structures are unusual in that they form circular elevations 80 to 100 meters in relief. Intended for college-level readers.

Jackson, M. P. A., D. G. Roberts, and S. Snelson, eds. *Salt Tectonics: A Global Perspective*. Tulsa, Okla.: American Association of Petroleum Geologists, 1996. A comprehensive presentation of the geologic means whereby bedded salt units are transformed into a variety of geometric shapes, including domes and diapirs. Written at the college level for anyone interested in the exploration of salt structures and their common association with economic reserves of sulfur, crude oil, and natural gas.

Kupfer, D. H., ed. *Geology and Technology of Gulf Coast Salt: A Symposium*. Baton Rouge, La.: School of Geoscience, Louisiana State University, 1970. This two-day symposium, conducted by nine scientists actively engaged in Gulf Coast basin salt-dome research, explored the origin, composition, and development of salt structures. This volume is of value in that it presents discussion of topics not commonly found in other references, such as cap-rock development, salt movements, and methods of salt intrusion. Written for the college-level reader, with numerous illustrations.

Lefond, S. J. *Handbook of World Salt Resources*. New York: Plenum Press, 1969. While this volume specifically discusses general salt resources of 196 continental and island countries, its documentation of the worldwide distribution of intrusive salt structures is invaluable to the student of salt domes and diapirs. The history of salt-resource utilization of each country is discussed, along with numerous charts showing chemistry, mineralogy, geographic location, and geology. Very suitable for high-school and college-level readers.

Murray, G. E. *Geology of the Atlantic and Gulf Coastal Province of North America*. New York: Harper & Brothers, 1961. A general reference to the geology of the coastal regions of the eastern and southern United States. Chapter 5, "Salt Structures," contains a thorough presentation of the salt domes and diapirs of the Gulf Coast basin. Though intended for the professional geologist, this volume should be intelligible to the general college-level reader.

Albert B. Dickas

Cross-References

Earth Resources, 2175; Evaporites, 631; Industrial Nonmetals, 1225; Oil and Gas Exploration, 1878; Precipitation, 2108; Seawater Composition, 2282; Sedimentary Mineral Deposits, 2296; Sedimentary Rocks: Chemical Precipitates, 2318; Seismic Reflection Profiling, 2333; Underground Mining Techniques, 1710.

SATELLITE METEOROLOGY

Type of earth science: Atmospheric sciences and meteorology
Field of study: Analytical techniques

Satellite meteorology, the study of atmospheric phenomena using satellite data, is an indispensable tool for forecasting weather and studying climate on a global scale.

Principal terms

ACTIVE SENSOR: a sensor, such as a radar instrument, that illuminates a target with artificial radiation, which is reflected back to the sensor
ALBEDO: the percentage of incoming radiation that is diffusely reflected by a surface
EL NIÑO: a periodic anomalous warming of the Pacific waters off the coast of South America; part of a large-scale oceanic and atmospheric fluctuation that has global repercussions
GEOSYNCHRONOUS (GEOSTATIONARY): pertaining to a satellite that orbits about the earth's equator at an altitude and speed such that it remains above the same point on the earth
NEAR-POLAR ORBIT: an earth orbit that lies in a plane that passes close to both the north and south poles
PASSIVE SENSORS: sensors that detect reflected or emitted electromagnetic radiation
RADIOMETER: an instrument that makes quantitative measurements of reflected or emitted electromagnetic radiation within a particular wavelength interval
SPATIAL RESOLUTION: the ability of a sensor to define closely spaced features
SUN-SYNCHRONOUS ORBIT: for an earth satellite, a near-polar orbit at an altitude such that the satellite always passes over any given point on the earth at the same local time
SYNTHETIC APERTURE RADAR (SAR): a spaceborne radar imaging system that uses the motion of the spacecraft in orbit to simulate a very long antenna

Summary of the Methodology

Satellite meteorology is the study of atmospheric phenomena, notably weather and weather conditions, using information gathered by artificial satellites. These satellites, unmanned spacecraft equipped with instruments that monitor cloud cover, snow, ice, temperatures, and other parameters, give scientists a continuous and up-to-date view of meteorological conditions and activity over a large area. Satellite data are an important tool not only for forecasting weather and tracking storms but also for observing climate change over time, monitoring ozone levels in the stratosphere, and studying other aspects of weather and climate on a global and ongoing basis.

The satellites from which meteorological measurements are made can be categorized by their orbits. Some weather satellites have a geosynchronous, or geostationary, orbit, meaning that they travel around the globe at an altitude and speed that keeps them above the same point along the equator. A near-polar, sun-synchronous orbit, by contrast, is a north-south orbit that passes close to the earth's poles and carries a satellite over any given location on the earth's surface at the same local time. Geosynchronous satellites have better temporal resolution: They provide updated information for an area every thirty minutes, while near-polar, sun-synchronous satellites may take anywhere from a few hours to several days to transmit updates. However, near-polar satellites have the higher spatial resolution—that is, they are better at providing images in which closely spaced features can be identified. Geosynchronous satellites provide images with comparatively poor spatial resolution because they must orbit at a greater altitude (at least 35,000 kilometers above the earth's surface). Examples of geosynchronous meteorological satellites include the U.S. Geostationary Operational Environmental Satellite (GOES) series, Europe's Meteosat series, Russia's Geostationary Operational Meteorological Satellite (GOMS) series, and Japan's Geostationary Meteorological Satellite (GMS), or Himawan, series. Near-polar, sun-synchronous meteorological satellites include the National Oceanic and Atmospheric Administration (NOAA) series of American satellites and Russia's Meteor series.

The various orbiting platforms carry different sets of instruments. The weather satellites launched in the 1960's and early 1970's included television camera systems as part of their instrument packages. Later satellites have relied instead on instruments such as specialized radiometers (instruments that measure the amounts of electromagnetic radiation within a specific wavelength range) and radar systems. Radiometers measure such parameters as surface, cloud, and atmospheric temperatures; atmospheric water vapor and cloud distribution; and scattered solar radiation. Radar-system measurements include satellite altitude and ocean-surface roughness. Television cameras and radiometers are examples of passive sensors, which record radiation reflected or emitted from clouds, landforms, or other objects below. Radar systems are active sensors, sending out signals and recording them as they are reflected back. The data collected by a satellite's sensors are transmitted via radio to ground stations. If a near-polar orbiter is not within transmitting distance of a ground station, its onboard data-collection system will store the information until the satellite passes within range.

The Advanced Television Infra Red Observation Satellite, or TIROS, and Next-Generation (ATN) near-polar orbiting satellites (NOAA 8 through 14), a series of American weather satellites, have carried an array of sophisticated instruments. Two of these satellites, NOAA 12 and NOAA 14, remained in operation into the late 1990's. All the ATN series satellites have included an Advanced Very High Resolution Radiometer (AVHRR), which detects specified wavelength intervals within the visible, near-infrared, and infrared ranges to generate information on sea-surface and cloud-top temperatures and ice and snow conditions; a TIROS Operational Vertical Sounder (TOVS), which measures emissions within the visible, infrared, and microwave spectral bands to provide vertical profiles of the atmosphere's temperature, water vapor, and total ozone content from the earth's surface to an altitude of 32 kilometers; and a solar proton monitor, which detects fluctuations in the Sun's energy output, particularly those related to sunspot (solar storm) activity. With the exception of NOAA 8 and NOAA 12, all these satellites have included the Earth Radiation Budget Experiment (ERBE), which uses long-wave and short-wave radiometers to provide data pertaining to the earth's albedo (the amount of incoming solar radiation that is diffusely reflected by the ground, water, ice, snow, clouds, airborne particles, or other surfaces). All but NOAA 8, NOAA 10, and NOAA 12 have carried the Solar Backscatter Ultraviolet (SBUV) radiometer, which measures the vertical structure of ozone in the atmosphere by monitoring the ultraviolet radiation that the atmosphere scatters back into space. Of the ATN series of satellites, NOAA 12 is the only one that has not also carried the Search and Rescue Satellite Aided Tracking (SARSAT) system, which detects distress signals from downed aircraft and emergency beacons from ocean vessels, then relays the signals to special ground stations.

The satellites of the U.S. GOES series that remained in operation in the late 1990's (GOES 8 and GOES 9) are geosynchronous orbiters with their own distinctive instrumentation. Instrumentation aboard GOES 8 (also called GOES-EAST) and GOES 9 (or GOES-WEST) includes a sounder, which uses visible and infrared data to create vertical profiles of atmospheric temperature, moisture, carbon dioxide, and ozone; a five-band multispectral radiometer, which scans visible and infrared wavelengths to obtain sea-surface temperature readings, detects airborne dust and volcanic ash, and provides day and night images of cloud conditions, fog, fires, and volcanoes; and a search-and-rescue support system similar to the ones flown on the NOAA near-polar orbiters. The GOES satellites are also equipped with a Space Environment Monitor (SEM), which uses a solar X-ray sensor, a magnetometer, an energetic particle sensor, and a high-energy proton alpha detector to monitor solar activity and the intensity of the earth's magnetic field. The GOES-EAST satellite is positioned above the equator at an approximate longitude of 75 degrees west, while the GOES-WEST satellite orbits above the equator at approximately 135 degrees west longitude. These locations are ideal: GOES-EAST can provide the United States with images of storms approaching across the Atlantic Ocean during hurricane season (June through November); GOES-WEST can monitor the weather systems that move in from across the Pacific Ocean, which affect the United States during most of the year. However, when instrument malfunctions impair a satellite's ability to provide data, the National Weather Service can use small rocket engines aboard the satellites to reposition a more functional platform to provide the desired coverage until a replacement satellite can be launched. After the imaging system on GOES 6 failed in 1989, for example, GOES 7 was relocated several times to compensate.

While operational weather satellites have generally carried radiometers, radar instruments have been part of the instrument package aboard experimental satellites and space shuttle flights. One of the best-known orbiters using active sensors is Seasat, a short-lived experimental craft launched in 1978 to monitor the earth's oceans. During its three months of operation, this earth-resources satellite provided a wealth of data for meteorological study. Its radar altimeter determined the height of the sea surface, from which data scientists derived measurements of winds, waves, and ocean currents. Its radar scatterometer yielded information on wave direction and size, measurements that in turn provided insights into wind speed and direction. The most sophisticated of Seasat's active sensors was a synthetic aperture radar (SAR), a radar imaging system that created a "synthetic aperture" of view by using the motion of the platform to simulate a very long antenna. Images of the ocean's surface were obtained from SAR data.

Satellite data have become indispensable to the meteorologist. From orbit, information is readily available from any location on the planet, regardless of its remoteness, inaccessibility, climatic inhospitality, or political affiliation. Satellites yield regular, repeated, and up-to-date coverage of areas at minimal cost. They make it possible to view large weather systems in their entirety, and facilitate meteorological observations on a regional or global basis. Satellites also provide a single data source for multiple locations, alleviating the problem of individual variance of calibration and accuracy that would be associated with separate ground-based observations for each location. However, it is important to note that ground-based stations can make more accurate and detailed observations of a small area; such details may be lost in a view from space. Important though it is to modern meteorology, the use of satellite data augments, rather than replaces, other methods of study.

Applications of the Method

Satellite meteorology provides a relatively inexpensive means for obtaining current and abundant information on temperature, pressure, moisture, and other atmospheric, terrestrial, and oceanic conditions that affect weather and climate. These data, collected in digital form, are readily processed digitally and integrated with other information. Through these ongoing observations from orbit, scientists gain insights into the short-term and long-term implications of major atmospheric phenomena.

Weather forecasting is the best-known application of satellite meteorology. Anyone who has watched a televised weather report is familiar with geostationary satellite images, a series of which is usually presented in quick succession to show the recent movement of major weather systems. Meteorologists use computers to process the vast amounts of data provided by satellites and other information sources, including ground-based stations, aircraft, ships, and buoys. Data processing yields such forecasting aids as atmospheric temperature and water-vapor profiles, enhanced and false-color images, and satellite-image "movies." Computer models of atmospheric behavior also assist the meteorologist in short-range and long-range forecasting.

Satellite images of cloud cover alone yield a wealth of information for the forecaster. By comparing imagery from visible and infrared spectral regions, meteorologists can identify cloud types, structure, and degree of organization, then make assumptions concerning associated weather conditions. For example, the tall cumulus clouds that produce thunderstorms appear bright in the visible range, as they are deep and thus readily reflect sunlight. These clouds show up in infrared images as areas of coldness, an indicator of the clouds' altitude. Clouds that appear bright in visible-range imagery but that register as warm (low-altitude) in infrared scans may be fog or low-lying clouds. Wispy, high-altitude cirrus clouds, which are not precipitation-bearing, appear cold in infrared images but may not show up at all in visible-range scans.

Weather satellites have proved particularly useful in the science of hurricane and typhoon prediction. These violent rotating tropical storms originate as small low-pressure cells over oceans, where coverage by conventional weather-monitoring methods is sparse. Before the advent of satellites, ships and aircraft were the sole source of information on weather at sea, and hurricanes and typhoons often escaped detection until they were dangerously close to populated coastal areas. Now, using images and data obtained from orbit, a meteorologist can track and study these storms from their inception through their development and final dissipation. With accurate storm tracking and ample advance warning, inhabitants at risk can evacuate areas threatened by wind and high water, thereby minimizing loss of life.

Meteorological satellites also provide scientists with a view of how human activity affects climate on a local, regional, and even global basis. Terrestrial surface-temperature measurements clearly show urban "heat islands," where cities consistently exhibit higher temperatures than those of the surrounding countryside. In images obtained from orbit, thunderstorms can be seen developing along the boundaries of areas of dense air pollution: The haze layer inhibits heating of the ground surface, leading to the unstable atmospheric conditions that produce rainfall. Satellite imagery has revealed that in sub-Saharan Africa, where the overgrazing of livestock owned by nomads has contributed substantially to the spread of desert areas, the resulting increase in albedo has led to a reduction in rainfall and a subsequent reinforcement of drought conditions. Studies of deforestation in tropical areas have incorporated satellite data in their efforts to determine whether replacing forests with agricultural land affects rainfall by reducing evaporation or altering albedo. Satellite data have also played a major role in the ongoing debates regarding how human activity has affected global temperature trends and the earth's ozone layer.

Satellite meteorology is useful for monitoring the climatological effects of natural occurrences as well. The 1991 eruption of Mount Pinatubo in the Philippine Islands marked the first time that scientists were able to quantify the effects of a major volcanic eruption on global climate. Satellites equipped with ERBE instruments tracked the dissemination of the ash and sulfuric acid particles resulting from the violent eruption. The larger ash particles more readily drift down into the lower portion of the atmosphere, where they can be removed by precipitation; the smaller sulfuric acid particles can remain suspended in the stratosphere for several years. The ERBE instruments measured the amount of sunlight reflected by clouds, land surfaces, and particles suspended in the atmosphere and detected the contribution of suspended particles, clouds, and trace gases such as carbon dioxide to the amount of heat that the atmosphere retained. The eruption was found to have brought about a uniform cooling of the earth, slowing the global-warming trend that had been observed since the 1980's.

Another natural phenomenon, El Niño, has also been the subject of satellite-based study. This periodic anomalous warming of the Pacific waters off the coast of South America is part of a large-scale oceanic and atmospheric fluctuation, in which atmospheric pressure declines over the eastern Pacific Ocean and rises over Australia and the Indian Ocean. These widespread pressure changes influence rainfall patterns around the world. Satellite measurement of sea-surface temperatures facilitates the early detection of El Niño conditions, and satellite observations on a global basis help scientists to discern the climatic patterns that make up this complex phenomenon.

Meteorological satellites have also been used to gather data pertaining to "solar weather." Using orbiting sensors that detect energetic particles from the Sun, scientists can monitor and predict sunspots and other solar activity. The ability to predict the increases in solar emissions that are associated with sunspots allows scientists to anticipate the resulting ionospheric conditions on the earth, the effects of which include magnetic storms and disruption of radio transmissions.

Context

Since the launch of the first experimental TIROS meteorological satellite by the United States in 1960, observing the earth's weather and climate from orbit has become an integral part of modern meteorology. Weather satellites gather a wealth of information covering a large area, in a digital form that facilitates subsequent computer processing. With this information, meteorologists learn more about the atmosphere's three-dimensional structure and the ways in which fronts, thunderstorms, hurricanes, typhoons, and other weather systems develop, move, and dissipate. The broad over-view satellites provide of the earth, its oceans, and its atmosphere helps scientists to gain a better understanding of the complex interrelationships between the various elements of weather and climate.

Continuing insights into how weather and climate work lead to ongoing improvements in the science of weather forecasting. More accurate forecasting is a convenience for the family planning a vacation; for the farmer hoping for rain or the ski-lodge owner lacking snow, it has economic implications; and for the drought victim or the coastal resident facing a hurricane, it may affect life itself. Improved prediction makes possible a more timely response to hazardous conditions. Information from meteorological satellites can save property and lives, whether it is used to track large, violent storms, assess flooding hazards, monitor extensive forest or grassland fires, or coordinate rescue efforts in various emergency situations.

Satellite meteorology has also influenced the public, political, economic, and scientific responses to long-term global concerns. Two climatological issues that have received considerable attention in the popular media are the depletion of the strato-spheric ozone layer that regulates the amount of harmful ultraviolet radiation reaching the earth's surface, and global warming resulting from the buildup of "greenhouse gases" in the atmosphere. Widespread concern over ozone depletion, fueled by satellite observations of an ozone "hole" over Antarctica, led to the 1987 Montreal Protocol on Substances that Deplete the Ozone Layer, an international agreement that restricts the use and manufacture of chlorofluorocarbons and other chemicals believed to damage the ozone layer. Similarly, a treaty calling for reduced emissions of carbon dioxide and other "greenhouse gases" was introduced at the 1992 Convention on Climate Change. The global overviews afforded by meteorological satellites are crucial to the ongoing study of the earth's ozone layer and global temperature trends.

Bibliography

Barrett, E. C., and L. F. Curtis. *Introduction to Environmental Remote Sensing*. New York: John Wiley & Sons, 1976. The chapter on weather analysis and forecasting discusses satellite systems and data applications. The following chapter deals with the earth/atmosphere energy and radiation budgets and other aspects of global climatology. Each chapter includes references.

Burroughs, William James. *Watching the World's Weather*. Cambridge, England: Cambridge University Press, 1991. This useful text focuses on the importance of satellite meteorology to an understanding of weather and climate on a global scale. It deals not only with satellites and instrumentation but also with the essentials of meteorology. Includes satellite images, a glossary, a list of acronyms, and an annotated bibliography.

Colwell, Robert N. *Manual of Remote Sensing*. 2d ed. Falls Church, Va.: American Society of Photogrammetry, 1983. Volume 1, *Theory, Instruments, and Techniques*, includes a chapter on meteorological satellites. Volume 2, *Interpretation and Applications*, contains a chapter dedicated to remote sensing of weather and climate. This thorough technical manual includes a glossary, copious references, and examples of satellite imagery.

Fishman, Jack, and Robert Kalish. *The Weather Revolution*. New York: Plenum Press, 1994. Provides a nontechnical explanation of the basics of meteorology and outlines the evolution of weather forecasting, before and since the advent of weather satellites. The chapter on the development of satellite meteorology discusses programs from TIROS through GOES.

Gurney, R. J., J. L. Foster, and C. L. Parkinson, eds. *Atlas of Satellite Observations Related to Global Change*. Cambridge, England: Cambridge University Press, 1993. Suitable for college-level readers, this volume includes articles on the stratosphere, the troposphere, the earth's radiation balance, ocean-atmosphere coupling, and snow and ice cover. Illustrated with satellite imagery. An appendix describes selected satellites and sensors.

Hill, Janice. *Weather from Above*. Washington, D.C.: Smithsonian Institution Press, 1991. This overview of U.S. weather satellite programs, intended for a nonscientific audience, includes a glossary of acronyms, a chronological list of meteorological satellites, and suggestions for further reading. Illustrations include photographs of weather satellites, many from the collection of the National Air and Space Museum.

Lillesand, Thomas M., and Ralph W. Kiefer. *Remote Sensing and Image Interpretation*. 2d ed. New York: John Wiley & Sons, 1987. The chapter on earth resource satellites includes a description of the U.S. NOAA and GOES series of satellites and the Air Force's Defense Meteorological Satellite Program. Earlier chapters provide detailed information on various scanning instruments.

Villmow, Jack R. "Application of Remote Sensing in Weather Analysis." In Richason, Benjamin F., Jr., ed. *Introduction to Remote Sensing of the Environment*. Dubuque, Iowa: Kendall/Hunt, 1978. This chapter includes case studies involving typhoons and hurricanes, snowfall, frontal systems, and other weather conditions as observed from orbit. Suitable for college-level readers.

Karen N. Kähler

Cross-References

Climate, 217; Clouds, 224; Earth Resources Technology Satellite (ERTS), 2904; El Niño, 2911; The Greenhouse Effect, 1004; Infrared Spectra, 1232; Ozone Holes, 3039; Remote Sensing and the Electromagnetic Spectrum, 2166; Volcanoes: Mount Pinatubo, 3150; Weather Forecasting, 2717.

SEASONS

Type of earth science: Atmospheric sciences and meteorology
Field of study: Heat flow

Seasons are the two (fair and rainy) or four (spring, summer, autumn, and winter) periods of the year that are distinguished by specific types of weather. Many plant and animal life cycles and periods of activity are based on the seasons.

Principal terms

AUTUMNAL EQUINOX: the day that the Sun shines directly over the equator and the season of autumn begins; in the Northern Hemisphere, the date is about September 21, and in the Southern Hemisphere, about March 21

EQUATOR: a line of latitude on the earth that is halfway between the North and South Poles

MONSOON: a wind system that results in an annual cycle of fair weather followed by rainy weather

PERIHELION: the point in a planet's orbit at which it is closest to the Sun

SUMMER SOLSTICE: the day that summer begins; in the Northern Hemisphere, it is about June 21, when the Sun is directly over the Tropic of Cancer; in the Southern Hemisphere, it is about December 21, when the Sun is directly over the Tropic of Capricorn

TROPIC OF CANCER: a line of latitude 23.5 degrees north of the equator; this line is the latitude farthest north on the earth where the noon Sun is ever directly overhead

TROPIC OF CAPRICORN: a line of latitude 23.5 degrees south of the equator; this line is the latitude farthest south on the earth where the noon Sun is ever directly overhead

VERNAL EQUINOX: the day that the Sun shines directly over the equator and the season of spring begins; in the Northern Hemisphere, the date is about March 21, and in the Southern Hemisphere, about September 21

WINTER SOLSTICE: the day that winter begins; in the Northern Hemisphere, about December 21, and in the Southern Hemisphere, about June 21

Summary of the Phenomenon

The seasons are the natural, weather-related divisions of the year. In some tropical areas, the seasons may be classified merely as "rainy" and "dry." In the North and South Temperate Zones of the earth, the four seasons are spring, summer, autumn, and winter.

The seasons and their weather patterns are all caused by energy from the Sun. The seasons change because, in places, this solar energy increases and decreases in an unending annual cycle. This cycle results from the earth's axis being tilted at an angle of 23.5 degrees, an angle formed by the axis of the earth and a line perpendicular to the plane formed by the earth's orbit around the Sun.

The earth makes a complete orbit around the Sun every 365 days, 5 hours, and 49 minutes. As the earth revolves around the Sun, the direction of the earth's axis does not appreciably change. Thus the north end of the axis tilts toward the Sun in June; six months later in December, when the earth has traveled in its orbit to the other side of the Sun, the north end of the axis tilts away from the Sun.

Light is most intense when it strikes the earth vertically, because its energy is then concentrated. Light falling at an oblique angle is spread out as it hits the earth and is thus less effective in heating the earth. When the North Pole tilts toward the Sun, more sunlight falls on the Northern Hemisphere than on the Southern Hemisphere. In addition, this sunlight is more direct; that is, it hits the earth closer to a vertical direction. In fact, it is exactly vertical at the Tropic of Cancer. This results in two factors that together cause the warmer weather of summer: the Sun is higher in the sky than it is in autumn and winter, and the number of hours of daylight is increased. The higher the Sun is in the sky, the more concentrated is its heat, and thus the warmer that part of the earth becomes.

A common misconception is that summer occurs because the earth is closer to the Sun. In fact, the earth is closest to the Sun (at perihelion) about January 3 of each year, which is winter in the Northern Hemisphere. The earth is farthest from the Sun about July 3. The orbit of the earth is an ellipse (an elongated circle), but the shape of this ellipse is so nearly circular that its effect (that is, the variation in distance to the Sun) is not as important a factor in Earth's weather as is the angle at which the sunlight hits the earth. This angle is greatest in the Northern Hemisphere in June, when the Sun shines directly over the Tropic of Cancer, and greatest in the Southern Hemisphere in December when the Sun shines directly over the Tropic of Capricorn. It takes an enormous amount of solar energy to warm the earth's atmosphere, lakes, oceans, and land, and thus the warmest part of summer does not occur on the summer solstice itself (June 21) but instead about a month later.

Latitude affects seasonal change in two ways. One of these is the number of hours of daylight. As one goes from the equator (0 degrees latitude) to either of the poles, the latitude increases until one is at the poles, where the latitude is 90 degrees. On the day of the summer solstice (about June 21), daylight is at a maximum for areas north of the equator and at a minimum for areas south of the equator. The farther north one goes on that date, the longer the daylight. At 20 degrees north of the equator (approximately the latitude of Mexico City), daylight on that date is 13 hours and 12 minutes long; at 40 degrees north (approximately the latitude of New York, Rome, or Beijing), it is 14 hours, 52 minutes; at 60 degrees north (approximately the latitude of Anchorage or Oslo), daylight is 18 hours and 27 minutes.

The opposite is true at the winter solstice. At 20 degrees north of the equator, daylight on that date is 10 hours and 48 minutes long; at 40 degrees north, it is 9 hours, 8 minutes; at 60 degrees north, daylight lasts only 5 hours and 33 minutes. Therefore, the closer one is to the poles, the more extreme the variations of daylight and darkness.

The other way that latitude affects seasonal change is the angle of incoming sunlight. As one goes north from the Tropic of Cancer (or south from the Tropic of Capricorn), the angle of incoming solar light decreases. Even though far northern areas have extremely long periods of daylight from May to July, the angle of sunlight is so low that the solar energy is spread very thin. Therefore, the earth there does not receive much heat, and thus summer temperatures in the region never get very high.

Two other common misconceptions are that the Sun is straight overhead at noon every day and that it rises due east and sets due west every day. In fact, the Sun is never straight overhead at any part of any day in any location north of the Tropic of Cancer or south of the Tropic of Capricorn. The location of sunrise and sunset changes with the seasons. In June, the Sun rises in the northeast and sets in the northwest, while in December it rises in the southeast and sets in the southwest. The exact location is dependent upon one's latitude. The only days on which the Sun rises due east and sets due west are the vernal and autumnal equinoxes.

Seasons are affected by other factors: altitude, nearby mountain ranges, ocean currents, and proximity to water. Mountains lose heat in a manner very similar to the way a person's fingers do on a cold day. Thus, the air at the top of a mountain is much cooler than at the bottom. A typical example is Mount Kilimanjaro in Tanzania, the bottom of which is located in a tropical rainforest, but the top of which is covered by snow and ice.

The Gulf Stream in the Atlantic Ocean absorbs much solar energy as it passes through tropical areas near Florida. It then flows northeastward, carrying its warm water to Western Europe. Western Europe is thus much warmer than areas of Eastern North America at the same latitude. The same process occurs in the Pacific Ocean, where the Japan Current carries warm water to the western North American shore near the states of Oregon and Washington.

Mountain ranges often denude air currents of their moisture and deprive downwind areas of rainfall. The Cascade Mountains, for example, force moist Pacific air upward as it passes over them to the east. This causes the air to cool, water vapor to condense, and rain to fall on the windward side of the mountains. When the air gets to the other side of the mountain range, much moisture is gone, and the potential for rainfall is much lower. These factors cause western Oregon and western Washington to get much more rainfall than most places in North America but leave Idaho and Montana with very little.

Lakes and oceans heat up more slowly than land areas do. As a result, land areas near large bodies of water do not experience the extremes of heat and cold that areas farther from the water do. For example, downtown Chicago, which is at the Lake Michigan shoreline, does not get as cold on a winter night as Batavia, Illinois, which is thirty-five miles west of the Chicago lakefront. For the same reason, downtown Chicago does not get as hot on a summer afternoon as does Batavia.

Many areas near the tropics do not experience the four seasons described above but rather have an annual pattern of dry and wet seasons. In southern Asia, for example, the lower angle of the Sun in the winter causes temperatures to cool below the temperature of the nearby warm Indian Ocean. This causes winds to blow off the land toward the ocean and results in several months of fair or dry weather. By summer, the higher Sun has caused the continent to warm a little above the temperature of the ocean, and the wind pattern is reversed. Moist, warm air then flows from the ocean to the land, causing heavy rainfall; this wind system is called a "monsoon." The name also is given to the rains caused by this system.

Methods of Study

The ability to predict the seasons accurately was important to early civilizations. Because of their dependence upon farming, ancient peoples had to know when a river would flood or when to plant their crops. Primitive peoples were able to note that the appearance of certain constellations, and the locations of sunrise and sunset, varied when warmer or cooler weather could be expected.

Several early civilizations, including those of Egypt, Babylon, India, and China, have left indirect evidence of astronomical writings as early as 2500 B.C. Stonehenge, built in southwest England about 1800 B.C., has a large stone that marks the direction of sunrise at the summer solstice. Medicine wheels made by Native Americans two thousand years ago also show the direction of the summer solstice sunrise.

A critical barrier in defining the seasons was the difficulty of determining the exact length of one year. For many centuries, astronomers and civil rulers tried to define the year based on a number of lunar months. The Egyptians, who needed a means to forecast the flooding of the Nile, may have been the earliest civilization to adopt a solar calendar. By the year 46 B.C., errors in the accepted calendar were so great that Julius Caesar redefined the year, entirely independently of the moon, as 365 days, with one extra day added every four years. The Gregorian Calendar, adopted in 1582 and still used today, corrected a small error in the Julian calendar by eliminating the extra day from would-be leap years that are divisible by one hundred but not by four hundred.

An understanding of the causes of seasonal change begins with an understanding of the shapes and relative motions of the Sun and the earth. In the sixth century B.C., Pythagoras theorized that the earth was a sphere resting in the center of the universe. Yet even though several of his students believed that the apparent movements of the Sun and the stars were caused by the earth's movements, that explanation was rejected by many persons, including Aristotle. The Greek astronomer Ptolemy confirmed Aristotle's geocentric views. His *Almagest* was the standard work on astronomy for 1,400 years.

In 1543, Nicolas Copernicus published his explanation of the Sun-centered solar system and a new explanation for the changing of the seasons. His text shows the position of the tilted earth in relation to the Sun at the two equinoxes and solstices.

Although Copernicus' heliocentric solar system and explanation for the seasons are commonly taught in schools today, his ideas did not win general acceptance for nearly two hundred years. Galileo Galilei's use of the telescope confirmed Copernicus' theories, as did Sir Isaac Newton's 1687 theory of gravitation. The last minor obstacle to universal acceptance of the Copernican system was the fact that the distant stars did not appear to move as the earth revolved around the Sun. That opposition disappeared after Friedrich Bessel's 1838 discovery of stellar parallax, which confirmed that those stars do move, albeit by very small amounts.

Context

An understanding of the seasons is just as important to modern civilization as it was to ancient ones. Today, the need for an understanding of seasons is more complex but just as vital. A knowledge of seasons and the length of a growing season still affects decisions about which crops can be planted in a given area. Certain crops require longer growing seasons than others and must be grown in southern areas; some perennial flowers, such as tulips, require a cold dormant period and cannot be grown in areas without a cold winter season. Homeowners who purchase trees and other living plants from landscaping catalogs need to know about their seasonal climates in order to buy plants suited to local conditions. Knowing how high the Sun will be in the summer can help a homeowner or a landscape architect to decide in the spring where to put shade-producing trees so that they do not interfere with a Sun-loving vegetable garden.

Seasonal changes of the Sun can help the environmentally conscious architect to decide where to place windows and whether to design roof overhangs. For example, in summer, when most new houses and office buildings will likely be using air conditioning, midday sunlight streaming in windows can drive up electricity costs. To minimize this, homes and other buildings can be designed with roof overhangs that shade the windows from direct sunlight. In winter, when the buildings could use this sunlight to keep down heating costs, the Sun will be further south and thus lower in the sky. If well designed, a roof overhang can shade windows from the high summer Sun while allowing in light from the low winter Sun.

Schools that have their main entrance on the north side of the building have a particular problem that can be solved with a knowledge of seasonal variations of sunshine. Many yearbook editors of such schools have looked for a decent picture of the front of the building with no success. During most of the school year (fall and winter), the Sun never shines on the north side of any building north of the Tropic of Cancer; therefore, most pictures of such buildings show the building in the shade. With forethought, however, sunlit pictures can be taken from May to July either in the early morning or the early evening—although this is not when most yearbook staffs are gathering pictures.

In the 1930's, William A. Wirt, superintendent of schools for Gary, Indiana, went so far as to insist that the front door of each new school building in the city face south and have a maximum of classroom windows facing the Sun. On the other hand, designers of art studios often design their buildings with windows on the north side, away from the Sun, in order to maximize shadowless light. In no case should valuable photographs be hung on walls that receive direct sunlight in summer or winter, as ultraviolet light from the Sun can make photos fade quickly.

Bibliography

Armitage, A. *The World of Copernicus*. Wakefield, England: E. P. Publishing, 1972. Originally published in 1947 under the title *Sun, Stand Thou Still*. A description of the state of astronomy before and during the time of Copernicus. The last part deals with the conversion of scientific thought from belief in the geocentric solar system to acceptance of Copernicus' heliocentric system.

Asimov, Isaac. *The Clock We Live On*. Eau Claire, Wis.: E. M. Hale, 1965. The earth's relation to the Sun and Moon form the basis for this detailed text about measuring seasons, years, and hours. Includes eighteen diagrams and an index.

Berry, A. *A Short History of Astronomy*. New York: Dover, 1898. Reprint, 1961. A comprehensive history of the science of astronomy. This 440-page book has excellent diagrams, including some reproduced from sixteenth century texts. Extremely well documented; includes both an index of names and a subject index.

Emiliani, Cesare. *Planet Earth: Cosmology, Geology, and the Evolution of Life and Environment*. Cambridge, England: Cambridge University Press, 1992. A large, comprehensive book containing basic information about matter and energy, many aspects of the physical and historical earth, and a large section about the earth's relationship to the universe. The last section is a brief history of the earth sciences.

Fisher, Leonard Everett. *Calendar Art*. New York: Four Winds Press, 1987. A collection of stories about thirteen calendars developed by Central American, European, Middle Eastern, and East Asian civilizations. Each calendar is reproduced in its own language. Very good, in spite of an error in defining the vernal equinox. Diagrams are in blue and white.

Gay, Kathlyn. *Science in Ancient Greece*. New York: Franklin Watts, 1988. A book about the philosophers, astronomers, and mathematicians of ancient Greece and their concepts of the universe. The text is supported by black-and-white photographs and diagrams. Indexed, and has a small glossary.

Goudsmit, Samuel, and Robert Claiborne. *Time*. Alexandria, Va.: Time-Life Books, 1980. A comprehensive discussion of the elements of time, from the establishment of the calendar, to the building of clocks, to the theories of relativity and carbon-14 dating. Color and black-and-white photographs and diagrams.

Lambert, David, and the Diagram Group. *Field Guide to Geology*. New York: Facts on File, 1988. A profusely illustrated book about the earth, its seasons, rocks, erosional forces, and geological history. Contains a list of "great" geologists (including Copernicus) and a list of geologic museums, mines, and spectacular geologic features. Indexed.

Neal, Harry Edward. *The Mystery of Time*. New York: Julian Messner, 1966. Especially useful for those interested in the historical development of the calendar. Contains sixteen pages of black-and-white prints. Bibliography and index.

Ronan, Colin. *The Practical Astronomer*. New York: Macmillan, 1981. A detailed description of basic astronomy along with ideas for experiments for the amateur astronomer. Very well illustrated with color and black-and-white photographs and diagrams. Glossary and index.

Kenneth J. Schoon

Cross-References

Atmospheric Thermodynamics, 2826; Climate, 217; Earth-Sun Relations, 399; Gulf Stream, 2945; Hurricanes and Monsoons, 1088; Solar Power, 2427; Weather Forecasting, 2717; Weather Modification, 3186; Wind, 2730.

SEISMIC TOMOGRAPHY

Type of earth science: Geophysics
Field of study: Seismology

Seismic tomography is a technique for constructing a cross-sectional image of a slice of the earth from seismic data. Measurements are made of seismic energy that propagates through or reflects from subsurface geological materials, and the measured time of travel and amplitude of this energy are used to infer geometry and physical properties of the geological materials, from which an image of the inside of the earth is generated.

Principal terms

AMPLITUDE: the maximum departure (height) of a wave from its average value

ATTENUATION: a reduction in amplitude or energy caused by the physical characteristics of the transmitting medium

IMAGING: a computer method for constructing a picture of subsurface geology from seismic data

INVERSION: the process of deriving from measured data a geological model that describes the subsurface and that is consistent with the measured data

LITHOLOGY: the description of rocks, such as rock type, mineral makeup, and fluid in rock pores

RESOLUTION: the ability to separate two features that are very close together

SEISMIC REFLECTION METHOD: measurements made of the travel times and amplitudes of events attributed to seismic waves that have been reflected from interfaces where changes in seismic properties occur

SEISMOMETER: an instrument used to record seismic energy; also known as a geophone or a seismic detector

TRAVEL TIME: the time needed for seismic energy to travel from the source into the subsurface geology and arrive back at a seismometer

Summary of the Methodology

Seismic tomography is a means of making an image of a slice of the earth using seismic data. "Tomography" is derived from a Greek word meaning "section" or "slice." Since the 1970's, seismic techniques have been used to create subsurface pictures. Although some methods that have been used in exploration geophysics for a number of years can be classified as tomographic, it is only since the mid-1980's that seismic tomography has been specifically developed for geophysical exploration and exploitation. The current interest in and promise of seismic tomography in geophysical exploration and global seismology is made possible by many factors, including interaction between different scientific disciplines, along with advances in seismic field-data acquisition, imaging and inverse-problem theory, and computing speed.

The basic idea of tomography is to use data measured outside an object to infer values of physical properties inside the object. This method was pioneered by J. Radon in 1917. Radon showed that if data are collected all the way around an object, then the properties of the object can be calculated. In fact, Radon derived an analytical formula that relates the object's internal properties to the collected data.

Since the mid-1970's, the ideas of tomography have been applied to a number of fields of study. Applications of tomographic techniques are found in fields as diverse as electron microscopy and astronomical imaging. In medicine, the process of computed tomographic scanning ("CT" or "CAT" scanning) has developed particularly rapidly since its inception in the early 1960's, and its use has been very important in diagnostic medicine.

Geophysicists have been attempting to apply techniques similar to those of medicine to geophysical problems. Since the early 1970's, interest and applications have been rapidly expanding, and a number of papers have been presented and written on the applications of seismic tomography since 1984. These range from attempts to estimate the internal velocity structure of the subsurface to formulations that provide a complete image of the subsurface geology. Since the late 1980's, tomographic reconstruction has become a standard technique in analyzing data between drill holes (crosshole analysis). Thus, while tomography is relatively new to exploration geophysics, it is a broad, powerful concept that is making a significant impact. Seismic tomography has led to many useful new applications as well as insightful reinterpretations of some existing methods.

Seismic tomography is a type of "inverse problem"—that is, measurements are first made of some energy that has propagated through and reflected from within a medium (in this case, the earth). The received travel times and amplitudes of this energy are then used to infer the values of the medium through which it has propagated. The parameters that are extracted are velocities and depths; therefore, a gross model of the earth's structure can be derived. Initially, this was considered the ultimate goal of seismic tomography, but it has become obvious that an accurate set of measurements can be used effectively for other purposes, such as constructing an accurate depth image of the subsurface.

In CT scanning, an X-ray source and a number of X-ray detectors are used to acquire data around the human body. The X-ray source sends out X rays, and the receivers record the transmitted X-ray intensity. This intensity is related to the attenuation of the X rays along their raypaths inside the object. In turn, the amount of attenuation is related to the density of the object encountered by the X rays. Thus, a CT scan is an actual estimate of the density distribution within a body. CT scans can be done over various parts of the body, and these scans can be put together to form a three-dimensional image. This kind of image can show with great clarity the structure or damage inside the body. Interpreting three-dimensional images of the body's interior is similar in many ways to interpreting the interior of the earth from three-dimensional seismic data.

The similar problem in geophysical exploration is determining from seismic data the velocities with which sound propagates through a section of the earth, as well as other properties of the earth, such as density and compressibility. Classical tomography is typically associated with transmitted energy and requires a distribution of sources and receivers around the object to be imaged. In imaging techniques, such as medical X-ray tomography, the source and receiver rotate all the way around the object to be imaged. In contrast, by far the most pervasive seismic measurement is the surface reflection survey. Its measurements are made on just the upper boundary of the medium of interest.

Since the first seismic detectors (seismometers or geophones) were placed on the surface of the earth near the end of the nineteenth century, seismic waves have been used to locate remote objects. The first applications involved the location of earthquake epicenters in faraway regions. Efforts during the World War I to locate heavy artillery by seismic means evolved later to the first exploration methods for oil and gas. The imaging technique in exploration seismics has been improved ever since. At first, it merely involved the interpretation of travel times of observed seismic pulses in terms of the depth and slope of reflecting surfaces. Beginning in the 1970's, complete seismic records were used, and imaging methods were developed that are firmly based on sophisticated mathematical techniques.

In a seismic survey, geophysicists typically arrange seismic detectors along a straight line and then generate sound waves by vibrating the earth. Earthquakes release the large amounts of energy needed to probe the deep layers (mantle and core) of the earth. Other methods can produce seismic waves that can be focused on the geologic features closer to the earth's surface. These waves can be generated by explosions, such as a charge of dynamite, or by dropping a weight or pounding the ground with a sledgehammer. To eliminate environmental risks associated with the use of explosives, a system called "vibroseis" is used. In this system, a huge vibrator mounted on a special truck repeatedly strikes the earth to produce sound waves. A seismograph records how long it takes the sound waves to travel to a rock layer, reflect, and return to the surface. The recorded data displays the amplitudes of the reflected sound waves as a function of travel time. Such a graphic record is called a "seismogram." The equipment is then moved a short distance along the line, and the experiment is repeated. This procedure is known as the seismic reflection profiling method.

Since seismic waves traveling in the earth readily spread, refract, reflect, and diffract, classical tomographic methods must be adapted to produce realistic seismic pictures, and effective software and interactive graphics are required to process the seismic data into a relevant image. It has taken some time for tomographic concepts to spread to the seismic experiment, for appropriate data to be acquired, and effective processing and interpretation techniques to be developed. Using a variety of computer programs, seismograms are processed to yield seismic sections that represent the earth's reflectivity in time. Geologists, though, would really like to have a lithologic picture illustrating such features as rock velocity, seismic wave attenuation, and elastic constants of the rocks as a function of depth. Reflectivity is a property associated with interfaces between rocks; a rock sample held in one's hand does not have an intrinsic reflectivity. Therefore, reflectivity is not an actual rock property, and it must be converted to some parameter that really describes the rock. In addition, seismic time data must be converted to depth measurements in the imaging process. Consequently, conventional reflection sections are being greatly improved by the use of tomographic techniques to produce subsurface images as a function of depth and to estimate rock properties from some of the images.

The basic procedure of seismic tomography is an extension of the notion of transmission tomography; this process can also be classified as a generalized linear inversion of travel times. The procedure is to locate reflected events on the raw seismograms; associate these events with the structure of a proposed or guessed geological model; use the laws of physics to trace raypaths of seismic waves through the proposed model from given seismic sources down to a particular reflector and back to the seismic detectors; compare the ray-traced travel times through the model with the travel times recorded on the seismogram; and update the geological model to make the ray tracing consistent with the observed data. Seismic tomography is distinct from classical tomography in that only reflected waves are used, and the source-detector coverage of the object or area of interest is far from complete. These aspects of the problem create difficulties, but the tomographic velocity determination is still very useful, especially in areas of significant lateral velocity variations. By including all available well data, as well as any other available geophysical data, in the tomographic process, the resolution and certainty of subsurface images can be greatly improved.

Imaging in global seismology (whole-Earth geophysics) has lagged behind the developments in exploration geophysics for several reasons. In contrast to artificial sources, earthquakes are uncontrolled, badly placed sources of seismic-wave energy, and the earth is only sparsely covered with seismometers. In addition, instrument responses were for a long time widely different, and recording was not in digital form. Thus, seismologists were faced with the paradox that the available data, despite the enormous volume, often contained crucial gaps.

In global seismology, the whole three-dimensional Earth is considered as an object to be imaged. Seismic energy generated by earthquakes travels through the earth and is recorded by a distribution of seismic detectors, such as the Worldwide Standard Seismographic Network. By examining the travel times of the propagating energy for a number of earthquakes and stations, a model representing the velocity structure inside the earth can be constructed. Likewise, by measuring the shapes and sizes of the amplitudes of the recorded energy, a seismic attenuation model of the earth can be estimated. Based upon these models, a three-dimensional tomographic image of the earth can be constructed.

Applications of the Method

Various survey geometries and tomographic constructions are used to assist in solving geophysical problems. Geophysicists can use the velocities of seismic waves recorded by a seismograph to determine the depth and structure of many rock formations, since the velocity varies according to the physical properties of the rock through which the wave travels. In addition, seismic waves change in amplitude when they are reflected from rocks that contain gas and other fluids. Sometimes the fine details of seismic records can be used to infer the type of rocks (lithology) in the subsurface. Some tomographic studies have used subsurface velocities determined from the inversion of seismic travel times to construct geological cross sections of the geology inside the earth, while other studies have used reflection amplitudes for the same purpose. Based on the characteristic geometries and amplitudes for oil and gas traps and for mineral ore deposits, these tomographic images are used to predict where oil, natural gas, coal, and other resources such as groundwater and mineral deposits are most likely to be found in the subsurface. The tomographic cross sections constructed from seismic data make the odds of finding such resources much greater than would be the case if exploration were based on mere random drilling.

In seismic tomography, various source and detector geometries are used, such as drill-hole-to-drill-hole, surface-to-drill-hole, and surface-to-surface. The greater the degree of angular coverage around the rock mass of interest, the greater will be the reliability of the constructed tomographic image. By making numerous measurements from various source-detector positions and analyzing the travel times and amplitudes from a number of source-detector locations, the velocity and attenuation of the intervening rock can be calculated from the recorded energy (reflected or transmitted). This technique has found applications not only in locating subsurface natural resources, but also in areas such as siting of nuclear-waste dumps and monitoring of steam floods, which are used to help produce hydrocarbons from a reservoir.

In many hydrocarbon development areas, adjacent drill holes may be available. In these situations, it is desirable to have a very high-resolution description of the rock mass between the drill holes. It is often effective to adopt crosshole tomography. A seismic source, such as dynamite caps or downhole air guns, is placed in one drill hole, and appropriate detectors are placed in an adjacent drill hole. The source is fired, and the resulting seismic energy propagates through the rock and is detected in the other drill hole. The travel times and amplitudes of seismic waves that have been reflected or transmitted through the rock mass between the drill holes are recorded. The source and detectors are then moved to another position, and the process is repeated. This procedure is continued until the region of interest is adequately covered by the propagating energy. Seismic crosshole tomography has been used for a number of applications of different kinds. Among these are mineral exploration in mines, fault detection in coal seams, stress monitoring in coal mines, delineation of the sides of a salt dome, investigation of dams, and mapping of dinosaur-bone deposits. The resolution of crosshole tomography is typically better than for surface reflection tomography.

The broad objective of geophysics is to produce images that represent the subsurface geology as accurately as possible, and tomography-based imaging algorithms provide seismic depth sections that are consistent with drill-hole data in regions of resource exploration and exploitation. Integrating drill-hole and surface seismic reflection data in a tomographic approach can provide a better, less ambiguous subsurface picture. This correlation holds considerable promise to increase knowledge of the subsurface. The resulting seismic depth sections assist in interpreting the structure (geometry), stratigraphy (depositional environment), and lithology (rock and fluid types) of potential and established hydrocarbon reservoirs and mineral deposits.

The geologic detail needed to develop most hydrocarbon reservoirs substantially exceeds the detail required to find them. For effective planning and drilling, a complete understanding of the lateral extent, thickness, and depth of the reservoir is absolutely essential. This can only be done with detailed seismic interpretation of three-dimensional seismic reflection surveys integrated with drill-hole data. A common practice in three-dimensional seismic reflection surveying is to place the seismic detectors at equal intervals and collect data from a grid of lines covering the area of interest. Based upon integrated seismic tomographic imaging of the drill-hole and seismic reflection data, more wells are drilled in the area, and the three-dimensional data volume evolves into a continuously utilized and updated management tool that influences reservoir planning and evaluation for years after the seismic data was originally acquired and imaged.

In whole-Earth geophysics, seismic tomography makes it possible to observe the form of heat convection in the upper mantle. Estimates can be made of the variation of seismic velocities inside the earth using seismic tomography, and these variations in turn depend upon the variations in composition, structure, and temperature of the materials inside. Mantle regions that are relatively hot have lower velocities compared to cooler regions at the same depth. This is because the higher temperatures reduce the values of the elastic constants of the mantle material. Since the velocity variations get smaller in the lower mantle, the hot and cold regions cannot be reliably mapped, and tomographic imaging of the lower mantle is rather poor. Seismic tomography supports a hybrid convection theory that postulates the existence of shallow, small-scale convection currents as well as of deep, large-scale convection currents in the mantle. In general, tomographic results show a strong correlation at shallow depths with present plate boundaries, such as fast movement under cold, old shields and in subduction zones, and slow movement under hot, spreading ridges and other volcanically active areas. Three-dimensional images of the earth's interior reconstructed with seismic tomographic procedures are having a major effect on the understanding of the structure and dynamics of the earth.

Context

Tomography is practiced in disciplines ranging from diagnostic medicine to petroleum and mineral exploration and exploitation to whole-Earth geophysics. The concept of recovering material properties from data collected around an object is broadly applicable and powerful. In geophysics, mainly because of the incompleteness of the collected data, seismic tomography is undergoing continued research and development. There are realms in which tomographic concepts are directly applicable, such as crosshole surveying, while other specialities, such as seismic reflection tomography, require generalization or reinterpretation of fundamental tomographic ideas. Cross-hole tomography is providing an important acquisition and analysis methodology. Seismic tomography is proving valuable with integrated drill-hole and surface seismic studies, primarily as a velocity-analysis method. The seismic problem of imaging subsurface geology in depth can be solved in a tomographic form.

A major problem in the area of hydrocarbon-reservoir evaluation and production is the realization of the complexity of most reservoirs, leading to large uncertainties in estimated total recovery, recovery rates, and recovery methods. Reservoir complexity is typically related to the significant spatial heterogeneity in porosity (pore spaces in rocks), permeability (ability for fluids to flow in rocks), clay content, fracture density, overburden pressure, pore pressure, fluid phase behavior, and other associated factors. The only feasible approach to obtaining these spatial variabilities is from remote geophysical measurements, especially seismic measurements and seismic tomographic processing. There is little doubt that seismic tomography will play a major role in helping to solve not only exploration problems but also production and recovery problems.

In many areas of hydrocarbon and mineral exploration and exploitation, much is known about geological structure. Large bodies of data have often been recorded; in some cases, a full suite of drill-hole data, rock core analyses, and three-dimensional seismic data are available. The tomographic technique can process and integrate all these data to give as accurate a view of the lithologic structure of the subsurface as possible. In summary, seismic tomography is a useful tool in providing structural velocity models, rock attenuation models, more accurate depth images, calibrated seismic inversion sections, high-resolution crosshole pictures, and three-dimensional Earth images.

Bibliography

Bording, R. P., et al. *Principles of Seismic Traveltime Tomography*. Tulsa, Okla.: Society of Exploration Geophysicists, 1986. Discusses the basic principles of tomography and how they can be applied to seismic data to create a velocity model of the earth from recorded traveltimes.

Lines, L. R. "Cross-borehole Seismology." *Geotimes* 40 (January, 1995): 11. Discusses applications of seismic tomography to the shallow subsurface.

Nolet, Guust, ed. *Seismic Tomography*. Boston: D. Reidel, 1987. Describes the methods and reliability of seismic tomography. Contains many qualitative discussions that will be useful to the general reader as well as more technical discussions for those with the appropriate background. Primarily discusses applications of tomography to whole-Earth geophysics, with some discussion of applications to exploration geophysics.

Poupinet, Georges. "Seismic Tomography." *Endeavour* 14, no. 2 (1990): 52. Good description of seismic tomography as it is applied to the study of the deep structure of the earth by integrated analysis of seismic wave patterns generated from earthquakes.

Russell, B. H. *Introduction to Seismic Inversion Methods*. Tulsa, Okla.: Society of Exploration Geophysicists, 1988. Discusses techniques used for the inversion of seismic data, including principles of seismic tomography. Good illustrations.

Stewart, R. R. *Exploration Seismic Tomography*. Tulsa, Okla.: Society of Exploration Geophysicists, 1991. Recounts the historical development of tomography. Reviews the fundamentals of seismic tomographic techniques and discusses applications of seismic tomography, mainly to exploration geophysics.

Alvin K. Benson

Cross-References

Earth's Crust, 518; Earth's Mantle, 555; Oil and Gas Exploration, 1878; Oil and Gas: Petroleum Reservoirs, 1909; Oil and Gas: Well Logging, 1915; Physical Properties of Rocks, 2225; Seismic Reflection Profiling, 2333; Seismometers, 2340.

STROMATOLITES

Type of earth science: Paleontology and earth history
Field of study: Sedimentology

Stromatolites are the most common megascopic fossils contained within ancient rocks dating to 3.5 billion years in age. In both the living and fossil form, they are created by the trapping and binding of sediment particles and the precipitation of calcium carbonate to the sticky surface of matlike filaments grown on a daily cycle by blue-green algae. Modern stromatolites are found throughout the world; they are of particular use in the creation of hydrocarbon reservoirs, in geologic mapping, and as indicators of paleoenvironments.

Principal terms

ALGAE: primitive, one-celled, chiefly aquatic plantlike organisms lacking stems, roots, and leaves

BLUE-GREEN ALGAE: any of the algae classified within the division *Cyanophyta*

CYANOBACTERIA: an algaelike bacteria commonly known as "blue-green algae"

FOSSIL: the remains, trace, or imprint of any plant or animal that lived during the geologic past

ONCOLITE: an organosedimentary rock structure, concentrically laminated, formed by blue-green algae and smaller in size than a stromatolite

ORGANOSEDIMENTARY STRUCTURE: a sedimentary rock feature developed by the life processes of blue-green algae

PALEONTOLOGY: the study of life and organic evolution throughout geologic time, based upon the collection and analyses of fossil plants and animals

PROKARYOTE: an organism characterized by simple protoplasmic structure and lacking a nucleus

STROMATOLITE: an organosedimentary structure formed by the trapping, binding, or precipitation of sediment upon the laminae surface of blue-green algae

THROMBOLITE: a stromatolite-like fossil characterized by an obscurely clotted, unlaminated internal structure

Summary of the Phenomenon

Stromatolites ("layered rock" in Greek) are organosedimentary structures associated with certain types of the sedimentary class of rock; they develop through the metabolic processes of plant microorganisms. Stromatolites can also be considered to be fossils; in this sense, they do not represent the remains of actual organisms but rather material deposited and collected by a living organism in a manner such that the original size, shape, and morphology of the organism is preserved.

The organisms principally responsible for the development of stromatolites are photosynthetic cyanobacteria, commonly referred to as "blue-green algae." Structurally, blue-green algae are among the most primitive of this class of life, lacking true stems, roots, and leaves. They grow on a daily cycle, in response to the rising and setting of the Sun. In response to this cycle, a sticky, filamentous, organic surface is produced in the form of wavy, matlike laminae. This mucus-coated mat traps and binds fine and coarse-grained sediment to its surface during daylight hours, increasing the thickness of the laminae. During evening hours and nighttime, new algae growth penetrates the sediment-coated layer, producing a new gelatinous filament that in turn will trap and bind more sediment during the following daylight period. As this process continues, a layered, or laminated, structure is built.

Blue-green algae are prokaryotic (prenuclear) microorganisms, as they possess neither a cell nucleus nor a specialized cellular organelle (that portion of a cell that functions as an organ). Blue-green algae are also asexual and thus restricted in degree of variability, resulting in many living species that are almost indistinguishable from species that lived more than a billion years ago. Because of this relative lack of evolution over geologic time, much of what is known regarding ancient stromatolites has been gained by the study of living stromatolites produced by blue-green algae. The mineral matter associated with extant stromatolites is primarily composed of calcium carbonate, although a few species are associated with siliceous material, as evidenced by stromatolites studied in Yellowstone National Park, Wyoming. In the fossil form, the original calcium carbonate content is sometimes altered through replacement by magnesium, iron, and silica.

Modern blue-green algae have a wide geographic distribution and grow in diverse aquatic environments, ranging from marine to brackish to fresh water and even moist soils. Some blue-green species thrive in hot springs and geysers with temperatures only a few degrees below the boiling point, while others have been collected in Arctic and Antarctic regions. Regardless of their aquatic environment, all modern blue-green algae depend upon sunlight for growth and survival. Because of this need for light, it was formerly thought that marine varieties were restricted to shallow waters near shore. Today, however, it is known that the photic zone, that region of the ocean penetrated by sunlight extend to depths approaching 150 meters, allowing growth of deep-water varieties.

Stromatolite-producing algae are found in aquatic environments that are generally hostile to grazing and burrowing invertebrates. Sharks Bay in western Australia, a classic site for the study of modern (living) stromatolites, is conducive to blue-green algal growth because the hypersaline environment limits the activity of grazing snails. In Yellowstone National Park, alkaline waters up to 59 degrees Centigrade in temperature present an environment supporting the development of unique siliceous stromatolites produced by bacteria rather than by algae. In the shallow marine environment of the Bahama Banks in the Caribbean, blue-green algae are abundant in supertidal channels with current flow too strong for the effective colonization of stromatolitic-grazing invertebrates such as gastropods and ostracods.

In the geologic record, stromatolites are the most abundant of fossils found in Precambrian rocks, that period of time from the origin of Earth (approximately 4.6 billion years ago) up to 570 million years ago. The oldest fossil stromatolites are contained in the 3.3-billion-to-3.5-billion-year-old Warrawoona Group of rocks in Australia. Close in age are the 3.4-billion-year-old stromatolites of the Swaziland Group of South Africa; somewhat more removed are those associated with the 2.5-billion-to-2.8-billion-year-old Bulawayan Limestone, also in Africa. All these examples originated in the Archean eon, the first recorded period of geologic history, extending by definition from approximately 4 billion to 2.5 billion years ago. During the Proterozoic eon, immediately following the Archean eon and extending to 570 million years ago, stromatolites became prolific. This Proterozoic expansion is probably reflective of the initial development of continental land masses and associated warm, photic continental shelf regions, as plate tectonics became a controlling process in the early development of Earth's crust.

Throughout the Archean and Proterozoic eons, blue-green algae underwent a steady and progressive state of biologic evolution, recognized today as the singular, common megascopic fossil of the Precambrian time period (the Archean and the Proterozoic eons). For this reason, the Precambrian is often referred to as the "age of algae," or, more specifically, the "age of blue-green algae." Throughout the Phanerozoic eon, defined as 570 million years ago to the present, blue-green algae underwent minimal evolution, probably because its evolutionary state had become adapted to a variety of environments, reducing the need for further diversification.

Stromatolitic-building algae maintained their dominance of the aquatic world during the Early Phanerozoic eon (570 million to about 460 million years ago). With the rather abrupt appearance, however, of shelled, grazing, and cropping invertebrates in the early Phanerozoic eon, blue-green algae began to decline in significance. Today, as compared to their Precambrian domination, they have on a relative scale become endangered.

Geographically, fossil stromatolites are ubiquitous to every continent, especially within sedimentary carbonate rock sequences older than 460 million years. On southeastern Newfoundland, stromatolites built by blue-green algae of the genus *Girvanella* are found in conglomerate and limestone strata of the Bonavista Formation (approximately 550 million years in age). In the Transvaal region of South Africa, delicately banded stromatolitic structures compose one of the most widespread of early Proterozoic shallow-water carbonate deposits in the world, extending over an area exceeding 100,000 square kilometers. In nearby Zambia, algal stromatolites are closely associated with rock sequences containing economic levels of copper and cobalt. Upper Permian (250 million years ago) stromatolite horizons can be traced over an area of northern Poland exceeding 15,000 square kilometers. Miocene age (15 million years old) algae of the species *Halimeda* compose the limestone-forming rocks of the island of Saipan in the Mariana Islands of the Pacific Ocean. In North America, fossil algal-bearing rocks include the 2-billion-year-old Gunflint (Iron) Formation of Ontario, Canada, and the well-developed stromatolitic horizons of Early Paleozoic era age (450 million years ago) composing the Ellenberger Formation of Oklahoma and Texas.

The classification and identification of stromatolites is often conducted on the basis of overall morphology, particularly the size, shape, and internal construction of the specimen. The relevant literature makes use of a variety morphological terms, including the adjectives "frondose" (leaflike), "encrusting," "massive," "undulatory" (wavelike), "columnar," "laminar," "domed," "elliptical," and "digitigrade" (divided into fingerlike parts). Through the study of modern blue-green algae, it is suggested that three environmental criteria are of importance in stromatolite geometry development. These are direction and intensity of sunlight, direction and magnitude of water current, and direction of sediment transport. As an example, the extant elliptical stromatolites of Shark Bay, Western Australia, are oriented at right angles to the shoreline as the result of strong current-driven wave and scour action. Under certain environmental conditions, cyanobacteria growth surfaces are not preserved, producing fossil algal structures characterized by a lack of laminae. These structures are termed "thrombolites," in contrast to laminar-constructed stromatolites.

While stromatolites are generally described as megascopic in size, discussion of specific dimensions relates both to laminae thickness and to overall size. Stromatolite laminae of the Precambrian-aged Pethei Formation, an outcropping along the shores of Great Slave Lake in the Northwest Territories of Canada, are both fine and coarse in dimension. The coarse-grained layers, formed of lime-mud pellets and calcium and magnesium carbonate rhombs, are principally less than 5.0 millimeters in thickness. The fine-grained laminae, composed of calcium carbonate clay and silt-sized particles, are, on average, only 0.5 millimeters thick.

In size, individual stromatolites can range from centimeters up to several meters. Fossils of the common Precambrian genus *Conophyton* occur in a range of sizes, from pencil-sized shapes to columns up to 10 meters in diameter. Subspherical varieties of stromatolite-like structures, formed by the accretion of successive gelatinous mats of blue-green algae and generally less than 10 centimeters in diameter, are termed "oncolites." Stromatolitic complexes in the Great Slave Lake district measure 80 meters long by 45 meters wide by 20 meters in thickness and can be continuously traced for distances exceeding 160 kilometers.

Methods of Study

During the first half of the twentieth century, the existence of life on Earth prior to 570 million years ago, while generally discounted, was an increasingly debated subject. The worldwide absence of shelled fossils in Precambrian rock strata was evidence to most paleontologists that this eon represented geologic time during which life had yet to evolve.

Prior to 1913, several brief reports discussing fossilized algae had been published, but the described examples were considered by many readers as either inorganic concretions or problemental organisms. The initiation of the serious study of calcium carbonate-secreting plants by geologists is closely associated with a presidential address on rock-building algae given by E. J. Garwood in 1913 before the British Association for the Advancement of Science. At about the same time, the North American paleontologist Charles Walcott described moundlike structures from the Early Proterozoic Gunflint (Iron) Formation of Ontario, Canada, proposing them to be fossil reefs constructed by algae, while demonstrating the presence of living marine plants during Precambrian time.

By the 1950's, stromatolites—a term introduced in a 1908 publication by the German scientist E. Kalkowsky—were drawing the attention of petroleum geologists worldwide. This interest focused on the economic value of cyanophytic carbonate rocks as possible reservoir strata for the accumulation of petroleum and natural gas, as indicators of environments of sedimentary rock deposition, and for use in the age-dating of rocks.

A benchmark 1954 publication by S. A. Tyler (University of Wisconsin) and E. S. Barghoorn (Harvard University) demonstrated that the discussed symmetrical fragments were of Precambrian age and were indeed the product of blue-green algal activities, eliminating any remaining skepticism regarding the existence of early life. The microorganisms were contained in dense, black, amorphous opal (a form of chert, composed of silica dioxide and water) of the 2-billion-year-old Lower Chert member of the Gunflint (Iron) Formation. The fossils were in the form of microscopic filaments believed to have been originally entrapped in a silica dioxide gel, which upon loss of water dehydrated to solid opal, producing a weathering-resistant matrix. Filaments were extracted from the opal by immersing the fossil-bearing rock in a hydrofluoric acid bath. The released organic particles were transferred to glass slides and examined under a microscope in both polarized and normal transmitted light.

In later years, further studies of the Gunflint (Iron) Formation by Tyler and Barghoorn included hydrocarbon analyses through destructive distillation of the opal rock and study of extractable organic residue under ultraviolet light.

In the field, lack of agreement exists among paleontologists regarding fossil algae classification. Most experts agree on classifications above the level of genera, but opinion can differ on classifications between the phyla and genera levels. In general, the greater the age of the fossil, the greater the uncertainty associated with its classification. Megascopic studies are based upon morphological character, principally size, shape, and apparent style of growth. Additional study includes chemical extraction of organic forms and thin-sectioning of slabs of the fossil host rock for microscope review.

Since the 1950's, the study of fossil lime-secreting algae has become of such significance that a new branch of paleobotany has come into existence. Today, stromatolites remain the fossil form most useful in the analyses of the Precambrian eon, that period of geologic time representing 88 percent of Earth history.

Context

While of great interest to paleontologists as examples of early life forms, and while they are important to the understanding of paleoenvironments, stromatolites also have practical and economic value, especially in the search for new reserves of metallic and nonmetallic natural resources.

Stromatolites are found associated only with the sedimentary class of rock. The emplacement and economic accumulation of a variety of natural resources in sedimentary rock is largely dependent upon the rock's porosity and permeability. Without a degree of porosity—a percentage of rock occupied by void space—a rock cannot act as host for a natural resource, whether it be petroleum, natural gas, or metallic ores. Without a degree of permeability—the quality of allowing fluids or gases to migrate through a rock—a natural resource cannot move within the rock to a site of optimum accumulation. As organosedimentary structures, stromatolites possess both porosity and permeability; in general, these properties are preserved, as the stromatolite structure resists compaction. When developed in colonies of extensive lateral distribution, stromatolites become potential reservoirs of great economic significance. For example, the largest gas field in China is composed of stromatolitic limestones.

The successful exploration for new oil and gas fields is dependent upon the ability of geologists to map sedimentary strata of the same geologic age over widely separated regions. Russian and African geologists have been particularly successful in using stromatolites to trace rocks over distances of hundreds of kilometers. In addition, certain stromatolite species are useful in the relative age-dating of sedimentary rocks. The presence of the species *Collenia* and *Cryptozoan* is indicative of a Late Precambrian to Early Ordovician age (1 billion to 500 million years ago) for the host rock.

Studies indicate that the overall shape and form of many stromatolites is directly related to the flow direction and intensity of the currents in which the living algae grew. By comparing different morphologies with paleocurrent data determined by other means, information about transitions in paleoenvironments can often be gained. A particularly interesting aspect of early Earth history involves the habit of certain stromatolites to be controlled by heliotrophism, the tendency of any plant to grow toward or away from the light of the Sun. Studies suggest some fossil blue-green algae were particularly dependent upon sunlight direction and intensity for development, resulting in the daily addition of one lamina growth influenced by seasonal change in the position of the Sun. In the Bitter Springs Formation of Australia, formed in the Late Proterozoic (approximately 850 million years ago), the growth axis of the stromatolite genus *Anabaria* is wavelike, rather than straight. Assuming that each wavelength represents a year of growth, the number of individual laminae composing one wavelength would represent the number of days making up the year. A count of *Anabaria* laminae indicates an approximate 422-day-year during the Late Proterozoic eon, evidence of a gradual lengthening of the day with the passage of geologic time.

Bibliography

Barghoorn, E. S. "The Oldest Fossils." *Scientific American* 224 (May, 1971): 30-42. An easy-to-read primer on the subject of Precambrian algae and bacteria up to 3 billion years in age. Of interest to the student of early life and evolution, as the author was instrumental in advocating and demonstrating that life forms evolved very early in the evolution of Earth itself. For the high-school level reader.

Barghoorn, E. S., and S. A. Tyler. "Microorganisms from the Gunflint Chert." *Science* 147 (1965): 563-577. This benchmark article was largely responsible for the elimination of skepticism among paleontologists regarding the presence of Precambrian life, and ultimately responsible for the acceptance of stromatolites as among the most ancient of known fossil organisms. Written at the undergraduate college level.

Dott, R. H., Jr., and D. R. Prothero. *Evolution of the Earth*. 5th ed. New York: McGraw-Hill, 1994. A well-illustrated textbook on the subject of the geologic history of Earth. Contains several sections on stromatolites, their significance to Precambrian history, and their role in the understanding of very early forms of life.

Flugel, E., ed. *Fossil Algae*. Berlin: Springer-Verlag, l977. Fourteen papers in this collection are dedicated to blue-green algae and stromatolites; included are discussions on their ecology, interpretation, environmental significance, and distribution. Of particular value is chapter 2, wherein historical and evolving conceptions on the nature and ecological importance of stromatolites is given. Suitable for college-level readers.

Gebelein, C. D. "Biologic Control of Stromatolite Microstructure: Implications for Precambrian Time Stratigraphy." *American Journal of Science* 274 (1974): 575-598. This lengthy paper discusses the various environmental factors, including water and wind currents, that affect the detailed structure of modern stromatolitic organisms. Such knowledge is useful in worldwide mapping of stromatolite horizons. Written for the undergraduate college student.

Johnson, J. H. *Limestone-Building Algae and Algal Limestones*. Boulder, Colo.: Johnson Publishing, 1961. A still-valuable reference on limestone-building algae. Contains details on more than 110 genera and a listing of representative genera of each geologic period. Profusely illustrated with drawings and microphotographs. A necessary volume for readers interested in the classification of stromatolites.

Levin, H. L. *The Earth Through Time*. 5th ed. New York: Saunders College Publishing, 1996. This college-level textbook discusses fossil stromatolites of the Proterozoic eon and their importance as heliotrophic rock structures. Chapters 6 and 7 place these fossils within the context of the evolution of prokaryotic organisms. An easy-to-read source complete with numerous photographs.

Stewart, W. N. *Paleobotany and the Evolution of Plants*. London: Cambridge University Press, l983. The first four chapters discuss the preservation, preparation, and age determination of fossil plants, the geologic fossil record, and the Precambrian eon, when stromatolites were common throughout the aquatic world. Suitable for college-level readers.

Walter, M. R., ed. *Stromatolites*. New York: Elsevier, 1976. Contains papers on zonation, paleoenvironments, environmental diversity, morphologies, origin, geologic significance, and distribution of fossil stromatolites. Several papers discuss modern algal stromatolites and the organisms that build them. A valuable reference for the serious student.

Walter, M. R. "Understanding Stromatolites." *American Scientist*, September-October, 1977, 563-571. An in-depth paper on stromatolites, thrombolites, and oncolites. Discusses means of development of differing morphologies, modern analogues, and uses in stratigraphic mapping of stromotolitic-bearing rocks. Contains a complete reference section. Written for the high-school science reader.

Albert B. Dickas

Cross-References

Archaebacteria, 78; The Archean Eon, 92; Biostratigraphy, 173; The Evolution of Life, 655; Fossil Plants, 753; The Fossil Record, 760; Fossils of the Earliest Life Forms, 782; Microfossils, 1674; Prokaryotes, 2115; Sedimentary Rocks: Biogenic, 2312.

SUPERCONTINENT CYCLE

Type of earth science: Geology
Field of study: Tectonics

Supercontinent cycles, which recur over periods of 400 million to 440 million years, are helpful in understanding the distribution of certain natural resources, fluctuations throughout geologic time of sea level and climates, the process of mountain-building, and the evolution of life.

Principal terms

CONTINENTAL DRIFT: an early theory of continental fragmentation and displacement causing the creation of new ocean basins and the formation of mountain ranges

CONVERGENCE: the second-half process of a supercontinent cycle, whereby crustal plates collide and intervening oceans disappear as a result of plate subduction

DIVERGENCE: the process of fracturing and dissecting a supercontinent, thereby creating new oceanic rock; divergence represents the initial half of the supercontinent cycle

OPHIOLITE SUITE: a unique vertical sequence of peridotite (very basic) rock overlain by gabbro, basalt (lava), and oceanic sediments representative of ancient seafloor material

PLATE TECTONICS: a modern theory describing the earth surface as composed of rigid plates continually in motion over the interior, causing earthquakes, mountain-building, and volcanism

SEAFLOOR SPREADING: the continual creation of new seafloor bedrock along mid-ocean ridges through the process of ascending thermal currents

SUPERCONTINENT: a single vast continent formed by the collision and amalgamation of earth crustal plates

WILSON CYCLE: the creation and destruction of an ocean basin through the process of seafloor spreading and subduction of existing ocean basins

Summary of the Phenomenon

One of the most persistent questions relating to the historical development of Earth concerns the processes whereby extensive mountain chains, such as the Himalaya, Appalachian, and Ural ranges, have been formed. During the nineteenth century, the planet-contraction hypothesis, supported by the doctrine of permanence of continents and ocean basins, suggested that such linear features of the earth crust were comparable to the wrinkles within the skin of a dried apple. After the discovery of radioactivity in 1896, studies suggested heat formed by radioactive decay of rock minerals approximately equaled heat lost to the atmosphere by the gradual cooling of Earth from its supposed original liquid stage. This balance of heat gain and loss did not support a shrinking-earth concept. With the additional knowledge that linear mountain ranges had formed during different stages of geologic history, rather than simultaneously, the contraction hypothesis gradually lost favor.

Between the publication of his 1915 book *The Origin of the Continents and Oceans* and his death during an expedition to the Greenland icecap in 1930, Alfred L. Wegener, a German meteorologist and geologist, gained international repute as the father and chief advocate of the theory of continental drift. Wegener postulated that mountain ranges were created by the collision of large blocks of continental crust moving through oceanic crust, following fragmentation and dispersion of the vast supercontinent he called "Pangaea" (Greek for "all lands"), surrounded approximately 200 million years ago by the universal ocean Panthalassa (from "thalassa," Greek for sea). An intriguing set of evidences supports this theory, including the unusual degree of geometric fit of present-day continents (especially South America with Africa) and, through the reassembly of Pangaea, the reconstruction of truncated salt, fossil-reef, glacial-deposit, and mountain-range trends. While many scientists at the time became "pro-drift," many others questioned what possible mechanism could displace solid continental crust through equally solid oceanic crust. Various Earth forces, ranging from centrifugal to tidal to rotational axis-wobble, were investigated and rejected as inadequate by physicists and mathematicians. By the 1930's, continental drift as a theory was no longer considered viable and was increasingly mentioned only within the context of the history of science.

Following World War II, a new era of Earth investigation began, focused primarily on the ocean basins. Employing newly developed military technology, including methods of water-depth sounding (fathometry) and magnetic-body detection, surplus military aircraft and surface-vessel equipment began to collect a wide array of information. By the International Geophysical Year of 1957-1958, ocean-floor depth-profile analyses confirmed the existence of a previously unknown, 65,000-kilometer-long global submarine mountain range system traversing the Atlantic, Pacific, Arctic, and Indian Oceans. This feature, identified almost five hundred years following the discovery of the Americas and the Pacific Ocean, defied immediate explanation.

During the same period, ocean-evaluation programs sponsored by both private and U.S. government interests began the routine task of measuring the magnetism of the ocean floor. By the mid-1950's, sufficient data had been collected off the west coast of the United States to reveal a repetitive north-south pattern representing alternate zones of above-average and below-average magnetism. Soon similar patterns were shown to exist in the Atlantic and Indian Oceans.

The discovery of these unexplainable phenomena prompted the collection of any form of additional data that would help to explain the existence of ocean floors dissected by a universal mountain range and masked by symmetrical magnetic patterns. New oceanographic programs gathered information on bedrock temperature, radiometric age, and ocean-sediment thickness and studied the worldwide distribution of earthquakes and volcanic eruptions.

By the early 1960's, broad-based analyses of these various forms of oceanographic data were being conducted in Canada, the United Kingdom, and the United States. Gradually, consensus began to form that perhaps at least some of the ideas of Alfred Wegener were worthy of reconsideration. Paramount among these resurrected ideas was that of the assembly of the supercontinent Pangaea. Rather than postulating continental crust as floating through oceanic crust, the revised continental drift theory, termed "plate tectonics," envisioned the outer layer of the earth as divided into a series of major plates, each composed of both continental and oceanic bedrock. As examples, the North American plate is made up of the continent of North America (including Greenland), the western half of the north Atlantic Ocean, and eastern Siberia, while the Indian-Australian plate is composed of the continent of Australia, the country of India, and portions of the Pacific and Indian Oceans. Major plate displacement was considered possible because of the movement of global thermal-convection cells, which form within the mantle of the earth and rise toward the surface until they are blocked by the presence of a supercontinent. The blockage of further transmission of heat, caused by the insulating nature of continental rock, divides the convection current into lateral, horizontally directed segments, which gradually dome by thermal expansion and then dissect the supercontinent.

As the new subcontinent begins to diverge, the separating void fills with high-density gabbro and basalt-type rock, which forms the floor of a newly developed ocean. Because the earth is neither expanding nor contracting in size, continuing divergence cannot proceed indefinitely without experiencing resistance caused by the convergence of antipodal plates. The effect of plate convergence depends on whether such plate margins are oceanic (basaltic) or continental (granitic) in nature. Where margins are oceanic, the more dense margin will subduct, or plunge under, the less dense margin. Where margins are both continental, subduction is unlikely, and the result is massive folding and faulting (earthquaking). Finally, where a continental margin converges with an oceanic margin, the latter, being more dense, will subduct beneath the former. In all three possible convergence cases, earth-crust shortening is accomplished. Rock volume harmony results, as the formation of new oceanic crust through plate divergence is matched by the destruction of older crust through the process of subduction.

Processes of divergence and convergence are believed to have been ongoing throughout a large portion of geologic time and to continue today. Divergence, accompanied by new-ocean development in region A, continues simultaneously with convergence in region B, resulting in the gradual destruction of region A ocean by way of subduction. Eventually, region A ocean will cease to exist, and the cycle of ocean birth and death will be complete. This sequence of events, during which it is estimated 2.6 square kilometers of ocean floor rock is created and destroyed each year, is termed a "supercontinent cycle" (also known as a "Wilson cycle," after the Canadian geologist J. Tuzo Wilson, an early advocate of the plate-tectonics theory). Conversely, the dispersion and amalgamation of continental crustal masses, as opposed to oceanic masses, constitutes the principle phases of what has been termed the "Pangaean cycle." The operation of plate tectonics continuously creates and recycles ocean basins, while continental regions increase in age geologically even as they are agglomerated and dissected by ongoing seafloor spreading.

A maxim of geology states that the validity of any hypothesis or theory is determined by the degree to which that concept can be examined through the analyses of extant geology. Where, then, might there be modern-day examples of a supercontinent cycle in its various stages of tectonic development? The Great Basin of the western United States has been portrayed as a model of very early continental rifting that may in the future separate the North American plate from a newly constituted Pacific plate. The approximately one hundred block-faulted mountains composing this geographic terrane are caused by the same extensional forces responsible for the early continental-rift stage of dissection of a supercontinent. Similar forces have formed the more structurally advanced rift structures of East Africa, the most illustrative of which are those broad-basin and steeply dipping escarpment topographies of Tanzania, Kenya, and Ethiopia, which continue to yield an ever-revealing record of mammalian and hominid evolution. The fresh waters that partially cover these rift valleys, such as Lake Tanganyika, are evidence of a late stage of continental rifting. To the north, the central valley or rift of the Red Sea is filled with salt water characteristic of an incipient ocean developing during an early stage of oceanic rifting separating the Arabian from the African plate. Finally, the Atlantic Ocean is the often-cited mature example of oceanic rifting representative of the midpoint of a supercontinent cycle. According to the concepts of plate tectonics, the Atlantic Ocean has been created through some 200 million years of seafloor spreading driven by extensional rifting of Pangaea. This stage, representing the first half of a supercontinent cycle, will in theory be followed by assembly of the world's continents over the next 200 million years into a new supercontinent. This assembly may have already begun, as India, an island subcontinent up to approximately 35 million years ago, has since that time been colliding with the Eurasian plate, resulting in the formation of the Himalaya Mountains.

If the above are examples of contemporary stages of a supercontinent cycle, what of past supercontinent cycles? Following the general acceptance of the plate-tectonic theory in the 1960's, many ideas have been advanced regarding the existence and nature of pre-Pangaea supercontinents. Since the supercontinent cycle not only creates but also destroys oceans, pre-Pangaea supercontinents must be reconstructed from continental geologic data that becomes, with increasing geologic age, more difficult to interpret. Certain criteria have been developed in the attempt to discern a pattern of supercontinent cycling since the earliest periods of geologic time.

Methods of Study

The convergence of continents will largely eradicate any intervening ocean. Such loss by subduction is seldom complete, as attested by the presence of remnants of pre-existing ocean floor rock contained within the deformed (suture) zone caused by plate collision. Basalt, gabbro, and olivine-rich rocks, termed an "ophiolite suite," are scraped off, or "obducted" from, the subducting ocean floor and thus preserved in the developing mountain belt. Obducted ophiolitic rock from the former Tethys Sea, which lapped onto the eastern shores of Pangaea, is present in the Alps and the Himalayas, while ophiolites within the Ural Mountains of central Asia are evidence of an ocean that was destroyed by the collision of Baltica and Siberia, continental masses that preceded the formation of Pangaea. The presence, location, and age-dating of ophiolite suites are helpful in the identification of former supercontinents.

Paleontological and high-pressure rock evidence collected from the Appalachian Mountains, created by the convergence of proto-Africa (the earliest form of Africa) with proto-North America, suggest the existence approximately 500 million years ago of a proto-Atlantic Ocean. The existence of this body of salt water, the Iapetus Ocean, attests the existence of an associated supercontinent.

The presence of exotic terranes (also known as a "melange," from the French for "mixture") forming the collisional edge of former crustal plates in Japan, New Zealand, and the Apennines of northern Italy is further evidence of former supercontinents and their cycles. These terranes, packages of rock possessing similar mineral and fossil character, are accreted to enlarging supercontinents by the same obduction process as ophiolites.

Using the above and other lines of reasoning, the existence of various pre-Pangaea supercontinents has been postulated. Obviously, the older the proposed supercontinent, the more conjectured its existence. As the theory of plate tectonics is but several decades old, little agreement exists on the naming and geologic age of pre-Pangaean supercontinents. The following discussion, however, presents two contemporary schools of thought regarding supercontinent cycles.

The oldest Earth specimen found to date is the 3.96-billion-year-old metamorphic continental rock forming a portion of the Northwest Territories of Canada. This and slightly younger rock terranes from Greenland, Antarctica, and Australia may have combined to form the first amalgamated continental masses. John Rogers, a professor of geology at the University of North Carolina, has proposed the existence three billion years ago of an early subcontinent he calls "Ur" (from the German for "original"). Five hundred million years later, a second subcontinent, Arctica (predecessor to Canada, Greenland, and eastern Russia) formed, followed another 500 million years later by Baltica (proto-Western Europe) and Atlantica (eastern South America and western Africa). One-and-one-half billion years ago, plate-tectonic forces formed the sub-supercontinent Nena (from the Russian for "motherland") through the merging of Baltica and Arctica. This lengthy chain of events culminated one billion years ago in the formation of the first supercontinent, Rodinia (also known as "proto-Pangaea"), as a result of the joining of Ur, Atlantica, and Nena. After a period of stability lasting some 300 million years, Rodinia subdivided, forming numerous proto-continents and Iapetus, the proto-Atlantic. Finally, the reassembly of these proto-continents and subsequent subduction of Iapetus brought about the creation of the second supercontinent Pangaea about 250 million to 300 million years ago.

A second school of thought differs principally in the suggestion that plate-tectonic processes did not begin until some 2.5 billion years ago, on the occasion of the development of the first distinct oceanic and continental crust. Prior to that time, the very high temperature of the earth and the relative thinness of primordial crust forestalled the onset of supercontinent-cycle processes such as divergence, convergence, and subduction. While differing in detail, both schools of thought generally recognize Rodinia and Pangaea as supercontinents.

The length of a typical supercontinent cycle is variously estimated at from 400 million to 440 million years. Such a cycle would constitute three phases. Once formed, a supercontinent would exist for 100 million to 120 million years before the accumulation of thermal convection heat initiated crustal dissection. During the second phase, lasting from 150 million to 160 million years, maximum dispersal of subcontinents would take place, with resultant development of new oceans. Finally, subduction would gradually destroy the intervening oceans over a period of 150 million to 160 million years, creating a new supercontinent and terminating the cycle.

Context

The concept of plate tectonics and the supercontinent cycle has been termed the contemporary unifying theory of earth history. The dynamics of the supercontinent cycle have encouraged geologists to create new exploration models establishing a scientific link between solid, liquid, and gaseous natural-resource deposits and plate-tectonics processes. Knowing the location and specific geologic conditions under which mineral deposits are formed is paramount to discovery and economic evaluation. Many metallic and nonmetallic minerals are formed by magmatism (relating to magma, naturally occurring mobile rock) at divergent and convergent crustal plate boundaries. The formation of fossil fuels is dependent upon changes in earth structure, sedimentation rates, and climate attributed to the varying stages of a supercontinent cycle. Even the role of water in crustal plate movements is necessary to an understanding of hydrocarbon migration and hydrothermal (subsurface hot water) processes.

The discovery in 1977 of "black smokers," mineral-rich hot springs with temperatures up to 450 degrees Centigrade, along the East Pacific oceanic ridge is believed to be evidence of metallic ore deposits in the early stages of formation. Black smokers precipitate iron-, zinc-, and copper-rich minerals on divergent plate borders during the first half of a supercontinent cycle. These deposits later become accreted onto continental borders through ophiolitic obduction during the final half of the cycle. Conversely, convergent borders are commonly associated with Kuroko-class (named from the location of discovery in Japan) sulphide ores of copper, lead, and zinc emplaced during subduction of crustal plates accompanying supercontinent amalgamation.

Eighty percent of known world oil and gas reserves are contained within sedimentary rocks deposited since the breakup of the supercontinent Pangaea some 200 million years ago. Much of this hydrocarbon is contained within offshore (shallow marine water) provinces resulting from plate-tectonic dynamics. Examples are the Gulf of Mexico, the North Sea, and the gigantic reserves of the northern coast of Alaska.

The distribution and economic grade of coal is also supercontinent-cycle-dependent. In the United States, the Appalachian coal fields are divided into a narrow eastern anthracite (high heat rank) and a wider western bituminous (lower heat rank) province. This distribution is directly related to compressional forces accompanying the assembly of Pangaea.

Finally, the understanding of the supercontinent cycle has proven most valuable in helping to provide a plausible explanation of the mass extinctions of organisms that have periodically occurred over the past 600 million years. The most famous of these extinctions marked the end of the Paleozoic era of geologic history 245 million years ago. The fossil record indicates a disappearance or severe reduction at that time of as much as 90 percent of all marine species; the supercontinent Pangaea had then completed its assembly. With the presence of one large continent, surrounded by universal sea waters, faunal diversity decreased as the result of loss of warm, shallow seas and the onset of colder, continental climates. Similarly, when a supercontinent dissects, this hypothesis would suggest an increase in faunal diversity, as newly developed shallow water seas and warmer climates expand the geographic area favorable to reproduction.

Bibliography

Dalziel, Ian W. D. "Earth Before Pangaea." *Scientific American* 272 (January, 1995): 58-63. An easy-to-read account of the nomadic wanderings of the North American plate prior to the assembly of Pangaea.

Davidson, J. P., W. E. Reed, and P. M. Davis. *Exploring Earth: An Introduction to Physical Geology*. Upper Saddle River, N.J.: Prentice-Hall, 1997. Chapters 6 through 11 are an excellent undergraduate-level introduction to the natural consequences of plate tectonics and their role in the supercontinent cycle.

Dietz, Robert S., and John C. Holden. "The Breakup of Pangaea." *Scientific American* 223 (October, 1970): 30-41. An interesting extrapolation into the next 50 million years of the present-day supercontinent cycle. Contains illustrations of the expected geographic locations of continents and ocean basins at that time.

Nance, R. Damian, T. R. Worsley, and J. B. Moody. "The Supercontinent Cycle." *Scientific American* 259 (July, 1988): 72-79. Combining specialties of tectonics, oceanography, and geochemistry, the authors discuss in a clear manner several supercontinent cycles and their effects on climate, evolution, and geologic changes.

Nicolas, A. *The Mid-Ocean Ridges*. New York: Springer-Verlag Berlin Heidelberg, 1995. A review presenting the European view of the construction and destruction of ocean basins. Written at the knowledgeable adult level.

Sullivan, W. *Continents in Motion*. New York: American Institute of Physics, 1991. The author, a science editor for *The New York Times*, presents a recommended compilation of the history and dynamics of plate tectonics. Suitable for the educated layperson.

Wegener, A. *The Origin of the Continents and Oceans.* New York: Dover, 1929. Written by "the father of Continental Drift," this volume presents the original thoughts and data sets used in the formulation of the first unifying theory of earth science.

Albert B. Dickas

Cross-References
African Rift Valley System, 2805; Continental Drift, 2863; Lithospheric Plates, 1387; The Ocean Ridge System, 1826; Ophiolites, 1954; The Origin of the Oceans, 1863; Plate Margins, 2063; Plate Motions, 2071; Plate Tectonics, 2079; Subduction and Orogeny, 2497.

VAN ALLEN RADIATION BELTS

Type of earth science: Atmospheric sciences and meteorology
Field of study: Geomagnetism and paleomagnetism

The Van Allen belts consist of two distinct regions of radiation that surround the earth and are contained within the earth's magnetic field. The particles that make up the belts are energetic electrons and protons that originated as particles of the solar wind plasma or as particles of cosmic radiation.

Principal terms

ELECTRONS: negatively charged subatomic particles
MAGNETIC FIELD: magnetic lines of force that are projected from the earth's interior and out into space
PARTICLE: a quanta or packet of energy, rather than a hard piece of matter
PLASMA: a sea of positively and negatively charged particles
PROTONS: positively charged subatomic particles

Summary of the Phenomenon

The Van Allen radiation belts consist of two toroidal, or doughnut-shaped, structures that exist within the earth's magnetic field. The inner belt begins at an altitude that varies between 400 kilometers and 1,200 kilometers, depending on latitude, and extends to an altitude of about 10,000 kilometers. This inner belt is made up of energetic protons and electrons. The outer belt extends from the boundary of the inner belt to about 60,000 kilometers. During times of extensive solar activity, it may expand outward to more than 80,000 kilometers. The outer belt also consists of protons and electrons, but they possess significantly less energy than do those in the inner belt.

The particles in the Van Allen belts spiral in a corkscrew-shaped path along the earth's magnetic lines of force. The spirals are small compared to the scale of the earth's magnetic field, and they curve to follow the field lines. As the lines of force converge toward a pole, the field becomes more intense. As a result, the particles travel in a tighter spiral as they approach the pole. Eventually, the converging tubes of magnetic force will cause the particles to be reflected back toward the equator and on to the opposite pole. The point of closest approach to a pole is the "mirror point" of the particle. The transit time between mirror points is about one second.

In addition to bouncing back and forth between mirror points, the particles undergo a slow lateral drift. The basic curvature of the path of a spiraling particle depends upon the local strength of the magnetic field. The particles in the inner belt have a tighter spiral, as the field nearest the earth is stronger. Since there is a slight difference in the curvatures of the spirals in the inner and outer belts, the particles drift laterally. Because the charges of protons and electrons are opposite, they spiral in opposite directions. The drift direction is also opposite; the protons tend to drift westward and the electrons eastward. This drift leads to a uniformity of the radiation belts.

At the end of each path, some particles penetrate through the mirror point and descend into regions of higher atmospheric density. These particles interact with particles of atmospheric gases. Particles of radiation lose energy as a result of these collisions, and after a period of days or weeks, they are lost to the lower atmosphere, only to be replaced by more particles from the Sun.

A large influx of particles from the Sun will, in turn, cause large numbers of particles to be "dumped" into the upper atmosphere. The resulting interactions with oxygen and nitrogen atoms produce the colorful auroras. In the Northern Hemisphere, this phenomenon is called the "aurora borealis" or "northern lights"; in the Southern Hemisphere, the display is called the "aurora australis" or "southern lights."

The auroral displays are usually pink, blue, and green streaks or curtains of light. The emission of light is the result of collisions between particles of radiation from the Van Allen belts and atoms of gas in the atmosphere. When a particle of radiation strikes an atom of gas, the orbiting electrons of the atom absorb the energy of the collision. They then jump to a higher energy level. After remaining there for only a fraction of a second, the electrons fall back to the lowest energy level, or the "ground state." When they do this, a burst of light is released that represents the difference in energy between the excited state and the ground state.

The Van Allen radiation belts exist because of three natural phenomena: the solar wind, cosmic rays, and the earth's magnetic field. As a result of the enormous heat in the Sun's upper atmosphere, atoms of gas are given enough energy to escape the Sun's gravity and move off into space. In other words, the solar corona is slowly evaporating. This phenomenon had been predicted by scientists since 1940, but was not actually confirmed until the advent of the space age in the late 1950's. The solar wind, as this phenomenon has become known, consists of a plasma with a temperature near 100,000 Kelvins. A plasma is a stream of charged particles consisting of protons, electrons, and ions of heavier elements, mainly helium. After the plasma escapes from the Sun's upper atmosphere, it flows outward into space. Since the plasma conducts heat well, the temperature remains high even after it has traveled a great distance from the Sun. The velocity of the solar wind increases as it expands radially outward. The speeds are near 300 kilometers per second at a distance of 30 solar radii from the Sun and nearly 400 kilometers per second at the distance of the earth.

At the earth's orbit, the density of the plasma is 5 particles per cubic centimeter at times of relatively little solar activity. This density changes considerably at times of peak solar activity. As the solar wind arrives at the earth, it encounters the earth's magnetic field. The edge of the magnetic field, the bowshock, deflects the solar-wind particles away from the earth, but many protons and electrons penetrate into the magnetosphere where they become trapped. It is these trapped particles from the solar wind that make up the bulk of the Van Allen radiation belts.

A less significant contribution to the radiation belts is made by cosmic rays. Cosmic rays consist primarily of protons and electrons and come to Earth from two different sources. Some are hurled into space from the surface of the Sun during violent eruptions such as solar flares; others come from the depths of space.

Solar cosmic rays are considered to be low-level radiation, not nearly as energetic as cosmic radiation that originates outside the solar system. This second type of cosmic radiation, known as "galactic" cosmic rays, may have originated with the big bang, the explosion that created the universe. These particles are accelerated in violent events such as supernovas and may be further accelerated by interactions with clouds of interstellar plasmas and shockwaves. When galactic cosmic rays were first discovered in 1912, they were thought to be some form of electromagnetic radiation. It is now known that these rays are made up of 85 to 90 percent protons, 10 percent alpha particles or helium nuclei, 1 percent electrons, and 1 percent nuclei of heavier elements such as oxygen, nitrogen, iron, or neon.

Some cosmic rays have energies sufficient to penetrate the earth's magnetosphere and reach the surface. Others collide with particles of atmospheric gas and release a shower of secondary radiation that is detected on Earth. The principles of the interaction of cosmic-ray particles with the earth's magnetic field are the same as for the trapped particles of solar radiation.

The lifetimes of particles trapped in the Van Allen belts are highly variable. Under conditions of minimum solar activity, some particles remain trapped for months or years. Since the radiation belt density is fairly low, collisions that would send particles out of the belt are rare. The individual particle's lifetime is therefore determined by the height of its mirror points above the densest part of the atmosphere. The higher the mirror points, the less chance that the particle of radiation will collide with an atom of atmospheric gas.

The mechanism of loss and replenishment of particles in the radiation belt is not well understood. There are several theories; however, none appears to be adequate alone. There is a good possibility that there are several mechanisms that work to distribute particles of various energies to different parts of the belt. The continuous supply of solar-wind particles from the Sun appears to be a necessity. Apparently, low-energy solar-wind particles enter the magentosphere and are accelerated to energies necessary to become radiation-belt particles.

Methods of Study

Radiation in space consists of electromagnetic waves from the Sun; highly energetic protons, electrons, and atomic nuclei that make up the solar wind; cosmic rays both from the Sun and outer space; and trapped particles within the Van Allen radiation belts. While on the ground, we are protected from these forms of radiation by the earth's atmosphere and its magnetic field. Astronauts flying in space however, have a much more significant risk. If a spacecraft is in orbit at an altitude lower than the altitude of the inner Van Allen belt, then there is no danger to the astronaut from the trapped particles of radiation. Although the radiation intensity of the inner belt is fairly constant, the intensity in the outer belt is much more sensitive to what is happening on the surface of the Sun. Activities on the Sun such as solar flares will result in a considerable fluctuation in the radiation intensity at this higher level. During periods of peak solar activity, the radiation in the outer belt could give an unprotected astronaut an exposure that could be fatal. The cabin of a spacecraft does offer some protection; however, when a particle strikes the spacecraft wall, it produces a shower of secondary radiation by a process known as "bremsstrahlung."

In modern X-ray machines, highly penetrating particles of radiation are created in the exact same way. The machine consists of two electrodes, one of negative charge (the cathode), and the anode, which is charged positively. A large electrical potential difference is set up between the two electrodes, the anode being several thousand volts positive as compared to the cathode. As the cathode is heated, the electrons leave and move toward the anode, accelerating rapidly and picking up great amounts of energy as they travel. They then slam into the anode, releasing a shower of X rays. A high-speed spacecraft traveling through the Van Allen belts can generate energy radiation just by making contact with a highly energetic particle of radiation, giving rise to the process.

High-energy particles are capable of creating damage in human organisms. High-speed, high-energy particles pass through the body, colliding with and knocking electrons out of atoms that make up the cells. The result is chemical changes in the cells.

On the surface of the earth, humans are subjected to a certain amount of background radiation. The cells of the body regularly absorb radiation, die, and regenerate. The body has acquired an immunity to this type of radiation. When the body is exposed to too much high-energy ionizing radiation, however, the cells may not be able to replace themselves because of damage to the nuclei that control the cell. Another possibility would be the uncontrolled reproduction of the cells and the spread of a cancer.

The best way to protect an astronaut from the effects of the Van Allen radiation belt is shielding, although shielding of the entire spacecraft may prove to be impractical because of the mass of the materials used in making the shield. It is generally more feasible to have a small portion of the spacecraft protected; the area must be large enough to provide a safe haven for the entire crew until the time of danger has passed. In August, 1972, a major solar flare occurred. A detailed study of the radiation released from that event showed that a shield of aluminum 0.2 meters thick would provide the necessary protection to keep astronaut exposure rates below the established limits.

During the Apollo missions, spacecraft trajectories were planned that avoided the regions of highest concentrations of radiation. Also, most of the missions were launched after the peak of the solar cycle. As a result of these precautions, the astronauts were exposed to about the same radiation dosages as someone would receive from a diagnostic X ray.

The inner Van Allen radiation belt interacts with the earth's upper atmosphere in the polar regions to produce the aurora borealis and the aurora australis. Although the auroras are sometimes seen over most parts of the globe, their regular and most frequent appearances are confined to the Arctic and Antarctic zones. The greatest frequency of the aurora in the Arctic region appears within a zone that lies from 15 to 30 degrees from the earth's north magnetic pole. Records from the Antarctic are too few for a designation of a maximum zone.

In the region of the auroral zone, viewing an auroral display can be a nightly event. The development of an auroral exhibition may be described by the following sequence. After sunset, a faint arc becomes visible in the northern sky. The arc remains quiet for hours, with only a slight amount of movement. Suddenly, its lower border becomes more intense, and the arc breaks up into a series of parallel rays. The rays increase in color and intensity, and bundles of rays move along the arc. The arc then splits up into rays and draperies that fill the sky with dancing movements. The entire display usually lasts only minutes before the forms fade away. The faint arc again becomes visible in the northern sky. This display may be repeated several times during the night. A faint luminosity covers the northern sky after a particularly powerful auroral display. This phenomenon has given the aurora borealis the additional name the "northern dawn."

These colorful displays are produced when low-energy electrons and protons drop out of the inner radiation belt and collide with atoms of atmospheric gases. The gas atoms are excited by these collisions; when they return to their stable forms, visible light is emitted.

The trapped particles that make up the Van Allen belts are held in close proximity to the earth by the earth's magnetic field. Geophysical studies have concluded that the earth's magnetism is generated within the liquid iron-and-nickle outer core rather than the solid inner core or the rock that makes up the mantle and the crust. The molten outer core flows at a rate of several kilometers per year in massive convective currents.

These currents, along with the rotation of the earth, create electrical currents. The currents in turn, create the earth's magnetic field. It has been found that other planets that have strong magnetic fields, Jupiter for example, also have radiation belts similar to the earth's Van Allen radiation belts.

Context

The history of the study of near-Earth radiation goes back to the early 1950's. During those years, scientists launched instrument packages into the upper atmosphere by using a combination of balloons and rockets. A balloon would lift a small rocket up to an altitude of fifteen or so miles, the rocket would then ignite and carry the package to an altitude of from sixty to seventy miles. The purpose of these tests was to monitor cosmic-ray intensities at high altitudes and latitudes. By doing so, scientists hoped to learn more about how cosmic rays are deflected by the earth's magnetic field and absorbed in the atmosphere.

In 1953, a rocket launched into the northern auroral zone yielded a radiation count far greater than expected. It was proposed that since other instrument packages launched into regions both north and south of the zone revealed no anomalous data, there must be a connection between the high radiation count and the aurora. It was believed that the auroras were caused when showers of particles from the Sun entered the earth's atmosphere along magnetic lines of force. During the International Geophysical Year (1957-1958), further tests were completed in the polar regions. The tests revealed that the radiation included energetic protons and electrons.

It was during the International Geophysical Year that a series of orbiting satellites were to be launched. It was decided that aboard these satellites would be placed radiation-detecting instruments. Before any American satellites could be oribited, the Soviet Union launched *Sputnik* I; moreover, the first American launch attempts, using the Vanguard rocket, ended in a dismal failure. In January, 1958, the Jupiter-C rocket successfully carried *Explorer* I into orbit. The satellite carried with it a cosmic-ray detector.

The first reports from *Explorer* I indicated that radiation intensity increased with altitude. The data was somewhat incomplete, as it could only be taken when the satellite was near a tracking station. A later satellite, *Explorer* III, carried a tiny magnetic tape recorder. This device could record data during an entire orbit and then send it upon receiving a radio command. The data from *Explorer* III confirmed that the radiation increased with altitude and eventually went to zero. Scientists eventually determined that the zero reading on their radiation counters was anomalous; the counters were actually being overloaded by radiation. The satellites had found a major new phenomenon: particles of radiation trapped in the earth's magnetic field.

Data from satellites and lunar probes carrying more advanced instrument packages eventually revealed the existence of two belts of trapped radiation. Since their discovery in 1958, the radiation belts have been thoroughly mapped by space probes. Knowledge of the Van Allen belts is essential for any space traveler. In the case of a low-orbiting spacecraft, the belts actually protect the craft from radiation. If the spacecraft should enter the belts, then there is the possibility of encountering ionizing radiation. Space radiation is one of the most important elements in space travel and long-term space habitation because of the effects of ionizing radiation.

Bibliography

Baugher, Joseph F. *The Space-Age Solar System.* New York: John Wiley & Sons, 1988. A well-written, well-illustrated volume on what has been learned about the solar system since the dawn of the space age. Suitable for the informed layperson.

Beatty, J. Kelly, and Andrew Chaikin. *The New Solar System.* Cambridge, Mass.: Sky Publishing, 1981. This well-illustrated, somewhat technical volume consists of a collection of essays by various experts in solar system research. Topics include the Sun, planets, moons, cornets, asteroids, and meteorites.

Damon, Thomas D. *Introduction to Space.* Malabar, Fla.: Orbit, 1989. A well-written, well-illustrated volume that covers various topics relevant to spaceflight. These topics include the history of spaceflight, propulsion systems, orbits, satellites, and living and working in space.

Harang, L. *The Aurorae.* New York: John Wiley & Sons, 1951. Contains detailed discussion of how the auroras form, their spectra, electromagnetic storms, and more. Well-illustrated with graphs and charts. The reader should have some basic knowledge of electromagnetism, spectroscopy, and advanced mathematics.

Plummer, Charles C., and David McGeary. *Physical Geology.* Dubuque, Iowa: William C. Brown, 1996. A general introduction to physical geology intended for use at the college-freshman level. Contains many tables, illustrations, and photographs; also includes a glossary and an index.

Shipman, Harry L. *Humans in Space*. New York: Plenum Press, 1989. A nonmathematical, very readable volume. The author deals with such subjects as living in space, space resources, and uses for advanced space technology.

Stine, G. Harry. *Handbook for Space Colonists*. New York: Holt, Rinehart, and Winston, 1985. A volume suitable for the general reader on the effects of spaceflight on humans. Such topics as space habitats, health and medicine, working in space, and social aspects of space living are discussed.

Tucker, R. H., et al. Stacey. *Global Geophysics*. New York: American Elsevier, 1970. Deals with topics in geophysics such as geodesy, seismology, and geomagnetism. Well-illustrated; however, the author does make liberal use of advanced mathematics. Intended for the college-level physics student.

Van Allen, James A. "Radiation Belts Around the Earth." *Scientific American* 200, no. 3 (March, 1959). By the scientist who designed the experimentation that discovered the radiation belts that bear his name. Contains both a history of the study of radiation near the earth and a technical description of the radiation belts.

Wentzel, Donat G. *The Restless Sun*. Washington, D.C.: Smithsonian Institutional Press, 1989. A well-written volume intended for the layperson that describes, in nonmathematical terms, internal and external solar processes.

Zeilik, Michael, and Elske V. P. Smith. *Introductory Astronomy and Astrophysics*. 2d ed. New York: Saunders College Publishing, 1987. A text for an introductory college course on astrophysics. Well-illustrated with graphs, drawings, and photographs. Includes problem sets at the end of each chapter; the author assumes some knowledge of advanced mathematics.

David W. Maguire

Cross-References

IMPACT VOLCANISM

Type of earth science: Planetology
Fields of study: Igneous petrology and volcanology

Impact volcanism is the process whereby a giant impact event has produced a huge crater along with a magma reservoir that will subsequently produce volcanic activity. Such cratering is clearly visible on the Moon, Mars, Mercury, and probably Venus. It is assumed that Earth had similar craters, but erosion has erased most of the evidence.

Principal terms

ACCRETION: a process in planetary formation whereby particles of various sizes hit and stick together to form a larger object

ASTEROID: a small interplanetary body made of rock or metal; most range in size from 100 feet to 10 miles across

BASALT: a dark-colored volcanic rock principally made from the silicate minerals pyroxene and plagioclase

CONDENSATION: the process by which a solid material is produced from the rapid cooling of a hot gas or liquid

LAVA: the molten material extruded from a volcano; lava will form into rock upon cooling

MAGMA: the fluid material that exists below a planet's surface; magma may erupt as a volcano or slowly cool and harden into rock

MARIA BASIN: a huge crater produced by the impact of an asteroid and later filled with volcanic lava

MELT: the fluid material that results from the melting of rock after a giant asteroid impact

SOLAR NEBULA: the gas and dust cloud that surrounds a newly forming star

VOLCANO: one of the resulting geologic features produced by the eruption of magma from beneath a planet's surface; it usually displays a cone shape

Summary of the Phenomenon

Impact volcanism is a direct result of the cratering process evident throughout the inner solar system. The effects of an extensive period of impact can also be seen on most of the moons of the Jovian planets and even on the two asteroids photographed by the *Galileo* spacecraft. Most planetary scientists agree that this extensive period of asteroid bombardment took place from about 4.5 billion to 3.5 billion years ago. The best evidence for this comes from the analysis of lunar maria rock brought back from the Moon by the Apollo astronauts. The most recent date from a maria basalt gives an age of approximately 3 billion years. It is assumed that the impact that produced this basaltic lava occurred several hundred million years earlier. It would require about that much time for a sufficient magma source to build up and later erupt on the surface, filling the crater produced by the impact. Since the period of giant impacts, the Moon and the other terrestrial planets have still received their share of impacts, but most are of a much smaller size and do not generate the immense quantity of lava that the earlier impacts produced.

The period of giant impacts that is recorded on the terrestrial planets is regarded by most planetary scientists as the final stage of planetary accretion. It is generally accepted that the planets formed from the gravitational collapse and subsequent condensation of the hot residual gases that surrounded the early Sun. Once this solar nebula cooled sufficiently to condense solid grains of metal and rock, the process of accretion began. At first, the process would involve micro-grains attracting one another to form larger particles; these in turn would attract one another to form still larger particles. This process would continue through larger and larger objects until the objects achieved the size of small asteroids. Collisions between these asteroids would then continue until planet-sized objects formed. After that, frequent collisions between the nearly formed planets and the remaining asteroids took place. It was during this period that giant impacts formed the maria basins on the Moon.

The best example of impact-generated volcanism can be seen on the Moon. Giant impact craters were first observed on the Moon by Galileo Galilei with his low-power telescope in 1609. Based on his observations, he thought that he was viewing large bodies of water, and he named these features "maria," from the Latin for "seas." For centuries after Galileo's initial observations, scientists pondered the nature of the maria. It was established early on that they were not bodies of water, but their true nature remained the subject of much debate. As late as the 1960's, scientists were not sure if the craters they were observing were volcanic or were impact generated. It was left to the Apollo missions to provide the necessary proof.

In modern geology, theories concerning the origin of the planets are based upon the interpretation of similar features that occur on Earth. For the most part, this is a valid approach that usually works very well. The problem with applying this method to features the size of the lunar maria, however, is that there are no terrestrial equivalents for detailed study. Although Earth has been hit by objects the size of those that created the lunar maria, the craters they produced have long since been removed by erosion. The most recent impact craters on Earth are small in comparison to the lava-filled craters on the Moon.

The thickness of Earth's crust also plays an important part in impact volcanism. The largest impact structures on Earth seem to be concentrated on the continents, where the crust is quite thick. In comparison, the oceanic crust is quite thin, and the probability of large impact features should be higher. Only recently have impact features of considerable size been found on the ocean floor, notably off the coastlines of Newfoundland and Maryland and partially on land in the Yucatan in Mexico. Unfortunately for researchers, the oceans tend to conceal impact structures quite well.

To understand the process of impact volcanism, one must look to the Moon for the best examples. A casual glance at a globe of the Moon shows two very different terrains dominating each side. The earth-facing side is characterized by the presence of maria, with an approximate ratio of 60 percent maria to less than 40 percent highland terrain. On the far side, this ratio changes to about 80 percent highlands to 20 percent maria. Clearly, there must be a reason for this striking difference in appearance. Although each face seems to have experienced a similar number of impacts, it is the crustal thickness that makes the difference. On the average, the crust on the earth-facing side is thinner than that on the far side.

The thickness of a planet's crust will have a definite effect on what type of impact structure will occur. In the case of an impact into thick continental crust, a crater will certainly result, but the chances of its becoming completely lava-filled are extremely low. A large impact will always produce a certain amount of melt at the point of impact, but not enough to fill the entire crater. Sufficient magma for that can be found only deep below the planet's crust. There, temperatures are usually sufficient to melt rock into magma, but high pressure keeps the rock solid. The controlling factor in generating a melt is found in the amount of pressure exerted upon the rock. An increase in pressure raises the melting point of any material. Conversely, as pressure is relieved, existing temperatures can easily convert rock into magma. When an extremely large impact occurs, huge amounts of rock are vaporized during the excavation of the crater. The elimination of such a large amount of rock causes a significant drop in pressure, and the existing temperature easily converts solid rock into magma. A magma reservoir has now been formed and may serve as a source for further volcanic activity.

Once a magma source has been formed, it still has to make its way to the surface. An impacting object fractures rock well below the floor of the crater it excavates. These fissures in the rock provide a pathway for the magma to work its way to the surface, as pressure periodically changes and chemical differentiation of the magma occurs. Once the magma reaches the surface, it can take on the form of an actual volcanic eruption, producing a conical structure, or it can extrude lava from a series of fissure outpourings. Taken to their maximum extent, these fissure eruptions can become enormous; notable examples include the Columbia River Basalt Plateau in the Pacific Northwest and the Deccan Traps in India.

On the Moon, the crust is considerably thinner on the Earth-facing side. When large impacts occurred there, they were able to punch deep into the Moon's crust and release huge amounts of magma. With time, these huge outpourings of lava completely filled structures such as Mare Imbrium (600 miles in diameter). In contrast, on the far side, a giant impact excavated Mare Orientale, forming a huge multiringed basin. Although a small amount of impact melt is present at the center of Mare Orientale, the structure is essentially devoid of lava. In its place are a series of concentric rims that define the entire structure. With a thick underlying crust, the impact was not sufficient to penetrate deep enough to generate the quantity of magma necessary to fill the structure. If one could drain Mare Imbrium, on the near side, it would very closely resemble Mare Orientale.

A close inspection of the lunar maria reveals many volcanic features such as rilles, wrinkle ridges, and chain craters typical of fissure eruptions. Clearly, volcanism has been an active geologic process on the Moon in times past. Samples returned by the Apollo astronauts include vesicular basalts that are essentially indistinguishable from those found on Earth. The basic difference between volcanism on the Moon and that on Earth is in how the magma, which feeds the volcanic activity, was generated.

On Earth, the planet's interior is sufficiently hot to maintain a certain level of fluidity at specific depths. As pressures change for various reasons, rising plumes of magma result and may break through to the surface as volcanic eruptions. The principal source of heat needed to maintain these high temperatures comes from Earth's own mass. The greater a planet's mass, the higher the interior temperature will be. Although other mechanisms will generate heat within a planet's interior, mass remains the critical factor. In the Moon's case, its lower mass is insufficient to maintain temperatures hot enough to sustain large magma bodies. It is assumed that by the end of the giant impact period, the interior of the Moon had cooled significantly and could no longer maintain large near-surface magma reservoirs. No matter; by that time, most of the objects capable of producing a large impact basin had already crashed into a planet, and only the smaller bodies remained. This can be seen in the apparent lack of large fresh craters on the Moon.

Impact volcanism is not restricted to the Moon but also occurs on Mars and Mercury. Based on the photographic data returned from the *Mariner* 10 mission, it appears that Mercury offers many examples of impact-generated volcanism. One reason why Mercury does not have as many volcanic features as the Moon is that its crust is uniformly thicker and thus is less susceptible to impact penetration. On Mars, there is considerable evidence of impact volcanism, but it is harder to discern because there is ample evidence of basic volcanic activity not related to impact. The fact that Mars is subject to extensive erosion makes it yet more difficult to distinguish incidents of impact volcanism. Older volcanic features have been worn away or covered by blowing dust. Mars is a geologically active planet, unlike both Mercury and the Moon, which are essentially geologically dead worlds.

Methods of Study

The methods of scientific investigation that are employed to gain an understanding of impact volcanism span the range of the geological sciences and merge with the techniques of astronomy as well. First, geologists seek to gain a complete understanding of the volcanic processes that occur on Earth, particularly those that involve basaltic volcanoes. The initial step is to understand the relationship of the various minerals that make up basalt and how they interact with one another. It is also necessary to learn about the various mechanisms that govern a volcanic eruption. The eruptive nature of a particular volcano is governed by the amounts of silica and water present in the initial magma. Based on those amounts, the volcanoes will either erupt with a relatively gentle flowing lava, like the Hawaiian volcanoes, or will explode violently, like Mount St. Helens.

The next step in understanding impact volcanism is to investigate the mechanics of high-velocity impacts. Based on the size and speed of the impacting object, different-sized craters will be formed. Almost every crater will attain a circular shape, but the actual size of the crater depends upon the impacting object's mass. Only the bigger objects will produce an impact melt, which may be found only at the impact point. Objects the size of asteroids in the 10-to-20-mile range are the ones that will produce maria basins such as those seen on the Moon. It is fortunate for life on Earth that asteroids of that size rarely approach the planet today.

Since impact-related volcanism is not well represented on Earth, scientists must look to the other terrestrial planets for evidence of these planet-shaping events; the Moon also serves as an excellent example of widespread impact volcanism. Scientists examined the Moon through indirect means for decades before the first astronaut set foot on its surface. Certainly, the rock and soil material brought back by the astronauts greatly increased the knowledge of impact events, especially in dating their occurrence with a high degree of precision. Data gained from lunar orbits also added greatly to what was known about the lunar surface. More recently, the unmanned probe *Clementine* completed a global geologic map of the lunar surface that characterized most of the major rock types and formations. Even after almost forty years of lunar exploration, however, there is still much to be learned about the Moon and its history of impacts, both large and small.

Beyond the Moon, space probes have visited Mars, Mercury, and Venus. On each of these worlds, they have detected evidence of giant impacts with subsequent volcanism. On both Mercury and Mars, the spacecraft were able to make firsthand observations, and the evidence was clear. On Venus, the situation is very different. Orbiting space probes rely on radar mapping to identify the various surface features. In many cases, impact volcanic features can be easily identified, since they are found among the largest structures on the surface. The limited data returned from the surface strongly suggests that the principal rock of Venus is basalt, like that of the other terrestrial planets.

Context

Impact volcanism is one of the fundamental planetary processes associated with the period of heavy meteoroid bombardment that followed formation of the planets. This period is also known as the final stage of planetary accretion. It was a time when the planets were frequently subjected to giant impacts by asteroid-sized objects. The result of these impacts produced supercraters measuring 600 miles in diameter. Shortly after the initial crater-producing events, magma began to flow out from impact-generated reservoirs deep within the crust. In time, these outpourings of lava gradually filled the craters and left behind the familiar maria as seen on the Moon today. Maria basins are seen on Mercury, Venus, and Mars as well. No doubt Earth had its share before erosion and plate tectonics destroyed all evidence of them.

What role did impact volcanism play in the evolution of Earth? Some theorists have suggested that it played an important part in mineral-deposit emplacement. There is a strong suggestion of this from the Sudbury impact structure located in Ontario, Canada. This is one of the world's richest deposits of nickel and cobalt, both of which are associated with basic meteorite mineralogy. If these metals are not the residue from an impacting object, they could have resulted from the upwelling of magma from the upper mantle following the impact event. In either case, the Sudbury mineral deposits have a direct relationship to an impact event and may serve as a model for the immense impacts of the past.

Understanding impact volcanism is important to modern planetary geologists. Maria basins are fundamental crustal structures, and they tell much about the impact history of a planet. It seems apparent that the original crust of the terrestrial planets was destroyed by the period of heavy meteoroid bombardment. In its place came the vast, smooth lava plains of the maria. How long did it take for these supercraters to fill, and is volcanism going on today? Planetary geology is a two-way street. Scientists take what they learn from Earth geology and extend it out to the other planets. In return, the knowledge gained from planetary exploration can be brought home to attempt a reconstruction of what the early Earth looked like.

The question of active volcanism on other planets is also significant for the future of human space travel and exploration. Where there is volcanism, there is usually water in some form. Perhaps rich mineral deposits will be found as well. Both will be needed in great quantities if humans are to survive on distant planets. A basic understanding of impact volcanism will certainly aid future space travelers in any efforts to establish a new home world. Such an understanding will also provide additional insight into where we have come from and how our planet evolved over time.

Bibliography

Basaltic Volcanism Study Project (1981). *Basaltic Volcanism on the Terrestrial Planets*. New York: Pergamon Press, 1981. Perhaps the most comprehensive single-volume work on basaltic rocks and magmas. Chapter 5 in particular deals with basaltic volcanism on the various planets. Essential to the understanding of impact volcanism.

Francis, Peter. *Volcanoes: A Planetary Perspective*. New York: Oxford University Press, 1993. Describes the essentials of volcanic activity in a thoroughly understandable manner. Provides the reader with a wealth of basic information concerning various volcanoes and related volcanic activity.

Greeley, Ronald. *Planetary Landscapes*. 2d ed. New York: Chapman & Hall, 1994. Intended to serve as an introduction to planetary geology. Concentrates primarily on the surface features of the various planets and their satellites. Chapters 3, 4, and 5 are useful in understanding impact volcanism.

Hamblin, W. Kenneth, and Eric H. Christiansen. *Exploring the Planets*. New York: Macmillan, 1990. A good general text that reviews the various planets in the solar system and their comparative characteristics. Chapters 3 and 6 are extremely good in presenting information concerning impact-related events on both Earth and the Moon.

Hartmann, William K. *Moons and Planets*. 3d ed. Belmont, Calif.: Wadsworth, 1993. One of the most comprehensive books on the subject of planetary science. Chapters

10 and 11 are valuable in their explanation of the various concepts and mechanisms involved in volcanic processes.

Lewis, John S. *Physics and Chemistry of the Solar System*. San Diego: Academic Press, 1995. A comprehensive survey of planetary physics and physical chemistry as it pertains to the solar system. Contains an enormous amount of information and has numerous references for further reading. Impact volcanism is covered in part in several chapters.

Melosh, H. J. *Impact Cratering*. New York: Oxford University Press, 1988. An excellent reference work that describes the mechanism of impact cratering and how it influences planetary evolution. An understanding of cratering events is essential to the understanding of impact volcanism.

Ragland, Paul C., and John J. W. Rogers, eds. *Basalt*. New York: Van Nostrand Reinhold, 1984. A comprehensive compilation of papers that deal with basalt. Basalt has been referred to as the "basic rock of the Solar System," and it is closely related to impact volcanism and the early stages of planetary evolution.

Taylor, Stuart Ross. *Solar System Evolution*. Cambridge, England: Cambridge University Press, 1992. An excellent work that describes the processes involved in planetary formation in great detail. Chapter 4 presents a comprehensive picture of the role giant impacts play in a planet's evolution.

Yoder, H. S., Jr. *Generation of Basaltic Magma*. Washington, D.C.: National Academy of Sciences, 1976. Basalt forms as the result of giant impacts, as evidenced by the surfaces of the terrestrial planets. In this classic work, Yoder provides chemical descriptions of basaltic magma generation. A fine reference work.

Paul P. Sipiera

Cross-References

INTRAPLATE VOLCANISM

Type of earth science: Geology
Field of study: Volcanology

Intraplate volcanoes are found at localized hot spots that are formed in response to hot columns of mantle material that originate near the earth's core and rise toward the surface. These hot spots initiate volcanoes and volcanic chains located far from the edges of the earth's tectonic plates. Long lines of extinct intraplate volcanoes provide a way of tracing the motion of the earth's lithospheric plates.

Principal terms

ASTHENOSPHERE: the shell within the earth beneath the lithosphere that yields plastically to stress; found at depths ranging from 5 kilometers beneath spreading ridges to 100 kilometers under continents

CONVECTION CELLS: movement of materials as a result of density differences caused by heating

CONVERGENT PLATE MARGIN: a plate margin where two crustal plates are moving toward each other

DIVERGENT PLATE MARGIN: a plate margin where two crustal plates are moving away from each other

LITHOSPHERE: the outer, cooler portion of the earth that behaves more or less rigidly; the lithosphere consists of the crust and the uppermost part of the mantle

MANTLE: the thick layer of the interior of the earth between the crust and core

MANTLE PLUME: a localized column of hot mantle material originating near the core-mantle boundary and rising to the base of the crust

PLATE TECTONICS: a theory that interrelates the internal and external processes of the earth and involves the interaction of lithospheric plates

RIFT ZONE: a long, broad trough bounded by faults on each side, formed by stretching the crust; common at divergent plate margins

SUBDUCTION ZONE: the linear belt at the surface of the earth where one lithospheric plate sinks beneath another; common at convergent plate margins

Summary of the Phenomenon

Planets may lose their internal heat by a number of different mechanisms that transfer heat from the hot, deep interior to the surface. The least efficient form of heat transfer is lithospheric conduction, which involves simple heat migration through solid rock. Rock is a very poor conductor of heat, and the conductive heat loss is extremely slow. Another method of heat transfer in planets is by mantle plumes, in which a rather narrow column of hot material, from deep within the mantle near the core-mantle boundary, rises toward the surface. Plumes of this kind are the most effective means of heat transfer from the deeper regions of a planet. In contrast, mantle convection, in which the plastic interior of a planet undergoes slow convective motion, is the mechanism by which the upper mantle loses heat. These convection cells, within the upper mantle, pull and push on the more brittle lithosphere of the earth. This movement of the mantle is responsible for breaking the lithosphere of the planet into mobile plates separated by narrow zones of upwelling mantle material and zones of downwelling mantle.

The earth's surface is broken into approximately twelve large (and several small) mobile, rigid, lithospheric plates that jostle about. The plates consist of 100- to 200-kilometer-thick slabs of relatively rigid crustal and upper mantle material over-lying lower plastic materials of the mantle. Convection cells in the mantle, below the lithosphere, drive plate motions at the surface of the earth. Ninety-five percent of the earth's volcanoes occur along the boundaries of these plates. At the spreading centers between divergent plates, large rift valleys are formed as plate margins are pulled apart. Melting in the mantle beneath the rift zone, caused by the upwelling hot mantle material and the decrease in pressure beneath the rift, gives rise to nearly continuous igneous activity, as basaltic magmas intrude along fractures in the crust to form new ocean crust and erupt onto the floor of the rift valley.

Where plates converge, one side of the convergent zone is pulled down and subducted into the mantle. The zone of convergence is marked by a deep oceanic trench flanked by arcuate chains of islands. As the plate segment descends, it is heated by the natural increase in temperature at greater depth in the earth. When the descending plate reaches a depth where the temperature is high enough to begin melting, part of the plate is assimilated into the mantle, and part is melted to form magma that rises toward the surface. Those magmas that make it to the surface form volcanoes aligned along the junction created by colliding plates. These active volcanic chains form island arcs such as the Japanese Islands, the Philippines, and the Aleutian Islands in the Pacific Ocean and mountain chains such as the Andes of South America and the Cascade Range of the northwestern United States.

In contrast to volcanoes on the edge of plates, some very prominent volcanoes are found within the interior of plates far from any spreading ridge or subduction zone. These intraplate volcanoes are driven by mantle plumes. Mantle plumes are concen-trated regions of hot upwelling mantle material that are independent of the plate boundaries and the convection cells associated with them. These plumes give rise to local hot spots at the surface, which are the homes of the earth's largest volcanoes. Mantle plumes are important components of the convection system by which the earth loses heat. Intraplate volcanism shows up as chains of volcanic islands, as seamounts on the ocean floor, and as flood basalts or isolated volcanic fields on the continents. More than one hundred mantle plumes have been active in the past ten million years. They occur in both oceanic and continental settings. The largest concentration of intraplate volcanoes is on the African plate.

Probably the best known of the intraplate volcanic systems is the Hawaiian Island-Emperor Seamount Chain situated within the Pacific Ocean plate. The volcanic activity of Hawaii builds very large volcanoes with gentle sloping sides; these are known as "shield volcanoes." Many of the older volcanoes of this chain have sunk below sea level and are now identified as "seamounts." Other intraplate volcanic trails are common in the Pacific, including the Line Island-Tumoto Chain and the Marshall-Gilbert-Ellice-Samoan Island Chain. Most of the intraplate volcanoes of the Atlantic and Indian Oceans are marked by seamounts and broad ridges or rises. The New England-Corner Seamounts and the Great Meteor Tablemount are sites of past intraplate volcanoes in the North Atlantic. Tristan Da Cuna of the South Atlantic, Reunion Island in the Indian Ocean, and the Tasmantid Seamount east of Tasmania are active volcanic centers associated with chains of extinct volcanoes on the ocean floor.

On the North American continent, intraplate volcanoes include the Snake River-Yellowstone Volcanic Province and the Columbia Plateau flood basalts. The one-billion-year-old basalts of the Lake Superior region represent a mantle plume that was responsible for erupting in excess of 400,000 cubic kilometers of flood basalts. In Africa, the isolated mountain ranges in the central Sahara, such as the Tibetsi, Hoggar, and Jebel Marra, are major intraplate volcanic complexes in which some of the volcanoes reach more than three thousand meters in height. In contrast to the Pacific plate plumes, the African plumes have remained active in the same locality for thirty million years.

The source of a mantle plume at the core-mantle boundary remains stationary over hundreds of millions of years. Therefore, as the earth's lithospheric plates move over the plumes, the plumes generate hot spot trails or chains of volcanic islands. Unlike the volcanic chains of the island arcs, which are active all along the arc, hot spot trails are only active above the mantle plume. The volcano located over a mantle plume becomes extinct as the moving plate moves it away from the source, and a new volcano forms over the plume. Thus, the volcanic rocks of the volcanic chain become progressively older with increasing distance from the hot spot. The age of the volcanic rocks of the chain can be used to trace absolute plate motions.

Hot spot trails are less obvious on the continents. A mantle plume that rises beneath the much thicker and insulative continental crust may give rise to magma that cools within the crust, known as a "pluton," or it may cause a regional bulge in the crust with accompanying stretching, thinning, and fracturing of the crust. The release of pressure at depth gives rise to great quantities of magma, which rises to pour out of great long fissures onto the surface as lavas. If eruption rates are high, fluid lava does not build a cone but spreads across the surface to bury the landscape under a series of massive lava flows. These "flood basalts" are the most extensive type of volcanic activity on the earth's continents. The one- to two-kilometer-thick Columbia River Plateau basalt covering an area of 200,000 square kilometers of southern Washington, northern Oregon, and western Idaho is an example of a flood basalt that erupted on the North American continent from six million to seventeen million years ago. This same mantle plume may be responsible for the basalts of the adjacent Snake River Plains and for the current activity of the Yellowstone region. The lavas of Yellowstone National Park, Wyoming, are rhyolitic rather than basaltic; nevertheless, Yellowstone is thought to represent a hot spot that incorporates much more continental rock in its magma than that of the Columbia River Plateau basalts.

By definition, intraplate volcanism is not associated with plate boundaries, yet the two cannot be completely separated. Some mantle plumes may fortuitously reach the surface at a plate boundary, and some hot spots under continents may evolve through time to initiate rifting. Many onetime continental, intraplate volcanic centers sitting above a mantle plume continue to develop along a characteristic pattern. The expansion of the crust over the mantle plume stretches the lithosphere to the point that normal faulting creates a down-dropped trough or rift zone. Magma, erupting along the faults, flows onto the floor of the rifts. Eventually, the faulted arch is thinned to the point that its crest founders. The floor of the rift drops below sea level and floods with water to become an embryonic ocean. As the rift widens with time, the once adjacent pieces of the continent are slowly pushed apart by the intrusion of more magma between them, and a new divergent plate margin is born. Often such rift zones begin with three radially divergent rift zones as a "triple junction." Such a triple junction can be seen where the Red Sea, the Gulf of Aden, and the East African Rift zone meet. Two of the arms of the junction (the Red Sea and the Gulf of Aden) have opened to form narrow arms of the ocean, while the third arm (East African Rift zone) has not yet collapsed enough for flooding. The East African Rift zone, which is the site of recent and current volcanic activity, was the site of earlier extensive flood basalt eruptions. In this way, a mantle plume that gave rise to intraplate volcanism has continued to develop until it initiated a spreading center that now defines the edges of tectonic plates.

Vast basalt accumulations, such as the Parana flood basalts on the eastern edge of South America and the Etendeka flood basalts of the western edge of Africa, began as continental, intraplate volcanic centers, but they are associated with the separation of those continents by the opening of the southern Atlantic Ocean 120 million to 130 million years ago. In like manner, the Greenland flood basalts and the Hebridean basalts of northern Scotland and Ireland once formed a single volcanic province that was split by the separation of the northern Atlantic Ocean sixty million years ago.

Iceland is the only part of the northern Mid-Atlantic Ridge to grow above sea level. Because of the large volume of basalt, it is suggested that Iceland is a hot spot that coincides with the ridge, and its volcanoes are of dual origin-mantle plume and spreading center. The diverse composition of lavas—an apparent mixture of ridge and hot spot compositions—would seem to support the theory of the composite origin of Iceland. Another hot spot that coincides with spreading centers includes the Rio Grande Rise and the Walvis Ridge of the south Atlantic Ocean, which has left symmetrical trails across the ocean floor on either side of the spreading center at Tristan da Cunha.

The great size of the volcanoes on Mars is attributed to the presence of mantle plumes and the absence of plate tectonics. Olympus, the largest volcano in the solar system at nearly 600 kilometers in diameter and 20 kilometers in height, owes its great size to continuous outpouring of lava at one spot. This long-term coupling of a magma source at depth has allowed Martian volcanoes to build over long periods of time, as long as the mantle plume was active—probably hundreds of millions of years. In contrast, the largest volcanoes on Earth, the Hawaiian Islands, do not grow to such large dimensions because they are cut off from their source as the Pacific plate continues to move over the hot spot. Although early models attempted to fit Venus to a plate tectonic theory, there is no strong evidence for large-scale crustal spreading or subduction. The distribution and shape of large volcanic features on the surface of the planet are more consistent with mantle plume-driven volcanism similar to that of Mars and with intraplate volcanism on Earth, as are the active volcanoes on Io, a satellite of Jupiter.

Methods of Study

The recognition of plate tectonics as a major explanation for the large-scale structure of the earth's surface largely grew out of attempts to understand the morphology and structure of the ocean floor. The ocean floor was the last and greatest unexplored terrain of the earth's surface, primarily because of its inaccessibility. With the advent of technology that would allow the depths of the ocean to be sounded following World War II, the physiography and geology of the ocean floor was exposed. What was once assumed to be a rather featureless abyssal plain was found to contain myriad features, including fracture zones, midoceanic mountain ranges, and seamounts. As the theory of plate tectonics grew, it became necessary to explain the isolated volcanoes, groups of islands and island chains that are not explained by plate tectonics and yet are obvious in the Pacific Ocean. J. Tuzo Wilson, an important figure in the development of the plate tectonics theory, first advanced the concept of hot spots in the early 1960's, and the theory was amplified by Jason Morgan in the early 1970's. Radiometric age-dating of the islands and seamounts of the Hawaiian-Emperor Chain was not completed until the 1980's.

Mineralogical and chemical studies have been employed to compare and contrast basalts of the oceanic islands to those of the midoceanic ridges and to continental volcanic materials. The plume-related volcanic rocks are much more diverse in composition than the spreading-center basalts, which suggests that the mantle is quite heterogeneous. Experimental crystallization studies and mantle xenoliths provide information regarding the composition of the mantle at the source where the magmas form. Phase studies indicate that intraplate magmas form at greater depths (60 to 100 kilometers) than those of the midoceanic ridges (20 to 40 kilometers). Geophysical data indicate that little or no melting actually occurs in the lithosphere immediately beneath the oceanic island volcanoes; this supports the idea that magmas actually come from deeper in the mantle. The development of techniques for seismic tomography, which allows a three-dimensional imaging of the location of seismic-wave velocity throughout the mantle, is providing a clearer picture of the distribution of temperatures within the mantle. It is now possible to image upwelling currents and descending slabs within the mantle as three-dimensional models.

Relative positions of the islands and radiometric studies of the ages of basalts on the various islands and seamounts of the Hawaiian-Emperor Chain provide a record of the Pacific plate motion over the last seventy million years. The big island of Hawaii is currently active. Volcanic rocks of Maui are dated as from zero to 1.3 million years old; rocks of Oahu are 2.3 million to 3.3 million years old; and those of Kauai are 3.8 million to 5.6 million years old. Midway Island, 2,400 kilometers to the northwest, is 27.2 million years old. The entire Hawaiian-Emperor Chain is 6,000 kilometers long and more than 70 million years old. The Pacific plate is drifting to the northwest at approximately 8.8 centimeters per year. A bend in the chain 700 kilometers northwest of Midway Island, which marks a change in the direction of plate motion, is dated at 43 million years. Other chains of the Pacific Ocean basin exhibit a progression of ages similar to that of the Hawaiian chain, as well as a similar shift in direction of motion. This date, associated with the bend, correlates to some tectonic events in western North America and to the time that the Indian subcontinent collided with Asia.

Context

An understanding of intraplate volcanism is important to understanding the internal mechanisms that continue to shape the ever-changing surface of the earth. Unlike igneous activity associated with continental margins, intraplate volcanism plays a minor role in the origin of tangible economic resources. The diamond-bearing kimberite pipes of South Africa may be associated with prerift arching over a mantle plume; however, for the most part, intraplate volcanoes are not associated with significant ore deposition. The volcanoes may be important as a local source aggregate and building materials; however, their economic potential is chiefly a function of secondary factors such as location, scenery, and habitat. The chief economic value of the oceanic intraplate volcanoes is tied to their location as way stations in the vast Pacific Ocean. The islands provide a source of fresh water and a habitat for terrestrial plant and animal life. The shallow waters surrounding the islands provide favorable conditions for a diverse marine ecology. Fringing reefs built by coral and other marine organisms in shallow water on the coast of volcanic islands survive as atolls enclosing shallow lagoons after subsidence of extinct volcanoes. Some coral islands rooted on foundered extinct volcanoes become nesting grounds for seabirds. The phosphate-rich guano reacts with limestone to form phosphate rock, a much sought after component used in fertilizer manufacture.

The lava beds of the Columbia River basalts are important groundwater reservoirs in the northwestern United States. Geysers and hot springs of the Yellowstone area are famous for their scenic qualities. Areas of active or recent volcanism are important as potential sources of hydrothermal energy.

Intraplate volcanoes are subject to the same volcanic hazards as any other volcanically active region. Earthquakes, landslides, and lava flows are potential hazards to inhabitants of such areas. Although intraplate volcanoes are less explosive than volcanoes associated with convergent plate margins, volcanic activity on the big island of Hawaii is, nevertheless, responsible for the destruction of roads, homes, businesses, and government buildings. On the positive side, recent eruptions are responsible for adding new land to the island.

Bibliography

Burke, K. C., and J. Tuzo Wilson. "Hot Spots on the Earth's Surface." *Scientific American*, August, 1979. A description of "hot spots" by one of the first proponents of the concept. The authors describe the occurrence and probable mechanisms of hot-spot origin and its relationship to continental rifting.

Decker, R. W., and B. B. Decker. *Mountains of Fire: The Nature of Volcanoes*. New York: Cambridge University Press, 1991. An extremely lucid description of Earth's volcanoes and their relationship to plate tectonics.

Francis, P. W. *Volcanoes*. Harmondsworth, England: Pelican Books, 1976. Written for the general reader, this book provides a clear description of volcanic phenomenon. Makes good use of eyewitness accounts of major volcanic events, ranging from that of Vesuvius in A.D. 79 to more recent activity.

Frankel, Charles. *Volcanoes of the Solar System*. New York: Cambridge University Press, 1996. Describes volcanism on Earth and proceeds to discuss the Moon, Mercury, Mars, Venus, Io, and the icy satellites of Jupiter, Saturn, and Uranus. The text is suitable for the general reader, but it contains enough detail for introductory earth science students.

Tilling, R. I., C. Heliker, and T. L. Wright. *Eruptions of Hawaiian Volcanoes: Past, Present, and Future*. Washington, D.C.: U.S. Geological Survey, 1987. Offers a comprehensive description of the world's most famous and most intensively studied hot spot.

René De Hon

Cross-References

Continental Rift Zones, 275; Earth's Mantle, 555; Hot Spots and Volcanic Island Chains, 1079; Lithospheric Plates, 1387; The Ocean Ridge System, 1826; Plate Motions, 2071; Seamounts, 2274; Volcanoes: Flood Basalts, 2630; Volcanoes: The Hawaiian Islands, 2638; Volcanoes: Plumes and Megaplumes, 3157.

VOLCANOES: MOUNT PINATUBO

Type of earth science: Geology
Field of study: Volcanology

The eruption of Mount Pinatubo in June, 1991, was the second most violent eruption of the century. The use of modern techniques of eruption prediction and danger assessment allowed the safe evacuation of nearly 150,000 people from the area adversely affected by the eruption.

Principal terms

ASH: small fragments of volcanic material less than two millimeters in diameter formed by explosive ejection from a vent

CALDERA: a large circular depression around a summit vent that typically forms by collapse when large volumes of magma are rapidly ejected

DOME: a small, steep-sided mass of volcanic rock formed from nonexplosive, viscous lava that solidifies in or above a vent

FUMAROLE: a volcanic vent from which only gases are emitted

HARMONIC TREMOR: a type of earthquake activity in which the ground undergoes continuous shaking in response to subsurface movement of magma

LAHAR: a volcanic mudflow resulting from the mixing of erupted lava and ash with surface water, rain, or melted snow

PYROCLASTIC FLOW: a turbulent, dense mixture of volcanic gases, magma, ash, and rock that is ejected from a vent and flows rapidly down the flanks of a volcano

STRATOVOLCANO: a large, steep-sided volcano consisting of alternating layers of coherent lava and explosively ejected fragmental material; also called a "composite volcano"

Summary of the Phenomenon

Mount Pinatubo is one of the nearly three hundred active volcanoes that rim the Pacific Ocean basin in a narrow belt called the "Ring of Fire." This stratovolcano had been dormant since the Philippines were first settled by the Spanish in 1541. The awakening of Mount Pinatubo was of considerable concern to the United States because Clark Air Base was located only 20 kilometers to the east of the summit, and the Subic Bay Naval Station was 40 kilometers to the southwest.

Pinatubo rumbled into activity on April 2, 1991, when a series of small explosions formed a row of craters 1.5 kilometers long just northwest of the volcano's summit. The explosions lasted several hours and deforested an area of several square kilometers. Villagers living on the volcano's flank reported hearing the explosions and awoke the morning of April 3 to find a row of fumaroles extending along the western side of Pinatubo. Civil officials evacuated a circular area in a 10-kilometer radius from the volcano's summit.

During all of April and the early part of May, Mount Pinatubo experienced dozens of small earthquakes each day as magma began to move beneath the volcano. Magma fractured the brittle rocks as it cleared a pathway upward to form a shallow magma body. The center of the earthquake activity was about 5 kilometers northwest of the summit and 4 kilometers below the surface.

During May, the earthquake activity increased, with more than 1,800 low-intensity quakes being recorded between May 7 and June 1. During the last two weeks of May, the fumaroles showed a tenfold increase in the emission of sulfur dioxide.

At the beginning of June, a second area began to experience a series of shallow earthquakes several kilometers closer to the summit. The magma was rising beneath the volcano, and it was forcing a conduit to form above the magma chamber. The rate of emission of gas reversed its May trend, decreasing from a production of 5,000 tons of sulfur dioxide on May 28 to a production of 1,800 tons on May 30; by June 5, the total had dropped to only 260 tons. Apparently, the rising magma had sealed the fractures that allowed the escaping gases to reach the fumaroles.

On June 3, a series of small explosions blew ash from the summit area, and the earthquakes moved into a type of activity called "harmonic tremor": a prolonged rhythmic shaking of the earth, in contrast to the single sharp jolts of earlier earthquakes. Harmonic tremor occurs when underground magma flows in a more continuous manner through established subsurface channels. On June 6, the summit region of the volcano began to bulge outward, with the upper flank showing a measurable increase in the slope of the land surface. As the tilting increased, there was an increase in earthquake activity, leading to a strong shock and explosion on June 7. This explosion sent a column of ash and steam to a height of between 7 and 8 kilometers. The explosion allowed the summit area to stop its inflation temporarily, and there was a brief period of reduced earthquake activity. Based upon these warning signs, the area of evacuation was extended to a radius of 15 kilometers.

Magma first appeared on the surface of the volcano the next morning, June 8. Observers reported that a small lava dome 150 meters in diameter was growing near one of the fumaroles just northwest of the summit. The vents associated with this dome emitted a series of weak ash clouds that rose only to the level of Pinatubo's summit over a three-day period ending on June 12. During this interval, harmonic tremors occurred almost continuously. An examination of the composition of ejected ash revealed that a new, very fluid magma had invaded an old magma chamber that contained residual magma from the last eruption nearly five hundred years ago. This intruding magma signaled the potential of a major eruption, and authorities extended the evacuation area to a radius of 20 kilometers from the volcano. On June 10, fourteen thousand U.S. servicemen left Clark Air Base along with their aircraft, never to return. They left behind three helicopters and a contingent of fifteen hundred security and maintenance personnel.

The first major explosion of Pinatubo occurred at 8:51 A.M. on June 12, signaling the final and most powerful phase of the 1991 eruption. This very violent phase lasted about ten days, with the most intense activity occurring on June 15 and 16. The June 12 eruption lasted thirty-five minutes and spewed a column of steam and ash to a height of 19 kilometers. A small pyroclastic flow traveled a short distance from the vent down the northern flank of the volcano into already evacuated villages along the Maraunot River. Clark Air Base evacuated six hundred maintenance personnel, and Filipino authorities extended the evacuation zone to a 30-kilometer radius. Ash from the eruption was so dense and spread so far that the airport in Manila, more than 50 kilometers away, was forced to close.

Similar explosions continued over the next few days, producing ash clouds that prevented visibility of the volcano. The arrival of Typhoon Yunya on June 13 meant that most of these explosions were completely unseen from the ground. The associated earthquake activity was recorded by seismic stations, and the presence of an eruption cloud was verified by military weather radar.

Beginning on June 14, the main, violent phase peaked in a three-day period with more than fifty short, violent explosions in which numerous vents erupted simultaneously. The intensity of the earthquakes generated by these eruptions was more than a hundred times greater than those recorded during May. These eruptions grew progressively more violent during this time, sending ash to a height of more than 40 kilometers. At 5:55 A.M. on June 15, the ejected ash switched from a vertical orientation to a more horizontal one. The onset of laterally directed explosions indicated that the summit region was beginning to collapse. Several pyroclastic flows erupted and traveled up to 13 kilometers from the summit. The remaining personnel at Clark Air Base were evacuated that morning.

At about 3:30 P.M. on June 15, the climax occurred. A series of strong earthquakes started, lasting all afternoon and throughout the night. The seismographic equipment on the volcano was destroyed during the night by a series of large pyroclastic flows. Pyroclastic deposits that exceeded 200 meters in thickness formed in many valleys around the volcano. A 2-kilometer caldera formed when the summit area collapsed, causing the volcano to drop by more than 300 meters in elevation. About 0.8 cubic kilometer of ejected material covered the west-central portion of the island of Luzon. The falling ash blanketed villages and buried crops around the volcano. Many rooftops collapsed under the added weight of the ash, causing the majority of deaths attributed to the volcanic eruption. The total volume of ash ejected was close to 5 cubic kilometers, most of which fell into the South China Sea.

The water runoff from the heavy rains associated with the typhoon mixed with the recently fallen ash and caused disastrous volcanic mudflows known as "lahars." The lahars swept down twelve river valleys, including the Abacan and Sacobia River valleys, where the town of Angeles City was completely destroyed. Seven other towns were damaged by these mudflows. The July monsoons caused secondary lahars, one of which inundated the city of Pabanlog along the Gumain River. All these lahars destroyed bridges and farmland along the floodplains and caused widespread economic and social disruption. Special early-alert systems detected the lahars and sharply reduced the loss of life. However, the region continued to experience secondary lahars caused by heavy rains, and this threat was expected to last well into the twenty-first century.

The cloud associated with the June 15 eruption released four billion pounds of chlorine gas and forty billion pounds of sulfur dioxide into the stratosphere. By June 25, satellite images showed that a 7,750-kilometer-long cloud of sulfur dioxide had spread across the tropical Northern Hemisphere.

The gases and ash combined to produce an aerosol that blocked both incoming sunlight and infrared radiation emitted by the earth. The loss of solar radiation causes cooling, whereas the absorption of the earth's transmitted infrared radiation leads to global warming. The two effects did not balance equally, and by 1993, measurements from the National Aeronautics and Space Administration's Earth Radiation Budget Experiment satellite provided the first conclusive evidence of a significant change in global energy as the result of a volcanic eruption. The net effect of a loss of solar radiation and a greater retention of infrared radiation resulted in a period of global cooling in which the average global temperature dropped by one-half degree Celsius (about one degree Fahrenheit). Approximately 2 to 3 percent of the Sun's energy was blocked out, counteracting prevailing global-warming trends and temporarily setting the earth's climatological clock back to the 1950's.

The gases also altered the chemistry of the upper atmosphere. Three months after the eruption, there was 50 percent less ozone in the tropical stratosphere over an area roughly coincident with Mount Pinatubo's volcanic plume. The ozone layer over the United States was 10 percent thinner than normal, translating to a 20 to 30 percent increase in the amount of cancer-causing ultraviolet radiation reaching the earth's surface. There was fear that an ozone hole might open over the populated areas of the Northern Hemisphere; by 1996, however, measurements of the levels of ozone-depleting chemicals had dropped to lower-than-average values.

After June 16, the eruption slowly grew less intense. There were occasional ash explosions into 1992 that sent ash columns upward of 10 kilometers in height. During July and August of 1991, a dome grew in the fuming caldera that was 300 meters across and nearly 100 meters high. With an average of more than twenty centimeters of ash covering the region around Clark Air Base, base personnel were unable to stop ash infiltration into the jet engines, and the base had to be abandoned.

More than 108,000 homes were partially or totally destroyed. The final death toll for the region was 722; of these, 281 died as a result of ejected material either as ash falls or pyroclastic flows, 83 died from primary and secondary lahars, and 358 died from disease related to the social turmoil associated with the interruption of the country's infrastructure. The loss of life was undoubtedly compounded by the typhoon that hit the island during the climax of the eruption.

The world's largest volcanic eruptions have all produced global climate and atmospheric changes. Fine volcanic ash and gases are blasted into the high atmosphere and dispersed around the world. Upper-level winds can keep volcanic ash suspended in the atmosphere for many years. The suspended ash from Mount Pinatubo's eruption produced colorful sunsets worldwide in 1991 and 1992.

Methods of Study

The successful evacuation of nearly 150,000 people during the Mount Pinatubo eruption required both successful short-term forecasting of eruption events and a well organized program of danger assessment. The activities that transpired during the ten weeks from the first steam explosion on April 2 to the culminating eruption of June 15 were a model of cooperation between scientific personnel, Filipino authorities, and the local citizenry. Immediately following the first gas explosion, volcanologists from the U.S. Geological Survey joined forces with other scientists from the Philippine Institute of Volcanology and Seismology to coordinate the scientific work of eruption prediction. They jointly established the Pinatubo Volcano Observatory (PVO).

Modern eruption prediction involves determining the nature of the volcano's past eruptions and monitoring the active volcano for any changes in its physical and chemical behavior. An array of scientific equipment must be deployed around the volcano and the active vents to measure earthquake activity, volumes and composition of emitted gases, changes in the slope of the land surface, changes in the horizontal distance across vents and fissures, and fluctuations in the temperature of the volcano.

Active volcanoes have sporadic eruptions that are separated by time intervals called "periods of repose." Most active volcanoes display a repetitive history in terms of their repose interval, their eruptive violence, and the kinds of materials that they expel. The nature of a future eruption can often be established by an examination of the geological record of previous eruptions.

The PVO team realized the value of knowing the previous eruptive history at Mount Pinatubo and did a rapid geological reconnaissance of the volcano during the month following the initial steam explosion. They found that three previous eruptions had occurred at about 500 years ago, 2,500 years ago, and 4,800 years ago. Each eruption had been dominated by highly explosive activity. Pyroclastic flows had swept down the volcano's flanks, leaving deposits more than 20 kilometers from the summit. Debris from lahars from these prehistoric eruptions were found in six river valleys leading away from the volcano for a distance of more than 40 kilometers.

On the basis of their geological study of past eruptions, the PVO team compiled a hazard map showing the regions that were likely to be affected by pyroclastic flows, ash fall, and lahars. The map was used by both civil defense officials and military commanders during the various stages of the eruption. A map of the areas affected by the actual 1991 eruption shows a remarkable correlation with the pre-eruption hazard map. A videotape depicting the various volcanic hazards was produced by filmmaker and geologist Maurice Krafft, and the film aired repeatedly on local television.

Danger assessment is a complex task that goes beyond the accurate forecasting of eruptions. For example, in 1985, the Nevado del Ruiz volcano erupted in a region of Colombia that was much less populated than the area around Mount Pinatubo. The eruption generated a mudflow that killed twenty-five thousand people. Although volcanologists were successful in predicting the eruption and recommended evacuation of the region, the civil authorities did not view the impending eruption to be particularly dangerous, and no evacuation occurred.

The PVO team worked closely with civil and military personnel to assess the level of danger posed by the various stages of the Mount Pinatubo eruption. Using the hazard map and the video, the Filipino scientists developed a five-level alert system. Alert level 1 was to be declared when low-level seismic activity was coupled with fumarolic emission. The level 1 alert occurred on April 3, when fumaroles developed in a row along the northwest flank of Mount Pinatubo. Alert level 2 was to be invoked when moderate levels of seismic activity occurred and there was positive evidence for the existence of subsurface magma. Level 2 was reached in late May, when 1,800 earthquakes were recorded within a three-week interval.

Authorities were instructed to interpret alert level 3 to mean that the magma was intruding into the volcano and could eventually lead to a major eruption. Level 3 was to be issued when high levels of gas emission occurred with simultaneous ground deformation. This level of danger was attained on June 5. Level 3 meant that a major pyroclastic eruption could occur within two weeks; it actually occurred ten days later. Alert level 4 was to be issued when extensive harmonic tremors indicated the magma was moving more freely beneath the volcano. Level 4 was announced immediately following the June 7 explosion at Pinatubo that generated the 7-kilometer-high ash column. Civil authorities were told that level 4 meant that a major pyroclastic eruption was possible within twenty-four hours. The highest level of danger assessment was alert level 5, which meant that an eruption was in progress. This level was issued on June 9, after a pyroclastic flow engulfed several evacuated villages on the northern flank of Pinatubo. The day after the level 5 alert was issued, the U.S. military evacuated fourteen thousand personnel from Clark Air Base.

Context

The violent eruption of Mount Pinatubo was classified as a magnitude 6. The largest recorded eruption has been classified as magnitude 7, and the largest geologically known eruption has been ranked as a magnitude 8. Such violent eruptions as these have historically caused high death tolls. However, as shown by Mount Pinatubo experience, the most dangerous volcanoes can cause far fewer deaths when proper surveillance is employed.

There are nearly three hundred active volcanoes that should be monitored for the eruption of pyroclastic flows and lahars, and many of these volcanoes are located in underdeveloped countries. Surveillance and risk-reduction programs are very expensive, requiring equipment, trained scientists, education programs for local populations, and development of cooperative military and civil planning. The expenses associated with such programs are beyond the capabilities of many less-developed countries. Consequently, the United States, Russia, Iceland, Italy, and Japan lead the world in this field of volcanology.

The United States has two facilities dedicated to monitoring active volcanoes, both staffed by geologists from the U.S. Geological Survey. The Hawaiian Volcano Observatory has been successfully predicting eruptions of Mount Kilauea for over forty years. After the eruption of Mount St. Helens in 1980, the Cascades Volcano Observatory was established to monitor magma amounts and movements beneath the active volcanoes in Washington, Oregon, and northern California. Japan has twenty-one volcano observatories.

It is very likely that Mount Pinatubo will erupt again, although the volcano has entered a period of repose that may last as long as a few hundred years. The volcano is located on the margin of two converging plates that have produced a very active chain of volcanoes. For example, Mount Mayon lies 300 kilometers to the south of Pinatubo and has had more than forty historical eruptions, with the last as recent as 1993. A key factor indicating continued life for Mount Pinatubo is that a 1996 study found that between forty and one hundred cubic kilometers of magma remained in a reservoir below the volcano's summit. This volume is the largest quantity of magma (by almost a factor of three) ever detected beneath any volcano.

Bibliography

Bullard, F. M. *Volcanoes of the Earth*. Austin: University of Texas Press, 1976. A good scientific treatment of volcanoes and volcanic products. Well written; does not require a geological background. The author, an experienced volcanologist, relies heavily on his own experiences, photographs, and drawings.

Francis, Peter. *Volcanoes: A Planetary Perspective*. New York: Oxford University Press, 1993. A thorough coverage written for the general reader. The book includes forty pages on pyroclastic flows and twenty-five pages on lahars. Well illustrated; gives numerous historic examples.

Robinson, Andrew. *Earth Shock, Hurricanes, Volcanoes, Earthquakes, Tornadoes, and Other Forces*. New York: Thames & Hudson, 1993. Chapter 4 is devoted to volcanoes and gives a humanistic accounting of many historic eruptions, interwoven with excellent scientific commentary.

Wolfe, Edward W. "The 1991 Eruptions of Mount Pinatubo, Philippines." *Earthquakes and Volcanoes* 23, no. 1 (1992): 5-35. The public report of the successful emergency response of the United States to the geologic danger presented by the 1991 eruption of Mount Pinatubo.

Dion C. Stewart

Cross-References

VOLCANOES: PLUMES AND MEGAPLUMES

Type of earth science: Geology
Field of study: Volcanology

A plume is a pipe that extends into the mass of hot rocks that exist in the mantle of the earth and brings them to the surface, forming a "hot spot." A megaplume is a supermass of extremely hot rocks that moves very slowly under the surface of the earth and influences the breakup of tectonic plates.

Principal terms

CRUST: the rock and other material that make up the earth's outer surface

GUYOT: a formation made by plume activity in the ocean that has a flat top that is wholly under water

HOT SPOT: a heat source fed by a plume that reaches deep into the earth and produces molten rock

MAGMA: molten rock generated deep within the earth that is brought to the surface by volcanoes and plumes

MANTLE: the part of the earth below the crust and above the core composed of dense, iron-rich rocks

PLATE TECTONICS: the theory that accounts for the major features of the earth's surface in terms of the interactions of the continental plates that make up the surface

SEAMOUNT: an isolated dome formed under the sea by plumes reaching a height of at least 2,300 feet

TECTONICS: the history of the larger features of the earth, rocks and mountains, islands and continents, and the forces and movements that produce them

Summary of the Phenomenon

There are more than a hundred regions of the world known as "hot spots," which are fed by plumes of hot rock rising from deep in the earth's mantle. These hot spots are responsible for a particular type of volcanic activity, which, unlike other active volcanoes, has its origins deep in the interior of the earth. Plumes are found far away from the most active centers of volcanic activity and are usually most active in flat landscapes or at the bottom of oceans rather than in mountainous regions, as is true of more-typical volcanoes.

The hot spots come from material found deep within the earth's mantle, the solid layer of rocks that extends to more than 3,000 miles below the earth's surface, just above the core. Plumes apparently arise in regions of the mantle that are stirred about as the large continental plates that cover part of the earth move slowly across the surface. This movement of plates has been going on since early in the earth's history, beginning at least 4.6 billion years ago, when the earth's crust was just forming. As the huge plates of rock that make up the continents formed, they were originally one giant mass, but they began breaking up and moving apart at a fraction of an inch per year. "Plate tectonics," as the study of these movements is called, describes how the continents reached their present locations; they are still moving apart, and still only by fractions of an inch every year. The plate movement helps explain the building of mountain ranges, for as the plates crash into one another, they push their margins up into mountains such as the Himalayas and the Andes. Plate movement also helps scientists to understand the activities of volcanoes. Most volcanic activity occurs in those areas where the six major plates that make up the earth's surface (the Eurasian, American, African, Pacific, Indian, and Antarctic plates) come together. At these margins of plate contact, the pressure of the plates pressing against one another creates fissures and breaks in the earth's surface, through which magma—the hot, molten material coming from deep in the mantle—can flow. The plates that form the continents are called "continental plates." Other plates are found at the bottom of the oceans; these are called "oceanic plates."

As the plumes of mantle material move upward toward the surface, they feed and create what are called "hot spot" volcanoes. These range in size according to how deep the plume has reached into the depths of the earth. The deepest plumes create the largest volcanoes. The material coming up through the plumes (magma) consists of gigantic blobs of melted rock. Plumes and the hot spots connected to them move much more slowly than the continents above them. When one of the continental plates crosses over a plume, the magma flowing upward creates a large structure that looks like a dome. Such domes are usually about 125 miles wide and can be hundreds of miles long. Approximately 10 percent of the earth's surface is covered with these domelike structures. As the magma continues to burst upward, the dome increases in size; as it does, cracks and small openings appear, and the hot magma flows through these openings onto the surface. The most well-known domes created by plumes are the Hawaiian Islands. Geologists believe that all of the islands in the Hawaiian chain were created from a single plume. As the Pacific plate passed over the hot spot, the islands popped up and out from the ocean floor, and the plume pumped huge quantities of magma into and out of the resulting dome.

Of the hundred or so hot spots, more than half are found on the continental plates, with about twenty-five found in Africa. The African plate has remained over these hot spots for millions of years. The shape of the continent, which is covered by hundreds of basins, domes, and ridges, was greatly influenced by the slow movement of the continental plate over these plume-fed hot spots. Hot spots are also found in great numbers under the Antarctic and Eurasian plates. It seems likely that hot spots are more likely to be found under slow-moving plates, since those continents moving more rapidly, such as North and South America, have only a very few areas of volcanic activity caused by hot spots.

One area in North America located over a hot spot is Yellowstone National Park. The hot spot below the park creates the many geysers, including Old Faithful, that are found in the region. Geysers are created when surface water seeps into the ground. When it comes in contact with boiling magma, the water is heated rapidly; it then boils upward until it explodes through cracks in the earth's crust.

Hot spots do have a limited life span. Typically, a plume feeding a hot spot cools off and disappears after about 100 million years. Their positions also change. The plume feeding the Yellowstone geysers originated farther to the north, around the Snake River in Idaho, 400 miles away, around 15 million years ago. Over time, the North American plate has slipped across it, putting the hot spot in its present location. Yet Yellowstone, too, is only a temporary home for this hot spot, and its slow movement to the southwest continues. The slow drift accounts for the volcanic activity in the area. Scientists believe that at least three major volcanic eruptions have taken place in this region during the last two million years. They predict that another massive explosion, hundreds of times greater than the huge Mount St. Helens eruption in 1981, will hit the area sometime in the next few thousand years.

Methods of Study

The hot-spot theory is an important contribution to the science of plate tectonics. Few geologists doubt the existence of these hot spots and the plumes that create them. One of the most intensely studied hot spots is the dome that makes up the North Atlantic island of Iceland. This megaplume, which was raised above the ocean floor more than 16 million years ago, lies across a formation known as the Mid-Atlantic Ridge. The dome is actually about 900 miles long, but only about 350 miles of it—Iceland—lies above sea level. To the south of the island, the dome tapers off gradually and dips below the sea. In 1918, a volcanic eruption under a glacier to the north of Iceland melted enough ice to create an oceanic flood of water that was twenty times greater than the yearly flow of the Amazon River, the world's largest river. Luckily, the floodwater did not hit land, or many islands and the European coastline would have been devastated.

Within the next few million years, a very short period in geologic time, the Mid-Atlantic Ridge will have moved away from the hot spot, carrying Iceland with it. This will dry up the source of magma supplying the volcanoes on Iceland. They will no longer erupt, and Iceland will become a cold, ice-covered, uninhabitable, island.

Most volcanic hot spots never rise above sea level and remain as underwater volcanoes. Magma erupting from these plumes forms structures called "seamounts." These are isolated, though they form into long chains along the surface of the oceanic plate. A few seamounts are found with extensive fissures and cracks; in these cracks, magma has cooled over hundreds of thousands of years, piling up thousands of magma flows, one on top of the other. A few of these are high enough to break through the ocean's surface. These seamounts become volcanic islands and dot various ridges in the crust, forming island chains such as the Galapagos Islands off the west coast of Ecuador. The tallest seamounts rise more than two and one-half miles above the sea floor and are found to the east of the Philippine Islands, where the crust is over 100 million years old. Generally, the older the crust, the larger the number of undersea volcanoes. The majority of seamounts are found in the Pacific Ocean, where there are between five and ten volcanic hot spots in every 5,000 miles of ocean floor. The Hawaiian Islands were created as the oceanic plate passed over a plume and formed the Emperor Seamounts, the name used by students of plate tectonics to refer to the Hawaiian Island chain.

Other plumes, in ancient geological times, formed undersea volcanoes called guyots (pronounced "ghee-ohs"). Dozens of these once rose high above the Pacific Ocean. Over millions of years, however, constant wave action eroded the tops of these guyots below the sea's surface. Guyots, over time, moved away from their sources of magma, the hot spots, and this also helps to account for their disappearance beneath the ocean.

In the Atlantic, volcanic islands formed from plumes are found along the mid-ocean ridge. The Azores and Ascension Islands appear on this ridge. The location of these island chains and hot spots can help scientists understand the movement of tectonic plates. The plumes appear to be fixed in relationship to one another and move at velocities of only a few millionths of an inch each year. Sophisticated measuring instruments can account for this movement, however. They also move in what appear to be well-established tracks, and as they move, their heat weakens the rocks above. Over time, these weakened surfaces begin to crack, causing rifts, or giant cracks in the earth. Some of these rifts become huge valleys, such as that found in the East African nation of Ethiopia.

The plumes described above are moderate in size and are considered to be a normal part of the earth's mantle. Some geologists are convinced, however, that once, millions of years ago, the earth went through an extremely intense period of volcanic eruptions. During this period, giant megaplumes exploded from deep within the earth, expelling huge quantities of molten material. These structures spread across the earth's surface, becoming ten times larger than average plumes. These "superplume" explosions were responsible for the volcanic activity that affected the ocean floor during the mid-Cretaceous period about 90 million to 100 million years ago. One result of this unusually violent activity was the creation of hundreds of seamounts in the western Pacific. Another area affected by these megaplumes was the Parana River basin in Brazil, where hundreds of rift valleys were created. It was also during this time that the Andes Mountains in South America and the Sierra Nevada in the western United States were formed.

Megaplume activity during the mid-Cretaceous led to a 100-foot rise in sea level and a 10-degree increase in the temperature of the earth's air. This increase was caused by the release of huge amounts of carbon dioxide into the air during volcanic explosions. A key result of this activity was an enormous increase in plankton, the microscopic organisms that drift in the oceans and are the first link in the ocean's food chain. As the plankton died, they devolved into huge deposits of oil. Perhaps 50 percent of the world's known oil supply dates to this period of megaplume activity. The volcanic activity of the giant plumes also brought large quantities of diamonds from the earth's interior closer to the surface, from which they are mined.

Context

Plumes and megaplumes have had a dramatic influence on the history of the earth. Plume activity has created islands, volcanoes, valleys, and mountains. The superheated rocks brought from far within the interior of the earth have helped to form geysers, oil deposits, and diamonds. Tracking the slow movement of hot spots can help scientists to predict future events, such as the possibility of volcanic eruptions or the creation of new rift valleys. The study of past volcanic explosions can help scientists to keep the public informed about the potential harm that can be expected from future eruptions of plumes. Volcanic eruptions have occurred periodically throughout the earth's history. From a geological point of view, periods of intense volcanic activity last for relatively brief spans of time, perhaps from 2 million to 3 million years. There are particularly intense periods of major activity every 32 million years. These latter periods—and the mid-Cretaceous period might have been one of them—coincide with mass extinctions of life, as volcanic gases flow into the atmosphere, releasing thousands of tons of sulphur and other dangerous chemicals. Some of the released gases are converted into acids that also have a devastating impact on living things. Hot spots and megaplumes expel huge amounts of ash, dust, and molten rock from their cracks and fissures. These materials absorb the Sun's radiation and can cause intense heating or cooling of the atmosphere. The dust can also shade out the Sun's light for long periods of time. The reduced sunlight can, again, cause mass extinctions of plants and animals because of the extreme cold produced. Intense volcanic activity can also produce acid rain, which could kill the leaves of plants and make the oceans and lakes unlivable. Scientists believe that the earth has been victimized by such violent activity at least three times in the past, the last time being about 65 million years ago. Hot spots and megaplumes were responsible for much of this violent volcanic activity.

Bibliography

Ballard, Robert D. *Exploring Our Living Planet*. Washington, D.C.: National Geographic Society, 1983. A well-illustrated guide to modern theories of continental drift, plate tectonics, and the activities of volcanoes. A good place to begin an investigation of the history of the earth's formation and the various forces that have created the earth's features. Includes pictures, maps, and an index.

Eicher, Don L., A. Lee McAlester, and Marcia L. Rottman. *The History of the Earth's Crust*. Englewood Cliffs, N.J.: Prentice-Hall, 1984. A brief introduction to plate tectonics and geological history. A good beginning for those unfamiliar with the topic. Useful illustrations, charts, and an index.

Erickson, Jon. *Plate Tectonics: Unraveling the Mysteries of the Earth*. New York: Facts on File, 1992. An excellent, well-written, easily understandable description of the forces shaping the earth's geology, including a detailed and illustrated discussion of plumes and hot spots. Megaplumes, however, are not described. A very good introduction to the subject. Illustrations, bibliography, index.

Kearey, Philip, and Frederick J. Vine. *Global Tectonics*. 2d ed. London: Blackwell Science, 1996. A textbook, written in somewhat technical language; nevertheless contains some good illustrations and a detailed discussion of megaplumes. Designed for college courses in geology. Index and up-to-date bibliography.

Seyfert, Charles K., and L. A. Sirkin. *Earth History and Plate Tectonics: An Introduction to Historical Geology*. New York: Harper & Row, 1973. A textbook for geology students, but easy to understand and well illustrated. Read this book after consulting some of the briefer descriptions of the formation of the earth's mantle and crust.

Sullivan, Walter. *Continents in Motion: The New Earth Debate*. New York: McGraw-Hill, 1974. A somewhat dated but still useful summary of the differing points of view of various theorists of the earth's formation and how such views have changed over time. Popularly written; easily understood without a technical background in geology.

Leslie V. Tischauser

Cross-References

WATER QUALITY

Type of earth science: Hydrology
Field of study: Analytical techniques

The term "water quality" refers to the fitness of water for a defined use, such as for human consumption, and is measured in terms of chemical, physical, and biological parameters. Standards against which the quality of water is compared are neither universal nor constant and depend upon who has established the standards and for what purpose.

Principal terms

CONCENTRATION UNITS: a way to report results of a chemical analysis or to present a standard against which the quality of water is compared; commonly used units include milligrams/liter (mg/L) or micrograms/liter (mg/L)

CONTAMINANTS: solutes introduced into the hydrologic environment as a result of human activity, without regard to degree of degradation

DETECTION LIMIT: the lowest concentration of a constituent that can be detected reliably

MAXIMUM CONTAMINANT LEVEL GOALS (MCLGs): nonenforceable health goals

MAXIMUM CONTAMINANT LEVELS (MCLs): enforceable standards for drinking water, established by the U.S. Environmental Protection Agency under the Safe Drinking Water Act

NATIONAL PRIMARY DRINKING WATER STANDARDS: the list of MCLs and MCLGs for organic and inorganic constituents; the list also includes various standards for asbestos fibers, turbidity, bacteria, viruses, and radioactive emitting constituents, established using less common concentration units

POLLUTION: contaminant levels at objectionable concentrations

STANDARD: any measure, principle, or rule established by authority

Summary of the Methodology

Pure water composed of hydrogen and oxygen and nothing else does not exist in nature. Even rainwater contains measurable dissolved constituents in the range of 10 milligrams per liter. Water is of acceptable quality for a defined use or purpose if, on analysis, constituents in it do not exceed prescribed concentrations. Water quality involves fitness or suitability of water for a specific use, based upon chemical, physical, and biological parameters. Significant differences have arisen among scientific and engineering disciplines and government agencies as to which indicators are appropriate to evaluate water quality. The results of an analysis of water are commonly presented as indicators of water quality without the provision of a context of use or standards.

Standards against which the quality of water is compared are neither universal nor constant and depend upon who has established the standards and for what purpose. Legal standards are legally binding, prescribe conditions not to be exceeded for a water resource, and allow penalties for violations. Standards are changed through time as more becomes known about health effects, as analysts are able to detect ever smaller quantities of contaminants, and as governments apply standards to more situations.

This methodology of listing constituents and concentrations that must not be exceeded has undergone constant evolution. Prior to the establishment of formal criteria, odor, color, taste, turbidity, and temperature were measures used by humans in assessing the desirability of a drinking-water source. By 1784, less direct chemical criteria, involving the ability of a sample to dissolve soap without forming lumps or a residue were applied to establish whether water was drinkable. Chemical criteria alone, however, are insufficient for establishing a water supply as both drinkable and safe. The relationship between disease and pollution by human and animal wastes had been suspected or recognized for centuries. An early method of measuring the bacterial quality of water relied upon observing for how long a stored water sample remained free of visible growths. This was replaced by techniques to count bacteria and to compare measurements to a standard.

The U.S. Geological Survey (USGS) first reported chemical analyses of natural waters in 1879, and by 1901 had published more than twenty-five reports on the geologic control and chemical and physical properties of natural water. At that time, many water sources were pristine, unaffected by human activity. The composition (quality) of waters from lakes, rivers, and wells resulted from reactions with gases in the air and minerals in soil and rock. The major dissolved constituents, those generally with concentrations of more than 1 milligram per liter, are calcium, magnesium, sodium, potassium, bicarbonate, carbonate, chloride, sulfate, nitrate, and oxygen; these constitute up to 99 percent by weight of the dissolved matter in pristine waters. Under less common natural situations, other constituents such as iron or fluoride may exceed 1 milligram per liter concentration. Minor constituents are detected in pristine natural waters if sought by analysis. Of the major constituents, only sulfate and chloride are included in either the current U.S. primary or secondary drinking-water standards. Other major constituents are listed in standards of other organizations, such as the World Health Organization or the European Community.

After 1901, the USGS expanded its activities to include pollution studies, recognizing that sewage and industrial wastes were degrading the quality of water and adversely affecting municipal water supplies. In 1905, the USGS began the first monitoring program to assess the quality of streams and lakes, efforts that led to estimates of the amounts of dissolved and suspended matter carried to the oceans by rivers.

The U.S. Public Health Service (USPHS) was established in 1912 and was directed to study sanitary water quality. The U.S. Geological Survey continued studying water supplies for public use and for agricultural and industrial purposes and maintained limited networks to evaluate trends in water quality. In the United States, formal chemical water-quality standards originated by action of the USPHS in 1914. Dissolved constituents believed to be harmful to humans were identified, and maximum allowable concentrations were established. Water exceeding the limits could not be used for food preparation or for drinking water on passenger trains (interstate carriers) crossing state lines. The USPHS standards were widely, although unofficially, regarded as the basis for acceptability of a water supply for human consumption. The standards were expanded both in number of constituents covered and in lowered permissible concentrations in 1925, 1942, 1946, and 1962. The final set of standards promulgated by the USPHS, issued in 1962, considered bacterial quality, physical characteristics of turbidity, color, and odor, chemical characteristics, some mandatory and others recommended, and radioactivity. In earlier times of pristine sources in protected watersheds, water that required no extensive treatment was available, and one set of standards was sufficient for both raw water and drinking water. By 1962, modern civilization had affected many water sources, and raw water from degraded sources had to be treated so that the standards for drinking water were met at the point of delivery.

By the 1960's, industrial manufacturing of new chemical products and by-products and generation of wastes had resulted in contamination and pollution, some materials being persistent in the environment and affecting surface and groundwater supplies. Efforts to restrict degradation of water sources were underway in specific geographic areas ranging from small drainage basins to interstate commissions for river basins. The Environmental Protection Agency (EPA) was established in 1970 and given the task of setting goals and standards and identifying sources of polluting effluents. Federal legislation, including the Water Quality Act and Clean Water Act, led to broadened activities in documenting quality, mandating treatment and recovery, and requiring the establishment of standards for discharged waters. The National Pollutant Discharge Elimination System (NPDES) was established for all point source discharges into U.S. waters, involving permits, reporting, and effluent limitation. For situations where the limitations were not stringent enough to improve quality of receiving waters, treatment was required. The EPA was charged with developing a wide array of water-quality standards. An understanding of the degree to which the nation's waters are contaminated and what the water quality trends are was seen as essential to management decisions. The USGS was thus brought back into the process of monitoring surface and groundwater supplies, looking at contamination to a greater extent than before. The agency established the National Water Quality Assessment Program (NAWQA) to systematically study U.S. water, stream basin by stream basin.

The first set of drinking-water standards to be established by the EPA became effective in 1977, under mandates of the 1974 Safe Drinking Water Act. Among the inorganic contaminants, fluoride and mercury were newly added to the earlier USPHS standards, nitrate became a mandatory rather than recommended standard, and radioactive sources were redefined. This came about in large part because of better information about risks and health effects. The standards have undergone changes and extensions since 1977, including modifications authorized by the Safe Drinking Water Act Amendments of 1996. A prior mandate to the Environmental Protection Agency to regulate twenty-five new contaminants every three years has been set aside, replaced by a mandate to review at least five contaminants for possible regulation every five years, looking at the following criteria: whether the contaminant adversely affects human health; whether it is known or substantially likely to occur in public water systems with a frequency and at levels of public health concern; and whether regulation of the contaminant presents a meaningful opportunity for health-risk reduction. In addition, there are provisions for monitoring unregulated contaminants, creating an accessible database, and disclosing violations to the public served by water systems as rapidly as within twenty-four hours.

Domestic use, including drinking water, is considered by many to be the most essential use of water, and standards for drinking water receive the greatest attention. Water quality requirements for other purposes may be more restrictive (for example, for high-pressure boiler water) or less restrictive (for example, for hydraulic cement manufacture) than standards for domestic use.

Applications of the Method

In the earth sciences, water-quality studies generally have a focus beyond determining whether a water source is suitable for a given purpose. Larger questions of regional water quality, such as determining how and why water of certain characteristics is associated with a specific rock type or recognizing how and explaining why groundwater evolves chemically as it slowly moves through an aquifer, are examples of applications that center on understanding natural processes. More recently, the contamination and pollution of water resources has drawn considerable attention, leading to studies of the transport by water of pollutants. One example of applications of the methodology from the earth sciences should illustrate the disciplinary perspective.

Of the major constituents in natural waters, only sulfate is listed in the national primary drinking water standards. Sulfate in drinking water produces laxative effects and unpleasant taste. It is listed in the unenforceable national secondary drinking water standards for taste and laxative effects at a concentration of 250 milligrams per liter and is prohibited by the Primary Standards at 400 to 500 milligrams per liter. The sources of the sulfate are listed as "natural deposits."

As a result of the Safe Drinking Water Act and using data from the U.S. Geological Survey, a series of state maps was compiled to show the regional variation in concentration of major dissolved constituents in well water. A zone of high-sulfate water extends from Lake Erie across northwest Ohio and into east central Indiana. Water from wells in this area is of generally unacceptable quality. From the perspective of the earth sciences, it was important to build upon the recognition of this zone in order to determine probable cause. Obviously, such a study cannot exclude areas from which groundwater just passes the standards. Results from this study provide an understanding of the geologic controls on the system. High-sulfate water is recovered from shallow wells in glacial deposits and also from wells in a deeper bedrock aquifer. The situation is explained in part by the presence of gypsum and anhydrite, calcium sulfate minerals, in a sedimentary terrain characterized by shale and dolomite units. Glacial activity eroded formerly exposed bedrock of shale and anhydrite, moved it, and redeposited it as unconsolidated material over undisturbed bedrock, also containing anhydrite and dolomite. High values of sulfate in the water, at some wells exceeding 1,000 milligrams per liter, would ordinarily not be possible because of the solubility limits of calcium sulfate minerals. In such waters, magnesium values were elevated, and calcium values lower than expected. The conclusion is that in order for such high values of sulfate to exist in the water, a process known as dedolomitization is taking place, in which dolomite, a calcium magnesium carbonate mineral, is dissolved, and calcite, a calcium carbonate mineral, is deposited, in effect adding magnesium and removing calcium from the water. Without this process, such high values of sulfate would not be possible.

Contaminated waters may or may not be safe to drink. In addition to the constituents derived from natural sources, these waters contain (by definition) constituents derived from a variety of human activities, such as improperly treated sewage, storage tanks that have leaked, improper disposal of hazardous wastes, and agricultural practices. Many of the chemicals involved are manufactured and do not occur in nature. Standards for safe drinking water for most of these constituents range generally from tenths to several hundred micrograms per liter.

Maximum contaminant levels (MCLs) are derived from studies of risk to humans consuming two liters of water a day over a lifetime of seventy years. Based upon extrapolations of animal studies for a given contaminant, an increased cancer risk to humans of one in one million over a lifetime leads to the standard. By statute, no cancer risk is to be tolerated, but technology is not available to eliminate totally the very small concentrations in water resources of many contaminants. The maximum contaminant level goal is generally zero for MCLGs and a small concentration for MCLs.

Other water-quality standards, including national effluent standards for limiting discharge of pollutants into surface waters, have been established or enforced as a result of a number of federal laws and resultant regulations, including the Clean Water Act, which addresses water pollution from point and nonpoint sources; the Comprehensive Environmental Response, Compensation and Recovery Act (the "Superfund" Act), which mandates cleanup of hazardous-waste sites and leaking tanks; the Resource Conservation and Recovery Act, which defines and requires tracking and proper disposal of hazardous wastes; the National Environmental Policy Act, which establishes the need for environmental impact statements for federally controlled or subsidized actions; the Endangered Species Act, which protects some habitats; and the Wild and Scenic Rivers Act, which limits development along some rivers. States in some instances have established water-quality standards, similar to or more restrictive than the ones put forth by federal agencies.

Currently, management of water quality for effluents takes place through regulations applied to discharges from or into three distinct sites. End-of-pipe standards specify levels that must be met at the point from which effluent is discharged from an industrial facility. Technology-based standards impose regulations on a discharging facility. Assimilative capacity standards define the water-quality conditions that a receiving body of water (stream or lake) must not exceed. Dischargers to the stream or lake are identified, and those causing the stream or lake to exceed standards are required to manage the quality of their discharges.

Context

Life cannot exist without water, the most abundant substance at Earth's surface. From rainwater to brine, the waters of Earth display a great range in chemical composition and concentration of solutes. Waters may be pristine or contaminated by human activity. "Water quality" refers to the character of a water resource, in terms of chemical, physical, and biological measures, and water-quality standards have been established to indicate whether a water source is suitable for a particular use. Is a water source safe to drink? Is it also palatable? Has a water source been degraded to the point that the aquatic ecosystem is stressed?

At any instant, waters of Earth are located in specific reservoirs: in the atmosphere as water vapor, in ice caps and glaciers, in lakes and rivers, as moisture in the soil, as shallow groundwater, in living things, in the oceans, and as underground brines. In general, the waters in these reservoirs increase in concentration of solutes in the order listed. Similarly, the suitability for a specific use of water from the several reservoirs varies dramatically. Ocean water and brine are undrinkable, but minerals may be extracted from them; shallow groundwater, lakes, and rivers provide most drinking water.

Nature, through the operation of the hydrologic cycle, powered by energy from the Sun and affected by gravity and rotation of Earth, provides a mechanism that both replenishes quantities of water on the land and also refreshes the quality of water as rain and the surface waters of the lands. This natural process of refreshment helps to minimize that contamination and pollution that results from human activity.

Before governmental assurances that water was safe to drink, humans relied upon sight, taste, and odor. Discolored or turbid water, water with an unpleasant taste, or water that had an odor was avoided whenever possible. These indicators of water quality were not entirely reliable in themselves, but they have been quantified and added to a greater number of criteria for water quality and are used today. Where they proved unreliable in history was with respect to unseen bacteria. More recently, water kept in a vessel for several days was observed for visible growths as a simple means of checking for bacteria.

Governments have taken on the responsibility for assuring a safe water supply through the development of water-quality standards and requirements for water analysis. If a water supply, upon analysis, has lower concentrations of contaminants than a prescribed set of standards, then it is suitable for the use to which those standards apply.

Despite the many efforts that have been made to improve the U.S. water supply, there are sections of the country that have poor-quality water, and extensive treatment is required in order to bring it into compliance with standards. Poor water quality in some of these areas results solely from natural processes, but in many other areas results from human activity.

Bibliography

Berner, E. K., and R. A. Berner. *The Global Water Cycle*. Englewood Cliffs, N.J.: Prentice-Hall, 1987. An interdisciplinary text that provides chemical characterization of water as rain, soil and ground water, river water, lakes, estuaries, and oceans, and reports the relative importance of natural and human processes in the cycling of elements through the hydrologic cycle.

Fetter, C. W. *Contaminant Hydrogeology*. New York: Macmillan, 1993. An applied text for hydrogeologists and engineers that presents technical information on the collection and interpretation of data from contaminated groundwater sites and options for remediation of those sites.

Hem, J. D. *Study and Interpretation of the Chemical Characteristics of Natural Water*. 3d ed. (United States Geological Survey Water-Supply Paper 2254). Washington, D.C.: U.S. Government Printing Office, 1992. The term "natural water" refers to water in a real-world environment such as a lake. This introduction to water chemistry was written to serve geologists and hydrogeologists who need to evaluate water quality. The author provides practical information about low-temperature aqueous geochemistry using real-world examples. Offers an extensive list of references.

McKee, J. E., and H. W. Wolf. *Water Quality Criteria*. 2d ed. (State Water Resources Control Board, Publication 3A). Sacramento: State of California, 1971. The authoritative compendium of information about water quality through the 1960's, including criteria by state and interstate agencies, judicial expression, quality criteria for beneficial uses, and descriptions of potential pollutants. Provides nearly four thousand references to articles in the field.

Nash, H., and G. J. H. McCall, eds. *Groundwater Quality*. London: Chapman and Hall, 1965. Twenty papers report groundwater quality studies worldwide, excluding North America. Unacceptable groundwater quality results most commonly from anthropogenic pollution of aquifers, saline intrusion, and naturally occuring problems.

Office of Water, U.S. Environmental Protection Agency. *The Quality of Our Nation's Water*. Washington, D.C.: U.S. Government Printing Office, 1992. This government report summarizes the extent of water pollution as compiled from reports from the states in 1990 and 1991 generated under the requirements of the Clean Water Act. The report defines water-quality concepts and uses and summarizes pollutants and sources.

Perry, J., and E. Vanderklein. *Water Quality: Management of a Natural Resource*. Cambridge, Mass.: Blackwell Science, 1996. A text claiming that water quality is basically a social and political concern. The authors present a nonmathematical but comprehensive treatment of the subject, addressing broad issues such as ecological responses to stress, cultural dimensions of water-quality policy, and global implications of change. The writers review the evolution of the concepts of water quality and management and provide a perspective that could serve as a framework for further changes. Extensive bibliography.

Tchobanoglous, G., and E. D. Schroeder. *Water Quality*. Reading, Mass.: Addison-Wesley, 1985. A text for civil engineers and physical scientists that is mathematically rigorous and comprehensive in presentation of water quality and quantity, analytical methods for water-quality management, modeling of water quality in the environment, and modification of water quality.

Robert G. Corbett

Cross-References

Aquifers, 71; Drought, 2897; Environmental Health, 615; Freshwater Chemistry, 795; Great Lakes, 2938; Groundwater Movement, 1020; Groundwater Pollution, 1028; Groundwater Pollution Remediation, 1035; The Hydrologic Cycle, 1102; Lakes, 1318; Seawater Composition, 2282; Surface Water, 2504; Water in Magmas, 1433; Water-Rock Interactions, 2462; Water Wells, 2708; Waterfalls, 3171; Watersheds, 3178.

WATERFALLS

Type of earth science: Hydrology
Field of study: Geomorphology

Waterfalls are created by the steep descent of a stream over an escarpment or cliff. The fall may be perpendicular and free from the rock surface or may run across the rock, frequently in a series of falls. Waterfalls attract viewers for their scenic and aesthetic qualities, but they also possess scientific value as an aid in the interpretation of Earth history, and economic importance as possible sites for the generation of hydroelectric power.

Principal terms

CASCADE: a small waterfall or series of small falls
CATARACT: most frequently, an overwhelming flood or a great volume of flow over a cliff; sometimes, however, the term is used interchangeably with "cascade"
GRADE: a hypothetical profile of a stream seeking to achieve quasi-equilibrium
KNICKPOINT: a break in the stream profile, generally caused by a resistant rock layer that retards the rate of erosion
RAPIDS: a turbulent flow in a stream caused by obstructions in the channel or by resistant rock layers
RIFFLES: a smaller version of rapids, a turbulent flow between calm pools, found in nearly all streams for hydraulic reasons
TECTONICS (TECTONIC ACTIVITY): vertical or horizontal movements in the earth's crust, displacing rocks, landforms, and stream gradients

Summary of the Phenomenon

Waterfalls are breaks in the relatively smooth profiles of streams. The break in slope may be minor and result in only a riffle, or slight roughening of the water surface. All streams possess riffles, which are part of the hydraulic adjustment that permits streams to carry sediment. Rapids are a more profound interruption of the profile, sufficient to block the passage of most boats; rapids serve notice that the streambed has encountered resistance in the form of bedrock, boulders, or other obstructions. Some purists maintain that true waterfalls exist only where water falls free of its bed, plunging downward through the atmosphere. Except for the largest and most spectacular falls, however, free fall is generally a function of the amount of discharge in the stream channel, and discharge varies with weather and climate. Most of the world's streams have dry spells every year. During those droughty periods, a free-falling waterfall may become a cascade, a cataract, or even a rapids. The Great Falls of the Potomac River dried up to very weak rapids during a late 1960's drought, but they were still an obstruction to navigation and a potential site for waterpower development, possessed scenic appeal, and presented evidence to geologists of the underlying rock structure and its place in deciphering Earth's history. These are the major reasons why people are interested in waterfalls, whether they are a thousand meters high or less than ten, and whether they are free-falling or are better described as cascades, cataracts, or rapids.

Streams, on their route to the sea, lake, or some other termination, cut downward through loose sediments and bedrock, eroding and transporting some of this material as their sedimentary load. If the earth materials through which they are downcutting are relatively soft or weak, the stream ultimately will achieve grade, denoted by a smooth, upwardly concave profile. Waterfalls are an indication that something has prevented the stream from achieving an equilibrium between its discharge, or quantity of flow, and the sediment load it is carrying. The cause may lie in the structure of the underlying rocks, with particularly resistant layers being encountered in the course of the downcutting. Frequently, the stream cannot achieve a smooth profile because of some aberration of geologic history, such as rapid tectonic uplift or glacial deepening of a major valley. Most of Earth's relief is a consequence of tectonic uplift in the past few million years. It comes as no surprise that this is insufficient time for streams to achieve even quasi-equilibrium or grade in the highlands of the world, where complex geology often exposes rocks of varying resistance to weathering and stream downcutting. Resistant rock layers may be sandstones, as in much of the Appalachian Mountains and Colorado Plateaus. Dolomite forms the Niagara Escarpment, over which the Niagara River falls. The Niagara story, however, is more complicated than merely the encountering of a resistant dolomite rock layer by the downcutting river. Continental glaciation of the eastern and central United States and Canada obliterated the pattern of preglacial stream drainage, and the roughly twelve thousand years that Niagara Falls has been in existence is insufficient time for the stream to achieve grade. Similarly, the head of navigation on the Mississippi River is at St. Anthony Falls in Minneapolis, Minnesota; upstream of the falls, the Mississippi flows on a new, postglacial course. The head of navigation of the Ohio River is the falls at Louisville, Kentucky, only a short distance upstream from the mouth of the Ohio, where it joins the Mississippi. This peculiar situation led geologists to search for the preglacial Ohio River, which was discovered buried by glacial sediments in northern Indiana and Ohio. Niagara Falls, St. Anthony Falls, and the falls of the Ohio at Louisville may be considered as large and dramatic knickpoints, or breaks in the smooth stream profile. Knickpoints migrate upstream as erosion proceeds on its path toward grade or quasi-equilibrium, eventually becoming smaller and smaller until they are eliminated as significant breaks in the stream profile. Thus, waterfalls represent unusual and temporary geologic circumstances and contribute to scientific knowledge both in the quest for explanation of each individual waterfall and in the contribution to understanding of the geologic history of a region. The largest number of waterfalls worldwide undoubtedly occurs in younger, recently uplifted mountains that have been subjected to alpine glaciation. Just as major rivers have greater eroding capability than their tributaries, so larger valleys are occupied by larger glaciers, capable of cutting deeper into the bedrock. The glaciers of tributary valleys are much smaller and have less erosion potential than those in the main valleys. After the glaciers melt, the streams occupying the tributary valleys are left hanging, and they descend to the main stream as waterfalls. Hanging tributary valleys also occur in unglaciated uplands, but they are far more common in the spectacular scenery of alpine mountains, especially in the world's major fjord regions: Alaska and British Columbia, Norway, Chile, and New Zealand's South Island.

The scenic appeal of waterfalls is the reason most people find them of interest. The sheer grandeur of the falling water inspires artists, photographers, and writers, whose products enhance the waterfalls' fame and encourage multitudes to experience the view personally. The attraction of waterfalls is a significant factor in decisions to visit state and national parks and even roadside waysides. As a consequence, a sizable fraction of the expenditures of tourists can be attributed to the existence of waterfalls. Tourist counts are notoriously unreliable, but it is safe to say that millions have visited Niagara Falls, owing in part to their location near the large population centers of the United States and Canada. By contrast, Victoria Falls on the Zambezi River in southern Africa, Angel Falls in Venezuela (the world's highest at 979 meters), the Iguazu Falls on the border of Argentina and Brazil, and Guaira Falls on the upper Parana River between Brazil and Paraguay all possess characteristics that encourage many writers to proclaim they are even greater, more attractive, or more spectacular than Niagara; however, they are located too far from large centers of population to be visited easily. There is even disagreement as to which waterfall has the greatest discharge. Unlike the height of a waterfall, which is static unless a catastrophic rockfall occurs, stream discharge is variable throughout the year, and from dry year to wet. Nearly all waterfalls occur in places with seasonal precipitation, or in environments where the winter precipitation is in the form of snow, leading to spectacular flows during the snowmelt season but disappointing conditions when the stream is chiefly ice. Niagara retains an appeal when it is frozen, but the weather outside is generally uncomfortable at that time of year, and most tourists visit during the warm season. Thousands of people annually register disappointment at the appearance of Yosemite Falls and the other falls of Yosemite National Park during the long, dry summers. This is a characteristic of waterfalls in regions of alpine glaciation; they are frozen in winter and are most spectacular during the short snowmelt season of spring and early summer. Tropical waterfalls, such as those of Africa, South America, and India may have tremendous discharges during the rainy season but much lower flows during the dry season. One of Niagara's great advantages as a tourist attraction is that it has huge natural reservoirs upstream in the form of the Great Lakes, which ensure an even and high discharge year after year, wet season and dry. The difference between average discharge and the peak discharges of rainy seasons and wet years probably accounts for much of the uncertainty as to which waterfall is the biggest.

Arguments concerning which waterfall among the giants is greatest frequently involve rating systems employing the height of the falls, its width, its discharge, and other quantifiable factors. Curiously, vista, or the opportunity to view the falls from a particular point, is often overlooked. Whereas Niagara Falls can be observed from several viewpoints, all of which overwhelm the observer with the perception of a tremendous amount of water flowing over the edge of the ledge, the wider Victoria Falls actually descends into a complicated narrow chasm or canyon; little of Victoria can actually be seen from one point on the surface. This is also true of Iguazu Falls, which is up to several kilometers wide and consists of as many as twenty cataracts. Aircraft flights are the best way to observe these giants—in fact, the only way to experience more than a small fraction of the falls. In a hypothetical rating system, should the amount of time a waterfall is in full flow each year be a factor? Should availability to the general public be a factor? Egalitarian considerations would force a vote in Yosemite's favor, as opposed to Angel Falls in Venezuela or several other competitors in remote regions. In addition, aesthetic considerations come into play. Which waterfalls are the most beautiful, or inspiring, or dramatic? These and other considerations can be important if a governmental decision must be made regarding the protection of a particular waterfall. Such scenarios, incidentally, confront many water projects, which must procure a favorable ratio of benefits to costs in order to survive. The allocation of limited financial resources increasingly involves such decisions. If waterfalls were forced to pay for themselves in terms of tourist revenues in order to be protected from destruction, few waterfalls other than Niagara and Yosemite would likely survive.

The height of waterfalls creates the third area of interest in this phenomenon: the potential for hydroelectric power generation. "Head" is the term used to describe the difference in elevation between the water level at the top of a fall and the bottom. The higher the head, the greater the potential energy of position, which can be converted into electrical energy as the water descends. It must be emphasized that the waterfall itself is not harnessed. Water flows through tubes to the bottom elevation of the falls, where turbines generate electricity. Niagara Falls was for years the world's largest single hydroelectric generating facility, and it is still among the giants. Most of the waterfalls of the tropics have a potential for power generation, but this has not yet been developed extensively. Europe, Japan, the United States, and Canada have the most fully developed hydroelectrical generating capacities. Regions of alpine mountain glaciation have particularly high potential. The economic benefits of this aspect of waterfalls can be enormously significant locally, and frequently nationwide, although highly industrialized nations with significant numbers of automobiles demand far more energy than waterpower can generate. Most hydroelectric power generation today is actually not from natural waterfall sites, but from what can be called "artificial waterfalls": the creation of head by building a high dam in a narrow valley or gorge.

At the beginning of the Industrial Revolution, before the development of electricity and its distribution through transmission lines, water-power sites furnished the energy for countless small factories and mills. Many of these were the sites of small waterfalls and rapids, such as along the Fall Line of the Piedmont of the southeastern United States. The Great Falls of the Potomac are an example of such a site. The development of electrical transmission lines freed industry from these locations near falls and rapids and allowed an expansion throughout the countryside. The smaller water-power sites fell into disuse, and only a few have been preserved for historic reasons. The larger sites, such as Niagara Falls, remain an important part of the economy.

Methods of Study

The methods used to study waterfalls are fairly simple from a technical point of view, forming part of a larger examination of the site and region. From a scientific viewpoint, the rate of retreat of the falls is of prime interest. Detailed geologic study of the stratigraphy and structure of the rocks at the site, including both downstream and upstream reaches, is essential. Stratigraphy involves the physical and chemical character of the rocks, including horizontal bedding planes and vertical joints, or fractures in the rock. These are the zones of weakness that accelerate weathering and erosion, particularly the breaking off of large slabs of caprock at the edge of the falls. Waterfalls in sedimentary rock typically include a resistant caprock of well-cemented sandstone or dolomite, underlain by softer and less-resistant shales or other sediments. The stratigraphy, or vertical variations in the nature of bedrock, must be identified both for the caprock and for the underlying beds, which provide the weaknesses in the column of rocks that speed or retard the retreat upstream of the falls. "Structure" refers to the arrangement of the beds or rock layers. Are they flat-lying, or do they tilt, and if so, at what angle? Engineering geology is also involved, which includes engineering tests of various rock properties related to strength. In crystalline rock areas, the requirements for study are similar, but such study may be considerably more complex because of the highly varied structure and the less-predictable arrangement of the rocks in three-dimensional space.

A study that seeks to unravel the geologic history of the falls will have similar requirements for information, but probably at a less-detailed scale. Recurrent or repeated surveys are especially useful. Over a period of years or decades, several series of aerial photographs may be available to document the position of the falls at different times. Downstream stratigraphic knowledge is essential if the purpose is to determine past rates of retreat (weak zones of rock should have higher rates of retreat; stronger or resistant zones should have lower rates of retreat). The same principle applies to upstream information, if the purpose is to predict what future rates of retreat will be, in order to provide controls. Observation even over the course of decades is generally insufficient for a long-term prediction, and other data may be called into play. In a number of instances, such as that of St. Anthony Falls, early surveys by explorers can extend the documented positions of the falls by two or three centuries. Since 1950, radiometric dating techniques have been available to add better resolution (a smaller margin of error, or a sharper picture) to the interpretation of geologic history of the region of the falls. These include, particularly, carbon-14 dating of organic matter buried by changes in the course of the stream, a technique that offers good resolution for postglacial environments. New radiometric techniques become available every year, some of which may be adapted to the study of particular waterfalls.

Beyond what has been discussed for scientific purposes, the study of waterfalls for scenic or aesthetic purposes is likely to involve social and political considerations rather than purely scientific ones. Most likely, these will include consideration of such matters as the predicted impacts resulting from reductions of stream discharge. Reduced flow results in a less aesthetic environment, and this can have profound impact upon the tourist industry; *Niagara Falls and the Glacier* (1976), by Glenn C. Forrester, provides an interesting case study. The study of waterfall sites for potential hydropower facilities is not unlike that for dam and power projects. Detailed engineering geology is necessary, and the requirements are similar to those outlined for scientific studies of waterfalls.

Context

The general public's interest in waterfalls primarily stems from the scenic and aesthetic attraction these sites offer; the public typically opposes alternative uses of water that would impair the appearance of the falls. Recent decades have seen acrimonious debate over the preservation of natural stream regimens and the ecologic systems of the streams. Waterfalls are a part of this general picture and would enjoy a fairly large measure of protection, at least in the United States. Nevertheless, streams move inexorably toward a state of quasi-equilibrium, wherein the most efficient means are sought for carrying sediment to the sea with the available stream discharge. This entails the eventual demise of waterfalls, cascades, cataracts, and rapids, all of which are temporary conditions on the scale of geologic time. The knickpoints of the Mississippi River at Minneapolis and the Ohio River at Louisville no longer retreat upstream; they have been encased in concrete, and other measures have been employed to navigate past these obstacles where it is desirable. Consider the scale of disruption to the economy, and to the environment, if Niagara Falls were permitted to retreat upstream and empty the Great Lakes. Cleveland, Toledo, Detroit, and Chicago would stand on bluffs, scores of meters above muddy flats bordering whatever stream systems would evolve where the lakes once sat. It appears that an informal cost-benefit policy has developed: In regions less touched by human hand, the scenic attraction of waterfalls outweighs most other considerations, and the falls must be preserved. Where population concentrations require order and a status quo, however, the falls themselves may disappear under concrete, as at Minneapolis and Louisville. Niagara Falls has it both ways. Permitting the falls to retreat upstream, or significantly lessening their flow, is seen to be contrary to the public interest. In the case of Niagara Falls, letting nature take its course would be both aesthetically and economically disastrous.

Bibliography

Easterbrook, Donald J. *Surface Processes and Landforms*. New York: Macmillan, 1993. A not-overly-technical discussion of how waterfalls and rapids relate to attempts by streams to achieve equilibrium and a graded profile. Suitable for college-level readers.

Fairbridge, Rhodes W., ed. *The Encyclopedia of Geomorphology*. New York: Reinhold, 1968. The entry on waterfalls, by Derek C. Ford, provides a succinct but illuminating classification of waterfalls and a brief description of rates of recession of falls, centering on Niagara with a comparison to the Nile. Suitable for college-level readers.

Forrester, Glenn C. *Niagara Falls and the Glacier*. Hicksville, N.Y.: Exposition Press, 1976. A highly readable account of the geological context of Niagara Falls, together with a discussion of the role of glaciation in the origin and development of the falls. Includes considerable information on hydropower developments and measures taken to preserve the falls. Well-illustrated, with photographs and diagrams. Suitable for high-school readers.

Snead, Rodman E. *World Atlas of Geomorphic Features*. Huntington, N.Y.: Robert E. Krieger, 1980. Includes a readable discussion of the nature of major waterfalls of the world, as well as a listing of more than seventy major worldwide waterfalls and more than thirty major U.S. waterfalls. Accompanying maps show the general location of each falls and, in addition, regions where smaller waterfalls are common. Suitable for high-school readers.

World Almanac. *The World Almanac and Book of Facts, 1997*. Mahwah, N.J.: World Almanac Books, 1997. Contains a succinct listing of the world's most famous waterfalls, including their heights and certain other characteristics.

Neil E. Salisbury

Cross-References

Alpine Glaciers, 960; Cascades, 2840; Continental Glaciers, 967; Great Lakes, 2938; Hydroelectric Power, 1095; Mississippi River, 3010; Nile River, 3024; River Bed Forms, 2196; River Valleys, 2210.

WATERSHEDS

Type of earth science: Hydrology
Field of study: Geomorphology

A watershed, or drainage basin, is a region that is drained by a stream, lake, or other type of watercourse. The earth is divided into millions of watersheds of varying sizes and shapes, all of which act as collectors of runoff that flow from higher to lower elevations. Most watersheds join other larger watersheds and eventually flow into the "ultimate sink": the oceans.

Principal terms

BASE FLOW: that portion of stream flow that is derived from groundwater

DISCHARGE: the volume of water per unit time that flows past a given point on a stream

DRAINAGE DIVIDE: the ridge of land that marks the boundary between adjacent watersheds

INTERIOR DRAINAGE: watersheds in arid areas where the runoff does not flow into the oceans

PERENNIAL STREAM: a stream that has water flowing in it throughout the year

RELIEF: the difference in elevation between the highest and lowest points of land in a particular region

RUNOFF: that portion of precipitation in a watershed that appears in surface streams

STREAM: water flowing in a narrow but clearly defined channel from higher to lower elevations under the influence of gravity

Summary of the Phenomenon

The term "watershed" has several meanings. The term is derived from the German term *Wasserscheide*, which means "water parting," or the line or ridge of higher ground that separates two adjoining drainage basins. This definition is also used in Great Britain, where "watershed" refers to a drainage divide between adjacent drainage basins. The usage of the term in the United States and by several international agencies has been modified to refer to the land area that is drained by, or that contributes water to, a stream, lake, or other water body. For this discussion, the term will refer to the region that serves as the collecting system for all the water that is moving downslope from higher to lower elevations on its eventual path to the ocean. In this physical context, which is governed by topography, the terms "watershed" and "drainage basin" are synonymous.

The relationship of watersheds to topography was recognized years ago. For example, Philippe Buache in 1752 presented a memoir to the French Academy of

Sciences in which the concept of the topographic unity of a watershed was outlined. This concept was followed by European cartographers of the late eighteenth and early nineteenth centuries who prepared maps that showed the major drainage basins of each country. Although these early cartographers would often exaggerate the height of the divides between watersheds, the basic concept was to show how the land was divided into a variety of drainage basins that acted as efficient collection systems for runoff that resulted from precipitation.

Watersheds transport water from upland areas to lower elevations in a variety of pathways. The most obvious path is by perennial streams that flow in channels. This form of surface runoff includes not only overland flow, which is the water moving over the ground surface, but also base flow, which comes from that portion of the precipitation that has infiltrated through the soil into the underlying groundwater that enters the stream at some downgradient point. Thus, surface runoff from a watershed is a mix of "stormflow" or "quick flow," which occurs right after a precipitation event, and base flow from groundwater, which takes a much longer time to join the surface water. The rates at which surface water and groundwater move through a watershed depend upon many factors, such as precipitation amounts and intensity, geology, soils, topography, and vegetation.

Just as stream channels vary enormously in length and width, from a channel that can easily be jumped across to a river such as the Mississippi, which is as wide as 1.5 kilometers before it empties into the Gulf of Mexico, watersheds also have an enormous range in length, area, and discharge. The largest watershed in the world by far is the Amazon, with a drainage area of 6,150,000 square kilometers, approximately one-third of the entire area of South America. The second- and third-largest watersheds in the world are the Zaire in Africa (3,820,000 square kilometers) and the Mississippi in the United States (3,270,000 square kilometers). Thus, the Mississippi River watershed, which includes the Missouri River, drains an astonishing 40.5 percent of the entire area of the conterminous United States.

The Amazon is also the largest river in the world by far in terms of discharge, averaging 6,300 cubic kilometers per year. The second- and third-largest dischargers in the world are the Zaire and the Orinoco in Venezuela (1,250 and 1,100 cubic kilometers per year, respectively). The longest rivers in the world are the Nile in Africa (6,671 kilometers), the Amazon (6,300 kilometers), the Yangtze in China (6,276 kilometers), and the Mississippi (6,019 kilometers). At the other end of the spectrum are innumerable small streams that are in the headwaters of their watersheds near the divides with lengths of only a few meters.

Although there is obvious variation in shape from watershed to watershed, most tend to be pear-shaped. This shape is the most probable one to occur, as ground slopes and branching stream networks become adjusted to dispose of the runoff and the sediment load in the water efficiently. Departures from the usual pear-shape are attributed to structural control by bedrock formations. For example, some basins are elongated in shape when they occupy long, narrow valleys; such valleys are often found in regions such as the Appalachians in the eastern United States, where long, resistant ridges of sandstone and quartzite run approximately parallel with less resistant valleys underlain by shale and limestone.

Most of the runoff in the humid land areas of the world eventually flows into the oceans via a series of hydrologically connected watersheds. Thus the waters and sediment load of the Missouri and Ohio Rivers join the Mississippi River at St. Louis, Missouri, and Cairo, Illinois, respectively, and eventually flow into the Gulf of Mexico below New Orleans. Another large-scale example is that of the watersheds for the Great Lakes, which furnish the water for the St. Lawrence River, which flows into the Gulf of St. Lawrence and the Atlantic Ocean. However, there are areas of the world where runoff flows into interior basins surrounded by high mountains that do not allow the stream to get to the ocean. This type of drainage system, called "interior drainage," is common in semiarid and arid climates. Major examples of watersheds with interior drainage include the Caspian Sea in Asia (3,626,000 square kilometers), the Aral Sea in Kazakhstan and Uzbekistan in Asia (1,618,750 square kilometers), Lake Eyre in Australia (1,424,500 square kilometers), and the Great Basin in Utah, Nevada, and eastern California (500,000 square kilometers).

The divides that separate watersheds vary from sharply defined ridges in mountainous terrain to poorly defined boundaries in glaciated landscapes, regions of low relief, and areas of limited topographic expression. For example, the highest land in the Everglades (12,950 square kilometers) in Florida is only 2.1 meters above sea level, which means that natural runoff (excluding canals) flows in directions sometimes governed more by wind than by topography. Another prominent instance of a poorly defined divide occurs in southern Wyoming, where the Continental Divide in the United States, which separates the waters that flow into the Pacific Ocean from those that flow into the Gulf of Mexico, splits into two divides that surround the "Great Basin Divide." This unusual situation means that anyone who drives along Interstate 80 in Wyoming, for example, will be able to cross the Continental Divide twice in an east-west direction.

Watershed divides, especially in mountainous areas, often have been used as political boundaries. Examples include the Andes between Argentina and Chile, the Pyrenees between France and Spain, and the Bitterroot Range between Idaho and Montana. Watershed divides also often serve as starting points for major cities. For example, Atlanta developed as a rail center in the nineteenth century because it was on the divide between the streams that flowed into the Gulf of Mexico (the Chattahoochee and Flint Rivers) and those that flowed into the Atlantic Ocean along the east coast of Georgia (the Ocmulgee River).

The drainage pattern or network of stream channels that develop within a watershed are related to local geologic and geomorphic factors. The most common drainage pattern that develops on horizontal and homogeneous bedrock or on crystalline rock that offers uniform resistance to erosion is called "dendritic," since it resembles the branching pattern of trees in plan view. All other types of drainage patterns reflect some form of structural control, such as the trellis pattern that is associated with the elongated watersheds in the "ridge and valley" regions in the Appalachians of the eastern United States. Rectangular patterns can develop in faulted areas where the drainage paths follow the lines of least resistance that develop along the fault lines.

Watershed size and flow can change either naturally or by anthropogenic means. Major natural examples include the deflection by continental glaciation of the upper Missouri River from Hudson Bay in eastern Canada to its present-day confluence with the Mississippi River, and the geologic subsidence and tilting that diverted the drainage of the Nyanza area in East Africa from the Zaire River (formerly the Congo), which flows into the Atlantic Ocean to Lake Victoria, which drains into the Nile and the Mediterranean Sea. The flow in the Florida Everglades has been substantially altered by drainage activities and canal building for agricultural purposes that started in the late nineteenth century and continued into the twentieth century. Water that used to flow into the Everglades and Florida Bay from Lake Okeechobee was diverted to the canalized Caloosahatchee River which empties into the Gulf of Mexico, and the Miami, North New River, Hillsboro, West Palm Beach, and St. Lucie Canals, which are connected with the Atlantic Ocean on the east coast of Florida. Another instance of anthropogenic intervention with watershed flow is illustrated by the diversion of water from Lake Michigan, which is part of the Great Lakes and St. Lawrence River system, to the Chicago Ship and Sanitary Canal, which is connected with the Illinois River, which flows into the Mississippi River. The purpose of the canal was to transport sewage from the Chicago metropolitan area away from Lake Michigan, which is used as a water source.

Methods of Study

Many disciplines are involved in the study of watersheds. On the physical and technical side, the study of the amounts of water involved in runoff and their variations as a response to precipitation events is done by hydrologists and civil engineers. Geologists and physical geographers study the role of streams in the processes of erosion, transportation, and deposition of rock material. Aquatic chemists and environmental scientists study the variations in water quality in the watershed from both natural background conditions and contamination from anthropogenic sources. These various studies are the primary function of the Water Resources Division of the U.S. Geological Survey, the major data-gathering agency of the federal government for water-related activities. This agency also acts in cooperation with state governments to obtain water quantity and quality information for major watersheds. Other federal agencies that study various aspects of watersheds include the U.S. Forest Service, which is concerned with runoff issues in national forests; the National Resources Conservation Service (formerly the Soil Conservation Service), which studies the relationship between runoff and soil erosion; the U.S. Army Corps of Engineers, which is concerned with water supply, flooding, and navigation in inland waterways; and the Environmental Protection Agency, which studies water quality issues such as point and nonpoint sources of pollution.

On the nonphysical side of watershed study, environmental planners, geographers, and political scientists are concerned with watershed management issues, because there is an inherent topographic and hydrologic unity to the drainage basin in the sense that what happens upstream will sooner or later affect downstream users. Lawyers become involved when there are issues relating to transfers of water from one basin to another (interbasin transfers) of either an intrastate or interstate nature.

One of the most important activities of the U.S. Geological Survey is stream flow measurement. The survey maintains more than seven thousand continuous-record gauging stations on the major streams and their tributaries. Discharge at a site is first calculated by multiplying the cross-sectional area of the stream by the average velocity of the stream, in accord with the equation of hydrologic continuity: discharge equals area times mean velocity. When a sufficient number of measured discharges at each site have been obtained, rating curves are constructed that allow discharge to be estimated directly from gauge height. This procedure facilitates computation of mean daily discharge for all of the gauging stations, information that is invaluable to watershed managers.

Another major function of the U.S. Geological Survey is to collect and analyze water-quality samples from more than two thousand locations in the nation's watersheds. The water-quality variables include instantaneous discharge, water temperature, pH levels, dissolved oxygen, hardness, calcium, chloride, total dissolved solids, and nutrients such as nitrates and phosphorus. Depending upon the particular stream and location in the watershed, sampling frequency varies from several times a year to monthly. The survey publishes the data in a series of annual reports.

Remote sensing has become a useful tool in watershed analysis. Remote sensing, which simply means obtaining information from an area without direct contact, includes aerial photography using either conventional film or special types of film such as colored infrared, which uses different parts of the electromagnetic spectrum. The active mode of remote sensing, as distinguished from the passive mode of remote sensing exemplified by aerial photography, includes radar-sensing systems that provide images of the earth that can be taken through cloud cover and at night. All the many forms of remote sensing provide important information about the vegetation, geologic structure, drainage networks, and land use within a watershed.

Context

The basic function of a watershed or drainage basin is to transport water and mineral matter from upstream areas to downstream areas in a variety of pathways. These pathways include perennial streams and groundwater. As development occurs, watershed functions change as the hydrologic pathways are affected. As previously pervious surfaces get paved or covered with buildings, surface runoff increases, and infiltration and groundwater recharge decrease. The entire hydrologic response of the watershed is changed dramatically as the volume and rate of runoff and consequent flooding potential increase in response to impervious cover spreading over the land surface. Urbanization and suburbanization radically alter the hydrologic regime of a watershed so that it becomes "flashy" in response to precipitation events.

Watersheds also play a crucial role in pollutant attenuation. Natural vegetative surfaces and soils can decrease the concentration of pollutants by physical filtration, microbial decomposition, and biochemical transformation. Land development inevitably leads to the diminishment of the capacity of a watershed to attenuate and assimilate pollutants. Accelerated runoff results in increased erosion and transport of contaminants at a higher rate and concentration than in undeveloped systems. Downstream areas and navigation channels may become clogged with contaminated sediment, which is the number-one pollutant in the United States.

Watershed impacts tend to occur incrementally and may go unnoticed for quite some time. For example, hydrocarbons, metals, and other pollutants are transported from paved surfaces every time it rains. With time, these pollutants accumulate in the downstream aquatic ecosystem, which usually results in long-term habitat deterioration. Since groundwater flows at a very slow rate (approximately 1.5 meters per day to 1.5 meters per year), any pollutant that gets into the groundwater of a watershed could take years or decades to exit the system.

Successful watershed management involves many disciplines such as hydrology, physical geography, civil engineering, geology, soil science, environmental planning, environmental science, and water law. There are a number of structural and nonstructural measures that could be taken to reduce the negative impact associated with watershed development. For example, flood-prone lands can be delineated and zoned for non-building purposes such as parks and recreational areas. Ordinances can and have been established at the local, county, or state level that require pre-development and post-development peak runoff to be equilibrated by the proper use and location of detention basins, wetlands, and recharge basins that are underlain by permeable soils. Vegetated buffer strips along streams can reduce bank erosion as well as providing protection for the aquatic habitat. Although there is continuing discussion over the most effective width for buffer strips, most studies suggest a minimum width of 8 to 10 meters from the stream bank. Water-quality improvements for both point and nonpoint sources of pollution include upgraded sewage treatment, minimum lot sizes for homes on septic disposal systems, detention basins, grassed filter strips, artificial wetlands, street sweeping, salt reduction in roadway deicing, and a variety of best management practices for agricultural areas such as manure management, restrictions on plowing too close to a stream, and management of fertilizer and pesticide application rates and quantities.

Bibliography

Albert, R. C. *Damming the Delaware*. University Park: Pennsylvania State University Press, 1987. An interesting history of two hundred years of water management for the Delaware River, which serves as a water source for New York City, Trenton, and Philadelphia. This is a good case study of the institutional factors that have resulted in a model interstate compact and the historical absence of dams on the main stem of the river.

Black, P. E. *Watershed Hydrology*. 2d ed. Chelsea, Mich.: Ann Arbor Press, 1996. A fine introductory book that presents in an integrated fashion the various hydrologic processes that occur in a watershed. The complex of interactions between climate, soils, vegetation, atmosphere, streamflow and channels, humans, and water-resource infrastructure are thoroughly discussed. The treatment is qualitative, with only minimal uses of quantitative methodology.

Dunne, T., and L. B. Leopold. *Water in Environmental Planning*. New York: W. H. Freeman, 1978. A comprehensive book about watershed hydrology (818 pages). In addition to the useful chapters on hydrology, the book has an extensive section (220 pages) on drainage-basin analysis, hillslope processes, stream channels and changes, and sediment production and transport. Many of the chapters conclude with solved sample problems involving basic hydrologic equations and methodology.

Hillel, D. *Rivers of Eden*. New York: Oxford University Press, 1994. An engrossing book about water shortages in the Middle East, set against the backdrop of competing territorial claims in a highly politicized and arid environment. The major watersheds selected for study include the Tigris and Euphrates, with headwaters in Turkey and downstream areas in Iraq and Syria; the Nile, with a source region in east-central Africa; and the Jordan River in Israel, Jordan, Lebanon, and Syria. This is a well-written and well-documented study of historical watershed mismanagement and the compelling need for cooperation and water-sharing arrangements if peace is ever to come to the region.

Leeden, F. V. D., F. L. Troise, and D. K. Todd, eds. *The Water Encyclopedia*. 2d ed. Chelsea, Mich.: Lewis, 1990. A huge compendium of information about virtually all aspects of water. Includes hundreds of tables and many maps covering surface and ground water, water use and quality, environmental problems, water resources management, and water law and treaties. An excellent reference work that contains a bewildering array of facts about water.

McDonald, A. T., and D. Kay. *Water Resources: Issues and Strategies*. New York: John Wiley & Sons, 1988. Chapter 8, "River Basin Management," provides short but useful examples of the Tennessee Valley Authority, the Senegal and Volta River basins in West Africa, and regional water authorities in England and Wales. The institutional factors pertaining to watershed management are stressed.

Marsh, W. M. *Landscape Planning: Environmental Applications*. 2d ed. New York: John Wiley & Sons, 1991. An interesting blend of the principles and processes in physical geography, planning, and landscape architecture as they pertain to environmental issues in landscape planning. Contains some very useful chapters on watersheds, land use, stormwater discharge and landscape change, soil erosion and stream sedimentation, and soils and development suitability.

Newsom, M. *Hydrology and the River Environment*. Oxford, England: Clarendon Press, 1994. Focuses on watersheds as the fundamental unit for water management. Although many of the examples discussed are from Great Britain, there is an inherent universality to the watershed analysis methodology. A very good set of pertinent references for each chapter is included at the end of the book.

Strahler, A. H., and A. N. Strahler. *Modern Physical Geography*. 4th ed. New York:

John Wiley & Sons, 1992. One of the best college-level texts in the field. Provides an excellent introduction to the geologic and hydrologic processes that govern watershed development and change. Notable for its numerous and exceptionally lucid diagrams.

Robert M. Hordon

Cross-References

Dams and Flood Control, 309; Drainage Basins, 384; Floodplains, 712; Floods, 719; Geologic and Topographic Maps, 869; River Flow, 2203; River Valleys, 2210; Sediment Transport and Deposition, 2290; Soil Erosion, 2387; Surface Water, 2504; Water Quality, 3163.

WEATHER MODIFICATION

Type of earth science: Atmospheric sciences and meteorology

Weather modification involves all the changes that can occur to the earth's climate at the local, regional, and global scales. These changes can occur naturally or by deliberate or inadvertent human intervention.

Principal terms

ALBEDO: the amount of electromagnetic energy reflected from the surface of an object, generally expressed as a percentage

ELECTROMAGNETIC ENERGY: energy that is radiated in wavelike form by any object that has heat; it goes through space at the speed of light

FOSSIL FUEL: the remains of ancient organic material that have been trapped in rock; coal, crude oil, and natural gas are examples

GREENHOUSE EFFECT: the buildup of heat in the lower portions of the atmosphere that occurs through the absorption of longwave radiation that is being reflected back from the earth's surface

LONGWAVE RADIATION: electromagnetic energy that is being given off by the earth

SHORTWAVE RADIATION: electromagnetic energy that is coming from the Sun

STRATOSPHERE: the layer of the atmosphere that is directly above the troposphere; it reaches a height of about 50 kilometers

TROPOSPHERE: the lowest layer of the atmosphere; it reaches a height of 12 kilometers at the poles and 15 kilometers at the equator

Summary of the Phenomenon

Climatic changes can occur naturally, as evidenced by the advance and retreat of huge continental ice sheets that covered large parts of North America and Europe during the last 2.5 million to 3 million years of the Late Pliocene and Pleistocene epochs (the "Ice Age"). These alternating series of glacial and interglacial periods may have been caused by plate-tectonic activity that shifted the location of continents on the earth's surface, by an increase in the frequency and severity of volcanic eruptions, by reductions in the output of solar energy, by variations in the astronomical relationship between the earth and the Sun, or by a combination of some or all of these factors.

Weather modifications can also occur as a consequence of human activity. Human impact on the climate began to be felt some five thousand to nine thousand years ago as part of the Agricultural Revolution. Wooded areas were cleared for tilling, and river valleys were irrigated in dry areas. Wind speed was increased in the small forest clearings and albedo was decreased, while relative humidity was increased in those areas where crops replaced desert scrub. These changes were locally important but had little effect beyond the immediate vicinity of the cultivated fields. Indeed, until the Industrial Revolution and more definitely until the middle of the nineteenth century, the human impact on the climate was confined to the local level.

From the mid-nineteenth century on, and in an accelerating fashion in more recent times, inadvertent human modifications to the atmospheric environment began to have effects on the regional and global scales. Global warming provides an excellent example of the nature of these impacts. There is growing evidence that human activities are causing a significant increase in the temperature of the earth, although some scientists argue that current trends are merely part of a natural climatic cycle. One mechanism that causes global warming is an increase in carbon dioxide. This gas absorbs longwave radiation from the earth's surface. Although carbon dioxide is a minute fraction (0.035 percent) of the total amount of gas in the atmosphere, it is especially important, as it absorbs radiant heat passing from the earth through the atmosphere and is therefore involved in the production of the "greenhouse effect." Carbon dioxide has been increasing from a concentration of 300 parts per million in 1860 to a current level of about 350 parts per million. This increase of 22 percent has been attributed to the burning of wood and fossil fuels (coal, oil, and natural gas), particularly after 1940, when the rate of increase became exponential.

Methane, nitrous oxide, ozone, and chlorofluorocarbon concentrations have also been affected by human activities. Since these gases along with carbon dioxide absorb longwave radiation that enhances the greenhouse effect, they are referred to as "greenhouse" gases. It is believed that an increase in these gases, even though they form a very small percentage of the atmosphere, is associated with an increase in world temperature.

The effects of global warming can result in many changes to the earth's environment. Sea levels can rise as glaciers and sea ice melt; indeed, there is evidence that this process is already happening. Tide-gauge records along the U.S. Atlantic Coast show a long-term trend of a rise in relative sea level of 2 to 4 millimeters per year over the last fifty years. The U.S. Environmental Protection Agency estimates that global warming will cause a 100 millimeter rise in relative sea level by the year 2050. Other investigators predict that sea level will rise 190 to 900 millimeters by the year 2100, with a best estimate of 480 millimeters. This increase in sea level means that 92 million people in low-lying coastal locations would face the risk of annual flooding.

Changes in the earth's climate could facilitate the wider distribution of insect-borne diseases such as malaria and also shift the boundaries between climatic regimes. Thus, some areas would become drier, while others would become wetter. The impact on agriculture and dependent human populations could be significant and serious.

An increase in climatic variability is a recent consequence of atmospheric warming. For example, since 1980 there has been an increase in the frequency of extreme meteorological events such as severe snowstorms, rainstorms, and ice storms. The increasing intensity and frequency of spells of hot and cold weather may also be associated with global warming.

Particulate matter (such as dust and smoke) in the atmosphere comes from natural sources, such as sea salt, volcanoes, and cosmic dust, and from anthropogenic sources, such as slash-and-burn agriculture and industry. Some sources, such as forest fires and wind-blown dust, can come from both natural and human activities. Using 1970 as a base year, the estimated amount of particulates injected into the atmosphere from human activities in 1880 was 25 percent of the total amount; this level has been projected to reach 158 percent by the end of the twentieth century. The rate of increase from human-induced sources is estimated to be as much as 4 percent per year. The increase in particulate matter is believed to result in a cooling of the earth's climate, although the effect depends upon the particle size and vertical distribution in the troposphere (the lowest layer in the atmosphere) and stratosphere (the atmospheric layer above the troposphere). The major effect of the dust is to intercept the shortwave radiation from the Sun and thereby diminish the amount of solar radiation that reaches the ground surface. Atmospheric dust also increases the earth's albedo, meaning that more solar radiation would be reflected back into space and, therefore, less would be available to heat the planet.

The percentage of solar radiation that is reflected by an object is called its "albedo." Albedos range from 0 percent for a pure black object that absorbs all radiation to 100 percent for a pure white object that reflects all radiation. The albedos of bright objects on Earth, such as clouds, fresh snow, and ice, range from 50 to 95 percent, as compared to a range of 5 to 20 percent for darker objects such as forests, fresh asphalt, and dark soils. Information about albedo is very important, since objects with low albedo absorb solar radiation and increase the amount of energy that is available to the surface and atmosphere of the earth, whereas objects with high albedo reflect the solar radiation out to space.

Human activities on the earth's surface can change the albedo. Studies have shown that overgrazing in semiarid regions, such as sub-Saharan Africa, can increase the surface albedo as much as 20 percent. This change may then result in rainfall suppression, which only serves to enhance the "desertification" process. Other investigators have proposed that surface albedo may be substantially increased by the deforestation that has occurred in tropical rainforests. Note that an increase in albedo is associated with a cooling of the climate, as there is less solar radiation reaching the surface of the earth. Supersonic aircraft and rocket exhaust add water vapor to the stratosphere, although the amount thus added is small. The water vapor leads to an increase in cirrus clouds, tending to warm the earth's climate.

Thermal pollution of the atmosphere is attributed to direct output of heat from human activities. The urban "heat island" is an example of this type of heating; in many cities, the downtown surface air temperature averages up to 2 degrees Celsius higher than in the suburbs. Large cities also affect precipitation, which may increase by up to 15 percent over downtown areas and up to 80 kilometers downwind. These climatic effects are locally significant but do not appear to have any regional or global importance.

Deliberate modification of the climate has been proposed on a regional and global scale and has been experimented with at the local level. Large-scale schemes have included proposals for damming the Congo River in central Africa and diverting the water to Lake Chad, which would be expanded from its present size of from 7,000 to

22,000 square kilometers to an area of 2,000,000 square kilometers. The new lake would presumably lead to an increase in precipitation in the region, although the creation of the High Aswan Reservoir on the Nile in Egypt, the third-largest reservoir in the world, has not resulted in any measurable increase in precipitation in the downwind area of the central Sahara.

The Russians have been interested for some time in reducing the amount of sea ice in the Arctic Ocean, a modification that might lead to a temperature increase in northern territories and open up new areas for human settlement and cultivation. An early proposal to facilitate this scheme was to spread carbon black and soot on the ice during the summer to speed up melting. Proponents argue that the regional exchange of heat and moisture would be radically altered if the Arctic Ocean were ice-free, thereby warming the polar climates of the Northern Hemisphere. Critics of the scheme note that the change could induce greater storminess in the region. An alternative and even bolder plan is the proposed damming of the Bering Strait between Siberia and Alaska, blocking the flow of water from the Pacific Ocean into the Arctic Ocean. Instead, proponents have suggested, 500 cubic kilometers of water per day could be pumped from the Arctic into the Pacific, thereby permitting relatively warmer Atlantic Ocean water to flow into the Arctic. Needless to say, the costs and climatic uncertainties associated with this large-scale scheme are enormous.

Attempts to induce precipitation have ranged from ancient ritual dances to nineteenth century efforts to fire cannons at the clouds to twentieth century cloud-seeding experiments. The cannon shots were meant to create shock waves that would lead to the formation of ice crystals, assisting in precipitation development. The same type of reasoning was applied in more recent times when experimental rocket explosions within clouds were tried to see if precipitation could be induced. The results were inconclusive.

More elaborate attempts to modify clouds and thereby induce precipitation began in 1946, when dry ice (frozen carbon dioxide) was found to be effective in cooling droplets to make ice crystals. Cloud seeding experiments with dry ice have had mixed and unpredictable results. A related method of inducing precipitation is to introduce minute particles of silver iodide into thick cumulus clouds. The silver iodide can be spread by airplanes or shot into the clouds by artillery shells. The particles form nuclei that facilitate increased condensation of water, which can lead to cumulonimbus cloud formation and heavy rains.

It is difficult to gauge the effectiveness of cloud seeding. In order to have a scientifically controlled experiment, two or more identical clouds would be required to enable researchers to apply different methods and observe the results. Since identical clouds are practically impossible to obtain, the alternative is to randomly select from a group of similar clouds and make some statistical comparisons of the different procedures. Claims for inducing precipitation by cloud seeding vary considerably and include instances of both increased and decreased precipitation. Cloud seeding has also been used to attempt to modify hailstorms and hurricanes. The results have been mixed and difficult to appraise.

Fog dispersal is another form of planned weather modification. Since fog is a surface form of cloud, seeding it with dry ice or liquid propane has been tried. The seeding experiments have indicated that such methods can work with cold fog that consists of supercooled droplets. These cold fogs, however, represent only a small fraction of all mid-latitude and high-latitude fogs. Research is continuing on warm-fog dispersal, since warm fogs are much more common and widespread. The benefits to commercial aviation would be considerable if fog dispersal could be achieved economically.

Weather modification at the micro level has been accomplished successfully in agricultural areas where killing frosts may occur. This condition can develop on calm, clear nights when longwave energy from the ground surface is radiated into the atmosphere. The net radiation becomes negative, and the ground surface cools. This situation is called a "low-level temperature inversion," since the ground becomes cooler than the relatively warmer overlying air; this is the reverse of the usual situation in which temperatures decrease with height. Farmers growing sensitive plants, often oranges and other fruits, then use oil-burning heaters or large fans to circulate the air in order to mix the cooler air at the ground with the warmer air above.

Methods of Study

Weather modification involves the study of climatic change. Scientists have developed a wide variety of instruments to measure the meteorological elements of temperature, precipitation, wind direction and velocity, and albedo.

Temperature is an easily obtained and widely measured meteorological parameter. It is reported in the Fahrenheit scale in the United States and in the Celsius scale throughout the rest of the world. Since air temperature can vary with height, it is measured at more than five thousand weather stations across the United States at a standard height of 1.2 meters above the ground. Thermometers at these stations are housed in louvered shelters to keep them out of the Sun's direct rays.

Precipitation is measured in nonrecording or recording-type rain gauges. They are cylindrical devices that vary in design from country to country. The standard nonrecording rain gauge in the United States is 79 centimeters high with a diameter of 20 centimeters. Precipitation is reported to the nearest 0.01 inch (0.25 millimeters) in the United States and in millimeters or fractions thereof elsewhere. Measurement errors at a single point are generally several percent for a single storm but can range up to 30 percent for a poorly located gauge in a large storm with high winds.

Wind direction is determined by a vane that is designed so that it is always facing into the wind. Wind speed is measured by an anemometer, a common variety of which has three funnel-shaped cups attached to the ends of spokes of a horizontal wheel. The rotational speed of the cups is proportional to that of the wind. Some anemometers have small electric generators attached, allowing the current generated by wind flow to be measured by a meter. Wind speed is reported in miles per hour in the United States and in meters per second in the rest of the world.

Albedo has traditionally been measured by instruments known as "pyranometers"; they are typically used in pairs, one oriented to the sky and the other to the ground.

Pyranometers measure solar radiation by responding thermally to the amount of incoming radiation. Thus, a pyranometer would record peak radiation at noon on a clear day when the Sun is highest in the sky and zero radiation at night. Photoelectric detectors, such as silicon cells, began to be used by the late 1960's for albedo measurements. They have the advantage of being able to detect rapid variations in incident radiation, facilitating high-resolution measurements, especially from airplanes and satellites.

Context

The alteration of the earth's surface by human activities has been going on for thousands of years. These alterations have had varying degrees of effect on the climate; historically, most such effects have been local in scope. However, the magnitude of alterations sharply increased during the Industrial Revolution and grew exponentially during the latter part of the twentieth century. Such effects can be observed worldwide. Destruction of the tropical rainforests has been widespread. Water is diverted from distant watersheds and transported hundreds of kilometers to large metropolitan areas, such as Los Angeles. Irrigation efforts have expanded, in some areas leading to the drying up of major bodies of water, such as the Caspian Sea and the Aral Sea in central Asia. Particulate matter has been increasingly released into the atmosphere, where it can serve as nuclei for condensation of water droplets and also block incoming solar radiation. The burning of fossil fuels has led to a marked increase in carbon-dioxide releases, contributing to the greenhouse effect and warming the planet. Chlorofluorocarbons damage the ozone layer in the stratosphere, leading to increases in the amount of ultraviolet radiation reaching the earth's surface.

The list of anthropogenic impacts on the atmospheric environment is virtually endless. Some of the impacts, such as carbon-dioxide emissions, have tended to warm the earth, while others, such as increases in atmospheric turbidity caused by particulate emissions, have tended to cool the planet. Until fairly recently, most of these impacts have been local, but the trend is now toward regional and global changes in climate.

Planned modifications of the weather, such as cloud seeding, fog dispersal, and crop protection from frost, have been mostly at the local level. However, several major schemes have been proposed, such as the creation of large lakes in Russia by diversion of Arctic-flowing streams, the damming up of the Bering Strait in order to reduce the sea ice of the Arctic Ocean, and the diversion of Canadian rivers to the dry southwestern United States. All these large-scale schemes would not only be enormously costly but would also hold substantial uncertainty as to their effects on the climate. Climatic modeling is an exceedingly complex exercise, even with supercomputers. The dynamics of the atmosphere, the incompletely known interaction between meteorological parameters, and the size of the modeling field—the whole planet—dictate that specific predictions of global climatic change be viewed with caution.

Bibliography

Baer, F., N. L. Canfield, and J. M. Mitchell. eds. *Climate in Human Perspective: A*

Tribute to Helmut E. Landsberg. Boston: Kluwer, 1991. Several essays deal with aspects of weather modification, such as "Five Themes on Our Changing Climate," by J. Murray Mitchell, and "Climate of Cities," by Timothy R. Oke.

Critchfield, Howard J. *General Climatology.* Englewood Cliffs, N.J.: Prentice-Hall, 1983. 4th ed. A well-written book suitable for an introductory course at the college level. The modification of weather and climate is discussed at length in chapter 17.

Hartmann, Dennis L. *Global Physical Climatology.* San Diego, Calif.: Academic Press, 1994. A thorough, fairly technical textbook on physical climatology. Requires some background in climatology, but includes a very good discussion of anthropogenic climate change in chapter 12.

Henderson-Sellers, A., and K. McGuffie. *A Climate Modeling Primer.* New York: John Wiley & Sons, 1987. The basics of climate modeling are covered at the advanced undergraduate and graduate levels. Readers with a background in fluid dynamics and numerical analysis will find the book somewhat easier to read, but others will find it useful for an overview of the modeling process.

Henderson-Sellers, A., and P. J. Robinson. *Contemporary Climatology.* New York: John Wiley & Sons, 1986. A standard textbook on the numerous aspects of climatology. Deliberate climate modification and the human response to climate are included.

Horel, John, and Jack Geisler. *Global Environmental Change: An Atmospheric Perspective.* New York: John Wiley & Sons, 1997. Global warming and stratospheric ozone depletion form the major topics of this readable book geared for beginning-level undergraduate students. An interesting feature is its discussion of the many Internet sites where graphics and information on global environmental change can be obtained.

Lamb, H. H. *Climatic History and the Future.* Princeton, N.J.: Princeton University Press, 1977. A classic, well-documented book covering many aspects of the earth's climatic history. Chapter 19 deals with anthropogenic changes in climate.

Oliver, John E., and John J. Hidore. *Climatology: An Introduction.* Columbus, Ohio: Merrill, 1984. A well-illustrated college-level book that covers at the introductory level all of the physical processes that govern climatology. The numerous maps are particularly useful. Good information about climatic change is included.

Strahler, Alan, and Arthur Strahler. *Physical Geography: Science and Systems of the Human Environment.* New York: John Wiley & Sons, 1997. A thorough, well-illustrated book containing considerable information about atmospheric processes and issues. Suitable for college students.

Robert M. Hordon

Cross-References

Acid Rain, 9; Air Pollution, 24; The Atmosphere's Evolution, 114; Atmospheric Ozone, 144; Climate, 217; Clouds, 224; Global Warming, 2932; The Greenhouse Effect, 1004; Precipitation, 2108; Weather Forecasting, 2717.

XENOLITHS

Type of earth science: Geology
Field of study: Igneous petrology

Xenoliths are blocks of pre-existing rocks within a magma. Consequently, xenoliths provide a sampling of materials through which the magma has traversed on its rise toward the surface. Some xenoliths originate within the mantle and provide the only means of obtaining samples of this elusive material.

Principal terms

ASSIMILATION: the absorption of chemical components of wall rock or xenoliths into a magma

COUNTRY ROCK: rocks through which a magma is intruding; also known as "wall rock"

DIATREME: a pipelike conduit in the crust of the earth filled with fragmented rock produced by gases-rich volcanic eruptions

ECLOGITE: rock composed principally of garnet and pyroxene that formed at high pressures associated with great depths

FELSIC ROCKS: igneous rocks rich in potassium, sodium, aluminum, and silica, including granites and related rocks

MAFIC ROCKS: igneous rocks rich in magnesium and iron, including gabbro, basalt, and related rocks

MAGMA: a naturally occurring silicate-rich melt beneath the surface of the earth

MANTLE: the intermediate zone between the crust and the core of the earth

PERIDOTITE: a class of ultramafic rocks made up principally of pyroxene and olivine, with subordinate amounts of other minerals

SEGREGATION: the concentration of early-formed minerals in a magma by crystal settling or crystal floating

ULTRAMAFIC: a term for any rock consisting of more than 90 percent ferromagnesium minerals, including olivine and pyroxene

Summary of the Phenomenon

Xenoliths are fragments of pre-existing rocks that have been incorporated in a magma as it makes its way into higher levels of the crust. The term "xenolith" is derived from the Greek roots *xeno* and *lith*, meaning "strange or foreign" and "rock." These rock fragments are pieces of previously formed rocks that become incorporated into the magma and perhaps removed from their source as the magma moves. The xenoliths may retain their original identity with minor alteration, or they may be greatly altered by attendant heat and fluids present in the magma. Xenolithic inclusions may be preserved near to their original sources along the borders of an intrusive magma, or they may carried for great vertical distances from where they originated. In this manner, fragments of deep crust and mantle material from as much as 200 to 300 kilometers below the earth's surface have been brought to the surface by volcanic eruptions.

Xenoliths represent fragments of the rocks through which a magma has moved to its site of final emplacement and crystallization. They may be found in products of explosive volcanism such as volcanic tuff and breccia, within crystalline igneous rocks as in lava flows, and within shallow and deep-seated igneous rocks. Explosive volcanic materials are ejected by highly gas-charged eruptions that produce diatremes and maar-type volcanoes. These are volcanic craters in the form of inverted conelike or dishlike depressions in the surface surrounded by a rim of ejected deposits. Xenoliths are found as angular or rounded blocks embedded in ash tuffs or volcanic breccia in the rim and in the pipelike conduit underlying the crater. In certain types of basalt and related magmas, such as kimberlite, that originate deep in the mantle, rare fist-sized fragments of mantle material are transported upward from near the source of the magma origin. Fragments may also be collected from rocks traversed by the magma along its path of vertical ascent through the crust. Xenoliths in crystalline igneous rocks are embedded within the rock and are not exposed until erosion exposes the xenolith by removing overlying material. Granite rocks typically contain large xenoliths of metamorphic or sedimentary rocks. Such xenoliths reflect the typical intrusive process that produces granites. In this process, subsurface magma chambers expand and move upward by physically plucking country rocks from the wall and roof.

Three basic varieties of xenoliths are recognized: wall-rock xenoliths, cognate xenoliths, and mantle xenoliths. Wall-rock xenoliths are represented by blocks and pieces of the adjacent country rock that have been incorporated into the magma. Cognate xenoliths are inclusion of chilled margins of the magma or comagmatic segregations in which early-formed crystals are segregated within the magma chamber and are later incorporated in more energetic magmatic motions. Mantle xenoliths are presumed to be pieces of the mantle that become incorporated in magmas that are formed by partial melting deep within the earth.

Magmatic intrusions make room for themselves by three processes: forceful injection, stoping, and assimilation. Stoping occurs when the magmatic front advances by injection into fractures and surrounding blocks of country rock. Theses blocks may sink or float in the magma, and they may be slightly altered or totally assimilated within the magma depending on the characteristics of the magma and the wall rock. Most wall-rock xenoliths in felsic magmas do not move far from their source. Xenoliths are abundant near the margins of most intrusions. Because the margins are more likely to be losing heat and cooling at rates faster than the interior of the intrusion, the magma is more viscous, and xenoliths are less likely to move very far from the source. In contrast, fast-moving magmas in volcanic conduits often carry a wide variety of xenoliths from country rock traversed by the magma. In this way, a wide variety of crustal rocks cut by the volcanic vent may be brought to the earth's surface.

Xenoliths usually show effects of the high temperatures to which they are exposed. Pre-existing minerals within a xenolith react to form new minerals that are in equilibrium with the magma. Thus, most xenoliths are brought to a high-grade metamorphic state unless they are composed of high-temperature refractory minerals to begin with or unless they are exposed to high temperatures for short periods of time. The German term *schlieren* is used to describe hazy, ill-defined streaks of nearly completely assimilated xenoliths. Materials caught up in low-temperature felsic magmas are more likely to be altered by reactive assimilation, in which there is an exchange of ions between the xenolith and the magma. Inclusion of large blocks of country rock may alter the composition of magma by enriching it with elements that were not originally abundant.

Buried salt beds are capable of plastic flowage in response to the weight of overlying rocks. Often the salt, which has a lower density than the enclosing sedimentary rocks, will rise many thousands of feet through overlying sediments to form salt domes or salt plugs. The rise of large masses of salt is very much like the rise of magma. Pieces of wall rocks and sub-salt rocks may be incorporated into the salt as xenoliths. In this manner, salt domes in the Persian Gulf have brought up blocks of sedimentary, igneous, and metamorphic rocks from great depths in the crust. Ultramafic igneous xenoliths in the Weeks Island salt dome in southern Louisiana are thought to be fragments of mantle-derived ultramafic intrusions emplaced along fault zones prior to deposition of the salt.

Cognate xenoliths, also called "autoliths," are xenoliths from parts of the magma that have previously crystallized. Magmas solidify over a wide range of temperatures. Large bodies of magma may require tens of thousands of years to crystallize fully. Material on the outer edge of the magma will cool and crystallize more rapidly than that of the interior, resulting in chilled margins. Elsewhere within the magma, early formed crystals in some magmas will either float or sink depending on the specific gravity differential with the magma. Feldspar crystals tend to float and collect near the top of the magma chamber, and mafic minerals such as olivine or pyroxene tend to sink to the bottom of the chamber. Some magmas undergo energetic degassing because of the reduction in confining pressure as they approach shallow levels in the crust. The rapid evolution of dissolved volatiles may disrupt previously crystallized portions of magma (chilled margins or crystal segregations) and mix solid cognate xenoliths with the mobile fluid phase.

Perhaps the most exotic xenoliths are those that originate within the mantle. The mantle lies at depths of five to forty kilometers below the surface and extends down to the top of the outer core nearly three thousand kilometers beneath the surface. No drill has penetrated to the mantle; therefore, these materials are completely inaccessible for direct sampling. A program to drill into the mantle was briefly attempted in the 1960's but was abandoned as infeasible. It was easier to go to the moon than to drill to the mantle—or, at least, the manned lunar landing was better funded. The probable composition and mineralogical makeup of the mantle is postulated from calculations of the density, pressure, and temperatures that exist at mantle depths and by comparisons with meteorites, which are pieces of asteroids that have been fragmented by collisions with other asteroids. The interior of asteroids are thought to reproduce conditions similar to those of the mantle. Fortunately, pieces of the upper mantle are delivered to the surface of the earth as xenoliths in some magmas that originate by partial melting deep within the earth. For these rocks to make it to the surface without significant alteration by the host magma, they must be delivered to the surface in a fairly short period of time. Thus, it is not surprising that mantle xenoliths are found in volcanic rocks associated with rift zones and interplate magmatic zones that allow rapid rise of gas-rich magmas to the surface.

Kilbourne Hole, New Mexico, is approximate thirty miles northwest of El Paso, Texas. This maar-type crater, similar to those of the Eifel Region of Germany, is approximately one mile in diameter. The floor of the crater is 150 feet below the level of the surrounding plain, and a raised rim of volcanic debris reaches up to 100 feet above the surrounding surface. A large part of the rim height consists of bedded volcaniclastic fine-grained materials—mostly quartz sands carried by volcanic gases from shallow depths beneath the crater interspersed with scattered blocks of basalt. Underlying this epiclastic material is a thick layer of volcanic breccia composed largely of mantle xenoliths, wall-rock xenoliths, and fine-grained, quartz-rich materials. The most common xenolith in this layer consists of rounded peridotite nodules ranging from an inch in diameter to the size of a football. In addition to these mantle xenoliths, inclusions of a variety of crustal rocks are also common.

Typical mantle xenoliths are composed of peridotite (olivine and pyroxene-rich rocks) incorporated in mafic volcanic rocks such as basalt. Basalts are formed from magma that originates by partial melting of mantle materials. They often incorporate xenoliths from their place of origin as well as fragments of crustal rocks torn from walls of the conduit along which they are rising. Most notable of these magmas are varieties of peridotites known as "kimberlites" and "lamproites." Kimberlites derive their name from the town of Kimberly, South Africa, which is near the location of the inverted cone-shaped bodies that were found in 1870 to contain diamonds. Prior to that time, diamonds had been recovered from stream gravels (India, Brazil, and Africa) and beach deposits, but the source rocks were unknown.

Kimberlite (mica peridotite) is a potassic ultramafic rock that occurs in intrusive pipes and plugs and in explosively formed volcanic craters that overlay them. Kimberlite is composed of phlogopite (a mica), magnesian olivine, and pyroxenes with minor amounts of potassic amphiboles, garnets, carbonates, oxides, and, rarely, diamond xenocrysts. Lamproite is a porphyritic, ultrapotassic ultramafic rock that occurs in dikes and small intrusions. It is distinct from kimberlite in that it contains preserved glass and lacks carbonate. Kimberlite and lamproite magmas are rich in the volatiles, water and carbon dioxide—which contribute to their rapid ascent to the surface as a result of violent degassing (boiling) of the magma as decompression causes gas to escape the magma. Kimberlites ascend at rates of 35 to 100 kilometers per hour from well within the mantle at depths of 120 to 300 kilometers. Often the original minerals in kimberlite are altered to serpentine, chlorite, and clays. Typically, these magmas contain up to 75 percent xenoliths and xenocrysts. Kimberlites contain abundant xenoliths of lherzolite—a mantle peridotite with magnesian olivine, pyroxene, and minor calcium-plagioclase, spinel, or garnet.

The range of xenoliths in basalt is more restricted than that in kimberlites, because basalts form at shallower levels of the mantle. Thus, basalts incorporate less of the upper mantle on their way to the surface. Spinel lherzolites are common in alkali basalts such as those found in Hawaii, Arizona, the Rio Grande Rift, and Central Europe. Basalts also contain xenoliths of harzburgite, dunite, and eclogite. Harzburgite (a peridotite with magnetite and spinel) and dunite (an ultramafic rock that consists of mostly olivine with minor chrome-bearing spinel as an accessory mineral) probably represent residual melts following fractionation of lhertzolite.

The occurrence of mantle xenoliths in volcanics is limited to intraplate magmatic environments such as oceanic islands (Hawaii and Tahiti) and continental volcanic provinces or rifts (the southern Colorado Plateau and the Eifel District, Germany). Kimberlite intrusions favor old, stable, thick continental crust (South Africa and central North America). These environments are characterized by simple plumbing systems in which magmas rise rapidly to the surface; otherwise, xenoliths would sink in the host magma. Xenoliths are more rare in complex systems found in interplate environments such as collisional magmatic provinces or island arcs.

Methods of Study

The mineralogical composition and textural relationship of minerals within xenoliths are studied with the aid of a polarizing microscope. In addition, chemical analysis is often used to determine the minor and trace-element composition, the partioning of various elements between minerals, and even the distribution of elements within minerals. Rare earth elements in mantle peridotites, measured in trace amounts, are considerably enriched relative to other ultrabasic rocks and to average chondritic meteorites. Isotopic studies, especially strontium and oxygen, are used to distinguish mantle rocks from crustal rocks.

The assembledge of minerals in xenoliths reveals a wealth of information about the chemical and mineralogical composition of the mantle. From a study of these rare rocks, various processes and conditions of the lower crust and upper mantle can be inferred. The mineralogical combinations serve as geobarometers and geothermometers. Controlled crystallization studies at a variety of temperatures and pressures are employed to characterize the stable mineral assembledge within differing crustal and mantle environments. A mixture of minerals or rocks exposed to elevated temperatures, as found in the lower crust and upper mantle, recrystallize into a mineral assembledge that is in equilibrium with the higher temperatures. Or, by examining altered rocks, such as some altered xenoliths, it is possible to determine their prior state before metamorphism by the magma.

The major mantle xenolith in kimberlites and lamproites is a variety of peridotite known as "lhertzolite." Postulated to constitute most of the earth's upper mantle, lherzolite is an olivine-rich rock with substantial orthopyroxene and minor chromium-bearing calcic-pyroxene. The chief aluminum-containing minerals in lherzolites are calcic-plagioclase, chromium-aluminum spinel, and magnesium-rich garnet. The specific aluminous mineral in any lherzolite is determined by the depth of origin. Plagioclase occurs at depths of less than 25 kilometers, spinels at depths of 25 to 60 kilometers, and magnesia garnets at depths below 60 kilometers. Diamond-bearing kimberlites have all three types of lherzolites, but diamonds are associated only with magnesia-garnet lherzolites. Further, graphite is the stable form of carbon above 30 kilobars pressure or 120 kilometers deep. Diamonds are the stable form of carbon at greater depths. Small amounts of silicon dioxide found with diamonds are in the form of coesite, which is stable up to 100 kilobars pressure or approximately 300 kilometers depth. At greater depths, stishovite is the stable phase of silicon dioxide. Therefore, diamonds probably form below 120 kilometers but above 300 kilometers.

Context

The chief scientific value of xenoliths rests in their being samples of materials collected as magma ascended through the earth's mantle and crust. Wall-rock xenoliths provide samples of country rock that remain close to their original source. More important, xenoliths in rapidly ascending, volatile-rich volcanic magmas may provide samples of crustal rocks from the walls of the conduit throughout its entire path. These materials are brought to the surface in relatively unaltered states. In addition to mantle xenoliths, some localities, such as Kilbourne Hole, New Mexico, and Williams, Arizona, contain significant xenoliths of granite gneiss representing crustal basement rocks. Xenoliths found at Kilbourne Hole include granite, gneiss, limestone, metamorphosed shale, rhyolite, and caliche. These rocks occur beneath this maar-type volcano at varying depths, from very near the surface to tens of kilometers below it. Cognate xenoliths provide information on the earliest parts of the magma to crystallize. Basalt, kimberlite, and lamproites contain xenoliths from the mantle. Distribution of nodule occurrences is not random. Siliceous basalts rarely contain nodules, whereas alkali basalts commonly contain eclogite and spinel peridotites. Kimberlites contain abundant nodules, including garnet peridotite. These differences suggest different depths of origin for the different magmas. Mantle xenoliths are the only means of obtaining samples of the mantle. From the study of these materials, it is possible not only to know the composition of the mantle but also to develop an understanding of its physical state and some of its processes.

The sole economic value associated with xenoliths and xenocrysts is as a source of diamonds that formed deep within the mantle. Diamonds occur as xenocrysts in kimberlite, lamproite, and in alluvial gravels derived from kimberlites. Diamonds form at very high pressures. Minimum conditions required are pressure greater than 40 kilobars, which is equivalent to depths greater than 120 kilometers, and temperatures of approximately 1,000 degrees Celsius. Diamonds are associated with magnesia garnet-bearing lherzolites and coesite.

Diamonds make up only one part in twenty million of a typical diamond-bearing kimberlite, and many kimberlites are devoid of diamonds. By far, most diamond production is from kimberlites in West Africa, South Africa, and Siberia, but diamonds are also mined in Australia, Brazil, and India. Small concentrations of diamonds have been found in kimberlite and lamproite bodies in Arkansas, Wyoming, Montana, Michigan, and Canada. After unsuccessful attempts to develop mining operations at the lamproite body at Murfreesburo, Arkansas, the area has been turned into the Crater of Diamonds State Park, where several small diamonds are found by tourists each year.

Bibliography

Dawson, J. B. *Kimberlites and Their Xenoliths*. New York: Springer-Verlag, 1980. A technical treatment of xenoliths and their scientific significance as samples of the mantle.

Legrand, Jacques. *Diamonds: Myth, Magic, and Reality*. New York: Crown, 1980. This amply illustrated book provides comprehensive coverage of diamonds, including their worldwide occurrence, geology, crystallography, mining, and cutting.

Morris, E. M., and J. D. Pasteris. *Mantle Metasomatism and Alkaline Magmatism*. Boulder, Colo.: Geological Society of America, 1987. This collection of papers presented at the Symposium on Alkali Rocks and Kimberlites provides a technical discussion of the chemistry, mineralogy, and petrology of the mantle as determined from mantle xenoliths.

Raymond, L. A. *Petrology: The Study of Igneous, Sedimentary, and Metamorphic Rocks*. Dubuque, Iowa: William C. Brown, 1995. This book, written as a text for undergraduate students, provides a comprehensive coverage of the field of petrology. Xenoliths are discussed in several places in the sections on igneous rocks.

Sinkanka, John. *Gemstones of North America*. Vols. 1 and 2. Princeton, N.J.: Van Nostrand, 1959 and 1975. These companion books, written for the amateur collector, describe gem-hunting localites in North America, including several diamond localites in the United States.

René De Hon

Cross-References

Diamonds, 362; Earth's Mantle, 555; Gem Minerals, 802; Geothermometry and Geobarometry, 922; Igneous Rock Bodies, 1131; Igneous Rock Classification, 1138; Igneous Rocks: Kimberlites, 1186; Igneous Rocks: Lamproites, 1200; Igneous Rocks: Ultramafic, 1207.

MAGILL'S
SURVEY
OF
SCIENCE

ALPHABETICAL LIST

CATEGORY LIST

INDEX

Page ranges appearing in boldface type indicate that an entire article devoted to the topic appears on those pages; a single page number in bold denotes definition of a term in the Glossary (volume 5).

Ductility, 297, 747, **2774**
Dune stabilization, 2263, 2264-2265
Dunes, 1347-1348, 2196, 2198, 2199, **2774**;
longitudinal, **2783**
Dust Bowl, 2897
Dust devils, 2527, 2530, **2774**
Dust storms, 886-887, 2390
Dust tail, 253, **2774**
Dynamic metamorphism. *See* Cataclastic
metamorphism
Dynamical extended range forcasting, 2717, 2720
Dynamo effect, 532, 534-535, 542-543
Dynamo hypothesis, 2589

Earth-emitted radiation, 1004
Earth observation satellites, 410
Earth Observing System, 2174, 3007
Earth Radiation Budget Experiment, 3153
Earth Radiation Budget Satellite, 3006
Earth Remote Sensing Satellite, 2907
Earth resources experiment package, 2375,
2378-2379, 2380-2381
Earth Resources Technology Satellite, 1358,
1364, 2377-2378, **2904-2910**. *See also* Landsat
Earth-sun relations, 150-151, 152-153, **399-406**,
416, 419, 550, 1819, 1995
Earth system science, **407-414**
Earth tides, **415-420**, 583, 584-585, **2774**
Earthflows, 1365, 1366, 2834
Earthquake engineering, **430-436**
Earthquake focus, 1261, 2079
Earthquake magnitudes and intensities, 438,
452-460, 927
Earthquake swarms, 2622, 2623-2635
Earthquake waves, 2882
Earthquakes, 301, **484-489**, 2340, 2500-2502,
2548, **2774**, 2863, 2882, 3069-3075,
3105-3112, 3123; distribution of, 162, **421-429**,
1262, 1266, 1382-1383, 2602; famous,
476-483, 2244-2245; hazards of, **437-444**,
2405-2406; locating of, 295, **445-451**;
man-made, 442; prediction of, 21, **461-468**,
867, 1085, 1385, 1568, 1837, 2345-2346,
2474-2475; prehistoric, 457
Earth's age, **490-495**
Earth's composition, evolution of, **496-503**
Earth's heat budget, 399, **496-503**, 1798
Earth's origin, **569-575**
Earth's shape, 416-417, **583-588**
Earth's structure, **589-595**
East African rift zone, 1174

East Pacific Rise, 1828, 2609, 2612
Echo sounding, 1788, 1795-1796
Eclipse, 2094
Ecliptic plane. *See* Plane of the ecliptic
Eclogites, 556, 1565, 1569, 3193
Ecological succession, 1718, **2774**
Ecology, 407, 1514, **2774**
Ecosystems, 1718, 1722-1723, 2259, 2651
Ediacarian fossils. *See* Fossils, Ediacarian
Effective temperature, 1004
Egypt, 3025
Einstein, Albert, 1749, 1772-1773
Einstein X-Ray Observatory, 2880
EIS. *See* Environmental Impact Statement
Ejecta, 106, 1393, 1394, 1397, 1480, 1500, 1508,
1528, 1625-1626, 2645, **2774**
El Chichón, 2690
El Niño, 134, 219, 221, 910, 1779, 1781, 1782,
2774, **2911-2917**, 3007, 3090
Elastic, 469, **2774**
Elastic behavior, 669
Elastic deformation, 297, 298
Elastic rebound, 461, 484
Elastic waves, 396, 431, **469-475**, 485, 1382,
1383-1384
Elasticity, 2225, 2226-2227
Electrical-resistivity surveys, 608-609, 610-611,
612
Electricity, 1095
Electrodialysis, 1037
Electrojets, 153
Electrolysis, 2058, **2774**
Electromagnetic energy, 3186
Electromagnetic radiation, 2166, 2333, **2774**
Electromagnetic spectrum, 150. *See also* Remote
sensing and the electromagnetic spectrum
Electromagnetism, 2876-2881
Electron microprobes, **596-600**
Electron microscopy, **601-606**
Electron shell, 596
Electronic lens, 601
Electrons, 3129
Electronvolt, 2876
Electrostatic charge, 2402
Electrum, 975
Element, 706, 2282, 2434
Elemental distribution in the solar system,
2434-2441
Elemental distribution in the earth, **391-398**
Elemental mapping, 598
Elementary particles, 2876-2881, 3129-3135

Greenstone belts, 95, 500

Greenstones, 92, 1162

Greisenization, 1601-1602

Ground penetrating radar, 608, 610, 612

Ground resolution cell, 2349

Ground state, 2744

Ground zero, 2918

Grounding, 1947

Groundmass, 1146, **2778**

Groundwater, 71, 384, 1012, 1020, 1042, 1342, 1351, 1494, **2778**, 2856. *See also* Artificial recharge; Groundwater movement; Groundwater pollution; Saltwater intrusion

Groundwater movement, 385, 916, **1020-1027**

Groundwater pollution, 943, 952, **1028-1034**, **1035-1041**, 1356, 2152, 2157, 2385, 2460, 2714; remediation of, **1035-1041**, 2714

Groundwater recharge. *See* Artificial recharge

Growing degree-day index, 2826

Guaira Falls, 3173

Guano, 707, 708, 1225

Gulf of Aden, 3146

Gulf Stream, 283, 1800, 1803, 2930, **2945-2951**, 3100

Gullies, 2387-2388, 2392

Gummite, 2580

Gunflint formation, 2116-2118, 3117

Gunflint fossils, 783

Gutenberg Discontinuity, 2884

Guyots, 1466, 1468, 2274-2275, 2278, 2279, **2778**, 3157

Gypsum, 196, 637-638, 2856

Gyres, 1779, 1798, 1799, 2945

Hadley cell, 121, 140, **2779**

Hail, 2110-2111

Half-graben, 2805

Half-life, 157, 275, 276, 561, 833, 840, 848, 855, 862-863, 1521, 1734, 1735-1736, 1749, 2136, 2143, 2150, **2779**, 2918

Halides, 1743, 1746

Halite. *See* Salt

Hall, James, 66, 899, 904

Halley, Edmond, 1052, 1057

Halley's comet, **1049-1058,** 1669; probes, 1049-1051, 1055-1056

Halobacteria. *See* Extreme halophiles

Haloclines, 1871, 1873

Halogens, 1059, 1248

Hamadas, 339

Hamilton, Sir William, 2670, 2672

Hanging wall, 157, 275, 676

Hardness, 2225, **2779**

Harmonic tremors, 2638, **2779**, 2844, 3150. *See also* Volcanic tremors

Haüy, René-Just, 1694-1695, 2370

Hawaiian Island-Emperor Seamount Chain, 3145, 3160

Hawaiian Islands, 836, 1069, 1081-1082, 1086, 1440, 2551-2553, 2615, 2620, 2621, **2638-2644**, 2684, 2686, 3160

Hazardous wastes, 599-600, 609, 800, 920, 1039-1040, **1059-1064**, 1355; disposal of, 322-323

Head, 1095

Head wall, 683, **2779**

Heat Capacity Mapping Mission, 2906

Heat sources and heat flow, 396-397, 536, 557, 571, **1065-1072**, 1265, 2067-2068, 2141, 2760, 2762

Heat transport. *See* Geothermal phenomena and heat transport

Heaviside layer, 131

Heavy metal, 1059

Hematite, 1254, 2219

Herodotus, 874

Herschel, John, 1053

Hess, Harry H., 693, 2064, 2065

Hess, V. F., 2877

Heterosphere, 128, 130

Hexahedrites, 1652

Heyerdahl, Thor, 2978

High Calcareous Alps. *See* Bernese Oberland

High-frequency seismic waves, 452

High-grading/low-grading, 2995

High-level wastes, 1758-1759, **2779**

Highlands, 1400, **2779**

Highwall, 1703

Himalaya, **1073-1078**, 1270

Hinge, 739

Hiroshima, Japan, 2919

Holmes, Arthur, 848, 879, 1522, 2083

Holocene epoch, 205-206

Holotype, 874

Homo erectus, 643-644

Homo sapiens, archaic, 644

Homogeneous accretion theory, 525

Homosphere, 128, 130

Hoover Dam, 388-389

Horizons. *See* Soil horizons

Hornfels, 1580, 1594, **2779**

Horns, glacial, 947

INDEX

INDEX